APOCALYPSE

APOCALYPSE

On the Psychology of
Fundamentalism
in America

CHARLES B. STROZIER

BEACON PRESS

BOSTON

Beacon Press
25 Beacon Street
Boston, Massachusetts 02108-2892

Beacon Press books
are published under the auspices of the
Unitarian Universalist Association of Congregations.

99 98 97 96 95 94   8 7 6 5 4 3 2 1

Text design: Christine Taylor
Composition: Wilsted & Taylor Publishing Services

LIBRARY OF CONGRESS CATALOGING-IN-PUBLICATION DATA

Strozier, Charles B.
Apocalypse: on the psychology of fundamentalism in America /
Charles B. Strozier.
p.   cm.
Includes bibliographical references and index.
ISBN 0-8070-1226-2
1. Fundamentalism.   2. End of the world—History of doctrines.
3. New York (N.Y.)—Religious life and customs.   4. Psychohistory.
I. Title.
BT82.2.S77   1994
277.47′10829—dc20   93-39540
CIP

For Christopher

CONTENTS

INTRODUCTION

This is a book about the apocalyptic in contemporary life. Because we all die, everyone reflects at some point about individual and collective endings. But what might be called endism, or the location of self in some future, ultimate narrative, pushes such reflection into a profoundly different realm, wrapping the future in magical projections that isolate it from meaningful, human connection with the past. My concern in this book is with the psychology, or mind-set, of endism, especially as it expresses itself in contemporary Christian fundamentalism, as well as its history, or where it comes from, and why it is now so significant in our culture. This study has no simple answers but some rather interesting questions.

"Apocalypse" is a transliteration of the Greek word *apokalypsis* meaning "to uncover or disclose." Within the Judeo-Christian tradition it means the specific ways in which God reveals himself or

1

herself to humans. For nonliteral Christians, such "revelation" of the ultimate can come close to what is called "insight" in psychoanalysis, or that profound understanding that connects thoughts and feelings at their deepest levels. Prophecy, in turn, is the form of our access to that apocalypse, though some scholars have distinguished the prophetic from the apocalyptic traditions. In prophetism, it is argued, we are called to a change of heart, to repentance in the present, to a new way of living. It is a call to efficacy and a challenge to change so that we can avoid catastrophe. In the apocalyptic, or the already-determined future, hope is deferred, which is why it is so often associated with the poor, the broken-hearted, the oppressed.[1]

The apocalyptic energizes contemporary fundamentalism, which in its many garbs has become a familiar global happening. It is not at all clear how one should properly define "fundamentalism," but all students of the subject, from Selma to Tehran, have noted that fundamentalism has a decidedly apocalyptic character. In its Christian form, fundamentalists believe that God will remake the world in a huge firestorm of destruction, that he will send Jesus back to rule for a thousand years, and that in the end the faithful will conquer death and live forever. The unsaved die once, and then are resurrected to face God at the final judgment, after which they are cast into the lake of fire for all time. It is a remarkable myth of violence, revenge, and renewal.

The apocalyptic is not new to human culture, and certainly not to the religious imagination. The apocalyptic has, however, taken on a new dimension in an age of real scientific threats to human existence. Many Christians who subscribe to fundamentalist end time theory differ on the exact sequence of events they envision as human history ends and we move into God's time. There are dogmatists, to be sure, but most fundamentalist Christians are more loosely apocalyptic and believe only that this earth will somehow be purged in the fires of God's anger, that Jesus will return, and that a new heaven and a new earth will be reborn. Many, especially African Americans, link such beliefs to a perceived human drama of oppression and look toward the Apocalypse with a unique sense of rebirth. Even more loosely, in the culture at large, endism of one kind or another, from New Ageism to nuclearism, is remarkably widespread. While my focus is on the Christian side of things—largely because of the distilled clarity of its apocalyptic vision—it would be parochial to isolate considerations of endism from its wider cultural context.

Apocalyptic myths are necessarily rooted in private dramas of great significance and pain. In various ways death and its equivalents, along with constant efforts to hold off fragmentation, play a central role in the self experiences of fundamentalists. Their passionate religious commitments are an authentic expression of Christianity, one that grips the imagination of many millions of Americans (though not my own). I am in no position to judge the truth claims of fundamentalists, their position on biblical interpretation, or their certainty of the return of Jesus. Nor is that my purpose. I do feel that there is generally something unsteady about fundamentalists and there are some worrisome aspects of the apocalyptic within fundamentalism. But my larger purpose in this book is to argue that we are all unsteady in an age of ultimate threats to existence; fundamentalism is simply one form of response, and a more interesting one than has been appreciated, to what can only be understood as a kind of collective illness in our contemporary culture.

In this book I explore lives in detail from which to cull such themes. For five years in different settings and with varying frequency, I visited carefully selected fundamentalist church environments as a participant-observer; I also had several researchers who worked in the churches under my supervision. In these settings I became familiar with the fundamentalist experience and got to know people well enough to interview them at least two times, often more, in taped, structured yet open-ended, psychological interviews. Perhaps these Christians merely "put on their worship faces" for me as an avowedly nonbelieving outsider, but I would like to think I spent enough time with them, was sufficiently empathic, and am psychologically astute enough to cut through such deceptions. I could, of course, be wrong.

I bring several disciplinary perspectives to bear on this study. I basically see things psychohistorically. My own background is as an historian: I am a professor of history at John Jay College, CUNY. I have written about Lincoln and the Civil War, but more recently I have turned my attention to issues of ultimate human extinction. I am also a practicing psychoanalytic psychotherapist and on the faculty of a psychoanalytic institute in New York (TRISP). Within psychoanalysis I have training and a special interest in self psychology (Heinz Kohut, with whom I did a book, was once a mentor). But out of necessity in the investigation of the fundamentalist subculture I had to become something of an anthropologist as well, taking elaborate field notes, keeping a journal, and tracking my own subjective reactions to my experiences (including my own dreams). Finally, of necessity I brushed up against religion and theology. It's a rather heady mix that is either creative or a witches' brew.

In structure, this book moves quickly into a discussion that is immediate and psychological. In chapters 1 through 6, I try to understand the individuals I interviewed within the fundamentalist movement in relation to their end time beliefs and in the context of the inner dynamics of their life experiences. Each chapter in the first part opens with the story of one particularly interesting and informative respondent, which begins with an account of their apocalyptic thinking and then fits those beliefs and attitudes into their life history. The second part of my inquiry reaches out to the more conceptual, historical, and comparative dimensions of my topic. I treat the detailed questions of the cultural reach of the apocalyptic, the meanings in general of getting close to fundamentalists, and the issue of community and totalism in fundamentalism (chapter 7). From there I explore the history of the apocalyptic in America (chapter 8) and the complex ways Jews and Israel have worked their way into the minds of fundamentalists in the last century or so (chapter 9). In chapters 10 and 11, I turn to two comparative cultural expressions of the apocalyptic in America: the Hopi Indians and New Age. Both show the broad influence of the Christian end time myth but also reveal alternate possibilities of imagining the ultimate within American culture. Finally, in a brief conclusion I try to end a book on the end by looking toward the future.

Christian fundamentalism in America at the end of the millennium is a mass movement that broadly describes the religious orientation of roughly a quarter of the population. In general, Christianity is, as

Frank Kermode has shrewdly noted, the "most anxious" of all the major religions of the world and the one "which has laid the most emphasis on the terror of death."[2] Christian fundamentalists, in turn, have a particular orientation toward biblical literalism ("inerrancy," or the idea that every word of the Bible is the authoritative voice of God); the experience of being reborn in faith as described in John 3 (especially verse 3: "Verily, verily, I say unto thee, Except a man be born again, he cannot see the kingdom of God"); evangelicalism (or the obligation to convert others); and apocalypticism in its specifically end time form. The polling data on American beliefs are startling. The historian Paul Boyer wisely cautions against too much reliance on polls, which have no way of probing the extent to which expressed attitudes about belief impinge vitally on daily life.[3] But even with that caution, the survey data suggest that some 40 percent of the American public believes in the Bible as the "actual word of God and is to be taken literally, word for word." That would approach 100 million people. Approximately 84 percent of Americans believe that Jesus is the son of God, and 80 percent said they were convinced they will appear before God on judgment day. The same percentage believes God works miracles, and half the population believes in angels. Nearly a third of all Americans firmly believe in the rapture. As Garry Wills puts it: "It seems careless for scholars to keep misplacing such a large body of people."[4]

There are, however, differing fundamentalist styles. Most studies of fundamentalism deal with its white, rural, Baptist, puritanical, southern face. But the way we look shapes what we see. I want to shift the ground of the debate about fundamentalism out of the South to its northern, urban, racially and ethnically mixed environment where the whole notion of one's response to modernism is profoundly ambivalent and developed not in fantasy from remote areas of the country but up close, in an often stagnating immersion in the city. When you live in Sodom you have no easy retreat from it into idealized rural passions. What seems to drive people instead is an apocalyptic yearning for renewal within the degradation and chaos of the city they know so well. New York City is a good place to test that idea, and that is where my interviews took place.

The most inclusive fundamentalist style is the evangelical, an umbrella term used to describe a broad spectrum of beliefs, churches, and organizations, not all of which could be considered fundamentalist. In much of Europe and the Middle East, the term "evangelical" is used to refer to the historic churches of the Reformation and is therefore synonymous with mainstream Protestantism. In the Americas, however, "evangelical" has quite different meanings and is associated with being born again, reading the Bible literally, personal evangelism, and apocalypticism. There are different wings within the evangelical movement, including the nonfundamentalist progressives (about 20 percent), represented by groups like "Sojourners" or, more interestingly, Bill Clinton, a firmly believing Southern Baptist who once regularly attended Pentecostal summer revivals. In order to keep my sights clear, the term "evangelical" in this book should carry with it the descriptor "conservative."[5] At its ideological center conservative evangelicals are those born-again Christians associated with Billy Graham, the National Association of Evangelicals, and Campus Crusade; with schools like Moody Bible Institute, Fuller Seminary, and Wheaton College; with publishing firms like Zondervan; and with magazines like *Christianity Today*, *Eternity*, and *Moody Monthly*.[6]

In my work, I encountered conservative Evangelicals in a richly endowed center for Bible study and outreach to business executives that I call Grady House (in naming the churches and church settings where I carried out my research, as with all the respondents whom I interviewed, I use pseudonyms). I spent nearly two years attending Bible study and the various programs at Grady House, which was located in a prestigious section of Manhattan. The people at Grady preferred not to call themselves "fundamentalist" and were at pains to stress that they were "neither a cult nor a club" (a line used by one of the staff leaders during a Bible study session); instead they described themselves as "historic Christians," which in my two years of active field work seemed a distinction without a difference, and reflected mainly their wish not to be associated with what they felt to be low-class fundamentalists. The orienting rituals of Grady House included Bible study and other on-site programs; direct evangelical outreach by the staff of missionaries to executives in the city; and free dinners for as many as seven hundred guests that included business leaders and members of the Social Register. The dinners were personally hosted by Mrs. Grady and were always held at special New York spots like the Plaza Hotel or the restaurant adjacent to the ice rink in Rockefeller Plaza.[7]

Pentecostals, whom religion scholar Martin Marty once said are difficult to get "in focus,"[8] define a second fundamentalist style. Pentecostals overlap with the Evangelicals in often confusing ways but also need to be considered as a separate fundamentalist style. The most important Pentecostal denomination is the Assemblies of God, though there are many independent white, black, Hispanic, and Korean Pentecostal churches. Their liturgical enthusiasms make Pentecostals most easily identifiable. They wave their arms in supplication and regularly speak in tongues. Their services run on for hours with responsive prayers and heartfelt singing. Partly due to their enthusiasms, Pentecostal leaders like Jimmy Swaggart or Jim Bakker have taken great falls with dramatic public confessions. Bakker's sprawling Heritage USA in North Carolina, including a giant water slide, was built on financial fraud, and he was drawn to liaisons with many women and even some men.[9] Swaggart, it turned out, had a passion for prostitutes, which was the basis for his fall. Most such leaders return in time to the church, or some church, even if chastened. It is not that sin is allowed but forgiveness is assumed. As people believe about faith healing, the instrument of God's power can be flawed and yet the action efficacious.

I spent a good deal of time with the Pentecostals, some of whom I encountered outside of a church. For the most part, however, my work with Pentecostals took place in two churches. The church I call Abiding Light, in midtown Manhattan, had a multicultural mix of whites, African Americans, and Hispanics, though historically it was a white congregation and the leaders remain white now. Abiding Light, which was declining in membership, sustained itself financially partly by renting out the church on Sunday mornings to a huge group of fundamentalist Koreans (who even hosted a full orchestra for their services). The Abiding Light congregation itself met in small Bible study groups early on Sunday afternoon and then gathered for a mid-afternoon service and some kind of evening dinner and prayer session. During the week there were other activities

as well, including a prayer meeting on Tuesday evenings, choir practice on Wednesday, special events on Fridays (like occasional all-
night prayer sessions), and outreach programs for poor adolescents
on Saturday led by the assistant pastor.

Abiding Light led me, indirectly, to Calvary, an independent African American Pentecostal church in Harlem that was self-styled as
"an end time church with an end time message."[10] In the early 1900s
Calvary had begun as a "church planting" of Abiding Light, but the
racist policies of the mother church in not allowing blacks to join the
church council led Calvary to split off and become independent.
Calvary remained small for many decades, indeed a storefront, until
its current charismatic minister, the Reverend Charles, took over in
the 1970s. They then grew dramatically in size (to about one thousand) and used their collective purchasing power to buy a large, old
building. Members of the congregation personally rehabilitated the
building, and it came to function as a thriving church and something
of a community center for its surrounding dilapidated neighborhood. The three-hour Sunday service—which was the most important event in a week crammed with other meetings, prayer services,
and activities—was quite a lively happening. Many brought their
own tambourines. They stood and talked in prayer as the spirit
moved them. They swayed to the music and sang lustily. There was
much clapping and ritualized saying of "Amens." Anyone praying
from the podium was answered from the congregation in a continuous and spontaneous dialogue. The singing was exquisite, and the
piano and electric organ, placed at opposite sides of the podium,
played along with a multi-piece drum set and several trombones.

The dominant fundamentalist style, however, that anyone would
agree to designate as "fundamentalist," consists of those now
largely southern and white Americans who most directly inherit the
fundamentalist traditions forged in the nineteenth and early twentieth centuries. Such believers are most visibly Baptists, but they
may also find their home within any Protestant denomination.
These fundamentalists are the actual literalists, as Erik Erikson
might say,[11] those whose certainty about faith borders on absolut-
ism. They are ambivalent about the somewhat looser standards of
belief of the conservative evangelicals and mock "holy-rolling Pen-

tecostals." Such fundamentalists believe in and talk about "inerrancy" and spend many hours of Bible study on the end time theory of "premillennial dispensationalism." In this theory God is revealed to humans through a series of dispensations, or stages, each with its own narrative sequence that ends in violent disruptions in the transition to the next dispensation (the expulsion from the garden, the flood, and so on). Inevitably in such a theory, we are at the end of the last dispensation before the violent end of human history and the opening up of the millennium. Furthermore, the "premillennial" part of the theory holds that Jesus returns to rule at the point of the transition as human history ends, or before the millennium itself, an idea that is also linked to the rapture of the faithful away from the violence of the end times. Any theory that brings the end closer at hand and puts its violence in focus lends end time chronicles a certain urgency. At the ideological core among fundamentalists, in other words, a new theory of ultimate death energizes the apocalyptic as it ripples through the mass movement of fundamentalism.

My direct experience with this fundamentalist style was in St. Paul's, an independent Baptist church in the northern reaches of Manhattan. St. Paul's was a thoroughly mixed congregation of whites, African Americans, and Hispanics with a white minister. They ran a variety of programs, including a soup kitchen, and aspired someday to build a new church building. St. Paul's kept close to its ideological commitments in its Bible study program and nurtured their version of the truth in the young they taught in the school. More than any of the churches I attended, St. Paul's was totalistic in the kinds of commitments it expected of its members and in the involvement of the congregation of all ages. The interviews with people in this church, furthermore, showed an unusual degree of ideological certainty, together with a marked suspiciousness of outsiders.

In my view, then, the fundamentalist movement in America includes three distinct, if overlapping, styles. Largely because the styles are so close and yet distinct, the movement is rife with what Freud called the narcissism of small differences.[12] Strict fundamentalists find the liturgical enthusiasms of the Pentecostals repugnant, who in turn speak with disdain of the rigidities of their brethren (many of my Pentecostal respondents talked of their "full gospel" beliefs as a "step forward" from the Baptists and one young African American woman, raised an Episcopalian, said the mainstream church needed to "get off this . . . social programs–type stuff"). The privileged members of Grady House dissociate themselves from vulgar street evangelizing. The members of Calvary still bristle at the insults they endured from the founders of Abiding Light four score years ago. And at the fringe the battle over end time ideas can be especially intense. Whole groups are formed around whether they believe Jesus will return to rapture the faithful before, during, or immediately after the seven-year period of tribulation that marks the transition out of human history, a distinction that might well seem both arcane and meaningless to outsiders, unless one appreciates its psychological significance. The survivalist groups in Idaho, for example, many of whom are Neo-Nazi or Aryan, tend to believe Jesus will rapture them into the clouds only in the middle or at the end of tribulation, because they first want to experience the violence directly and fight it out with the beast.[13] The distinctive characteristic of Jehovah's Witnesses is their reading of Revelation 7:4–8 and its mention of the 144,000 who are "sealed," an idea that also obsesses other ideologues in relation to the ingathering of the Jews, which some mainstream Evangelicals dismiss out of hand.

The noise of difference, however, should not obscure the underlying unities within the fundamentalist movement. All within it would agree with the inclusiveness of what a middle-aged man, Otto, told me ("My definition of a Christian is someone who has a personal commitment to Jesus Christ"), and the location of the outer boundaries of the movement as defined by another man, Isaac, who scorned the "easy believism" of "nominal Christians." The strict "fundamentalists" may be the chief carriers of the idea of inerrancy, but it is a term frequently used in Pentecostal churches, in Bible studies, and by individuals when talking about scripture. It is in the discourse, one might say. Furthermore, what defines the movement psychologically is its unique Christian commitment to the apocalyptic. The ideologues place the greatest emphasis on premillennial dispensationalism, but I found that virtually all my respondents carried often large, if somewhat undigested, parts of the theory with them.

Images of the rapture, tribulation, Antichrist, the beast, and Armageddon are quite universal, if by no means always the same, in the minds of fundamentalists. Calvary, remarkably enough for an African American Pentecostal church, required of new members in the congregation that they study premillennial dispensationalism in special classes. The apocalyptic is more than subtext. It is the ground of fundamentalist being.

I do not presume to pretend that I was a fly on the wall in this study, removed from the intense religious experiences into which I rather unwittingly threw myself. My formal psychoanalytic training and involvement in clinical work perhaps justify such avowed subjectivity, though any observer of fundamentalism needs to account to the reader for his or her special connection to the subject. That this almost never happens is a commentary on the false positivism that prevails in much of the academy. Throughout this book I use my own reactions as a vital source of data, while studiously trying to avoid the luxury of self-indulgence. I wrote extensive field notes after every service, Bible study, interview, or encounter I had in the churches over some five years. In these notes I tried to capture the externals of the setting and the mood, the songs and prayers and general happenings, as well as what was happening to me inside in response to these events. My reactions are woven into the text, but I will begin with a specific word on my own religious origins, which I realize now were an important, if only partly conscious, influence on my decision to undertake this study, as well as my curious first encounter with fundamentalism.

I was raised as an Episcopalian on the South Side of Chicago, near the University where my father was a professor of French literature and a dean. He had been born and raised in Georgia, where I was also born. My paternal grandmother, an ardent Methodist, practiced her form of Protestantism in a simple, whitewashed church directly across the street from their house in a small Georgia town. After her husband's death at the turn of the century, she was left in near-poverty with six children to raise. Her faith helped keep her strong. A rich aunt sent my father through school, though when she died all the money went to the Methodist Church. In his thirties, studying at the University of Chicago, my father married up. My mother was a doctor's daughter from Colorado who had had servants as a child and had spent a year in a finishing school before college. At thirteen she had become an Episcopalian. That became our family church as well, reflecting in part the social aspirations of my father, though he also used to joke that he sometimes missed singing "Beulah Land" from the pews of our incense-drenched church.

We attended church every Sunday and on all important holidays, like Good Friday, as well as some of the lesser holy days. Before dinner we always held hands and said a lengthy prayer. We sang Christmas songs together in our living room after dinner, and I have fond memories of nestling close to my father on an old brown felt couch as we sang from a worn songbook. Everyone in the family gave up something for Lent (chocolate, desserts, whatever); I would worry about what I was going to give up for weeks each year before Ash Wednesday and feel a large dose of guilt if I ever broke my vow. All these rituals that bound our family to the church gave us a sense of togetherness. We never actually talked of God per se and certainly never read the Bible or made reference to heaven, hell, or even, really, to Jesus.

None of this was artificially imposed on me. I was an active partner in our relationship to the Church of the Redeemer that was at the end of our block. For one thing, I was an earnest and, at least for my mother, an angelic choirboy singing soprano solos in our traditional (and paid) men and boys choir from about the age of seven until my adolescence. That involved two long practices after school on Tuesdays and Thursdays and before the Sunday service, monthly performances for shut-ins, concerts that required extensive preparation, and long hours of services during Christmas and Holy Week. Besides regular Sunday School, I was also an altar boy through these years. I would thus serve at the first Sunday service, attend a class on some innocuous topic, grab a roll at the coffee hour in the basement, go to choir practice, and then sing at the larger 11:00 A.M. service. I also got up on Wednesday mornings at 6:00 A.M. to attend the minister in a service in the chapel. I even confessed my sins, such as they were, three times a year, kneeling alone beside the minister in the small chapel.

I guess I was marked for some future role in the church, for I was also recruited early into a number of special activities and programs. For several summers I attended a church camp, which I remember as distinctly unpleasant and quite removed from anything to do with religion. I also had a special relationship with our minister (who later became a bishop). He seemed to want me as his acolyte at both the Sunday services and at the Wednesday morning chapel. He also decided to put me on the fast track for confirmation. At all of eight years old I was therefore enrolled in the training program to be confirmed four years ahead of schedule. I dutifully learned the rules and expectations of a true Christian, which were in any event hardly burdensome and lightly shared, and worked hard to memorize the Lord's Prayer and the Nicene Creed. These I had to recite before Father Moorehouse, alone, in his office. I was terrified. I did okay with the Lord's Prayer, but the Nicene Creed got mixed up with some phrases rattling about in my brain from my Cub Scout activities: "And I believe," I said, "in the Father, the Son, and the Holy Ghost, and the Republic for which it stands." I was confirmed, but Father Moorehouse also had a good laugh about my examination with my father over a stiff glass of bourbon.

Religion was serious but not oppressive. Family and ritual mattered much more than Jesus and God. The Bible was hardly opened. Sunday School dealt with issues of ethics and life, not spirituality or religion. I never owned a Bible as a child, never took one to church, and was never expected by anyone in my world to know anything about biblical stories. We sang to the glory of God and filled our church with incense but never once mentioned anything about what happens to infidels, let alone something as coarse as hell. The sermons were intelligent and witty. They were not particularly profound, but they were blessedly short. I was never inspired but also never offended. Besides, my main concern in any service was my role in singing or carrying the communion materials to and fro.

At thirteen I left the church with a sudden realization that life inside Christianity could be insidious, if not evil. It was 1957 and we had moved to the very old South in north Florida, where my father became president of Florida State University. Although I had been born in Georgia, I really knew little of southern ways until then.

Naturally, we started attending an Episcopal church. One Sunday, not long after our move, I sat astonished through a sermon that argued for "negro" racial inferiority based on biblical passages. I decided something was seriously amiss with this church and probably church in general. Besides, I cared then about football and girls, and worried about pimples.

For the next twenty-five years I hardly went to church, except for an occasional Christmas Eve service and a few weddings and funerals. After my father died when I was sixteen I went through a spiritual crisis and decided to read the Bible straight through. It had some meaning for me but also got frankly boring somewhere in the middle of the Old Testament and after the Gospels in the New Testament. I lost that Bible at the end of my summer's reading. The closest I came to continuing my childhood involvement in religion was when I attended conservative Jewish services at Harvard with my devout roommate. I liked the singing, the mystery of the Hebrew, and the friendly ecumenical spirit in which none of the Jewish students objected to the presence of a tall, blue-eyed, blond WASP in their midst.

I raised my first pack of three children without any church in their lives. I was living on an old farm in central Illinois, trying to make it in my first teaching job at the nearby university, Sangamon State. I was in analysis and doing my psychoanalytic training in Chicago, as well as writing my first book. My marriage was troubled, there was never enough money, and my horses kept breaking through my makeshift fences and eating my neighbor's corn. Church seemed an unnecessary luxury, something I might get to in another decade of my life, but certainly not vital. Besides, I considered myself an agnostic of major proportions and it seemed hypocritical to raise children in a faith in which I did not believe. A part of me remained nostalgic about the church, especially its sense of mystery and ritual, and the way it had worked in our family to build cohesion. As my marriage crumbled, that image gained some renewed vitality, especially through several years of single parenthood with my three boys.

In the mid-1980s I came to New York with a new wife in a newly reconstituted family to take a new job at the City University. Perhaps it was the change and the opportunities it offered for remaking myself (or maybe it was having just turned forty), but I decided to search out a church. Powerful Christian images that contributed to my social and political passions had clearly never left me during my years away from the church. My new wife and growing boys were only mildly interested in my project, so I decided to find a church first, then try to lure them into it. While jogging I spotted an Episcopalian church not far from where I lived in Brooklyn and noted the time of the Sunday service. I wondered whether I could really go home again, but I certainly was not prepared for what had happened to Christianity since my departure at thirteen.

It looked familiar at first, as the robed minister at the altar busied with the chalice and stacks of wafers for communion and other tasks preparing for the beginning of the service. I felt a warm glow looking at the stained glass windows. Maybe the church could in fact reinvigorate the moral principles that my Christian upbringing had instilled. There was nothing pretentious about the church and the large number of people filling the pews suggested an active and vital congregation. I was also pleased to see that the congregants were thoroughly integrated. The church reflected the social and ethnic diversity of the community.

My first sign of change came when a man sat next to me and asked if I would like a "prayer partner." It was clear he expected to "help" me through the service. I wanted to explain that I could manage quite well, thank you, but sensed something peremptory about his demeanor that made him someone who was not going to be deterred from sitting at my side as my "prayer partner." I realized I would just have to go with the flow that morning and see what this church would bring. The man suggested I might want to keep a pencil and paper ready at hand, along with my Bible, when the priest spoke, for "He really roams quickly through scripture." I explained that I had none of those items with me. The man looked surprised but quickly produced paper and pencil and moved close to share his Bible.

Everything from that moment on was completely outside of my experience. The service was interminable and at least twice the length of anything I had ever attended as a child. The congregation belted out hymns more like "Beulah Land" than Bach, reading from a screen in front of the altar on which the words were projected.

Most parishioners raised their hands with palms open, presumably to let in the Holy Spirit, a gesture I had only once seen in a TV broadcast of some Billy Graham revival. The sermon mentioned innumerable biblical passages (as my prayer partner quickly flipped through his Bible to locate each reference and share them with me) and talked about them with a literalism I found strange.

But the most disorienting experience of the morning was the communion. I never questioned that I would participate; I was, after all, confirmed in the church. I had always thought of taking communion as a way of celebrating membership in a congregation and perhaps opening oneself up to a spiritual process the end of which was murky indeed. Taking communion had something to do with faith, to be sure, but one could be a long way from certainty about belief and still be eminently qualified to participate. Not so in this church. As I walked to the railing to take communion, I saw a number of those assisting the minister look alarmed and whisper among themselves. As I knelt three people surrounded me. One asked if I was confirmed but seemed not to believe me when I replied in the affirmative. They then encircled me, touching my shoulder and arms, praying intensely for (and they thought, with) me. When they felt I was ready, to my great relief they moved on and the minister brought me the bread and grape juice (as a child we always used real wine).

After communion I felt inclined to just walk down the aisle and out the door. This was not a form of Christianity with which I was familiar. It was literal, exclusive, intense, and, for me, quite alien. Part of me wanted to flee and never return. Perhaps I should have. But for better or worse the anthropologist in me took over. I stayed that day, and though I only returned once to that particular church, which in any event only bears a "family resemblance" to fundamentalism,[14] I went to many like it over the next five years.

That stunning first encounter with fundamentalism in the Brooklyn church connected with a conversation I was then (1987) beginning with my colleague Robert Jay Lifton about how ordinary people imagine ultimate threats. In time, with MacArthur Foundation funding, our common interests led to an elaborate interview study of which fundamentalism was a part. From these shared beginnings,

I took off in my own idiosyncratic directions to complete the research for this book.

I limited my work on fundamentalists to New York City, because it was a domain in which they had not previously been studied and was available for my personal involvement. Fundamentalism as I understood it as shaped in three styles determined the types of fundamentalist communities I wanted to locate: conservative Evangelicals, Pentecostals, and more doctrinaire fundamentalists who would probably be Baptists. Within those styles I also felt it was important to include representation of the racial and ethnic diversity of New York fundamentalism, to the extent possible given language constraints. Consultation with authorities familiar with the New York church scene generated some five or six possible communities for each of the styles. I then visited churches (and Grady House) to find the best ones for my purposes. I sought churches in which I was made to feel welcome; in which the minister seemed accessible; in which the number of parishioners was neither too small to be suffocating nor too large to feel lost; in which the diversity of the city was reflected and one African American church because of its special importance for understanding the subject; and in which there existed an active program throughout the week into which I could fit myself.

The selection of respondents for interviews was a rigorous and exhausting process. Sometimes the pastors helped identify members of their congregation whom they felt would be interested in the work and good to interview. But in general I found respondents on my own within the churches as the logical extension of my active participation in services, Bible study, prayer meetings, and other activities. Respondents were people who had to feel sufficiently comfortable with me to be willing (and sufficiently articulate) to talk. I had to begin the dance, or courtship, and it could take anywhere from several weeks to as many months to convince a respondent to agree to formal interviews, which then might take another month or so to conduct.

In my work I sought to be empathic with my respondents and their world and yet never lose sight of my research purposes. On the one hand, I had little trouble entering into most fundamentalist rituals. I sing well and thoroughly enjoy a spirited service, though I never took communion again after my experience in that Brooklyn church and was never able to raise my arms in supplication with the Pentecostals. I came to tolerate the innumerable Bible study sessions I attended, which I more or less accepted (or rationalized) as filling a gap in my education. I found a certain spiritual nourishment in all my church-going and Bible reading that touched my early experience and deepened my ethical commitments. On the other hand, I never lost sight of my identity as a researcher nor my sense of personal discomfort with the religious attitudes of most fundamentalists. I tried not to be false to myself or to my respondents. I never pretended to be reborn, or even Christian for that matter. I readily shared my doubts about faith but always focused on my quite genuine interest in understanding what other people believe. I know outstanding scholars of fundamentalism who were raised as fundamentalists and move delicately at the edges of the experience; others like myself who had a religious background in mainstream churches feel a deeper ambivalence about the potential totalism of contemporary fundamentalism; still others have conducted good, though usually antagonistic, work from the outside. Each stance has its merits. What does matter is honesty in understanding oneself in relation to the experience itself.

My self-presentation, however, had some important consequences in the very ambiguity it presented fundamentalists. They feel acutely the scriptural commandment to evangelize. "God has no grandchildren" is the phrase I often heard, meaning that each generation has to be converted, each person born *again*. Otto was quite clear about the evangelistic purpose of fundamentalism. Nonbelievers must be reached, because "We're mandated by scripture to take the gospel to every creature." Now, of course, "We're losing the battle," but we must struggle on. God wills it. Everyone must have an "opportunity" to know God, whatever they then do with that knowledge. If they refuse the word, they die, not once but twice. "If you believe the Bible, you have to believe that." In fact, however, except for such deeply committed individuals (besides Otto I might also mention Monroe, Sam, Mary, Frank, and Reverend Charles in my study), and certain marginal fundamentalist groups like the Jehovah's Witnesses within which all individuals fiercely spread the word, most fundamentalists do little actual work converting people.[15] But they believe they should evangelize, and my unusual presence offered special opportunities. I was the perfect target. I came to services, Bible studies, and talked with them over coffee. They had repeated chances to work on me. I was a self-confessed nonbeliever but knew a lot about their beliefs and deepest commitments and was both sympathetic and genuinely interested in them and their world. A kind of nonverbalized contract came to cover my work: I was granted interviews in exchange for making myself available for conversion. This contract was not without its psychological stress, though it also had its moments of humor and absurdity. And for my part it was not a devil's bargain. The offering of myself for conversion was genuine. Otherwise I would have felt dishonest in the dialogue. I listened carefully to their pitch, and made every effort to let it enter my own spiritual imagination. Besides, how could I know for sure how the repeated evangelical onslaught to which I subjected myself would turn out? At some level I had to keep open the option that they would succeed.

In the churches themselves, which are hierarchic institutions, I could never expect to interview without the tacit approval of the pastor. The procedure therefore was first to attend Sunday services for a while to get known and somewhat legitimized. But before too long one had to talk with the pastor and explain the purposes of the work. The responses varied, but it is a mark of the relative openness of most fundamentalist churches that tentative approval from the pastor in no way assured contacts and certainly not interviews with individuals in the churches; it simply removed the veto at the top. For the rest, I was on my own, meeting people and generally immersing myself in their lives. But it was never easy getting close. I courted Otto at Abiding Light, for example, for months. We both attended Ian's Bible study, and I took every opportunity to talk with him, ask questions, and generally make myself a familiar part of the surroundings. I sensed in him a valuable respondent for my study but also a vague distance that would make it difficult to set up a formal interview. Even after I finally asked him for an interview it took several frustrating weeks to find a time and place to conduct it. He always returned to New Jersey immediately after the 2:30 P.M. Sunday service and arrived for the 1:00 P.M. Bible study just as it began. But it turned out that on one Sunday he was staying through the evening for a 7:30 P.M. Christian movie at Abiding Light and agreed to an interview between the end of the service and the movie.

It was hard at first to find a place to set up. The sanctuary would have been inappropriate and I was not close enough to the minister to ask to use his office. That left some corner of the basement, which was bustling with activity. After some indecision, during which I could feel Otto's suspiciousness mounting, I at last found two chairs in a corner of one room with a third between us on which I could place the tape recorder. It was clear he could not understand the need for such privacy, and I had not anticipated the fear that filled Otto's eyes as he saw me handling the tape recorder. He visibly pulled back, and asked again what my study was all about. I said I was studying what people believe, especially about end time things. He paused but then suspiciously agreed to go ahead. Quickly, however, he warmed to the subject, and was even enjoying himself by the end. He was surprised an hour and a half had passed, said, "Time flies when you're having fun," and warmly invited me to visit his church in Jersey and agreed to a second interview. I think he felt listened to, even though it had taken months of fieldwork to get him to talk.

Another researcher, Laura Simich, working in Abiding Light, attempted to interview a white woman named Nan who was in her early seventies. Caustic, chronically depressed, and in pain from arthritis, Nan played very hard to get. She had only converted in her early sixties after a lifetime of loneliness and various treatments for her depression (including some electroshock therapy). Since then, however, the church had become the mainstay of her existence. She spent most days in bed mobilizing herself to come to the church for something in the evening. Laura even took on the task for several weeks of escorting Nan to church from her apartment, riding with her on the bus. Nan told some of her history in informal chats and made abundant references to end time concerns. But when it finally came time for Laura to ask her if she could interview her more formally with a tape recorder, Nan suddenly grew highly suspicious. She withdrew for a few days and resisted any contact. When she next saw Laura she said the Lord had told her not to talk into a tape recorder. This honest answer, as far as one could tell, showed a typical aspect of fundamentalist thinking: the shift in agency. She was a passive agent in divine hands. God willed that she not give the interview. His instructions freed her from responsibility for the refusal, or for facing in herself why she was afraid to grant an interview. Whatever dangers Laura represented were kept at bay.

For most of the first six to eight months, in church rituals and in interviews my ambiguous status sustained my work. Interviews proceeded well, which deepened my relationships with at least some members of the congregations. But the commitments of fundamentalists eventually led them to see me as a highly suspect presence. One man who actually agreed tentatively to an interview pretended, the next time I asked him about it, not to hear me. When I repeated my question, he waited nearly five minutes (during which time I thought it would not be wise to ask again) before turning to me with a nervous smile and said, "We'll see." One time Nan, at Abiding Light, referred to me as "that tall, blond fellow" who is "not impressed with us" because he is not converted.[16] Why was I not converting despite their most earnest efforts? How could I know so much about the Bible and not believe it as they did? Perhaps I was a fraud, a spy, or worse, an agent of the devil sent to undermine their own faith? Now I should stress that I never encountered anyone who was openly hostile and was never asked to leave any church. On the other hand, you are never left alone by fundamentalists, who check regularly on the status of your beliefs. After about half a year, and certainly by nine to ten months, whatever benefit there was in my continued presence was more than offset by the ambiguity of my persistent nonbelief. The antagonism I began to feel was subtle. Heads turned, no one granted interviews, and I felt shunned.

There were some exceptions. I had long since passed the ten-month mark and was in fact into my second year of Bible study at Grady House. I had not completed my interviewing and so, despite the discomfort, needed to continue attending Bible study. I returned to a meeting after a month's absence, which had reflected my own ambivalence. At first, I had to endure a number of critical comments about my absence, especially by Monroe, Luke, Larry, and Sam, all of whom I had interviewed at least once by then and I suspected felt somewhat betrayed that I would leave after I had them on tape. But with that backdrop, we finally got into the Bible study. At this meeting, somewhat unusually, we were asked a series of set questions from a pamphlet that asked you to relate belief to your personal life. Everyone in our small group had to give some kind of answer to each question. I managed nervously to stay with generalities in answering questions like "Who is Jesus Christ to you?" (a religious leader of great significance who redefined human ethics, I mumbled) but knew there was no escape from the last question, "What does it mean to you now to have Jesus living within you?" I happened to be the last person to answer and thus followed seven sincere statements of belief. I said I respected those answers but that it was difficult if not impossible for me to answer the question. I had been raised a Christian but had never made a decision to accept Jesus into my heart, which would make it inauthentic to describe the ways in which my life had been changed by having him within me. There was an extended moment of silence in the group, after which, to my surprise, I immediately became the object of devoted attention. Luke commented on his own struggles with accepting Jesus, and others assured me it was normal to have doubts (I did not think it was necessary to respond that doubt understated my stance regarding my faith). Then, during the final prayer, Sam said: "If I may be so presumptuous, I would ask your prayers for Chuck in his ongoing search for Jesus, and may he continue his search and end up finding you, Lord, in his heart." When we broke up the meeting, several people gathered around me and were solicitous of me and talked in an overly friendly and earnest way.

I had a number of complicated feelings in response to this sequence of events. Initially, I felt that my need to be honest made me a pariah among the faithful. My immediate thought when members of the group drew toward me was that now I had my perfect opportunity to secure some additional interviews I needed (and in fact the experience in the Bible study gave me the opportunity to get my second interview with Luke and my fourth and final one with Monroe). On the other hand, and at a different level, the scene left me feeling invaded and exposed. I felt swallowed up by the oppressive goodness and decidedly uncomfortable when Sam prayed for me. It all made me think of the "love bombing" of the Moonies. At the same time, I was left with a sense of emptiness and a longing for the security they all talked about finding with Jesus. I wished quite genuinely I could have their beliefs. It was as though two parts of myself were carrying on a dialogue. One part said I should accept Jesus and take comfort in him as my friends advised, while the other said how ridiculous such feelings were. The very fact of my split feelings gave me insight into the incredible power of using the human need for love and acceptance within a group as a tool for conversion. I was clearly the outsider to this group, and they were reaching toward me to pull me into their magic circle.

I based my interview style largely on Lifton's approach that modifies the psychoanalytic model. The interview data consist of fifty-four different interviews with twenty-five respondents divided between the four churches or church settings in which I worked. Some of the interviews were conducted by talented researchers working closely under my supervision; all were taped and later transcribed. Structured yet open-ended interviews are perhaps the only way to uncover the deepest understandings of the self. Such psychological conversations aim to identify relevant images and themes that can emerge in this narrative form. It is a search for meanings in a life history, in a whole self whose story is still unfolding. The conversation is process oriented and, though carefully structured by means of a protocol, moves with the respondent in terms of thoughts, fantasies, feelings, even dreams.[17]

In this kind of qualitative and psychological research, one nagging question that always arises is whether the respondents were "typical." In one sense, no one is typical. Any life explored in depth is unique, even extraordinary, and if told at all well anyone's story is unusual. But were the people I chose to interview colorful in other ways and so far out of the ordinary as to distort my findings? Were these bizarre people who gave voice to their endism in ways that cannot be said to be "representative" of the larger movement of fundamentalism? I believe not. For one thing, the psychohistorical themes and images of significance for my work appeared with regularity in most of my respondents, who were otherwise remarkably different people and members of completely separate congregations. The churches in which I decided to work were also in no way out of the ordinary (to the extent that there is something ordinary about fundamentalism). Except for the ministers, all the respondents were typical members of the various churches or communities in which I worked. Some figures were immediately striking in visiting a church, but on the whole the people I talked with were quite like the other members of their churches. None of their peers, and certainly not I, saw them as odd or disturbed. In fact, in the few cases when an initial encounter produced visible stress in a respondent he or she was immediately left alone and the research taken elsewhere. That is part of one's ethical obligation in this kind of work.

But interviews, however central to my work, were only part of my data. Singing hymns and joining in Bible study with fundamentalists was an equally significant part of my research, as was the systematic exploration of my own feelings about what was happening to me in the churches or during the interview process. I also only began to comprehend endism in a larger sense as I deepened my historical and comparative study of the subject. Abraham Lincoln and the Hopi, who enter significantly into this book, were not incidental parts of my work but central to my emerging understanding. Such a blend of psychological and historical perspectives that led to this book is what I at least mean by the psychohistorical method.

ONE

THE
PSYCHOLOGY OF
FUNDAMENTALISM

1

THE
BROKEN
NARRATIVE

ARLENE. The first time Arlene revealed her end time self to me came after she had told me her story up to the point of her most recent arrest and incarceration. She was talking about her feelings of being a prostitute, particularly her guilt, and the way it connected to her relationships with men. In the course of her description of the period just before going to jail, I asked her what she felt about her continued work then as a prostitute. "I didn't want to do it anymore," she said, "but it was the only way to survive." That statement, however, was somewhat disingenuous, for Arlene needed easy money at odd intervals only because she was then drinking heavily and into crack. At some level Arlene was aware of her own contradiction, for she next shifted time quite dramatically in her associations. She asserted: "I didn't like it. I, in fact, I rebelled, I resisted, that's where the battery came in, I didn't want to do it."

I was confused. She had been talking about the period just prior to her arrest but had suddenly reverted to the previous year with her abusive lover, "dirty dog" James. She seemed to be listening now to an inner voice that had entered our dialogue for the first time. Any open-ended interview has a certain looseness to it, but up to this point in my discussion with Arlene I had been impressed with the coherence of her self-presentation, despite the horrors of the experiences in her life. Suddenly I felt far less connected to her. Something had intruded and broken our bond. That new voice seemed to me to be coming from deep within her.

Arlene began to elaborate on how James had wanted her to work as a prostitute and bring money home. When she refused he beat her up. "I just wouldn't do it." The issue, she explained, was money and self-respect. "I'm this kind of person that I have to see something for my money. . . . I wasn't seeing anything for the money." She said the main objection she had to James was his drug dealing, though in another context she had made quite clear that the real issue was his other girlfriend. "I never ever worked [as a prostitute] and said I'm going to give it to a drug dealer, no. That's a no-no. I'm not supporting any drug dealer." She wanted to see her money buy something visible like a car or a home. For that "I'll pound the pavement twenty-four hours a day." Then Arlene mentioned her sister who works a regular office job, and has to struggle for such a long time to acquire something like a down payment for a house. Arlene got that kind of money in six months. The thought of houses and her sister brought Arlene back again into the present. "See what I'm saying?" she asked me. "I wanted to re-establish, and once again, that basis I didn't have, I went and I got myself a house in six months. I went and got myself a car," both of which were quite true. "That's why you hustle," she added with less conviction but obvious pride at her success. She was now almost sad at her train of thought, which trailed off into illogic. "Otherwise, you wait for the five years of the down payment. And those are the only reasons why I do, you know, it now."

At that point a whole new self took over, one that sharply condemned her work in prostitution, and flooded her with guilt. "Being a believer, of course . . . it's against my beliefs, and, and, when God has a plan . . ." Now I felt on familiar ground. "What do you think God has as his plan for you?" I asked. "Good things," she replied warmly. "You know, there are certain, um, biblical promises, and if we live by God's laws and principles, I find that he's just and he's faithful to, to these things . . . and he's fulfilled all his promises [to me]. Any of the promises that I stand on, he fulfills them." She found in her faith that she was learning more about herself and growing daily in knowledge. Her faith in God even had a metaphoric shape to it. "I can actually feel it," Arlene said. Since her conversion, she had become sensitized to things in her life, more receptive to her own thought processes, more receptive, finally, to divine intervention. "Your spiritual eye becomes clearer," as she evocatively put it.

But the world is a sad and terrible place. People are mean and stupid. Everything seemed without rules, both within herself ("I really don't have any boundaries") and in the world. Chaos reigned supreme. We need a ruler, Arlene said, another Martin Luther King, maybe even Jesse Jackson ("if he just got his eye off that presidency"). "It's time for a revolution," Arlene asserted, with a note of political awareness and a sense of efficacy. She was too much in and of this world, too committed to change within herself to give up altogether on trying to radically alter for the better the course of human affairs. "Let's start a revolution against the drug dealers," she said angrily. They are destroying our children, and our sisters are being ruined by thirteen or fourteen. "Nobody is taking care of the children." There are no rules, she says repeatedly. "It's hari kari."

Such political reflections and healthy assertiveness proved fleeting. "It's all part of the end time and the approaching Armageddon," she said without apparent reference to the world but clearly speaking in the context of her inner text. What we've seen is bad, but there is much more to come. There are the signs, such as AIDS. "That's a plague. It's a plague. *Literally*. And there's *no* cure for it." Even syphilis is back on the rise and running rampant. It's another plague. Another is illiteracy. It's terrible. Then there is the greenhouse effect. "It's God trying to get our attention." We are marching toward the Apocalypse, she said with certainty. History will end and we will be healed, and "with history ending, all those things, it won't matter. Nothing will matter." Right now, Arlene believed, earth is under the rule of Satan and *his* angels. "He is loosed, he is loosed," she said, "he's having a field day" (evoking Revelation 20:2–3: "And he laid hold on the dragon, that old serpent, which is the Devil, and Satan, and bound him a thousand years, / And cast him into the bottomless pit, and shut him up, and set a seal upon him, that he should deceive the nations no more, till the thousand years should be fulfilled: and after that he must be loosed a little season"). Even though Arlene tried not to slip into too much demonology—the chaplain advised against it, she confided—she felt the presence of the devil against whom she has to valiantly struggle. Sometimes, at least, she was successful, as with her intravenous drug use. In overcoming that habit, Arlene felt she won one specific victory over the devil.

Arlene was aware that some people have always said the end is at hand and feel that what they are experiencing is the worst in history. But what's happening now, she believed, was unlike anything else that has ever occurred before. It is much worse. She was convinced that Jesus will return soon—in her lifetime—and rapture her and the believers before retaking the earth for his millennial rule. "When the rapture comes, there'll be no doubt in our minds that God is involved, okay? That'll separate the believers from the unbelievers." It's like with the Jews in the old days, Arlene said. They were very disobedient and had to go through much suffering. But in the end God heard their prayers. "We're praying [now] for his kingdom to literally come so this can be over with."

Within her largely conventional fundamentalist schema, Arlene inserted some creative and idiosyncratic variations. She had, for example, an image of God as an old black woman. Black women, she said, are the "nurturers of this earth," the caregivers and helpers. They keep things together, even to the second and third generation. Her endism also had a refreshing note of ambiguity to it. "I don't know what's in store," she said about the future. "But I *do* have a tomorrow. I'll always have a tomorrow." Nor will human error or folly be the instrument of human destruction. "I don't see the nuclear bomb or misuse of that as being our end." She did not preclude the possibility of nuclear war, or even of New York being wiped out in some kind of nuclear exchange. But that won't be part of the end of the world. That would be too much in our control, too "attributed" to humans, as she put it. The end of human history, in other words, will be beyond human comprehension. We will be responsible for it, but we can't make it happen. God may use us, but we cannot control his plan. The end is absolutely at hand (certainly in her lifetime) and yet she hoped for tomorrow and lived partly committed to a human future. It was inconsistent, and fully human.

The way Arlene worked out such contradictions was to carry within her at least two opposing ideas about ultimate violence, in particular the explanation for the transition into the millennium. One such image was a magical vision of destructiveness at the end that was both grand and grim, a violent and total cleansing that will purge the earth of sin and suffering. In this vision, Arlene evoked Sodom and Gomorrah, as well as the flood of Genesis, to explain her thinking. She noted once, for example, in a rather menacing way: "Like whenever there's an act of God, you're going to know this is an act of God." In this frame of mind the devil was a real and terrible thing (*He* is not, she said, a "beautiful angel of light" but epitomizes evil and "looks like black lungs filled with cancer," a horrible monster, rather "like the AIDS virus under a microscope").

On the other hand—and at different points in our discussions—Arlene stressed that between now and the end things will get worse but that the actual transition into the millennium will be peaceful. "We don't have to wipe out this earth to get a new one, we don't have to." God will simply "transform the earth," and make it over into something resembling her childhood in Jamaica. That will be "our New Jerusalem." Everything will grow abundantly and no one will have to toil on the land. It will be beautiful. We'll all walk around like Adam and Eve. There won't be black or white; we'll all just commune with each other. There will be no diseases, or robbery, or greed. All that will be gone. The weather will be perfect, and when it rains the sun will keep shining. We won't even need houses. There will be "flora and fauna" everywhere, and when you need fruit all you'll have to do is reach out and take some. "The name of the Lord is a tower where the righteous can run and be safe," Arlene said. We must hope for that. "I know where to go to get peace, and I have joy in this, as a believer." She can get peace with God, more peace than anything else. "Peace of mind, peace of my spirit, even my body." But without hope life is terrible. You'll commit suicide. One must hope for tomorrow, for deliverance. "It suits my personality just perfect," Arlene said. "It gives me order, it gives me discipline." When you've known tragedy, "you can learn from it," it can make you strong.

I met Arlene on Rikers Island, the huge New York City jail located just northwest of La Guardia Airport. In each of the four long interviews I conducted with her over a two-and-a-half-month period, we talked in the small but private office of the Catholic chaplain. The bedlam of prisoners moving about outside, laughing, talking, smoking, sometimes fighting was cut off from our little world of temporary peace. When Arlene first walked in, I was not at all sure that she was an inmate. She moved quickly and had an air of confidence as she set down a stack of papers on the desk and turned to greet me. As an (as yet) unsentenced inmate, she wore civilian clothes and seemed so much in charge of her environment that I thought maybe she was a staff member coming to get something in the office.

Arlene was a thirty-one-year-old woman at the time of the interviews. The beatings at the hands of her most recent boyfriend (including a deep scar on her arm from a knife wound and a somewhat distorted left jaw where it had been severely broken) and the effects of overeating had left their imprint. She was highly intelligent and articulate, able to express complex feelings in clear, evocative terms. She had an excellent vocabulary that far exceeded the bounds of her limited formal education. She was also self-reflective. She had had some therapy both in and out of prison that had clearly nourished her natural introspection, and made her receptive to the interview process.

Arlene was born in Jamaica. When she was very young her mother left her father and moved to New York. Arlene came to stay with her mother when the mother sent for four of the eight children. She spent a year in America, but was then sent back to Jamaica until she was eleven. At that point Arlene left Jamaica for good and came to live with her mother in Brooklyn. Arlene's father was a construction worker in Jamaica who once made pretty good money. "I had a father," she said remotely, "[who] was an alcoholic and he slept around and wasn't there, and was just difficult." He was "abusive" to Arlene's mother, who came to America to get away from him. But Arlene adored her father. "I thought he was the greatest." "He was this magical guy," she said. "Those are the most impressionable years," she said of the time before she came to America, "things I can remember . . . all these outings to the beach, and my father as a swell guy, all my happy moments, the happiest time of my life, I associate with my father."

Arlene hated her mother as a child, especially after coming to America. "I hated her," Arlene said, "because I didn't like America." The mother was distant, rigid, moralistic, and demanding. She also seemed to be unhappy, especially at the treatment she had received from her husband. The mother clearly sought allies in her various struggles and spent a good deal of time trying to turn Arlene against her father. The result, however, was only to create bitter resentment on Arlene's part toward her mother and deepen her yearnings for her father in faraway and somewhat mythical Jamaica.

Meanwhile, Arlene's stepfather began to sexually molest her, at first hesitantly but soon with abandon, fondling and kissing her regularly. Arlene feared to tell her mother, for she believed, reasonably, that her mother would deny it and claim it was Arlene's fault. Later, in fact, when she did tell her mother about the stepfather that is exactly what happened. Arlene felt abandoned and hopeless. Her mother kept saying she was going to send her back to Jamaica, but it was a lie and she said it only to quiet Arlene. "I cried, I cried, I wouldn't eat, I cried, it was terrible," she said. Twice Arlene tried to commit suicide. Once she jumped out of a third-story window but only sprained her ankle when she landed on a rose bush. A second time she took a bottle of aspirin and spent a day vomiting but was otherwise unharmed. The mother denied both attempts. She simply ignored the aspirin sickness and rationalized the jump from the window as an accidental fall. "My mother has a knack for that," as Arlene put it. "Anything that happens, she changes it." Arlene's life was in a shambles, and no one knew or cared. Of the responsible adults in her life, one lived in a remote world of self-centered fantasy, and the other was trying to seduce her. Even potential helpers, like neighbors, compounded her troubles. The man across the street raped her when she was twelve. It was her first sexual experience. "I had little white panties with bows all around it, with blood all over it and I just threw the panties away." She never told her mother.

Arlene was running out of options. Somehow she had to get out, escape, be free. She would consider anything, even prostitution, which a friend of hers suggested to her at fourteen. It didn't take much persuading. In a matter of hours Arlene was recruited by a pimp who whisked her away. For the first time since she had come to America, Arlene felt appreciated, even at the cost of turning herself into a commodity. She was treated well and made friends. Men often picked her up and went out for the evening, did things, went to a show, had dinner. She felt wanted. She had a number of regular dates, "nice people," she says, men she got attached to and saw every week. "I was on top of the world, I had the world at my tail," she said with enthusiasm (and without irony). And the money was important. It was a "representation of just how good you were, so you tried hard and made more money."

Part of the pleasure Arlene took in her work as a prostitute was the knowledge that it would drive her mother crazy to know what she was doing. It seems the whole family spent a good deal of time looking for Arlene that first year she worked as a prostitute. All her brothers roamed the streets trying to find her. "I used to see them looking for me," she said, curiously, since she was some distance from Brooklyn. It seems, however—and Arlene was vague about the sequence of events here—that she returned fairly often to Brooklyn "for bookings," and used the opportunity to visit her old haunts, walk the familiar streets, and observe her family and mother from a distance. Eventually, her mother hired a detective who located Arlene and insisted that she return. She was just sixteen. It was a moment of decision for her. To go back would have meant a renunciation of self at many levels, a return to an impossibly childish role for someone who was now highly experienced in the world, and an admission of guilt that would have established her mother as morally superior. Arlene instead chose to marry Alex, whom she had met on one of her Brooklyn bookings.

Alex was a pimp. He wanted Arlene to stop having so many outside dates and instead work a house in Bed-Sty. It was supposed to be the best in town, where the "mayor's friends" visited. Alex, however, seemed largely motivated by a complex blend of love, jealousy, and a need to control. He wanted Arlene safe and free to work her trade, but he also sought to insure that she would not have fun at it and most of all not develop relationships with her clients. As she said: "It was unfortunate he met me in that profession. He just never trusted me [*laugh*]. And I wasn't doing anything wrong." Arlene made a valiant effort to make her marriage work. Her earnestness was a central part of her personality, as was her deep and abiding desire to be accepted, recognized, and honored. After a year or so she quit prostituting and went back to high school, which she finished in record time. Together Arlene and Alex opened a small business. She also got pregnant and decided to have the baby, even though her first response was to have an abortion. Some things were finally working out for Arlene.

But Alex never lost his suspicions. He became obsessed with Arlene, jealous of her every move, fearful she was out whoring. He "wouldn't leave me alone," she said with irritation, especially since she was dutifully playing the role of the loyal housewife. Arlene was then eighteen. She decided she had to get out of her marriage. It could only lead to continued heartache. Besides, she felt she could never raise a child in the grubby world of pimping and prostitution. She secretly got an apartment and fixed it up for herself and the baby to escape to after the birth.

Part of Arlene's character, as she realized with a vengeance, was that she could not live without a man, and that she had only been able to change her life at crucial times by changing men. At this point in her life, feeling stifled in her first marriage, Arlene's solution to her dilemma was to set out to find a new husband. This time, however, she was more cunning than the first time around and determined to find someone who would open up new financial and social opportunities for her. After the birth of her baby, whom she basically turned over to her mother to raise, Arlene did in fact leave Alex to live in the apartment. Then she set out to find someone white, secure, older, and rich. She was very calculating about it, and did exactly what Alex most feared: She worked her "wiles," as she put it, on Long Island, in a house that she somehow found out about. It didn't take long for Arlene to find what she was after. When she first saw Ben she knew he was just right. He was fifty, widowed, Jewish, and had lots of money.

Arlene soon moved in with Ben, who seemed decent and in love with her. Within two years they were married and settled down to live in an upscale community on Long Island. "He was a very, very good husband, and he loved me because I was a good wife." But it was not a happy time. Suddenly this young woman with experience only in Caribbean American, working-class culture was the lover, then wife, of a rich and respected Jew in a New York suburb. Class, race, culture, and a thirty-year age difference opened up a vast chasm between them. Ben remained absolutely devoted to Arlene throughout these trials and tribulations of their relationship. The only tension came when she got pregnant early on when they were dating. He insisted she have an abortion, which she undertook reluctantly. But he did everything else he could to make her happy. He doted on her, bought her clothes, took her out, and insisted she not work. He also fiercely defended her blackness and broke with many of his white friends who objected to the relationship. But Arlene never adjusted. She was deeply troubled by all the rejection of her, including, to her surprise, rejection from many of her black friends. In her culture—by which she meant Jamaican—she said it is not uncommon or frowned upon for a black woman to find someone white to marry. Besides being rich, she wanted someone kind and gentle, which for her meant someone white. "I'm not a rough person," she stressed, as she sought to explain her feelings to me. "I didn't like being black," she said, "so I considered myself . . . Jamaican." American blacks, she thought then, were a "disgrace" (her mother's favorite word). They didn't work, lived off welfare, and the men were all in jail. Arlene's empathy was later considerably expanded. "I'm learning I have to consider the plight of black Americans because it affects me." And she concluded mournfully in terms of our own black-white interaction: "You don't see that I'm Jamaican, you don't see that I'm different."

Arlene had found her white man in Ben, but she had also come up against the full force of American racism, not to mention her mother's continued chagrin over her life. She began to get into drugs seriously for the first time in her life. She would drive to Harlem to buy cocaine with her black girlfriends, sneaking away from Ben. She felt numb about everything in her life. It all seemed pointless. She also experienced fresh trauma: her two closest brothers were killed in a robbery. She had grown up with these two brothers in Jamaica. One was slighter older, one younger. The breakup of the family had thrown them on each other for support. Arlene adored them both. The older one was a master craftsman who could fix anything; the younger one was to be an engineer and had just received notice of a full scholarship to college. The death of Arlene's brothers was utterly senseless and brutal. It also simply faded into the tapestry of violence in East New York: the police never came up with a suspect, in fact hardly investigated the crime.

The renewed loss, the closing down of options, and the rejection by family and neighbors made Arlene feel life was worthless. Once again she tried suicide, this time very seriously indeed. She took an overdose of valium, cut her wrists, and climbed into the shower, where Ben found her. She woke up in the hospital, tied to the bed, her wrists bandaged and wires and tubes everywhere. Recovery came slowly, and the scars remained. As a gesture, Ben bought a huge house for Arlene's mother and extended family in New Jersey. He also nursed Arlene back to health. But problems remained. Ben continued to be caught up in his own problems losing friends and dealing with the censure of neighbors; he also had an angry break with his daughter over Arlene that led him to take his daughter out of his will. Arlene meanwhile struggled to make sense of feeling a kind of misplaced responsibility for all these problems. She had always felt she should make everyone happy; now she blamed herself for Ben's loss of friends, her own loneliness, even the despair in the world. She took everything onto her own shoulders.

Among her other problems, she was also bored. Though Ben did not want her to work, he eventually relented and helped her set up a small women's clothing business that she ran part-time. Arlene tried school, but that didn't fill her needs. Sometimes she cavorted with her friends. Ben saw that things were hard for her in their suburban community, so he tried as much as possible to take her away. He was in semiretirement anyway, for his business was pretty much in the hands of his stiff and distant son. Ben and Arlene traveled all over

Europe, to the Caribbean islands, indeed all over the world. It was all she had dreamed of; it was also empty. She started drinking with a vengeance. Arlene had drunk before when working as a prostitute but only occasionally to excess and never on a regular basis. But she and Ben soon worked themselves into an alcoholic pattern: two large drinks at home at cocktail hour, another one or two at the restaurant before dinner, a bottle of wine, perhaps also some champagne, with dinner, an after-dinner drink, and a nightcap. "That's a lot of alcohol on a daily basis," Arlene said.

And then a strange thing happened. Someone robbed their home and Arlene was accused of masterminding the heist. It took me some time in our talk to get the facts of this robbery straight, for Arlene obviously felt guilty about it. But after much hemming and hawing she finally explained what had occurred. Her partner in her clothing business was in deep financial difficulty and conceived of robbing Ben's house with Arlene's permission and knowledge. Arlene claimed her friend was only supposed to take a few items, but "it went awry" and the friend cleaned out the house when they were away. She then shamelessly implicated Arlene. Three times the district attorney tried Arlene in an effort to convict her of masterminding the robbery; finally he succeeded, and she got eight and one-third to twenty-five years.

Not surprisingly, the case drew tremendous publicity as well as racist approval from the community. But Ben never abandoned Arlene. He stood by her, paid her huge legal fees, and did everything humanly possible to keep her out of prison. But something had broken between them. As she admitted to me, Arlene had in fact helped her friend rob her own husband of his possessions, even though she never expected to be cleaned out or that she would be punished if the robbery was discovered. It was a betrayal of Ben at many levels, and she knew it. Arlene seemed to need to find some way out of a stifling relationship that was complicated by issues of race and class and the determined adoration that Ben lavished on her. "I was always trying to find myself, and he was always keeping me," she said. "I didn't want a relationship with this old white man anymore." Though Ben visited her regularly in prison, after a couple of years she asked for a divorce. She regretted it, however. "I numbed it while it was happening, I numbed it out afterwards. I refused to think about it, you know."

Prison life, as Arlene soon discovered, can have some decided advantages. "It's easy to survive on the inside," she said. She got all kinds of "positive input from everywhere." Group therapy and a "lot of stuff" helped her orient herself and get her life together. Jail gave her back a sense of future, and stirred hope. "When I was [upstate in prison] you know . . . I had five-year plans and year plans and everything else." "It is so structured," she said with enthusiasm. She didn't have to pay rent and got her own private room. Outside, she was dependent on a man to support her. Inside the jail "I have *my* room," and three hot meals a day. On the other hand, Arlene was too smart not to know that free food and a room were not the real issue. For one thing, when she was in prison she was full of guilt and shame at what had happened to her. "Those of us in jail," she told me, "are the lowest spectrum." What she welcomed were the controls, the limits, the clear boundaries. "Sometimes you do need that healing, you just, you do need to stop running and just be still. Especially when you've done a lot of running when you're out there, you're actually glad for the rest." The jail for Arlene was a holding environment in which the chaos of her inner self could be stilled.

Prison also brought new experiences in love and sex with other women, something not without its complications for Arlene. Against much resistance, she confided that she had actually had a series of affairs in prison. She never considered herself "gay." True lesbians, in her view, "have an identity crisis." She was just "having a little fun." The problem for her was that she saw homosexuality, even masturbation, as a sin. "Sin is sin," she told me with the confidence of her current fundamentalist view of these past matters. "I don't believe there's a first-degree and a second-degree sin with God. Sin is sin." Arlene's ethical dilemma with her relationships grew out of the fact that she went through a conversion experience in prison and was born again. She saw her acceptance of Jesus as a turning point in her life. She had been something of a Christian as a child, but in prison she embraced faith more earnestly, symbolized by a full immersion baptism. Her trauma in her life, however, was only beginning to move toward healing.

Once out of prison, Arlene jumped parole. She went south on the run with her new lover, James, "no-good, low-down scoundrel, I mean, dirty dog. Lower than a dog." In an attempt to hold onto her faith, she joined a church in Georgia and renewed her commitment by a second full immersion baptism. But she was unable to do any serious work, because she feared that by signing W-2s and other paperwork she would be traced via her social security number. She therefore fell into menial and unsatisfying jobs that left her hard up for money. She began to commit various petty robberies to stay afloat, and entered into the "subculture" of crime and drugs that took her further "outside of the norm." Not surprisingly, she got arrested while in Georgia for prostitution and some kind of assault charge. The authorities sentenced her to two years, but they never figured out she was on the run from New York State authorities. They told her they would not put her in prison if she would leave Georgia.

She came back to New York angry and depressed. "I had a death wish," she said. "I had no hope . . . I didn't want to go on." In no time she was drinking and had fallen into crack use, about which she was quite analytic. "Crack changes you," she said. "I mean, you can tell the personality of a crack addict. You're brash, you're very, very aggressive. You turn into this crazy person . . . a literal monster." Her "drug of choice," however, was alcohol. "I've been alcoholic all these years, and finding more and more about alcoholism and myself, I realize that with alcohol not in my body, I'm a rational human being that you're talking to. But that drinking, I'm off and running."

New York City, as Arlene knew, is not a good place to wander alone through the night, especially as a woman. Somehow she never got hurt. She moved in with a man named Henry but seldom spent much time with him, even though they were engaged in theory. There was a fierceness to her, a mean streak of pure violence that often found expression in attacks on people who irritated or threatened her in any way. She told me, for example, of attacking one man with a baseball bat and seeing his head "busting all over the place." Nor was that her only experience with violence that year. Another time she hit someone with an axe. She also stabbed someone. "I just kept stabbing and stabbing till I got him twice in his arm, his forearm." She understands all this violence as partly a response to the crack, which made her crazy, and as a way of working out the ferocious anger she felt after all the battering she had received at James's hands (James, for example, cut her on her arms just the way she attacked the man with the knife). But she could make little sense of her uncharacteristic anger and cynicism that year. Normally, she wanted to "do the right thing."

Arlene got so bad that her girlfriends insisted she get away. They packed her, barely conscious, onto a bus with a one-way ticket to South Carolina. Once there, Arlene temporarily came to her senses and got one job waiting tables and a second managing a small store near where she found an apartment. She was not in treatment but for the next six months managed to stay off crack. She enjoyed the hard work, the regularity of her life, the new people. But perhaps inevitably she could not make it alone so far from what she knew as home. That fall she returned to Brooklyn and moved back in with Henry, who seemed eager to help her. He was a born-again Christian who attended a well-known fundamentalist church on Flatbush Avenue in Brooklyn (which had a charismatic white minister and a huge African American and Hispanic congregation). Henry prayed constantly for her, which she believed was what made the difference. He was also long-suffering in his determination to help. She cut his face a number of times and once broke his foot. He had no use for drugs himself, but told her that he was so devoted that he would be willing to sell crack himself to support her habit if that would keep her home. He repeatedly searched through an endless series of crack houses to find her and bring her back. He insisted she was a good person; he even wanted to bring her home to live with his mother. The only real anger he ever showed her was when she once insulted his mother and he slapped her. She grabbed a knife and stabbed him twice. Many other times he let her beat him up ("You see he can't beat me, he has never beaten me. As a matter of fact I have abused *him*").

In the end it was raw jealousy that pushed him over the line rather than crack. Arlene and Henry had fought early in the evening. She stabbed him and he bled all over the room, on the drapes, on both sides of the window, everywhere. "Do you know that all this is my blood," he kept telling her, trying to get through to her feelings. But she was numb. All she knew was that she wanted to get high but wasn't comfortable doing it around him. He just sat there and wept. She started drinking and got some sushi, then returned to sit on the street corner. Suddenly, he insisted on knowing whether she had slept with one of her drug contacts. She denied it but he kept "picking and picking."

They moved the fight inside the room where they circled warily for a time. Arlene felt Henry was fed up with her for the first time. Perhaps it was the jealousy, perhaps he had just lost hope in his crusade to save her. She in turn felt an awesome sense of death in the room. She told him to stop moving about, to be still, but he refused. As though in a movie she could see that one of them was going to die that night and it could be her, "because he was tired of being defeated in these battles." He kept telling her she held nothing sacred. "Baby, baby, don't sleep with my friend." She told him to go outside and cool off, walk down to the pub at the corner and have a beer, but he was afraid she would sneak off and get high. He wouldn't leave. She got enraged and picked up a lamp and threw it at him, then a jar of pickles, then a hammer. To her surprise he threw the hammer back at her. She went berserk, both in fear and anger at this sudden turn of events. The all-suffering, ever-loyal Henry seemed so full of righteous indignity at her supposed infidelity that he could well kill her. With a sudden move—"I can be fast"—she picked up a can of kerosene and poured it all over him. She pondered whether to light him.

At that crucial moment, reason prevailed. She called the police and asked for help. She said she was turning into a monster and desperately needed treatment. That got her into jail, for the police noticed that she was wanted for breaking her parole. I saw her first a few months later after a renewal of her faith through daily work with a devoted chaplain.

THE DIVIDED SELF

The most general psychological observation about fundamentalists one can make is that they demonstrate inner divisions that find expression in their beliefs. *All* fundamentalists I met described their personal narratives as broken in some basic way. Before rebirth in Christ they described their lives as unfulfilled, unhappy, and usually evil. Their stories were discontinuous and full of trauma; faith healed them. That moment of finding a "personal relationship with the Lord," as they put it, was the great divide in their lives. It would be wrong to say that fundamentalists *only* thought about their pre-Christian selves as bad because the dogma of conversion demands a self-transformation (John 3:3: "Except a man be born again, he cannot see the kingdom of God"). A biblical passage cannot impose trauma on the self. But it is fair to say that fundamentalists experience trauma and then find a way to talk about it in the rhetoric of literal Christian belief. That rhetoric, in turn, builds on divisions. Satan opposes God; only a remnant of the faithful survive the end times; violence pours out on the ungodly; ordinary church life moves toward totalism; and our bad, discarded, pre-Christian selves are washed away in the apocalyptic transformation of the rapture.

Not all fundamentalists, however, experience the revelation of Jesus as a blinding moment of truth that transforms their lives. Very broadly speaking, I found two categories of fundamentalists: those who are raised in the church and those who come to it later in life, usually in their late adolescence or early adulthood (almost never old age). For those who come to fundamentalism later, there is the enormously significant moment of being saved, which can take many forms but is always a transformative personal experience. For those raised in the church, being saved usually has rather different meanings, for it occurs so early as to be without much conscious or symbolic significance. Sometimes, as with Mary (a thirty-year-old Pentecostal from Abiding Light) or Nigel (a twenty-eight-year-old Wall Street broker from Grady House), an early salvation was followed by an adolescent period of "falling away from God" (Mary) that ended in a rather dramatic return to the faith. For others the continuities were more evident. Harriet, widowed and in her early sixties, never seemed to drift from the church; her total identity was fused with it. Her grandparents joined Abiding Light when it opened. For the next several decades it was a thriving congregation, and Harriet was raised within it, saved there as a child, regularly attended the church's summer camp with its tents and sawdust floor revivals, raised her children in it, and buried her husband there. She has spent her life quietly working in the church, preparing for the "soon coming" of Jesus. "As a result," she said, "I never was out in the world." Another member of Abiding Light congregation, middle-aged Otto, also never experienced a dramatic break with conversion. He stressed that, of course, he wasn't an "angel" as a child. "I used to get sent down to the principal's office, you know, but that's not the worst of it." He even had trouble defining what it meant to be reborn or saved. He ended up distinguishing between the two in a very idiosyncratic way. He said he was born again at five or six, as best he could remember, but only saved at thirteen. In this way Otto reserved for himself at thirteen the choice he never experienced at five or six.

But no matter how conversion is experienced, an overlay of human evil from deep within Christian tradition always permeates the fundamentalist sense of their stories. Humans are born bad, in this view, and even the saved remain open to the workings of the devil. It is a constant struggle. Even if you are saved at five, you were born an evil person. Most of mainstream Christianity has found ways to soften this harsh, Manichaean view of human nature, but contemporary fundamentalists keep the notion very much alive. Reverend Matthew, patting his Bible, said (quoting Jeremiah 17:9 almost verbatim from memory), "The heart of man is deceitful above all things, and desperately wicked." This theological claim to evil works together with whatever happens psychologically in fundamentalist individuals *and* with the forms of badness and violence in the world. Fundamentalists fight to hold on to their God-given virtues. They know Satan was once within and could return; certainly he is about in the world. Life is dangerous, scary, and fragile.

Such divisions in the self, however, are relative. We all have them to a degree. Some difficult thoughts and ideas are truly repressed, as Freud argued, but for the most part the self functions under stress by splitting off aspects of troubling feelings and experiences that then become dissociated memories. We know of them but not completely. They are disavowed, as Michael Franz Basch has put it.[1] It is quite rare that memory is really blank. If encouraged, most people can recall aspects of even traumatic experiences, though they may well filter out much of what happened at first in the process of remembering and certainly separate out the feelings from the memories to mute the suffering. In more extreme cases of trauma, however (say of long histories of sexual abuse), dissociation serves to protect the self against fragmentation. Most victims of such violation report the sensation during the abuse itself of leaving their bodies and watching the unfolding encounter happen from some safe, unfeeling distance.[2] Repeated trauma then requires repeated dissociation, and the patterns of separateness in the self take on a structure, with its own memories and feelings (or history, one might say).

The challenge in talking with fundamentalists is to locate the appropriate meanings of whatever divisions exist, without ever describing their lives as pathological. I am not arguing in this book that fundamentalists are crazy; at least they are no more so than anyone else in our culture (including myself). Categories of pathology, in the first place, are meaningless in trying to figure out the psychology of a mass movement.[3] As William James knew well, there is also something ethically obtuse in using reports of religious transformation against the committed. What is valuable (and what James demonstrated as well as anyone) is that one can learn a great deal about the phenomenology of religion from the direct reports of the faithful about their experiences.

Fundamentalists' broken narratives profoundly distort time, a break that is rooted in experience. The past is separated off, to be remembered only as an object lesson. You recall to forget. Except for the testimonial, so important in converting others, the past might not be remembered at all. The present, in turn, is profoundly degraded and full of evil. God is furious, and about to end it all. The handful of the faithful must keep struggling, but they are persecuted and doomed to failure. Things can be delayed but not solved. There is no redemption in human purpose. Culture is rotten. The only hope lies in the mythical transformation of the future, in the remaking of the world during the millennium and the ultimate salvation in heaven after the final judgment. Such a profound reconfiguration of historical time and a dramatic move into the magical as the means of salvation reflect the extent of trauma in the lives of fundamentalists.

If all that seems a bit arcane, perhaps a parable will help, one told to me by a theological friend, Karen McCarthy Brown of Drew University.[4] Most of us, if we made a movie of our lives, would have it circle back on itself after death and show the ways in which we leave pieces of ourselves in our children and family and work and communities. We remain embedded in the past. Our imagined future is part of our experienced past. With fundamentalists, however, the movie camera would stay with the individual after death and move into the misty heavens.

DEATH

The sources of the kind of trauma I've just described in the pre-Christian selves of fundamentalists I encountered, while as varied as human experience, centered on themes of real or symbolic death. These fundamentalists divided their lives into a period of psychological deadness, or virtual nonexistence, and a revival through faith into life, vitality, and hope. The religious dogma of rebirth requires such notions of death, or at least of non-self, in pre-Christian existence. You are *saved* from death, according to the theory, and salvation in the kingdom of God brings eternal life. All badness is overcome. Deborah, a forty-five-year-old single woman from Abiding Light, literalized the idea of being "born again" in her image of a "spiritual birth canal." Hearing fundamentalists' born-again testimonials surely fills one's own story of a spiritual journey with borrowed elements and evocative descriptive phrases. But the pain of death and deadness that creates trauma in the lives of fundamentalists is not fictive. Death and rebirth operate on a collective level among fundamentalists, and individual stories reveal such larger "shared themes," as Lifton calls them.[5] In the fundamentalist world these themes then get organized according to conventional religious rules.

Life before Jesus for fundamentalists is remembered as death-imbued, empty, lonely, depressed, and often meaningless. Sam, the executive director of Grady House, presented himself to the world as a secure member of the upper class he spiritually tended. He dressed in tailored and expensive suits with subdued ties and wore shoes with little tassels. The handkerchief in the outside pocket of his suit coat was carefully folded. Sam and his wife lived in the rent-free, elegant apartment on the top two floors of the Grady mansion; they also owned a house that his wife had inherited in a posh resort on Long Island. Since he both lived and worked in the mansion, Sam moved comfortably through its rooms with an air of ownership. I conducted my interview with him in one of the second-floor meeting rooms that was once a parlor. The walls were covered in a beautiful wallpaper. An ornate mantel along one wall held vases containing dry flowers. Along the wall to my right were two windows covered with fine, soft, embroidered drapes. In front of the couch was a glass coffee table with six Bibles on it, a small plastic glass of pencils, and three copies of a pamphlet, "The Christian and the Abundant Life."

On the surface Sam had led a happy, middle-class life into his early forties. He was successful in his advertising business and his children were moving through school without apparent distress. He lived in an expensive home in a good section of an eastern city. He was always under pressure in his business but seemed to be making the necessary moves upward at the right times. But in ways that this tense man ("I've always been a worrier," he said several times) only suggested, there was great distress underneath. His work itself was flat and without any ultimate purpose; working every waking moment to sell pet food was Sam's image of all that was wrong with his life before Christ. But as he talked it became clear that his sense of the fatuousness of advertising was only part of a much deeper life crisis in which he found himself. For one thing, he missed a crucial promotion at his agency, and the suggestion was made that he might well stagnate as an account executive and never become a partner. He also went through a personal tragedy: his depressed wife committed suicide. It was almost more than he could bear (and in fact he only mentioned it in passing, with pain on his face).

In the middle of this crisis, Sam attended an evangelical dinner for businessmen. Sam had always gone to church but never with much enthusiasm or committed belief. At the dinner he heard the testimony of a prominent lawyer from California who talked about the new sense of "peace and direction" he had found in his life after "establishing a relationship with Christ." Sam was impressed, but in his typically cautious way (that is perhaps also appropriate to his class position) he never experienced a moment of blinding truth when the scales fell from his eyes. He simply got closer to Jesus and an inner truth the longer he stayed with it. He started attending Bible study sessions and learned about a new approach to Christianity. "I always thought, you know, that you got [to heaven] through being a good person and keeping your nose clean and giving turkey to the poor at Thanksgiving. I don't mean that it's not important [to do those things], but that's not biblically how you get in a relationship with the Lord." He kept reading and talking to people, seeking guidance for his troubled soul. One night his new commitments came together: He prayed to Jesus alone in his bed, asking him into his life. Even then he hedged, for he added something like "So, let's see how this works out."

After that, however, things began to change more rapidly for Sam. His potential leadership was recognized, as well as, perhaps, his availability for a fundamental change in his life course. He began working with the national organization with which Grady House was affiliated and was soon selected to begin some evangelical work with businessmen. He found that he was good at talking with well-to-do business leaders whose spiritual quest paralleled his own. For nearly four years Sam continued in this middle level of commitment, reading, learning, and changing. He also found a wife whose beliefs were as deeply felt as his own and who warmly supported his changing life course. When asked to head up Grady House, Sam was ready to make the leap. He quit advertising to serve the Lord full-time, though he was refreshingly frank about the irony of living as such a privileged missionary.

Sam's dying self found perhaps the most graphic kind of expression in the actual death by suicide of his depressed wife. More conventional forms of Christianity, which Sam knew well, for he had been raised as an Episcopalian, seemed not to offer the kind of radical transformation he sought. To be born again, however, and get locked into the absolute security of biblical literalism, was more attractive. "I feel that the major question in life which is what happens at the end, has been answered for me," he said. And the answer came not through being good but just by believing. That was God's great gift to him. With the knowledge of eternal life, Sam could then live his life in a "triumphant way." He was secure on many levels. His daily life and work gained meaning. He became well known for his intelligent, witty, and compassionate lectures on the New Testament. His own empowerment made the staff at Grady House more confident. I would be hard pressed to name a person I encountered in my work who seemed to derive more personal rewards from his faith. Only the occasional haunted look in his eyes revealed the torment that still lingered in his soul.

The middle-aged Sam had his counterpart in the adolescent past of the Reverend Dean of Abiding Light. Reverend Dean had experienced a personal crisis that led him to leave the church in his early adolescence. The first topic Reverend Dean brought up about himself was how "rebellious" he had been, his use of drugs, and the difficulty he had then of accepting Jesus. He described a scene of going to the altar at twelve to accept Christ, but "rather than being led in any sort of a sinner's prayer or any sort of form of repentance, or encouraged to trust to Christ for salvation," he was simply signed up for a water baptism. He felt he should have been "better handled, instructed" by the adults in his congregation. He seems to have felt abandoned, ignored, as though the baptism he did in fact go through with was merely conventional and without meaning. Not long after his baptism, he stopped going to church, he said, though he later added a qualification that he attended fitfully for a couple of years before stopping altogether.

Reverend Dean recognized that his personal crisis occurred in the broad context of the cultural revolution of the late 1960s and early 1970s: "Maybe everybody feels this way about their high school years or their childhood but it doesn't seem to me that there has ever been a period of time quite like that one." His first experience with fundamentalism was when, just after graduation from high school, a born-again friend invited him to attend an Assemblies of God service. He was very moved. He found it "free flowing" with "a lot of love" and "expressive" in its forms of worship. The people were happy and sincere and "had a joy on their face that I had never seen anywhere." He felt none of the "blank stare" of the "cultish thing" but only a "genuine warmth that was very appealing." After he had left the church, he had been at odds with himself, adrift, psychologically fragmented. Drugs were probably an attempt to mask the pain of fragmentation but seemed only to worsen his feelings. When he found Jesus, on the other hand, he felt reintegrated.

The kind of inner deadness that Sam and Reverend Dean felt prior to conversion can have physical correlates in the sense of bodily deterioration. Arlene was raped at twelve, an alcoholic before she was twenty, and a crack addict less than a decade later. Isaac, an actor in his thirties from St. Paul's, was locked in a ferocious struggle with cocaine that left him always fearful of backsliding into his deadened life before being born again. For others this process of decay was more symbolic and its dread purely psychological. Monroe, a missionary to executives in his forties from Grady House, worried about being overweight and spent an extraordinary amount of time in my interviews with him musing about what he will look like during the millennium. According to the theory, the faithful are eternal by the time of the millennium, but there is no dogmatic position about what one will actually look like, or feel. It is left largely to individual fantasy to conjure up one's appearance after death is conquered. That conundrum provided Monroe with all kinds of opportunity to give indirect voice to his underlying fear of disintegration back into his pre-Christian self.

Family crises (sometimes hints of sexual abuse) also stirred a pervasive sense of guilt and despair in the imagination of fundamentalists. Deborah reported a happy childhood but in a dreamy-eyed tone that seemed based more in denial than fact. She described how her "compassion for others" came from her training and her "secure" position as the youngest child who was always pampered. She talked of all her siblings and how close she was to them as an adult, and how that more than made up for the loneliness she sometimes felt in being single. But there was something deeply sad about Deborah and she had a too-eager need to portray the difficulties in her life as not significant. The only clue to some of the deeper sources of trauma she may have suffered emerged in the second interview when, presumably feeling greater trust in the process, she revealed that her father had been an alcoholic. She immediately added that he wasn't "mean," but noted how painful it was when he started drinking again when she was eighteen (he had stopped when she was five).

The sense of deadness in the lives of fundamentalists before conversion seemed usually to be symbolic but could become directly suicidal. Larry was raised in a large working-class Catholic family in a midwestern city. He was always outgoing and articulate, hammed things up, and found that he was the actor in the family. Besides three other siblings, Larry had an identical twin brother with whom he had an almost mystical unity.[6] That brother also ended up in New York and seemed to have had the same spiritual strivings as Larry. The ethnic Polish community in which Larry grew up was surrounded by the worst of urban decay. "It was crumbling all around us," Larry said, "going black," while his neighborhood got increasingly narrow and constricted geographically; the image of constriction perhaps described his inner life as well. As a child Larry always attended church, but "mainly because it was something I had to do. There was really no true understanding," he said. In the parochial high school he attended, Larry was always at the top of his class and won a merit scholarship to a local college, as well as a starring position on the football team. He was in fact still fit and athletic looking when I knew him. The college he first attended, however, proved unsatisfactory. He was majoring in theater, and he found the program limited and unimaginative. Besides, he dreamed of bigger worlds.

He came to New York at twenty to make it as an actor. He felt it was then or never. He was an experimenter, a player of roles, yearning for cohesion. At first he found the New York acting scene quite enjoyable, including the "side benefits of booze, sex, and drugs." But he soon realized that he was not going to make it in New York as an actor. "There might have been some potential," he said of himself, "but I was just so tied up in knots of tension. Why, I was just scared, just so scared, no confidence." He felt the pressure of people expecting him to make it, and the unusual experience of failure for the first time in his life. In one of his first attempts to speak some lines before a small group of twenty people, "I couldn't stand up and speak a word without getting [nervous], it coming out so miserably." And he never really could relax. He could barely talk. "My voice would shake so miserably," he said in a way that made me feel the pain he must have been going through.

Things began to close in on Larry. He withdrew from the acting school he was attending and separated himself from the world of the theater. He was regularly drinking a six-pack of beer and then Scotch on a daily basis and fighting his erupting anger. His relationship with Ellen, whom he had known as a child and who was also acting in New York, was on the rocks because he was unfaithful to her. He felt trapped. He had no friends and no one to talk to about his problems. Even at his day job at a local retail clothing store he ended up in the stock room all by himself. He started planning his suicide. He intended to jump off the Queensboro Bridge. It has a walkway he had scouted out and knew was high enough to knock him out on impact with the water, after which he would surely drown. He planned his note for loved ones that would have explained how "I just didn't like the person I was becoming."

As his crisis intensified, Larry began to attend a fundamentalist Baptist church in Manhattan that was easily accessible from his work. He was not yet born again, but he found the service congenial. The church's abundantly varied programs gave him a lot of choices. He began to talk with people, hesitantly but genuinely. One Sunday afternoon, hanging around the church after the morning service, he watched a famous Christian movie about the end times, "A Thief in the Night," by Mark IV Productions (the New Testament has six references to Christ returning unawares as a thief; the one most frequently quoted by fundamentalists is 1 Thessalonians 5:2: "For yourselves know perfectly that the day of the Lord so cometh as a thief in the night"). After the interview, I rented the movie and watched it myself. It is set in the early 1970s, and portrays the agony and terror of those not raptured. Its dramatic appeal turns on not sleeping through the Lord's alarm. "A Thief in the Night" has proven the most durable of Christian videos over the years and has become a kind of underground Christian classic known to most fundamentalists.

Larry was transfixed by the film. He was instantly filled with the Spirit and accepted Jesus into his heart at that very moment. He has never strayed since. He got out of acting and into accounting, returned to school, and eventually married Ellen. He kept his faith cohesive by regular attendance at a church he and Ellen found but more importantly by their intense work at Grady House. He could not believe his luck. He kept waiting for the day when he would wake up to find things had changed for the worse. It was all too good to be true. Somewhat curiously, however, given the role of "A Thief in the Night" in his conversion experience, Larry had trouble talking about and was distinctly uninterested in issues of the end times. "I'm not future oriented," he said. He even claimed to have no fear at all of death, individual or collective. With a self-satisfied grin on his face, one that contradicted his words, he even said he had never feared death as a child. Once his grandmother died but it was "no big deal" for him. He said he "just doesn't care about such issues" as death, the return of Jesus, or tribulation. He immediately added, playing student to me as professor, that he wanted to learn more about these issues and planned to take a Bible course on Revelation before too long. But that was an afterthought. In fact, the end times did not play in Larry's head. It seemed he was too young, now too full of his own promise in business, too happy with the relief at being saved from the icy waters of the East River and saved again by his faith in Jesus.

Death of the self for fundamentalists, however, is more than a personal experience. The world is also dying. The personal and collective become mirrors of mutual despair. It is a profoundly painful existential dilemma. Cynthia, a Baptist in her late thirties from St. Paul's, grew up in a Christian home with parents she idealized. She accepted Jesus at eleven. She said that actually she was aware of her need for the four or five years before that. Every night the family prayed together and the parents read Bible stories to the kids. She thought constantly of God. "And so when I lay in my bed at night there would be times that I would be really fearful and I know now that it was the Spirit of God that was convicting me and showing me my need." Cynthia's dread of death, of "not knowing my destiny," had, as well, a connection to fears of ultimate human endings. She felt drawn to Jesus as a way out of these fears, of finding meaning. She had a fear of being "eternally lost" and of "eternal death, a sense of dying never ending." "It's torment," she said directly.

What was existential for Cynthia was more explicitly communal for Reverend Dean. For the most part this appealing minister based his motivation for conversion in personal issues of vitality and rebirth. But in a subtle way Reverend Dean felt deeply ultimate issues of human survival. A month before his conversion he chanced on a magazine with articles by leading end time commentators like Hal Lindsey. The message at first terrified him—he "had some thoughts about suicide" which could have been in part a reaction to his mother's unspecified sickness that year—but it also opened him up for conversion. Lindsey links the symbolic end time rhetoric in the book of Revelation with the more immediate political world of the early 1970s, the cold war, and the threat of nuclear annihilation. His work makes the metaphorical concrete. The end could be imagined. Those images of collective death, working together in the various dimensions of his personal crisis, finally brought Reverend Dean to his knees. It was an existential crisis. He was then ready for the full impact of the Pentecostal community into which he happened to be thrown a month later. He was saved and got his life together and has served in the church ever since.

Nigel, in turn, stressed that the actual experience of death was something he, like any sane person, feared. But death itself will be transcended in his mind through the return of Jesus, he said. And that could happen tomorrow, or anytime, he added, "through the advent of my death," a phrasing that suggests a linking of himself with God. Since the return of Jesus marks the end of human history, its image freed Nigel from death in quite concrete ways. "That was really the motivation behind my getting serious with God," he noted. Not only because he felt a "deep sense of emptiness" in his life, "but knowing that, you know, Christ is coming back at some point and I don't want to stand before him and say, you know, I'm sorry about this and I'm sorry about that, you know. I wanna stand before him having, at least to the best of my ability, lived the life that he would want me to have lived." Conversion united the separate strands of Nigel's self into a meaningful cohesive whole.

The broken narrative is the defining characteristic, spiritually and emotionally, for fundamentalists. The past is bad and worthless, even tainted with death. One yearns for transformation. The individual believer struggles with personal sin, a struggle expressed collectively as a cosmic battle between the forces of good and evil. The converted claim to find salvation from their suffering in the born-again experience. But radical divisions in the self are grounded in trauma, which can operate in personal and idiosyncratic ways but can also be based in collective experience. The born-again experience, which is an attempt to heal the broken narrative, is also a direct religious response to our common traumas.

2

ULTIMATE
THREATS

MARY. Mary was a thirty-two-year-old white woman who had lived in New York City for a little over a decade at the time of my interviews with her. She had a beautiful singing voice and was the lead singer in the tiny Abiding Light choir. Mary stood erect on the podium as she lifted her hands in supplication and lustily praised Jesus in song. She often threw back her tousled blonde hair when she was carried away by the Spirit. Sometimes her dress also got thrown in disarray from her vigorous movements both in song and prayer. No one sang louder or prayed harder than Mary.

Mary seemed frantic to straighten out the narrative sequence of end time things, to clarify the meaning and inner logic of human history. The thought of Jesus' return, for example, reminded her of the signs of his second coming, which in turn means the end of human folly, sin, pain, and death itself. If you can read scripture with the

Holy Spirit in you, she said, you would see not just the famines, the wars and rumors of wars, and the earthquakes—those specific "signs" mentioned in Matthew 24:6–7—but also the "change in human nature that's occurring." As she said in a (somewhat confused) torrent of thoughts: "Human nature in the twentieth century has taken on a distinctly more with existentialism on downwards, there's been a plunge . . . you know, and also, it seems, that man, as an animal, has more to his plus than ever before, but his decided minus, his atrocities, man-to-man, are blossoming." And she continued: "Men will be lovers of themselves, boasters, they will be high minded, they will be traitorous, the love of many will grow cold, they will be disobedient to parents."

"In this world," Mary lamented, "you will have tribulation," a thought that led her to identify another sign, namely that people are so full of despair and fear that they are flocking into psychiatry and psychology. "If this country gets invaded, we'd lose because all the man force is lying on a couch somewhere being counseled." We have lost our resolve. We are all "into ourselves." If we had to call up recruits they would all be "wimps." Maybe there's a "fighting tiger" hidden deep inside the American soul, but she doubted it. The sins of modern culture abounded in Mary's mind as further signs. "In America we are just fat cats." It's just like in ancient Greece and Rome, where they had pedophilia, homosexuality, an advanced state of art and culture, and "vomitoriums." Her idiosyncratic sequence of horrors reflected her own concerns, for she added: "I have a weight problem, I know." Man is not magnificent, she said. Just go take the subway at 42nd Street and watch people claw each other getting onto the train. "That's really a good sign. You go and examine people at rush hour." They're even eating children in California, she said in an extraordinary associative leap. "Sacrifices . . . we look forward to the end."

These end times will be excruciatingly violent in Mary's scheme of things; she never lost sight of the central role of the violence that will be necessary to overthrow human history and move into God's redemptive time. On all issues Mary spoke with authority, for knowledge of scripture and prophecy gave her more than a hint of divine intention. She was at one with God's knowledge and grand plan. Yet her very psychological closeness to God created a dilemma for Mary: she tended to shape God in her own uncertain image. Mary thus seemed to doubt whether God actually knew what he was up to. He was anxious about the onrush of events, unhappy with human evil and the course of history, but somewhat confused about what to do and when to do it. Even his knowledge of the future was not much greater than Mary's. He knew "the end of things from the beginning" and had "foreknowledge," and yet, though he would have peace, he seemed unable to prevent imminent nuclear destruction.

Nuclear threat worked in Mary's imagination in complicated ways. Her Christian fundamentalist ideology served to absorb and contain the terrors of ultimate destruction that she had so actively let into her thinking. A clue to this arcane connection lay in the way she contradicted her end time story as her feelings about nuclear threat changed in different interviews. That threat first emerged early on in my first conversation with her. She then seemed quite clear about the certainty of nuclear war. As one of the "signs" of the approaching end times, Mary mentioned "war materials" that now make it possible for us to "annihilate" ourselves. I asked her about her choice of verbs, and she said spontaneously that she expected World War III and a nuclear holocaust. "I definitely believe it," she said. "I believe it with all my heart." For one thing, a depression greater than that of the 1930s is threatened (which had some kind of special meaning for her), and "I see a lot of baby boys born, Chuck, I see baby boys being plopped out all over the place."

Astounded, I put the logic of her thought into more general terms: "You think," in other words, that "the Lord is bringing more boys [into the world] because there's going to be a war?" She said, "Absolutely," and continued, "There's going to be a great fight." Humans are not going to push the button and blow up the world, but we will come close to it. "I believe there will be contained nuclear warfare." "There are going to be a number of nuclear wars," she said, though the "big one" at Armageddon is not necessarily going to be nuclear. It will be when Jesus will finally "triumph over evil," and it will be violent in ways we cannot even conceive. As reborn Christians we are "aliens in the scripture," said Mary in her expressive way. We are not of this world, only in it. We are born "from above" in the "Spirit of God." Our bodies will either "rot in the ground" or "get blown up." But we also have spirits. And these are eternal, even there now, "seated in heavenly places." We already have "conversations that are in heaven."

Mary's apocalyptic language was generally laced with nuclear allusions. She referred once, for example, to Ezekiel's prophecies of "flesh coming off bone, eye sockets—eyes dissolving in the eye socket, and this sort of thing—and you look at a nuclear poisoning victim, someone who has been through a—even Chernobyl—you know if you were standing nearby, see what you get in a nuclear warfare." This vivid description of the effects of nuclear poisoning in a text several thousand years old evoked for Mary the return of Jesus in prophecy. "You see the Lord's return as it is prophesied," she said. "He will return to Mount Olive [in present-day Israel]," which will also be the site of the "great and mighty" battle against Antichrist. And the "primary catalyst" for all these developments, she continued, leaning forward earnestly, is oil. It complicates everything in relation to Israel and centers world tensions on the Middle East. Russia has a "keen clear eye on this whole Persian Gulf area." It is a "hotbed of dissension and unrest" and has been that way for centuries. The battle is for water, for land, and for oil. All the forces are going to "converge" there, because we are depleting, "you know, we just deplete."

One could say Mary's end time rhetoric was in a nuclear key. In one tumult of associations about the end times, she noted, evoking Ezekiel 22:20–22 and 2 Peter 3:10, that the Lord will "destroy this world and heaven by fire, melt it down, and there will arise a new city, the new Jerusalem." At another time she noted that there have been endings of civilizations but not yet an "ultimate, final end." On the other hand, she added astutely, "there has never been an atomic age." We live in a hard time when "little winds of war start whispering" (her own version of Matthew 24:6) and small conflicts become big ones and we risk blowing up the whole world. In general, Mary's mind turned on "huge battles" and "nuclear holocaust that's going to blast off everybody." Such thoughts vividly occupied her imagination. Her prophetic and redemptive vision was nuclearized. There is going to be "suffering," she said typically, "suffering, and many calamities."

There was, however, no simple way that nuclear violence intersected with Mary's sense of the future revelation of God's purpose. Without doubt she had fully taken in the violence of nuclear threat and given it a place in her end time story. In her first pass at these issues, Mary argued that some kind of nuclear conflict is inevitable and will mark the process of transition out of human history and into God's time. That battle at Armageddon will, however, be a "showdown in the OK Corral in Israel," violent in ways that we cannot even comprehend. Nuclear war, in other words, begins the process of God's final revelation but cannot conclude it. Mary made it clear that God needs to preserve the earth for Jesus to rule over during the millennium; he cannot allow a complete holocaust. She was clearly relieved when she sorted all this out, connecting Antichrist and the end of human history with limited nuclear war, and preserving the final battle for God's mysterious ways. Things seemed in order, and she was calm.

And yet during her second interview, Mary contradicted her earlier account of the certainty of nuclear war. In discussing Antichrist then, for example, she noted that part of his deception of the world in his self-presentation as a man of peace will be that he will purposely avert World War III and a nuclear holocaust. She even easily changed her mind about God's destructive attitude toward humanity at one point. She described God's fury at the way man (or subtextually, the Jews) broke his promises and allowed Jesus to endure "untold sufferings." Then why not just wipe out humanity? she asked herself. It is because "God restrains himself." He is willing to wait for a faithful people who will worship him. He has always been seeking that, "from the time he taught Adam to worship in the Garden."

Psychologically, this contradiction and conflict are part of the same inner thought process. For Mary, the image of nuclear destruction both demands a central place in her end time story as a way of taming it, and yet is so terrifying that it cannot stay put. Nuclear images, which "fit" the destructive images of the book of Revelation so accurately, feed apocalyptic musings. But the anxiety caused by these death-related imaginings can easily force a reworking of the end time story to calm fears. Mary's future vision, which is full of nuclear imagery, thus alternated between normalizing nuclear threat (a limited nuclear war will occur but God's violence at Armageddon will be greater and will not destroy the earth for Jesus) and reworking her idea of Antichrist to take out nuclear war altogether from her end time story. In her decidedly human contradiction lay the deepest level of a psychological attempt to bring together apocalyptic faith and an awareness of nuclear threat.

I asked if she was afraid of all the horrible things that are to happen in the end times. She said she feared only for all those who will suffer and die. For herself she feared nothing. She would be delighted at being a martyr and having her hands sawed off. ("You know, the gift of martyrdom" to which she was drawn: "Peter, you know, he blundered, he made dreadful mistakes, he put his foot in his mouth all the time, but after the baptism in the Holy Spirit he was able to get up and preach and then go and get crucified upside downwards for the Lord and [not] deny him then.") Mary's faith made her confident that she would reign supreme with Jesus. She felt she had been persecuted some for her faith and therefore knew what it was all about, even though she had not shed any blood. But she stood prepared: "In the end times there are going to be many persecuted for his name."

Mary was raised in Georgia as a Baptist. Her mother was the apparent source of strength in the family, and Mary's own religiosity seemed to connect her to her mother in special ways. As a strictly observant Baptist, the mother never washed clothes, worked, or allowed Mary to play in any way on Sundays. Mary expressed some ambivalence about the fact that she was never taken to the beach or the movies on Sundays but then immediately praised the way the sabbath was observed in her family.

Mary's father was an alcoholic. It clearly pained Mary to talk about this fact of her family life, and it only emerged in the context of relating how he was not saved and required her constant prayers. Immediately after saying it, however, she rattled off his positive aspects ("He's the most intelligent man I ever met"; "He's the funniest man I know"; and "He says some shrewd things"). It seemed Mary did not want to acknowledge her anger or disappointment in him, though these found reluctant expression. After she said he was not a Christian, I asked her if that bothered her. She said no, but a minute or so later, in another context, indicated that "he doesn't believe like I do." Her father was not even a "nominal Christian" but a complete heathen. But she had hope for him. She was convinced he would be reached, "as difficult and downtrodden as he is." We can be certain of that, she said, an idea that switched on her believing self. "He [God] knows us by name. He knows the hairs on our head," she said, alluding to Matthew 10:30. "He knows. He's intimately acquainted with the way, your fabric, your emotional framework, and he will reach that."

Mary's early life seemed full of terrors. Her feelings about her father and her ambivalent identification with her mother filled her life with stress. From an early age she was full of apocalyptic dread that of course drew energy from her southern Baptist environment and which she connected with events in the world. She related, for example, feeling certain the world would end during the Cuban missile crisis and recalled hiding under her grandmother's dining room table at age six as protection against the bombs raining in from ninety miles off the coast of Florida. "I thought we were going to get bombed. Cuba's not far away. It's right off Florida. You know, this is it. This is the end. I was terrified."

During her adolescence, Mary fell away from the church in what she described as a period of "self-indulgence" and "fascination with herself" as she discovered her abilities as a singer. She became a "cynic." She was ambitious, self-absorbed, and a "Sunday School drop-out." In fact she had quite a remarkable mezzo-soprano voice that ranged widely and could subtly explore nuances of musical expression. She performed often in local theater and became well known regionally. She aspired to an opera career; it is indeed easy to imagine her as a blonde diva, wrapped in purple robes, singing her swansong as she lay dying in some nineteenth-century Italian opera. From her perspective now, however, the discovery of her voice brought a large degree of narcissistic absorption that took her away from God. The classic definition of sin for believing Christians is just such a separation. Mary felt it keenly, as she drew away from religion and the oppressive closeness of her parents, even though she never entirely (and certainly never formally) left the church. But in such a strict Baptist world that defined boundaries so narrowly Mary pushed up against the limits of what was possible. Mary's mother fought vigorously against her daughter's move away from faith. When Mary told her mother at thirteen that she didn't believe in the Noah and the Ark story, the mother "fell on the floor and screamed and cried before Sunday dinner and said, 'I created an atheist.'"

Singing brought Mary to New York and the Juilliard School, a long way from west Georgia. Juilliard is a part of the Kennedy Center for the Performing Arts and is widely recognized as probably the best conservatory of music in the country. Singers come there to study from all over the world. It is a highly competitive and decidedly secular world, very much a part of the frantic art scene in New York. During her training things seemed to go well for Mary and she showed promise. She even got "some debuts and some works with some orchestras and things." She dreamed reasonably of getting one of the 125 or so jobs in opera in the city upon her graduation, even though she realized New York has at least five thousand good singers. She didn't make it.

Mary's failure to make it as an opera singer caused the great trauma in her life. Everything she had aspired to for over a decade was a failure. Life seemed worthless, and she was completely adrift. "God was taking me out in the desert and tumbling me and humbling me," she said. Without a career she also had no means of support, and soon fell into working as a maid. She ended up "cleaning toilets for millionaires on the Upper East Side" to survive. She wasn't singing, she had no career, she was far from home and family, she was working at humiliating tasks just to eat, and she was alone and alienated in a great big, terrifying city.

She resolved that crisis in her life when she was reborn and became a "follower of Jesus" in the October following her June graduation from Juilliard. The Holy Spirit "buckled" her by the "scruff of the neck" and brought her the "blessing" of her life. It was a blinding moment of truth for her. That was when she found Abiding Light, her sacred home from which she has not since strayed. She kept free

of what she called the "New York Christian revolving door thing."
During the week (besides the Tuesday evening prayer service at her
church) she also attended and sang in the choir of the "Jews for Jesus" ministry; participated in the "Arabs for Jesus" at times; and
was the pianist of a small church on Sunday morning.

Her dream was to become a full-time minister. She already held a
"Christian Women's Permit." She was not certain she wanted her
own congregation but was sure that she wanted to "itinerate as an
evangelist." She had already visited seven countries and she went
every year to the United Kingdom with the "Billy Graham Mission
England." She had, she said, a "deep burden on my heart for this
particular country." What drew her to England is that it has had a
"massive, culture-transforming revival" every century for eight
hundred years—except in the twentieth century. This absence
weighs "heavy" on Billy Graham's heart; he's been leading revivals
in England for some thirty years and has not seen a change. Mary
felt chosen to join in his efforts there.

There was an important continuity of self in the reborn Mary.
Singing still defined her life. She had to give up dreams of opera but
found abundant opportunity for creative self-expression and even
performance in the church and in "religious gigs" in the city, as well
as some summer stock throughout New England. Even in the millionaires' homes where she worked her new centeredness brought
her back to familiar territory: she stopped cleaning toilets and became a kind of nanny and piano teacher for the children of several
families.

Mary's subjective sense of change at her religious rebirth, on the
other hand, was quite dramatic. She contrasted her Christian status
as a "nominal adherent to a congregation" before being reborn with
becoming a "real Christian" afterward, which related to the whole
issue of being "saved." She connected what might be called her sense
of an "authentic self" with her childhood innocence. What she was
doing today, she said, was like what she did between three and five,
when she was a "very pure child" and "loved singing, playing the
piano, doing plays." It was as though, in finding Jesus, she had found
herself as she once was, a self she had lost in her ambitions to become

an opera star but one that continued to exist and, with God's help, could be expressed.

Mary's shifting from bad to good selves with her conversion and a rediscovery of something authentic in her earliest experience could not always hold off the demons. She let slip once that, since her conversion, "I'm a much worse person." She then explained that her increased awareness of the majesty of Jesus made her more conscious of her own insignificance, which seemed to express a basic self-loathing. After a lengthy discussion of the sins of modern life and the signs of the end everywhere, for example, she noted how humans are depraved. "I don't believe there is one good thing in me," she said. Then she told a story that probably has elements of fantasy in it and may have served her as an improvised parable. She was once acting in a play, she said, and, as a part of her role, she wore a cheap ring that she didn't bother to take off between performances. Evidently, her skin reacts powerfully to the chemicals in such metals. One day she was ironing and smelled something awful. Her first thought was "good grief, no deodorant today." It seemed to affect the whole apartment. She decided to go wash, and while scrubbing her hands accidentally loosened her ring. In horror (but for some reason without any pain) she saw that her flesh under where the ring had been was literally rotting away. The smell had been from her decaying body.

Mary drew a religious message from the story: "Our bodies decay while the spirit lives on." But the image that stayed with her was that her body was worthless and going to rot. "You, me, even Joan Collins, will all rot." This body is going to stink. Our righteousness is but "filthy rags." We bring nothing to our redemption (which she repeated). And yet in that salvation lay her hope for renewal and eternal life, which for her moved with apocalyptic urgency. It is "imminent, really imminent," though "we might have one hundred fifty or two hundred more [years]." Who knows or really cares, she asked rather falsely, for in fact she cared a great deal. But, like other fundamentalists I talked to, she covered her predictions of immediacy in order not to seem to be speaking for God. "He knows all generations," she said. He knows when to return. And he is "always on time." Whenever it is "right" he will return. Until then we only "occupy" and do what he told us to do by going into the world to preach his word.

Still: "Not a day goes by that I don't think about it [the return of Jesus]," she said, which suggested the separateness of what might be called her end time self, a split-off part of her being that is grounded in the Christian tradition. This split-off part of herself was projected forward into her image of the millennium, which was not a place with "clouds, harps necessarily, and angels with big floppy wings." It was instead a city for those "redeemed people of God, where the whole light of the place is the light of Jesus Christ." If you receive his gift, if the Holy Spirit comes and dwells within you, then you have the promise of millennial renewal and eternal life. But if you reject that gift, she said ominously, you go where the "worm never dies."

NUCLEAR AND ENVIRONMENTAL THREATS

Many of my fundamentalist interviews were conducted in the waning years of the cold war, which partly explains the emphasis in them on images of nuclear threat, something Daniel Yankelovich (using a different method) emphasized in 1984 was firmly rooted in the culture.[1] With many people I talked with, however, I also uncovered a subtle shift in the late 1980s from nuclear to environmental concerns.[2] This shift suggests to me that fundamentalists are oriented to collective death, which they describe in terms of their theology and their specific personal concerns. Their beliefs, in part, neutralize the threat. In their groping attempt to relate their beliefs to ultimate dangers, they are at least dealing with authentic issues—unlike most of our culture, which foolishly acts as though the end of the cold war has wiped out nuclear threat, even though tens of thousands of warheads remain in the hands of a widening circle of unsavory characters and even though nuclear power (including the waste it generates) continues to present the greatest of all environmental threats. To end history slowly, choking from pollution or dying early from unnatural cancers, poses threats of the same kind of absurd death as nuclear war. Thus, nuclear issues in my interviews are only seemingly dated; the psychological processes and spiritual beliefs that underlie Mary's nuclear vision remain as relevant now as they were six years ago. Were I to conduct interviews today, though, I believe environmental threat would probably occupy the imagination of fundamentalists with greater salience, though in fact both nuclear and environmental threats are closely related images of ultimate destruction, and in the case of nuclear power (Chernobyl) they become one and the same.

The range of imagery and the depth of fear I encountered about ultimate destruction, particularly by nuclear weapons, was quite remarkable. Mary, although unusually evocative, was hardly exceptional in this regard. For example, Reverend Dean noted that "The potential [for destruction exists] . . . *more now than ever.*" The end is imminent, the "time is ripe." Reverend Lester, the mid-thirties pastor of St. Paul's, said: "It could happen anytime, everything is in place. . . . All the prophecies are fulfilled for this to happen. . . . We have nuclear weapons." And: "Satan is coming with the missiles," as he said in one sermon. The Reverend Charles of Calvary Church linked his nuclear themes to contemporary developments in the Middle East: "Now we've got a situation and it's a key thing to watch, what's happening in the Middle East. Those Palestinians are not about to stop throwing rocks and the Israelis are not about to stop shooting them down. . . . And what they say is the worst kept secret, that Israel has the bomb. . . . It could be the fuse[3] that lights the whole thing." The specter of nuclear war cast a dark shadow. Such war seemed all but inevitable. "I don't think there's any stopping it," said Isaac, from Abiding Light. "Look around you. There are women who kill babies when they think the baby is the devil. We kill young people because there are too many people on this earth." Besides, he continued, nuclear war is close at hand. It "almost happened" several times during Reagan's years, Isaac added darkly. The nuclear concerns of fundamentalists were diverse and often touched issues more central to the post–cold war era. Nigel located his imaginings primarily in terms of proliferation: "I'm sure that some third-world country is going to let one loose somewhere."

Much of the Bible, as they saw it, confirmed a sense of an imminent nuclear end. Reverend Lester, for example, in the middle of an interview, noted that "the Bible is explicit about bombs," as he reached for his well-worn book and quoted 2 Peter 3:10: "The heavens shall pass away with a great noise, and the elements shall melt with fervent heat, the earth also and the works that are therein shall be burned up." It's talking here about the "scientific word," he said. "We are talking about hydrogen bombs. We are talking about atomic bombs, nuclear warheads." Ordinary believers as well found the same confirmation of their nuclear imaginings in the Bible. Isaac specifically connected the discussion in Revelation about the "sores on a man's body" and the "skin coming off" with radiation sickness. "Even Carl Sagan," he said, "talks about the earth burning up and the ashes rising to form a shadow over the earth. That's in Revelation." Sam added that "the Bible talks about heat and fire . . . [which] clearly fits in with our capacity to blow ourselves up nuclearly." Wilma nervously declared, "I believe [nuclear weapons] are part of the end time scenario. . . . He said it won't be by water, it will be fire and I believe that's going to happen." The Bible doesn't say it's going to be a nuclear war, she added, but it's "going to burn." It "could be a bomb, because the Bible says the earth shall burn with fire. Could be a bomb."

The end time process, based as it is in apocalyptic texts, makes special sense in terms of nuclear destruction. The book of Revelation reads for many fundamentalists as a handbook of nuclear themes. The book's prophecy of doom ends in a great judgment (Chapter 20) that finally separates out good from evil and rewards believers with a secure place in heaven. The logic of the theology, therefore, makes destruction the necessary precursor to salvation. But destruction has to be justified. Here the theory turns to human sin and our evil ways. The signs are everywhere, though once again they are often nuclearized. For example, "these weapons are being advanced so fast," Deborah said, "we're more or less going down the road of destruction." Otto even suggested that "the bomb has caused an acceleration of all that's going on." Everything seems to be happening at once in his troubled mind, and the creation of the bomb lies at the center of the chaos. "All these things are just coming together and getting worse."

Fantasies about Antichrist, as well, spark thoughts about world government and nuclear destruction, an association that runs throughout popular fundamentalist texts. "The Bible speaks of one world government at the time of his [Jesus] coming back and I think the world is heading toward that," said Otto. "That may be a very important sign. We're getting to the place where people are saying, 'Well, we need just one person in control of everything.' So we eliminate the possibility of nuclear war, [have] equal food distribution, these things." The fear of nuclear war, in other words, makes "people" turn to one strong ruler who staves off nuclear conflict but also uses his power to take control of everything else, including "food distribution." Such world government, by centralizing everything, ends up creating something far worse, a monster who can then manipulate the end time events. In Otto's vision: "First you centralize the world, the technology and the government and that's what allows the Antichrist."

It is, of course, inherent human evil—aided in obscure ways by the devil working in history—that both creates nuclear weapons and threatens their use. Destruction results from our "increased wickedness," said Isaac. "Man has incredible evil in him," he continued. "We all do. And if the Christians are gone, if the people who keep telling the world about the value of man are gone, then I'm afraid to see the evil that will be unleashed [*he bangs the table*]. . . . Man will just rise up and destroy everything. For the first time in history we have the ability to destroy ourselves." Nuclear war cannot be prevented. The signs of it and of the end in general are much too pervasive. Furthermore, the corruption and moral deadness of human society works for evil and destructive purposes in the world. Frank mused, weaving nuclear weapons into the message in Revelation 21:1: "At some point there will be a new heaven and earth . . . the old heaven and earth just passing away completely. . . . Nuclear war, to a certain extent we can picture it happening. There are real possibilities." As Wilma said, in her quietly dramatic tone: "Burning will cleanse the earth."

Chernobyl, in turn, was the environmental image of nuclear power gone awry, the disastrous and unsuccessful attempt to harness the knowledge of the atom. Among fundamentalists, though important, it was less often evoked on its own terms than as part of an overall image of environmental destruction. As Isaac astutely put it: "I don't even know if God needs nuclear weapons, but we do see a period in the history right now that man can destroy himself, he can destroy a third of the earth, he can destroy." Isaac's third part of destruction was an obscure reference to the successive waves of violence that unfold in Revelation in what might be termed a "biblical genocide."[4] Otto had a haunting sense of pressing toward the Apocalypse, which he was sure will bring worldwide death and destruction. He calculated precisely the rolling waves of death in Revelation. "It [the Bible] talks about one place where He sends out judgment over one quarter of the earth to kill. That means to kill one quarter of the earth. At another place it talks about . . . killing over one third of the earth, so if you take one quarter, you have three quarters left, and if you take one third of three quarters you have half the population gone." I asked him how the idea of all those people dying made him feel. He answered calmly: "Concerned, I guess, in a way, and yet, at times, I think the way the scripture points, brings it out, is that when it happens, it will be a judgment that is just." Those who refuse to accept Jesus into their hearts, in other words, shall justly die. Nearly everyone on the earth has had an opportunity to know Christ; even in grass huts, Otto said, there are portable TVs on which they can watch Billy Graham or Jimmy Swaggart. Everyone has the chance to believe. "Then it's up to them," he said darkly, "whether they accept or not."

Otto's embrace of end time violence, as it was with most fundamentalists I met, had an oddly dissociated quality. He was personally a gentle man, yet he nourished in his mind a stirring cauldron of images of end time destruction. After my first interview with him in which he laid out the violence of the end justified by human sin and disbelief, Otto told me a touching story of the crib death of one of his children. It was just after he was out of Bible school and he had a milk route. His wife thought for once she was getting a chance to sleep in. The baby was nineteen days old. By the time she found the baby it was long since dead and was already turning blue. He said that only now, some twenty years later, can he tell the story without emotion, and for years it affected his and his wife's ability to sleep easily without constantly checking the other children. This same man can have God wipe out 2.5 billion people without blinking an eye because they are not saved.

But even Otto did not think God would let humans destroy the earth in a nuclear holocaust. "I really don't think man's going to blow this world up," he said. "Because the scriptures speak of God judging it. And I feel there has to be something for God to judge [*he laughed*], so I don't see how . . . I really don't . . . the book of Genesis talks about God judging Sodom and Gomorrah. He didn't need a nuclear bomb to pour out fire and brimstone on Sodom and Gomorrah." Mary also moved easily back and forth between nuclear and environmental imagery of destruction. No one had more nuclear themes in their end time story. But even she believed that the battle of Armageddon between the forces of good and evil at the end of the period of tribulation would be somehow *even worse* than nuclear war.

In fact, most fundamentalists show considerable equivocation about the end, mixing a very human kind of hope that the world will not self-destruct with a conviction that the end is prophetically assured. In this respect they sometimes suggested that God would prevent the end of the world. A kernel of this idea lies in Isaac's statement that "I don't even know if God needs nuclear weapons." Similarly, Nigel saw nuclear weapons as superfluous to God's plan: "If he wanted to destroy this earth, he could do it in a second. He doesn't need nuclear arms. . . . He created it all, he could certainly destroy it all." Otto commented: "He could use nuclear bombs, no question, but I don't think he needs that." Reverend Dean also cautioned against dwelling on the nuclear end time scenario: "When you emphasize to what extent nuclear activities take place, that's strictly speculation." Yet he implied that humans can do little to alter the end time course when he said: "Again God's plan is going to be perfected regardless of what weaponry man may have."

Some people expressed the hope that God would step in to prevent complete destruction. Reverend Dean stated: "Well, I don't think the planet is going to be annihilated because God, he made it, he'll take care of it." Frank suggested that "when things get to the point where it is utterly and completely hopeless, at least as far as the Bible teaches, that's when Jesus returns . . . and intervenes at what seems like the moment of utter despair for the planet." Yet, as he also admitted, "It's hard in our natural understanding to picture God coming down out of the sky, invading, and stopping the ultimate war. Some people would laugh at that, you know." Deborah echoed this idea: "He knows what our potential is to destroy ourselves and I think even with all these nuclear plants and everything else . . . you know, exposure to radiation and all that . . . he realizes . . . he sees everything, but things we don't even think about he can see the danger. . . . I think that's why he'll come back soon. . . . He wants to curtail that. . . . We're going to destroy ourselves if God doesn't escalate the time," she said.

All these equivocating images of nuclear and other related forms of violence are part of a pervasive ambivalence on the part of fundamentalists toward end time violence. It is simply not the case that they actively want nuclear war, suffering, and widespread death to bring Jesus back sooner, which one might infer from the logic of their theology. I find reports from other researchers regarding fundamentalists' violent wishes highly suspect.[5] They seem, instead, to have an anticipation of destruction, but it is a kind of half-wish from which, once expressed, they quickly back off. The closest anyone in my study came to expressing a direct (but still qualified) desire for a nuclear war to hasten the return of Jesus was Reverend Lester: "So I'm kinda looking forward to all this stuff [nuclear destruction], to the whole thing because once the rapture takes place the church is glorified." But most fundamentalists responded, when asked, as Wilma did: "No, I don't look forward to the end. I want to live, don't you? I love life. I always thank God for life."

There was, however, a good deal of confusion about the place of nuclear violence in their end time musings. "I don't think it scares people anymore, you know," said Deborah in an ambivalent tone. "Weapons are being advanced so fast it's almost like you become hardened. Like if it's going to happen, it's going to happen. What can you do about it by worrying about it? Maybe people don't think about that, but in the papers now, how can you not." And Sam replied, when asked whether he was frightened by nuclear destruction: "Not a great deal . . . uh . . . you know obviously, [I'm] going to go in twenty or thirty or forty or whatever number of years. . . . And I think that the world is going to end at some point. I would rather have it later than sooner, for my [*nervous laughter*] for the sake of my children and now one grandchild, but I don't stay awake at night or anything like that, worried and concerned about, you know, the world being blown up. It might be a lot quicker way to go than cancer, but [*and he laughs again*] . . ."

Having let in the terror, even if partial and numbed, my respondents struggled constantly with issues of efficacy. How should one live in the end times? How does one prepare? What obligations exist toward one's fellow humans? What difference does life make? For many, especially white fundamentalists, a political quietism prevailed, except on selected issues that they would designate "spiritual," like abortion, pornography, and prayer in the schools. On the whole, one does not generally associate social action with fundamentalists, though some are involved intermittently in politics (the 1992 Republican National Convention, for example). An important exception, as we will see in a later chapter, was Reverend Charles, who found a special kind of hope in these end times. For him the sense of being on the brink was enormously vitalizing. It gave life a sense of permanent urgency, and the chance of "reaping an end time harvest." He should, perhaps, have been in a state of despair and hopelessness. In fact, exactly the opposite was true. "This is the time to get *involved*," he said with enthusiasm.

But for most fundamentalists nuclear threat had a deadening effect, even if a certain excitement was also mixed with the fear. Reverend Dean believed the effects of nuclear threat have been to wipe out a sense of future. "We have a generation of young people," he said, "that for the first time feel that they don't have a future." The young don't think they will grow up to marry and have children, and "in many cases" they don't even think "they'll live through high school." It was a grim image.

Frank, from St. Paul's, likewise related the pain of living with nuclear threat. He talked of his childhood and how wrenching it had been when both his paternal grandfather and maternal grandmother died within a few weeks of each other when he was fifteen. Both had been vital in his life, almost more important than his parents. His grandfather had been a spiritual model. And his "Nana" had cared for him for many years after school because his mother worked. Oddly, though, when Frank talked of his grandparents and their almost simultaneous deaths, he seemed impatient to get on to other topics: "I don't know where this is really going in terms of the past, but that's [all there is]," he said, letting his sentence trail off. He also had a friend who had been killed, though he was just as numb to that.

The death that really haunted Frank, a man of unusually intense spiritual longings, was collective death. "What is it that so fascinates me about atomic bombs?" he asked himself. "I mean, even when I was a kid, I would go to the library and look at the pictures and read the stories about it. And it was horrible. It was horrible . . . there's something so powerful about it that it just evokes fear and awe." It seemed Frank's search in the library followed his first encounter with nuclear issues, which was some unit in fourth or fifth grade dealing with Hiroshima and Nagasaki. Somehow that touched a powerful chord in him. Even today, when he sees a clip of something nuclear on TV, it has a huge effect on him.

Yet for all the images of nuclear and environmental violence that are integral to the end time story, for all the death and destruction during the period of tribulation that marks the end of human history, fundamentalists still grapple with ways to soften the story, even to the point of contradiction, and force their narrative to yield hope for the earth where it seems most unlikely. For many it is a question of emphasis: the violence of tribulation during which the blood will run up the bridles of horses or the regenerative image of Jesus descending from the clouds to a cleansed but preserved earth over which he will rule with the faithful. The difference in emphasis corresponds in large part to the class position of respondents. Sam and Monroe, both well educated, once successful, and still financially secure men, moved relatively quickly through the violence of the end times to images of hope in the millennium and in heaven. In contrast, Otto, Mary, and others dwelt on the violence of the end, and often got stuck on it. Their lives at the bottom of the social scale were full of struggle and the forces of society and history often seemed to work against their best interests. It was interesting, however, that they, too, sought to embrace images of the earth's renewal. Mary beamed with excitement as she described the millennium, and Otto expected to be raptured within the decade.

3

THE
NEW SELF

MONROE. In Monroe's apocalypticism, the millennium was a kind of Christian Wall Street. The first thing he said about it was that during the thousand years of Jesus' reign the earth is going to have "super productivity." Believers who will rule with Jesus then will have bodily form as Christ did after the resurrection; they will also "do work, will perform work." The GNP during the millennium will be "astounding."

Such fantasies are not really so surprising. The concept of the millennium for fundamentalists lends itself to highly subjective constructions, since it is not literally biblical; that is, the literal form of the millennium is nowhere explicitly described in the Bible (compared, for example, with the Garden of Eden). It is necessarily left to imagination how earthly life continues with Jesus as the ruling king, whether there is money and work, and whether something like the subway system continues. Monroe was perhaps more concrete than most in the projection of his own experience into his imaginings about the millennium, but the way he extended his world into God's space in no way compromised the boundaries of fundamentalist ideology. Nor was Monroe altogether a new Christian phenomenon in this regard. Augustine, in *The City of God*, details a remarkably unequal distribution of "grades of honour and glory" in the Heavenly City. There will definitely be such distinctions, he says, "of that there can be no doubt."[1]

The explicitness of Monroe's future narrative was an integral part of the doubts he harbored about the meaning of life that had led to his conversion experience in the first place. He had to tie down the apocalyptic, because everything else closer at hand was so problematic. But the same doubts that had forced his radical midlife transformation carried over into his thinking about end time issues. As he described the rapture to me, for example, he said the "saints" will be called to meet Christ in the air (which is the conventional definition). In this way, he said, they avoid the death and suffering of the tribulation. I asked him then what happens to someone who accepts Jesus after the rapture but during the period of tribulation. He said, nervously, that some people will convert during tribulation and live into the millennium itself. These new Christians will then continue to have children, and to die, though the "resurrected saints" (who return to earth with Jesus after the tribulation) will do neither. But even as he said it he realized his answer only restated the problem, which addressed the finality of the rapture. Once history as we know it is over with, can there even be such a thing as a *new* Christian? If one can convert once the terrors of tribulation commence, can such Christians later be saved from death? If so, the whole system begins to crumble, especially the absolute necessity of conversion now, which was, of course, the whole focus of Monroe's life work. Indeed, he mused in some confusion, why would new Christians who convert after the rapture hold onto their faith without any hope of heavenly reward or an end to their separation from the "saints" who rule with Jesus as king? His effort to describe the Apocalypse in concrete detail had backfired and he quickly backed off from his speculations: "How all that works out, I'm not certain."

This confusion in end time details threw Monroe into a small state of panic. If he was wrong about converted Christians, maybe he was wrong in other ways too? Maybe death is not conquered? Maybe the theory of premillennial dispensationalism itself is mistaken? In the room where we talked, he leaned forward intensely and knitted his brow in deep thought. He tried again to go through what happens, but this time he got even more confused. For a man who was not articulate in the best of circumstances, Monroe became barely intelligible. "My understanding," he said, is that there is not going to be sickness and "those kinds of things" and "there's not going to be death." But right away he added: "It doesn't mean some people can't die." But that in turn led to a *non sequitur* that showed a latent authoritarianism: "Christ will rule [with] an iron hand. People will be punished for doing wrong." Monroe then tried again to deal with this troubling issue of Christians who die during the millennium, and in stating the issue realized there was yet another thorny issue to face: What about the children born to these mortal Christians? Can the children be saved? Who is going to convert them? All of these concerns and questions were compressed into an otherwise confused statement: "Christians, or those Christians that made it through [to] the millennium and then through birth, people are going to be not Christians in that period because they'll be born and they'll have a choice to make."

Monroe then tried to escape his confusion by returning to a much earlier question I had asked, namely how the idea of Christ's second coming and the end of human history affected his daily existence. He said vaguely how much of scripture is revealed, and how prophecy is fulfilled. "God put it [the prophecy] there by design" as a "motivational factor." That's it, he said twice, that's it. "It's a motivational factor in my life," by which he meant prophecy motivates him as a Christian. "Okay?" he asked me and himself. "The more that I believe it, the more that my life will really be committed to Him in obedience to Him." Now Monroe was on firmer ground. He had stated a basic issue of faith and gotten away from exploring the details of his end time imagery. At last he felt a measure of security. He added: "I guess that about answers it."

In general, Monroe's literalism kept his anxiety in check. He could discuss the horrible death and destruction of the end times with marked detachment, as long as he felt he was elaborating on scripture and thus quoting God. He often introduced descriptions of violence with "It [the Bible] tells about what's going on." I felt he could almost see the passage, and I had the idea, when Monroe said this kind of thing, that immediately after the interview he would go back to the Bible and reaffirm himself in it.

> The thing that's so incredible to me, after going to school and spending all that time in the Bible, [is] that I had real confidence in taking God at his word [about] what happens when I die. . . . And when I looked at the supernatural things that he has done just in the prophecies alone in the Old Testament . . . just incredible. It's through faith, but also, faith is based on how God has operated before. I really believe Christ is going to return like he said. . . . I really think it could happen in my daughter's lifetime.

Monroe always sought to turn the metaphorical, the mystical, the poetic into the concrete. His was more than an abstract belief in "inerrancy." His belief governed how he read the Bible and taught him how to understand life after death and how to deal with daily life. During my fourth and last interview with him, when we knew each other quite well, he told me how his dying father told him that much of life is wasted on things that don't count. Monroe's response was to launch into a literal counting of his years left, translated into a count of the number of days left for him (9,000, he estimated), and what he planned for himself so that he didn't waste time. To make things count became, for Monroe, an actual counting, a way of mastering death in meaningful days. It seemed to take the pain out of death. Security thrived in the literal.

On the other hand, literalism presented Monroe (as it did Mary) with exactly the dilemma he sought to avoid. The fear of death motivated his literalism, but the imagery of destruction in the Bible that was so much a part of his life stimulated his worst fears. The torrent of violent images in Revelation holds death back from consciousness by abstracting it, except that the very experience of entering into it could, and often did, flood him. Then the personal joined the theological. The result was terror.

The apocalyptic cannot stay completely dissociated if it is to continue grounding the self and act, as Monroe put it, as a "motivator." But as soon as the end time images are let into the experience of the self, one is confronted with what the "end" really means in a personal sense. Monroe, it might be said, moved from easy dogmatism to pained confrontation. Ultimate violence was a well-grounded idea for him. We think of God as a God of love, he said, but he is also a "God of justice." When God sent Jesus he gave humans a certain time frame in which to act and make that revelation apparent to the world. But it's not going so well. "When he looks down at New York City, I honestly don't know why he doesn't just wipe it out." This thought put Monroe on a roll. They do things to each other in Times Square, he said, that animals don't do to each other. The city is filled with all these gays and lesbians, an image that made him squirm. We have to deal with the impact of the New Age movement and people like Shirley MacLaine, he said with disgust, puckering his mouth. Even so-called Christian churches are repugnant. Some don't even believe Christ is God. "It's amazing to me that God hasn't ended it."

But soon he will. And then justice will be meted out. Satan will run wild. With the saints gone (in the rapture) the rest of the people will be left to their own devices. There will be "pandemonium" and "tremendous destruction." "They'll fall by the sword," he said enthusiastically in another interview, "their little ones will be dashed to the ground, their pregnant women will be ripped open." In the tribulation, it will be worse than "you've ever seen," "beyond imagination." This deferred violence and shift in agency from himself to God allowed Monroe to separate himself from responsibility for his intense loathing for sinners, especially gays and lesbians. He didn't have to kill anyone. He could remain a relatively gentle and genial person. God punishes sinners, and he does it worse than anything we can devise, for he does it twice and forever. The apocalyptic for Monroe thus served as a vehicle for his own violence toward those whom he felt threatened his fragile self and, at the same time, protected him from having to own these feelings in any real emotional sense. Punishment was in the hands of God, who will carry it out with terrible vengeance after history ends.

When I first met Monroe at Grady House he was a handsome man in his forties with neatly trimmed hair. He wore tailored clothes and with his suit on looked the part of the top executive he once was. He had smooth skin, even features, and a highly appealing boyish enthusiasm. He greeted everyone warmly and genuinely. His hearty laugh at Bible study could often be heard across the room. Yet he could be surprisingly naive. He often acted like an older student and talked about himself as still learning the ropes in his new role as a missionary to the rich.

Monroe was somewhat overweight, which he complained about; he said it had to do with getting used to New York. At our four breakfasts together he talked each time about losing weight, his special cereal, and his concern with the calories in the cream cheese on the bagels and in the butter on the toast (as he devoured each time what struck me as surprisingly large meals). As in other spheres, Monroe longed to control his body, harness it for higher purposes, make it serve God. He also wanted to continue looking good. There is no doubt he was one of the most handsome middle-aged men in the Bible study groups. He even had money, despite his austere lifestyle.

Monroe came from a family of five in an upscale neighborhood in western Massachusetts. His father had several small but successful businesses. The family was reasonably close, certainly comfortable, together, and without any manifest problems or crises. Monroe went to a military college because he had always wanted to be a general in the army. He ended up pursuing that goal for seven years, including stints in Germany and Vietnam. After a while, however, Monroe recognized in himself that he was too money oriented and not doing everything he should to stay on track to become a general. He was not "maxing out" on his efficiency reports. It was pretty clear to him that he would have a decent career but would never make it past colonel. That was not enough. "I did not want to be a colonel in the military," he said. It was second-rate, not worth his considerable talents. He had always intended either to be a general or make a million dollars. It was time to move on and make money.

He left the army and moved to New Orleans where he had some contacts. He was recently divorced, but not long after moving south he married a beautiful woman with whom he was very much in love. He established a small business that grew quickly into a multi-million-dollar enterprise. Some thirty people worked for Monroe. He bought a magnificent home with 5,000 square feet outside the city, a 450 SE Mercedes, and began taking long vacations. It seemed on the surface that he had fulfilled all his dreams. But underneath he was deeply troubled. He was also alone. His second wife had left him.

Then one morning several Christian friends took Monroe to breakfast at an elegant restaurant in the French Quarter. They confronted their colleague bluntly: "What would happen to you if you died?" He was struck dumb. Despite all his outward success, he could not answer the question, for he had no sense of anything beyond what seemed to him his utterly meaningless existence. Monroe's friends shared certain key biblical passages, like John 14:6, when Jesus says: "I am the way, the truth, and the life: no man cometh unto the Father, but by me"; and 1 Corinthians 15:26, "The last enemy *that* shall be destroyed *is* death." In such passages Monroe discovered what he believed to be the power of Jesus and the mastery of death. Only in that faith could he find sense to life. It changed everything for him.

After he let Jesus into his heart at that breakfast, Monroe sold his business and his home and car and packed off to Dallas Seminary, the Harvard of fundamentalism, for training to become a missionary. He said even he was daunted by his new enterprise. "We always think of a missionary in Africa going around with shorts or, you know, tramping through the jungle." His parents wondered why he could not keep his business going and attend a seminary on the side in New Orleans. The final straw for his parents was that at some point not long after his conversion he had a good job offer that would have allowed him more or less to maintain continuity between his new and former selves. It was an offer to head up a group of executives in the city who had all been reborn and now wanted to run their businesses according to the teachings of the Bible. His job would have been to advise these rich and powerful businessmen on what it means to run a Christian business, to do something useful and Christian with the valuable resources God has entrusted them with. His "church" would have been CEOs in a crucial part of the new South, a small but select "congregation" that directly influenced the lives of thousands working for them. Monroe, as a former member of this small club of CEOs, would have had a good salary and could have kept his house and connections. It would have been respectable, and not only kept him out of short pants but in his dark suit.

Instead Monroe threw off everything of the world, went to seminary, and volunteered to serve out his life with a Christian organization that has evangelical programs all over the United States and the world. Monroe fantasized he would end up somewhere exotic like Russia. In any event, he would have to work as a true missionary wherever he was sent, and he would have to raise his own salary. His parents were aghast. He was once worth millions; now he would be begging. But it was precisely the totality of the change that had the most appeal for Monroe. He had been stuck in his life. Everything had failed him. Two wives had left him. He felt worthless in a mansion of plenty and utterly lonely in his fancy car. Jesus' story of the camel hit home (Matthew 19:24: "It is easier for a camel to go through the eye of a needle, than for a rich man to enter into the kingdom of God"). For Monroe it was not enough to change inside. His conversion breakfast brought him new life, he felt, but that was only the beginning. He then had to make over everything else, purge himself, be renewed. His life had to have consistency or it would have no integrity. There could be no compromises. His commitment had to be total. He "let" Jesus in and was "saved" and "reborn"; in return he "gave back" to Jesus everything he possessed.

As it happened, however, not as much changed in his financial security or relative status in society as he might perhaps have wished or secretly fantasized. He liquidated his substantial wealth but then put all the money from the sale of his business, home, and possessions into personal savings and CDs at a time of high interest rates.

He was even to remain comfortably associated with business leaders. When he graduated from seminary, he wrestled for a while with whether to go to Eastern Europe where he felt he might be effective. But then he interviewed with Grady House and felt "like, for who I am, this is the place the Lord wanted me to go." Monroe, in a phrase typical with fundamentalists, said he would "do whatever the Lord asked me to do"; that seemed to be with business executives in New York City. Although he was obliged to raise his salary through the contributions of those he converted and spiritually touched—and had strict limits on what he could draw on from his savings—he was given special permission to use the money from his savings to buy an apartment and get himself established in the city. What Monroe purchased was a beautiful one-bedroom apartment in an elegant high rise. Monroe's life and soul were full of contradictions.

That is not to say he was a hypocrite. Monroe had given his life to Christian service. His "work" was to spread the message to executives, and he put in long days making contacts, having lunches, and following up on those he converted. His apartment was lined with various multivolume commentaries on the Bible, and he spent most evenings and all his free time poring over biblical texts and pursuing their subtler meanings. On a washstand in his bathroom was a stack of daily prayers for Christians around the world, each card for a separate country. Card #53 implored the believer to pray for the faithful in Vietnam to remain true in the face of persecution; for the pastors and others now in prison there for their faith; for the growth of a "missionary vision" despite the difficulties; for the planting of churches among "tribal peoples" who have been responsive to the gospel; for the conversion of Vietnamese who have had to flee to other lands; and for the radio broadcasts beamed daily into the country. No moment was wasted. Monroe was only saved from suffocating earnestness by his self-effacing posture and warm, hearty laugh.

The contradictions in Monroe's life were, finally, what made him an interesting, complicated, and appealing figure. He was not making much money, but he also had not divested himself of his significant wealth. He once moved as a nonbeliever making money in a world of secular executives; now he continued in that world in the same costume and with many of the same rituals (lunches in fancy restaurants, golf, vacation retreats) as a missionary seeking to awaken in his colleagues a faith in and understanding of Jesus. He looked and, in most external respects, acted like any other powerful CEO in New York. In New York, he had reduced the square footage of his home but vastly increased the value of each inch of floor space. He had no car, but that is hardly uncommon in New York where it is easier to take cabs than search endlessly for parking places. And he was still without anyone to love in his life. All alone he cooked and ate and prayed in his apartment overlooking Manhattan, just as he once rattled around his huge house all by himself.

But he felt different inside. He wasn't empty; God was within. His life had a purpose, a direction. Most of all, Monroe did not dread death. Like any sane person, Monroe feared sickness and the experience of actually dying, something he went through with his father between my third and fourth interviews with him. I shared with him then my terrible feelings of loss when my father died suddenly when I was sixteen, and how it took me some fifteen years to get over it. Our mutual loss helped bring us together and bridge the gap between the fundamentalist Christian and nonbelieving researcher. Monroe talked at length of his father, what he looked like toward the end, and the joy he felt that his father had converted on his death bed. For Monroe death was not the end of everything but the beginning of meaning. He looked forward eagerly to a future filled with God, his own eternal life, and some reasonable reward for his suffering on earth. Monroe still doubted himself and would forever wonder whether he was performing as well as others. But he remained confident that in the long run things surely would work out.

I asked Monroe why he seemed so acutely concerned with ultimate meanings in his forties both before and after finding Jesus, and what, especially, was the background for his intense sense of emptiness that had resulted in his conversion experience. "Men," he said in reply, "go through, as women go through, a change of life." For the first time in his life he had been troubled by a lack of motivation. He felt "low." He was searching. All the earlier goals he had set for himself he had met (or, in his relationships, realized he would never succeed at). A lot of what he was going through right then was probably brought on by the death of a father, he added parenthetically, though it seemed mostly to come from the larger sense of being halfway through life. And "I'm halfway, by golly," Monroe said in his idiosyncratic way.

Even after becoming a Christian, Monroe told me with an evangelical edge, things don't change overnight. You have to search and study. By way of explanation he reached over for his Bible and quoted to me 1 Corinthians 2:14: "But the natural man receiveth not the things of the Spirit of God: for they are foolishness unto him: neither can he know *them*, because they are spiritually discerned." This passage was extremely important for Monroe—and for many I met and talked with at Grady House. These were generally well-educated people who read their texts seriously. Somehow they want to explain the feeling of greater understanding they have of the words of God after being reborn. They can read and comprehend what the Bible says before their conversion but they cannot fully "know" it unless in the act of reading they are filled with the Spirit; and even then it takes unending effort and continued study to "mature" in belief, to move further along what Monroe called the "spiritual journey." "This will sound hokey," he said, but all you have are words when you read the Bible as a non-Christian. There is no "supernatural sense," no "full understanding of that till you become a Christian."

The Christian world was tightly closed for Monroe in the magical power of the sacred word. When he shared "spiritual-type things" with me as a nonbeliever, "the amount of revelation that is revealed . . . is limited." The sacred word marked the boundaries of the self. Inside of that line for him lay true knowledge, fulfillment, and happiness; outside lay only ignorance and despair. This Manichaean view of things was reassuring at many levels. It defined the possibilities of the new self. Belief brought you into direct communication with the Almighty; it empowered action and banished doubt. A new world of ethics and end time hope opened up. At the same time, nonbelievers can read the same Bible and not take the same truth from it. It's only words for the nonbeliever, while the believer reads with the lens of the Holy Spirit. "It's incredible," said Monroe to me, "how passages and things in the Bible really come together after you've trusted Christ. It's a phenomenon." He really wanted me to see that, to give something to me: "When you come to place your trust in Jesus Christ," he told me with enthusiasm, "you'll remember that and you'll look back on that" and understand.

DOUBLINGS

The early psychoanalyst Otto Rank first introduced the concept of "the double" into psychoanalysis, and it has been a popular idea ever since, especially for literary theorists.[2] In psychiatry, however, it was not until Robert Lifton's work with Nazi doctors that the idea of doubling actively re-entered psychological imagination. As Lifton uses the concept, doubling means "the division of the self into two functioning wholes, so that a part-self acts as an entire self."[3] There is, of course, nothing magical about doubling. Along with several other concepts that have emerged in self psychology in recent years as either new ideas or revitalized older ones (including disavowal and splitting),[4] doubling is used in trying to describe the divisions in the self that are the consequence of dissociation. The self is, almost by definition, a holistic concept. Even in multiple personalities, there remains an essential communication between competing selves. Certainly, in most of human experience the separateness of aspects of experience is a relative concept. "I" am one thing, one person, one being, something William James clearly recognized, even if Freud tended to forget it. But life can seem in parts, even as we yearn for wholeness. "Man is born broken," says Brown toward the end of Eugene O'Neill's *The Great God Brown*. "He lives by mending. The grace of God is the glue." This apt characterization, which was one of Heinz Kohut's favorites, may express the dilemma of contemporary humans.[5] In any event, fundamentalists turn away from their broken, fragmented selves toward a fully separate self that is born anew with its actual baptism.

The reborn self that fundamentalists proclaim grounds their existence. The creation of a new self at the moment of conversion marks a profoundly significant psychological realignment, as Larry demonstrated when he found Jesus instead of jumping into the East River. It brings a new code of ethics, and it changes the style of one's life, as two pastors, Dean and Lester, found in getting beyond their drug-filled adolescence. It brings a new self-concept, as Monroe found in remaining alone and in his suit but filled with God. And it brings a new future in the idea of the millennium, as Otto and Mary imagined, one of goodness and virtue and social equality.

But most of all the reborn self brings salvation from death. Indeed, the transition from old to new selves, as fundamentalists imagine it, is itself a kind of death experience conveyed in the language of rebirth. Whatever else transpires in this vale of tears and hereafter, that new self is eternal and will eventually rest in peace with God. Cynthia thus felt protected against sin in her reborn self. "I'm never tempted to read smut," Cynthia gushed, "because I know that my mind is impressionable," even though she acknowledged watching TV movies and being horrified by all the swearing. "When you accept Christ that gnawing feeling, that uncertainty, that impending fear is gone, is replaced with peace and the guilt is gone and that is the beauty." But death remains. "There is a real freedom in being a Christian. Number one you say I don't have to worry about death and my eternal destiny. . . . But death isn't so bad when my eternal destiny is secure. Right [which she repeats, as if to reassure herself]. Right. I don't fear death anymore. It doesn't mean I want to die. Let's be real. But I don't feel fear is the ultimate." She had, in fact, radicalized the relation between life and death. She once said that as a child she feared the unknown, but "Now I don't fear the unknown, I don't fear death in the same way that I did. But I don't see that second coming of the Christ as death." The return of Jesus is not death, of course, except in a subtextual sense, that is, to save believers from death. Cynthia continued: "But I just see it as an exit out of this life to be with Christ." The return of Jesus, in other words, somehow washes away death and makes her immortal. Cynthia wanted that desperately.

In fundamentalist theory, all important things happen twice. You are born full of evil, separated from God. To enter the kingdom you must be "reborn" in a dramatic act of self re-creation. Jesus returns to earth at the end, making good the promise of ultimate redemption. It will be his second trip. True Christians who have died will be resurrected at the rapture. They will then live again on earth during the millennium, and forever in heaven. A crueler doubling is reserved for nonbelievers. Their sinful bodies are obliterated in a wash of violence during tribulation and their souls rest for a thousand years while the faithful rule the earth with Jesus. They are then resurrected as a kind of living presence to be judged by God and brutally cast forever into the lake of fire. (Revelation 20:13–14: "And the sea gave up the dead which were in it; and death and hell delivered up the dead which were in them: and they were judged every man according to their works. / And death and hell were cast into the lake of fire. This is the second death.")

More than anything else, these doublings distinguish fundamentalism from mainstream Christianity. There are at least three reasons for such marked differences in basic doctrine. First, fundamentalists seem to have to be doubly sure of the apocalyptic precisely because it is so fraught with uncertainty. Repetition relieves uncertainty, and yet reveals an aching doubt that prompts the repetition or doubling in the first place. Faith, for fundamentalists, is not just a part of our being in relation to a transcendent power. On the contrary, "real" faith must be a visible part of self-transformation as we define a personal relationship with God and become a new person. Similarly, one can never be quite sure that nonbelievers will not get away scot-free, so they must die and die again. Maybe then they will really be dead.

Second, the repetition of important things makes difficult and transcendent ideas much more comprehensible for ordinary people. End time theory is democratic, accessible, and imaginable in its literalism, while also being highly evocative in its mysticism. To dismiss fundamentalist theology as the kind of fanciful imaginative scheme fit only for comic books is an elitist judgment that reflects more than anything the anger of mainline Christians who have seen their churches emptied by the message and enthusiasms of fundamentalists. Accounts of faith, Jesus, the end times, the afterlife, and reward make the fundamentalist story immediate and concrete. These are not the concerns of erudite theologians but the narratives of popular culture. Fundamentalists, for example, talk and worry about where Jesus will appear in the clouds at the rapture and whether the Mount of Olives will split when his foot touches it at his descent. One need not learn Greek or Aramaic to reflect on these kinds of problems, and many millions find it religiously rewarding to work their faith at this level of explicitness.

Finally, the doubling in fundamentalist theory touches individual and collective death. Ideas such as the double death of nonbelievers weave the true threats to human existence into the Christian story. Fundamentalist theology is, in this sense, an authentic, maybe even realistic, adaptation to the modern world. If all the bombs go off or we choke ourselves in a haze of pollution, the human story will die in ways that make little sense in a theology based on the compassion of the Sermon on the Mount. The focus on violence by way of tribulation gives the traditional Christian story the edge it needs to fit our crumbling and maybe dying world. As Kathryn, an African American woman in her mid-thirties, said, "You cannot go over it, you cannot go alongside it, but you must go through it. You must go *through the blood*."

Fundamentalists live with a stark contrast between eternal souls and degraded bodies. Christianity, of course, has always taught such a dualism, but the fundamentalists literalize it in their end time views about double resurrections and deaths. The intermediate period between the final end and the termination of human history—the tribulation and the millennium—imposes similarly contrasting fates on the souls of the faithful and the infidels. Nonbelievers, of course, suffer and die in great numbers during the tribulation, while at the rapture believers are either raised from the dead or taken directly from life to be with Jesus in the clouds and then to rule with him from Mount Zion. During the millennium these "resurrected saints" look, as Monroe said, like Jesus after the resurrection.

The way dualistic death concerns worked their way into the interview process could be surprising. Mary's loose talk of mass death and Otto's numbed counting of those who die during tribulation frankly appalled me at the time; only in writing this book and with distance from the actual interview was I able to gain more empathy for the human pain behind such an easy acceptance of collective violence. In one interview with Reverend Lester, he launched into an hour-long lecture about how people build their security around a wife, husband, or whatever and then collapse when those fall apart.

The gospel, on the other hand, provides a permanent identity and inner peace. Reverend Lester thus set up a contrast between domestic and spiritual peace, a dualistic tension that carried over into a diatribe about the apocalyptic in which he distinguished between those who get the sign during the tribulation and those who do not; the latter are persecuted and hounded and judged and "actually killed."

For fundamentalists, the nonbeliever is death tainted. It must never be forgotten that the nonbeliever (in the eyes of the faithful) lives a constricted life and suffers the pain of death without hope of redemption. There are, in other words, severe consequences for refusing to accept Jesus in one's life. In the immediate and visible present the effects show themselves in a failure to understand the Bible. To the fundamentalist, the nonbeliever is like a preverbal child (1 Corinthians 13:11: "When I was a child, I spake as a child, I understood as a child, I thought as a child; but when I became a man, I put away childish things"). Words are little more than babel. You need time and lots of help to discern meanings, coherence, and grammar. But the larger significance of nonbelievers' failure transcends issues of cognition. Those who refuse Jesus are not only dumb but also different, dangerous, and possibly contagious. The believer is obliged to rub up against the taint in the commandment to convert, which implies a conquering of death. But to stay with that death too long can be a dangerous affront to the self.

Such thinking can lend itself to potentially dangerous stereotyping. People like Monroe tend to believe the Lord is with him in his reading of the Bible and that God speaks directly to him through his word, while all others are doomed to ignorance (and, subtextually, eternal damnation). The difference between self and others is sacralized, which provides a totalistic framework for dismissing all those who do not fit into the holy world in which the fundamentalist is blessed. The fundamentalist's chosenness defines the nonbeliever's abandonment, the one's salvation the other's ultimate punishment. Nonbelievers are rejected by God and thus in some inexplicable way are only tentatively human. As such, nonbelievers are dispensable. If they intrude in the believers' world, the psychological conditions exist to make it possible for believers to accommodate violence toward nonbelievers. I must stress that for most fundamentalists, and certainly for all I met, such violence was nowhere near being realized. But the fact that the potential exists is best illustrated in its occasional realization at the radical fringes of fundamentalism, as, for example, with the survivalist, Aryan, or Neo-Nazi groups in Idaho and elsewhere, or with David Koresh and the Branch Davidians.

Two important factors, however, one religious and the other psychological, mitigate the dangers of fundamentalists acting on or realizing the potential for violence that exists within their belief system or within themselves. Religiously, the fury of doctrinal certainty is softened by an evangelical commandment that fundamentalists take quite seriously (though some much more so than others): One has an obligation to reach and convert others, to help them, to recognize their weakness, to bring them to Christ. Such an impulse within Christianity tends to expand fundamentalist empathy out of necessity and may explain why Christian fundamentalism (as opposed to its forms in some other religions of the world) has so far, except for dramatic episodes on the radical fringe, been relatively free of violence. Monroe, for example, gave his whole life over to saving souls for Christ; during the time I knew her Arlene was actively planning a full-tub baptism for scores of the reborn in the gymnasium of the quarters for women on Riker's Island; and Mary spent hours each week with Jews for Jesus *and* Arabs for Jesus. The evangelist cannot afford a life-style of pristine ideological purity, even if he or she is emotionally drawn toward monastic retreat or violent engagement. The world cannot be disdained. It must be entered or no one will ever be converted.

Equally significant, the fundamentalist shares a specific psychological connection with the nonbeliever that goes beyond the mere fact of their common humanity: The nonbeliever symbolizes the believer's pre-Christian, earlier self. For Monroe I had the distinct feeling that I represented the way he saw himself prior to accepting Jesus into his heart at that New Orleans breakfast. As such I was the discarded part of his being, something that no longer fit as he grew in faith and found new robes in which to dress. The danger, of course, in such symbol-systems is that one will turn on these discredited and abandoned fragments of the self with violent renunciation. The reformist's zeal can be harshly condemnatory; enemies of the state are often purged after the revolution; the newly rich may disdain the poor as lazy; and the recovered alcoholic all too often scorns spineless drunks. But the more tentative approach of Monroe also remains. He looked back with sadness on his life before coming to know Christ, and at times that spilled over into the way he treated me with a note of condescension. He knew me, or at least thought he remembered that part of himself that he saw symbolized in me, and connected empathically with me, despite our rather large differences in background and values.

Don DeLillo, in his apocalyptic novel *Mao II*, notes: "The nice thing about life is that it's filled with second chances." In one sense, this is a thoroughly upbeat statement that reverberates with the American dream. There is hope in our potential for self-refashioning. But DeLillo's comment also touches a certain dread, for second chances are premised on our failing the first time. Who knows what will happen the next time around?

THE LITERAL SELF

Perhaps since the first century, Christians have had a sense that God's intentions and the story of Jesus are directly communicated to humans through scripture. As a result committed believers have always tended to literalize those words. But it was only in the nineteenth century that a theory of inerrancy emerged, arguing for the absolute integrity of every word in the Bible as God's complete truth and thus casting a long tradition of literalism into dogma. Inerrancy, however, does not require that the Bible be taken as literally true in theory or in practice. The erudite (and non-fundamentalist) theologian James Barr has written extensively on this seeming contradiction. His basic point is that, while inerrancy is a "constant factor" in all of interpretation of scripture, literalism may vary "up or down."[6] Clearly some biblical passages must be interpreted symbolically, something fundamentalists generally recognize and accept as part of the complexity of understanding the text. When asked about whether a born-again Christian has to accept the Bible literally, Reverend Dean hedged and said a Christian should read it literally "where possible." He added that he was not a creationist, believing in a literal reading of the story of creation—a belief in fact held to by only a minority of ideologues in the movement. But what the Bible is not, in the view of fundamentalists, is just a great story or a series of theological reflections. There is a "plain" or "right" meaning to any passage that God means to convey in it, even if it is difficult for humans to ascertain that meaning. That meaning may not be literally true but it will be the actual truth of what God said.[7]

The matter of literalism among poor and largely illiterate believers, however, is a bit more complicated than these theological distinctions would indicate. Can one really apply a theory of inerrancy, developed by highly privileged white Victorian Presbyterians at Princeton Theological Seminary, to the educationally disadvantaged masses? If you are illiterate and cannot appreciate the text in its full meaning, can you be a fundamentalist, or, as they might put it, a real Christian? Belief is the first and greatest step; it takes only a leap of faith. But belief is the beginning rather than the end of Christianity in the minds of fundamentalists. At a minimum, you also have to lead a moral life; proclaim the word to others; and learn the word and study it carefully. Reverend Lester, for example, said, "There are 1,700 churches in New York City. Few apply the Bible as a living book. Few teach the Word of God to common people," which was his mission from the first moment of his "church planting."

Intimate acquaintance with the Bible is, in fact, an important goal of the Bible study sessions that are such an essential element in the activities of any fundamentalist church. At Grady House a high level of education was assumed among the participants, and the issue was to walk a fine line between simplistic, literal reading and something approaching what they called "historic Christianity." At Abiding Light, on the other hand, where the congregation consisted of poor whites, blacks, and immigrants from various countries, nothing in the way of literacy or background knowledge could be assumed. Ian, the leader of the Bible group I attended, was particularly good at reminding members of such basic information as who the Jews were, what difficult terms meant, and where key places were located. He often had different people read passages aloud, and then would lead a discussion of their meanings. For the newly or partially literate (and perhaps especially for those for whom English is a second language), this kind of Bible study is highly educational, and spills over into their lives generally in significant ways.

Learning how to read, however, in the context of a belief system that stresses the theoretical notion that every word in the Bible is inerrant tends to reinforce the literalism of the movement in a naive but often touching way. I never met a fundamentalist in the various study groups in which I participated who was too poor not to have his or her often expensive Bible wrapped in a leather case with a zipper. These cases are carried as badges of honor. They protect the sacred text from rain and damage, and ensconce it in what I often felt was a mystical wrapping. A distinctive sign of a fundamentalist on a subway, for example, is the unzipped case with the open Bible on their lap. For many the Bible is the first, and remains the only, book they have really read. Even without a theory of inerrancy, one tends to treat such volumes with special meaning.

Such a learning process by rote with public reading and discussion as its core experience tends to move one toward ever greater literalism. Teachers of Bible groups are necessarily more educated and—at least with Ian, who did not have a dogmatic bone in his body—may be more moderate in their views. He simply passed over troublesome passages (like those dealing with the need for wives to be subservient to their husbands), and never tried to comment on thorny issues of theology. Ian's students, however (that is, the regular members of the congregation of Abiding Light), had a much more literal understanding of the text, which they asserted in discussion. Ian often brought in articles clipped from the *New York Times* to illustrate themes that he felt were raised in the biblical passages under review in a given week. Members of the group, on the other hand, were generally not interested in referring to sources outside of the text itself. If they had a question about 1 Corinthians, they wanted to know what it said in Isaiah on the same issue; or in talking about Revelation how it related to Daniel. Only in extreme cases were they interested in connecting the text to the larger cultural and historical world. The fall of Jimmy Swaggart thus caused great consternation at Abiding Light. It fell to the gentle Ian in Bible study to find biblical passages that could make some sense out of the tragedy. It was, after all, an Assemblies of God church, and several people I met had been converted by Swaggart at a revival he led once on Long Island.

But why is it, one can well ask, that learning to read one book carefully should make one a literalist? Abraham Lincoln learned to read a few books (including the Bible) by rote; he even read out loud in the "blab" schools of the American frontier, but he was hardly a literalist. Most highly educated people, in fact, begin somewhere by careful attention to words, and may have one or a few books to which they remain specially attached. Liberation theology, furthermore, purposely uses its Bible instruction as a form of instruction, and turns the process to political advantage and empowerment of the masses. But with fundamentalism that same process of biblical instruction yields exactly the opposite results. The difference lies in the theory behind the reading and the goals that the instruction serves. Inerrancy, one has to say, matters, and the way it undergirds Bible study always returns the discourse to its literal origins. The process tends to discourage interpretive change; it always returns to the self-referencing text that is imbued with the mystical knowledge of God.

Speaking more generally and psychologically, the move toward literalism and away from metaphor defines the religious experience of the fundamentalist. Literalism means control over sin and badness and ultimately control over death. Anxiety over those issues requires the literalism. Whether one can truly find eternal life in faith, or what happens during tribulation to a believer's nonbelieving children, or how nuclear violence fits into the end time story, reflect the kinds of concerns of greatest intensity for fundamentalists and therefore become the theological areas in which literalism most visibly operates.

The impulse toward literalism leads the more creative fundamentalists into some poignant dilemmas. Frank, for example, lived with his own special terror regarding the second death, the final judgment, and hell. "The worst part about hell," he said, "is what is described, it is a lake of fire, it is torment, but I think the worst torment of all would be having briefly experienced the presence of God [that is, at the moment of the final judgment] and the wonderful, the wonderful personal God he is, and forever being deprived of him."

The literal impulse also prompts fundamentalists to reflect on the concrete future history of the soul. Our body dies and rots but the soul, our divine essence that connects us with God, lives on forever.

Some eastern religions and New Ageists argue that this soul is repro-cessed in successive lives until it reaches some kind of exalted state. In Christianity things are more teleological (or directional). The soul is our spark of the divine and somehow at death joins with God in heaven. For the stricter traditionalists such (re)union of the hu-man soul with God requires faith during life, just as they would ar-gue that the soul of nonbelievers dies off, or somehow disappears. But in most of mainstream Christianity, and certainly in all its pro-gressive forms, notions of damnation are blurred, if not explicitly eliminated. We are all open to God's love, and the move is toward theological inclusiveness rather than exclusiveness.

Not so with fundamentalists. They wallow in the details of salva-tion and damnation. Such a position toward the future has gener-ated not only a whole library of books on the course of the end time (Hal Lindsey's, for example), but also detailed graphs and charts of the apocalyptic that are the stuff of endless hours of Bible study. As with any ideology, people also disagree over specifics, often with doctrinal certainty.

Fundamentalist explicitness about the end time, grounded as it is in difficult biblical texts, requires "experts" at interpretation. You must read prophecy, especially the book of Revelation, correctly or you will not understand the future course of events. That explains the many sermons and handbooks and videos and tapes and Bible studies on the subject. If you learn enough, the most specific details about your future life can be known. How exactly will human his-tory end, who will be the false leader, where will the big wars take place? What can you expect during tribulation? Where and with whom will you be living during the millennium? What will you look like? What will God be reading at the final judgment? What can you expect in heaven? You will also understand the dark side with the proper study. Who does not get raptured to be with Christ in the clouds? How many die and by what methods during the tribulation? How does life proceed for surviving nonbelievers during the millen-nium? And what really is the lake of fire?

The damnation of nonbelievers offers renewed hope for believers ("The last enemy to be destroyed is death," Otto said, quoting 1 Co-rinthians 15:26). For it is taught in the churches and endlessly repeated at the level of ordinary parishioners that there is nothing you can do to recover yourself if you die without accepting Jesus. No prayer helps the dead along. No amount of good work will offset a lack of belief. I asked Otto once about Mother Theresa (would she be saved?). He replied hesitantly that, well, he didn't know about her relationship with the Lord, but he repeated that only the saved, or those Christians specifically reborn as described in John 3:3, can ensure their future in heaven.

4

DIVINE
COMMUNION

WILMA. "Anything that holds your head together is of God,"
Wilma said. "Anything that confuses you is of the devil." Wilma led
her life with the constant knowledge of God's presence. He spoke to
her as she walked down the street, instructed her, helped her make
the right choices. He talked directly into one ear. The Holy Spirit, for
example, would tell her to stop watching so much television, because "thou shalt have no other gods before me." But Wilma also
wrestled with the power of the devil. He spoke into the other ear.
You have to be constantly aware that Satan is a "very strong force."
He is "just like the Lord" because he was once the archangel and got
to know all the secrets of God. But Satan got proud and was banished to hell where he continues to wreak his havoc. Earthly atheists
and agnostics, like Satan, set themselves above God. You can't tell
them anything, she lamented. They confuse you, like Satan. "He's

the author of confusion," Wilma added. You have to read God's word, memorize it, "hide it in your heart." The word of God is sharp, Wilma said, "sharper than a two-edged sword [her version of Revelation 1:16]. It cuts asunder."[1]

The literal struggle between the Holy Spirit and the devil for Wilma's soul reflected the immediacy of God's unfolding plan in the mind of this fragile woman. "Without hell, God would not be just. Where are you going to put all those people who refuse?" she asked. One must hold on. "He that endureth to the end shall be saved," Wilma quoted, seeking reassurance in a familiar phrase. For her that end is close at hand. Plenty of signs "point to the culmination of an age" and "every two thousand years there's a change." What we are living in now is just like the world before it was destroyed by water. Remember Noah? Wilma asked. "Everybody was doing what was right in their own eyes. That's what's happening today. More and more and more."

A member of Abiding Light, Wilma was a slightly built woman in her sixties who had the appearance of a fragile porcelain vase. She was near to tears throughout most of her two interviews, and once actually began crying when she described the experience of waking up from an emergency operation and thinking she was in hell. Wilma had straight gray hair and wore almost no make-up. During the winter she wore a simple black coat and hat that practically made her invisible.

Wilma's father came from Russia in the early part of the century. He was a Baptist, in fact a lay minister, but as a young man visiting a church with some friends he was once filled with the Holy Spirit and fell down speaking in tongues; this was in the early days of Pentecostalism as it swept the country after its beginning in San Francisco in 1903. That experience prompted her father to join the newly established Pentecostal church, Abiding Light. After his marriage Wilma's father worked hard at various unskilled jobs through decades of struggle. The family barely saw him. But whenever he was around in the evening, he would gather the family together to pray and read the Bible together. Wilma remembered those sessions fondly.

Abiding Light then was a large and active congregation with a charismatic ministerial team that tended the flock. An orchestra played as back-up to the organ. Wilma's father played the violin in that orchestra and later passed the violin on to Wilma for her high-school graduation. She in turn gave it to her eldest daughter but has it back now and does not know what to do with it. The passing of the violin into untrained hands seemed a metaphor for Wilma of the decline of Abiding Light itself from hundreds of enthusiastic worshippers to the few score who come to services now. In her typical way Wilma (as did other old-time members in this church) connected that decline with cosmic purposes: They saw it as a sign of the end because "it is written" that the number of Christians will decrease prior to the return of Jesus. "In the last days," Wilma said, "the love of many shall wax cold."

Wilma had very sentimental memories of her "beautiful" mother who died from a severe stroke after Wilma was grown with a young child of her own. She thought her mother must have been half Jewish, for Wilma remembered that her mother "koshered the meat," though why that proved she was "half" Jewish was unclear, just as it was left unexplained why her mother kept kosher after conversion to Christianity. Wilma's most distinct memory of her mother was praying. "Every time I came in the house, I found her on her knees. She just loved to pray." Her mother also imposed herself on Wilma. She taught her to avoid social conversation, "idle chatter," she called it. She was taught to read the Bible and concentrate on sharing the Lord's word. There was nothing else of significance to talk about. At the end of the interview Wilma gently chided the interviewer (a young woman) for letting her talk too much. She explained that she needed more direction. "I like to be a follower, you see. That's why I loved my mother so much. She was so strong, ooh! She made me afraid."

Most of Wilma's adult life was filled with sadness. She mistakenly married a man with a good job rather than the musician whom she loved. That marriage "ruined my life." Wilma cried all day before the wedding and her mother even suggested she might call it off. That was clearly a portent for Wilma. The husband turned out to be a complete cad, often leaving her alone and finally abandoning her, forcing Wilma to return to work to support her young children. She even had to suffer the criticism of others at church ("Why isn't Wilma living with her husband?" they asked behind her back). No love was between them, and worst of all the husband had no interest in her religion or her church. "We were unequally yoked," Wilma put it (referring to 2 Corinthians 6:14: "Be ye not unequally yoked together with unbelievers").

Wilma's family provided few alternative satisfactions. At one point she mentioned two children but only told stories of her adult daughter, giving the impression that a boy died. The daughter was a constant trial for Wilma. Her sanity seemed in question. "She went into astrology," Wilma said, distressed. In fact, she went into all kinds of religions, suffered serious emotional problems, and lived on her social security disability. She was "very emotional" and "nervous," Wilma said.

For all her submissiveness, meekness, and piety, another side of Wilma struggled for a voice in the interviews. "I do not trust what I am capable of doing," she said once out of context, and immediately referred to the grace of God. Her reasoning seemed to be that a side of her, one fed by the devil, strived for expression and independence. The constant surging of such feelings only reinforced her sense of badness. All her life Wilma had fought back such feelings. To illustrate them she told a story of rebellion as an adolescent. She had demanded that her poor parents purchase a new three-piece suit for her to wear to a party. It became a prized possession, though she berated herself for proving somewhat later to be a "complete ingrate." At a church party with some friends of her parents at which she was also wearing the suit, Wilma was asked to play the piano but instead sat under a tree and refused to budge. She was disobedient. As she saw it, predictably, the devil had gotten hold of her, but perhaps she simply wanted to be something that the strict demands of her faith would never allow.

Whatever that small voice was it died years ago, though not without a struggle. Wilma told another story of feeling guilty as a young woman when she played popular music on the piano. "My heart condemned me," she said. And then, without a break in her associations, she told a dream: "I saw a branch of a tree. And I saw the bark about this big, but the branches were very crooked. One went this way, one went this way. It was orderly, but it was so crooked. None of them [the branches] seemed to be going the same way. One this way, one that way, one that way. And yet the trunk was so even. And I was wondering, how could a tree be so, so diversified. And then on top, in gold, pure gold, on top of the bark with all the branches all around, no leaves, just the branches: 'The will of God' in gold. So beautiful, so even." Wilma's dream seemed to capture the central dilemma of the young woman who felt guilty even playing the piano outside of church, and since it stayed with her through the decades the dream seems also to have spoken to her continuing conflicts over her self-definition. Wilma yearned for the straight and even trunk that reached upward and touched the golden will of God. But in fact she spent most of her life in the twisted and crooked branches.

THE REACH OF PRAYER

No one prays more fervently than fundamentalists. Prayer is one of the central experiences of their faith commitments and is elaborately ritualized in the rhythms of their daily lives. Luke, a young executive who attended a Pentecostal church on Sundays and Grady House for Bible study during the week, lived alone in New Jersey. He rose every day at 6:00 A.M. and sat in his living room facing a large picture window with his heavily marked and underlined Bible on his lap open to a passage from a guide to daily scripture that he reflected on and prayed about, slipping always, he said, into tongues. Any church function begins and ends with prayer, and services themselves return constantly to individual and collective prayer. At Grady House (where Luke was more restrained in his self-presentation), there were four distinct periods of prayer in the course of an evening's activities: before and after Bible study and, with Sam, before and after his sermon/lecture. At Abiding Light, at least once each year members of the congregation gathered for an all-night prayer session, though even the earnest Ian told me he had trouble staying awake. At Calvary each Sunday one of the remarkable sights in Christendom is six to seven hundred people speaking in tongues at one time with all the fervency of black Pentecostalism.

The Lord hovers closely for true believers. They ask God for guidance in matters large and small in their lives, and expect concrete answers. If in their lives it turns out they have chosen badly after asking

God for help in a decision, they reason that the devil has spoken. It is not that their faith is weak, just that Satan has great power. Nevertheless, they see—or convince themselves they see—enough evidence of God's majesty in the world but most of all in their lives to fully justify their confidence in their continued personal relationship with Jesus.

I often wondered, given fundamentalists' belief in the reach of prayer, what were its limits. Clearly, much of what one asks for is denied, from the trivial to the ultimate. This denial is not new to fundamentalists, but fundamentalists, because of what they believe is their closer form of contact with God, seem never to doubt that they are in communion with the divine. The failure of prayer is thus quite personal. It may result from inadequate sincerity in the asking or from God's inscrutable ways that may be temporarily confusing but always have a purpose.

Otto told me of the extraordinary powers he ascribed to prayer. At several points in his life he had such severe chest pain that he thought he was going to die. But at those times, he did not go to a doctor or take any medication. He prayed. And he did not consider that an avoidance or denial of the problem. He was taking creative action. Otto did not even take aspirin for the eight or nine days of acute pain. With prayer, "I was healed from it. It all just completely cleared up." Otto explained to me why prayer could not solve all the problems in the world in terms of God's mystery and our willful ways:

> Okay, God gave us a free will when he created us, and Genesis says, "Let us make man in our own image." I believe that involves intellect, the ability to learn, create things, emotions, so we can feel, love, hate and if you can't hate, you can't love. You've got to be able to have all emotions. And the will to choose. Now God could have made us robots. So that we all live righteous [lives], we never do anything wrong. But God gave us a will, and that involves the ability to choose wrongly.

The intimacy of the fundamentalist's relationship with God, as shown in this attitude toward prayer, shapes much of the subtext of fundamentalism. God is neither remote nor an immanent power in the universe. He is a part of one's life. He cares for the most minute details of our existence and ultimately watches out for his flock, even if he purposely lets things go somewhat awry along the way. In prayer we approach God directly. A bit of God rubs off, and we ourselves become sacred. In the best of senses, this extension of the divine into daily life enormously enhances a believer's self-esteem and nurtures the capacity to live a Christian life. From the moment of faith the fundamentalist says "I believe" and draws closer to God.

But such proximity to the divine can be audacious, if not arrogant. Reverend Lester fully expected to have God on call. "My ultimate purpose is to be like Jesus Christ in my inner character, the qualities that Jesus had," he said. Isaac illustrated a related but somewhat different grandiosity that was common among those fundamentalists I got to know. The line in Isaac's mind blurred between what he thought God might do in his apocalyptic fury and Isaac's vision of what he would do in God's place. Isaac talked, in other words, with God-like omniscience when he described end time issues. He spoke in the rhetoric of Revelation, and filled his speech with phrases from the apocalyptic. He spoke with the certainty of one who has fully divined prophecy: "They [believing Christians] will be spared [at the rapture] because God said he put the seal on them and they will be the witnesses to the world. You see God always has witnesses—even if he takes the church out, he leaves a remnant." He spoke with confidence about matters that even fundamentalist theologians tread on lightly (like what happens to Christians who convert during tribulation), because he somehow felt his intimacy with the divine gave him special license.

GUILT TRANSFORMED

Nigel stressed that life changes when one believes in God and is in intimate communion with him. You don't need to wake up and worry about paying bills next week (said this affluent Wall Street trader) or dealing with tragedy in your life. "In putting your life in God's hands he takes care of those things and he provides for you." We cannot know what's in the future, but if we believe we can relax in the knowledge that "he has designed the future," including "everything that happens in our life." It's all taken care of.

For Nigel one of the added benefits of such close communion with God was relief from guilt over what he considered his abundant sins during the decade when he strayed from the church. During these years after his parents' divorce, Nigel drove sports cars, took drugs, and dated lots of women. When I asked him if he felt regret now over those years, he replied that his only regret was in losing all that time with the Lord. God doesn't punish us for past sins, he stressed. "He doesn't bring it up, and there is no reason why I should either," he said in a quite extraordinary statement about the closeness he felt to God.

In a psychological sense Nigel's understanding of God's involvement in his life served to reverse the shame-guilt mechanism. Normally we feel ashamed or guilty about bad thoughts or actions. Such feelings of shame or guilt help prevent us from straying too far away from the internalized norms of our culture. Conscience, in this sense, serves to regulate behavior in any social setting. But for those who believe in a fundamentalist God, the pangs of conscience fade after they are saved, or so they claim. God absolves them of their sin and frees them from guilt. Such relief is a crucial part of the personal gain that believers attest to in being saved. "Christianity," Nigel said, "is the only faith that offers atonement. There is no other religion that offers atonement for our sins as human beings." At the final judgment, the Lord is not going to look at you and say, "Chuck, you dropped the ball on February 28 at two o'clock in the afternoon when you lusted after this person." That gives you "sort of a license," though you are commanded to be obedient. But then Nigel concluded with the thought that really tormented him: "One of the big things that I look forward to in going to heaven is the end of that struggle against the flesh."

Perhaps they protest too much their escape from shame and guilt. Nigel spent much of his interview with me rehashing his time of troubles and describing in what struck me as loving detail his manifold sins. Fundamentalists often seem to fool themselves about their relief from sin and guilt. In this they are not really hypocrites (though sometimes their self-righteousness can be suffocating). They fully acknowledge continuing temptation in the reborn self, and theologically assume that as long as the soul remains in the wicked vessel of the body, the possibility for sin exists. That was the point of Mary's story about the rotting flesh under her ring. The victory over sin and death is complete in an ultimate sense but more tentative in the immediate human context. The struggle remains. Yet the relative release from sin, even from the point of view of the fundamentalists themselves, is remarkable. As far as I could tell in my exchanges with fundamentalists, they *are* free from sin (as it is normally understood in the Judeo-Christian tradition). If hardly free of guilt, they are at least released from torment, expiating guilt by the constant processing of it in prayer.

The amount of guilt felt, however, often had little to do with actual behavior. A huge difference exists between the subjective experience of guilt and the actions and thoughts that prompt it. Wilma berated herself for playing the piano as an adolescent just for the pure fun of it. One could see Nigel's "sins" that have caused him so much pain as the normal behavior of a college student.[2] Isaac, on the other hand, had been a cocaine addict, and Arlene had been a prostitute, crack addict, and had actually tried to kill her lover at one point. Yet all these fundamentalists struggled in similar ways with their transgressions by collapsing radically different behaviors into the common mold of their pre-Christian, sinful self that they remade in the experience of being saved.

Guilt and shame, in other words, occupy the minds of fundamentalists to a rather extraordinary degree irrespective of the actual behavior that apparently occasioned it. They feel that they were completely sinful at one point but totally freed of guilt after conversion; only their constant harping on the past suggests its continued presence in their lives now. Much of the motivation for conversion lies in getting free of these feelings. Certainly it matters that the saved universally claim to feel different about themselves and to have experienced a transformation of self in relation to guilt and shame after being saved. But where is all that guilt and shame after conversion?

The answer is complex. The effort to reverse the guilt-shame mechanism never fully succeeds, and fundamentalists (like the rest of us) spend a lot of time in self-laceration and expressions of guilt and shame. They also create a *new* source of guilt and shame in their lives in trying to match the extraordinarily high ideals they set for themselves. But to a significant degree, it seems, fundamentalists do free themselves from much of the haunting residues of guilt through a process of externalization. God takes over one's sin. With God's forgiveness, one can forget about sin and trust, as Nigel did, that God will not recall it. This attitude presupposes an intensely personal relationship with God, one that can only be continued by a sense of communion with him as an immediate part of one's daily life. God has to enter into matters that most people would never imagine him caring about. That is the heart of the "personal relationship" with the Lord that fundamentalists constantly evoke.

But shame and guilt, then, become an integral part of the apocalyptic. A striking aspect of the fundamentalist system is that just as individual guilt and shame diminish, collective evil increases. The badness, one might say, shifts its venue. Fundamentalists believe that the number of true Christians will decrease as we approach the end of time, for evil will increase everywhere else. The world implodes on itself from the weight of all its evil. End time violence is the indirect expression of all that accumulated sin, and it helps maintain individual purity as it unloads destruction. Such is the effect in fundamentalist theology of transforming guilt. The purer Christians are, the more sinful nonbelievers become.

5

THE END
AT HAND

———

ISAAC. Isaac represented the extreme edge of end time commitments. Underneath his veneer of good humor and geniality lay a tormented soul. He continued to wrestle with drugs. He had to suppress his own violence and he was always toying with leaving the church in an act of rebellion. The "solution" Isaac found to the dangers within was a kind of cosmic projection. He completely embraced the violent end times and neatly shifted agency. It was not his violence but that of God. It was God who punished pornographers, and God who rained down desolation and made the blood run to the bridles of the horses. The end time script proved useful for Isaac, the actor, as a vicarious expression of his inner conflicts. His immersion in end time destruction served to control his own violence. Antichrist was a useful carrier of Isaac's projections, and he was drawn to the tension created by living on the cusp of destruction without knowing exactly how soon it will occur. The shifting of agency in a very real sense played an important healing role for Isaac. Through faith he had given up his drug addiction, gotten his and his mother's life back together, and found a community in St. Paul's Church. But Isaac's new faith commitments represented a perilous and fragile new set of self structures, something well short of a transformation. As his interviewer keenly felt, despite his friendly facade there was a disturbing readiness for violence in his obsessive attraction to the details of destruction in the end time story.

Isaac was in his late thirties when he was interviewed. He was balding, which made him look older, but fit from his frequent weight-lifting. He was unusually outgoing and an actor who had appeared in various bit parts on TV and in commercials. He was particularly respected by other members of the St. Paul's congregation for his knowledge of the book of Revelation. He even taught a course on prophecy. Isaac had a good sense of humor and could be disarming in his frankness (at one point he described himself as "cocky and arrogant"). When he made announcements at the Sunday service he usually had the entire congregation laughing. But there was also a suppressed violence in Isaac. Tension pulled at the corners of his mouth, contradicting his professed happiness. During one interview Isaac talked at length about the serial killer Ted Bundy (even he "wanted love"). Isaac seemed unduly interested in Bundy, whom he said "represents something in all of us." Isaac was himself a cocaine addict before being saved and he spoke with feeling of the rage the drug can cause.

Isaac grew up in Florida. He was raised a Methodist and was very active in his church. He was president of his Methodist fellowship and during the summers went to youth camp. The religious beliefs he was taught, however, were "watered down" and without much integrity. At least in retrospect, the mainstream Christian church failed to provide that ideological core of commitments that Isaac yearned for. After high school Isaac went into the army. The Vietnam War was winding down, however, and he was not sent overseas. At twenty-one he started college in Florida, but he later transferred to a west coast university. In both schools he majored in acting and proved to be quite accomplished; since he was prematurely bald he was always cast as the grandfather.

Isaac spoke about end time issues with authority. He knew the book of Revelation well and enjoyed rambling on about topics like the ingathering of the Jews, the exact nature of tribulation, the seven trumpets and seven vials, and the plethora of symbols that clutter the texts of prophecy. Isaac attached great significance to the book of Revelation, which along with Genesis are the two books "the devil attacks." Isaac saw the world as a place of marked decay. As in the days of Noah, he saw people drinking and eating and not noticing what was going on right in front of their eyes. But he clearly saw that the signs of the end are everywhere. It is all intensifying, including the vast expansion of knowledge. Along these lines, Isaac seemed particularly impressed by computers, which for him were an integral part of end time process.

Isaac was influenced by people like Hal Lindsey (whom he mentioned specifically at one point) who take the end time grid and apply it to contemporary events. During the cold war, Russia and China played out the Gog and Magog roles in Lindsey's hugely successful books, while the Gulf War brought Saddam Hussein into focus as Antichrist and aroused great passions among fundamentalists about Israel and the Jews.[1] Isaac's special concern in the construction of such apocalyptic narratives was the identification of Antichrist. This charismatic contemporary leader, who wears the facade of peace but is inhabited by the devil and is the instrument of great destruction because he fools people for so long, perhaps symbolized the inner tensions Isaac himself felt.

Isaac had strong views about the liberal drift of politics and ethics in America. He mocked those who insist on access to pornography as a right of free speech and yet turn around and deny fundamentalists the right to worship in school or even educate their children at home. That represents a disintegration in values, according to Isaac, one that marks the end times (and which Antichrist will take maximum advantage of at the end). "I wouldn't want to be you or someone like you," Isaac said to the interviewer, whom he knew to be Jewish and who had steadfastly resisted conversion despite months of fieldwork in St. Paul's. You, he said, speaking both generally of nonbelievers but more specifically of the interviewer herself, will be part of the armies that go up against Jesus when he touches down from heaven and splits the mountain and laughs at the assembled hordes.

Isaac liked the image of that haughty laugh of Jesus, as he did anything that suggested violence. He searched out the bloodiest of biblical passages to quote (which in the book of Revelation is not too difficult). "It says" was a refrain of Isaac's. It says "he called the birds to come and eat the flesh of mighty men"; It says "the battlefields will be covered almost up to the bridles of a horse with blood, that's how deep you can feel the blood will be, you know." Isaac truly lived psychologically in the violence of the end, that time when a third of the vegetation of the earth will be burned up and a third of the water poisoned. He also added his own creative images to more familiar ones about end time events. "The sky," he said, "is going to literally reel up like a scroll, almost like a Venetian blind, and boom!" People will have sores all over their bodies, he continued, because the ozone will be completely gone, and they will stand there helplessly shaking their fists at heaven, demanding God help them, as though he was working the heavens as a short-order cook. Isaac warmed to his topic, leaning forward across the table where the interview was being conducted, pounding the table, hoping to impress his nonbelieving interviewer.

Isaac segued from end time violence into drugs and his own tormented experience with cocaine. All you have to do is look at crack, he said, and you get addicted. It must be "out of the pit of hell, you know." And then he gave his testimony, his experience of degradation that led to his conversion. It came four years ago. He was a cocaine addict at the time, doing two or three grams a day. He went back home, partly to get away from New York but also to see his mother. What he found was awful. She had become almost a bag lady. She had stopped bathing and the house was full of trash. There were rats in the house. He turned from the sight at first, not wanting to get involved because he knew it would take a deep level of commitment to help her.

That was the turning point in his life. Almost absentmindedly, he picked up a Bible and found suddenly that the text was speaking directly to him. He had never experienced those words before in that fashion. He faced what he considered his own evil ("I'm not basically a good man, I'm basically a bad man," he said once, and like Satan he was a "very vain creature"). But somehow the words of the Bible worked on Isaac. He returned to his mother and coaxed her out of her house and into a hospital where she could be treated properly for her diabetes. He then stayed with her for six months and got her—and himself—back in shape. Somewhat later, he moved to stay away from the New York drug scene he knew too well. He found a large fundamentalist church (with ten thousand members) and was baptized. He spent lots of time reading, trying to catch up on his religious education. He was quickly recognized as a good communicator and was asked to teach a course on religious fundamentals. He said it helped him solidify his own faith.

For all this time he stopped his drug use as well, though he added, somewhat ruefully, that he had "slipped" several times. "Becoming a Christian doesn't mean you're going to stop sinning," he said, rationalizing. It only means you will sin less, a sanction he found in Jeremiah: "The heart is deceitful above all things." And he acknowledged in himself: "I'm entertaining sin in my life, I'm entertaining thoughts of rebellion." In general Isaac said of himself that his move into Christianity was a "slow burn" rather than a "bolt of lightning." He constantly struggled with himself, with doubt, with desire. He gets "antsy" and feels he wants to walk away from the church (and probably back into drugs).

And yet Isaac testified to the power of prayer that holds his latent violence in check. He told a story at one point of being home with his mother and sister and her family recently. His brother-in-law was an alcoholic and into drugs. On Easter he totaled his jeep while drunk. Isaac was enraged and told his brother-in-law he wanted to "deck" him but refrained from physical violence and prayed instead. The next day the brother-in-law got into a rehabilitation program. For Isaac it was proof positive of the place of God in our lives.

THE TIMING OF THE END

The Bible reports that Jesus explicitly told his followers he would return, both before his death (Matthew 24:27–31) and during the forty days after his resurrection but before his ascension (Acts 1:4–5). This promise is referred to many times elsewhere in the New Testament (especially in the expansive readings of the Bible by fundamentalist theologians like John Walvoord[2]). Since the apostles watched Jesus ascend into the clouds (Acts 1:9), believers have waited eagerly for his return. But it is not to be talked of; Jesus was quite clear about that (Matthew 24:36: "But of that day and hour knoweth no *man*, no, not the angels of heaven, but my Father only"; and Acts 1:7: "It is not for you to know the times or the seasons, which the Father hath put in his own power"). This dual message of immediacy and uncertainty, of hope deferred, of dreams that may not be mentioned explicitly, creates the central tension in the apocalyptic for fundamentalists. Mainstream Christians tend not to worry too much, if at all, about the Second Advent; fundamentalists are obsessed with it. They want it now and move toward it psychologically, but they also must avoid naming a date. Paul Boyer, in *When Time Shall Be No More*, details the long history of such date setting and its agonized rationalizations from those actually involved in such activity.[3] My fieldwork and interviews reveal a somewhat different picture, for I avoided the noisy leaders of the movement or those at the radical fringe. Among ordinary people, I found more confusion and hesitancy about the world's end, combined with a deep longing. The timing of the end is a complicated matter, but much can be learned about the fundamentalist movement and individuals within it from the way they position themselves emotionally and spiritually in relation to the return of Jesus.

The Second Advent, it should be remembered, is by definition for fundamentalists the event that marks the end of human history and inaugurates the sufferings of tribulation that are then followed by the hope of the millennial rule of Jesus on earth. The "end" stops our historical time and ends evil, but it marks as well the "return" of Jesus and the "beginning" of the millennium. These discrete (and magical) aspects of the end time process can easily merge, however, in the minds of fundamentalists. For their own reasons, fundamentalists focus differently on endings, beginnings, death, renewal, despair, and hope, but all agree that the expectation of the return of Jesus defines their existence. It may be that those who are most agitated about their own death are also the most immediate about the apocalyptic end. The end time process, precisely because it involves so many different events, allows for much variation in self-expression.

For Arlene the end was misty, just as her images of the millennium recycled her memories of her childhood in Jamaica. Reverend Charles brought a much greater sense of urgency to his reflections on the end but also steadfastly avoided any hint of date-setting. Sam was somewhere in between. He put little emphasis on the idea of the return of Jesus or the end of the world, either in his interview or in his sermons at Grady House. He clearly believed in the Second Advent, but he laughed at the idea of setting a precise date for the return of Jesus and saw no significance in the year 2000. What mattered for Sam was that he will appear before Christ whenever he comes (though it was not clear Sam had the final judgment or the rapture in mind). In fact, Sam got quite confused talking about these issues and acknowledged that he just does not pay much attention to the theology of the end time. He does keep straight "the really important things," namely that Christ will return, that there is both a heaven and a hell, and that only those who accept Jesus are "headed in the right direction."

Reverend Dean was a bundle of fascinating apocalyptic contradictions. His ideas were incompletely formulated and conventional; they were also appealingly human. Though a minister, he was not at all interested in or informed much about the theory of premillennial dispensationalism. He was only vaguely apocalyptic. Contrary to all expectation, he once described a "harmonic convergence" New Age celebration held in Central Park with interest, by way of noting that other people as well felt "great changes are occurring." At another time, he referred to Hal Lindsey's *The Late Great Planet Earth*, which he said was a "credible" statement, even though he said at another point that he didn't "see" nuclear war in the Bible (which is the whole point of Lindsey's book). Christians, Reverend Dean said, have always believed in the end itself. "Every generation since Christ," he said, "has believed that they were living in the last days. . . . We live that way because we want an open, active relationship with God. Love compels us to go on." Reverend Dean's apocalyptic style was in general decidedly gentle. He made it clear that he did not like the rabid patriotism of Jerry Falwell but greatly admired Billy Graham.

Deborah asserted that the end times play a very important role in her thinking, though she gave it a typically personal twist. For her living in the end times gave life an "urgency." There is no guarantee, she said, "that we are going to live another day." As proof, in a sense, she told a story of a woman she had met handing out tracts on a bus. Deborah introduced herself, and discovered the woman had stomach cancer. Deborah was impressed that the woman seemed at peace with herself. Deborah concluded: "Here she [the woman] is, who knows how many days she has, if the Lord heals her, but we also have to think of it in [terms of] the time that the Lord is returning." The point seemed to be that end time urgency connected with daily life by making death more real and apparent. God's purpose was apparent at many levels. The threat of actual death sharpened life's focus, as with the woman on the bus. But the awareness of the end times does the same for the young and healthy, like Deborah. We are all living with the equivalent of stomach cancer in the certainty of individual death, but we must also realize the equal certainty of end time finality for human existence. Deborah's small story of human suffering evoked for her cosmic endings, indeed God's purpose.

The end times for Reverend Lester are right around the corner, but what he really cared about was God's judgment at the end. "The judgment has got to come as the sun has got to rise." There is also moral rot everywhere. In fact, if God doesn't bring judgment on America, he is going to have to "apologize to Sodom and Gomorrah" (which led him into a tirade against abortion, and the murdering of 25 million babies). Asked once whether it changed his life in any way to believe the end is imminent, he replied: "No. I'm living one day at a time anyway, giving a hundred percent to whatever it is that God wants me to do." But the image of the end he lived with was terrifying. "The heavens will pass away with a roar, and the elements will be destroyed with intense heat and the earth and its works will be burned up." And he added: "We are talking about hydrogen bombs, we are talking atomic bombs, nuclear war heads."

Such knowledge posed problems for Reverend Lester about how to lead his flock. If he talked too much about the end times in his sermons, he felt people would either get "smug" about their own salvation and the fact that everyone else is damned (it "just puffs people up" knowing that they will have eternal life, he said), or be frightened away. "You have to share truth with love," that is, somehow not ignore the end time message but present it in the context of a ministry of the love of Jesus. Reverend Lester's subjective sense was that he muted discussion of the end in his sermons, which was in marked contrast to the impression I got from his sermons, and most of all from the powerful apocalyptic themes that emerged in the interviews from his church members. The apocalyptic was also expressed throughout Reverend Lester's ministry, sometimes in small but significant ways. After his second interview, for example, Reverend Lester gave his interviewer a six-page newsletter on the church that was prepared for new or prospective members. The newsletter speaks primarily of the loving model of Jesus, whose teachings are a guide for the living and whose death has saved us from sin. But tucked away at the end of the little brochure, in one strategically placed half column, is the note: "Some will enter the kingdom prepared for them from the foundation of the world. Others will not."

Within all this diversity on the timing of the end, I did find one consistent element in the way fundamentalists of different classes view the apocalypse. Working-class fundamentalists, whether African American or white, male or female, tended to see the end within sight and some even connected it to the approaching end of the current millennium. The upper-class fundamentalists I got to know pushed the end well beyond their own lifetime. The poor and disenfranchised, in other words, whose lives approximated the suffering of the early Christians, yearned for the transformation and renewal so basic to apocalyptic theory.

Otto was as specific about the significance of the year 2000 as anyone I talked with, though even he hedged ("I'd be surprised if we reached the year 2000 before he comes back") and told me in quite a different context that he did not expect to die, for he would be raptured first. Certainly, no one I encountered matched Otto's obsession with end time death and resurrection (though Harriet and others also talked loosely about the year 2000 and suggested as well that they expected the rapture imminently). Otto, however, lived in and for the return of Jesus to a remarkable degree, even for fundamentalists. Yet he pressed toward the Apocalypse with dread. There was persecution, war, and suffering at hand on the horizon, and Otto had thought through what all that meant for himself and his family. "Ah," he said sighing, "Well, my youngest is thirteen. I've got two married, one that's on his own, he's twenty-one. So hopefully they won't be in the part [of their lives] where they could be drafted in some war or something. I don't know. It concerns me, yes." But at least he sees a "light at the end of the tunnel." There will be persecution, Otto said, but it won't last long. Nor will it kill everyone. Many will die, including Christians in the vast persecutions,[4] but there will also be purification. "The best and truest will survive."

On the other hand, the fundamentalists from Grady House delayed the end in their religious imaginations. They saw it as vulgar, not to mention blasphemous, to even think about a human dating of God's purpose. One might say they were certain about *an* end but unsure about *the* end. The men in my Bible study group, for example, laughed with scorn at Elizabeth Claire Prophet who dared to make a concrete prediction that the end would come in April 1989; Nigel made unflattering comparisons of her with the Millerites, a group that predicted the end in the 1840s. The end for this group of rich fundamentalists was only imaginable as a real but remote possibility. Their empowered class position in the society appeared to spill over into their spirituality.

The idea of the end for them, however, was not at all one that assured a human future; in this aspect of the apocalyptic they had much more in common with working-class believers than with other upper-class mainstream Christians. Their suits and Mercedes and houses in the Hamptons could be deceptive. They lived with a clear sense of the outer limits of the time left for human history. They were loosely but absolutely apocalyptic. They talked about history not lasting past the time of their children or their children's children. Everyone I talked to in-depth at Grady House dated the end, even if vaguely, along such lines. Two generations, it seemed, was as far as any fundamentalist could see human history lasting.

On that continuum from half a decade to roughly a century, however, there was a crucial point of psychological significance that further distinguished categories of fundamentalists: the point of their own death. Arlene, Otto, and the others, whether or not they attached significance to the year 2000, all believed the end would occur before they died; Sam, Nigel, Monroe, and the members of Grady House saw the end as coming sometime after they died. The moment of one's personal death served as a kind of metaphor for a collective ending, even, perhaps especially, for the disenfranchised. It actually mattered much more than the year 2000 in figuring the apocalyptic.

"We don't have much time," said Ivan, an African American fundamentalist of thirty-three who worked two jobs to survive but lived in a shelter for the homeless. "We don't, you, me, my children, your children, and anybody else's children." At the most "we have thirty to forty years" (which is what he could reasonably expect to live), but even that could be shortened "if things keep increasing at the rate they're increasing with the drugs, the larceny, the murder, the mayhem, it's not going to last that long." Later in the interview, however, Ivan seemed to contradict himself. In thinking about his future he imagined himself "thirty years from now" with a nice home in the country somewhere, a fantasy that transcended the effects of the prejudice he encountered in contemporary America. But he added quickly "if there's a country," which took him back into the apocalyptic. "God knows all the shit that's going on. He knows the good that's going on, what little good there is, and he knows all the evil that's going on. He knows."

Monroe, on the other hand, dated the end in the second generation. In a general discussion of the return of Jesus, he noted the urgency of conversion for all, especially his daughter Jennifer. He was concerned that his daughter be "prepared." He wanted her to have a "commitment equal or greater than mine," and was concerned that her faith was weak. He did not want her to waste her first forty-three years, "like I did." For there is no joy or happiness in life, he added, outside of belief in God. Although banal in one sense, Monroe's ideas about the end were not quite as simple as they seemed. He had only a vague idea of the end in Jennifer's lifetime, which was part of his continual immersion in end time prophecies. He was keenly aware that history seemed to be hurrying along, which he felt could be God's way of announcing that the end was at hand. He said: "There are so many of those prophecies that are starting to be fulfilled in the last thirty, forty years at a rapid rate." The creation of the state of Israel was "the big one" for him, but "there's so many." There are "a lot of things going on" that are highly "significant." What Monroe slid away from was the implication for his daughter of human history ending during her lifetime, and what that meant in terms of her loving, or having children, or doing anything else that committed her to this life, indeed to human existence. Instead, he only addressed the importance of faith in general. It was not easy for Monroe to think about the implications of his end time thinking for himself or those he loved. He could only think about the apocalyptic in the abstract. He was not dogmatic, in other words, but he also was not without his convictions about the approaching end of the world. In this he was quite unlike those who trust, even if ambivalently, a human future. Monroe counted out his own days and envisioned a life for his daughter. But he had no image of his own symbolically immortal self lasting through her and unto the generations.

Mary had some of the same confusions as Monroe. True to form, she stressed that Jesus' return is "imminent, really imminent" and noted that "I don't think there's going to be that many more generations. I honestly don't." In everything Mary said, Jesus seemed to hover over her life, ready to drop in at any moment. However, the only actual date she gave me for his return was one hundred fifty to two hundred years, which seemed a rather long way off for someone as thoroughly immersed in the apocalyptic as Mary. She herself could not really understand it all, but the divine, she said, seemed to have remarkable patience with human evil. God has a "long fuse," she said. Perhaps as well she felt the need to be "historical" with me—she referred several times in the interviews to my profession as an historian—and to appear knowledgeable like her own father, whom she once said was the most informed man on historical events she ever met. But perhaps she also simply changed her mind without conscious awareness, responding to internal cues and various stresses in her life that gave shape to her apocalyptic notions.

THE RAPTURE OF THE CHURCH

"Then we which are alive *and* remain shall be caught up together with them in the clouds, to meet the Lord in the air: and so shall we ever be with the Lord" (1 Thessalonians 4:17). The rapture is probably the single most significant theological innovation in contemporary fundamentalism. It gave new meaning to and helped reshape premillennialism in the nineteenth century and was a crucial part of theologian John Nelson Darby's overall end time schema. It is based on only this one biblical passage, but it is an idea that unlocks many other prophetic mysteries.[5] Obviously, a powerful note of escapism is sounded in the idea of the rapture. The rapture lifts the faithful out of end time destruction, including (as most imagine it) nuclear war, rivers running with blood, strange beasts stalking the land, and general mayhem. The confidence of protection from these disasters in turn profoundly affects the way many fundamentalists think about social responsibility, and contributes to a tendency to opt out of involvement in political and social matters and into a privatized, separatist world. Democracy is not well grounded in the lives of the 60 to 70 million Americans (conservatively estimated) who believe in the rapture.

The escapism inherent in the end time doctrine is also deeply personal. The rapture represents the great triumph of faith for those who consider themselves God's chosen people and in direct communion with him; the rapture justifies the wait and makes everything worthwhile. From the moment of the rapture, eternal salvation is absolutely secure; indeed, as Monroe put it, the "resurrected saints" (that is, the raptured souls of the faithful dead) actually look like Christ after his resurrection. Further suffering and death await the world and all its inhabitants, but true Christians need never worry again. They are on a sure path. Even the brief loosing of Satan (Revelation 20:7) at the end of the millennium for one final battle in no way threatens their royal road into heaven.

But the rapture has a dark side: As the key event on the very cusp of the end of time, it saves the faithful but also represents the point beyond which there can never, ever, be hope for nonbelievers. They may live through tribulation, perhaps survive a while during the millennium, even have children who will make a life and have their own children for many generations. But nothing they do can ever alter their ultimate fate at the final judgment. The moment of greatest hope for fundamentalists is simultaneously one of eternal damnation for nonbelievers. It is quite grim, for it simultaneously means personal salvation and eternal separation from nonbelieving loved ones (Harriet, for instance, was truly haunted that her middle child, who had strayed from the church, would not be raptured).

Mainstream Christians and secularists in general tend to mock the idea of the rapture as a magical, nonbiblical idea harbored by religious enthusiasts. But such attitudes fail to appreciate the centrality of rapture doctrine for fundamentalists, at least as far as I could tell from my work in the churches and from my interviews. The rapture is not just a vague idea that floats in the air; it is a linchpin of the fundamentalist belief system, for it explains why it matters so much that Jesus will come back at one specific point and not another (before tribulation to save true saints or believers for the millennium itself), which in turn is crucial to the concept of phases in the revelation of God. The end of each such revelation, or dispensation, ends in violence, and the last (which is, of course, ours and the one we care most about) must have massive violence—the tribulation—but must also preserve the faithful to remake the world with Jesus as the anointed king. The rapture bothers many informed literalists, precisely because it is not specifically mentioned in the Bible and has to be inferred from the passage in Thessalonians.[6] But in the popular mind the rapture is appealing at many levels, and the longer it remains central to the theory the more sheer weight of historical tradition accrues to it.

What I found particularly interesting in my work, however, were the different ways fundamentalists shape (and sometimes modify) rapture doctrine. One of the more famous, though for some obscure, ideas during the cold war (which sometimes found expression in bumper stickers) was that as the bombs come down the faithful go up. That notion is an example of the general way fundamentalists locate images of the rapture in a decidedly modern context, which can seemed strained to an outsider—and is not always easy or clear for fundamentalists themselves. Cynthia, for example, had reflected anxiously about the specifics of what might happen to planes that were in flight at the moment of the rapture. Some would crash after the pilot was lifted out of the cockpit, but others might keep flying because the plane would be on automatic pilot, which would allow the co-pilot to take over. "Of course, now we've automatic pilots so you know maybe they'll end it. And how is it going to be explained [*pause*] away [*pause*] I don't know?" Clearly, Cynthia was speaking out of a private voice at this point, struggling in a realm within her end time self that was cut off from the interview process.

The rapture has also gotten sexualized in the minds of fundamentalists. Reverend Lester was not unique in this regard; he was only unusually expressive. He was asked in one interview to define the rapture: "There will be, according to scripture," he said, stumbling a bit at first, "we will be with the Lord." Then he was on a roll, relating his version of Revelation 21:2 ("And I John saw the holy city, new Jerusalem, coming down from God out of heaven, prepared as a bride adorned for her husband") and 7:4 about "sealing" the tribes of Israel: "It will be almost like a honeymoon, Jesus the bridegroom comes for the church, the bride, this is the beautiful symbolism used here, and he takes those that are his from every tribe of the earth up to the heavens." The passage in 1 Thessalonians (and a more obscure one in Revelation 1:7) simply locates the Lord in the clouds. But in the imaginative realm of fundamentalism, "the Lord" becomes "Jesus," who is then transformed into the bridegroom of Revelation 21:2 with the church as a waiting bride. Their meeting in the air, which is textual, subtextually becomes a kind of heavenly sexual intercourse. The passively waiting, virginal, and submissive female church gets "snatched up" (a common fundamentalist expression to describe the rapture) by Jesus standing erect in the clouds, which is how he is almost always pictured in popular representations. Reverend Lester, however, pushed beyond even this imagery, and went into a discourse on intimacy. Such closeness with God necessarily precedes intimacy with others, as he put it, and the rapture is like the "ultimate of intimacy." He then made reference to Ephesians on the proper roles in a marriage for husbands and wives (Ephesians 5:22–23: "Wives, submit yourselves unto your own husbands, as unto the Lord. / For the husband is the head of the wife, even as Christ is the head of the church: and he is the saviour of the body"). In this whirlwind of associations, Reverend Lester brought the dialogue full circle, folding a sexualized rapture theory into domestic relations.

But by far the most fascinating commentary on the rapture that I found was from Deborah, a perfectly ordinary believer who struggled valiantly to bring together her decency with the rapture's harshness. For those nonbelievers who miss the rapture, she said blithely, "they still have another chance." Since "every eye will see him" (Revelation 1:7), Deborah concluded that the rapture will surely be on television. "I do believe they're going to maybe record it on film or something. Somebody might get it on film." And she added the *New York Times* already has a headline prepared.[7] Through these media the rapture will be made available to the world just after it occurs. Nonbelievers who missed the rapture the first time around will be able to watch it on TV or read about it in the *Times* and even then accept Jesus and join the church; that is their second chance. Deborah was vague about the details of what can only be called a second phase of the rapture. This wonderfully original notion that bent theory, to put it mildly, and softened it considerably at a crucial juncture, was in the interests of extending the opportunities of salvation for nonbelievers. It would seem she simply refused to fully take in the harsh, apocalyptic doctrine that had been forced on her all her life. She had the main ideas in her head, but they had been quite drastically modified in an age of mass media to suit her more humane purposes.

Nor did Deborah stop revising end time theory with the rapture, part two. She was equally expansive in her understanding of the further opportunities that would be available during the millennium. Her basic image of the millennium was conventional. She described how during it the government, run by Jesus, will work the way it is ideally supposed to, and there will be peace and contentment on the entire earth. But Deborah added a rather significant twist. People, she said, will be so astounded at how good things are that they will finally recognize the majesty of God and accept him as their Lord: "There, again, they'll have that opportunity to make a decision." This *third* chance for nonbelievers, furthermore, would actually be practically open-ended, for the millennium, after all, lasts a thousand years. Deborah even argued that the chances for salvation only begin to diminish at the end of the millennium when the devil is loosed "for a little season" just prior to the final judgment. In her ruminations Deborah was particularly concerned with those children born during the millennium. It was beyond her comprehension that such innocents would not have an opportunity for salvation. So she made one up. Children, she said, will be witness to "the wonderful way things are being done" and "there's another chance for them, too." One can only wonder how many Deborahs lurk in the fundamentalist ranks, humanizing the tyrannical ideas of (largely male) theologians mapping out what they believe are God's destructive plans for a wayward humanity. Her adaptations may suggest a uniquely female use of the magical elements in fundamentalist theory.

GENDER AND FUNDAMENTALISM

I am in a position to offer only a few tentative generalizations about the gender differences I found among fundamentalists. When I was doing fieldwork it was not a conscious concern of mine to search out such differences, and I had no questions specifically about gender in my interviews. It was only later, almost as a kind of secondary analysis of my data (and prompted by the questions of several feminist friends) that I became increasingly aware of some interesting points I could make about gender and fundamentalism. Nevertheless, I offer these findings with caution, and hope they will contribute something to the work already being done in this area by others.[8]

In the broadest possible sense, the men I encountered tended to imagine the end as an extension of their traditional hierarchic and patriarchal Christianity. They often reflected male fears of the breakdown of social and sexual roles in society, and their images of nuclear and end time destruction in general were harsh. Most women, on the other hand, deflected end time violence onto more immediate human concerns like personal salvation and morality. They tended, in other words, to skip over tribulation and move directly into the millennium. Men, it seemed, planned the death of the world at the side of God; women prayed that their children would accept Jesus so that they would have eternal peace with God in heaven.

Otto laid claim to an assertive, macho brand of Christianity with a paranoid certainty. He evoked images of persecution of Christians and had complicated schemes of punishment worked out for non-believers prior to their ultimate damnation in the lake of fire. The end was close at hand for Otto, and he certainly expected to be raptured before his own death. Other, somewhat stereotypical male, themes entered into the imagery of fundamentalist men. Monroe's homophobia, for example, was so extreme he even mocked himself at one point about it. Nigel's form of sexual obsession had to do with a search for the ideal mate and a rigid puritanism. This well-heeled and ambitious Wall Street bond dealer lived an intense celibate life as he sought the perfect Christian mate who would never leave him. Nigel spent two nights a week in Bible study groups besides his church activities. He kept himself under strict control and reined in his lurching desires, which he renounced after his conversion.

Grady House, in turn, provided an institutional setting for pairing true Christians who toed traditional gender lines. The House, among other things, was a kind of Christian singles club. On a given evening, there was plenty of opportunity to mingle before Bible study began (though the study groups were segregated by gender), and a lengthy break with coffee and cookies before everybody from the various groups gathered on the main floor for announcements, a selected testimonial, and the lecture/sermon/biblical commentary that Sam, the executive director of Grady House, gave. Once at announcements, two gorgeously dressed young women urged people to sign up for an upcoming ski trip Grady House was sponsoring. They both giggled a lot as they emphasized the fun and fellowship of the trip but especially the opportunities it would provide for meeting good-looking Christian men. One said that last year there had been three executive ministry marriages that came out of the Aspen trip. The unmarried men I got to know well at Grady House—Monroe, Nigel, and Luke—were all actively looking for mates. I learned indirectly that Monroe married someone from Grady House after I stopped attending. For Luke it was quite a trip to come to the House for Bible study, since he had to return to a rather distant town in New Jersey late in the evening when it was over. When I asked him why he attended, he said honestly and without apology that he sought a Christian mate. What was left unsaid, however, is that such a mate would also be well educated, probably rich, cultured, traveled, and exquisitely dressed. For a boy off the farm and the graduate of a midwest Christian college, even though he was doing well in his business activities and had the prospect of getting rich himself, such a mate represented a rather large leap into the upper middle class.

There was, however, an important male theme that broke from the stereotype. Many men, almost despite their fundamentalism, were complex, ambiguous, vulnerable, quizzical people. Most such men seemed uncertain about their sexuality and lonely (which partly explained the intensity of their involvement in church life). Ian was an ascetic man who played the organ at five services each Sunday in two different churches and was involved in various church activities most other days. He did not care at all for issues of dogma or ideology (he could not remember whether he was to be raptured up before or after the millennium), but built his whole life around preparing for that time with Jesus. In the mid-1980s Ian had been positive enough about the future to put his money into a long-term investment program. Later, however, after the fall of Jimmy Swaggart, he got depressed about the world and how much longer the Lord would tarry. He felt Swaggart's fall was surely a sign that the end would come before the year 2000, and so transferred his money into a savings account with less interest earned but no restrictions on withdrawal. His reflections drew him into end time musings. He looked out the window as he talked of the death and destruction foretold in Swaggart's fall. He grew pensive and sad. He noted how tragic it is that the treasures of the Met and the glorious music of Bach are all of this world and will be wiped away in the tribulation. But, he said, almost as an afterthought, our hope is in Jesus. That makes it all worthwhile.

Women, for their part, tended toward a conventional form of Christian self-presentation. All accepted without question church teachings on issues of morality, and nodded in affirmation when Bible study discussion turned to Ephesians 5:22–23, about how a wife should be to her husband as he is to God, or 1 Peter 3:4–7, about how wives, as weaker vessels, should be in subjection to their husbands. The various ministers' wives I encountered were all dutiful, quiet, supportive women who served as role models to the congregation.

The fundamentalist women I met were also generally more gentle in understanding the apocalyptic. Kathryn turned her attention to the violence of the end times with some reluctance in the interview. She said such violence was "ugly and horrible" and that she found thinking about it "dismayed her." Thelma said she detested the book of Revelation. "I don't understand it," she said with certainty. "I don't think I want to understand it because I think I'd get too caught up [with it] *and* I'm fearful of the thing. And it sounds like an ugly book." For her part, Wilma expressed great interest in the approaching end of the millennium and the many signs that prove we are at the end of the dispensational age and that Jesus is about to return. But she also grew impatient with a question that sought to tease out the logic of her points and tie down a date for the end. "I'm not too concerned about that," Wilma said, "because there are a million interpretations. Everybody has his own interpretation. So I don't go into that too much," even though in fact she lived her life around end time expectations. Deborah, finally, illustrated a distinctly female voice in modifying end time theory altogether, especially regarding the rapture, to soften its harsh treatment of salvation. Deborah also had a wonderful reason why the battle of Armageddon could never be nuclear. The Plain of Jezreel, near Megiddo south of Haifa in contemporary Israel, where the battle of Armageddon will be fought, is too small for a big battle, she said. "It will be difficult to bring heavy military equipment onto the plain of Armageddon."

Among some women, there was as well a sexualization of their relationship with God. Cynthia, who was single, began to cry as soon as she talked about her personal relationship with God. She was too tender, she said of herself, and "his love is so wonderful." She also spent an inordinate amount of time in the interview talking about all the pornography and smut in the world and how she was not tempted to go down to 42nd Street. Wilma, in turn (and also in tears), said in an eruption of associations that we all need to "make love to Jesus." The connection between the individual and the divine is so concrete and immediate in fundamentalism that it lends itself easily to personalization, even sexualization, in the needy. This process is particularly apparent in women, since the figures in the pantheon are all men and the discourse patriarchal.

There were, however, some interesting variations on the female apocalyptic. For some the totalism of the church environment and the literalism of their religious commitments caused them to strive toward a mythical image of purity. Harriet's monastic life was perhaps the most interesting I encountered in this regard. A quite different female variation was illustrated by Mary's muscular Christianity, which came close to a mocking of the male style. Her special obsession with the signs of our decay, the nuclear and other violence of the end times she evoked with such vigor, and her imagery of a reborn millennial world were much more typically male in the fundamentalist world. Mary adopted this male style in an aggressive way that made her the leading end timer in her church, the analogue of Isaac in his congregation. Mary, also, in her appropriation of the Christian male role, was disdainful of America's men. All our men are on the couch, she complained, wimps and helpless beings who could never repel a Russian invasion. Psychiatry has destroyed us, Mary concluded. Kathy, in turn, a severe young woman interviewed in a Christian bookstore, relished the most phallic of patriarchal images. Jesus, Kathy said, would keep absolute peace during the millennium because he would rule with a "rod of iron." Anybody who disobeys or does anything wrong will be "zapped," she said. "And that's it."

Finally, the women in Calvary Church in Harlem clearly represented an altogether different female style. For one thing, their gritty lives made some of the concerns of wealthier white women seem trivial. They told stories of AIDS and drugs, absent and murdered husbands and sons, and fierce struggles to keep their families and neighborhoods together. These proud women seemed to have weathered trials that prepared them for God's mercy. They had already suffered tribulation; they are the surviving remnant. There was nothing separatist about these women. They adored their charismatic preacher, Reverend Charles, and prayed with remarkable enthusiasm. They were clearly the heart and soul of their church and reached out from it to include men. They pulled their children along by the scruff of their necks and applauded their men if they made it to church. But it seemed clear to me that from this congregation, it will be the women who lead the faithful into the millennium.

THE END
AT HAND

6

THE
WORLD
AND ITS EVILS

REVEREND CHARLES. The story Reverend Charles had found
to make sense out of his life history and commitments was that of
Jonah. This "first and greatest evangelist" was a messenger of God
sent to warn the citizens of Nineveh that they risked destruction unless they repented of their evil ways. Jonah, who at first resisted carrying out God's commandment by fleeing (just as Reverend Charles
delayed his "calling" to the ministry), eventually accepted his responsibility. He then reached Nineveh in time and convinced its inhabitants of their impending doom and the urgent need for them to
repent of their sins. The citizens of the city fell down and worshipped, and even the king put on sackcloth and sat in ashes. Similarly, Reverend Charles saw his role as that of warning a doomed
people of the need to beg God's forgiveness. "I think one of the roles
of our church or any end time church is to make people aware." They

then must change their "life-style and their attitude toward life, and their attitude toward God, and their attitude toward each other." It is only the pressure of destruction that can force such a radical transformation; standing at the edge of the Apocalypse, Reverend Charles felt, was a powerful motivator.

The ironic end of the biblical story, however, which was hardly lost on Reverend Charles, is that Jonah's success and the repentance of Nineveh only bought some time. As the book of Nahum, which is the sequel to that of Jonah, makes clear, after about a century God in fact carried out his destruction of the city so totally that it disappeared from the face of the earth. For Reverend Charles, who commented on this final end of Nineveh in a near whisper of terror, such is the paradox of faith and action. He sought to instill hope within awareness, or soon someone without "God in his heart" will "push the button." At best we can only buy time, and even that takes a huge effort and commitment. But we cannot give up, even though our ultimate destruction is assured. We must and can only act in a godly way to make a human future worthy of muting God's fury. It is an ambiguous lesson, it seems to me, but perhaps it is the only spiritually honest position in an age of real and evil threats to human existence.

Reverend Charles had a wonderful sense of humor, was articulate, and kept his vast church together as a dynamic force in the neighborhood. His hour-long sermons each Sunday were masterpieces of performance and conviction. His timing was perfect as he mocked his own sleepiness while once driving a bus (as a way of waking up the congregation), or mimicked the turning of the microphone head as an imaginary camera to keep the Lord "in focus." One could feel the expectancy in the air as his sermon approached, and the great sense of joy people took in having listened to his words and shared in his message. He had profound influence over the lives of his parishioners but used it to bring them out, to help them realize themselves, never to demean them. Reverend Charles was a consummate leader harnessing the collective will of his followers for the glory of God and the good of this deeply troubled and threatened community. These general assessments were made after some five years of my own intermittent participation in his church and three supervised interviews with Reverend Charles by a young African American researcher.

Born in 1930, not three blocks from the building that was the current home for the church, Reverend Charles was a taut and wiry man. At the time of his interviews, he was in his late sixties and had strikingly large and intense eyes. During the interviews he stared so closely as to seem almost glaring. "My folks were poor," he said. In his crowded family and later at school Reverend Charles seemed to have been particularly active and full of mischief. "I was the least likely to succeed, not because I didn't have brain matter, but I was prone to get into mischief and trouble, and my parents came back and forth more often than any parents should." Yet he carried a kind of secret mark, a special relationship to God, for his mother converted while he was in the womb. He seemed to see that as a kind of magical blessing, like being born under the caul. "I couldn't conceive that I would maybe have a hand, some small part in helping to up-build this community," he continued, "and that's the thing that marvels me at what God is doing and has established me here three blocks from where I was born and spent over twenty-odd years, almost thirty years of my life, and then bring me back and then put me in a position where I can help to bring about some change."

Reverend Charles was brought up as a Christian, and most members of his family seem to have been believers, but sometime in his youth he himself strayed from the faith. He related this falling off to the influences of his environment. "I came up in a rough block," he said "a rough area, a rough environment and you know the right way but I'm saying get caught in the tide, and you know, I got caught in the tide for a while." As a child it became clear to him quite early that he would never succeed and get an education unless he worked. Throughout his childhood he held a succession of jobs, including tarring roofs and working in the electroplating field. At twenty-one he was drafted into the Army during the Korean War. During the training period of the war he revealed some of his significant leadership skills and was put in charge of a training program. He found he derived a good deal of satisfaction from this experience, even though he found the racism in the army at that time detestable.

For thirteen years, Reverend Charles held a succession of jobs trying to find one that would give him some satisfaction. As he noted, "I was never ever fired from a job in my whole entire life. But I went from one job to another, because I just didn't feel this was it. I didn't find that fulfillment." At last he was "called" to become pastor at the church, something he accepted with great enthusiasm, despite the fact that it meant a significant loss of income.

Reverend Charles was an impressively well-read man on current affairs and about events in general. He read the *New York Times* every day, along with two or three news weeklies to which he subscribed. His conversation and sermons were factually accurate about world affairs, and when he discussed events as signs he brought to them a subtlety of thought and imagination that was indeed impressive. He also qualified everything. He believed the end was imminent, that it could even occur before the end of this century; he also had printed on the front of the church's program (at least during the 1980s) the slogan that Calvary was "an end time church with an end time mission." But he added in his interview: "God has the prerogative to take us into the twenty-fifth century, to the thirtieth century if he wants to."

Reverend Charles's immediate family life seems to have been relatively stable and without much death or loss. The exception was an aunt, whose death when he was quite young hurt him keenly. "My aunt, she was a missionary and she had given so much of her time. I said Lord, let her live. Our family was close because two sisters married two brothers and lived together and my aunt was like my second mother. I was raised with two fathers and two mothers. I called my aunt, Momma, and called my mother, Mother. I said, "Lord why did you allow her to die? God, what kind of God are you to take a sheep?" But despite the relative stability of his family life Reverend Charles came into frequent and immediate contact with death as a part of his experiences in his world of Harlem. As he said painfully: "I watched a lot of people around me die."

He recounted that as a child he was almost killed in three different incidents. In one of them he was hit on the head and had to have a number of stitches over one eye, while in another incident that he vaguely described he was caught in the hallway while some sort of fight went on around him. He also had an extensive experience with fighting in the "clubs" or gangs that flourished in his neighborhood. He had to take "unto myself" a kind of "survival violence" to make it to school each day with his lunch money. He soon internalized the violence. "It was easy for me," he said, "to destroy."

With his gang he often beat people "to a pulp," because that's what he was trained to do as part of the "club." He was under tremendous peer pressure to act violently. "Something that takes place [and] you've got to go out there, you've got to get out there, with the rest, when they call 'let's go to war council.'" Then you "lie to your mother," and "do whatever you have to do and be down at the spot and they'd outline, 'well this is what we're going to do down here.'" No matter how reluctant you might be, you have to follow what the gang leaders tell you to do. It breeds violence in you. You learn how to "crunch a dude," which becomes easier and easier each time you do it. "So, you begin to think violently. Let's change this thing *violently*, you know."

Death, as well, haunted his existence in the gang. Everywhere there was a sense of killing, violence, and death from which he felt he was spared only because he accepted Christ into his life. "As I look back and watched what was happening to my contemporaries, the fellows I was running with, the fellows and girls, I knew then beyond a shadow of a doubt that I had made the right choice [that is, accepting Christ]." Looking back at them, he saw that most of them were not only dead but that they died violently. Others died as a result of drugs, and the rest were just "empty shells waiting to die." And he reiterated the saving power of his faith: "My survival depended only on Christ coming into my life, my receiving him."

Much of the sense of destruction and death that Reverend Charles felt was fueled by racism, a theme that resonated in the lives of his congregation. He mentioned it often in his sermons, often by allusion, not to stir up anger but to give voice to the real and in the end to move toward some kind of healing. Reverend Charles was also quite concerned with the way whites are buying up Harlem and pushing blacks out. In the long run the process was a direct threat to the future of the church, and he felt it keenly. Such real threats to existence at so many levels lent Reverend Charles an emotional tone of uneasiness tinged with marked suspiciousness toward the outside world: "I feel that *they* let it [Harlem] run down like this," Reverend Charles concluded. "That gets rid of most of the blacks, that disperses most of the blacks." Such a keen sense of danger kept Reverend Charles in a state of preparedness that made him alive and vital, but it was not without its psychic consequences.

Reverend Charles's fears ran deep. "I watched drugs," he said, "take more and more of a grip, and a generation of promising, promising young people [get] wiped out." It seemed to have no end. "There's been times I've felt in my heart that this drug thing is a planned genocide by the white man to just wipe us out." Despair grips the community. "Our fathers and our husbands are in jail . . . out in the streets." It's hard to know when it will stop. "Our black men," he said, "will not live past their forties." The world of Harlem is also clearly getting worse, fast approaching the end time: "I feel its end and end time. And I feel whatever I must do, [I must] do it quickly, do it with all my might." Jesus may not choose to come for another hundred years. That's his choice. It is not within human province to dictate the time of his coming to God. But Reverend Charles did feel, in the light of what he's seen "as a lad" and watched from the time he was "old enough to understand," that "these things have just grown increasingly worse." People seem unusually brutal and inhuman. "We have crimes and deaths now that we've never heard of," Reverend Charles said with feeling. "I mean folks cutting people up in little pieces, stuffing them in plastic bags. Man's hard, man's turning almost worse than animals."

From Reverend Charles's perspective the signs of the end of human history were evident. "On all fronts, it looks dark, it looks dark." Things seemed to be getting even worse than he knew as a child. "I don't know how we're going to survive to the year 2000 at the rate things are going now, unless some things really take hold." Something must happen. "In the light of what I see and read, I feel that we're nearing the end." There is only one solution, and that is for "Christ to return and bring about an end to all the chaos." We have every "conceivable plague," especially now with AIDS. "They say the nearest solution they see may be ten, fifteen years down the pike, and they say 'we have no idea as to the depth of this epidemic.'"

The signs are grim as well in the world as a whole. There is unrest in Israel as well as in South Africa. "There's turmoil, tension, you just sense that the world is headed for a climax."

In a typical sermon, in January 1991, Reverend Charles discussed the Middle East and the issues of the Gulf War then in progress. He noted that with the war we were hearing more about the Apocalypse. It's all part of the "signs of the times." The war sets the stage for World War III, he said, and "even ungodly folk" are talking about Armageddon. The nations are being "positioned" for the end time. The time is short, he noted repeatedly, "perhaps shorter than we think." Jesus is about to come back, the harvest reaped. The segment of the sermon dealing explicitly with apocalyptic and end time issues followed a reading from the Bible in Mark 9:30–37 and bracketed what was to occupy most of his sermon on the biblical passage.

In the verses from Mark, the disciples talk among themselves about who is the greatest after Jesus tells them of his coming death and resurrection. Reverend Charles talked at length about this problem of losing focus on what matters and straying from real concerns. He referred often to the signs of a deteriorating world and of our own sins within it. He noted the circumstances of the community where God had planted Calvary Church, namely in a world full of drugs and crime and despair. His message was that God had entrusted this congregation with a "special mission" by placing it there. "There are souls for us to reach before the end comes," he noted with a passion.

The apocalyptic ran through Reverend Charles's sermon like a red line. It was there in the biblical passage when Jesus tells his disciples about his approaching death and resurrection; it was there in the framing comments about the end times and the current war; and it was there often in the references to the people dying around us in hopelessness and despair in Harlem. And yet, despite his end time themes, I never heard Reverend Charles give a sermon that lacked hope. Somehow he used the apocalyptic to energize his congregation rather than deaden it. Surely his own skill and humanity played a role in this remarkable transformation. But, as I suggested earlier, perhaps the more one's current life approximates the original experience of oppression that led to the book of Revelation, the more apocalyptic themes can authentically speak to personal renewal and transformation.[1] Life in Harlem fit the bill. Despite all Harlem's despair, Reverend Charles maintained a curious and hopeful sense of efficacy and commitment to the human experiment. As though he was energized by standing on the brink of the end, he seemed to draw strength from the approaching Apocalypse. His response was not to be passive or to withdraw (in contrast to many white fundamentalists), but to be highly engaged and connected with life now precisely because of the imminent threat of collective death. As he said: "While I've got the people we are out on the streets, the whole building, everything is dedicated to trying to reap this harvest, because I am gripped with a sense that it is not as much time as we think." And he continued: "This is the time to get *involved*. I'm not saying, well, I've got insurance, I plan ahead, I plan for twenty years from today if I never live to see that Jesus comes next month, next year. I continue to occupy, but I occupy with a sense of urgency."

This urgency bred a spirit of social activism throughout the church. The building, which had been taken over and refurbished by the congregation, was ideally suited for a variety of programs serving the community, including day care programs, a soup kitchen, and an adolescent youth center. Reverend Charles believed with a passion that he must combine saving souls, building bodies, and revitalizing the community. He told the story of a woman whom he helped find God. She had been a hopeless drunk until he brought her into the church. She was living in the park "from pillar to post, stinking up the place." He helped her find a job and a home, and the drug support group in the church gave her new confidence. "Here she has a car in the street, [and before she was] a hopeless drunk. She has a six-room apartment, money in her pocket, money in the bank that God—the Lord has allowed her to lift not just her soul out of sin but the whole mold." She herself then became an active convert and helper in the community. "She's walking straight now, she's working in the program to help folks who are drug addicts and so forth that want to get squared away, putting them into programs, getting them jobs, rehabilitating the whole mess."

At the same time, even Calvary had an intolerant side when certain issues were touched. In the fall of 1992 in New York City an intense debate took place over a proposed new curriculum for first and second graders that in part sought to enhance tolerance for gays and lesbians (stories about having two mothers, for example). Two weeks before Thanksgiving I attended the church to see how the debate was playing out in this congregation. Calvary had lined up solidly against the new curriculum, presumably because the biblical injunction against homosexuality is simply too explicit (Romans 1:27 and especially verse 32, which notes such "sin" is "worthy of death"). One of the assistant pastors gave an impassioned plea for everyone to sign a petition against the curriculum after the service. Other speakers followed (Calvary always had some four to six assistant pastors on the stage with Reverend Charles), and one conducted a prayer for "homosexual sinners." It was for me, frankly, a painfully ironic show to watch. My experiences with Calvary's members had led me to think that they would have been able to show greater tolerance for other oppressed groups and been able to distinguish tolerance for homosexuals from an endorsement of their life-style. The proposed new curriculum did exactly that, and also included multicultural awareness and sensitivity as a much more prominent part of the changes it recommended than anything to do with homosexuality. Calvary, I felt, had gotten suckered into the wrong fight. It was interesting, however, to note that Reverend Charles himself never said anything. Some years earlier (1987) I had heard a sermon by Reverend Charles in which he stressed concern, compassion, consecration, and contact of the Christian for sinners, some of whom—"like drug addicts and homosexuals"—will be difficult to deal with. Perhaps he felt some ambivalence and left it to subordinates to oppose the curriculum.

Reverend Charles always interpreted the Bible for his literal believers in ways that connected it with their lives in Harlem as disadvantaged blacks in a privileged white world. In one sermon, for example, he took the image of the raven—a black and usually disdained bird—and turned it to his purposes. He took an Old Testament passage in which the raven played a helpful role feeding Elijah, who was hiding by the River Cherith (1 Kings 17:2–7), to explain more generally why the Lord sometimes uses the evil raven as the bearer of good. He said he had once been hit by a car and was on crutches (as he began to limp around the stage). Before the settlement came through, he was desperately short of cash and unable to work. He was out trying to exercise his leg and stopped by Big John's Candy store for a cup of coffee. A pregnant pause at this point and raised eyebrows brought instant recognition to the congregation of the nature of "candy" sold at this store. Reverend Charles noted that he knew Big John from his days driving a bus, when he would stop on his route to chat and also then have coffee. Big John, in sympathy for his old friend on crutches, gave him $100. Reverend Charles hesitated to take the money, for he knew well the source of the funds from the real activities in the back room of the store. He went through various contortions to demonstrate his ambivalence but in the end grabbed the money from the imaginary hand of Big John and limped quickly away across the stage. Sometimes, he concluded, the Lord sends gifts via the raven. We at Calvary cannot pretend not to be a part of Big John's world. We cannot retreat into our sanctuary and expect to remain a vibrant congregation. We are part of the community and we must reach out into it. Besides, he suggested by ending his story with taking the money, such interaction can be personally rewarding.

As he was well aware, Reverend Charles's program in the church and his beliefs distinguished him from most other fundamentalist churches that focus much more closely on ultimate issues to the exclusion of social and especially political concerns. Reverend Charles's end time message, on the other hand, explicitly included what is traditionally called "social gospel" *and* a commitment to long-term change in the surrounding black community: "You know," he said of his goals for the congregation, "this is really black power. I can't tell the members [of his church] that because they would back off. It is biblical. Everything that we're doing is based on scripture. But it is [also] black power. We're pooling our resources and helping each other." The black church, he said, "has always been our strength. It's been our rallying point." This sense of Reverend Charles's end time ministry as a form of black power drew on what was clearly part of his early political activism: "Had I not made a commitment to Christ," he said "I would have been a revolutionary."

SIGNS OF THE END

Just as fundamentalists are obsessed with the timing of the Second Advent, so, too, they search everywhere around them for signs that the end is at hand. The concept of such a search is biblical. Jesus thus tells the doubting Pharisees and Sadducees: "O *ye* hypocrites, ye can discern the face of the sky [that is, tell what the weather is]; but can ye not *discern* the signs of the times?" (Matthew 16:3). The world, in other words, is collapsing around us, and if our eyes are open, it should be easy to discover the truth. But if people are enjoying themselves (though falsely and full of evil), that also is a sign of the end (Matthew 24:37–39). In fact, nearly everything is a sign of the end, when Jesus will return to defeat evil and bring salvation. That is the hope in the apocalyptic. Again and again, throughout my interviews, I was struck by how dread and hope are intimately connected in the Christian apocalyptic.

Fundamentalists talk of "signs" with disarming ease and frequency. There are two levels of such signs, natural and human, a complexity that exists in the single most popular biblical passage on the subject (and, in my experience with fundamentalists, one of the most commonly quoted passages in the Bible): "And ye shall hear of wars and rumours of wars: see that ye be not troubled: for all *these things* must come to pass, but the end is not yet. / For nation shall rise against nation, and kingdom against kingdom: and there shall be famines, and pestilences, and earthquakes, in divers places. / All these *are* the beginning of sorrows" (Matthew 24:6–8). These signs detailed by Jesus in response to his disciples' question, "What *shall be* the sign of thy coming, and of the end of the world?" (24:3), range from the purely political (nations rising up against nations) to demographic, social, and economic catastrophes (famines and pestilence) to purely natural disasters (earthquakes). The specific mention of earthquakes in Matthew is why fundamentalist anxiety rises immediately after any major earthquake or other natural disaster. But of equal interest among the signs Jesus mentions are the more political examples of kingdoms rising up against kingdoms (which are more urgent than wars) and what might be considered by-products of political discord (famines and pestilence). Signs, of course, must be interpreted, and in the modern context the search for understanding has generated an expansive attitude toward technology. In this regard fundamentalists are hardly backward. In their search for empirical evidence of the unknown, which feeds their hunger for symbols, they stay abreast of modern technological culture and all aspects of the mass media revolution.

For Deborah the single most important sign was abortion. It's "pagan" and "uncivilized." And yet it continues unabated. "In our day and age, we are supposedly civilized people, and we're allowing people just to openly commit murder." Abortion, it is worth noting, is universally opposed by fundamentalists and regarded as the murder of children with eternal souls—before they have a chance to hear the word and be saved. As a result abortion is often mentioned in the same breath with wars and earthquakes as an important sign. There appears to be no room for compromise on this issue, which makes abortion quite unique, and different, for example, from the debate over creationism. Only the ideologues (like Otto in my study) insist on the teaching of evolution in the schools as a sign; I never heard anyone else mention it. A moderate position allows fundamentalists to accept the theory of evolution ("days" are metaphors in the creation story), which is consistent with the theory of inerrancy as it took shape in the 1880s. At the moment, however, given the way the debate over abortion has taken shape in the last two decades, it is difficult to imagine a biblical position on the subject (and, given the orientation of fundamentalists, any argument would have to have a biblical grounding) that would allow for the emergence of a moderate fundamentalist stance on abortion analogous to the range of views that exist within the movement regarding creationism. For progressives on this subject, the primary task at hand, it seems to me, is to identify just such a biblical rationale for a pro-choice position. It would have enormous political implications.

In any event, the fundamentalist stance on the world in general is that it is deceptively appealing because Satan works within it. Cynthia argued that you must never let down your guard as a Christian, and you must look under every rock to locate signs of the end, like earthquakes and wars, AIDS, pornography, child abuse. But Cynthia also talked vaguely of the Common Market and associated it directly with the Beast of the tribulation, which, she said, "will have everyone's identity" and put the 666 number on their foreheads. Now that's "really interesting," she said darkly, "because right now in Brussels, Belgium, the huge computer system there that controls the Common Market and everything is called 'the Beast.'"

A sign, however, can be a process as well as a thing. One such phenomenon is the quickening pace of change in the world. Brother Heflin, from a black church (he was a visitor at Calvary when interviewed), said such acceleration was one of the clearest signs. "You know you'd have a major event that might take place once in a month. Now you have major events that take place once a day almost." Frank echoed this fundamentalist response to the *rate* of change in the world as much as the evils within it. The quickening pace stimulates the apocalyptic. Frank lived with the conviction that "things are not going to get better but worse," and "there is a pattern there of things getting progressively worse and worse and worse." His metaphors in this regard were both sublime and ridiculous: he noted that microwave ovens can now cook a turkey in an hour and forty-five minutes, on the one hand, and nuclear power and aerospace technology may change our universe, on the other. "The progress we've made, it's exponential, it's beyond just gradual growth." Soon Jesus will return, he said, because things are "utterly and completely hopeless."

Otto gave this idea of the quickening pace of modern life as a sign an interesting historical twist: He argued that it began with Hiroshima and the beginning of the nuclear age. He was careful not to say with certainty that Hiroshima marked the beginning of the end times, but with that qualification, which really served merely to cover himself against overly precise statements about God's actions, the beginning of the nuclear age was definitely when Otto saw the breakdown of things begin, when human history began its downward course. He seemed to understand that ultimate issues became something forever different with Hiroshima, that nuclear power in all its dimensions altered the very shape of contemporary life. In a curious way, Otto's view reflected Robert Oppenheimer's famous statement that physicists knew sin in creating the bomb.[2]

Sam, from his position of privilege, saw the main problem in the world as the move toward a "secular and humanistic point of view where God is looked at lightly." Nigel, for his part, got visibly angry in talking about the agnostic idea that the universe began by accident rather than as a willful creation of God. It is unbelievable, he said, that someone would try to pass off such an idea. "It takes a lot more faith to believe that than to believe that God created the world." The seriousness of the challenge posed by humanism was not related to the upper-class world of Sam and Nigel, for it struck fundamentalists at all social levels. Kathryn said in this regard: "I think we have come to a culmination here of seeing just number one as being all important. Humanism is based on number one being all important. That New Age sort of thing. Seeing how you can develop the inner self to its fullest. Develop the self. So that you can become like God." Humanism, in their eyes, is the direct opposite to true belief, which takes you out of yourself and connects you with God. Humanism is selfish, inner-directed, and, as Kathryn suggested, grandiose ("So that you can become like God"). It is also linked to the New Age movement, which to their mind gives it an organizational base, a kind of church, from which it can reach out to infect the society as a whole.

One sign of so much evil in the world is that Christianity is on the decline in America. "We are very quickly losing influence," Otto said. If "we" were more powerful, "I think we'd see more righteousness in this nation." There would certainly be less drug use, fewer killings, less pollution. We might even be able to stop the "abortion crime wave." It's not church and state that is separated in Otto's view but the separation of "God from state activities." The world presses in with all its evil ways, and true Christians keep losing power and authority, though the persecution of the church is a biblical part of the end times. Otto was systematic and even scientific in his search for empirical evidence of the end. "Never just accept something because someone tells it to you. Prove it," he said, fondly quoting one of his engineering professors in college. I pushed him on why he thought the end was so close at hand. He responded: "Well, I think the scripture in Timothy says that in the last days perilous times would come. Then it lists a whole bunch of things, like lovers of self, boastful, unthankful, unholy, different things, that I'd say were getting worse roundabout us.[3] I remember growing up on Staten Island. We never locked the door, my dad left his keys in his truck. He's got locks on every window now, and even then he's been broken into."

One response to the signs proliferating in the world is to erect barriers against the world. Reverend Lester thus complained bitterly of the inadequacy of the school system to teach children how to live their lives. There are no values taught, and the system itself is loaded with drugs, crime, and corruption, he said. That's why he started the K through 12 school attached to the church. But the school was only part of the protected and sacred space Reverend Lester hoped to create at St. Paul's. He saw false prophets everywhere (alluding to Matthew 24:11), which aroused great fears in him. The evil ones are out there now "becoming part of the system," pocketing money. They are even "representing God," which was a rather nasty dig at the mainstream church. Reverend Lester's goal was to create as self-contained an environment at St. Paul's as possible. It is not possible to be hermetically sealed from the world in New York City, but one can tighten the bonds within to ward off the perceived dangers without.

Analogously, an acknowledged objective of the operation at Grady House was to encourage the rich and powerful to make their businesses Christian after their own conversion. The theological and practical issues were complicated. Jesus was quite clear about the need for the rich to give up their wealth and distribute it to the poor (Matthew 19:21, 24), though a whole discourse (based more on 2 Corinthians than on Matthew) was developed arguing that the biblical commandment was only to abandon the love of money, not money itself. The figure held up by Grady House as the epitome of evil in this regard was Donald Trump. Instead of loving money, you were to use your money and power to spread the word of God, even though evangelism in their world presented its own special problems. One highly successful midtown dentist who gave his testimonial one evening in early 1989 described with self-congratulation how he had made his practice Christian by hiring only believing assistants and working only with converted colleagues. He was vague, however, about whether he intended to put his hands into the mouths of infidels. A more interesting ambiguity emerged in a discussion I once had with a man named Morgan, whom I got to know in my Bible study group but never formally interviewed. He had made a fortune in his merger and securities business but was left feeling a tension between his faith and the godless world of Wall Street. He had made the decision to make his business Christian. I genuinely wanted to understand the specifics of what it meant to create a Christian merger and securities business, but probably questioned him too directly when he was himself in doubt about what he was creating, for he literally backed away from me and my questions. As far as I could tell, what he meant was that he would employ only Christians in his business (like the dentist) but also use his profits largely for Christian purposes. He had no intention of only consummating Christian deals, which would have been impossible anyway. That reasonable business decision made him aware of the highly limited impact his new commitments would make on Wall Street. I think he felt unclean and saw me as an accuser; in any event, he turned away from me in our group and left the mansion immediately after Bible study.

At a personal level, fundamentalists feel the dangers of the signs of the end acutely, and their lives alter accordingly. Commonly, some retreat from the world (though many more than is recognized also move into the world); others intensify their own ethical commitments to stay pure in the very face of the world's corruption. As a child, Deborah's life was often confused by the need to maintain her religious morals and her desire to fit into the sinful world at large. She refused to take square-dancing lessons at her school, for example, because there was doubt in her mind whether she should be dancing. She was allowed to study in the gym by herself during those periods. "I do think I missed out on some things," she acknowledged. Even as a forty-five-year-old woman Deborah positioned her life in opposition to contemporary American culture. She had lived

in New York City for a decade and a half and only seen two movies.
One was *The Last Emperor*, and "they could have left some of [the
trash] out."

Such attitudes have led to the common perception that fundamentalists are separatists, withdrawn from a society they see as cor-
rupted. At the extreme edges of the movement such separatism is total, as with groups like the Branch Davidians, or the Church
Universal and Triumphant led by Elizabeth Claire Prophet, or in quieter ways with many smaller church groups in communities around
the country. But to label Christian fundamentalists generally as separatist would be wrong. There are, in fact, many exceptions. As I
mentioned before, Calvary was a very socially involved church, with
its programs for adolescents and drug addicts, its soup kitchen and
counseling. And it was not alone. Most members of Abiding Light
and St. Paul's (two lower-middle-class and working-class churches
with many African American and Hispanic members) worked with
the poor and the homeless. St. Paul's ran a soup kitchen, Abiding
Light ran a special program for kids in the projects, and generally
ministered to homeless people. Abiding Light also regularly had
special collections for a drug treatment center for adolescents it ran
elsewhere, and often the rehabilitated (and saved) kids came to sing
and testify at services.[4]

Even at the upper end of the social spectrum I found some evidence of involvement in the world that went beyond evangelical
work. It is true that most of those who attended Grady House de-
plored New York as dirty and dangerous, a city of sin from which
they escaped to the Hamptons whenever possible. Many whom I
knew directly worried no more about the world than the dentist who
reported making his practice a Christian one. But a few people I got
to know at Grady felt rather more empathy for the poor and sought
to reach them. Larry struggled to define a world of modest social action for himself that went beyond the boundaries of Grady House.
"Your faith without works is death," he said, trying to remember in
his uncertain way where the commandment is in the Bible (in James
2:14: "What *doth* it profit, my brethren, though a man say he hath
faith, and have not works? can faith save him?"). I asked him what
constitutes "works" and he listed feeding people who are hungry for

food and fellowship, visiting the sick, relating to the depressed. And he made his commitments real. Every other Sunday afternoon he and his wife went down to a mission in lower Manhattan to work and minister. It was a form of social activism that overlapped with his evangelical commitments, but it also went beyond merely saving lost souls. It was a fairly substantial amount of time for a busy broker who was in school and active in both his church and at Grady House.

ANTICHRIST

Despite these efforts toward good "works," though, the world remains corrupt, full of "false prophets," deceivers, and evil of all kinds. The obvious signs of evil for fundamentalists—crime, abortion, pornography, AIDS, humanism, the acceleration of change itself, the existence of weapons of mass destruction—resonate with scripture and serve as direct reminders of the approaching end. But even beyond such signs the real evil in the world is that which lies unseen or masked by apparent goodness or harmless pleasures—the devil, about whom fundamentalists have a lively image. The devil is at hand, speaking, as Wilma said, in one ear while God speaks in the other. Isaac, in turn, believed the devil is the "most beautiful creature ever created in God's universe." In Ezekiel he is described as a "beautiful cherub, one of God's highest angels." Some people think he was the "choir director" of heaven, but in any event he is a "very powerful, powerful creature." And he is nobody's fool. Never underestimate him, Isaac warned. He will come as the "angel of light," not as some "deformed thing with a red tail." Deborah noted: "And I believe there is a real devil. It's not just a, you know, a way of saying, 'This is good and this is bad.' This is God at war."

The devil manifests himself in human form most concretely as Antichrist, who comes as the great deceiver, the messenger of peace. Most fundamentalists believe he has already been born, and, like Monroe, allude to 1948 (the creation of Israel) as the beginning of the end times in which Antichrist plays such a crucial role. In the scheme of things, Antichrist makes world peace, including most of all with Israel, before revealing himself in all his horror. The subtextual message is beware the peacemaker. The greater the world leader, and the more he speaks to global issues of peace (for example, Gorbachev), the more he is ultimately to be feared as the probable Antichrist. One day, Cynthia said, people will turn on their TV and this "great leader" will appear to tell them everything is okay. They will be fooled into accepting his message. Thelma noted (referring obliquely to Jeremiah 6:14): "The Bible warns us that when men cry peace, peace, then sudden destruction [is certain]. I'm not interested in world peace because I know it's not what God says will be. He has never lied. His prophecies have come true. They're written down." Reverend Matthew had an expansive understanding of Antichrist that included the institutions within which he worked: "Now, the man [Antichrist] again, who, as I said, could be a system, but could well be both: a man with a system, a system that is so subtle that it sounds logical. For example, even the financial structure . . . the World Bank and all the things that are focusing on getting things with some brain, so-called, behind it. And one who can befriend everybody, no enemies. The best way to judge Antichrist is to recognize he is the opposite of Christ."

Carl Jung, in his perceptive ruminations on Antichrist, begins with the idea that the image of Christ parallels the psychic manifestation of the self. In that sense, Antichrist corresponds to the shadow of the self, the "dark half of human totality." The psychological concept of the self cannot omit the shadows, for without it the archetype of Christ lacks "body and humanity." He adds: "In the empirical self, light and shadow form a paradoxical unity." But the self, as expressed in the archetypes of Christ and Antichrist, is "hopelessly split" between the irreconcilable halves that find expression in the metaphysical dualism of the "kingdom of heaven and the fiery world of the damned." Antichrist is the "counterstroke of the devil." It only became Christ's adversary after the rise of Christianity. The image of Christ is so sublime, so perfect, so spotless, that it "demands a psychic complement to restore the balance." If you speak of high, there must be a low, of right and there must be a left, of good and there must be a bad, of the one and there must be the other. The devil is necessary to the image of Christ; in early Jewish-Christian circles the devil was seen as Christ's elder brother.[5]

Perhaps Christians in general but certainly fundamentalists in

particular need the idea of Antichrist to balance the absolute goodness embodied in their image of Jesus. They make abundant use of
Antichrist in this psychological and spiritual sense. Fundamentalist
images of Antichrist can be quite varied and creative, partly because
the two direct references to him (1 John 2:18, 22 and 2 John 7) and
the two indirect ones (2 Thessalonians 2:9 and 1 Timothy 4:1) are
thin. As a result, these references have been fleshed out with other,
vaguer ones, especially Matthew 24:24 ("For there shall arise false
Christs, and false prophets, and shall shew great signs and wonders;
insomuch that, if *it were* possible they shall deceive the very elect"),
and made into a wonderfully picturesque, malevolent figure.

Cynthia stressed that Satan as Antichrist appears as an "angel of
light," which is why he is so confusing. We believers know "who the
final deceiver is going to be," she said—not according to script—but
everyone else is bound to be fooled. Isaac, for his part, said Antichrist would be like John F. Kennedy or Adolf Hitler, both "amazing
men." Antichrist will be so powerful as to mesmerize us. He may
have telekinetic powers. Searching for another metaphor, Isaac said
Antichrist will be like a slum landlord who lets everything get run
down. "But the real owner is going to come back." Brother Heflin,
finally, as most fundamentalists, believed Antichrist has already
been born. In him all sin and chaos unite. Furthermore, he will set up
his kingdom right here in New York at the United Nations, with
branches in Europe (the Common Market) and a third in Jerusalem.

Otto felt that Antichrist works through religion. He uses false
faith, in other words, to draw people in, "then, after he consolidates
his power, then he will outlaw all religion and just say 'I am God, if
you're going to worship someone, worship me.'" The "religion"
that concerned Otto was less secular humanism than the New Age
movement, to which he ascribed some rather surprisingly malicious
motives. For one thing their goal, he said, is to reduce the world's
population to 2.5 billion people by the year 2000 by using euthana-
sia and forced abortions and encouraging homosexuality. In time,
Otto feared, "they may decide Christians are not useful if circumstances were right."

Things were always ominous for Otto. He thus had some quite
specific fantasies about how Antichrist will subtly take over. It will

begin with a consolidation of all the numbers in our lives—social security, bank, license, car—into one computer chip that "they" can put in the back of your hand, "and then just put you under a scanner, or whatever they use, and it could tell who you are, how old you are, where you live, how much money you have in the bank, what bank do you work with, and all these things." Perhaps, he said, they could just as well use a "laser-type tattoo." But since "it talks about not being able to buy or sell with that mark" it will pose a severe problem for believing Christians. Antichrist will not allow you to live in the world without the mark, but Christians will know they cannot take it on. Reverend Lester, like Otto, believed that during the end times people will have to take on signs on their foreheads to buy or sell anything, "almost like a credit card." He had even thought through the bureaucracy of the beast. "Instead of carrying a plastic card you'll go to some place and you'll get a number on your forehead that can be read by some machine. It won't be visible, I don't think, but it will be very clear that that's your numerical entry into buying and selling. It's like having credit cards."

Such modern concreteness about the passage from Revelation brings the end times into direct connection with modern technology in an almost humorous way. It is exactly such contextualization that makes end time imagery real and evocative for fundamentalists. Once the metaphor is literalized, it makes psychological and even spiritual sense to ground it in the specifics of the known world; at the same time, the dimension of absurdity that adheres to literalized end time ideas within a modern world may begin to undermine the whole elaborate structure.

PSYCHOSOCIAL PERSPECTIVES

7

THE
PROBLEM
OF ENDISM

THE REACH OF ENDISM. Endism, it could well be said, is the shadow side of our firm belief in renewal and second chances. It is our counter-narrative that competes with the boundless optimism we have in the future and our remarkable confidence in the capacity of our political system to correct itself for its own excessive enthusiasms.[1] Endism, which demands a special hearing as we approach the *end* of this millennium, opposes such optimistic commitments, foolishly perhaps, but always with conviction. It cares little about adjusting for small swings from center right to center left, or making more equitable use of resources, or allowing creative forms of expression, or, indeed, about sacrificing today to build a human future for the sake of our children's children. The Christian apocalyptic, as one expression of endism, seeks renewal through ultimate violence and God's cleansing of the earth, through faith rewarded and evil punished, and most of all through the miraculous return of Jesus.

The principal apocalyptic text of Christian fundamentalist culture, the book of Revelation that so many of my respondents quote, is also the one written last, in A.D. 95, after the destruction of the Temple and the Roman massacre of as many as a million Jews. God's revelation, as disclosed to John of Patmos, comes in the form of a violent and destructive end of human history, followed by some kind of parenthesis that fundamentalists read as the millennium, and the great climax of the final judgment which sorts out those who go to heaven while nonbelievers are thrown into the lake of fire. The apocalyptic, in other words, relates the specific forms of our forthcoming destruction, including the seven-year period of tribulation with its ferocious and unfolding violence of trumpets, seals, and vials that ends with the great battle of Armageddon between the forces of good and evil on the Plain of Jezreel near Megiddo in part of what is present-day Israel. One might say, following Revelation, that the apocalyptic connotes the violent, the redemptive, the vengeful, and the hopeful.

But the term "apocalyptic" also has a series of looser and more secular meanings that have accrued to it over the centuries that, like it or not, have become part of its associative meaning. Thus the apocalyptic is also the predictive (as that which foretells what will happen), the terrible (or any imminent disaster or final doom), the grandiose (or any wild and unrestrained predictions), and the climactic (or anything that is ultimately decisive). In this broad sense the Civil War, Hurricane Andrew, and the return of Jesus can all be quite accurately called apocalyptic, or, more broadly, endist.

Endist thinking, in other words, moves in many directions—including, most of all in America, race relations. The Los Angeles riots of 1992 struck terror in this country. "The City of Angels," said John Singleton, producer and director of *Boyz N the Hood*, the morning after the rioting began, "is turning into the City of Armageddon."[2] And New York has its own brooding tensions. In the Crown Heights section of Brooklyn a Hasidic Jewish fundamentalist group of Lubavitchers lives uneasily among Caribbean and African Americans. In the summer of 1991 a young rabbinic student, Yankel Rosenbaum, was stabbed and later died in a riot after a car in the entourage of the Lubavitcher Rebbe, Menachem Schneerson, hit and killed a young black male. Some radical Jewish leaders complained later that the police were instructed to go easy on rioting blacks, a complaint that was given new life when the person accused of stabbing Rosenbaum was acquitted. The accusation was that Mayor David Dinkins created a climate of fear about black riots after Los Angeles that made it impossible for a jury to convict Rosenbaum's accused killer. Even more specifically, former mayor Ed Koch sharply criticized Mayor Dinkins for talking about the danger of black backlash. When Dinkins makes such statements, Koch said, "he's threatening us with violence."[3] In this case the apocalyptic worked its way into the terrain of fear and code-words that make up American race relations. With a phrase a Jewish former mayor conjured up the Holocaust and pogroms and the whole scenario of racist imagery about black violence for political use against an African American mayor trying to control just such tensions, to stave off further violence, and to prevent white flight. The Los Angeles riots have altered the racial climate in New York and across the country, as fear of racial violence has itself become part of the apocalyptic, renewing the deeper hatreds and fears that always lurk below the surface of American culture.

Endism is deeply rooted in human experience and human history. Henri Focillon, in his brilliant historical and avowedly psychological study, *The Year 1000*, notes that the decline in cultural and artistic activity in the monasteries toward the end of the tenth century was "an evening of the world" (*mundus senescrit*) in people's imaginings.[4] The conclusion of the first millennium seemed too precise a fulfillment of *millennial* anxiety. It took no elaborate calculations, or year-day equivalents, or any special knowledge to feel secure in the approaching end of history. The end (followed by renewal) had long been associated with thousand-year cycles and was in fact known to *all* the ancient peoples "as a basic element of their religion or philosophy." The only change Christianity introduced via John of Patmos was to be specific about the thousand years (Revelation 20:4: "And I saw thrones, and they sat upon them, and judgment was given unto them: and I *saw* the souls of them that were beheaded for the witness of Jesus, and for the word of God, and which had not worshipped the beast, neither his image, neither had received *his* mark upon their foreheads, or in their hands; and they lived and reigned with Christ a thousand years"). In medieval Europe's thoroughly biblical culture, and one brimming with superstition and general illiteracy, the apocalyptic had a kind of democratic flavoring. No experts were required to foretell its coming. Most people (at least as far as one can tell from the fragmentary evidence available) assumed the world was about to come to its logical conclusion. A "nameless fear gripped mankind," a dark mood fell on the age.[5]

When nothing happened there was at first confusion (was the date wrong when Christ was born?), then astonishment, and finally a dawning sense that it was not going to end after all. A great weight seemed to be lifted. The monk Glaber wrote: "About three years after the year 1000, the world put on the pure white robe of churches."[6] Life began anew, especially in the monasteries where virtually the only written evidence of the change in attitude then existed. Dutiful monks who had stopped copying manuscripts resumed their tasks. Men thought again about religious and ethical issues. Long-delayed architectural projects were renewed, which in turn required money and spurred economic activity. Many factors fed into the great awakening that came to be called the Renaissance, and its full flowering was several centuries off. But its early stirrings in the eleventh and twelfth centuries make no sense except as part of a renewal of the human spirit after the grip of the apocalyptic was broken. The extent of the renewal serves indirectly to suggest the degree of psychological bondage in the apocalyptic experienced by a whole generation before the year 1000.

Focillon further argues that the more broadly secular meanings of the apocalyptic arose in the series of crises in the late medieval and early modern period in Europe that included the Reformation but also brought recurring plagues, witch burnings, and seemingly endless wars that dragged out over decades. "We may say," Focillon concludes from a look at the endist imagery in that period of history, "that every time mankind is shaken to its depths by a political, military, or moral cataclysm, it will evoke the Apocalypse."[7] Focillon also notes that there might well appear to be a contradiction between the humanism of the Gospels, which breathe love and peace, and the apocalyptic violence of Revelation. In fact, however, "each of the two satisfies certain needs of the human soul, and it may even be said that they complement each other."[8] Love and hate, one might say, as well as their extensions into peace and violence, are both potentials of the self.

The diverse meanings of endism, however, should not obscure the fact that we know of it directly because we all die. We are the only animals with such knowledge, even though it keeps fading away. It can well be said that human culture itself depends on the struggle to become aware of death. A primary task of religion is to provide some meaningful sense of endings and beginnings (which is why images of the millennium so often draw on those of the Garden of Eden, or, as Freud put it, our images of the future are molded by our indestructible wishes from the past).[9] Our children and forms of work symbolically immortalize the self. And all types of art, but especially literature, seek to define continuities and at some level are always about what Frank Kermode calls the sense of an ending.

No one argues more strenuously than Kermode for what I might call eternal endism.[10] He dismisses as "childish" any attempt to attach special significance to the terrors of our modern age, arguing that apocalyptic thinking is too firmly rooted in human experience. Only the naive, he argues, would privilege one's own time as uniquely dark and set it off as a cardinal point in time. The anxiety itself is not new. Cultures since the Mesopotamians have been dealing with it. Only the patterns of creative response to that anxiety have been different.[11] Kermode would also dismiss as heated imaginings the brooding anxiety aroused by the approaching end of the millennium. It would seem a form of "centurial mysticism," or, as Don DeLillo calls it, "millennial hysteria."[12] To the extent that we feel we now live in a state of perpetual transition, Kermode argues, we elevate our period of ambiguous ending into an "age" in its own right.[13]

Much wisdom lies in such a deep appreciation for the enduring, human attachment to the end. It has been part of culture since its beginnings some six to eight thousand years ago. Most scholars would agree with Focillon's discussion of the decline in creative activity in the half century before the year 1000 (though the evidence is inevitably thin and has occasioned heated controversy).[14] Norman Cohn has shown how widespread the manifestations of the apocalyptic were in social and religious movements throughout the Middle Ages.[15] And much in modern life continues these diverse forms. Apocalyptic eruptions reminiscent of tenth-century France or nineteenth-century New York state (the Millerites) often puncture our sense of calm, from those who mark the end (Elizabeth Claire Prophet in 1990; the Mission for the Coming Days, which forecast the rapture on October 28, 1992),[16] to those who claim divinity (Menachem Mendel Schneerson and David Koresh in early 1993), to the more simply, if terrifyingly, psychotic (Jim Jones). Modernism, it might be said, merely alters the shape of endism. It becomes democratic and somewhat chic, especially in a time of mass communications.

But such continuities may be misleading. To note only the eternal aspects of endism may prevent an appreciation for its more specific historical manifestations, compromising in the process specific moral and psychological insights. Based on the interviews I did for this book, I would argue that our historical moment is fraught with a new kind of dread, for we live with the real, *scientific* possibility that either through nuclear warfare, or choking pollution, or vastly increased rates of disease, especially cancer, we could actually end human existence. Millennial anxieties were quite real in the latter part of the nineteenth century—the term "fin de siècle" originated in the 1880s—and were grounded in the pervasive dread of a transforming modernism.[17] Yet Americans remained optimistic, expansionist, and assertive about the great virtue of their newly forged political institutions. But in the last half century things have begun to change in society, in the family, and most of all in the self. One can no longer trust in a human continuity; it matters that such an ending is scientifically possible. We no longer need poets to tell us it could end with a bang, or a whimper, or in the agony of AIDS.[18] Consciousness of endings haunts the psyches of quite ordinary people.[19] This is what Robert Lifton has called the "shadow" of nuclear threat. It changes nothing in particular but influences everything, and it is surviving astonishingly well after the cold war (just as nuclear threat preceded the beginnings, in the late 1940s, of the cold-war phase of American-Russian rivalry).[20] Before the nuclear age, conjuring up an idea of the actual end of humanity took a leap of imagination. But human endings now lurk in everybody's minds. No one can escape it; indeed, to completely ignore the forms of our potential destruction itself requires an act of imagination.

Furthermore, the emergence in the last half century of a mass movement of Christian fundamentalism, energized by the apocalyptic, has moved the endist impulse into the center of our culture, where it works directly on large numbers of Christians and spills over in unpredictable ways into other cultural forms. The task of the next chapter is to understand specifically how we arrived at this mass movement of apocalyptic fundamentalism. But for the moment, I want to further reflect on the larger implications of fundamentalism for American culture, and how the experience of fundamentalism can work on each of us.

COMMUNITY AND TOTALISM

It is by no means obvious what "being saved" means to ordinary members of fundamentalist churches. Cynthia literalized the metaphor: "You can't possibly know the answers to spiritual life until you're born again." And at another point: "You can't expect to see and understand things of the Spirit until you are born again." And a third pass: "You can't possibly expect to have all the answers when you are still in the birth canal; you have to be born again." All of these versions of the same idea came in one of Cynthia's breathless harangues, and were not dissimilar in content from Monroe's earnest efforts to convince me that only through belief could I get answers to my questions about end time things, or the grounds on which Mary finally refused me a third interview (I could learn more by talking directly to Jesus, she said). As discussed in earlier chapters, the idea that you truly understand what is in the Bible only after being saved is quite conventional among fundamentalists. The words of God are readily available. Anyone can buy a Bible and read them. But those words will be without meaning, or integrity, until you read them as a believer. Then the ideas become clear, the mysteries are solved.

Born-again reading thus casts most discussion of the Bible into a mystical framework, with some important consequences. Many fundamentalists, even recent immigrants for whom English is a second language, insist on reading Scofield's King James version of the Bible with its beautiful but old-fashioned English phrasing. The KJV overall is in a distinct minority among Bibles actually read by fundamentalists (there are some four hundred fifty English-language versions on the market),[21] but it remains the standard in their minds, the ideal to be reached if at all possible. In born-again reading you simply let the text wash over you, bathing your soul. Your task as a believer is to enter into the deeper sense of the words, which represent God talking directly to the reader. If you believe by definition you understand, which is not exactly the hermeneutics we try to teach in the university, and why it took me so long to figure out that my innocent questions about the meaning of difficult passages were often experienced by fundamentalists as intrusive and threatening.

Mystical reading of the Bible also binds the fundamentalist to the community of the church in ways that can be distinguished sharply from most other social institutions in America. They are all born again, and the kind of reading and understanding that they believe flows from that experience grounds their rituals of togetherness. There are, of course, personal and psychological factors in the born-again experience, but accepting Jesus also brings the believer firmly into a tightly cohesive community, which I suspect is as much a motivation for as a consequence of conversion. Friends, entertainment, ethical guidance, and personal integrity all meet in the community, which in turn shapes a parishioner's sense of self. In a world of often intense loneliness (perhaps exaggerated in New York City) and disintegrating families, the vitality of the communities created in the fundamentalist churches is one of their more salient features. At a place like St. Paul's, for example, parishioners often ate together, they spent much of Sunday and at least three nights during the week together, and their children attended the church school. Pastor Lester also played a fatherly role toward them, and he and his wife often had people over for meals. He advised them on minute details of their lives. From the outside it all seemed rather suffocating and infantilizing, but for the members of that community it clearly provided a togetherness that gave meaning to their lives. Even at Grady House, the involvement in the affairs of the community could extend to several days a week including special events like the ski trips for singles or religious retreats over whole weekends.[22]

But the dissolution of self in community can have an apocalyptic downside. At Abiding Light, something was seriously wrong, since from a once huge congregation in the first five or six decades of this century, by the late 1980s Abiding Light was a decidedly dwindling institution. That decline struck terror into the hearts of many parishioners who found it difficult to simply move on, or to understand such changes in anything but cosmic terms: the decline of the church, as everyone who was interviewed told me, was yet another sign of the end. The psychological investment in the church was too great. Its decline made no sense. God must be willing something, revealing his majesty through such ironic means. In this way, a kind of greatness (and mystery) returned to the church. God would never idly let one of his precious institutions disappear.

The mere fact of spending time together means virtually nothing in terms of the psychological experience of participation in a group. It is easy to be lonely in a crowd, or, conversely, to feel richly connected in the mutuality of a close relationship with one person. What defines the fundamentalist church experience is the intensity of its group interaction and the way it draws the individual into its rituals in an active way. Participation is never casual. If during a service you try to sit in the back unseen, there will suddenly be someone at your side, who will afterward take you to the coffee hour and invite you to Tuesday Bible study and Wednesday prayer meeting. At that coffee hour you will be asked directly where you stand with Jesus, along with many facts of your personal life that relative strangers in most group situations would wait months to ask about.

The benefits of such a strong, cohesive community are significant. Friendships are often intense. One is assured support in times of personal crisis. There are as well enhanced feelings of self-worth from participation in religious rituals. I learned quickly in my interview work that one good entry into a person's story was to ask them about how they found Jesus. Frequently, at the end of the interview people would give me a tape of their "testimony." Finally, it matters to one's sense of personal worth that the experience of the divine is shared. Otherwise, it suffices to stay at home and watch a televangelist.

On the other hand, many are repelled by such close encounters and dismiss the group experience in fundamentalist churches as cult-like, though the term "cult" is perhaps so loaded today that it may be losing its significance. A better conceptual question might be whether the fundamentalist experience is "totalistic" in the mind-numbing ways defined by Robert Lifton. Based on his interview work with "brainwashed" dissidents in China during the 1950s, he developed a number of criteria for defining the totalistic environment. These include the control of communication so that the balance between self and world is disrupted; manipulation of the individual around basic issues of trust and mistrust; the demand for absolute purity, which is contrasted with an outside world of pure evil; the obsession with personal confession as the vehicle for obtaining purity and merging the individual with the community; the maintenance of an aura of sacredness around basic dogma; loading the language with highly reductive, definitive-sounding phrases that can be easily memorized and repeated; the subordination of the individual to the claims of the doctrine; and drawing a sharp line between those who have a right to live and those whose lives can be dispensed with in the name of the movement.[23]

There are, to be sure, totalistic enclaves in contemporary fundamentalism. In David Koresh's Branch Davidian compound near Waco, Texas, for example, four or five score followers of this self-proclaimed messiah moved in a trance-like state as they gave over their lives (and the women and girls their bodies) to their leader's extravagant fantasies. The group was cut off from the evil world and armed to the teeth to ward off its potential intrusions, fears that in the end proved quite realistic. Koresh himself developed rituals of immersion into his dualistic world, as when he divided his followers into two groups, the first of which said, "Who's gonna destroy the Babylonians?" and marched three steps in place, to be answered by the second group, "We're gonna destroy the Babylonians." Certainly, Koresh's apocalyptic ideas were sacralized, his language loaded, and evil outsiders were to be dispensed with in the climactic events he foretold. David Koresh was unusual in his charisma, in his disregard for the psychological or sexual separateness of his followers, in his violence, and in the immediacy of his apocalyptic aspirations. But as the leader of a fundamentalist cult he was not alone, nor even that unusual. There are anywhere from 1,000 to 1,500 mostly nonviolent but separate and totalistic cults in contemporary America.[24] The actual number depends, of course, on how you count, but no one with experience in this area would claim the number is negligible.

But is the Branch Davidian sect in Waco—or Jonestown, or the more extreme survivalist and end time groups in places like Idaho[25]—the appropriate model to use in analyzing the typical fundamentalist church? It would be easy to do so, especially if one had a desire to malign the movement, to collapse its wings and use the totalism of Waco as the standard for defining fundamentalism everywhere. It would also be wrong, and certainly contrary to my experience in the churches. Fundamentalist dogma has a totalistic core, even if one has enough breathing space to live in the world as well. But what sustains that core can be complex and very human. Most of the time in my fieldwork I actually enjoyed myself. In all the churches I became friendly with a number of people, and felt I touched lives in a real, human sense as I developed enough closeness to conduct interviews in a private space with a tape recorder. I was invited into their homes, fed, and told of their deepest fantasies about end time matters. I often felt assaulted by their relentless efforts to convert me, but it soon got easy to endure "the pitch" as something their faith required of them. It would be highly dishonest to suggest that I experienced fundamentalists in any way as mindless, thought-controlled cultists.[26]

At the same time, it is important not to be fooled by the ordinary. Significant areas of continuity exist between the mainstream fundamentalist movement and its more extreme manifestations. In terms of ideology, in fact, little separates the two. The Branch Davidians in Waco were firm believers in the theory of premillennial dispensationalism (as are most survivalist, Aryan, or Neo-Nazi groups, whatever else they are). In terms of the rapture, Koresh and his followers were "mid-tribbers." In other respects, David Koresh understood the return of Jesus in ways quite familiar to mainstream fundamentalists, though to be sure, he added a few wrinkles to the end time story. His name, which was the Hebrew version of King Cyrus of Persia, connected with various apocalyptic themes in the Old Testament (it was in the third year of the reign of Cyrus that Daniel had his vision and Isaiah defines Cyrus as an instrument of God), and Koresh in general placed a great deal of emphasis on his symbolic tie to Jews and Israel. A flag with the Star of David on it flew over the compound, and as the flames consumed the buildings one of the last visible images was that of the flag falling into the fiery apocalypse. Koresh also believed that the House of David would be reestablished in Jerusalem when Jesus returns.

In tracking my feelings in the churches, I also noted, often reluctantly, that the pull toward totalism always exists in fundamentalism. When the ideological basis of their belief system is so apocalyptic, it matters that fundamentalists spend so much time together in worship, study, and prayer. The world, they believe, is an evil place to be resisted, and it is in any event on a sure path toward imminent destruction. Everything about their experience tends toward a psychological closing down. After extended contact, I often experienced such attitudes as oppressive. I personally have a lot of hope for the world. For all its suffering and gloomy potential, it is a wonderful creation that we have a responsibility to preserve for future generations. Fundamentalists believe otherwise, which I respect but found distressing and frankly irritating in large doses.

I had even more difficulty accepting the forced immersion of children into the fundamentalist world. Adults make the beds they lie in, but I always felt a pained empathy for the gloomy apocalyptic that surrounded the lives of the children in the churches. Philip Greven, in *Spare the Child*, argues that the authoritarian tradition in Christianity itself finds new vigor in the violence and abuse against children in fundamentalist families, which in turn creates the psychological conditions that attract damaged selves to the apocalyptic.[27] Although he exaggerates, Greven has identified an important psychosocial dimension of contemporary fundamentalism. Even if it is not expressed in physical violence, a violation of children's wills occurs in forcing on them an ideology that makes the world an evil place, in dragging them into a closed faith system without exit from an early age, in loading them with guilt, and in insuring that conversion occurs early enough so that they are bound to the community of believers before they are really ready to make free choices.

There is also a potential for violence in fundamentalism that I often found troubling. As we have seen, violence often defines their discourse. They talk and sing of washing their robes in the blood of the Lamb (Revelation 7:14), and warm to the cascading images of destruction and death in Revelation as trumpets are blown, seals opened, and bowls emptied in the heavens. These waves of violence form a rising and interconnected spiral, for the seventh of each includes and opens up to the next, until it all culminates in the final judgment. The churches themselves are awash in this imagery.

With most fundamentalists, however, this violent undertow remains an unseen counterforce beneath a relatively calm demeanor because of the shift in agency to God. The violence is ultimate rather than proximate. It comes from the heavens rather than from within us. Believers alone will be saved and all others killed. Believers are pure in faith. And in that faith they can overcome death *and* the sins of everyday life. Such a shift in agency allows individual fundamentalists to separate themselves from the violence that suffuses their ideology and present themselves as decent, kind, law-abiding citizens with enduring family commitments. But I found that at important psychological levels they move toward the violence that distinguishes their elaborate system of belief. Under individual or social duress that violence can turn from latent to overt forms. A group like the Branch Davidians in Waco represents that potential realized.

These general considerations, which constantly occupied my thoughts in and out of the churches, found personal meanings in my encounters. In Ian's Bible study, for example, I once let slip that I was married and had three children. Up to then I had studiously avoided mentioning my family. I sensed such knowledge would somehow be used to invade my privacy, indeed my separateness as a person in the interests of trying to convert me. It was. From that moment I was asked on a weekly basis about my family and strongly encouraged to bring them to church. It was suspect that I never brought them to church with me, especially as I clearly was not converting. Why was I there? What was I up to? One day I made yet another mistake and indicated my wife was pregnant. That piece of personal news opened me to the insistent intrusions. Ian immediately asked the group to pray earnestly for the unborn baby, for its future salvation, for the life of its mother, for me, for my faith, and for all unborn babies whom ungodly folk abort. I was appalled at what I had gotten myself into, and found myself praying against Ian and the group and all their dangerous ideas, vowing to myself that if something happened to my unborn baby I would hold them accountable. It was one of the few times I actually prayed in all my fieldwork (and, alas, in this study, prayer usually had this defensive quality for me). I was genuinely scared by the intrusiveness of the group and the danger of potential taint they seemed to pose at that moment in a matter of such enormous personal significance. (The baby, a beautiful little girl, was fine.)

Clearly I have no simple conclusions about the fundamentalist encounter from this analysis. The fundamentalist experience ranges across a continuum from Waco to Harlem, from complete surrender of the individual to the demands of a totalistic group and a charismatic leader to the empowered experience of building self-cohesion and salvaging community, with every kind of nuanced variation in between. Most fundamentalist churches are not totalistic. Believers are too much in the world and themselves to imagine they are under some mind-bending system of control. People come and go from these churches easily (sometimes to the consternation of the ministers). Adults entering the churches make free choices about participation. The vibrant and large fundamentalist congregations are well led and tightly organized. Others, like Abiding Light, are dwindling and often rather pathetic in their failure to attract people. But for all that the potential to move toward totalism still remains. Social crisis, or a big war, or a disaster like nuclear terrorism could transform the movement overnight into a potent and active apocalyptic force, and so transform the American political and social landscape. The consequences of such a transformation are unpredictable, but it is probably not unreasonable to guess that they would not be welcome.

8

A HISTORY OF
AMERICAN ENDISM

Endism is not without a history. Its medieval roots were suggested in the last chapter. In America, the story begins around 1820, though of course it has antecedents: the colonists' struggles to create the city on a hill in the seventeenth century encountered truly great odds;[1] and our own revolution was more radical than most people realize.[2] One could also note that the very discovery of America began in a kind of phallic apocalyptic. The feminist theologian Catherine Keller thus deconstructs the image (from her school days) of a blond, blue-eyed Columbus gazing out at the oceans as a masculinity looking forward, "penetrating its own future, piercing horizons," a gaze that will "render the planet endlessly available to cartography, to conquest, to control, to commodification." Basing her study on his *Professies*, only recently published in Spanish and not translated into English until 1991, Keller notes that in fact Columbus harbored extravagant apocalyptic dreams about the Americas and his relation to them. By his own calculation the world was to end in 1650, an imminence that lent urgency to his "discoveries." He was also the "Christ-carrier," as he began signing letters during his third journey in 1498, selected by God to fulfill ancient prophecies. "He would be the one to rescue Christianity before the Apocalypse," Keller notes, summarizing Columbus's *Professies*, "by spreading Christianity to the unsaved pagan populations around the world," finding the gold "for financing the crusade to recapture the Holy Sepulcher from the infidels." He was to be the new Christ who would discover Eden and rejuvenate the faith at the moment of the world's transformation into the millennium. At some level Columbus confused the line between himself and Jesus.[3]

But endism as we know it in contemporary America, specifically in its Christian form but equally in its broader cultural expressions, began to take clearer shape in the early nineteenth century. Any such historical—or psychohistorical—dating is arbitrary. One could begin elsewhere, and certainly emphasize different dimensions of the story. I have chosen here to narrate the historical unfolding of the Christian apocalyptic in the last century and a half. This narrative began in our crisis over slavery, was forged in war, took ideological shape within Christian theology as a response to modernism, was turned into dogma in the early twentieth century, and became a mass movement in the nuclear age.

LINCOLN AND THE CIVIL WAR

Antebellum America was obsessed with apocalyptic anxieties. This era of rapid social and economic change seemed to spawn great confidence, and yet, as de Tocqueville and many other European visitors noted, the boisterous claims made for the superiority of American life and land and democratic institutions had a distinct note of insecurity to them.[4] Underneath everything lay the great moral blot of slavery that at last began to push many whites to feel radical social change was necessary (or at least inevitable, even if regrettable). The sensitive founders, especially a Virginian like Thomas Jefferson, had recognized the immorality of slavery and the contradictions of their slave-owning lives as they wrote impassioned documents of human freedom. After the 1820s such tortured hypocrisy was a thing of the past, as the institution of slavery itself changed in the first half of the nineteenth century, gaining a new economic vitality and bringing vast wealth into the South. Its apologists became increasingly brittle. In the North the voice of dissent gained new moral ground, connected in part to the spirit of intense revivalism and religious fervor that swept the land from the 1820s on. Preachers like Charles Grandison Finney had remarkable evangelical successes in upstate New York and whole new religions (like Mormonism) appeared in the country. It was also a time of widespread apocalyptic predictions. William Miller, the most famous such prophet, had fifty thousand devoted followers and may have had as many as a million people more loosely associated with his movement in the early 1840s, though after his failed prediction of the return of Jesus on October 22, 1844—called the Great Disappointment—his movement rapidly disintegrated.[5]

The wait for some kind of dramatic resolution to the crisis affected peoples' minds and souls, and profoundly influenced the shape of politics. The antislavery movement, for example, beginning in earnest in the 1830s, reacted with moral outrage and a mounting sense of frustration to the continued existence of slavery. With the identification of slavery as a national sin, the antislavery movement brought a new earnestness and zeal to the political process.[6] During the 1830s a strong religious fervor encouraged abolitionists to commit themselves to a variety of reform movements (especially temperance) and remain peaceful, even pacifist, in their means.[7] But after the war with Mexico and the huge land grab in 1848 seemed to open up the country to domination by a white-led South based in slavery, abolitionists felt the struggle for radical but peaceful social change was being lost. Moral persuasion was not working. The old pacifism gave way to accommodation to violence as the only way to end slavery. For example, John Brown's attack on some proslavery settlers in 1856 at Pottawatomie in Kansas reshaped attitudes and prepared the ground for his attempted raid on Harper's Ferry in 1859. That raid, said the leading African American intellectual, Frederick Douglass, "has attacked slavery with the weapons precisely adapted to bring it to the death. . . . Like Sampson, he [Brown] has laid his hands upon the pillars of this great national temple of cruelty and blood, and when he falls, that temple will speedily crumble to its final doom, burying its denizens in its ruins."[8]

An underlying dread pushed the culture to extremes. There was almost a war in 1850, especially over the return of fugitive slaves. Some, like Lincoln, reluctantly accepted the great compromise measures of that year ("I confess," he said, "I hate to see the poor creatures hunted down . . . but I bite my lip and keep quiet.") Others, however, were much more vehement in their denunciation. "Let the President drench our land of freedom in blood," said Joshua Giddings of Ohio, "but he will never make us obey *that* law."[9] Throughout the rest of the decade there was much apocalyptic rhetoric about the "irrepressible conflict" (William H. Seward), the "impending crisis" (Hinton R. Helper), more loosely of the great fight to come, and of course Lincoln's own imagery of the "House Divided" in 1858 (which resonated so widely partly because it was imagery drawn from three of the four Gospels):[10] "It will become *all* one thing, or *all* the other," Lincoln said from the floor of the House of Representatives in Springfield, prophesying a climactic end to the great issue facing the nation.[11]

As the crisis over slavery deepened in the next three years, so did the sense of inevitability, North and South, about the approaching war. For the first time in the country's history, voters faced stark presidential choices regarding secession and slavery: the southern wing of the Democratic party openly favored secession against a Republican candidate widely perceived as an active enemy of the South determined to abolish slavery. Even the centrist Stephen A. Douglas blamed the Harper's Ferry raid on the "doctrines and teachings" of the Republican party.[12] Nevertheless, as Don Fehrenbacher has recently noted, it remains surprising that the South should have taken such an apocalyptic view of the perfectly legal election of Abraham Lincoln. Somehow Southerners had come to feel that the Republican party was a "hostile, revolutionary organization bent on total destruction of the slaveholding system."[13] And so, mysteriously it seems to me, the Confederate States of America squandered whatever moral authority they might have possessed in their attempt to build a new nation and fired the first shot at Fort Sumter.

Arthur Schlesinger, Jr., has said that the end of slavery in America is a good example of the triumph of the rational in our history.[14] If true, it is an odd characterization of the rational. Slavery itself was grounded in wild fantasies on the part of Europeans about Africans;[15] the antislavery movement, from the moment of its active beginnings in the 1830s, drew its entire inspiration from biblical images of moral reform, and when it turned toward an accommodation with violence in the 1850s generated apocalyptic (and sometimes mad) leaders like John Brown, while even its moderates, like William Lloyd Garrison, thundered with Mosaic certainty: "Ardently as my soul yearns for universal peace, and greatly shocking to it as are the horrors of war, I deem this a time when the friends of peace will best subserve their holy cause to wait until the whirlwind, the fire and the earthquake are past, and then 'the still small voice' may be understandingly and improvingly heard."[16] The forces that the war set loose pushed the sluggish system toward radical change;[17] and the great jubilee of emancipation itself inspired apocalyptic rhetoric in almost all observers, including in that seemingly rational man of action whom history pushed to actually free the slaves.

The Civil War shattered the dream of infinite progress that Americans had long nourished. De Tocqueville noted, with grudging respect but more than a little irritation, that Americans possessed a complete confidence that they rode the wave of the future and that their democratic institutions would eventually triumph over the tired monarchies of Europe. Ideas about American millennial purpose reached a kind of apotheosis in the notion, first formulated in 1845, of our "manifest destiny" in the world. Such exuberance in both the North and South cloaked imperialistic (and genocidal) motives while at the same time expressing a genuine sense of chosenness. The South felt entitled to create a nation in its own image while the North felt virtuous in its condemnation of the extension of slavery and its commitment to keeping the Union intact. Perhaps clashing forms of self-righteousness were required for such a bloody civil war to result. The special forms of our mission had been taking shape since the seventeenth century, when some ministers began calling their congregations "our Israel" and culminated in the northern idea of the Civil War as "ennobling."[18] Such attitudes led a man like Matthew Simpson, a confidant of Lincoln and champion of the Union, to comment during the war that, "If the world is to be raised to its proper place, I would say it with all reverence, God cannot do without America."[19]

War also gave reality to images of apocalyptic horror. Americans before the 1860s, to a large degree, had been insulated from the violence of war. The Indians were uprooted and pushed west with relatively small contingents of regular troops and only rarely engaged in actual battles. On the edges of American life, an edge that kept pushing west, of course, there was some experience of violence and fighting. Otherwise, despite the violence of slavery, in our systematic destruction of Native American life and culture, violence in the family, in the newly emerging cities, and, one might say, in the soul of Americans,[20] Americans had been pampered in relation to war before the 1860s. We simply had no idea what it meant for hundreds of thousands of people to die in vast battles on our own soil. The Civil War prompted powerful yearnings among whites and, as far as one can tell without a written record, blacks as well, for an apocalyptic cleansing in the fires of war. War would purge the virus of rebellion and remove the blot of slavery. This idea was clearest among abolitionists, who talked of American sin in slavery with every breath and urged the battalions onward to redeem the land. Lydia Maria Child said that she abhorred war, "yet I have become so desperate with hope-deferred, that a hurra goes up from my heart, when the army rises to carry out God's laws."[21] And George Ide, a noted preacher, seemed to justify any destruction as part of the war's higher purpose: "The cause of our country and the cause of religion, the cause of humanity, the cause of eternal Right and Justice, are so intimately blended in this crisis, that you cannot separate them. The triumph of the Government will be . . . the triumph of pure Gospel."[22] Some, like Lincoln and a few of his more timid or humane generals, were appalled at the carnage, but most seemed to revel in it.

An extraordinary number of Civil War generals, most notably

Stonewall Jackson, were self-defined as Christian soldiers marching onward, and only slightly more secular types, such as William T. Sherman, often sounded like Old Testament prophets.[23] In general, as Charles Royster has noted, northern military, political, and spiritual leaders talked loosely of a policy of extermination and repopulation of the South that would have to precede any regeneration of it in a way that set no limits on the destruction necessary to accomplish such goals. Both sides descended into "visions of purgation and redemption, into anticipation and intuition and spiritual apotheosis, into bloodshed that was not only intentional pursuit of interests of state but was also sacramental, erotic, mystical, and strangely gratifying. This process of taking the war to heart, believing that it would change everyone, worked as strongly as any other influence toward making it more inclusive and more destructive."[24]

Even Robert E. Lee worked from within an apocalyptic script. Lee's misplaced sense of "honor" led him to pursue the war long past the time he was personally convinced it was lost. As Alan Nolan has thoughtfully argued, Lee despaired more than has been recognized in the summer of 1863 after the defeats at both Gettysburg and Vicksburg, though he could reasonably cling to a shred of hope in northern opposition to the war. After the siege of Petersburg began in June 1864 (a full ten months before Appomattox), Lee characterized the certainty of southern defeat as "categorical" and "unqualified." He then lost even the remotest hope for the Confederate States of America with the reelection of Lincoln in November 1864, which was still five months before the final surrender. As Nolan points out, military leadership is not just a private matter. To continue a lost cause means that thousands more must die, or be maimed, or suffer.[25] Why did Lee keep fighting when he knew it was hopeless? Certainly he was insensitive to his obligations as a general not to waste lives. But in all other ways Lee seemed to care greatly for the welfare of his soldiers, who reciprocated with a blind worship of him. The issue would appear to be a more complicated one psychologically, one that is common to leaders—military, political, business, whatever—in many situations of looming defeat, namely the enlargement of their own grandiosity so that they can no longer distinguish between their own failure and that of the world (or army, or government, or business); indeed, that if they go down to defeat the world ends in an apocalyptic sense. For those with a paranoid cast, like Hitler, suicide is the preferred route at such a final moment. Lee, being sensible, instead built a protective myth of the "Lost Cause" that shielded him and the South in general from facing the moral and political consequences of his disastrous leadership in the bloody war.

But perhaps only defeat could satisfy the South, which lacked the morale to win due to their uncertainty about their identity, the peculiar circumstances that created secession, and doubts about the validity of their cause. They were economically and militarily ill-equipped for a long war, but much more importantly they were not spiritually or ideologically ready to fight one. There was much bravado. Alexander Stephens, Vice President of the Confederate States of America, said at the outset of the war: "Lincoln may bring his 75,000 troops against us. We fight for our homes, our fathers and mothers, our wives, brothers, sisters, sons and daughters! . . . We can call out a million of peoples if need be, and when they are cut down we can call another, and still another."[26] But in fact most white Southerners "could not persuade themselves," as Kenneth Stampp has argued, "that slavery was a positive good, defensible on Christian and ethical principles." Abolitionism, as they recognized at some level, was the "echo of their own conscience." It was a $2 billion investment and white Southerners dreaded the consequences of living with four million free blacks in their region. But they also knew it was basically wrong to keep Africans enslaved. It was an impossible dilemma. Only defeat served their purposes, something they embraced, probably unconsciously, on the road to Appomattox.[27]

Lincoln, in turn, was not always helpful in taming the apocalyptic impulses in the culture. In his first inaugural address he talked loosely about secession as the "essence of anarchy," and soon after characterized the firing on Fort Sumter as an attempt to "end free government upon the earth" (July 4, 1861), which became, by the end of 1862, a war to defend our fragile democracy as the "last, best hope on earth." The apocalyptic, in fact, was everywhere in Lincoln's rhetoric: in military strategy ("I think to lose Kentucky is nearly the same as to lose the whole game");[28] in his ready embrace of unconditional surrender as the goal of the fighting;[29] in his transmutation of individual soldiers' mortality for the nation's immortality in the Gettysburg Address;[30] and in his characterization of the war as a "fiery trial" through which we must pass.[31] As David Hein has noted, Lincoln surely used this phrase in conscious knowledge of its biblical origins in 1 Peter 4:12–13, where the experience of the fiery trial is that of martyrdom, or participation in the sufferings of Christ.[32]

Americans moved easily and quickly into this imagery of a purging through violence. As James H. Moorhead has noted, for example, the Civil War was the first time (and I would add the last) in our history that there was a virtually unanimous feeling among northern ministers that the war was hastening the day of the Lord and was a "climactic test of the redeemer nation and its millennial role."[33] By the second year of the war soldiers were singing that apocalyptic favorite, "Mine eyes have seen the glory of the coming of the Lord," who is "trampling out the vintage where the grapes of wrath are stored," not to mention the implicit theme of sacrifice in their song, "We are coming Father Abraham, We are coming, We are coming." Horace Greeley spoke from within the violence of the apocalyptic when he wrote on July 7, 1864: "Our bleeding, bankrupt, almost dying country longs for peace—shudders at the prospect of fresh conscriptions, of further wholesale devastations, and of new rivers of human blood."[34]

Many thoughtful observers have been mistaken in their strenuous efforts to rationalize Abraham Lincoln and take him out of this cultural apocalyptic in which he thrived and to which he gave such powerful voice. He was himself undogmatic, cautious, forgiving, ambiguous, and always sensitive to the inscrutable ways of God. One has to be impressed by the subtle irony of someone who could call Americans the "almost chosen people."[35] Furthermore, Lincoln's avowed use of apocalyptic rhetoric is always tempered with a human touch of doubt and forgiveness. The stark choices for the country he lays out in the first inaugural address culminate in an appeal for us all to be touched by the better angels of our nature. His passionate commitment to democracy was grounded in his belief that only free government can insure justice. He talked of fiery trials but moved quickly toward compromise about reconstruction in Louisiana as early as 1862. He insisted on the defeat and surrender of southern armies in the field but strictly avoided himself using the rhetoric of unconditional surrender and never talked of purging any land with blood.

And yet Lincoln defined the policies that created the war and formulated the specific apocalyptic language that gave it meaning for a Bible-drenched culture, from the image of the "fiery trial" in 1862, to that of the sacrificial redefinition of the nation's purpose at Gettysburg in 1863,[36] to God's purposes in ending slavery about which he spoke in his second inaugural address:

> If we shall suppose that American Slavery is one of those offences which, in the providence of God, must needs come, but which, having continued through His appointed time, he now wills to remove, and that He gives to both North and South, this terrible war, as the woe due to those by whom the offence came, shall we discern therein any departure from those divine attributes which the believers in a Living God always ascribe to Him? Fondly do we hope— fervently do we pray—that this mighty scourge of war may speedily pass away. Yet, if God wills that it continue, until all the wealth piled by the bond-man's two hundred and fifty years of unrequited toil shall be sunk, and until every drop of blood drawn with the lash, shall be paid by another drawn with the sword, as was said three thousand years ago, so still it must be said "the judgments of the Lord, are true and righteous altogether."[37]

The most extraordinary development of the apocalyptic in the Civil War, however, occurred in connection with the death of Abraham Lincoln. Shot on Good Friday and dead the following morning, Lincoln immediately became, in those 1865 Easter Morning sermons, a modern Jesus whose blood sacrifice fulfilled prophecy.[38] This "terrible tragedy," said the Reverend C. B. Crane of Hartford, Connecticut, is the "blackest page save one" in the history of the world and is an "after-type" of the passion of Jesus. It was "meet" that Lincoln should have been shot on Good Friday. "Jesus Christ died for the world; Abraham Lincoln died for his country."[39] The Reverend Rolla Chubb, in turn, noted: "On that sacred day, made holy and consecrated to the freedom of our race, by the crucifixion of Him, who died to redeem mankind from the thraldom of Sin and the slavery of the Devil, we were called as a nation to mourn the martyrdom of the great emancipator of four millions of slaves from the vilest bondage that ever saw the sun." The parallel was not exact, he recognized. And yet the spiritual joining of Jesus and Lincoln was virtually complete: "Those who thought to crucify the spirit of Freedom, will behold it roll away the stone from the sepulchre, and visit with a pentacostical effusion its disciples, inspiring them with a faith that shall revolutionize the world."[40]

The analogy with Jesus helped explain God's purposes in the war. The "serene Providence" gave us Lincoln, said Ralph Waldo Emerson, to direct the country through the war.[41] And Henry Ward Beecher added that, "His life now is grafted upon the Infinite, and will be fruitful as no earthly life can be."[42] In the minds of at least his northern contemporaries, including some of its intellectual and moral leaders, Lincoln thus carried out divine intention. This keen sense of American mission in the immediate wake of both Lincoln's death and Lee's surrender at Appomattox was cast in millennial terms. "In blessing our Abraham," Theodore L. Cuyler said, "God blessed our regenerated country, and the whole household of humanity." And the noted historian George Bancroft opined in his sermon that, "Heaven has willed it that the United States shall live. The nations of the earth cannot spare them."[43] Through Lincoln God revealed his plan. "The great battle of Gog and Magog," said Chubb, "is being fought on the gory field of Armageddon, which is the American Republic—a contest between freedom and oppression, liberty and slavery, light and darkness—and O how that conflict has raged during the past four years!"[44]

The sanctification of the Union was essential in constructing the Lincoln/Jesus myth. On the day Lincoln was shot but without knowledge of the assassination, the Reverend George Dana Boardman, speaking at the "re-establishment of the flag at Fort Sumter," described the American Republic as not a league but a nation, not a confederacy but a people, not a congeries of states but a Union. It is a "vital, throbbing, indivisible organism" and secession is more than subtraction or amputation but a "vivisection, suicide, murder, a death." And now with peace "a millennium awaits the groaning, travailing creation" that we call this Union. The celebration at which Boardman spoke marked the return of the fort where the fighting began and, by extension, of the Union itself. At the ceremony the actual tattered flag that had been lowered in defeat four years earlier was raised to the salute of one hundred guns.[45] It was a moment of great significance for the Union; and within hours Lincoln lay dying. This eerie, almost mystical, sequence of events was hardly lost on contemporaries, which is why the Boardman sermon on April 14 got published together with his Easter Sunday sermon on the assassination two days later; why the Reverend Theodore L. Cuyler talked of the "resurrection" of the flag at Fort Sumter in his Easter sermon;[46] and why the Reverend S. S. Guthrie could say: "His [Lincoln's] soul took its flight amid the echoes of solemn praises which accompanied the raising of the old flag over Sumter. Both are significant. The nation has completed its atonement; let the New Man and the People see to it that the New Dispensation shall come."[47]

There was, of course, a good deal of variety in the sermons and many regional and denominational idiosyncrasies. The eastern as opposed to the western, and the Unitarian and Congregational as opposed to the Baptist and Methodist, sermons tended to be more literate and less likely to fall into extravagant comparisons of Lincoln with Jesus, except by allusion and context. But in the end the *common* themes in the sermons are more striking than the variations. A great American secular and religious myth took shape almost instantly in the pews that Sunday morning. The historian and minister William E. Baron noted in the 1920s that there probably had not been a Sunday in American history when as many people attended church.[48] "Certainly history," noted a Boston preacher, "furnishes no case in which death has so instantly invested its victim with the sanctity of an approval more spontaneous and universal."[49] The Reverend W. E. Guthrie noted that Lincoln's death was his "apotheosis" and that he was now "The American Martyr."[50] "These trappings of sorrow," noted a Massachusetts minister, "—this sable, fringing and shadowing the nation's flag—these wailing Misereres that rise in the place of the joyful Easter Jubilates that we thought to sing—they are but poor symbols of the grief that lies too deep for tears. What has he not been to us—this high priest of Freedom—murdered at the altar."[51]

The most hopeful version of the apocalyptic was explicitly joined to images of Lincoln's own generosity and spirit of forgiveness[52] and expressed the transformative power of the bloody sacrifices of the war. The war, said one minister, "baptized our land with blood."[53] But God caught us up short in our moment of victory and took Lincoln. God hopes that Lincoln's death will bring Americans to their knees in a pious sense of their dependence on the Almighty. We will then become, through the sacrifice of Lincoln, fully aware of God's gift.[54]

Many sermons also developed transformative images of Lincoln as Moses, leading blacks out from slavery and glimpsing the promised land but not actually inhabiting it. Lincoln's identity as the Great Emancipator made such a comparison almost inevitable. Furthermore, the rhetoric of most preachers when they did refer to Lincoln as Moses slipped almost unconsciously, and sometimes unbiblically, into images of Jesus. The Reverend Charles S. Robinson said blacks expected Lincoln, and had been waiting for him, as the Israelites did Moses. "They prayed he would come. They waited for him to come. And then he came! . . . He seemed to them and their children a second Messiah." This "world's Redeemer" became then for blacks "*their* Messiah" (though one has to wonder about the patronizing way Robinson speaks so grandly for African Americans), "the seed of the woman [Mary], appointed to bruise the head of the serpent, in whose folds so many generations of their race had been crushed." In the end Robinson adopted an explicit note of apocalyptic hope: "Over the sad pall that covers our buried hopes bloom the bright flowers of resurrection."[55]

But for all the bright and hopeful—if extravagant—images in these sermons, there was as well a violent and vindictive theme that expressed the passions of a country just emerging from four long years of civil war. The assassination itself (America's first) was darkly evil in the minds of many ministers. As the Reverend James Douglas noted: "We mourn, in our deepest humiliation, the disgrace inflicted on our national character, in the most odious crime known, not only to civilization, but to barbarism."[56] No one doubted where ultimate responsibility lay for the assassination. A relatively unknown but quite typical minister, the Reverend James DeNormandie, rhetorically asked, Who killed Lincoln? It is said a man named Booth did it, he replied to himself. But that man was only an instrument. The true cause lay in those who supported slavery for two hundred years.[57] In most cases, in fact, the sermons gloss over the person of John Wilkes Booth, who on that Sunday was still at large. All felt that Booth would surely be caught and his co-conspirators hanged. The larger issue was whether the South would somehow reassert itself and restore slavery, which, some darkly noted, was by no means fully eradicated since the Thirteenth Amendment, though passed in Congress, had not been adopted in a number of states.

This vindictive endism erupted in the sermons even though most ministers recognized it was out of character with Lincoln himself, as well as with the spirit of renewal and joy in the resurrection of Jesus on Easter Morning. Those who developed this theme searched biblical texts for a rationale that would ground the theme of retribution. The Reverend John Chester, for example, quoted 1 Samuel 15:23, which equates rebellion with witchcraft, and Exodus 22:18, which says that witches should not be allowed to live. His conclusion was that the South had a "sinful complicity with slavery," was then rebellious, and like witches must die. Now they have murdered Lincoln. In dealing with their crime, there should be no "undue leniency," especially with the leaders of the Confederacy. "If this people let this sin of rebellion go unpunished, they will repent it in sackcloth and ashes."[58] The Reverend William Chaffin emphasized as well that those who murdered Lincoln were seeking to restore slavery. "Not to punish them with memorable penalties, is to set a premium on treason and bid for a recurrence of rebellions in the future. It is but right that we should be roused to a state of terrible indignation, for our uncompromising severity will, in the end, be the greatest mercy."[59]

There are those, said Charles Robinson, who were "nurtured under the hot debasements and vile luxuries of the slave system, sojourning here on our charitable sufferance, in order meanly to escape the perils of the ruinous war they have helped to incite, who clap their hands in applause of this murder! I think, in serious self-defense, we are to see that this thing is ended. This wickedness clamors for retributive judgment, and invokes the wrath of God." Although Lincoln himself demonstrated forgiveness in much of his life, Robinson thought that forgiveness was inappropriate in light of what the nation faced at this moment. "Let it be said, in reply [to the call for forgiveness], that the tidings of this murder, going into the ranks of rebellion, will be hailed with a howl of gladness and satisfaction, equal to the yell of Pandemonium, when Satan seduced Adam, and buried a race in ruin." Ultimate issues were at stake. The very existence of the Union, indeed of humanity, seemed in the balance. We do not want revenge but retribution, he concluded: "Let judgment follow on as implacable as doom."[60]

FUNDAMENTALISM AND THE APOCALYPTIC

"Strange (is it not?)," wrote Walt Whitman, "that battles, martyrs, blood, even assassination should so condense—perhaps only really, lastingly condense—a Nationality."[61] There is no question that the war, however terrible, brought some good and perhaps had to be fought; the end of the obnoxious institution of slavery has to be judged as a positive outcome of the war. But what is the nature of that millennium for which all those people, black and white, died? And what is the meaning today of having forged, but not discarded, the apocalyptic as the core experience of our nationality?

The great disappointment of it all was the huge letdown when it was over. The American character had been "tempered in the furnaces of war"[62] without much to show for it except missing limbs and a broken heart. The expectations of freedmen were dashed in the wake of a white southern backlash and a feeble national effort to protect the gains of the war.[63] Whole cities were destroyed, families broken, social and political institutions were in chaos. The Apocalypse had not brought the millennium. The story remained unful-filled, the script only partially enacted. The Union was secure, but the war shattered the dream of infinite American progress. We could no longer fully trust a human future—and this loss of faith in the ground of our being was to find deeper resonance in the ultimate threats of the twentieth century.

The war that seemed to settle so much for the future—the secure institutions of a national government and the end of slavery—in fact left open, bleeding wounds. Out of it came a postwar culture rent by the discords of modernization. The old patterns of communal life were breaking down. Basic changes in the infrastructure (especially those fostered by the railroad) were changing the very face of America. New cities sprang up everywhere, and old ones altered beyond recognition in the wake of huge population shifts from South to North and East to West, along with the largest influx of immigrants ever in American history. A new phase in industrialization took shape by the end of the century, one that some have called a second industrial revolution grounded in the new industries of oil and electricity and fed by the systematic expansion of scientific knowledge.[64] In addition, a widespread cultural insecurity, as Elaine Showalter has argued, "was expressed in fears of regression and degeneration, and the longing for strict border controls around the definition of gender, as well as race, class, and nationality." The terms "feminism" and "homosexuality" both came into existence in the 1890s. The anxiety then, she argues, parallels our contemporary fears about AIDS and homophobia that have prompted a return to patriarchy and celibacy.[65]

The conventional view of the formative influences in the shaping of fundamentalism keeps the analysis tightly within the boundaries of religion. This religious view holds that certain doctrinal developments occurred that fed the popularity of a seductive new approach to scripture. "Fundamentalism was primarily a religious movement," says George Marsden in the very first sentence of his authoritative monograph on the origins of American fundamentalism between 1870 and 1925.[66] Even Timothy Weber, in his excellent study of premillennialism, which acknowledges the apparent relationship between it and the rise of industrialization and the disintegration of American society, asserts: "Premillennialism's rise cannot be explained on environmental or even psychological grounds." His view, on the contrary, is that it arose "as an authentic part of the conservative evangelical movement at the end of the nineteenth century that gained popularity among those conservatives who favored a rather literalistic interpretation of Scripture and who recognized in premillennialism a way to remain both biblical and evangelical under difficult circumstances."[67]

Such an approach, which passes over the Civil War as a mere backdrop, privileges the heated theological and doctrinal disputes of the era and downplays the significance of their cultural context. But the whole period from the 1830s to the 1880s was one of radical ideological change within Christianity, and the appearance of premillennialism only became a movement of any significance after the Civil War. The key ideas of this emerging theory—dispensationalism, the rapture, and the "new" premillennialism (new because it was associated with these other ideas as part of a larger theory)—all dated from the 1830s, with sources in much earlier thinking.[68] The only subsequent development at the level of theory that mattered was the notion of inerrancy that forged a long tradition of loose biblical literalism into dogma.[69]

The key figure in this process of ideological change was John Nelson Darby, who was born in London of Irish parents and had been ordained in the Church of England before he broke from it in the 1830s, first to join the Brethren, and then in the 1840s to lead a faction within that group called the Plymouth Brethren (or Darbyites).[70] Darby's theory of "premillennial dispensationalism" included the idea of the rapture as the way Jesus returns before his millennial rule, and his idea of dispensationalism, which placed us in the last days without having to predict the actual time of the end, was a substitute for the kind of end-time arithmetic of William Miller. While Darby's theory was a new mix, it is worth pointing out that many of the individual strands of his ideas had earlier sources: his basic apocalypticism evoked that of the early Christians; the notion that Christ would return before the millennium was well established, especially in America; the essential idea of dispensationalism is at least as old as Joachim of Fiore's three Ages (the third of which, the Age of the Spirit, lies in the future) from the twelfth century; and glimmerings of the rapture doctrine can be seen in Increase Mather's thinking from the seventeenth century.[71]

Nevertheless, earlier sources are not the same as final formulation. The seven dispensations Darby worked up fit the biblical story well and are much more concrete and evocative than Joachim's amorphous Ages. The rapture in Darby's hands became a central idea in his prophetic system: it was the moment of separation of the faithful from human time, the spark that starts the end time clock ticking, rather than a mere possibility in the apocalyptic margins of Mather's thought. Darby also came up with some completely new prophetic notions, especially regarding the Jews and Israel, that had enormous consequences later. Darby, in other words, created a whole ideological system out of some existing strands of thought and some that he added. This whole was much larger than the sum of its parts, of sufficient depth and breadth and adequately enough based in scripture to ground the subsequent mass movement of fundamentalism.

It took the Civil War, however, before the culture began to be receptive to these new ideas—and even then things moved slowly. Darby himself was a tireless promoter of his ideas. He preached often outside the British Isles and was particularly influential in the United States, especially after 1859 (between then and 1877 he made at least six major tours in this country).[72] In these years Darby's ideas joined with the more homegrown theory of biblical "inerrancy" that took shape in the 1870s and 1880s. What is often lost in historical discussions of the origins of the idea of inerrancy is that from the outset the motivation for creating a systematic theology of biblical authority was apocalyptic. Spiritually and emotionally it is relatively easy to be literal about the sores on Job or Jonah's whale. It can be quite problematic, on the other hand, to take literally and theologically the complex symbols in prophecy. And that is what inerrancy was all about. What people really wanted to know was how to make sense of the seven weeks of Daniel, or the millennium of Revelation. If God loosed Satan from the bottomless pit, does that mean hell must be at the center of the earth? Where are the books of life and death that are opened at the final judgment? Are the wars and rumors of war in Matthew portents of an imminent return of Jesus?

Biblical literalists emerged out of a history of what is called Scottish Common Sense Realism and near reverence for the philosopher Francis Bacon.[73] In this value system (or discourse), the world presented itself in relatively simple, direct form, and the task of the observer was to gather evidence of its meaning. Enough carefully selected facts on a given problem yielded an answer that amounted to truth. In the spiritual realm, the search for Truth was subject to the same method. Close biblical analysis of a text thought to be without error proved the scientific validity of God's revelation to humans. Blind faith was unnecessary. One only needed to accept the validity of the scientific method. The most advanced and modern of approaches could prove the ineffable. Belief seemed ever more certain, grounded, secure.

Such literalism, of course, sometimes bordered on the absurd, as it does sometimes today, and spoke mainly to the observer's lack of sophistication, or education, or lack of psychological flexibility. But it was a comfortable academic setting that provided the crucial institutional framework for the development of a *theology* of literalism. The Princeton Seminary, founded in 1811, proved remarkable in this regard. Its most famous professor was Charles Hodge, a voluminous writer and editor. His magnum opus was his *Systematic Theology*, published in three volumes in 1872 and 1873. Hodge built something of a dynasty at Princeton (and immortalized his scheme of biblical interpretation), since two of his sons and one grandson all held chairs in the seminary. Other figures at Princeton, such as Benjamin B. Warfield, were important in the new theology, but none had the commanding influence of the Hodges. Within the ivy walls of Princeton, seemingly insulated from the outside world but in fact directly and interdependently connected to it, these Calvinist scholars pored over the Bible and its meanings in an attempt to formulate a theology relevant for the new world of postwar uncertainty.

The notion of inerrancy took concrete shape in the 1870s. Charles Hodge, in his *Systematic Theology*, argued that all of scripture, every book and every word in every book, was divinely inspired, based on his reading of Jeremiah 1:9: "Then the Lord put forth his hand, and touched my mouth. And the Lord said unto me, Behold, I have put my words in thy mouth." How God actually put his words into the mouths of humans remained inscrutable, but as Hodge once said, biblical writers "were controlled by Him in the words which they used," a formulation that has not unreasonably led to the persistent idea among literalists that God dictated the Bible to his oracles.[74] Hodge himself could easily allow for errors in biblical texts ("No sane man would deny that the Parthenon was built of marble, even if here and there a speck of sandstone should be detected in its structure"), but his son, A. A. Hodge, and colleague, Benjamin Warfield, pushed his ideas to new heights of certainty. In an 1881 article, the two argued that "all the affirmations of Scripture of all kinds whether of spiritual doctrine or duty, or of physical or historical fact, or of psychological or philosophical principle, are without any error." And Warfield wrote: "A proved error in Scripture contradicts not only our doctrine, but the Scripture claims and, therefore, its inspiration in making those claims."[75] In the theory of inerrancy, in other words, literalism became dogma.

However, one key problem in the theory that threatened to undermine the new theology needed to be solved. Careful research, especially by German scholars, was continually unearthing contradictions in the texts of the Bible. Since Charles Hodge stopped short of an absolute theory of inerrancy, he could airily dismiss such apparent errors as sandstone specks in the marble, but once his son and colleague had turned his ideas of literalism into dogma, the issue of mistakes in the biblical texts could not be avoided. So they came up with the convenient idea of "original autographs," or the notion that the only truly inerrant texts were the first ones written. Since then, with all the copying and translations, errors have inevitably crept in. It was a convenient theory, since the original texts have long since been lost, but it also created further problems of its own for which there was no easy or logical solution. What an inerrant believer has to accept in reading the Bible is that it is a surviving text that is simultaneously seriously flawed and yet perfect. Ernest Sandeen rightly sniffs with disdain at such a "scholastic" argument.[76] It is worth noting, however, that psychologically inerrancy at its core has a mystical grounding: The perfect text can only be imagined, not seen; must be believed, not read; worshipped, but never directly encountered. Perhaps any literalism, whether Christian or Marxist, requires such an intellectual and spiritual adjustment. Biblical literalism makes mystics of the whole fundamentalist movement.

In the remaining decades of the nineteenth and the early years of the twentieth centuries, the new movement gained a wide audience. It sometimes named itself premillennial but is better seen as a loose coalition of like-minded conservative evangelicals who drew loosely on Darby, the Hodges, and others. It would be an historicist fallacy to portray the movement as unified in theory, practice, or membership, but nevertheless a movement was taking shape. Regularly held "prophecy conventions" were hugely popular; the *New York Tribune* issued the 1878 sermons from one such meeting at the city's Holy Trinity Episcopal Church in a special "extra" of 50,000 copies.[77] Dwight Moody in turn created a number of institutes, the first of which was in Chicago in 1888, that trained "gapmen" to "go into the shops and meet these bareheaded infidels and skeptics" in order to appeal to them "in the name of Jesus Christ." Moody dispensed with laborious training in Greek and Hebrew in his institutes. He wanted to graduate evangelists, not exegetes, as he put it. Hundreds graduated each year from his institutes (which numbered fifty by 1900), and many more attended for brief courses of study. In a matter of a few short years and largely via this new institutional vehicle, premillennialism transformed the missions field.[78]

The waning years of the nineteenth century was a time of religious enthusiasms on a variety of fronts. Some new sects appeared (for example, Christian Scientism), while Seventh-Day Adventism, founded in 1863, gradually shed its dismaying Millerite background and became an important premillennial group. Charles Taze Russell founded the Watchtower Bible and Tract Society (Jehovah's Witnesses) in 1884, which was explicitly built on the predicted end of the world in 1914 (needless to say, it developed some new ideas about the end after that). A surge in revivalism in the early part of the twentieth century furthered these prophetic developments. The most famous was the Los Angeles revival in 1906 that led directly to

Pentecostalism and its leading denomination, the Assemblies of God, founded in 1914.[79]

The fundamentalist movement also acquired grounding in two texts that became the basis for a new canon. The first was Cyrus I. Scofield's edition of the Bible that was published in 1909 and sold as many 10 million copies by 1967 and since then 2.5 million more copies of a revised edition.[80] It had long been a convention in the Judeo-Christian tradition that notes and commentary on the Bible should be published separately from the text itself. Scofield, an ardent premillennial dispensationalist, broke that rule and incorporated both into his edition of the King James Bible. In the Scofield Bible each book is introduced with a brief essay that provides some basic background about the author and the premillennial dispensational meaning of the text. The tone of this version of the Bible is clear in the first textual note, which *precedes* the first word of Genesis: "The Bible," that note states with authority, "begins with God, not with philosophic arguments for His existence." Each of God's dispensations is explained with great care, and anything obscure or relevant to the larger theory is explained with forward and backward references. Most of all the prophetic texts are interpreted in elaborate detail. The mention of "tribulation" in Revelation 7:14, for example, calls forth a note that begins: "Although God's people may expect tribulation throughout the present age (Jn. 16:33; Acts 14:22), the word 'tribulation,' as here, is also used specifically of a future time (Mt. 24:21, 29; Mk. 13:24).

"Since our Lord links the abomination of desolation spoken of by Daniel with this time of tribulation (Mt. 24:15–21; Mk. 13:14–19), it is evident that the tribulation is to be connected with the seventieth week of Daniel (Dan. 9:27). Furthermore, the biblical references have in common an allusion to unprecedented trouble (Jer. 30:7; Dan. 9:27; 12:1; Mt. 24:21–22)." The note continues for four long and turgid paragraphs.

The Scofield Bible *is* the inerrant text of God in the minds of many unsophisticated fundamentalist believers. One man with whom I attended a Bible study class for two years had well over half of it highlighted with various brightly colored markers and never seemed to have it out of his hands. Another related a complicated story from the end of Revelation in the course of one of my interviews with him and confused a note with the text. Indeed, that is exactly the power of this edition, which for the first time incorporated a whole interpretive framework into the notes on the Bible. The notes come to assume a canonical quality. The Bible is a difficult book, written over the course of more than a millennium with many different authors in different languages and styles and even beliefs. It is more like a library than a book. Comprehending the Bible understandably raises a good deal of anxiety among mostly naive believers who have been told there is only one right way to read it—and that way is not always readily apparent. With the Scofield Bible, little is left obscure. One evidence of its amazing authority is that most popular fundamentalist books are either slightly revised versions of the Scofield notes, or adapt his theory to contemporary events.[81] It may well be that the Scofield Bible has touched the lives of more people than any other single book published in this century.

The second text, actually a series of twelve paperback pamphlets named *The Fundamentals* published between 1910 and 1915, codified the dogma of the emerging movement. A Christian philanthropist, Lyman Stewart, with some help from his brother, Milton, provided $300,000 for the dissemination of three million free copies of the pamphlets. Milton, who regularly supported the Moody Institutes and helped underwrite Cyrus Scofield's edition of the Bible, was motivated to reply to those "infidel professors at Chicago University." He selected the well-known and contentious evangelist, the Reverend A. C. Dixon, to lead the effort. Dixon in turn appointed an editorial committee that conceptualized the topics to cover and selected the numerous authors to write for the series. All the leaders of premillennialism in the country participated in the effort, including Arno Gaebelein and Cyrus Scofield, as well as leading academic figures like Benjamin Warfield from Princeton. Compared with the stridency of later battles, the authors of *The Fundamentals* took a fairly moderate position on most issues (except that of inerrancy). On Darwinism, for example, *The Fundamentals* allowed that the days of creation may have lasted a long time, allowing for some evolution during those intervals. The volumes were primarily conceived as a defense of the faith against the "higher criticism" of the Bible that dominated the seminaries of most major universities and the modernism in the culture of which it was a part. The most surprising aspect of the volumes is that their contemporary impact was far less than their historical role marking the consolidation of ideas that were to ground the fundamentalist movement. Few journals even reviewed the volumes, and certainly they failed to close the floodgates of modernism. Mostly, it seems, they were ignored, to be noted later as marking something they never did at the time.[82]

In 1920 this movement, with its diverse history, apocalyptic concerns, dogmas, emerging institutional grounding, and texts, got a name. Curtis Lee Laws, an editor of a Baptist newspaper, said a fundamentalist was someone who was willing to "do battle royal" on behalf of the fundamentals of the faith. "It was both a description and a call to action," says Nancy Ammerman, "and the name stuck."[83] Fundamentalism, however, soon faced a great test—and lost, or so it seemed, profoundly altering its history for the next half century. John Scopes, a high school biology teacher in Tennessee, decided to test the state's law against teaching evolution. He was prosecuted for breaking the law. In the dramatic trial that was the century's first true media event, two of the nation's greatest trial lawyers and orators lined up on opposite sides of the case. Henry Mencken, the caustic reporter for the *Baltimore Sun*, attended the trial and wrote of fundamentalist "boobs." The *New York Times* ran daily coverage on its front pages. The case quickly turned into a struggle of the old versus the new, of the twentieth versus the nineteenth centuries, of progress versus obscurantism. Clarence Darrow and the ACLU lost the case but won the war for public opinion. William Jennings Bryan, who won, appeared to be a beaten and humiliated man in the arguments with Darrow, something Bryan's death shortly after the trial only made more real.[84]

That at least is the official version, encrusted now with tradition. In fact, it is not so clear that the fundamentalists lost, or even felt they were defeated. Smart-aleck modernists like Mencken, who were not in the daily reading of true believers anyway, failed to change the face of emerging fundamentalism in Tennessee, or anywhere else, for that matter. The trial crystalized the lines of opposition in the country. It showed just how far apart the two worlds had gotten by 1925. But the Scopes trial hardly marked the defeat of the "boobs." For various reasons, fundamentalists after Scopes went into a period of retreat and relative quiescence. Those in the ranks who had imagined taking over the citadels of power for the faith had to plot a more modest, sober course of action. But most ordinary believers simply returned to their local concerns, churches, and institutions, unrepentant and unbowed, without shame or even a sense of having been defeated. This alternating rhythm of engagement with and withdrawal from modern culture has characterized fundamentalism for most of the twentieth century. The contrast between the fundamentalist activism of the 1980s on the national stage and its current involvement in the 1990s with local fights compares with the period before and after Scopes. Unlike then, however, no secularist of any sound judgment would now argue that fundamentalism is over with.

FUNDAMENTALISM TRIUMPHANT

In the two decades after 1925 the movement reorganized in various self-contained institutions, like the Moody Bible institutes, Wheaton College, and the Dallas Theological Seminary.[85] Somewhat later the Fuller Theological Seminary and Bob Jones University became important fundamentalist centers.[86] Various special publications emerged, and Christian schools, often directly associated with individual churches, proliferated. This subcultural network had little to do with the increasingly secular world of colleges and universities, which continued to dismiss it, unwisely, as a largely Southern, atavistic irrelevance. That is why the surprise was so great when Jerry Falwell and Ronald Reagan burst on the scene.

An important structural change, however, did occur within fundamentalism in the 1940s and 1950s: The looser, more moderate, less ideological evangelicals assumed a personal and institutional identity separate from the harsher and less numerous fundamentalists. Until the early to mid 1940s, "evangelical" and "fundamentalist" had been used interchangeably; after that they came to represent distinct styles within a larger movement. In retrospect the differences were apparent well before the 1940s, but they had little significance in the minds of believers or outside observers. Without the ideological clarity that developed in fundamentalism between 1880 and 1920, a schism was not possible because there was no moderate position to define in opposition to a more dogmatic one. But by 1942, with the founding of the National Association of Evangelicals, a breach opened up in the movement.

The evangelical/fundamentalist split was, and remains, a difference in degree, not kind. D. H. Watt has recently argued that the evangelicals sharply turned fundamentalism away from end time concerns to "private matters" of family and related issues. By the 1970s evangelicalism, Watt argues, presented quite a different picture from the 1930s. "Postwar evangelicals have not abandoned the doctrine of the Second Advent," he says, "but, on the other hand, not many evangelicals have meditated on it day and night." The family became the central concern of the Billy Graham Evangelistic Association, for example. Graham talked about it constantly from the late 1940s on, and half his mail dealt with family matters. In the late 1960s and early 1970s, as well, there were many vast evangelical congresses on the family, which Watt compares to the important prophecy conferences in the latter part of the nineteenth century that played such an important part in defining the emerging movement.[87]

Watt's distinction, however, may be more apparent than real. Conservative evangelicals, as I tried to show in earlier chapters, have much more in common with their fundamentalist brethren than with mainstream Christians. Watt also fails to incorporate into his analysis the important issue of the numbers of people involved in the competing fundamentalist styles. As far as one can judge, the most important change that occurred in the 1940s and into the 1950s is that a once marginal movement became mainstream. The evangelicals hardly "turned" fundamentalism inward. The old ideologues remained firmly in place in the Bible schools and places like Wheaton, Bob Jones, and Dallas. What happened is that a vast *new* group of believing Christians moved toward them, incorporating their essential apocalypticism without all the theoretical trappings. This much larger group of evangelicals brought with them concerns and commitments, especially about the family, that are not always in full agreement with the fundamentalists. The two groups have been fighting it out ever since. As Bob Jones and Billy Graham quarreled in the 1950s, so Jerry Falwell and Jim Bakker became rivals in the 1970s. But it is a fight within one family, more a sibling rivalry than a generational struggle or a basic disagreement over belief.

My point in this book is that the enormous enlargement of the movement, from the margins to now a quarter of the entire U.S. population, is what stands in need of explanation. In the middle of this century a powerful anti-modern group with a clear Christian end time ideology rather suddenly became a mass movement.[88] It is not surprising that differences in emphasis over issues of doctrine and practice emerged, or even that the further one moved from the ideological core of the movement the less passionate was its apocalypticism. It is more surprising that so many people choose to live their lives with a sense of the urgency of Christ's return. As late as the 1960s the significance of what was happening eluded some good observers, for example Harvey Cox, whose book *The Secular City* might have made one think humanism reigned supreme in America.

The purpose of this chapter, however, is not to rehearse the now-familiar story of the rise and demise of the Moral Majority; the great falls of people like Jimmy Swaggart; the recent and dramatic role of the Christian Coalition; the institutional rhythms of change in the fundamentalist subculture; or most of all the recent history of prophecy writing in America.[89] It is instead to understand the historical origins within the American experience of the contemporary mass movement of fundamentalism. The one piece of Darby's nineteenth-century theory that I have thus far left largely undeveloped is a set of ideas that has entered into the imagination of twentieth-century fundamentalists with a vengeance; they concern Jews and Israel, and the way both are part of a process that paves the way for the return of Jesus. These ideas, to which I turn in the next chapter, are of more than historical interest, for they continue to exert enormous influence on the minds of fundamentalists.

9

JEWS, ISRAEL, AND THE PARADOX OF THE INGATHERING

■

THE BLOOD TAINT. Beginnings matter. Matthew 27:1–26 tells us that the chief priests and the elders of the Jews took counsel against Jesus. They bound him and carried him before Pontius Pilate. Pilate, seeking escape from the dilemma of not wanting to condemn Jesus, asked the assembled multitude of Jews whether they would accept a substitute for Jesus in Barabbas. But the multitude cried out for Jesus: "Let him be crucified." Pilate, feeling guilty for condemning this righteous man, washed his hands and claimed he was innocent of Jesus' blood. To which the crowd replied, "His blood be on us and on our children." Then he released Jesus to them for crucifixion.

This blood taint has haunted relations between Jews and Christians for nearly two thousand years. The image of Jews as Christ-killers lay behind the medieval legal institutions that restricted Jews to certain professions. It was the underlying basis for enduring popular anti-Semitism and periodic pogroms, and it shaped the anti-Semitic thinking of theologians like Martin Luther, which fed into the many forms of Protestantism after the sixteenth century. Such ingrained hatred for the Jews provided the basis for the emergence, during the late nineteenth and early twentieth centuries, of "scientific" anti-Semitism, or the modern version of anti-Semitism that was grounded in evolutionary thought. This "social Darwinism" postulated a biological basis for the notion of a hierarchy of human races extending from Jews to Aryans and has had a significant global impact, particularly in the hands of Hitler.[1]

But were the Jews in fact complicit in the death of Jesus? There is no question that the Romans carried out the actual punishment. They ruled the land, Pontius Pilate was a Roman judge, and Roman authorities erected the cross and nailed Jesus to it. Haim Cohn, in an exhaustive study, even concludes that the Jews, in fact, "took no part" in the trial and death of Jesus, "but did all that they possibly and humanly could to save Jesus, whom they dearly loved and cherished as one of their own, from his tragic end at the hands of the Roman oppressor." Cohn argues that the stories of Jewish guilt for the death of Jesus were motivated by the desire to portray Jewish suffering after the destruction of the Temple as God's punishment for killing Christ,[2] and to the extent it is true is a distortion based in apocalyptic yearnings with fateful consequences.

Not all would agree. The story of the trial told in Mark (14:53–65), which is generally regarded as the oldest Gospel, and echoed in Luke (22:63–71), talks more darkly of Jewish complicity, of false witnesses, and condemnation to death by the Jewish authorities. At this late date, there is no easy way to sort out historical truth in a story so laden with conflicting meanings and passions. It would seem, though, that the conventional anti-Semitic view, now weighted with two millennia of tradition, that blames Jews for the death of Jesus and casts the blood taint on them, is inaccurate. The Romans killed Jesus, and, as Cohn emphasizes, they were the imperial power in a position to control all minorities under their rule. On the other hand, it is facile not to recognize that *some* Jewish leaders were coopted by the Romans and participated in the condemnation of Jesus, which made the trial and execution of this local, religious troublemaker much easier.[3]

For most of the last two thousand years the relationship between Jews and Christians has been at best ambivalent and often fraught with misunderstanding and violence. But in the last half century, with the widespread secularization associated with modernism, the creation of Israel as a state, and global ecumenism, relations between most Jews and Christians have been put on a new footing. Particularly in the United States, mutual acceptance is part of the social fabric. But in the florid imagination of the fundamentalists, which returns to the oldest of views of the crucifixion of Jesus,[4] a new, post-Holocaust chapter has opened.

HISTORICAL EXPERIENCE

Historically, Jews are one of America's many stable immigrant ethnic groups, though they have often had to contend with special religious antagonisms based ultimately on the blood taint. Some argue anti-Semitism has been steadily declining in America during the last forty years. Jerome Chanes, in a recent review of the relevant literature, enthusiastically concludes that anti-Semitism "is simply no longer a factor in American life." Chanes argues that there is broad acceptance of intermarriage and of Judaism as a faith (Unitarian Universalists generally rank lower in respectability in some polls), as well as a decline in stereotypical images of Jews and a decoupling of ambivalent attitudes toward Israel from feelings toward Jewish neighbors. Black anti-Semitism remains a haunting mystery, Chanes says, but he argues that it is mingled with class resentments and general anti-white sentiment.[5] Others, understandably, question such upbeat sentiments and worry that the deteriorating relations between African and Jewish Americans are basically rooted in religion and that often negative attitudes toward Israel overlap American domestic relations.[6]

Fundamentalists, for their part, feel no special guilt about the Holocaust, and treat it as something perpetrated by other people in a distant land.[7] They typically have little knowledge of what actually occurred, and what they do know is distorted by their theology. Fundamentalists' general feeling about the Holocaust is that the Nazis were agents of God's judgment against his rebellious people, and that the vast persecution and death of so many Jews could have a positive outcome in pushing Jews toward conversion. As one scholar puts it, summarizing the fundamentalist view, "God was using the Nazi horror to bring the Jews to faith in Jesus Christ and to rekindle their desire for a homeland in Palestine."[8] Furthermore, the Holocaust joins fundamentalist prophecy: It created the historical conditions necessary for the founding of the state of Israel. Hitler served God's purposes, as fundamentalists generally understand it.

Evocative Holocaust imagery, however, operates at many levels for fundamentalists, whose theology lends itself to images of shared suffering. One particularly subtle level is the opportunity the Holocaust offers fundamentalists to identify with Jewish suffering, persecution, and genocide. Otto, for example, drew his image of Christian suffering in the end times directly from the Holocaust. "Jews," he said, "as they were being brought into these cattle cars or into the concentration camps were crying out 'Messiah, Come!'" And Christians, too, whom he believed already suffer ridicule and abuse for their faith, will continue to face mounting persecution in these end times. Things are much better for Christians than for Jews, whose tragic deaths in the ovens found no fulfillment in God's intervention in human history. "So I mean," Otto said, "it's threatening, it'll be purification. But it won't necessarily be something like the Holocaust where, at least I don't think it would be, where just all Christians are put together and gassed or put in the oven, or mowed down with machine gun fire or something."

Such identification with Jewish persecution and genocide connects generally with the fundamentalist multifaceted response to Jews and Judaism. Many fundamentalists have a powerful, if somewhat abstract, respect for both Jews and Judaism. As people of the book themselves, fundamentalists revere Jews as chosen by God. Their story begins with Jews, and they feel they share a common narrative, and a common God. In this sense Jews are central to the Christian experience. As Deborah put it: "The Bible definitely tells us to pray for the peace of Jerusalem and for his people, for the Jewish people." This sentiment was warmly echoed by Isaac: "I find anti-Semitism one of the most horrible things . . . because I've read a lot of Jewish history. I pray for the country of Israel, I pray for it because they had the oracles of God given to them, our basic fundamental laws, right and wrong are based on Judeo-Christian traditions."

Jews and Christians share a common experience in the apocalyptic. Jesus was, of course, the Jewish Messiah (as understood by those Jews who accepted him), and the book of Revelation, in one sense, as the Christian prophetic story, merely updates its Jewish analogue, the book of Daniel. It may be that Jewish messianism has been more thoroughly secularized (Freud and Marx), which makes it only more apparently distant from its Christian analogue. And the affinity continues. In Jewish tradition, there are two views of what occurs just before messianic time: Either great evil and destruction occur, or things get so good that there is a natural enlargement of the human to encompass the divine. The parallel with Christian premillennialism and postmillennialism is exact. Jews and Christians mirror each other in their messianic ruminations, but differ in which messiah they await.

THEOLOGICAL ABSTRACTIONS

Below the surface, however, things are more complicated. One must begin with an examination of some important distinctions in dispensational theology that help shape the contemporary fundamentalist attitudes toward Jews and Israel. The leading theoretician of these ideas, indeed of most fundamentalist ideology, is John F. Walvoord, the former chancellor of Dallas Theological Seminary, who carries the mantle of John Nelson Darby for all literalist Christians in the late twentieth century trying to figure out the mysteries of the second advent. Walvoord's special concern has always been Jews and Israel in prophecy, which he has been writing about for some three decades.[9] Alert to nuance and well informed, Walvoord has clarified (as much as anyone can) the fundamentalist argument about Israel and the Jews and shaped a whole generation's thinking on these matters.

Walvoord argues that God's promise to the Jews covers both the natural descendants of Abraham (his "seed") and the spiritual children of God, or those Jews who followed the laws, but accepted Jesus as Christ. This crucial distinction has defined fundamentalist thinking since Darby.[10] Israel and the church move in separate directions, for it is a given that some kind of transcendence occurred with Jesus, some shifting of God's covenant. In the fundamentalist discourse, God is pursuing two distinct purposes. One purpose, with the Jews, is earthly, while the purpose with Christians is heavenly. Within certain bounds Jews can expect God's blessing, but that cannot be confused with his ultimate purposes regarding true Christian believers. "This is probably the most basic theological test of whether or not a man is a dispensationalist," says the fundamentalist writer Charles C. Ryrie. "A man who fails to distinguish Israel and the Church will inevitably not hold to dispensational distinctions; and one who does, will."[11]

Despite the potentially deadly dualism of the language in this distinction between Jews and Christians, the key fundamentalist point is to stress that Jews qua Jews (that is, unconverted ones) remain chosen and special in God's eyes. They were by no means simply discarded when Jesus came along, which is the older, simpler, and pre-Darby form of literalist prejudice against the Jews. But the question is, what are they chosen to do when and how? If God does not abandon the Jews, how will he use them? How can the explicit promises in the Old Testament be reconciled with the mission of Jesus *and* his prophetic return? What is the Jews' "future or continuance as a nation"?[12] Fundamentalists have been wrestling with this central question since Darby and others in the nineteenth century. The question as well as the answer is premised, of course, on a particular reading of the texts and assumes that Old Testament promises, interpreted literally, must be reconciled with prophetic reckonings in the book of Revelation. The creation of Israel and the ingathering of the Jews thus serve God's ultimate purposes in the second coming of Jesus.

Walvoord stresses that God promised the land to Abraham and his seed. "Get thee out of thy country," God tells Abram in Genesis 12:1, "and from thy kindred, and from thy father's house, unto a land that I will show thee." There is nothing figurative about this "land" for Walvoord. God meant the "literal land of Canaan," the proof of which leads Walvoord in a march through Genesis and Isaiah with a great leap forward into Hebrews.[13] The argument is that the covenant with the Jews is everlasting. Israel is forever theirs. And Israel, that nation of Jews, must be located in exactly the same place as promised to Abraham. Israel is not an idea in the minds of Jews. It is a sacred space with definite boundaries in the Middle East.[14] Since he takes scripture literally, Walvoord worries about the inconsistency of God, who made promises to Abraham and his seed, only to be broken once Jesus comes along. Genesis 17:7–8, for example, declares that the covenant with Israel is an everlasting one, a commitment that is repeated both to Isaac and to Jacob and is "constantly referred to throughout the Old Testament."[15] And "God never breaks his promises," as I heard often from fundamentalists.

When the modern state of Israel came into existence in 1948, fundamentalists felt it was a great confirmation of *their* prophecy. "[Revelation] required Israel to be a nation," Isaac said. "With the Jews back in Jerusalem," as Otto put it, "back in Israel, their own nation again, different things the prophecy has said about them have been fulfilled." And Frank: "God has good plans for Israel." In fact, it is fair to say that no other event of the twentieth century has had the same significance in the belief system of fundamentalists as the creation of the state of Israel.[16] The year 1948 marked—and continues to mark—"the winding down of the prophetic clock," as fundamentalists like to put it. I encountered this idea (and phrase) repeatedly in the churches. "The nation of Israel's existence is an important sign," said Mary. Otto added: "Jesus doesn't really return until the Jews are gathered back in Israel." And Elaine (Reverend Matthew's wife) noted: "Jesus says that they would be brought back to their land and that has taken place."

Otto and Elaine were referring, of course, not just to the creation of the state of Israel but also to the ingathering, or the return of the Jews to Canaan. The two are inseparable parts of the same process, which in turn marks the beginning of the end times that will culminate in the millennium and the return of Jesus. "The present regathering being witnessed by our generation," Walvoord says portentously, "is the largest movement of the people of Israel since the days of Moses."[17] The single most important text for the millennial significance of this ingathering is Isaiah 66:20 ("And they shall bring all your brethren *for* an offering unto the Lord out of all nations upon horses, and in chariots, and in litters, and upon mules, and upon swift beasts, to my holy mountain Jerusalem, saith the Lord, as the children of Israel bring an offering in a clean vessel into the house of the Lord"), but Walvoord also calls on Isaiah 11:1–12, 14:1, 27:13, 43:5–7, 60:21; Jeremiah 16:14–16, 31:21–40, 32:37–44; Ezekiel 11:17, 20:33–38 and 42, 37:21–22, 39:25–29; as well as more obscure passages from the minor prophets Joel, Amos, Obadiah, Micah, Zephaniah, and Zechariah.[18]

The ingathering moves inexorably toward Armageddon. The ingathered Jews who survive the violence of tribulation and the false peace engineered by Antichrist *must* all convert before Jesus returns to rule over his millennial kingdom. Again, since John Nelson Darby, this notion of a surviving remnant of Jews who will accept their long-rejected Messiah has been a cornerstone of fundamentalist theology.[19] The text here is the baffling reference in Revelation 7:4 to the so-called remnant of Israel: "And I heard the number of them which were sealed: *and there were* sealed an hundred *and* forty *and* four thousand of all the tribes of the children of Israel." Walvoord does some fancy footwork with this text: "Out of the total number of Israel, a representative group of 144,000 are sealed and thereby protected from destruction in this period [of the tribulation]. In Revelation 7, they are enumerated with their respective tribes. In Revelation 14, they are depicted on Mount Zion with the Lamb at the close of the tribulation, still intact and singing praises to the Lord. They form therefore the core of the godly remnant which will be awaiting Christ when he returns to set up His millennial kingdom."[20] It is an article of faith among premillennial dispensationalists, from Darby to Walvoord, that the rapture occurs before the tribulation, and removes the faithful from the suffering of that period. The remnant of converted Jews, however, who are "still intact" at the end of tribulation on Mount Zion awaiting Christ, survive because they are "sealed" before the suffering begins. Converted Jews are not raptured but survive as believers whose only purpose seems to be to make up for past sins by proclaiming the glory of Jesus' return.

It might seem that *converted* Jews would lose their death taint for fundamentalists because they affirm, rather than threaten, the fundamentalist belief system. Fundamentalist theologians try to be generous. During the millennium itself, for example, Walvoord allows for the inclusion of converted Jews. He thus argues that all are equal to participate in that kingdom, Jew and Christian alike, who are "joined by the baptism of the Spirit, placed in Christ, born again of the Spirit of God, and indwelt by the triune God."[21] But we should keep in mind that Walvoord's criteria of inclusion would exclude most Christians, let alone Jews, from "participation" in the millennium. Furthermore, premillennial dispensationalism in general, and Walvoord most especially, targets Jews for special suffering. Besides the extraordinary idea that converted Jews are not raptured, most converted Jews do not even live, for they suffer an appalling rate of destruction during the tribulation. "During the Grand Tribulation," Walvoord says, "two out of three of the Jews in the land attempting to flee their persecutor, the future world leader [Antichrist], will perish, and only one-third will escape and be waiting for Christ when He comes."[22] There is an important technical question that arises here, even a contradiction: How can a third of the Jews survive the tribulation if only 144,000 of them are "sealed"? Presumably those not "sealed" will shortly die a natural death and suffer eventual damnation (along with other nonbelievers who make it through the tribulation). In other words, of some twelve million Jews worldwide all but 144,000 will die during and shortly after the end time events, according to Christian fundamentalists.

It should be noted that many end timers—from Baptists to Jehovah's Witnesses—vigorously dispute the meaning of the figure 144,000 mentioned in Revelation 7:4. But for most fundamentalist Christians, the meaning of that sacred number centers on the notion that surviving and ingathered Jews, one way or another, *will be* converted in the end times. The ingathering is the precondition for the second coming, and in a mystically significant sense it is the massed presence of Jews that forces Jesus to return. "Jews for Jesus," interestingly, see themselves as the vanguard in this process, an evangelical idea warmly embraced by Mary. She believed the figure 144,000 in Revelation describes the horde of Jewish evangelicals who will lead the way in the conversion process. As she colorfully puts it:

"There are going to be 144,000 [Jewish] Billy Grahams running around the world."

JEWISH INSTRUMENTALITY

Jews, in other words, are instruments of fate in the minds of fundamentalists. The only historical role for Jews is to prepare for the arrival of Jesus. It is, needless to say, not a role most Jews accept. Most feel it is demeaning, even infuriating, to be fitted into a theological system to which they do not ascribe. Irving Kristol, a neo-conservative Jewish writer and editor, however, gives some pragmatic reasons for accepting fundamentalist attitudes: "This real world is rife with conflict and savagery. . . . We are constrained to take our allies where and how we can find them."[23] In regard to fundamentalist support for Israel, Kristol writes: "Why should Jews care about the theology of a fundamentalist preacher when they do not for a moment believe that he speaks with any authority on the question of God's attentiveness to human prayer? And what do such theological abstractions matter as against the mundane fact that this same preacher is vigorously pro-Israel." And he adds: "It is their theology, but it is our Israel."[24]

There are costs to this friendship. At the very least, the instrumentality of Jews in the minds of fundamentalists can mean that Jews are the object of intense scrutiny and evangelizing. New York City fundamentalists are fascinated with the large number of Orthodox and Hasidic Jews in the city. Monroe, for example, told me earnestly of his near success in "bringing in" a Jewish owner of a clothes factory in the city that would have meant his three hundred employees would be open to conversion as well. Mary conducted a series of special services for Jews at her church, which often featured guest speakers who minister and witness to Jews. One fundamentalist radio station in the city directs its broadcasts at the Hasidim in the Williamsburg section of Brooklyn. The station director made an emotional appeal to Mary's congregation, prior to a special collection, for their support in the effort to "save" even one Jew. The Jews "are all going to come back [to] Israel," Mary said.

At Abiding Light, largely as a result of Mary's initiative, there were a number of special outreach activities for Jews whom she felt were approachable because they were only "partially hardened" (Romans 9:18 and 10:14–21). At the beginning of Hanukkah one year, for example, she devised a skit to be performed for various groups in the city. With the menorah lit up, Mary began singing, "O, Holy Night." She had donned a dark wig and covered it with a black head scarf. A mock dialogue between two neighbors, a Mrs. Finklestein and a Mrs. Jones, followed the song. Mary played the role of Mrs. Finklestein. Using a Yiddish accent, she related how the two women met at the grocery store and became friends. The fictional Mrs. Finklestein talked about how impressed she was with Mrs. Jones. She said something had been missing in her life, and how gradually she began to understand that Mrs. Jones's peace and stability came from Jesus. The monologue was carried on with folksy humor, meant to convey how strange Christians must seem to a Jewish housewife. The presentation also included several songs, which seemed to represent the stories and feelings of diverse biblical women. For each song and each character, Mary changed head scarves.

The instrumentality of the Jews for fundamentalists is, in general, based on a lack of understanding or concern for the other and can carry within it the potential for violence. For most fundamentalists I talked with (as with theologians like Walvoord), the specific instrument of the violence against the Jews will be Antichrist, who will "strike at" the Jews first, said Reverend Matthew. Reverend Matthew's verb "strike at" is ambiguous in terms of the intentions of Antichrist toward the Jews. The verb could mean attack with intent to kill, but it could also simply suggest "get to and act upon" or, in other words, convert. But Reverend Matthew's latent meaning is clearer in a later statement: "The Antichrist will seek to make peace with the nation that needed most to be destroyed." Reverend Lester added his own twist about Antichrist to these violent images of destruction of the Jews. For him Antichrist will appear in the world as a "powerful orator and leader out of Europe." He will deceive people into thinking he is the Messiah, the ultimate savior. The certain proof of his secret deception is that Israel in fact will sign a treaty with him, but then three and a half years into the treaty they are going to realize their mistake. Then there will be a tremendous judgment.

But why does Israel need to be destroyed? The easy answer, that biblical prophecy foretells its destruction, fails to satisfy even the fundamentalists themselves, who uneasily combine abstruse points of theology with old-fashioned prejudice. Otto, for example, is fascinated by what he perceives as the warp and woof of Jews' relationship with God: "Someone has said that the biggest proof that there is a God [is that] the Jews are God's chosen people. There has never been a people that time and time again someone has tried to destroy and been unsuccessful in doing so. . . . I believe . . . they have been in rebellion against God. God protected them to the degree they sinned. God hasn't [forsaken] them, but punishes them." And yet, as Frank (a "Jew for Jesus") said, Assyria's invasion of Israel was an "instrument of judgment against Israel" for their "horrible abuses" against one another, their "inhumanity" toward each other, their "idolatry," and their "forsaking" of God. Elaine was more mundane: "Israel disobeyed God . . . they didn't follow his teachings . . . and they were scattered." "Problem is Jews have a set image of the Messiah as political," said Nigel. "They were wrong." Otto added: "Jews had these problems because of their idolatry in the past. . . . They would sacrifice their children to these altars." But the ultimate mark against Jews is, as Nigel said, "[because of their] refusal to accept Jesus."

Even fairly moderate evangelicals can be surprisingly severe in their attitudes about Jewish conversion. A group of fifteen evangelical Protestant theologians in 1989 issued a statement warning that creating a dialogue with Jews cannot substitute for converting them. The theologians noted that the only historical purpose of the Jews was to prepare for Jesus, and that after the resurrection God had broken his covenant with them. The Jews, the statement said, are "branches of God's olive tree" that have "broken off" (a reference to Romans 11:17–20). Contemporary Judaism in no way "contains within itself true knowledge of God's salvation." At the same time, the group of evangelical theologians condemned anti-Semitism and stressed the need for Israel to secure its existence and borders. There should be no "coercive or deceptive proselytizing."

But Christians must not compromise on God's purpose in relation to the Jews. As the chairman of the group put it, "We are under a New Testament mandate to carry the Gospel to all people, including Jews."[25]

This evangelical statement epitomizes the ambiguities of the more fervent Christian image of the Jews. Jews are abandoned children of God, fallen branches from his olive tree. They may find salvation *only* through the good evangelical efforts of Christians. Once exalted and chosen, Jews now are relegated to the margins of God's purpose in history. They sinned against God once too often. They continue to exist as a people and to retain a measure of his divine providence, but only because God does not go back on his promises. The new Israel is created, not the Israel of old, but an Israel in desiccated political fragments. The Jewish state, which fulfills the ancient promise, exists only as a sacred arena for the ingathering of Jews and the site from which Jesus will rule during the millennium. During the end times, which again it must be stressed we are *in*, Jews must be vigorously converted. God has given a great sign of his purpose in the creation of the state of Israel; now Christians must obediently fulfill his evangelical commandments, while Jews themselves await the worst kinds of suffering. Generally, then, fundamentalism is theologically pro-Jewish and at the same time anti-Semitic. Jews are special targets, something that is clear in the theology, as well as in the minds of ordinary believers, and their suffering rounds out a history of God's wrath from the Exodus to the Holocaust. Theologically, one might say, God saves Israel for Jesus while at the same time he destroys the Jews. At the end, Mary said, there will be a "showdown in the OK Corral in Israel."

Fundamentalists, in the end, have little empathy for Jews. They talk about "them" in the abstract and move quickly from discussing the seed of Abraham to Antichrist. It is important in this context to distinguish blatant anti-Semitism from the more subtle and pervasive forms of ambivalence and confusion about Jews that exist in the theology and in the minds of ordinary Christian believers. Fundamentalist writers themselves often react with sarcasm to the charge of anti-Semitism, stressing that they are "ardent supporters" of Israel and the Jewish heritage. They "chuckle inwardly" at the way Jewish intellectuals court liberal Protestants, who are in fact the enemies of both fundamentalists and Jews.[26] But as we have seen, the fundamentalist support for Jews and the state of Israel is much more complicated. For nearly all fundamentalists, instrumental images of the Jewish contribution to the end times make them and their state of Israel worth support only to fulfill apocalyptic visions. In the last analysis, fundamentalists find little of spiritual merit in contemporary Judaism, and most have in their minds a notably derogatory and devalued view of Jews as people. Ancient Christian prejudices find renewed life in this context.

The lack of genuine empathy that fundamentalists have for Jews has many consequences. Jews tend to be either idealized or debased but seldom perceived as people. Mary weeps when she sees the flag of Israel, a rather peculiar response for a thirty-year-old woman born in Georgia and raised a Baptist. For her it is important *only* that the flag waves over the land where she believes the resurrected Jesus will soon rule. Such pieces of Jewish experience have no authenticity in and of themselves. Mary's odd weeping at the sight of the Israeli flag is rooted in the basic Christian principle that God extended his promise from the Jews to Christians after Jesus. In the last analysis, for fundamentalists, "There is no kingdom for Israel apart from the suffering Saviour as well as the reigning King."[27] Even if muted, as it is in mainstream Christianity, it is clear that if one believes Jesus is the Messiah then some kind of transcendence of God's promises to the Jews has occurred in history.[28] That notion changed the cultural history of the west. It introduced the idea that Jews have been superseded by divine intervention in history, or abandoned by God altogether, depending on the theological interpretation. This notion of God's abandonment of the Jews, taken together with the taint of their assumed role in killing Christ, has resulted in the profound victimization of Jews for centuries. Even in a liberal democracy like the United States and in an age of secular humanism, the free-floating idea that Jews are somehow bad is not easily abandoned.

Clearly, in the extreme case of Nazism, the potential for violence in the western encounter between Jews and Christians was cruelly realized. Nor can one be entirely sanguine about the future. Despite a century and a half of writing, and much tragic history, it is fair to say that premillennial dispensational theology as well as most fundamentalists themselves are still confused about the Jews. Yet there are reasons to hope fundamentalists could in time soften and humanize their views of Jews. At the very least, it is worth noting that in all my work in New York I never once heard a fundamentalist say anything that would suggest images of actually rounding up surviving Jews on the Temple Mount and forcing conversion (or in any way threatening death to those who refused). But healthier images might also evolve out of the more ambivalent ones that currently prevail. Fundamentalists are part of the larger American society that many feel is moving toward a postmodern reconciliation of cultural and ethnic tensions. More specifically, fundamentalists may be saved eventually by the very confusion of their own ideas about Jews, Israel, and the ingathering. Their theology is quite inconsistent about basic issues such as whether Jews can be truly saved (as noted, converted Jews cannot be raptured), and ordinary believers often seem almost unconscious of their contradictions as they espouse a great love for Jews while talking numbly of their annihilation in the end times. More self-critical participants in the movement, especially younger people, might find it difficult to live with such tensions.[29] There is some room for cautious hope in these very contradictions about Jews and Israel.

10

THE HOPI WAY

THE HOPI APOCALYPTIC. It would be difficult to imagine a people more unlike Christian fundamentalists than the Hopi. The Christians are literalists, dogmatic, oriented to suffering and guilt, focused on ultimate violence, and often deeply dissociated in their personalities. The Hopi, on the other hand, are peaceful, gentle, non-dogmatic and non-literalistic (their language is not even written), and they purposely blur the line between the sacred and the profane. One is alienated from the world, from nature, from themselves. The other is at one with the universe, and their sense of the sacred infuses the most mundane of daily acts. The Hopi are even deeply psychological. Dreams, especially bad ones, must be recounted at breakfast or the spirits will be disturbed and the dream will come true.[1] And yet both Christian fundamentalists and the Hopi are apocalyptic. The Hopi live quietly on the three mesas overlooking the Painted Desert in what is now Arizona as they have for nearly a thousand years.[2] They plant their maize in the traditional way and perform the remarkable cycle of ceremonial kachina dances. Despite "Anglos" invading their world in RVs, they cling to their sacred Hopi way and ancient traditions. They also await the end of this, the Fourth World, when Pahana, the true white redeemer from the east, will appear with the broken piece of the tablet.

All Hopi prophecy concerns the coming of the "true white brother," Pahana, the redeemer, at which time all evil will be purified and the world remade. There are many versions of this story. In one Maasaw, the ruler over the Fourth World, just before he became invisible, gave the Fire Clan a tablet with instructions to migrate to their permanent home where, after a time, they would be conquered by a strange people. But he instructed them to remain faithful, for he assured them they would be delivered by Pahana, their lost white brother, who would return with a piece of the tablet that Maasaw had broken off before giving it to them.[3] In another version, the prophesied white man catches up with the Hopi and tests whether they have been true to tradition. If not, he will shake a Hopi by the ear and they will become like whites. But if the Hopi have been true, Pahana will go to an ash heap and kick an old shoe, after which whites will become Hopi.[4] And in yet another version the true white brother will return and slay all Hopi Two-Hearts (or false Hopi) and the races will unite.[5]

Perhaps such stories that center around deliverance by a good white man are simply apocalyptic accretions. But some evidence suggests the autonomy of the Hopi myth. One reason Cortés and the Spanish soldiers so easily defeated Montezuma's advanced Aztec civilization after they arrived in 1519 was the Aztec belief that they were descendants of their complex god, Quetzalcoatl. This beneficent deity with many mystical meanings had disappeared to the east some years earlier. It happened that the culture was actively waiting for the return of Quetzalcoatl when the Spanish arrived from the east. By the time Montezuma and his councillors awoke to their mistake it was too late.[6]

The Hopi by legend are direct descendants of the Aztecs. It may be that the Hopi were a special religious community at the northern edges of Pueblo civilization. Quetzalcoatl is not in the Hopi pantheon, but it is quite possible that the Hopi theme of waiting for the redeemer from the east was spiritually informed by connection with Aztec belief. Their subsequent experience with the Spanish dispelled Hopi faith in white-faced redeemers and also made them permanently hostile to Christianity. For a time in the first decade of the twentieth century, Americans required Hopi attendance at Christian churches, though the reaction was so negative the rule was eventually lifted. Although only about 2 percent of Hopi are Christians,[7] the impact of white Christian culture is far greater than such a statistic suggests. Schools that purport to be secular, for example, are outposts of a largely Christian culture and carry its assumptions and values. Hopi language, the carrier of religious traditions, has thus never been taught in the schools. And needless to say modern texts treating science, history, and literature that children on the reservation are required to read directly contradict and undermine the Hopi way. But it seems the Hopi have never given up on their prophetic assumption that the "true white brother" will be the instrument of the remaking of this world.

The Hopi have also incorporated into their end time discourse many apparently Christian elements. They talk of a "remnant" that has survived each of the previous worlds and will presumably make it through to the next, which is a familiar and important concept in Judeo-Christian apocalypticism.[8] The Hopi have an appointed "Last Day," called Nuutungk Talongvaqa, which is hauntingly like its Christian counterpart ("Last Days").[9] Their kachina dances, as well, which connect past and future, have been profoundly influenced by white and Christian themes.[10] The Hopi even talk about "signs" of the end. One informant told the researcher John Loftin, who has written an excellent book about the Hopi, that "by taking note of prophecy and recognizing the signs of its fulfillment, people can adjust their lives in accordance with the ways of the universe, and by doing so, prolong the existence of this world."[11] Another white researcher shared additional recent information on Hopi attitudes about the "signs" of the end. These include: various weather reversals; the blooming of certain yellow flowers in the winter of 1991; and further back in time, the dropping of the atomic bombs and the assassination of John F. Kennedy.[12] Unlike the Christian apocalypse, what is suggested in these signs for the Hopi, indeed in the end itself, only repeats something that occurred much earlier. That is why the most spiritual among the Hopi, those who still know the myths and legends of the past, also embody the greatest knowledge of the future.

In one sense, there are two primordia in Hopi conception that correspond to what we might consider mythic and historical time, though the Hopi themselves would never think of it in these terms. In the first is the creation, destruction, and recreation of the world through three stages of mythic imagination. Historical time occurs only in the Fourth World—our own—when myth approaches the remembered past. All Hopi images of the future are built, in large part, on the stories of the past, for apocalyptic endings and new beginnings are an essential element in Hopi cosmography. It is therefore worth outlining the story of creation in some detail.

All of the first three worlds were underground. The Creator, Taiowa, or *a'ni himu*,[13] who embodies the infinite, conceived of the finite. First he created a nephew, Sotuknang, that is, a kind of incarnated presence of the ineffable, to carry out his wishes. Sotuknang shaped the earth. But then he said he needed a companion, a mother of the world to come, a web to unite it all. And so the Creator made Spider Woman. Taiowa also created two spirit twins, who were to look after, protect, and inhabit the world. All four—Sotuknang, Spider Woman, and the twins—were to participate in the creation of humankind, but they had to have a song to do it. The younger twin wrote the song:

From the four corners of the universe:
From the East, for red is its color;
From the North, for white is its color;
From the West, for yellow is its color;
And from the South, for blue is its color;
In the counterclockwise motion of Tawa Taka, the Sun Father.

Come the four colors of the races of humankind,
each with its leaders,

each with its destiny.
Soon they will fight, as it is prophesied,
but someday they shall unite.
Then they will remember
that Taiowa is their Spirit Father;
that Sotuknang is their adoptive one;
and the Spider Woman is the web
which unites them all.[14]

Out of the power of the song people of all races and colors were created. Their one responsibility was to sing the Song of Creation, a song they were never to forget or they would lose the way. At first things went well and there was harmony everywhere. There was no sickness, no evil, and the people multiplied. They enjoyed the world and their bodies. But in time most forgot to sing the Song of Creation. Only a few remembered, and this "remnant" gathered into the home of the ant people while Sotuknang destroyed the world by fire. After that Sotuknang hesitated in his disappointment to create the world again but finally overcame his reluctance. But before letting the survivors come forth from the ant people he told them to remember their pledge to sing the Song, not to be greedy, and to respect themselves and Spider Woman.[15]

The world this second time around was even more plentiful. The plants were lush and strange new animals roamed about. People were happy. They built villages and sang the Song of Creation. But, alas, some of the men got greedy and fought each other for more possessions and for the women. In one version of the myth, Lavai-hoya, or the Talker, came among people as a mockingbird and convinced them of all the artificial racial and social and economic differences among them, leading to jealousies and alienation from the animals and from nature. Again, Sotuknang was furious. He gathered together the few who still lived by the laws of creation and remembered the Song. To them he gave safe haven once more with the ant people. Then he froze the earth solid from pole to pole, and even stopped it from spinning for a while.[16]

The story of the Third World repeats the pattern of the first two worlds but also introduces some important variations in its apoca-

lyptic ending. People at first emerged from the anthills and pros-
pered all over the earth. They built large cities, even civilizations and
boxes (or shields in another myth) that flew in the sky. But they became so powerful that they tried to dominate each other, waging
war and annihilating each other with their advanced weapons. Spider Woman, who at this point in the creation story begins to assume
greater significance, was distraught. She went to Sotuknang and
asked how she could save all the wayward people. He told her to
gather the few holy ones and seal them in the reeds, or hollow stems
of tall plants, while he destroyed the earth by flood. After the flood,
however, the survivors did not come out from their sealed reeds into
a new world but entered the same old one flooded over.[17]

At this point the myths proliferate and become complex, for in
fact the Hopi are more interested in the emergence into the Fourth
World than they are in the details of the creation of life and the story
of the first three worlds. Harry James, for example, who spent fifty
years in close contact with the Hopi, does not even mention the first
three worlds in his account of their creation myths. He concerns
himself instead with the story of the emergence into the Fourth
World through the *sipapu*, the point of entry into the Fourth
World.[18] As Loftin points out, the emergence through the *sipapu*
marks the separation for the Hopi between myth and history, life
and death, the here and now, and the world and the underworld,
though at the same time everything in Hopi religion dissolves these
dualities and contradictions.[19]

For my purposes, what is most interesting is that the apocalypse
at the end of the Third World is not complete. When the survivors
come out from their reeds the world is still there, just flooded over.
In various accounts, they wander in boats searching for access to the
new creation of Sotuknang, and go first north then south before
hearing Maasaw's footsteps on the ceiling of their world. That ceiling turns out to be the crust of the earth as we now know it. The survivors summon various birds to try to locate the entrance into that
world. In time the hole is found, but it is almost impossible to reach.
Finally, a chipmunk is summoned who urges the people to say their
prayers as he plants a special reed and then encourages it to grow up
to the hole.[20] The people crawl through that reed and emerge

through the *sipapu* into the Fourth World; this event is recreated in the emergence of each baby from a darkened hut after twenty days, in countless prayers during the ceremonies in the kivas, and is sacralized in reverse at the death of each Hopi.

The first being the people encounter is Maasaw, whom the Creator had put in charge of the Fourth World, since as master of the Under, or Third, World he had gotten arrogant but had been given a second chance. Maasaw tells them they may stay, but if they go back to their evil ways he will take the earth from them. In one account he says:

I am going to delegate some of my responsibilities to you,
I am going to leave the Earth and all living things on it
in your care. I appoint you guardians of this new world.
Take care of it, protect it from pollution. It is your home.
If you watch over it, it will feed you, clothe you,
and keep your children and grandchildren healthy and happy.
There will be hard times, when you will doubt.
But never lose faith that what I told you today is the truth.[21]

In other stories, both Sotuknang and Spider Woman also implore the people to avoid evil and sing praises to the Creator. Spider Woman especially assures them she will protect and nurture them from conflict. She also assigns different tasks to men and women to encourage harmony and prevent dissension.[22] With such blessings, the people undertake their new life. They begin, of course, with a vast store of knowledge, for memory of the achievements of people in their previous world is necessarily the beginning point in the minds of the remnant that survives. That knowledge, however, is of evil as well as of good. And the pattern is clear: Each time "the paradisaic situation is destroyed through disobedience, evil magic and sexual immorality."[23] The Creator destroys the world and creates a new one for the surviving few who have not strayed from holiness.

A crucial part of the creation myth, and one often talked about in Hopi legends and ceremonies, concerns the migrations that followed the emergence. Maasaw told the people they must first wander over the earth until they found the right place to settle. Maasaw detailed the elaborate pattern of their migration in a number of sacred tablets he gave different clans of the Hopi.[24] Interestingly, this sequence of legend merging into history corresponds with archaeological data that suggest the Pueblo people wandered for thousands of years, began to concentrate roughly in what is now Arizona after A.D. 700, and then, due to various droughts and other crises, began to congregate in larger communities and settle on the three mesas after the twelfth century.[25]

In the Hopi myths describing the making and unmaking of the four worlds, our own imaginable earth retains its ecological integrity. Fire, ice, and flood wipe out most living creatures (except for the ant people at the end of the first two worlds and then those tightly sealed in reeds at the end of the Third World). But in each case, the earth itself remains and is then repopulated with survivors from the previous world in another effort by the Creator to have a decent and holy people inhabit his creation. Indeed, the first three worlds as experienced by their inhabitants continue in a topographic and symbolic sense as the underworld; the earth as we know it now is simply an overlay, joined with these previous worlds through the *sipapu*. Just as life and death are a continuous process for the Hopi, the earth itself endures, while human culture goes through three waves of destruction. Those genocides, however, turn back on themselves in a cyclical pattern of recreation. Many die at the point of an old world's end, but life itself continues, and the earth's potential to nourish the fondest hopes of the Creator always remains in place. One might say the Hopi imagine an apocalypse of hope.

THE LITTLE PEOPLE OF PEACE

I came to the Hopi relatively late in my work on fundamentalism. I was finished with my fieldwork among the Christian fundamentalists and writing this book. But I kept coming back to the Hopi. I could not get the image of this peaceful group of Indians who were waiting for the end out of my mind. My interest increased as I read everything I could get my hands on and talked with people familiar with their culture and beliefs. But the Hopi baffled me. Who were these people who numbered less than ten thousand but whose culture and religion seemed of world-historical significance?[26] Who were these *Hopitu-Shinumu*, the Hopi self-designation as the "little people of peace"?[27] Were they really as mystical as they seemed? How did their sense of the apocalyptic fit into their culture? What did they believe comes after the end? These and many other questions seemed worth investigating.

Besides reading, I needed to undertake a brief period of additional fieldwork with the Hopi and discover my own sense of these unusual people. If I could have done so, I would have gone to Hopiland for six months. As it was, I gathered whatever insights I could manage in an intensive week of observation in the summer of 1992. I thought of it more as a pilgrimage than fieldwork, though I was in short pants and kept elaborate notes and a personal log. I had no specific agenda and no illusions that I would have the time to develop contacts to conduct formal interviews. I camped by myself on the Second Mesa and wandered the various villages throughout the reservation. I talked with everyone I could, though always informally, given the Hopi dread of tape recorders and cameras, and was even allowed to observe one of the major kachina dances, which are almost always closed to outsiders.

The Hopi have become highly suspicious of whites, who refuse to honor their sense of privacy and the sacred. Everything that matters is secret for the Hopi. The large sign at the entrance to Kykotsmovi speaks for all the villages. It says please take no pictures, don't use any kind of recording device, and don't pick up anything up from the ground to take with you. At Old Oraibi you are handed a piece of paper in the gift shop with a similar message, only it adds that you are not to walk on the roofs of the kivas, the underground ceremonial rooms with a distinctive ladder sticking up out of the entrance. At the back of Old Oraibi I strayed too far afield by accident, when a mean black dog lurched out at me from under a pick-up truck and chased one terrified white researcher back toward the Arts and Crafts shop at the entrance to the village. I felt properly chastened.

Most kachina dances, which go back some seven centuries, have been closed in recent years.[28] The First Mesa tribal chief published a statement in December 1990, closing off all dances on First Mesa to outsiders and had it posted throughout the reservation. On the other mesas, the ban seems to be more informal but equally universal. Sometimes individual dances are open, because the sponsor, or the village, wants it that way. Yet some ceremonies, like the Shalako dance that was going on while I was in Hopiland, even exclude other uninitiated Hopi. In part this extreme trend toward self-containment and separation from whites, however understandable, is something of a contradiction for those who embrace all people of peace into their spiritual world. But, sadly, outsiders too often secretly photograph or tape the dances. To reveal Hopi ceremonial secrets, including the preparatory prayers that go on in the kivas for days before the dances, is a sacrilege.[29] Nothing less than cosmic order is at stake. Secrecy is even built into the meaning of the dances. If a kachina takes off his mask, for example, the whole dance is compromised and the consequences for the Hopi can be enormous. And according to one story the end of the Fourth World itself will occur when the clown acts in a certain way in the plaza during the dance.[30]

The ultimate sense of the sacred infuses Hopi life at all levels. They live apart from modern, materialistic, urban, media-drenched America. In their self-contained rituals and communion with nature they express the belief that God and the world are one. Seeds are not future plants but spirits that, properly nurtured, bring forth sustenance. Seeds, in other words, are not "responsible" for the growth of plants. "Rather," John Loftin says, "seeds tell May'ingwa, the underworld god or manifestation of germination, which kind of plant is desired."[31] The cycle of dances from December to July harmonizes humans and nature. Then the spirits are sent off to the San Francisco Mountains to rest. If there is concordance between the spiritual and earthly, the rains and crops follow. At death the Hopi's breath rejoins *a'ni himu.*

The Hopi world is full of paradox and humor. It is an axiom among the Hopi that all humans are clowns.[32] The clown was the first Hopi to emerge from the underworld through the giant reed that led to the opening called *sipapu.*[33] Clown Youth and Clown Maiden were furthermore the direct ancestors of all humankind. When the sun failed to people the earth during the Third World, the task was given to the clowns. They wanted to escape the immorality and decadence of the Third World and heard the complex and mysterious god Maasaw "up there" walking around.[34]

Clowns play a particularly important role in Hopi rituals. In the Home Dance I saw, for example, some thirty kachinas danced for hours with great solemnity to the beat of drums and their haunting music. At the end of each sequence, however, fifteen or so clowns would rush into the plaza where the dance was being held, mock the kachinas and sometimes goose them, pull women from the audience, try to kiss them, and pour water on their heads. They also acted out scatological skits among themselves. As Louis Hieb notes, clowns usually speak English purposely to mock the religious seriousness of Hopi, and in their play might loudly note that they had no time for preparation for the dance in the kiva ceremonies.[35] One function clowns always play is to distribute food to the people watching the dance. These days, this is as likely to be loaves of Wonder Bread as stalks of maize, a substitution which is itself ironic.

Hopi cultural and religious ideas themselves are also full of contradiction and paradox. For example, Maasaw, who owns the Hopi lands, is the god of both death and fertility. In death one returns to the underworld, which is also the spiritual source of life. What endures is the breath and moisture, for the underworld is the source of rain. The Hopi petition their dead ancestors to bless them with rain. The Hopi word *gatungwu* means both human corpse and a harvested corn plant. In one legend, at the harvest Maasaw appears to farmers just as they finish stacking corn in heaps. He dresses paradoxically in an old woman's dress put on backwards and wears a mask of bloodied rabbit skin. He chases the men away from the corn. They run in terror, for if hit with his club they will die since he is the god of death. Yet his most important act at this moment is to touch the corn to mark his ownership. That provides a blessing of fertility.[36]

Hopi love to tell stories about Maasaw. He brings together the apocalyptic with life and sex. An unusually ugly and frightening looking god, he is the guardian of Old Oraibi. Each night he circles the village four times to protect it from danger, even though he himself is the embodiment of ultimate danger. Maasaw frequently changes into human form in order to court some beautiful maiden. In one such story Maasaw forgot about his disguise as he broke into song—and in the lyrics mentioned his festering and bony shins. The maiden fainted away dead. Maasaw then waited by her grave on the fourth day when, according to custom, she emerged from the grave. At that point Maasaw told her how much he loved her and how he wanted her to die so that she could marry him. She responded to his entreaties, and they "lived" happily ever after.[37] In another tale, Maasaw took on the skin of an old woman so that he could get close to her granddaughter. He then seduced the girl by telling her that old women always grow a penis; it is their appointed task to copulate with young maidens. Later, when Maasaw gives back his skin to the old lady and the grandmother returns, a funny scene occurs when the maiden turns to her expecting sex. The grandmother realizes in horror what has happened, though at the end one has a sense that the switch is laughed off as a joke, and certainly there is no regret on the part of the maiden.[38]

Hopi attitudes toward sex in general have always been tolerant. The best source on these issues is Mischa Titiev, whose work describes Hopi life in the 1930s. Lacking an authoritative update on Titiev's research, one has to assume the customs and attitudes he describes remain more or less in place. Parents and often many children sleep together in tiny rooms, and no taboo restricts parental intercourse, except during ceremonial preparation when the husband sleeps in his kiva. Children encounter sexual issues early. It is common to soothe babies by stroking their genitals. In clown skits little boys are taught racy behavior, and it is not uncommon during skits for adult women to simulate copulation with pre-adolescent boys. Sexual topics are discussed openly. Courtship is particularly unencumbered by restriction. Soon after puberty girls move into a separate room from their parents, while boys sleep together in the kivas and roam about at night as they please. Covering their faces with their blankets, they call on girls who decide whether to receive them. If a girl takes the boy in, they spend the rest of the night together. The custom is called *dumaiya* and is only interfered with by parents if a girl gets attached to a boy whom they feel is unworthy of her attentions. But in most cases girls and boys have multiple partners and parents stay out of the courtship ritual. Eventually, of course, the girl gets pregnant, though often without knowing the identity of the father. It is her prerogative, however, to choose her husband from among her suitors (though she may be rejected), irrespective of who the actual father of her child is.[39]

Hopi sexual customs, at least traditionally, even seem to include an easy acceptance of homosexuality. Mischa Titiev, the most reliable scholar on the Hopi, is somewhat hesitant about dealing with this subject. In his monograph he merely mentions that there was once widespread homosexuality among the Hopi, but that it appears to be less prevalent now. That "now" was the 1930s, and Titiev's point is supported by the later ethnographic work of Armin Geertz in the late 1970s, who says there is a strong Hopi taboo against homosexuality.[40] In his diary, however, Titiev is much clearer about the way the kachina dancers, and especially the clowns, explicitly embody and express themes of bisexuality.[41] The white historian Martin Duberman (himself an acknowledged homosexual) has unearthed references to some clown skits portraying men sucking penises and a general attitude of acceptance by the Hopi toward homosexuality. Duberman's work, perhaps not surprisingly, occasioned the loud protests of some white researchers, but the scholarship on which he relies seems beyond reproach.[42]

The Hopi, in terms of future directions, are granted a degree of latitude in choosing their own path.[43] They seem to have, in other words, a degree of conscious choice in relating to prophecy. The Hopi live in intimate communication with their gods, even though *a'ni himu* is ineffable. One would expect this godly people to direct their path toward mysterious communication with divine forms in a way that rediscovers the past. Such a vision is the antithesis of Christian end time theology, which envisions a return of Jesus and the creation of an altogether new world in the millennium, a final judgment, and eternal bliss for believers in heaven that bears no relation to anything before it. The Christian image of the end is directional, or teleological, awash in warlike and patriarchal symbols (for example, the appearance of Jesus with a suggestive sword coming out of his mouth).[44]

The Hopi, on the other hand, whose sense of future narrative is not at all clear, seem to envision in prophecy a future world that would either be something we have already known, or an extension of the Fourth World into a Fifth, or Sixth, or whatever. The pattern of creation, destruction, and re-creation is fairly well established in their myths and legends. There is no need to speculate on what might await us. One lives with the sacred as its meanings unfold. On the one hand, as Loftin points out, Third Mesa Hopi believe that the kachina dances will be the last to die, which is why they struggle to keep them going, while, on the other hand, "at the level of mythic continuity" these Hopi have no doubt that "the sacred essence of the ceremonies remains unchanged and always will."[45]

I talked with a man selling kachina dolls who bemoaned the frustrations that Hopi face. They are poor and only a few jobs exist on the reservation, though he himself chooses a marginal economic life in his village, rather than moving to Flagstaff or Phoenix where he might work in construction but would have to stay in the city. But the major dances are dying out, the young are not learning the ceremonies, and fewer and fewer are properly initiated into the culture. "People now fuck it up," he said. "Then they get sick or disappear." Still, he had not lost his hope. There was no question in his mind his people will endure. Things simply change. He was even baffled at my question whether he thought the Hopi would survive into the future. My question, it seems, ran counter to an apocalyptic mind-set that recycles future cultural forms from past experience. His view was echoed by the woman who guided me through Walpi. She had two years of college in Phoenix but got lonely and returned home, as she says 90 percent of all Hopi do who leave the reservation. She also saw many intrusions into the traditional way of doing things. She objected to the ugly public housing project in Polacca that we could look down on from the mesa heights of Walpi. She strongly felt that Hopi language and culture should be taught in school. And she quietly took swipes at the progressive tribal leadership, which would abandon the old for assimilation. But she remained hopeful. "Our people," she said, "will make it."

11

THE AGE
OF AQUARIUS

■■■■■■■

There is little doubt that "New Age" is a slippery concept. Most would agree that *A Course in Miracles* is New Age, but others would question how to connect Sun Bear's *Black Dawn, Bright Day, Path of Power*, or *Bear Tribe's Self Reliance Book* with Budd Hopkins's interest in UFOs (*Missing Time, Intruders*). Native American traditions have been a crucial influence on most New Agers, especially in their emphasis on the sacredness of the earth, though many Native Americans themselves, along with those more intimately familiar with their culture, feel trendy New Agers corrupt traditions that go back hundreds, if not thousands, of years. Christopher Lasch argues that the New Age seeks to "restore the illusion of symbiosis, a feeling of absolute oneness with the world," and is to Gnosticism what fundamentalism is to Christianity, "a literal restatement of ideas whose original value lay in their imaginative understanding of human life and the psychology of religious experience."[1] Not all New Agers would buy into notions like the harmonic convergence (August 16–17, 1987, when, according to Jose Arguelles, the New Age dawned) or astral projection (the experience of viewing the world from outside one's physical body). Some believe in only specific ideas or aspects adopted by the New Age (like holistic medicine), while others seek to define whole new theologies and life-styles from within its spirit, as Starhawk does in her popular books on Witchcraft (which she capitalizes): *The Spiral Dance*, *Dreaming the Dark*, and *Truth or Dare*. The number of New Agers is also impossible to measure. It appears that one in five Americans believe in reincarnation, while the figure for British is 30 to 35 percent.[2] Some, tongue in cheek, might include all Californians in the New Age count; in any event, it is certainly a movement of great cultural significance.

New Age is a decidedly middle-class and white movement. There are few African Americans and hardly any Hispanics. As a religious movement it is open to everything except people who are genuinely different.[3] Many disgruntled professionals are in its ranks, along with the full range of white-collar workers (and what used to be called the housewife). Some read *A Course in Miracles*, while others are more likely to pick up the *National Enquirer*, but neither extends the discourse to accommodate minorities who are outside of mainstream cultural assumptions. This class and racial focus gives New Age an identity often lacking in the murky waters of the multicultural world of Catholic and Protestant churches; it also puts constraints on its potential for future development.

New Age is easy to mock. Prediction of the future in palm reading or Tarot cards runs counter to western traditions of scientific rationality. Middle-class and middle-aged women and men in white robes on mountain tops chanting pagan tunes strike many as ludicrous. The absence of ideas of evil, the devil, or hell, along with a conflict-free psychology, can make much of New Age seem mushy and cloying.[4] Some aspects of the New Age movement have also gotten highly commercialized, absorbed into the American tendency to turn the new into the chic. Well-known figures such as Marianne Williamson, Shirley MacLaine, or Sun Bear before his death lead workshops at which people pay hundreds of dollars for a few hours of instruction in reincarnation, the mysteries of *Miracles*, astral projection, survivalist techniques, meditation. You can make big bucks off the spirit.[5]

The specifically religious ideas of New Age can seem outlandish. Take astral projection. This idea assumes the division of the cosmos into etheric, astral, and physical dimensions. It is an old idea, given new meanings in current thinking.[6] We live in the physical world, while ghosts and other spirits dwell in the astral plane. The highest level of existence (the analogue of heaven) is the etheric plane that extends infinitely into space. Our beings, it is believed, can depart this body and life through the proper meditation and either inhabit our double (a "parasomatic" experience), or travel without a body, just "be" (an "asomatic" experience). Several levels of proof are offered for such out of body experiences, often referred to simply as "OBE." The most frequently cited are near-death experiences,[7] though many would also say we actually travel while asleep. Freud's psychologizing of such events into "mere" dreams, it is argued, obscures the reality of psychic and spiritual life.

But many religious ideas, if deconstructed, can seem odd. In the mainstream Judeo-Christian world, God speaks to Hebrew prophets out of burning bushes, while Jesus raises the dead and heals the sick, before he himself is resurrected. It is at least ungenerous for someone who ascribes to such a belief system to label as laughable the New Age belief in reincarnation, especially given its significance in eastern religions. In the fundamentalist world, furthermore, God and the devil speak to the tormented believer in separate ears. As we've seen, the details of the end time scenario almost defy rational observers to take it in. Between torrents of violence pouring out of heaven, there appear disguised forms of Satan, confusing images of the Lord with a sharp two-edged sword coming out of his mouth, and Jesus rapturing believers into the clouds before touching back to earth.

In addition, the New Age has a general integrity that warrants more than cursory attention. In certain areas, it has had a profound impact. The environmental concerns of recent years draw much energy from New Age people and ideas. Holistic medicine, which has been virtually taken over by New Age, is altering the way we think about our bodies and how to heal its forms of illness. The self-help movement, including Alcoholics Anonymous and the plethora of 12-step programs, which fed into the creation of New Age and is now almost synonymous with it, has proven a durable and often remarkably effective alternative to some of the deadening abuses of medical psychiatry. New Age thought, which in many ways is making it up as it goes along, is at least trying to figure out some new beliefs about our understanding of ourselves, our world, and the cosmos. It may be, as Erikson once suggested, that our world-images have become corrupt because they have been left to ecclesiastic bureaucracies.[8] "The New Age must begin in fantasy," says Michael Grosso, "for the old age is dying of reality."[9]

In New Age there are no dogmas, no set texts, and certainly no orthodoxies. Unlike the Hopi, there are not even agreed-upon stories that define certain parameters of faith. The *Course in Miracles* inspires some (and in the hands of Marianne Williamson has enjoyed a renaissance of late), but others are put off by its earnest Christianity.[10] Some do, and some don't, believe in UFOs. The more theoretical New Age adherents read Carl Jung and his disciples. He is their source for myths and legends, and their philosopher of the psyche who opens up the ego to transcendental experience. Jung was open to the parapsychological and, in religion, to the mystical. He spent many years investigating alchemy, not to figure out how to make gold but to understand the secrets of mystical researchers. His interpretation of dreams connects the individual unconscious experience of desire with collective memory. It is not an anti-rational psychology but neither is it rationalistic in the tradition of Freud. God enters into the Jungian world of interpretation and healing.

New Age discourse has a Jungian cast to it. People talk of "living archetypes" and the "collective unconscious" with a breezy familiarity. Any New Age bookstore worth its name includes some, often many, books by Jung, as well as his more important contemporary interpreters, James Hillman and Robbie Bosnak. Jung, as well, grounds New Age practice. Clarissa Pinkola Estes, a Jungian analyst, has written a best-selling book, *Women Who Run with the Wolves*, that advises women to get in touch with their "wild woman archetype" by sipping jasmine tea, taking long baths, and dancing at night on bare earth.[11] A therapist advertising "Wholeness Meditation" explains that, through deep breathing and "staying the moment," one can "make the Deep Self connection."[12] *New Age Magazine*'s 1992 "Sourcebook" included an article on all the current New Age books, cassettes, and workshops that treat "Meeting your dark side." The article mentions Robert Bly's *A Little Book on the Human Shadow* (1988), along with his two-cassette program, "Meeting Your Dark Side," as well as W. Brugh Joy's *Avalanche: Heretical Reflections on the Dark and the Light* (1990) and his 12-Day Workshop, "The Dark Side: Death, Demons, and Difficult Dreams." Many, in fact, deride New Age exactly because it relies so heavily in its philosophical foundations on the work of Jung, a psychoanalytic renegade. But the effort to connect the exploration of deep spirituality with the writings of Jung adds a measure of continuity with western thought in this radical psychological and religious movement.

New Age terrain is constantly changing, as writers introduce new ideas and approaches that gain appeal, then rapidly fade away. One year Tarot reading is in, the next it's UFOs. Things are loose, ambiguous, unsystematic, even disorganized, but they are also creative. I would suggest an ad hoc, purely phenomenological definition of New Age: whatever books you find in a good New Age bookstore mark the contours of the field of inquiry. This is a definition from the bottom up. New Age ideas do not quite constitute an ideology and certainly are not yet a complete religion. It tends to reject tradition rather uncritically and is certainly murky about its myth of origins or its ethic. But New Age, if nothing else, has one thing about it that is utterly clear: it has an apocalyptic.

NEW AGE APOCALYPTICS

The New Age apocalyptic works in many unsettled modes that have yet to converge around a common story. There is a modified Christian version, a variant for witches, one that draws inspiration from Native Americans and connects with the environmental movement, another rooted in astrology, and the wildest of all in recent work on UFOs. A movement in search of religious grounding requires an apocalyptic, but in something as diverse as New Age there is no simple revelation we await, no one disclosure that can be easily predicted. The diversity of stories, however, is the key. As in so many other areas, New Age holds everything as possible. No white male, even a mystical one on Patmos, can dictate a vision of endings to control our cultural strivings.

The apocalyptic holds center stage in the spiritual imaginations of New Agers. The very term *New Age* has an apocalyptic flavor to it and implies a transformation of the world that is not necessarily conveyed in some of its component activities or sub-groups (like holistic medicine). The movement is larger than the sum of its parts.[13] If William McLoughlin is correct, it may presage a move into a "Fourth Great Awakening."[14] J. Gordon Melton stresses the transformative character of New Age ideas. "The New Age Movement can be defined by its primal experience of transformation. New Agers have either experienced or are diligently seeking a profound personal transformation from an old, unacceptable life to a new, exciting future. . . . Having experienced a personal transformation, New Agers project the possibility of the transformation not of just a number of additional individuals, but of the culture and of humanity itself."[15]

In a very general way, three forms of the apocalyptic compete in New Age discourse. These forms overlap in the minds of many people, and in typically open New Age fashion many take in all three without worrying about being consistent. But for heuristic purposes it helps to define the field by getting a clear sense of how *different* each approach is to the revelation of New Age. The three apocalyptic styles can be generally characterized as catastrophic, magical, and efficacious.

Catastrophe

Many believe the New Age will dawn in violence and destruction. Ruth Montgomery, for example, who dominated the New Age scene in the 1970s and into the early 1980s, may be the best-known prophet of doom. Once a journalist and columnist, Montgomery found her true voice as a guru in some ten books that describe channeling, walk-ins (where a historical figure, often of great renown, actively inhabits one's body), and the dawning of the New Age. Her writing is highly accessible to a mass audience. She takes esoteric topics and turns them into understandable, if still mystical, themes for the committed to ponder.

Montgomery's model (and that of many others) is that the coming of Jesus Christ marked the beginning of the Piscean age that has now reached its culmination. We await the age of Aquarius, which will realize the millennium spoken of in the Bible (at least as Montgomery conceives of it). That millennium will be a time of love and brotherhood. Schools will be unnecessary, for our expanded consciousness will allow us to tap directly into the minds of others and vastly expand our knowledge. We will be able to read books at a glance. Souls will be able to reach perfection, and not have to keep returning to human bodies to confront the same temptations of avarice, greed, and lust. Walk-ins bring messages of the end, and other "signs" that foretell the future millennium. With the environmental movement, for example, Montgomery sees a tremendous surge of collective empowerment in people simply refusing any longer to let big government control their lives and destroy the planet by moving back to the wilderness, using herbal remedies, and growing their own food. "The emphasis is on individual effort, rather than mass society, and on freedom of choice," she writes.[16]

The way into this millennium, however, is full of violence. The great change into the Aquarian age has begun to take place, she argues, but will not be "fully recognized" until the "shift of the axis has eradicated some of the evils of the present age." Such phrasing avoids naming exactly how many die in the transformation. Montgomery, however, leaves no doubt that the greedy and lusting are among those to be "eradicated" in the New Age. The next two decades will be a "strenuous" time for "Mother Earth," and many souls will wish "they had not chosen this particular time for rebirth into the flesh." We face the certainty of World War III, which she hints will be nuclear and will certainly generate famine and riots. Montgomery even suggests an ethic for the New Age: it will be "fraught with peril" for those not adequately prepared in spirit. In a directly fundamentalist way, Montgomery also argues in several books that Antichrist is now in college in an eastern seaboard state and will reveal himself at the end of the century as the final shift of the axis occurs.[17]

The active presence of and role for Antichrist in the minds of some New Agers, not to mention images of the millennium and "signs" of the "end times," suggest some of the many ways Christian fundamentalist imagery has worked its way into New Age ideas of catastrophe. One UFO abductee reported that her experience left her with one strong thought: "By the year 2000 the world would be totally different than we know it, but it would be only for the young and strong."[18] David Solomon, as many others, uses the idea of the "end times" to refer to the end of this present age of Pisces.[19] Others, like Nada-Yolanda, make the notion of living in the end times concrete. For her the period 1960 to the year 2000 is the most important span of time in the history of the solar system, or at least of the last 26,000 years. In this period, all of history must be "reexperienced, renewed, reevaluated and discarded." To be cleansed in this period, one must demonstrate the "I Am Consciousness," which will make us more self-reliant. The "sixth-phase rending of the seventh veil" ran from 1988 until the end of 1992. A "severe" cleansing period ended in 1988 but much more is to come. It will be painful but eventually beneficial. And we must learn about it and how to move the changes forward creatively by encounter with the cosmic law. All else, especially our "erroneous theories," are entirely misleading and confusing.[20]

In general, both among fundamentalists and New Agers, one consequence of any concrete dating of the end is that it tends to be associated with more violent images of destruction. There is something about naming catastrophe that brings it closer to hand, rather like the difference between those who talk generally about suicide and those who give details of their planned death. As therapists learn from bitter experience, the latter has far more dangerous meanings. Fundamentalists, of course, have only one date to be concerned about, the return of Jesus. Their question is how specifically one can locate that mystical event in time and space. New Agers, on the other hand, have a looser set of images that control their sense of renewal. The transformations leading to the creation of the New Age of Aquarius come in stages, in a kind of serial apocalypse.[21] Phases of it may already have dawned and the rest will unfold in steps. But the transformations are also potentials within us, which we can influence and shape; indeed, we have an obligation (though to whom or to what is not always clear) to get ahead of the apocalyptic and direct it.

That obligation, however, is fraught with danger. The "11:11 Doorway" movement claims that we are now in a twenty-year period of opportunity to end the earth's period of duality and conflict between dark and light. In this interval, there must be a "cleansing," after which we will find ourselves on a new earth. The "doorway" of opportunity opened on January 12, 1992, and will close on December 31, 2011. Opening the doorway could open a "major planetary activation" and the participation of (the Revelation-inspired number) 144,000 "Activated Star-Borne [united] together in conscious Oneness world-wide" to bring about "our mass ascension into new realms of consciousness." The 11:11 symbol itself, according to a self-appointed seer, Solara, was "pre-encoded within our cellular memory banks, long, long ago, prior to our descent into matter, under a time release mechanism, which when activated signified that our time of completion is near." This knowledge of the symbol somehow came to Solara looking at digital clocks. The 11:11 Doorway is, for its adherents, much more important than the "harmonic convergence" that Jose Arguelles identified. As Solara puts it: "It's moving onto a patterning of octaves, not dimensions anymore, under a template of oneness, aligned with a great central sun system. This signifies our graduation into mastery and freedom."[22]

As with fundamentalists, however, the issue of failed prophecy for those who name a date, even a vague one, lurks in the background for anyone working with the apocalyptic. New Agers have so far handled this problem by talking only very generally of being in a still-unfolding period of transformation, or with a vague retreat into the mysteries of astrological understanding. The "11:11 Doorway" movement, for example, since 1986 has mentioned five major and three minor periods of potential planetary alignments that could usher in a transformation of human evolution.[23] The potential for change is not quite a prediction on the order of William Miller (and others before and since) predicting the return of Jesus on a certain day, but it pushes up against concrete prediction, as does most of such discussion in New Age.

If Ruth Montgomery and others combine Christian apocalyptic imagery with astrology, Sun Bear brings his sense of the approaching catastrophe together (loosely, as always in New Age) with Hopi and other Native American traditions. This controversial figure was the son of a Chippewa father and a mother of German-Norwegian descent. He grew up on the White Earth Indian Reservation in northern Minnesota and received an eighth-grade education. After being drafted into the Korean War, he became a deserter for reasons of conscience. For many years he was an activist in Indian causes. He also founded the Bear Tribe Medicine Society, which has a national following and sponsors "medicine wheel gatherings." At such gatherings, Sun Bear evolved a variety of rituals that connect New Age with Native Americanism, including sweat lodge purifications and crystal healing ceremonies.[24]

Sun Bear's message is the conviction that Earth Mother is a living being now in the midst of what he calls a "deep cleansing." Earth is in tribulation. She is sick from all the poisons she has absorbed from humans. "It's plain to see," he said in 1983, "with the volcanoes, the earthquakes, the changes in weather patterns." His medicine wheels are a vehicle for getting people to connect with the earth. Hug a tree, he advocates, to begin your healing. "Trees are conductors of energy between the heavens and earth. When you hold and hug a tree, you feel the energy and it can be like a blood transfusion."[25]

Sun Bear notes the significance of prophecy in human history from the Hopi through the books of Matthew and Revelation in the Bible. He argues that we need to listen to those who can hear the future. He offers himself up as such a person, a shaman to be listened to. Sun Bear says he has had dreams of things that happened and those that will come to pass. He has organized his Bear-tribe as a rural-based community because he foresees major destruction in the cities. Those in the greatest danger are the ones near nuclear and chemical plants. He sees piles of garbage, breakdown of services, race riots, wars, and destruction on a vast scale.[26]

Sun Bear's image of change involves great violence and destruction. "The planet will survive, even though perhaps millions of people will perish."²⁷ (Or, in a more folksy apocalyptic image, he says the Earth is like a big shaggy dog full of testy fleas. When the dog gets sufficiently annoyed he scratches and shakes at the creatures. "Well," Sun Bear concludes, "there is going to be a lot of shaking and a lot of frightened humans during the Earth changes."²⁸) The only human survivors he sees are "small bands of people living very close to the earth."²⁹ What will end is the Fourth World, which specifically evokes the Hopi tradition, and one fourth of the world's population will survive, which is one way of calculating the destruction in the Book of Revelation.³⁰ The outcome of all this violence, however, is regenerative and hopeful: "All those who do survive will come through with a higher level of consciousness." There will be great spiritual leaders. "So this is a time of cleansing."³¹ There are many bad things going on, things on "many levels" that will no longer be around when the cleansing is completed.

The "period of change," furthermore, is upon us. "Between now and the year 2000 is the time span in which most of the major changes are going to be happening," Sun Bear says.³² Everything is accelerating and happening "so rapidly" that he has to update his examples weekly, even daily. These examples are changes in the earth (quakes and other natural disasters), as well as the effects of destructive pollution. It is this rending of the earth that most tore at his soul. *Black Dawn, Bright Day*, in a sense, is a great lament for the earth, which for him is a "living, intelligent being."

Sun Bear is ambivalent on the question of human efficacy. The earth changes cannot be reversed; they have gone too far. He asked Spirit that once and learned that, "No, the changes are sealed."³³ But Sun Bear also stresses that humans are not powerless in "beginning to bring about a solution." You can, he says, "help heal the Earth and yourself."³⁴ Much of *Black Dawn, Bright Day*, in fact, consists of detailed and pragmatic advice on survival during this period of change. Be prepared for unexpected weather changes, for example, and take both extra layers and a sun hat and umbrella when you travel; support education about birth control as well as pro-choice politicians; try bathing and washing your hair in five gallons of water you heat on a wood stove; move away from the coasts, especially California.[35] His sacred world on what he calls "Vision Mountain" seeks to create just such a safe refuge.

The *only* survivors will be those who make a conscious decision to change "in the way they look at life, in the way they understand things, and in their actions toward all creation."[36] You must be awakened to "true reality," which is the spirit within and in the earth. They can only be healed together. Humans and the earth must be in harmony.

Magic

New Age is a world of ghosts and spirits, not entirely explained but also not ignored. In a chapter on "A Typology of Helping Apparitions," Michael Grosso, for example, in *The Final Choice*, discusses much material from paganism, Christianity, and popular culture about the world of spirits. In one typical story a woman reported stopping at an intersection. As she started up, she looked down briefly at the cigarette lighter. When she glanced up the long-dead figure of her mother stood directly in front of her car. The woman slammed on her brakes, just in time to avoid a semi truck running a red light in front of her. Was the figure a projection of the woman's unconscious? asks Grosso. Or was it the saving act of the ghost of her mother? In fact, Grosso finds something of a middle ground: "Let us just say that these phenomena are signs of the Extended Self—the total or subliminal Self, the 'higher' or 'true' Self."[37] The Cartesian notion of a limited and rational self will not work, argues Grosso. There is just too much that happens to make such claims to rationalism false. The New Age conclusions to such ideas are not always clear, but all would agree that we can only begin to improve, indeed to save, our world by getting in touch with these dimensions of self experience. It could well be that these areas of the unknown extend to communication with aliens from space, which is not that far removed from the notion of ghosts and spirits returning to save the living from car wrecks and our own souls reincarnating in another body after a period of transformation in the astral realm.[38]

Grosso analyzes the significance of nuclear threat to human existence and concludes that "only a radical spirituality, a new metaphysics strong enough to command a new kind of courage and solidarity, will overturn the system of the nuclear warriors."[39] He finds some hints of the possibilities of such "radical spirituality" in the near-death experiences, and notes with encouragement that many have such transformative imagery even apart from actual death. "By analogy," he concludes, "the vivid premonition of catastrophe [in the collective psyche] might activate the reordering mechanisms of the deep psyche; we might then escape our bad fate and buy a lesson in enlightenment cheaply."[40] Grosso talks of the collective unconscious as being in a "state of unrest" as "The Bomb" stirs "Mind at Large" into action. The mechanism for that transformation, Grosso says in a chapter titled "The Morphology of the Apocalypse" is through the "archetype of death and enlightenment" and its adaptive capabilities, revealed, it seems, in UFO contacts and visions of the Blessed Virgin Mary.[41] "There must be light at the end of the tunnel," Grosso asserts. The prophetic visions, whether Marian or UFO, signal the end of an age and the dawning of something new, something beyond the smoke and rubble.[42]

The Marian visions represent for Grosso the "general awakening" to the "energies, the qualities, the sensibility, associated with the multiplex archetype of the feminine." Specifically, "the Marian experience resuscitates the earth goddesses of antiquity; the Marian age reconnects modern spiritual sensibilities with the age of Eleusis—the ancient mysteries, a world in which the divine was experienced in relation to certain collective feminine realities."[43] Put more succinctly: "The process of empowering the feminine archetype, if carried out authentically, would exert a powerful influence on planetary life."[44] Similar factors are at work with UFOs. In near-death visions, Grosso says, the soul sends up messages of guidance and consolation. The information addresses the transpersonal, or the collective, which is both response and warning at the level of archetype. UFO sightings, for example, vastly increased after 1947, which for Grosso is part of the response to the threat of nuclear war. Sightings "register perturbations in the collective psyche."[45]

The whole UFO phenomenon has become almost trendy of late in America. Frequent sightings are reported, and it is estimated by those in the field that some 700,000 to 3.5 million people have been abducted.[46] The pioneering and zealous, almost evangelical, work of people like Budd Hopkins has convinced large numbers of people that something real might be happening to which serious attention should be directed. On the five-hundredth anniversary of the birth of Christopher Columbus, the United States government recently turned a huge, 100-million-dollar dish to the heavens to receive messages. A noted Harvard psychiatrist, John Mack, leads UFO support groups, interviews abductees, and is writing a scholarly book on the subject.

The most famous observer of UFOs, however, is undoubtedly Budd Hopkins. In the clear, dispassionate prose of his two books (*Missing Time* and *Intruders*), Hopkins has described his astounding findings over the last several decades. A hallmark of his work is that he stays close to the available, if not quite empirical, evidence. He is scrupulous about not tainting his respondents with information from what he hears from others, about using witnesses, about taping interviews, about not jumping to explanations too quickly. He readily admits his findings are remarkable, indeed "unbelievable." He talks about the BB-like implants in the abducted, and attempts several possible explanations, but backs off from them quickly. "I do not wish to dwell on any of these paranoia-inducing theories. Perhaps these BB-like objects have some other, as yet unimagined purpose or purposes. Whenever we consider these large, theoretical questions about the ultimate nature, source and intention of the UFO phenomenon, we must admit that we still have no final answers."[47]

Hopkins takes his respondents seriously. He gets to know them, hypnotizes them, and talks for seemingly endless hours with them on the phone. He pays attention to details, like the reports of abductees being cold as they enter the UFO crafts or the exact nature of the scars people report (which he also photographs). He also studies the phenomenon with the care of a scientist, and includes in his book long transcripts (and excerpts where relevant) from his taped interviews. Without question Hopkins is a believer in UFOs, but he tries to maintain the distance of the serious scientific investigator, albeit a committed one. Hopkins may well be wrong but he should not be dismissed.

In the historical literature on abuse in the beginning of psycho-analysis, most now feel that Freud had it right the first time, and that psychoanalysis took a decided turn for the worse when Freud de-cided his early hysterical patients had only fantasized the seductions by their fathers that they remembered as real when adults.[48] In the same vein, the evidence Hopkins and others have assembled about UFO abductions is quite impressive about something, though it is not entirely clear what. He has uncovered all kinds of remembered traumas in otherwise relatively normal people, physical evidence, and converging stories.[49] Some kind of apocalyptic vision is at work (which could have some common roots in various forms of abuse).

The question, of course, is what the aliens want from us and why they would bother conducting their research on so many individuals over such a relatively long period of time, not to mention implanting things that mark abductees (or extracting semen from men and sex-ually abusing women). Some report a simple plot to conquer and destroy us. But other abductees report far more complicated and in-teresting communications from the aliens. The sexual experimen-tation, for example, they say appears to be in the interest of creating hybrids in breeding pools, which the aliens see as one way of saving something on earth before the final destruction. Indeed, that de-struction appears to be the central concern of the aliens, and from what they tell some abductees the aliens cannot understand why we would be so earnestly trying to destroy earth. The purpose of their interventions, in this view, is to offset the destruction of the planet by humans, to save us from ourselves, in other words, or at least be-come part of a process of co-creation in a transformed new age.[50]

Among other New Age thinkers the magical apocalypse takes some extraordinary twists and turns. Augusta Almeida brought to-gether UFOs, Jesus, and the rapture.[51] She claimed that Jesus was an extraterrestrial and the commander of a large force he has already brought with him to earth, many of whom still remain. Almeida claims that the earth is to be "evacuated" between 1993 and 1997 so it can be repaired; then Jesus will return. She names this process of repair the "Grand Lift" and says it will begin in the Philippines; in fact, she recommends some specific churches where those wanting to be saved should go for that purpose. After the "repairs" the earth will be a paradise again. People will then be returned to live in peace on it for a thousand years.

For her part Virginia Essene reports (from a channel) that we might be uncomfortable enduring the transition to the coming age, which is millennial in tone and feeling. That discomfort will be due to our interdependence with cosmic forces. As Essene puts it, we are each a "cosmic pattern, a template of celestial potential," and we are all precursors of a "new human species." The change itself is thought of as "waves of energy and light" that will "shower earth."[52]

This kind of idea has influenced New Agers to develop an evolving network of rituals that is gradually defining its own spirituality. From a loose and individualistic beginning that included massage, palm readings, and crystal wearing, and progressed into more organized and communal forms with workshops, lectures, and rebirthing weekends in hot tubs,[53] New Age has begun to formalize things. Some meet in nonconventional but organized ways to share and worship as they understand that concept. Witches regularly gather in covens and occasionally meet for special ceremonies for which they have become famous. New Age conventions are held frequently in large cities in central hotels and can draw thousands. Some groups strive at least to draw in huge audiences for their rituals. Solara, for example, instructs participants in 11:11 Doorway events to gather in the largest groups they can manage and perform prescribed movements in synchrony. Worldwide, these rituals must involve at least 144,000 people and are to be performed at 11:11 A.M. and P.M. local time.[54] In the spring of 1992 DaVid announced his presidential candidacy of the Human Ecology Party at a New York nightclub. DaVid timed the announcement to coincide with an 11:11 event. He was surrounded by followers with raised hands (a symbolic way of stopping time) greeting each other with a chant: "I offer you peace. I offer you friendship. I offer you love. I hear your needs. I see your beauty. I feel your feelings. All wisdom flows from a higher source. I salute that source. Let us work together."[55]

Channeling (which emerged in 1952 among UFO contactee groups to describe the nature of the communications they were receiving from the inhabitants of the alien spacecrafts) is central to the magical apocalypse.[56] The underlying concepts of channeling are often left vague, though the basic idea is that "cosmic awareness" is a force that has revealed itself through Jesus, Buddha, Krishna, Muhammad, and Edgar Cayce, and is now speaking through other, anonymous channels helping to guide us through the change to the Age of Aquarius.[57] William H. Kautz and Melanie Branon, in *Channeling: The Intuitive Connection*, tell us that "Ye who merge the mind, the body and the spirit shall experience greater longevity," that in fact by the year 3000, "Ye shall have fulfilled the thousand years of brotherhood—physical immortality."[58] A figure like Nada-Yolanda describes in detail her communications with Sanada/Jesus and how she has helped reinforce "the special new shield around the United States, with its dome at the top." She has broken through to new levels of consciousness and come to accept her responsibility as a cosmic relay from the "Hierarchical Board." She has had the sound "Om" implanted in her which has activated her light body. Her meditations on Easter, 1992, included "a loud, crunching crack. A boulder, the size of my forehead, tore across the front of my head. And I realized that my brain was . . . the inside of a cave or tomb." It might be said that this meditation is a kind of New Age form of the Resurrection, as the Christ-self is realized in each of us.[59]

The question of agency in channeling is a fascinating one. In a preface written in 1977 for the second edition of *A Course in Miracles*, Helen Schucman notes how she received the material in the *Course* from the Holy Spirit. A "little willingness" is sufficient, she says, "to enable Him to use any situation for His purposes and provide it with His power." Sometimes it is vaguer who is actually sending the information and why it is being sent, as in automatic writing. The key thing is to be in the grip of a higher power who communicates through you in some way that defies rational explanation. For Helen Schucman, who was a professor of medical psychology at Columbia University's College of Physicians and Surgeons in New York City, she heard "the Voice." As she put it: "It made no sound, but seemed to be giving me a kind of rapid, inner dictation which I took down in a shorthand notebook." You never quite know why you are being contacted, but clearly spiritual forces for good are attempting to transform the earth's evil ways by communicating messages of change, uplift, and hope.[60]

Personal Efficacy

For many New Agers neither catastrophic nor magical images of revelation dominate their thinking. Instead, they place the creative and efficacious role of human action at the center of any possibility for transformation in a New Age. In this view, the New Age is coming, perhaps inevitably, but in fits and starts, and without our push it may descend on us with tragic consequences.

A Course in Miracles urges personal responsibility to liberate the spirit from the guilt and sense of badness in the Judeo-Christian tradition. For some, the Course is too specifically Christian, in its feeling almost like a Bible (with the breakdown of chapters and the numbered sentences or verses), and in its use of Holy Spirit, of Christ, of God and His Son. The language is curiously old-fashioned and sexist, since the Course was published in 1973, just before the language change brought on by feminism. But its essential message is that we must be free to be human, and to be in God's eyes: "The veil across the face of Christ, the fear of God and of salvation, and the love of guilt and death, they all are different names for just one error; that there is a space between you and your brother, kept apart by an illusion of yourself that holds him off from you, and you away from him." And a little later: "To everyone has God entrusted all, because a partial savior would be one who is but partly saved."[61]

Douglas Grant works such Course ideas into his own writings about channeling and rituals of prayer. Grant argues that we are all to fulfill our own second comings by "reviving" our "inner Christselves" in preparation for the return of Christ. Only our own negativity and low self-esteem prevent this realization. We must become channels and take responsibility for what we receive. We must speak and live for God, and filter out our own desires and interpretations. Prayer thus precedes channeling, and we must be prepared for years of study and personal preparation. What we receive is prophecy, which prepares people in times like these of cosmic change. We are not helpless, however, in the face of approaching disaster. All events are influenced by human thought and desire. We become aware of disaster in order to enable us to avoid or forestall it. Just as we attempt to channel Christly energies we will "attract energies and entities of the same Christ level of vibration and beingness" and repel "lesser energies in our force field . . . caus[ing] new levels of purification to be achieved." This process multiplied raises the planet to a "new level of spiritual expression."[62]

Environmentalism draws New Agers into the world of politics. The basic idea in New Age thought is that we are somehow already in the process of transformation, and that an awareness of the environment is essential to the process. What is involved is a recognition of the "Oneness of Life." We are "kin" not only to all the animals on the earth but to stars and subatomic particles. And consciousness always evolves to higher levels and a "more inclusive integration."[63] There is seldom the kind of joining of prophecy and current events that one finds in the work of someone like Hal Lindsey. But the end of the cold war, perhaps because of its magnitude, contradicts the political insularity of New Age. It lends itself easily to the vision of transformation so central to New Age apocalyptic yearnings. Capitalism is dying of its own polluted weight, and communism clearly has proven to be a worthless form of social engineering. What is left is the "progressive transformation of human culture" in an "evolution toward divinity."[64]

Like many fundamentalists, many New Agers are apolitical and withdrawn from the mainstream political process in America (though there has been no study of this fascinating phenomenon), except for the active involvement of New Agers in the environmental movement. Aside from widespread individual action, some take part in the Human Ecology Party, which proposes a 15 percent across-the-board tax that can be itemized by the citizen. They foresee that the result would be a vast downsizing of government, especially the military. They would create a huge corporation to invest the funds taken from the military that would develop energy in harmony with the laws of nature, introducing the solar age. They would build a global peace center on Alcatraz Island in the shape of a hexagram to broadcast Artainment video to the global family.[65] Although there is no devil or hell in New Age, those who despoil the earth, those polluters who have subjected Mother Earth to sacrilege, may suffer.[66]

One suspects that the neo-pagan leader Starhawk would agree, as would Sun Bear and those interested in Native American beliefs, who tend to talk about our personal responsibility for the earth's destruction. The ethics in such a message are collective and communal. The individual must survive (and Sun Bear provides quite detailed information on how to live out the period of change we are in), but our ethical obligation is to the planet, to the human race, and to all living creatures.

Witches in turn, Starhawk argues, are bound to serve the life force. Some killing must occur for survival (for "life feeds on life"), but the wanton destruction of the environment contradicts all ethics. The Goddess may be immanent, "but she needs human help to realize her fullest beauty," as Starhawk puts it. Meditation is a spiritual act in Witchcraft but not as much as cleaning up garbage or marching on a nuclear test site. We are all interdependent, and both need one another and have responsibilities toward one another. To harm one is to harm everyone.[67] "What you send, returns three times over," say witches, which Starhawk sees as an "amplified version" of "Do unto others as you would have them do unto you." Our growing awareness of ecology, the impending environmental apocalypse, has forced on us a realization of our interconnectedness with all forms of life, which is one of the bases of Goddess religion.

Our changing cultural attitudes toward sexuality are influencing New Age spirituality as well.[68] In this regard, Starhawk asks a "hard-headed, critical question" about eastern religions: Are they not also hierarchical, denying sexuality, and demeaning women in many of the same ways as western religions? Eastern religions seem good for men. They open them up to cooperative, interdependent ways. For women, however, they seem only to offer further passivity and are "playing the same old song." We do not need messiahs, martyrs, or saints, she says. Instead, we need to find our own reality, inner and outer, to become fully human, "fully alive with all the human passions and desires," and the "infinite possibilities." Sexuality is a powerful and wonderful force for Starhawk. It is the "expression of the creative life force of the universe," and in orgasm "we share in the force that moves the stars" (though Starhawk adds that one has to be aware that the sexual revolution has generally meant the easy marketing of women's bodies).[69] Xaviere Gauthier supports this connection between witchcraft and sexuality. Why witches? she asks: "*Because witches dance.* They dance in the moonlight. Lunar, lunatic women, stricken, they say, with periodic madness. Swollen with lightninglike revile, bursting with anger, with desire, they dance wild dances on the wild moors. Wildwomen, uncivilized, as the white man says of other races; wildcats, as the government and the unions say of some strikes; as they say of some of our schemes. The witches dance, wild and unjustifiable, like desire."[70]

Witchcraft is a powerful affirmation of efficacy for women. The Goddess, Starhawk says, is manifest in humans and thus it is contrary to the spirit to deny the human. The task of "feminist religion" is to learn the simple things. It is easier to be celibate, for example, than fully alive sexually, to withdraw than to be in the world, to be a hermit than to raise a child, to repress feelings than to feel them, to meditate than to communicate, to submit to authority than to trust oneself. "In order to truly transform our culture," she concludes, "we need that orientation toward life, toward the body, toward sexuality, ego, will, toward all the muckiness and adventure of being human."[71]

The three "core principles" of Goddess religion are immanence, interconnection, and community. Immanence means that we are the "manifestation of the living being of earth," and that all forms of life in its diversity are sacred.[72] Starhawk does not *believe* in *the* Goddess; "We connect with Her," she says, "through the moon, the stars, the ocean, the earth, through trees, animals, through other human beings, through ourselves. She is the full circle: earth, air, fire, water, and essence—body, mind, spirit, emotions, change."[73] Interconnection expresses our link with "all of the cosmos as parts of one living organism." And this Starhawk interprets both ecologically (the felling of tropical forests affects our weather) and politically (the crying of a homeless child upsets our well-being).[74] Community, finally, speaks to the collective dimension. The goal is not individual salvation or enlightenment. "Community" also includes animals and plants, and is both personal and global.[75]

New Age images of transformation operate in their most salient form at the personal level. Self-help and empowerment govern its ethics, its style of spirituality, and its apocalyptic. This dimension of New Age lends it a cultural and healing power that a trendier movement like that of the Jesus People entirely lacked.[76] The sense of sacred healing gives New Age a remarkable potency. In this regard nothing has been more significant among the sources of inspiration for New Age than Alcoholics Anonymous, and the related 12-step programs for a variety of addictions in a troubled age that have sprung from AA's original principles. AA's astonishingly successful self-help program for alcoholics has shaped New Age ideas of empowerment and its commitment to leaderless groups.

AA was founded in 1935 by Bill W. in Akron, Ohio.[77] Bill had been a successful trader on Wall Street and a gregarious, friendly man. For years he drank to excess and could never find a way of curing his addiction as he watched his life and work crumble before his eyes. At the depths of his despair he was visited by an old drinking buddy who was now straight, well groomed, and sober. The friend, named Ebby, was a member of a zealous religious sect called the Oxford Group that had helped him overcome his drinking problem. The Oxford Group encouraged open confession from its members and guided its followers in assembled groups. Ten of AA's twelve "steps" were carried over directly from the Oxford Group.[78] Bill's first ally was a Dr. Bob, who was also a recovered alcoholic. The organization expanded rapidly, and now is worldwide with 58,576 chapters in over ninety countries and over a million members as of 1985.[79]

The genius of AA's organizational structure is its completely democratic character in what Marc Galanter has called, after Max Weber, a "routinization of charismatic leadership."[80] The crucial first step in membership is the entirely free selection of a sponsor (who can also be changed at will) who takes the inductee through the twelve steps and provides help in "working the program." A series of rituals govern AA attendance, such as always introducing oneself as "My name is _____, and I am an alcoholic" to mark the end of denial, along with expectations such as daily attendance at meetings for the first three months ("ninety meetings in ninety days"). Nevertheless, the actual membership of any given AA chapter is in constant flux, there are any number of possible meetings one can attend, and nothing prevents a member from withdrawing from the organization altogether and possibly returning later. Each chapter is autonomous and decides on its own format and rules. There are no dues, and funds for chapters to cover the cost of rental space (if not free) and pay for the ever-present coffee come from small contributions of those attending any given meeting. No money is ever taken as a gift from nonalcoholics. The name of AA can never be used for any kind of endorsement, commercial or political. The movement keeps itself focused on only one purpose and never gets involved in other causes, though individual members may do what they want politically with the rest of their lives.[81] The skeletal AA national office is run by volunteers.[82]

Galanter argues that AA healing has a cult-like quality with its public confessions, tight cohesion, shared beliefs, and behavior strongly influenced by the group.[83] It is a given in AA, for example, that "personal recovery depends on AA unity" and that members must "adjust, temper, and discipline" their own freedom to protect AA itself.[84] Galanter grants that AA, because of its effective structure, has avoided the faults of groups like Synanon but nevertheless heals its members of their alcoholism through their abject submission, public confessions, strict attendance, and subtle control of dissenting opinions (such as controlled drinking, which is gaining favor among some researchers but is denied as even possible by AA). Most AA members end up socializing with others in the organization, which can put stress on some marriages and old friendships, and fill their language with AA buzzwords that reflect the enthusiasm of a new member of a religious cult.

Certainly, AA rituals and ideals are strongly influenced by evangelical Christianity. The first step in AA is an affirmation of one's utter helplessness before alcohol that parallels the depravity of one's unsaved self before conversion. The second step accepts the exis-

tence of a "Higher Power," an ecumenical (though euphemistic) de-
notation that makes clear its Christian origins in the revelatory experiences that make up AA literature, in the way all AA participants
talk about it, and in the famous prayer of Reinhold Niebuhr that is
invoked at the beginning of every meeting: "God grant me the seren-
ity to accept the things I cannot change, courage to change the things
I can, and wisdom to know the difference." In the third step you are
to turn over your will to God as you understand him. Other steps require various forms of self-surrender, personal improvement, public
confessional, and prayer. The final step returns to the fundamentalist, evangelical model in requiring those who have had a "spiritual
awakening" and healing through following the previous eleven steps
to now take their message to other alcoholics. Faith without works
is dead, says Bill W. in the "Big Book."[85] From rebirth and conversion to personal transformation to sharing the word, AA adapts
Christian forms to its secular task of healing alcoholism.

AA traditions of self-surrender, confession, deep spirituality, mutual support and empowerment, nurturing relationships (especially
in the tradition of the sponsor), equality of members, and the structure of leaderless groups have profoundly influenced the values and
life-styles of many New Agers. It is difficult to imagine feminist
consciousness-raising groups, or most communes, or witches' covens, or UFO support groups except in an age of the self-help movement shaped by AA. New Age spurns medical psychiatry and Freud-
ian psychotherapy as highly suspect in their rational scientism and
embedded patriarchy, though they are drawn to less conventional
forms of talk therapies. They believe we must recognize and submit
to a "Higher Power." Healing in the New Age comes from a spiritual
process of personal transformation. We need to be nurtured and
touched, often literally as in massage.

The transformative character of the 12-step/New Age healing
process reveals its apocalyptic subtext. In Bill W.'s famous and now
archetypal story, he describes his conversion as "the fourth dimension of experience."[86] From a long tradition of mystics to New Age,
the "fourth dimension" has become a buzzword to evoke the ground
of spirituality that transcends the self. The revelation according to
Bill W. is script for AA, built as it is on stories of sin and redemption

that reveal inner truths. Martha Morrison, for example, was a talented and hopelessly addicted doctor in Arkansas in the 1970s who shot up vast quantities of hard drugs besides consuming whole bottles of Southern Comfort. After reaching bottom, Morrison had a religious experience on the banks of the Chattahoochee River in Georgia. At that point she "came to understand and to concede that I had to stop trying to dominate other people and situations. Then, and only then, did I begin to grow."[87] And grow she did into a successful doctor once again, this time helping other addicts, while marrying the son of her mentor and founder of Talbott Recovery Systems, G. Douglas Talbott. Her new self reveals the power of God, and her well-written book, *White Rabbit*, is one way of "witnessing" to others.

The apocalyptic is at the center of New Age. Not as a movement of mystics and fellow travelers; nor as an eclectic blending of Carl Jung and Native Americanism; nor as a therapeutics that rivals scientific medicine; nor least of all as a religion in formation can New Age begin to make sense or cohere without understanding its images of personal and collective transformation.

Clearly, the New Age apocalyptic evokes fundamentalist notions of the end times. Specific images from fundamentalist end time theory—like that of Antichrist, tribulation, even the rapture—creep into New Age thinking. More generally, Catherine Albanese has argued that New Age as a movement has some striking similarities with Christian fundamentalism. Both seek a personal transformation that must find its reflection in the transformation of society; both hear voices rather than see visions and clothe their mysticism as ongoing revelation; both stress healing and what the Puritans once called the "outer signs of inner goodness," or the spiritual benefits of material prosperity; both are literalists (one in terms of biblical scripture, the other in terms of reincarnation); and both espouse a democratized spirituality that looks forward into visions of the millennium.[88]

Perhaps both New Age and fundamentalism are plowing the same apocalyptic ground. We are in it, and it is in us. It cannot be escaped, though there is much uncertainty about our responsibilities toward it, and the role of violence in the move from the old into the new. But what opens up at the other end for New Agers is quite a different picture of the millennium from that of the fundamentalists. In the *inclusive* utopian images of the New Age, global justice and equitable distribution of resources prevail. The sacredness of "Mother Earth" is respected. There are neither executioners nor victims in a world of peace. And instead of a present God or resurrected Jesus leading the faithful, each individual is an empowered and fully realized human being.

CONCLUSION

There is no easy way to conclude a book like this. There are too many stories, and my interpretive points are imbedded in them. I can only underline some ideas that seem particularly significant, and look toward the future of endism and fundamentalism in American culture.

First, endism is a part of all our lives at some level, and has always been woven into religious imaginings at least since culture emerged. But until the last half century endism has been mostly a marginal phenomenon, as best we can tell, and the important task of imagining the end has been assigned to the deeply spiritual, the artistic or creative, and the psychotic. Endism has ebbed and flowed in significance within the self and culture, depending on historical circumstance. Now, however, in our postmodern age when it is a scientifi-

249

cally real possibility that human history could end in a bang of nuclear destruction or a whimper of environmental degradation, it takes an act of imagination *not* to ponder end time issues. The true craziness we live with is the way life itself has been transformed by the continuing presence of absurd threats to the human experiment, which could only make a "pointless apocalypse,"[1] not the varied and sometimes confused human responses to those threats. Fundamentalists speak in a rhetoric that is out of sync with contemporary secular culture; they also touch the real, and give voice to our underlying dread. It was something of a historical accident that Christian apocalypticism emerged in clear ideological form in the nineteenth century out of the crisis of war and as a response to the stirrings of modernism. But once clearly articulated in dogma by 1920, fundamentalism (which even then was at the edges of society), was uniquely well positioned to become a mass movement later in the century. End time theology and the scientific reality of prospective human endings were made for each other.[2] But those ultimate threats affect all of us, not just the fundamentalists. As we have seen, many others besides Christian fundamentalists in our culture have found ways to imagine the end. The Hopi Indians locate elements of hope in their notions of cultural transformations that manage to preserve the ecological integrity of the earth, while New Agers struggle in a variety of secular modes to explain the changes that they believe are upon us. In this broader sense, then, this book is both an interpretation of Christian fundamentalism and a comment on modern life.

Endism in our culture embraces many forms, and partially touches everyone's life in its connection with death. Endism is an attitude as much as a myth, a sense of foreboding as much as a given story, an orientation to ultimate concerns as much as a commitment to a specific end time narrative. Endism describes the future location and deepest yearnings of the self. Endism is process and vision. It cuts against all logic, is usually mystical, and may become magical. Endism stirs hope, which can inspire the dispossessed but can also come to serve as yet another instrument of control for the rich: consider, for example, the involvement of Mrs. Grady in right-wing causes. Endism surely has roots in trauma in the self, but that individual, psychological perspective must be broadened to locate the self in the historical crises of the twentieth century. As a result, there is a paradoxical, or dialectic, relationship between endism and our human future. Something is broken, and it is not even clear God is the glue. To be alive and even reasonably aware at the end of the millennium requires us to ask of ourselves, of our families, of our leaders: Will the human experiment continue?

The most troubling dimension of endism is its relationship to violence. In the endist imagination, transformation out of our present misery—however differently that is understood by people—occupies a central place. The result of the change is inevitably a new age, whether millennial or Aquarian, one that is radically and profoundly different from the present. Fundamentalists generally believe that this transformation can only be accomplished violently, and that the move from our time into the next requires mass death and destruction. Yet it is possible to be future-oriented and nonviolent. Much religious thinking about ultimate issues, from Jesus to Gandhi, purposely rejects violence in constructing images of future redemption, and it is important to take firmer hold of these traditions as we struggle to build utopias that continue a human future. But the more passionate forms of endism I encountered in this study seem to require violence to produce the transformation that will end what is experienced as the tormenting ambiguity and pain of human existence, indeed of time itself, and re-make history. That is the point of the biblical genocide described in the book of Revelation.

But ordinary people do not take in ultimate threats or absorb the grand or violent myths in their culture or religions in simple ways. In its Christian fundamentalist form, which occupies most of my attention in this book, endism (or the apocalyptic) varies enormously with different individuals. There are certain key ideas people take from the theory—like the idea of the rapture or the general notion of tribulation—but most fundamentalists bring their own concerns into their end time reflections and reveal in their apocalypticism projections of the self. Such a process of exchange always occurs in the transaction between the individual and his or her forms of faith. But fundamentalist theory is especially well suited for such end time projections; it is much more immediate in this regard than the impossibly far-off notions of heaven in traditional Christianity.

The immediacy that fundamentalism brings to the traditional Christian message, however, has its potential costs. The apocalyptic tends to undermine personal efficacy and a commitment to human purposes. That can raise ethical and political concerns. The reborn self can isolate the fundamentalist individual from complex social interactions. The intimate communion with the divine (and the devil) realigns moral responsibility in the fundamentalist mind, and can result in a withdrawal from participation in solving social problems. Moreover, the faith commitments of fundamentalists are thoroughly dogmatic; they believe *that* something is true, rather than *in* a transcendent God whom one can only know as immanent in our lives.[3] Something important is lost as fundamentalists shift the Christian emphasis from the Sermon on the Mount to the book of Revelation. Their ideology, to rephrase Diana Trilling, is the sterner face of the Christian myth.[4] The effects of such religious attitudes are readily apparent in the political realm, for certainty about ultimate issues lends ideological clarity to proximate concerns like gender equality, free speech, sexual choice, and curriculum change. For opponents, the certainty of fundamentalists can be vexing and seems to run counter to the dynamics of compromise in a democracy.

Pervasive dualisms and exclusivism are central to fundamentalism. Otto said of the end that, "He [God] is coming back for his people first." God has "his" people, those who have accepted him and believe in him. At the end they will be rewarded in their faith, for he will come back for them first. But such a notion of a chosen people excludes everybody else, especially given the suffering outlined for these "others" in fundamentalist theology. As Erik Erikson observes:

> *While man is obviously one species, he appears and continues on the scene split up into groups (from tribes to nations, from castes to classes, from religions to ideologies) which provide their members with a firm sense of distinct and superior identity—*

and immortality. This demands, however, that each group must invent for itself a place and a moment in the very center of the universe where and when an especially provident deity caused it to be created superior to all others, the mere mortals.[5]

Part of the power of Erikson's insight is his recognition that destruction between groups can only make sense with a spiritual grounding. We cannot value ourselves and degrade and ultimately kill the other unless we call God onto our side in the struggle. In the same way, the genocidal impulse is grounded in perverse forms of idealism and deep yearnings for spiritual purification.[6] Individuals kill others for many reasons, including greed and malice. But mass death, or genocide, though it may embody many motivations, must aim primarily at renewal and transformation of a particular group.

That is the danger. America is an affluent land with a stable political system and a long tradition of absorbing radical social movements into its vast middle. But fundamentalism, largely because it so directly touches ultimate issues, may resist any taming, and remain positioned to expand rapidly in the face of crisis. And it would be foolish to believe that we will always remain immune to crisis. The apocalyptic sense that thrived in and found renewal from the Civil War is enough part of American identity to prompt risky undertakings (like Bush's Gulf War). Protracted fighting abroad or racial war at home, large-scale terrorism, environmental disaster, or whatever, could easily prompt the eruption of the apocalyptic within fundamentalism.

Much, however, works against these dangers. James Davison Hunter, in careful survey work accompanied by interviews, has shown that the younger generation of fundamentalists are generally more moderate in their beliefs and more open in their life-styles than their parents. They think only loosely about the rapture or tribulation, which makes them open to other, modifying influences. Younger fundamentalists are much less likely to be creationists, for example, than older ones. They also seem to feel little compunction about sex before marriage (with someone you love and intend to marry), and have a much more complicated interaction with the media and mass culture than their parents. It may be that Hunter has merely uncovered a blip in the demographic sequence from the 1970s to the 1990s, but he may also have documented a more profound transformation in the making.[7]

There is also hope in the very diversity, even the confusions, of fundamentalists, which end time theory attempts to suffocate. Such a powerful system, with its own boundless sense of immortality, *requires* the search to eliminate all hints of alternative images. But alternative images lurk beneath the surface and demand expression, which in turn calls forth the invocation of Satan to explain them and the difficult work of overcoming them. The fundamentalist psychological process never fully succeeds in carrying out its agenda of purification.[8] The best evidence of these complex tensions is the way fundamentalists make up or bend theory as they go along to fit their own experience. Deborah, who taught a Bible class in her church, rewrote rapture theory to allow for open-ended salvation up to the moment of the final judgment, and God for Arlene was an old black woman.

At a different level, the Christian apocalyptic, even in its most rigid ideological form, provides renewal and hope in the lives of the socially, economically, and spiritually disadvantaged. That is why Reverend Charles and Calvary Church in general were so important in my study. This congregation, which toed the premillennial dispensational line as strictly as any white fundamentalist church, combined their fundamentalism with a significant degree of social activism. They also drew hope from the apocalyptic, into which they stared as deeply as anyone. Reverend Charles, as Jonah in the Bible, knew Nineveh would eventually be destroyed. In the meanwhile, he drew psychological sustenance for himself and his parishioners from the increased sensitivity to ultimate threats to human existence. Apocalyptic hope is cautious at best, but it can be real.

Many complex social, political, and religious factors are drawing fundamentalists into mainstream culture, which may also be a reason for hope. They are themselves masters of media and increasingly attend secular schools at all levels. They are also joining the political mainstream. Jerry Falwell, for example, to the chagrin of many fellow fundamentalists, struck elaborate deals in forging powerful political alliances on key issues during his years of leadership of the Moral Majority. Falwell eventually disbanded the Moral Majority but hardly abandoned his dreams of influencing American politics; he just changed the venue. He now takes the long view and plans to work through education, especially his own Liberty University in Lynchburg, Virginia. "As far as I'm concerned," Falwell has said, "Liberty University is one of the best ways that I can [have an] impact [upon] the course of the country. I foresee creating for political conservatism what Harvard has done for political liberalism."[9] One suspects Falwell, in his grandiosity, may be failing to appreciate that education often works in mysterious ways. Pat Robertson's Christian Coalition, which had some striking political successes in the 1992 elections,[10] is perhaps more doctrinaire but, like the Moral Majority, will almost certainly be forced to compromise with secular humanists as it attempts to take over school boards and other local centers of power throughout the country.[11] What may matter most in the long run is that Falwell and Robertson have brought fundamentalists into the process of compromise that makes up American politics.

Finally, the separatism of fundamentalism can be exaggerated. At times their world can move toward totalism, but in general fundamentalism is basically a variant of Christianity that pushes up against all aspects of American life. Whatever their images of redemption, New York fundamentalists still have to take the D train in from Brooklyn.

NOTES

INTRODUCTION

1. Martin Buber, "Prophecy, Apocalyptic, and the Historical Hour," in *Pointing the Way*, ed. Maurice Friedman (New York: Books for Libraries, 1957 [1954]), pp. 192–207. Note also Harvey Cox, "Christianity and the Apocalypse," presentation at the second conference on the Apocalypse in Providence, Rhode Island, organized by Robbie Bosnak, June 14–17, 1990, comments summarized by Michael Perlman; and Paul D. Hanson, *The Dawn of the Apocalyptic: The Historical and Sociological Roots of Jewish Apocalyptic Eschatology* (Philadelphia: Fortress Press, 1979).

2. Frank Kermode, *The Sense of Ending: Studies in the Theories of Fiction* (New York: Oxford University Press, 1967), p. 27.

3. Paul Boyer, *When Time Shall Be No More: Prophetic Belief in Modern American Culture* (Cambridge, Mass.: Belknap Press of Harvard University Press, 1992), p. 2.

4. Garry Wills, *Under God: Religion and American Politics* (New York: Simon and Schuster, 1990), p. 15. The most recent Gallup data is found in George Gallup and Jim Castelli, *The People's Religion: American Faith in the 90s* (New York: Macmillan, 1989), pp. 56, 58, 61, 63, and 75. The figure about the rapture is from Marlene Tufts, "Snatched Away before the Bomb: Rapture Believers in the 1980s" (Ph.D. diss., University of Hawaii, 1986), p. vi.

5. It should, however, be noted that the conventional scholarly view would not consider conservative evangelicals as fundamentalists. Note Nancy T. Ammerman, "North American Protestant Fundamentalism," in *Fundamentalisms Observed*, ed. Martin Marty and R. Scott Appleby (Chicago: University of Chicago Press, 1991), p. 4. Other scholars see conservative evangelicalism and fundamentalists as part of a continuum. See Douglas Sweeney, "Fundamentalism and the Neo-Evangelicals," *Fides et Historia* 24, no. 1 (Winter/Spring 1991), pp. 81–96.

6. David Harrington Watt, "The Private Hopes of American Fundamentalists and Evangelicals, 1925–1975," *Religion and American Culture* 1 (1991), p. 155. See also David Harrington Watt, *A Transforming Faith: Explorations of Twentieth-Century American Evangelicalism* (New Brunswick: Rutgers University Press, 1991); and the work of Erling Jorstad, especially *Holding Fast, Pressing On: Religion in America in the 1980's* (New York: Praeger, 1990).

7. Grady House was the epitome of the modern transformation of millenarianism, as noted by political scientist Michael Barkun (*Disaster and the Millennium* [New Haven: Yale University Press, 1974], p. 211), from a rural movement historically rooted in disaster and crisis to an urban one that has become "the creature of those who seek power and dominion." The apocalyptic, or, as Barkun calls it, "the idea of the millennium," taken from those who most require it, "now animates those who need it least." This phenomenon was also reported by Nancy T. Ammerman in *Baptist Battles: Social Change and Religious Conflict in the Southern Baptist Convention* (New Brunswick: Rutgers University Press, 1990), esp. pp. 146–49. An earlier treatment of the urbanization of sectarian fundamental-

ism can be found in John B. Holt, "Holiness Religion: Cultural Shock and Social Reorganization," *American Sociological Review* 5 (October 1940), pp. 740–47. I also want to thank Dana Fenton, who is writing her Ph.D. dissertation on Grady House under my direction, for confirming my suspicion about the systematic use of the Social Register by Grady House staff for culling names to invite to the dinners. The parent organization of Grady House, it is worth noting, has also sponsored the Christian Embassy in Washington.

8. Martin Marty, *Religion and the Republic: The American Circumstance* (Boston: Beacon Press, 1989 [1987]), p. 297.

9. The best book on Jim Bakker is by Charles E. Shepard, *Forgiven: The Rise and Fall of Jim Bakker and the PTL Ministry* (New York: Atlantic Monthly Press, 1989).

10. One can see African American fundamentalism on television in the person of Frederick Price. The congregations of the white televangelists can be observed to have many African Americans in them. David Edwin Harrell's classic work *White Sects and Black Man in the Recent South* (Nashville: Vanderbilt University Press, 1971) documents the presence of African Americans in many churches that are considered fundamentalist. See also Thomas Byrne Edsall, "Political Changes in the South: Black Majority, White Men and Fundamentalists," *Dissent* 34 (Winter 1987); and Samuel D. Procter, "The Black Community and the New Religious Right," *Foundations* 25 (1982), pp. 180–87. A minority view is that African Americans, because of their "distinctive style" of worship and their "relationship to society," cannot be considered within the family of fundamentalists. Note Ammerman, "North American Protestant Fundamentalism," p. 3.

11. Erik Erikson, *Insight and Responsibility* (New York: W. W. Norton, 1964), pp. 159–215.

12. Sigmund Freud's first reference to what James Strachey translates as the "narcissism of minor differences" is in "The Taboo of Virginity" (1918), in *The Standard Edition of the Psychological Works of Sigmund Freud*, ed. James Strachey et. al., 23 vols. (London: Hogarth Press, 1955–1962), vol. 11, p. 199. He later returned to the idea in *Group Psychology and the Analysis of the Ego* (1921),

Standard Edition, vol. 18, p. 101, and in *Civilization and Its Discontents* (1930), *Standard Edition*, vol. 21, p. 114.

13. James Aho, *The Politics of Righteousness: Idaho Christian Patriotism* (Seattle: University of Washington Press, 1990).

14. Martin Marty regularly used this phrase in his fundamentalism project at the University of Chicago (in which I participated for a while as a consultant). It is a useful way to capture the aspects of Christianity at the edges of what might not fit into a stricter definition of fundamentalism.

15. Nancy Ammerman also documented this in *Bible Believers: Fundamentalists in the Modern World* (New Brunswick and London: Rutgers University Press, 1987), pp. 147–67. Jehovah's Witnesses believe that only 144,000 Christians will be saved in the end, and they are judged partly on the basis of their evangelical successes, which explains their unusual intensity in their efforts to convert non-Christians. As usual in these matters, however, such pieces of harsh theology frequently get softened in actual experience.

16. Nan made the comment to Laura Simich, who was also working in the church then and trying to convince Nan (unsuccessfully) to grant her a formal interview. It is worth noting that Nan and the woman I call Mary were close friends and lived near each other. Mary granted me two useful interviews but refused a third. I think Nan probably influenced her decision.

17. Erikson says it well: "One can study the nature of things by doing something *to* them [human beings], but one can really learn something about the essential nature of living beings only by doing something *with* them or *for* them" (*Insight and Responsibility*, p. 229). For a more detailed discussion of method, see the article I wrote with Michael Flynn, "Lifton's Method," *The Psychohistory Review* 20 (1992), pp. 131–44.

1. THE BROKEN NARRATIVE

I borrow the term "broken narrative" from B. J. Lifton, my friend and Ph.D. student, who uses it in her forthcoming book, *The Adopted Self* (New York: Basic Books).

1. Michael Franz Basch, "The Perception of Reality and the Dis-

avowal of Meaning," *Annual of Psychoanalysis* 11 (1982), pp. 125–53. The first use of the term "disavowal," however, was by Sigmund Freud in his short paper, "Fetishism": see *The Standard Edition of the Psychological Works of Sigmund Freud*, ed. James Strachey et al., 23 vols. (London: Hogarth Press, 1955–1962), vol. 21, p. 153.

2. The most interesting empirical discussion of these issues is by a former student in a dissertation I supervised: Jennifer Manlowe, *The Grains of Loss: Psychological and Theological Reflections on Eating Disorders and Incest*, unpublished Ph.D. diss., 1993, Drew University. Nicholas Humphrey and Daniel Dennett also wrote a relevant paper, "Speaking for Our Selves," *Occasional Paper*, Center on Violence and Human Survival, New York, 1990. Diane Lunt, a psychoanalyst at the Training and Research Institute in Self Psychology (where I am on the faculty), also shared with me her as-yet-unpublished case of a multiple personality she has been treating for many years. A good recent discussion in general of these issues is Judith Herman, *Trauma and Recovery: The Aftermath of Violence—From Domestic Abuse to Political Terror* (New York: Basic Books, 1992).

3. There are many ways, other than biography, of understanding history psychologically. The issue has often been debated intelligently in the pages of *The Psychohistory Review* (of which I was the founding editor in 1972). I also wrote, with Dan Offer, a history of psychohistory that addresses this issue: *The Leader: Psychohistorical Essays* (New York: Plenum Press, 1986). Robert Jay Lifton has noted the evolving and overlapping psychohistorical styles (including his own) since Freud in *The Life of the Self: Toward a New Psychology* (New York: Simon and Schuster, 1976).

4. Karen McCarthy Brown, personal communication, March 3, 1989.

5. Robert Jay Lifton, in collaboration with Charles B. Strozier, "Psychology and History," in *Psychology and the Social Sciences*, vol. 2 of *Psychology and Its Allied Disciplines*, ed. Marc H. Bornstein, 3 vols. (Hillsdale, N.J.: Lawrence Erlbaum, 1984), pp. 164–84, esp. pp. 171–75.

6. I use "mystical" in this book, following Webster, to describe

spiritual meanings that are neither apparent to the senses nor obvious to the intelligence and that involve a direct subjective communion with God.

2. ULTIMATE THREATS

1. Daniel Yankelovich, the head of the Public Agenda Foundation, in collaboration with The Center for Foreign Policy Development at Brown University, found that 39 percent of the adult population in America believed that "when the Bible predicts that the earth will be destroyed by fire, it's telling us about a nuclear war" (*Voter Options on Nuclear Arms Policy: A Briefing Book for the 1984 Elections* [New York: Public Agenda Foundation, 1984], p. 40).

2. This discovery was by no means mine alone, but part of my own John Jay College Center on Violence and Human Survival research group's collective awareness in analyzing interview material from many different groups. It will be carefully documented in a volume in preparation by myself, Michael Perlman, and Robert Jay Lifton, *Nuclear Threat and the American Self*.

3. The idea of Israel as the "fuse" in the Middle East is a conventional one in fundamentalist thinking. See John F. Walvoord, the eighty-year-old dean of premillennial dispensationalism, who in December 1990 (that is, in the middle of the Persian Gulf crisis) cranked out an updated version of his 1974 book *Armageddon, Oil, and the Middle East Crisis* (Grand Rapids: Zondervan, 1990 [1974]). In 1991, a year with a Middle East war, the book sold 713,827 copies; see *Publishers Weekly*, April 6, 1992.

4. Robert Jay Lifton and I jointly came up with this term and first used it in "Waiting for Armageddon," *New York Times Book Review*, August 12, 1990.

5. A. G. Mojtabai, *Blessed Assurance: At Home with the Bomb in Amarillo, Texas* (Albuquerque, N.M.: University of New Mexico Press, 1986), pp. 142–83, esp. pp. 148, 178–79. Mojtabai is actually quite cautious on this issue. Other journalists, arguing more out of the logic of the theology than actual contact, charge fundamentalists with some extraordinary positions.

1. Augustine, *The City of God*, trans. Marcus Dods (New York: Modern Library, 1950), p. 865.

2. Otto Rank, *The Double: A Psychoanalytic Study* (Chapel Hill: University of North Carolina Press, 1971 [1925]). Note also Rank, *Beyond Psychology* (New York: Dover, 1958 [1941]), pp. 62–101.

3. Robert Jay Lifton, *The Nazi Doctors: Medical Killing and the Psychology of Genocide* (New York: Basic Books, 1986), p. 418.

4. The significance of "dissociation" and "splitting" was quite clear to the early, especially French, workers on hysteria from the 1880s well into this century, especially Pierre Janet. Even Sigmund Freud and Joseph Breuer grant the importance of splitting (*Studies on Hysteria* [1895], in *The Standard Edition of the Psychological Works of Sigmund Freud*, ed. James Strachey et al., 23 vols. [London: Hogarth Press, 1955–1962], vol. 2, pp. 227, 230ff). A good recent discussion of this early history is Bessel A. Van Der Kolk and Onno Van Der Hart, "The Intrusive Past: The Flexibility of Memory and the Engraving of Trauma," *American Imago*, special two-volume issue, "Psychoanalysis, Culture and Trauma," ed. Cathy Caruth, 48 (1991), pp. 425–54. For much of the twentieth century, however, Freud's stress on repression came to crowd out these early insights. The first thinker to begin actively recovering their meanings for the self was Heinz Kohut, especially his first book, *The Analysis of the Self: A Systematic Approach to the Psychoanalytic Treatment of Narcissistic Personality Disorders* (New York: International Universities Press, 1971). Kohut's favored term was "splitting," which was most clearly articulated in his model of the self in 1963: with Philip F. D. Seitz, "Concepts and Theories of Psychoanalysis" in *The Search for the Self: Selected Writings of Heinz Kohut*, ed. Paul H. Ornstein, 4 vols. (New York: International Universities Press, 1978 [1963]), vol. 1, pp. 337–74.

5. Heinz Kohut, *The Restoration of the Self* (Madison, N.J.: International Universities Press, 1977), p. 287.

6. James Barr, *Fundamentalism* (London: SCM, 1977), p. 51.

7. Ibid., p. 52.

4. DIVINE COMMUNION

1. Wilma used this image from Revelation but also said firmly how much she detested and never read the book itself. Such use of apocalyptic language by a woman who disavows the key text of the movement reflects how deeply such imagery has worked its way into the discourse.

2. A latent violence nevertheless seemed to haunt Nigel. He told me two chilling driving stories during his "wild period." In one he was driving on Highway 95 from Boston to New York in his sports car. Someone pulled in front of him and deliberately braked for whatever reason. Nigel moved at high speed into the passing lane, chased the car down, and purposely forced it off the road. Luckily, no one was killed. In the second story Nigel was blocked by a car and he pushed into it and forced it into the median where it crashed. He drove off into the night at high speed. "These are things that I would never do today," he said, "because I'm a different person."

5. THE END AT HAND

1. Hal Lindsey, with C. C. Carlson, *The Late Great Planet Earth* (Grand Rapids: Zondervan, 1970); John F. Walvoord, *Armageddon, Oil, and the Middle East Crisis* (Grand Rapids: Zondervan, 1990 [1974]). I also gave a paper, "Christian Fundamentalism, Nuclear Threat, and the Middle East War," Uppsala, Sweden, February 25, 1991, that was later published in *The End in Sight? Images of the End and Threats to Human Survival*, ed. Roger Williamson (Uppsala: Life and Peace Institute, 1993), pp. 49–58.

2. John F. Walvoord, *Prophecy Knowledge Handbook: All the Prophecies of Scripture Explained in One Volume* (Wheaton, Ill.: Victor Books, 1990). Note also Dwight J. Pentecost, *Things to Come: A Study in Biblical Eschatology* (Grand Rapids: Zondervan, 1958).

3. Paul Boyer, *When Time Shall Be No More: Prophetic Belief in Modern American Culture* (Cambridge, Mass.: Belknap Press of Harvard University Press, 1992), esp. pp. 1–79 and 190 on date setting.

4. Otto is a "post-tribulationist," for he believes that Christ only returns *after* the period of tribulation. What that means concretely

for Otto is that Christians first have to experience the horrors of God's destruction before being redeemed in the returned Christ.

5. Walvoord, for example, in *Prophecy Knowledge Handbook*, in his twenty references to the rapture, weaves it into the background of all sorts of crucial Gospel stories that touch on prophecy and the return of Jesus. Compare Hal Lindsey's breezy book *The Rapture* (New York: Doubleday, 1983). A study that puts the rapture in historical perspective is Timothy P. Weber, *Living in the Shadow of the Second Coming: American Premillennialism, 1875–1982* (Chicago: University of Chicago Press, 1983).

6. The question of the timing of the rapture before or after tribulation was also one of the first major sources of serious fragmentation in the evangelical movement at the turn of the century, and led to the disintegration of the Niagara Bible Conference in 1901 and the cessation of the prophetic conferences of the next decade. Note George Marsden, *Fundamentalism and American Culture: The Shaping of Twentieth-Century Evangelicalism, 1870–1925* (New York: Oxford University Press, 1980), p. 93.

7. A man at Calvary, a Brother Heflin, who runs an end time camp, went a step further in explicitness. He thought the headline was already printed and it said, "Millions Missing" in the largest type the *Times* has ever used.

8. Among the excellent studies of women in Protestant fundamentalism of all varieties are: Margaret Bendroth, "The Search for Woman's Role in American Evangelicalism, 1930–1980," in *Evangelicalism in Modern America*, ed. George Marsden (Grand Rapids: William B. Eerdman's Publishing Company, 1984), pp. 122–34; Kathleen M. Blee, *Women of the Klan: Racism and Gender in the 1920s* (Berkeley and Los Angeles: University of California Press, 1991); Virginia Lieson Brereton, *Training God's Army: The American Bible School, 1880–1940* (Bloomington and Indianapolis: Indiana University Press, 1990); Betty A. DeBerg, *Ungodly Women: Gender and the First Wave of American Fundamentalism* (Minneapolis: Fortress Press, 1990); James Davison Hunter and Helen V. L. Stehlin, "Family: Toward Androgyny" in James Davison Hunter, *Evangelicalism: The Coming Generation* (Chicago: University of Chicago Press, 1987); Rebecca Klatch, *Women of the New Right*

(Philadelphia: Temple University Press, 1987); Susan Rose, "Women Warriors: The Negotiation of Gender Roles in an Evangelical Community," *Sociological Analysis* 48 (1987), pp. 244–58; Susan Rose, *Keeping Them Out of the Hands of Satan: Evangelical Schooling in America* (New York and London: Routledge and Kegan Paul, 1988); Susan Rose, "Gender, Education, and the New Christian Right," in *In Gods We Trust: New Patterns of Religious Pluralism in America*, 2d ed., ed. Thomas Robbins and Dick Anthony (New Brunswick and London: Transaction Publishers, 1990); and Judith Stacey, *Brave New Families: Stories of Domestic Upheaval in Twentieth-Century America* (New York: Basic Books, 1990).

6. THE WORLD AND ITS EVILS

1. Catherine Keller, personal communication, January 27, 1993.

2. Robert Jay Lifton, *Death in Life: Survivors of Hiroshima* (New York: Vintage Books, 1967), p. 224.

3. Otto's memory was pretty good. 2 Timothy 3:1–5: "This know also, that in the last days perilous times shall come./ For men shall be lovers of their own selves, covetous, boasters, proud, blasphemers, disobedient to parents, unthankful, unholy,/ Without natural affection, truce-breakers, false accusers, incontinent, fierce, despisers of those that are good,/ Traitors, heady, high-minded, lovers of pleasures more than lovers of God,/ Having a form of godliness, but denying the power thereof: from such turn away."

4. *Religion Watch* (September 1992, p. 6) reports on a study at the Center for Survey Research at the University of Virginia showing that evangelicals and fundamentalists have a strong concern for poverty and other social issues and that they are among the most generous segment of the population. In the survey, "helping the poor in America" was the number-one concern of this group, and on the average they gave 10 percent or more of their income to such issues (though the article noted, without comment, that their giving to "such issues" included gifts to the church). The more fundamentalist the respondent, however, the more likely he or she was to rate converting people as the more significant goal of a Christian.

5. Carl G. Jung, *Aion: Researches into the Phenomenology of the*

Self, trans. R. F. C. Hull, in *The Collected Works of C. G. Jung*, vol. 9, pt. II, ed. Sir Herbert Read, Michael Fordham, Gerhard Adler, and William McGuire (Princeton: Princeton University Press, 1959 [1951]), pp. 42–45, 61.

7. THE PROBLEM OF ENDISM

1. Arthur M. Schlesinger, Jr., "The Turn of the Cycle," *New Yorker*, November 11, 1992.

2. John Singleton in an interview with Bryant Gumbel on "Today," May 1, 1992.

3. Martin Gottlieb, "Police in Crown Heights: A Holding Approach," *New York Times*, November 19, 1992.

4. Henri Focillon, *The Year 1000* (New York: Frederick Ungar, 1969), p. 53.

5. Ibid., p. 40.

6. Ibid.

7. Ibid., p. 50.

8. Ibid., p. 47.

9. Sigmund Freud, *The Interpretation of Dreams* (1900 [1899]), ed. James Strachey, 1-vol. paperback edition (New York: Basic Books, 1965), p. 660. Compare Freud's other comment on this issue, ibid., p. 278: "Paradise itself is no more than a group phantasy of the childhood of the individual. That is why mankind were naked in Paradise and were without shame in one another's presence; till a moment arrived when shame and anxiety awoke, expulsion followed, and sexual life and the tasks of cultural activity began." The specifically "Edenic" idea is a personal communication from Catherine Keller.

10. Frank Kermode, *The Sense of Ending: Studies in the Theory of Fiction* (New York: Oxford University Press, 1967), p. 16. Compare, however, Paul Boyer, *When Time Shall Be No More: Prophetic Belief in Modern American Culture* (Cambridge, Mass.: Belknap Press of Harvard University Press, 1992), pp. ix and 337. Boyer by no means mocks the contemporary popular concern with prophecy (as does Kermode) but tends to stress that its current emphasis blends "age-old themes" that will keep prophecy belief alive well into the next century. I generally agree with Boyer and would only

268

mass movement that is grounded, somehow, in ultimate threats to
human existence.

11. Kermode, *Sense of Ending*, pp. 95–96.

12. Don DeLillo, *Mao II* (New York: Viking, 1991), p. 80.

13. Kermode, *Sense of Ending*, p. 28.

14. Lincoln Burr, "The Year 1000 and the Antecedents of the Crusades," *American Historical Review* 6 (1900), pp. 429–44, argues that the "panic of terror" in the latter part of the tenth century actually originated in the mind of the fifteenth-century abbot Johannes Trithemius, is entirely legendary, and now exists only as a "nightmare" of modern scholars. The evidence Burr rightly discounts, however, is of a popular panic that some nineteenth-century historians used to explain the crusades. He does not address the more interesting evidence that Focillon used from the monasteries. Burr, of course, wrote a half century before Focillon.

15. Norman Cohn, *The Pursuit of the Millennium* (New York: Oxford University Press, 1957).

16. See the ninety-nine-page pamphlet of the Mission that was handed out on New York City streets during the summer of 1992.

17. Elaine Showalter, *Sexual Anarchy: Gender and Culture at the Fin-de-Siècle* (New York: Viking, 1990).

18. Susan Sontag, *AIDS and Its Metaphors* (New York: Farrar, Straus, and Giroux, 1988).

19. A number of empirical studies over the years have studied the effect of nuclear threat on people. See T. R. Tyler and K. M. McGraw, "The Threat of Nuclear War: Risk Interpretation and Behavioral Response," *Journal of Social Issues* 39 (1983), p. 186; Thomas A. Knox, William G. Keilin, Ernest L. Chavez, and Scott B. Hamilton, "Thinking about the Unthinkable: The Relationship between Death Anxiety and Cognitive/Emotional Responses to the Threat of Nuclear War," *Omega* 18 (1987–88), pp. 53–61; Raymond L. Schmitt, "Symbolic Immortality in Ordinary Contexts: Impediments to the Nuclear Era," *Omega* 13 (1982–83), pp. 95–116; Scott B. Hamilton, Thomas A. Knox, William G. Keilin, and Ernest L. Chavez, "In the Eye of the Beholder: Accounting for Variability in Attitudes and Cognitive/Affective Reactions toward the Threat of

NOTES

Nuclear War," *Journal of Applied Social Psychology* 17 (1987), pp. 927–52; and Jerome Rabow, Anthony C. R. Hernandez, and Michael D. Newcomb, "Nuclear Fears and Concerns among College Students: A Cross-National Study of Attitudes," *Political Psychology* 11 (1990), pp. 681–98. See also the collection of essays in Lester Grinspoon, ed., *The Long Darkness: Psychological and Moral Perspectives on Nuclear Winter* (New Haven: Yale University Press, 1986); this volume includes a scientific essay by Carl Sagan on nuclear winter and an essay reflecting on that image by Lifton. Another interesting—and controversial—area of research on nuclear threat in the 1980s was done on children. See Sybil K. Escalona, "Children and the Threat of Nuclear War," in Milton Schwebel, ed., *Behavioral Science and Human Survival* (Palo Alto, Calif.: Science and Behavior Books, 1965), pp. 201–9. See also Milton Schwebel, "Nuclear Cold War: Student Opinion and Nuclear War Responsibility," in Milton Schwebel, ed., *Behavioral Science and Human Survival*, pp. 210–40. But the most important work on children and nuclear threat, much of which was conceptual and clinical, was done by John Mack, William Beardslee, and their colleagues at Harvard: John Mack and William Beardslee, "The Impact on Children and Adolescents of Nuclear Developments," in R. Rogers, ed., *Psychosocial Aspects of Nuclear Developments*, Task Force Report No. 20 (Washington, D.C.: American Psychiatric Association, 1982); J. Mack, W. R. Beardslee, R. M. Snow, and L. A. Goodman, "The Threat of Nuclear War and the Nuclear Arms Race: Adolescent Experiences and Perceptions," *Political Psychology* 4 (1983), pp. 501–30; William R. Beardslee, "Perceptions of the Threat of Nuclear War: Research and Professional Implications," *International Journal of Mental Health* 15 (1986), pp. 242–52; and John E. Mack, "Resistances to Knowing in the Nuclear Age," *Harvard Educational Review* 54 (1984), pp. 260–70. The most bitter (and polemical) criticism of this work was C. E. Finn and Joseph Adelson, "Terrorizing Children," *Commentary* 79 (1985), pp. 29–36. Note also F. Butterfield, "Experts Disagree on Children's Worries about Nuclear War," *New York Times*, October 16, 1983.

20. Charles B. Strozier and Robert Jay Lifton, "The End of Nuclear Fear?" *New York Newsday*, November 13, 1991.

21. Randall Balmer describes the annual trade show of the Christian Booksellers Association as "one of the largest trade shows in the nation, with more than 350 exhibitors consuming more than 275,000 square feet of space." See Randall Balmer, *Mine Eyes Have Seen the Glory: A Journey into the Evangelical Subculture in America* (New York: Oxford University Press, 1989), p. 72.

22. Ammerman notes that active members of Southside Church were involved in at least Sunday morning and Wednesday night services as well as Bible studies set up for various age and gender groups, Sunday School, choirs, and various committees; Ammerman, *Bible Believers*, pp. 34–37.

23. Robert Jay Lifton, *Thought Reform and the Psychology of Totalism: A Study of "Brainwashing" in China* (New York: W. W. Norton, 1961), pp. 419–37.

24. Rick Branch, research director, "Watchmen Fellowship," Arlington, Texas, personal communication, August 8, 1993; and Ted Daniels, "Millennium Watch Institute," personal communication, August 8, 1993. Branch noted, however, that from an "evangelical" point of view (that is, from within a fundamentalist perspective that would include New Age channeling groups, as well as the Mormon Church, for example) there are easily six to seven thousand cults in America.

25. James Aho, *The Politics of Righteousness: Idaho Christian Patriotism* (Seattle: University of Washington Press, 1990).

26. It should be noted, of course, that I worked in New York City. I have had some distinctly different reactions to some churches I have visited in Georgia (where I have relatives), and, perhaps ironically, one fundamentalist church I visited three times in Sweden.

27. Philip Greven, *Spare the Child: The Religious Roots of Punishment and the Psychological Impact of Physical Abuse* (New York: Knopf, 1991). I discuss Greven's book in more detail in a forthcoming essay, "Suffer the Children," *Psychohistory Review*.

8. A HISTORY OF AMERICAN ENDISM

1. The most interesting discussion of the underlying psychological tensions in seventeenth-century America is John Demos, *Entertaining Satan: Witchcraft and the Culture of Early New England*

(New York: Oxford University Press, 1982). Note also Richard Slotkin, *Regeneration through Violence: The Mythology of the American Frontier, 1600–1860* (Middletown, Conn.: Wesleyan University Press, 1973).

2. Gordon Wood, *The Radicalism of the American Revolution* (New York: Alfred A. Knopf, 1992).

3. Catherine Keller, "De-Colon-izing Paradise: A Quincentennial Passage," unpublished paper, quoted with permission of the author.

4. Edward Pessen, *Jacksonian America: Society, Personality, and Politics* (Homewood, Ill.: Dorsey Press, 1969), chap. 1.

5. Ronald L. Numbers and Jonathan M. Butler, eds., *The Disappointed: Millerism and Millenarianism in the Nineteenth Century* (Bloomington: Indiana University Press, 1987). Note also Malcolm Bull and Keith Lockhard, *Seeking a Sanctuary: Seventh-Day Adventism and the American Dream* (New York: Harper and Row, 1989); and Paul Boyer, *When Time Shall Be No More: Prophetic Belief in Modern American Culture* (Cambridge, Mass.: Belknap Press of Harvard University Press, 1992), pp. 80–86.

6. Hazel Catherine Wolf, *On Freedom's Altar: The Martyr Complex in the Abolition Movement* (Madison, Wis.: University of Wisconsin Press, 1952), p. ix.

7. Lawrence Friedman, however, persuasively argues that the degree of genuine pacifism that infused the abolitionists in the 1830s is open to some question. See Lawrence Friedman, "Antebellum American Abolitionism and the Problem of Violent Means," *Psychohistory Review* 9 (1980), pp. 26–32. The basic question the abolitionists failed to grapple with was whether violence was acceptable if used defensively. The test case was the shooting of Elijah Lovejoy in Alton, Illinois. See Charles B. Strozier, *Lincoln's Quest for Union: Public and Private Meanings* (New York: Basic Books, 1982), p. 188.

8. Frederick Douglass, *Life and Writings of Frederick Douglass*, ed. Philip Foner, 5 vols. (New York: International Publishers, 1950), vol. 2, pp. 460–63.

9. Quotations from Geoffrey C. Ward with Rick Burns and Ken Burns, *The Civil War* (New York: Knopf, 1990), p. 19.

10. Matthew 12:22–28; Mark 3:22–26; and Luke 11:14–20.

11. Strozier, *Lincoln's Quest for Union*, pp. 182–87; compare Don Fehrenbacher, *Prelude to Greatness: Lincoln in the 1850s* (Stanford: Stanford University Press, 1962).

12. Stephen B. Oates, *To Purge This Land with Blood: A Biography of John Brown* (New York: Harper and Row, 1970), p. 310.

13. Don Fehrenbacher in Ward, *The Civil War*, p. 84.

14. Arthur Schlesinger, Jr., "The Opening of the American Mind," *New York Times Book Review*, July 23, 1989.

15. Some of the large number of studies that have dealt with this issue are: Joel Kovel, *White Racism: A Psychohistory* (New York: Pantheon Books, 1970); Robert Jay Lifton, *Death in Life: Survivors of Hiroshima* (New York: Vintage Books, 1967); and idem, *The Broken Connection: On Death and the Continuity of Life* (New York: Basic Books, 1979).

16. Peter J. Parrish, "The Instruments of Providence: Slavery, Civil War and the American Churches," *Studies in Church History* 20 (1983), p. 299.

17. Barbara Jeanne Fields, *Slavery and Freedom on the Middle Ground: Maryland During the Nineteenth Century* (New Haven: Yale University Press, 1985). Note also Fields's short and provocative essay in Ward, *The Civil War*.

18. Ernest Lee Tuveson, *Redeemer Nation: The Idea of America's Millennial Role* (Chicago: University of Chicago Press, 1968), pp. 195, 208.

19. Parrish, "The Instruments of Providence," p. 294.

20. Richard Slotkin, *Regeneration through Violence*; ibid., *The Fatal Environment: The Myth of the Frontier in the Age of Industrialization, 1880–1890* (Middletown, Conn.: Wesleyan University Press, 1986); and idem, *Gunfighter Nation: The Frontier Myth in Twentieth-Century America* (New York: Macmillan, 1992). One could also note the famous President's Commission, *Violence in America: Historical and Comparative Perspectives: A Report to the National Commission on the Causes and Prevention of Violence, June, 1969*, Hugh Davis Graham and Ted Robert Gurr for the President's Commission, eds. (New York: Signet Books, 1969).

21. Parrish, "The Instruments of Providence," p. 299.

22. Ibid., p. 304.

23. Sherman said it was all hell as he and Grant crossed some perilous lines that have led others to make total war in the twentieth century. Note Charles B. Strozier, "Unconditional Surrender and the Rhetoric of Total War: From Truman to Lincoln," Occasional Paper of the Center on Violence and Human Survival, John Jay College, City University of New York, 1987 (republished in *Military History Quarterly* 2 [1990], pp. 8–15). Compare William Tecumseh Sherman, *Memoirs of General W. T. Sherman*, ed. Charles Royster (New York: Library of America, 1990); Ulysses Grant, *Personal Memoirs of U. S. Grant and Selected Letters*, ed. Mary Drake McFeely and William S. McFeely (New York: Library of America, 1990). Two recent books on Sherman are quite useful in terms of these issues: John F. Marshalek, *Sherman: A Soldier's Passion for Order* (New York: The Free Press, 1993); and the extraordinarily interesting study by Charles Royster, *The Destructive War: William Tecumseh Sherman, Stonewall Jackson, and the Americans* (New York: Alfred A. Knopf, 1991).

24. Royster, *Destructive War*, pp. 82, 241.

25. Alan T. Nolan, *Lee Considered: General Robert E. Lee and Civil War History* (Chapel Hill: University of North Carolina Press, 1991), pp. 112–33, especially pp. 119 and 126.

26. Ward, *The Civil War*, p. 55.

27. Kenneth Stampp, "The Southern Road to Appomattox," in *The Imperiled Union: Essays on the Background of the Civil War* (New York: Oxford University Press, 1980), pp. 246–69, quotes from pp. 252, 260–61 respectively. Note also two recent books edited by Gabor S. Boritt that deal with the question of Lincoln's wartime leadership and why the South lost: *Lincoln, the War President* (New York: Oxford University Press, 1992), and *Why the Confederacy Lost* (New York: Oxford University Press, 1992).

28. Don Fehrenbacher, ed., *Lincoln*, 2 vols. (New York: The Library of America, 1989), quotes from vol. 1, pp. 220, 250, 415, and 269 respectively.

29. Note Strozier, "Unconditional Surrender." Cf. James M. McPherson, "Lincoln and the Strategy of Unconditional Surrender," in *Lincoln, the War President*, ed. Gabor S. Boritt, pp. 29–62; this

paper was first published in pamphlet form at almost the same time as my own. McPherson and I have overlapping but also quite different perspectives on the issue of unconditional surrender during the Civil War.

30. Royster, *Destructive War*, p. 151.

31. "The fiery trial through which we pass, will light us down, in honor or dishonor, to the latest generation." Fehrenbacher, *Lincoln*, vol. 1, p. 415.

32. Hans J. Morgenthau and David Hein, *Essays on Lincoln's Faith and Politics*, ed. Kenneth W. Thompson, 4 vols. (New York: Lanham, 1983), vol. 4, p. 145.

33. James H. Moorhead, *American Apocalypse: Yankee Protestants and the Civil War, 1860–1869* (New Haven: Yale University Press, 1978), p. x.

34. James M. McPherson, "American Victory, American Defeat," in *Why the Confederacy Lost*, ed. Gabor S. Boritt (New York: Oxford University Press, 1992), p. 40.

35. Fehrenbacher, *Lincoln*, vol. 2, p. 209.

36. See Garry Wills, *Lincoln at Gettysburg: The Words that Remade America* (New York: Simon and Schuster, 1992).

37. Fehrenbacher, *Lincoln*, vol. 2, p. 687.

38. Moorhead, *American Apocalypse*, pp. 174–75. I speak of "Easter Morning sermons" rather loosely in this analysis. I am particularly interested in those given that Sunday morning, April 16. In some cases, however, I draw on sermons from Lincoln's Washington funeral on April 19 and even from those of Sunday, April 23, when some ministers, such as Henry Ward Beecher and Theodore L. Cuyler, gave their sermons because they had been at a ceremony at Fort Sumter on Friday, April 14, and had been unable to return to their churches for Easter by April 16. In the larger body of "assassination sermons"—though I avoid quoting from them—there were also many sermons on May 4, the date of the Lincoln funeral in Springfield, and June 1, the national day of mourning proclaimed by President Johnson. The further one gets from the actual death of Lincoln, the more conventional and "canned" become the sermons.

39. C. B. Crane, *Sermon on the Occasion of the Death of Presi-*

dent Lincoln (Hartford: Press of Case, Lockwood and Co., 1865). Unless otherwise indicated, i.e., as separately published in a book, the sermons I read were from the collection in the Illinois State Historical Library. I used as a key to the collection Jay Monaghan's *Collections of the Illinois State Historical Library: Bibliographical Series, Volume IV: Lincoln Bibliography, 1839–1939*, vol. 1 (Springfield: Illinois State Historical Library, 1943). I also benefited from the assistance of Thomas Schwartz, the curator of the Lincoln collection of the Library, and Mark Johnson, a research historian with the Illinois Preservation Agency. As far as I can tell, some three hundred sermons survive in various collections around the country (though the Illinois State Historical Library has by far the greatest number of the sermons). I read about one hundred of them.

40. Rolla H. Chubb, *A Discourse upon the Death of President Lincoln Delivered at Greenwich M. E. Church*, June 1, 1865, p. 3.

41. Ralph Waldo Emerson, "A Plain Man of the People," in *Building the Myth: Selected Speeches Memorializing Abraham Lincoln*, ed. Waldo W. Braden (Urbana: University of Illinois Press, 1990), pp. 33–34.

42. Henry Ward Beecher, "A New Impulse of Patriotism for His Sake," in Braden, *Building the Myth*, pp. 37–46.

43. Theodore L. Cuyler, "And the Lord blessed Abraham in all things. Gen. 29:1," and George Bancroft, "Oration," in *Our Martyr President, Abraham Lincoln. Voices from the Pulpit of New York and Brooklyn* (New York: Tibbals and Whiting, 1865), p. 389.

44. Chubb, *A Discourse*, p. 7 (Illinois State Historical Library).

45. Abraham Lincoln, *The Collected Works of Abraham Lincoln*, Roy P. Basler et al., eds., 8 vols. plus appendix and supplement (New Brunswick, N.J.: Rutgers University Press, 1953), vol. 8, p. 375 n. and pp. 375–76. There was some confusion in the hectic weeks toward the end of March about the actual date Fort Sumter had fallen. On March 27 Secretary of War Edwin Stanton telegraphed Lincoln at City Point detailing the problem, namely that the surrender had been agreed to on April 13, 1861, but that the northern troops had only filed out of the fort the next day. Lincoln replied that he thought there was "little or no difference" which day was se-

lected on which to hold the ceremony. Stanton obviously chose April 14, which came to have much more meaning than he ever could have imagined.

46. Cuyler, "And the Lord blessed Abraham in all things. Gen. 29:1," in *Our Martyr President*, p. 159.

47. S. S. Guthrie, *In Memoriam: Abraham Lincoln* (Buffalo: Matthews & Warren, 1865).

48. William E. Baron, "The American Pulpit on the Death of Lincoln," *The Open Court* 37 (October 1923), p. 514.

49. A. A. Littlejohn, "Know ye not there is a prince and a great man fallen this day in Israel. 2 Sam. 3:38," in *Our Martyr President*.

50. W. E. Guthrie, *Oration on the Death of Abraham Lincoln* (Philadelphia: John Pennington & Sons, 1865), p. 9.

51. E. S. Atwood, *Discourses in Commemoration of Abraham Lincoln*, April 16 and June 1, 1865 (Salem: The Salem Gazette, 1865).

52. Lincoln was noted for his pardons of deserters who had been condemned to death by his harsher Secretary of War, Edwin Stanton. Lincoln also did things like moving quickly to prevent retaliation after the southern massacre at Fort Pillow on April 12 and 13, 1864, with the comment that "blood can not restore blood." Lincoln, *Collected Works*, vol. 7, p. 345.

53. Chubb, *A Discourse*, p. 9.

54. Henry W. Bellows, "Sorrow hath filled your heart. Nevertheless, I will tell the truth. It is expedient for you that I go away; for if I do not go away, the Comforter will not come unto you; but if I depart I will send him unto you. John 16:6, 7," in *Our Martyr President*, pp. 59–60, 62.

55. Charles H. Robinson, "He was a good man, and a just. Luke 23:50," in *Our Martyr President*, pp. 91–92.

56. James Douglas, *Funeral Discourse on the Occasion of the Obsequies of President Lincoln*, April 19, 1865 (Pulaski, N.Y.: Democrat Job Press, 1865).

57. James DeNormandie, *The Lord Reigneth: A Few Words on Sunday Morning, April 16, 1865, after the Assassination of Abraham Lincoln* (Illinois State Historical Library). See also Isaac E. Carey, *Discourse on the Death of Abraham Lincoln, April 19, 1865*

(Illinois State Historical Library); and John Chester, *The Lessons of the Hour. Justice as Well as Mercy. A Discourse Preached on the Sabbath Following the Assassination of the President* (Washington, D.C.: Washington Chronicle Print, 1865).

58. Chester, *The Lessons of the Hour*, pp. 11, 13.

59. William L. Chaffin, *A Discourse on Sunday Morning, April 23d, 1865* (Philadelphia: King & Baird, 1865).

60. Robinson, "He was a good man, and a just. Luke 23:50," in *Our Martyr President*, pp. 97, 99, 100.

61. Ward, *The Civil War*, p. 393.

62. Parrish, "The Instruments of Providence," p. 318.

63. Eric Foner, *Reconstruction: America's Unfinished Revolution, 1863–1877* (New York: Harper and Row, 1988). Note also Albion W. Tourgee, *A Fool's Errand, By One of the Fools* (New York: Fords, Howard, and Hulbert, 1879).

64. See Geoffrey Barraclough, *European Unity in Thought and Action* (Oxford: B. Blackwell, 1963).

65. Elaine Showalter, *Sexual Anarchy: Gender and Culture at the Fin-de-Siècle* (New York: Viking, 1990), pp. 3–4.

66. George Marsden, *Fundamentalism and American Culture: The Shaping of Twentieth-Century Evangelicalism, 1870–1925* (New York: Oxford University Press, 1980), p. 3.

67. Timothy P. Weber, *Living in the Shadow of the Second Coming: American Premillennialism, 1875–1982* (Chicago: University of Chicago Press, 1983), pp. 41–42.

68. Boyer, *When Time Shall Be No More*, pp. 80–112.

69. Note especially Weber, *Living in the Shadow*. Compare Ernest Sandeen, *The Roots of Fundamentalism: British and American Millenarianism, 1800–1930* (Chicago: University of Chicago Press, 1970).

70. Note especially Boyer, *When Time Shall Be No More*. Compare Marsden, *Fundamentalism and American Culture*; and Weber, *Living in the Shadow*.

71. Boyer, *When Time Shall Be No More*, p. 88.

72. Ibid., p. 90.

73. Marsden, *Fundamentalism and American Culture*, pp. 55ff; Nancy T. Ammerman, "North American Protestant Fundamental-

ism," in *Fundamentalisms Observed*, ed. Martin Marty and R. Scott Appleby (Chicago: University of Chicago Press, 1991), pp. 11ff.

74. Sandeen, *Roots of Fundamentalism*, p. 125.

75. Ibid., p. 126.

76. Ibid., p. 128.

77. Boyer, *When Time Shall Be No More*, p. 92.

78. Weber, *Living in the Shadow*, pp. 33–35.

79. Boyer, *When Time Shall Be No More*, pp. 92–93; Weber, *Living in the Shadow*; Marsden, *Fundamentalism and American Culture*; and Ammerman, "North American Protestant Fundamentalism," pp. 3–4, 13–14, 53.

80. Boyer, *When Time Shall Be No More*, pp. 95–96.

81. This can certainly be said of much of Hal Lindsey's *The Late Great Planet Earth* (Grand Rapids: Zondervan, 1970), but equally and more subtly of John F. Walvoord's *Armageddon, Oil, and the Middle East Crisis* (Grand Rapids: Zondervan, 1990 [1974]).

82. Marsden, *Fundamentalism and American Culture*, pp. 118–23; Sandeen, *Roots of Fundamentalism*, pp. 188–207.

83. Ammerman, "North American Protestant Fundamentalism," p. 2.

84. Garry Wills, *Under God: Religion and American Politics* (New York: Simon and Schuster, 1990), pp. 108–14.

85. Ammerman, "North American Protestant Fundamentalism," pp. 18–22, 27–34. See also Joel Carpenter, "Fundamentalist Institutions and the Rise of Conservative Protestantism, 1929–42," *Church History* 49 (March 1980), pp. 62–75.

86. George Marsden, *Reforming Fundamentalism: Fuller Seminary and the New Evangelicalism* (Grand Rapids: Eerdman's, 1987).

87. David Harrington Watt, "The Private Hopes of American Fundamentalists and Evangelicals, 1925–1975," *Religion and American Culture* 1 (1991), pp. 162–65.

88. Robert Wuthnow, asking a different question, comes to a surprisingly similar conclusion; Robert Wuthnow, *The Restructuring of American Religion: Society and Faith Since World War II* (Princeton: Princeton University Press, 1988).

89. The latter especially has been masterfully traced by Boyer in *When Time Shall Be No More* (1992), and continues to be updated by Ted Daniels in his encyclopedic newsletter out of what he calls his "Millennial Watch Institute." Interesting historical perspectives on fundamentalism have also been provided by Wills, *Under God* (1990). The evangelical subculture has in turn been well described by Balmer in *Mine Eyes Have Seen the Glory* (1989). Finally, Christian fundamentalism in global and comparative contexts, along with massive bibliographies, has been richly developed in The Fundamentalism Project at the University of Chicago under the direction of Martin Marty.

9. JEWS, ISRAEL, AND THE PARADOX OF THE INGATHERING

1. Note Lifton, *The Nazi Doctors: Medical Killing and the Psychology of Genocide* (New York: Basic Books, 1986). See also Benno Mueller-Hill, *Murderous Science: Elimination by Scientific Selection of Jews, Gypsies and Others, Germany, 1933–1945*, trans. George R. Fraser (New York: Oxford University Press, 1988).

2. Haim H. Cohn, *The Trial and Death of Jesus* (New York: Harper and Row, 1967). The quote is from page 331.

3. The early sources for what later became full-fledged anti-Semitism are explored in Richard Rubinstein, "Religion and the Origins of the Death Camps: A Psychoanalytic Interpretation," in *Thinking the Unthinkable: Meanings of the Holocaust*, ed. R. S. Gottlieb (New York: Paulist Press, 1990), pp. 46–63. Note also Richard Rubinstein and J. K. Roth, *Approaches to Auschwitz* (London: SCM, 1987). C. H. Dodd takes a balanced view of the matter: Jesus' claim to be the Messiah, which translated into "King of the Jews," could not be taken lightly by the authorities. See C. H. Dodd, *The Founder of Christianity* (London: Collins, 1971), p. 159. Other scholars follow this argument: see S. Neill and T. Wright, *The Interpretation of the New Testament, 1861–1986*, 2d expanded ed. (Oxford: Oxford University Press, 1988), p. 393; David J. Goldberg and John D. Rayner, *The Jewish People: Their History and Their Religion* (New York: Viking, 1987), pp. 76–77; Pinchas Lapide, *Warum kommt er nicht: Judische Evangelienauslegung* (Gutersloh:

Guterssloher Verlagshaus, Gern Mohn, 1988), p. 82; Humphrey Carpenter, *Jesus* (Oxford: Oxford University Press, 1980), pp. 87–88; William M. Thompson, *The Jesus Debate: A Survey and Synthesis* (New York: Paulist Press, 1985), pp. 206–9; E. P. Sanders, *Jesus and Judaism* (London: SCM, 1985), pp. 317–18; and F. F. Bruce, *Jesus and Christian Origins Outside the New Testament* (London: Hodden & Storighton, 1974), pp. 32–41. Note also Marc H. Tannenbaum, Marvin R. Wilson, and A. James Rudin, eds., *Evangelicals and Jews in an Age of Pluralism* (Lanham: University Press of America, 1984), pp. 257–67.

4. Joel B. Green, *The Death of Jesus: Tradition and Interpretation in the Passion Narrative* (New York: Coronet Books, 1988).

5. Jerome Chanes, "Antisemitism in the United States, 1992: Why Are the Jews Worried?" *Jerusalem Letter/Viewpoints* 255 (May 15, 1992), pp. 1–6.

6. Arthur Herzberg, "Is Anti-Semitism Dying Out?" *New York Review of Books* 40 (1993), pp. 51–57.

7. Richard John Neuhaus, "What the Fundamentalists Want," in *Piety and Politics: Evangelicals and Fundamentalists Confront the World*, ed. Richard John Neuhaus and M. Cromartie (Washington, D.C.: Ethics and Public Policy Center, 1987), p. 15.

8. Timothy P. Weber, *Living in the Shadow of the Second Coming: American Premillennialism, 1875–1982* (Chicago: University of Chicago Press, 1983), p. 199.

9. Three of John F. Walvoord's books relating to Israel and Jews have been brought together in one paperback edition, *The Nations, Israel, and the Church in Prophecy* (Grand Rapids: Academie Books, 1988 [1967, 1962, 1964]). In 1974 Walvoord published *Armageddon, Oil, and the Middle East Crisis* (Grand Rapids: Zondervan), which was brought up to date in 1990 for the Gulf War (and in the course of seven months sold nearly eight hundred thousand copies), with the suggestive subtitle: "What the Bible Says about the Future of the Middle East and the End of Western Civilization." The new edition of the book included a small picture on the cover of an F-15 landing on a suggestive desert landscape. Besides books on *The Holy Spirit, The Thessalonian Epistles, The Blessed Hope and Tribulation, The Millennial Kingdom,* and *The Rapture Question,* Wal-

voord's magnum opus is *Prophecy Knowledge Handbook: All the Prophecies of Scripture Explained in One Volume* (Wheaton, Ill.: Victor Books, 1990).

10. Weber, *Living in the Shadow*, pp. 17–18.

11. Charles C. Ryrie, *Dispensationalism Today* (Chicago: Moody Institute, 1965), p. 45.

12. Walvoord, *Israel*, p. 58 (see note 9 above).

13. Ibid., pp. 64–66.

14. Needless to say, this attitude has had, and continues to have, important political ramifications for Middle East politics. See, for example, Bernard Lewis, "Muslims, Christians, and Jews: The Dream of Coexistence," *New York Review of Books*, March 26, 1992, pp. 48–52.

15. Walvoord, *Israel*, p. 48 (see note 9 above).

16. Note Weber, *Living in the Shadow*, pp. 204–26. Compare Paul Boyer, *When Time Shall Be No More: Prophetic Belief in Modern American Culture* (Cambridge, Mass.: Belknap Press of Harvard University Press, 1992), p. 187.

17. Walvoord, *Israel*, p. 73 (see note 9 above).

18. Ibid., pp. 66–71.

19. Boyer, *When Time Shall Be No More*, p. 89.

20. Walvoord, *Israel*, p. 112 (see note 9 above).

21. Ibid., pp. 36–48.

22. Ibid., p. 332.

23. Irving Kristol, "The Political Dilemma of American Jews," *Commentary* 18 (1984), pp. 23–29.

24. Kristol, "The Political Dilemma," p. 25.

25. Peter Steinfels, "Evangelical Group Urges Conversion of the Jews," *New York Times*, May 21, 1989.

26. David A. Rausch, "Paranoia About Fundamentalists?" *Judaism: A Quarterly Journal of Jewish Life and Thought* 28 (1979), p. 304.

27. Ryrie, *Dispensationalism Today*, p. 163.

28. Needless to say, there are many intelligent, liberal theological answers to this quandary of apparent totalistic separation between Jews and Christians (or Christians and those of any faith, for that matter). Most of these answers revolve around reminding Christians

of John 4:22: "Ye worship ye know not what: we know what we worship: for salvation is of the Jews."

29. James Davison Hunter in *Evangelicalism: The Coming Generation* (Chicago: University of Chicago Press, 1987) notes the anti-Semitism of evangelicals in the past (pp. 124, 129), but anticipates a general softening of boundaries as evangelicals move up socioeconomically (pp. 203–13).

10. THE HOPI WAY

1. Ernest and Pearl Beaglehole, "A Note on Hopi Dreams," *Hopi of the Second Mesa, Memoirs of the American Anthropological Association*, no. 44 (Menasha, Wis.: American Anthropological Association, 1935), pp. 15–16.

2. The Hopi are one of the Pueblo people who have been living in the southwest for thousands of years. See E. Charles Adams, "Synthesis of Hopi Prehistory and History," National Park Service, July 31, 1978; and his book, *The Origins and Development of the Pueblo Katsina Cult* (Tucson: University of Arizona Press, 1991).

3. Frank Waters, *The Book of the Hopi, with Drawings and Source Material by Oswald White Bear Fredericks* (New York: Penguin Books, 1963), p. 31.

4. John D. Loftin, *Religion and Hopi Life in the Twentieth Century* (Bloomington: Indiana University Press, 1991), p. 116.

5. Don Talayesva, *Sun Chief: The Autobiography of a Hopi Indian*, ed. Leo W. Simmons (New Haven: Yale University Press, 1942), p. 379.

6. Harry C. James, *Pages from Hopi History* (Tucson: University of Arizona Press, 1990), pp. 34–35.

7. Armin Geertz, "Book of the Hopi: The Hopi Book?" *Anthropos* 78 (1983), p. 551.

8. The term occurs ten times in the King James translation of the Bible. One reference fundamentalists often quote is Ezekiel 6:8: "Yet will I leave a remnant, that ye may have *some* that shall escape the sword among the nations, when ye shall be scattered through the countries." Compare Revelation 19:21.

9. Armin Geertz, "Prophets and Fools: The Rhetoric of Hopi In-

dian Eschatology," *European Review of Native American Studies* 1 (1987), p. 36.

10. Frederick J. Dockstader, *The Kachina and the White Man: The Influences of White Culture on the Hopi Kachina Cult* (Albuquerque: University of New Mexico Press, 1985).

11. Loftin, *Religion and Hopi Life*, p. 115.

12. Dan Budnik, personal communication, March 18, 1992.

13. The term *Taiowa* is used by Frank Waters, *Book of the Hopi*, and Robert Boissiere, *Meditations with the Hopi* (Santa Fe: Bear and Company, 1986). Loftin, probably the better authority, speaks of *a'ni himu* in *Religion and Hopi Life*. The difference in terminology may also reflect different myths on the three mesas, and/or the non-written character of the language, and/or deliberate confusions to keep knowledge of the ultimate secret from outsiders.

14. Boissiere, *Meditations with the Hopi*, p. 31; used with permission. Compare Waters, *Book of the Hopi*, pp. 3–6; and Harold Courlander, *The Fourth World of the Hopis* (New York: Crown Publishers, 1971), pp. 17–18.

15. Boissiere, *Meditations with the Hopi*, p. 33.

16. Ibid., pp. 33–34. Compare Waters, *Book of the Hopi*, pp. 12–14; and Courlander, *The Fourth World of the Hopis*, pp. 18–19.

17. Boissiere, *Meditations with the Hopi*, pp. 35–37; and Waters, *Book of the Hopi*, pp. 17–20.

18. James, *Pages from Hopi History*, pp. 2–8; a photograph of the *sipapu* is given on p. 7.

19. Loftin, *Religion and Hopi Life*, p. 58.

20. James, *Pages from Hopi History*, pp. 2–8; Boissiere, *Meditations with the Hopi*, p. 41; and Courlander, *The Fourth World of the Hopis*, pp. 19–26.

21. Boissiere, *Meditations with the Hopi*, p. 42; used with permission.

22. Waters, *Book of the Hopi*, pp. 20–22; and Boissiere, *Meditations with the Hopi*, pp. 41–43.

23. Armin Geertz, "A Reed Pierced the Sky," *Numen* 32 (1984), p. 220.

24. Waters, *Book of the Hopi*, p. 31.

25. Adams, "Synthesis of Hopi Prehistory and History."

26. Harry C. James notes that there were under four thousand Hopi in 1968; see James, *Pages from Hopi History*, p. 16. A decade later E. Charles Adams said there were a total of 7,000 Hopi, with five to six thousand on the reservation; Adams, "Synthesis of Hopi Prehistory and History." I was told by several informants that there were some ten thousand Hopi, but that figure seems high. Most of the villages were tiny, though quite a few settlements are strung out along the three mesas and one can see in the distance many individual homes and trailers in the farther reaches of the reservation.

27. James, *Pages from Hopi History*, p. xii.

28. Note Adams, *The Origins and Development of the Pueblo Katsina Cult*.

29. Talayesva, *Sun Chief: The Autobiography of a Hopi Indian*, p. 363.

30. Tom Tarbet, personal communication, May 20, 1992.

31. Loftin, *Religion and Hopi Life*, p. 7.

32. Ibid., p. xxi.

33. This entrance to the underworld is located at the bottom of the canyon of the Little Colorado River above its juncture with the Colorado River. A visit to the site is of some significance for the Hopi. See James, *Pages from Hopi History*, p. 7, for a good picture.

34. Louis Albert Hieb, *The Hopi Ritual Clown: Life as It Should Not Be* (Ph.D. diss., Princeton University, 1972), p. 146.

35. Ibid., pp. 172–83.

36. Loftin, *Religion and Hopi Life*, pp. 11–12.

37. Ekkehart Malotki and Michael Lomatuway'ma, *Stories of Maasaw: A Hopi God*, vol. 10 of American Tribal Religion series, ed. Karl W. Luchert (Lincoln: University of Nebraska Press, 1987), pp. 3–12.

38. Ibid., pp. 65–71.

39. Mischa Titiev, *The Hopi Indians of Old Oraibi: Change and Continuity* (Ann Arbor: University of Michigan Press, 1972), pp. 309–10. Note also Titiev, *Old Oraibi: A Study of the Hopi Indians of Third Mesa* (Albuquerque: University of New Mexico Press, 1991 [1942]).

40. Geertz, "A Reed Pierced the Sky," p. 224.

41. Mischa Titiev, *The Hopi Indians of Old Oraibi*, pp. 99–100, 153, 158, 214–15, 293, 299, 303, 309–10.

42. With the help of astute archivists, Martin Duberman in the 1970s uncovered some remarkable affidavits taken from the Hopi between 1914 and 1921 in New Mexico and Arizona. The affidavits had lain uncatalogued and unnoticed for half a century in the National Anthropological Archives of the Smithsonian Institute. Duberman first published the material, along with critical commentary from two well-known authorities in Hopi studies, as Martin B. Duberman, Fred Eggan, and Richard Klemmer, "Documents on Hopi Indian Sexuality: Imperialism, Culture, and Resistance," *Radical History Review* 20 (Spring/Summer 1979), pp. 99–130; he later republished the most interesting and controversial documents in his more readily accessible *About Time: Exploring the Gay Past* (New York: A SeaHorse Book, Gay Presses of New York, 1986), pp. 97–106. The debate among Duberman and Eggan and Klemmer over the meaning of the documents was continued from issue 20 of *Radical History Review* to "Hopi Indians Redux," *Radical History Review* 24 (1980), pp. 178–87.

43. Loftin, *Religion and Hopi Life*, p. 115.

44. In Revelation 1:13–16, the Son of Man appears in a garment down to his feet and wrapped in a golden girdle, his head and hair white like wool or snow, his eyes flames of fire; in his right hand he holds seven stars, "and out of his mouth went a sharp two-edged sword: and his countenance *was* as the sun shineth in its strength."

45. Loftin, *Religion and Hopi Life*, pp. 34–35.

11. THE AGE OF AQUARIUS

1. Christopher Lasch, *The Culture of Narcissism: American Life in an Age of Diminishing Expectations* (New York: W. W. Norton, 1979), pp. 245, 247.

2. James R. Lewis, "Approaches to the Study of the New Age Movement," in *Perspectives on the New Age*, ed. James R. Lewis and J. Gordon Melton (Albany: State University of New York Press, 1992), p. 4.

3. The exceptions may be palm readings and faith healings, signs for which are on many streets in black neighborhoods in New York

City. The largest New Age bookstore in New York City is Wiesner's on 23rd St. and Lexington Ave., which has a section on African American spirituality. Note also the New York Open Center on 83 Spring St. in Manhattan, whose most recent (1992) catalogue is a cornucopia of workshops, courses, and lectures on New Age, which in no way excludes minorities but also includes nothing specifically designed for them. This whole question of minority involvement (or lack of involvement) in New Age is a subject worthy of deeper exploration.

4. Witches, however, include a Horned God, often black, in their pantheon. Starhawk argues he is the god of sexuality, and existed long before Christianity (or Judaism, for that matter). "He is gentle, tender, and comforting, but He is also the Hunter. He is the Dying God—but his sexuality is a deep, holy, connecting power. He is the power of feeling, and the image of what men could be if they were liberated from the constraints of patriarchal culture." It was only the medieval Christian church, Starhawk argues, that turned this god into the devil. See Starhawk, *The Spiral Dance: A Rebirth of the Ancient Religion of the Great Goddess* (San Francisco: Harper and Row, 1979), pp. 107–21 (quote is on p. 108).

5. Note Deborah Sontag's description of the New Age Convention in New York City in October 1992 that drew 21,000 people to midtown Manhattan: "Resonance and Rigidity in the New Age," *New York Times*, October 5, 1992.

6. See Papus, *Reincarnation: Physical, Astral and Spiritual Evolution*, trans. Marguerite Vallior (n.p.: Roger A. Kessinger, 1991), p. 13. Compare its New Age adaptation in Gari Gold, *The New Age: A to Z* (Albuquerque: ZIVAH, 1991), pp. 13–15.

7. See, for example, Betty Eadie, *Embraced by the Light* (Placerville, Calif.: Gold Leaf Press, 1992).

8. Erik Erikson, *Gandhi's Truth: On the Origins of Militant Nonviolence* (New York: W. W. Norton, 1969), p. 39.

9. Michael Grosso, *The Final Choice: Playing the Survival Game* (Walpole, N.H.: Stillpoint Publishing, 1985), p. 325.

10. Marianne Williamson, *A Return to Love: Reflections on the Principles of A Course in Miracles* (New York: HarperCollins, 1992). Williamson has also produced more than fifty tapes of her

lectures on subjects ranging from "AIDS/Radical Healing" to "Forgiving When It's Difficult/Illusions of Loss." The tapes are distributed by Bodhi Tree.

11. Clarissa Pinkola Estes, *Women Who Run with the Wolves* (New York: Ballantine Books, 1992).

12. Brochure for Sandy Gilbert's "Wholeness Meditation," 137 South Main St., Pennington, N.J., n.d.

13. Lewis, "Approaches," pp. xi, 5.

14. William G. McLoughlin, *Revival, Awakenings, and Reform: An Essay on Religion and Social Change in America, 1607–1977* (Chicago: University of Chicago Press, 1978), pp. 179–216.

15. J. Gordon Melton, *New Age Encyclopedia*, quoted in Lewis and Melton, *Perspectives*, p. 7.

16. Ruth Montgomery, *Strangers Among Us* (New York: Fawcett Crest, 1979), pp. 31–35.

17. Ibid., pp. 30, 38, 52, 64, 191–205, 220–21; compare Ruth Montgomery, *The World Before* (New York: Fawcett Crest, 1976).

18. Budd Hopkins, *Intruders* (New York: Random House, 1987), p. 12.

19. David Solomon, "Prophecy Update: Are We Living in the End of the Times?" *Fellowship Life & Lifestyles* 18 (1992), p. 3. Ted Daniels, editor of *Millennium News* (a publication of The Millennium Watch Institute, P.O. Box 34021, Philadelphia, PA 19101-4021) and an indefatigable researcher, graciously shared with me his background notes on New Age apocalypticism from the depths of his hard drive. For material from this research I will refer to "Daniels, Notes."

20. Nada-Yolanda, Note to Nova/Angelika, "No Hiding Place," *Main* 117, no. 7 (1988), pp. 10–15. Daniels, Notes.

21. Ted Daniels, personal communication, April 3, 1992.

22. Ashtar Command, "11:11 Doorway," *Connecting Link*, n.d.; "Spiritual Counterfeits Project," *SCP Newsletter* 10 (1991); and Swami Nostradamus Virato, "11:11 Doorway to the Cosmos: Interview," *New Frontier* 12 (1991). Daniels, Notes.

23. "Spiritual Counterfeits Project," *SCP Newsletter* 10 (1991). Daniels, Notes.

24. Catherine Albanese, *Nature Religion in America: From the*

Algonkian Indians to the New Age (Chicago: University of Chicago Press, 1990), pp. 156ff.

25. Ibid., pp. 160–61.

26. Sun Bear, *Black Dawn, Bright Day* (New York: Simon and Schuster, 1992), esp. pp. 27–49.

27. Ibid., p. 52.

28. Ibid., p. 92.

29. Ibid., p. 32.

30. Compare Otto's calculation, in chapter 2 of this book, that half the world's population will be destroyed in the events described in Revelation.

31. Sun Bear, *Black Dawn, Bright Day*, p. 37.

32. Ibid., p. 57.

33. Ibid.

34. Ibid., p. 148.

35. Ibid., pp. 149–57, 159ff, 197.

36. Ibid., p. 60.

37. Grosso, *The Final Choice*, p. 218. Compare Grosso's discussion of shamans, who he says are individuals who traditionally link the tribe with the "Mind at Large" (Aldous Huxley's phrase, which Grosso adopts) and become adept at "mapping and mobilizing the helping powers. . . . Shamans are individuals who, for different reasons, are susceptible to the creative forces of the deep psyche" (p. 210).

38. For a good discussion of the role of the astral realm in reincarnation, see Papus, *Reincarnation*, pp. 11–19, 60–69.

39. Grosso, *The Final Choice*, p. 301.

40. Ibid.

41. Ibid., p. 303.

42. Ibid., p. 310.

43. Ibid., p. 311.

44. Ibid., p. 312.

45. Ibid., p. 314.

46. John Mack, personal communication, October 9, 1992.

47. Budd Hopkins, *Intruders* (New York: Random House, 1987), pp. 59–60.

48. Compare Sigmund Freud's paper "The Aetiology of Hysteria" with his reasons for changing his mind in his letter to his friend Wilhelm Fliess; Sigmund Freud, "The Aetiology of Hysteria" (1896), in *The Standard Edition of the Psychological Works of Sigmund Freud*, ed. James Strachey et al., 23 vols. (London: Hogarth Press, 1955–1962), vol. 3, pp. 187–221; and Sigmund Freud, letter of September 21, 1897, in *The Complete Letters of Sigmund Freud to Wilhelm Fliess, 1887–1904*, trans. and ed. Jeffrey Moussaieff Masson (Cambridge, Mass.: Harvard University Press, 1985), pp. 264–66. The furthest most psychoanalysts will go in criticizing Freud on this point is from Heinz Kohut: "Freud, for example, often used the example of the hysterical patients whose seduction fantasies he originally believed. We have come now to realize that the hysterical patients were right, in a way. They didn't describe real seductions, it is true; Freud had to recognize he had been misled in his credulity. But he went much too far in saying the parents had nothing to do with their children's hysteria, that only fantasy is relevant." See Heinz Kohut, *Self Psychology and the Humanities: Reflections on a New Psychoanalytic Approach*, ed. Charles B. Strozier (New York: Norton, 1985), p. 230. In much of the recent literature on Freud from outside the psychoanalytic community, the change in Freud's thinking about child abuse has been sharply criticized (and most now feel Freud had it right the first time). Note Jeffrey M. Masson, *The Assault on Truth: Freud's Suppression of the Seduction Theory* (New York: Farrar, Straus and Giroux, 1983); and Frank J. Sulloway, *Freud, Biologist of the Mind* (New York: Basic Books, 1979). A recent view that is also critical of Freud but takes account of the political and cultural context of Freud's struggles is Judith Lewis Herman, *Trauma and Recovery* (New York: Basic Books, 1992).

49. The relative psychological normality of abductees, except in the area of their remembered trauma, is a point stressed by John Mack in his work, and Mack, as a psychiatrist, is well positioned to make such an assessment. I have had the opportunity to hear two of Mack's presentations on his work in the fall of 1991 and again in the fall of 1992, and have talked with him more informally.

50. John Mack at an informal presentation on his research at the Wellfleet Psychohistory Meetings in the home of Robert Jay Lifton, October 30, 1992.

51. As reported in *The Manila Bulletin*, May 18, 1992. Daniels, Notes.

52. Virginia Essene, "New Cells, New Bodies, New Life," *New Millennium* 3 (1992), pp. 1–3. Daniels, Notes.

53. Leonard Orr and Sondra Ray comment about deep breathing during just such weekends: "Hyperventilation is the Breath of Life attempting dramatically to free itself from a lifetime of unconscious neglect." Leonard Orr and Sondra Ray, *Rebirthing in the New Age* (Berkeley: Celestial Arts, 1977), p. 174.

54. Swami Nostradamus Virato, "11:11 Doorway to the Cosmos: Interview," *New Frontier* 12 (1991). Daniels, Notes.

55. Ibid., pp. 5–6.

56. J. Gordon Melton, "New Thought and New Age," in Lewis and Melton, *Perspectives*, p. 19.

57. Paul Shockley, "Cosmic Awareness Communications," *Revelations of Awareness: The New Age Cosmic Newsletter* 4 (1992). Daniels, Notes.

58. William H. Kautz and Melanie Branon, *Channeling: The Intuitive Connection* (San Francisco: Harper and Row, 1987), pp. 153–54.

59. Nada-Yolanda, *Mark-Age News from the Desk of Nada-Yolanda* 6 (1992). Daniels, Notes.

60. *A Course in Miracles*, 2d ed. (Glen Ellen, Calif.: Foundation for Inner Peace, 1992), pp. vii–viii.

61. Ibid., p. 664.

62. Douglas Grant, "Who Is a Prophet? I Am. Through I Am Self, We Are Modern-Day Prophets," *Main* 117, no. 7 (1988), pp. 2–9. Daniels, Notes.

63. Lucis Trust, "Transformation and the New Environmental Awareness," *Triangles Bulletin* 100, no. 6 (1992). Daniels, Notes.

64. *Prout: A New Voice for All Living Beings*, undated pamphlet from a group based in Los Altos, California. Daniels, Notes.

65. Human Ecology Party, "A Global Political Party Dedicated to 'Health and Freedom for All,'" pamphlet, 1992. Daniels, Notes.

66. Noree Liang Pope, "Letters from Spirit," *The Messenger* 12 (1992), pp. 17–21. Daniels, Notes.

67. Starhawk, *Spiral Dance*, p. 27.

68. Ibid., p. 207.

69. Ibid., pp. 206–8. American Buddhist women have also made this point. Note Sandy Boucher, *Turning the Wheel: American Women Creating the New Buddhism* (San Francisco: Harper and Row, 1988).

70. Xaviere Gauthier, "Why Witches," in *New French Feminisms*, ed. Elaine Marks and Isabelle de Courtivron (New York: Schocken Books, 1981), p. 199.

71. Starhawk, *Spiral Dance*, p. 209.

72. Ibid., p. 10.

73. Ibid., pp. 91–92.

74. Ibid., p. 10.

75. Ibid., pp. 10–11.

76. It is this healing dimension of New Age and its intimate links to feminism and other ideologies of empowerment that make it likely that the New Age will endure and perhaps cohere as a religion. Note, however, the opposite view in Melton, "New Thought and New Age," p. 16.

77. See "Bill's Story," in *Alcoholics Anonymous* (New York: AA World Services, 1976 [1939]), pp. 1–16. This book is affectionately referred to in AA circles as "the Big Book."

78. Marc Galanter, *Cults: Faith, Healing, and Coercion* (New York: Oxford University Press, 1989), p. 177.

79. Ibid., p. 178.

80. Ibid.

81. Galanter points out that many AA members have been drawn to feminist concerns in recent years, but the constraint against involvement of AA in anything but alcoholism has prevented the growth of formal alliances. Ibid., p. 183.

82. The AA message is divided into twelve steps of individual recovery and twelve traditions that describe the history and organization and purposes of AA itself. The two are intimately connected, and much of "working the program" in meetings consists of learning the steps and traditions and how they relate.

83. Galanter, *Cults*, pp. 176–90.

84. *AA Grapevine*, April 1992, p. 32.

85. *Alcoholics Anonymous*, p. 14.

86. "Bill's Story," *Alcoholics Anonymous*, p. 8.

87. Martha Morrison, *White Rabbit* (New York: Berkley Books, 1989), pp. 217, 248.

88. Catherine L. Albanese, "Religion and the American Experience: A Century After," *Church History* 57 (1988), pp. 337–51.

CONCLUSION

1. Robert Jay Lifton, *The Broken Connection: On Death and the Continuity of Life* (New York: Basic Books, 1979), p. 351.

2. A. J. Weigert makes this point, though it was very much in the air throughout the 1980s; A. J. Weigert, "Christian Eschatological Identities and the Nuclear Context," *Journal for the Scientific Study of Religion* 27 (1988), pp. 175–91. Note Lifton, *The Broken Connection*, p. 340; Michael Barkun, "Nuclear War and Millenarian Symbols: Premillennialists Confront the Bomb," paper delivered at the annual meeting of the Society for the Scientific Study of Religion, 1985; Ronnie Dugger, "Does Reagan Expect a Nuclear Armageddon?" *Washington Post*, April 8, 1984; A. G. Mojtabai, *Blessed Assurance: At Home with the Bomb in Amarillo, Texas* (Boston: Houghton Mifflin, 1986); and even Jerry Falwell, *Nuclear War and the Second Coming of Jesus Christ* (Lynchburg, Va.: Old Time Gospel Hour, Inc., 1983).

3. Gabriel Marcel, *The Mystery of Being*, 2 vols. (Chicago: Regnery, 1960), vol. 2, chap. 4.

4. Diana Trilling, *Mrs. Harris: The Death of the Scarsdale Diet Doctor* (New York: Penguin Books, 1981), p. 9.

5. Erik Erikson, *Gandhi's Truth: On the Origins of Militant Nonviolence* (New York: W. W. Norton, 1969), p. 431.

6. See Robert Jay Lifton, *The Nazi Doctors: Medical Killing and the Psychology of Genocide* (New York: Basic Books, 1986), which is as much a study of surviving physicians who carried out genocide as it is an historical interpretation of the Holocaust. Note also the book Lifton did with Eric Markussen, *The Genocidal Mentality:*

Nazi Holocaust and Nuclear Threat (New York: Basic Books, 1990).

7. James Davison Hunter, *American Evangelicalism: Conservative Religion and the Quandary of Modernity* (New Brunswick, N.J.: Rutgers University Press, 1983); and ibid., *Evangelicalism: The Coming Generation* (Chicago: University of Chicago Press, 1987).

8. Robert Jay Lifton, personal communication, May 12, 1992.

9. Matthew C. Moen, *The Christian Right and Congress* (Tuscaloosa: University of Alabama Press, 1989), p. 169.

10. The Christian Coalition, headed by Ralph Reed, is the political organization of Pat Robertson. Since 1988 it has been targeting local elections instead of focusing all its efforts on the presidency. In the November 1992 elections, according to People for the American Way (which monitored the elections), the Coalition seems to have won 40 percent of some 500 selected and representative elections. The fiercest battleground was in California, but the Coalition also scored successes in Iowa, Kansas, Florida, Texas, and Oregon. People for the American Way estimates there are thousands of "stealth" candidates throughout the country whose affiliations cannot be determined. See "Christian Conservatives Counting Hundreds of Gains in Local Votes," *New York Times*, November 21, 1992.

11. Al Ross of Planned Parenthood and a close student of the Christian Coalition was much less sanguine, in a presentation at the conference on the New Religious Political Right, University of Uppsala, Sweden, December 7, 1992. He argued that Robertson is out to create a "theocratic fascist state" and has allied himself with old and new Nazis, not to mention leaders of the KKK. Many Coalition leaders as well want the death penalty for abortion. Needless to say, I feel Ross misses the forest for the trees, though I respect his point that many local elections are up for grabs (at least for a while) since it is often the case that only 10 percent of the registered voters actually bother with most local races. Note also the Institute for First Amendment Rights, Great Barrington, Mass.

ACKNOWLEDGMENTS

The journey of this book has been an intensely personal one and changed me in ways that I never would have predicted. Many friends came along with me.

I have no adequate way to thank Robert Jay Lifton for his role in this book. The idea of studying fundamentalists at all first emerged in conversation with him. He guided me in my interview style; read and commented on early drafts of papers and chapters; provided endless support when it seemed the writing would never end; and then read the final manuscript through and made enormously helpful suggestions. I have also learned much from our dialogue in a course on the self we have been co-teaching for six years at the CUNY Graduate Center.

I draw heavily in these pages on the excellent work of researchers who assisted me: Ayla Kohn, Laura Simich, and Willie Tolliver

ACKNOWLEDGMENTS worked in three of the churches I describe and conducted some of the interviews I use in this book (I wrote with Ayla Kohn, "The Paradoxical Image of Jews in the Minds of Christian Fundamentalists," *Journal of Social Distress and the Homeless* 1 [1991]; with Laura Simich, "Christian Fundamentalism and Nuclear Threat," *Journal of the International Society for Political Psychology* 12 [1991]). Michael Perlman provided much insight over the years analyzing interviews, and read the final manuscript with care. Peggy Boyer researched fundamentalism at the beginning of my project. The late Archie Singham, whom I loved dearly, nourished me and everyone in his world. Pam Miller and Nick Humphrey were part of the research group that analyzed these interviews (and many others in a larger study). Michael Flynn read the manuscript in many drafts as it emerged and helped me understand what I was writing. And Dana Fenton helped me put together the notes to the text. This team of researchers was all part of a project funded by the MacArthur Foundation, whose support I gratefully acknowledge.

Others as well helped shape this book by careful reading and critical comments. My brother, Robert M. Strozier, first spotted the structural flaw (and other problems) that led to a re-write of the manuscript. Diane and Geoffrey Ward read several versions of my work over the years, and Diane's contacts with Dan Budnik proved crucial for my Hopi chapter. Paul Boyer and Michael Barkun both visited the Center on Violence and Human Survival at different times, and I found our conversations helpful and stimulating. As Boyer generously noted in his book, *When Time Shall Be No More*, our work overlaps in quite fascinating ways. I have also learned much over the years about the apocalyptic and contemporary politics and culture from conversations with Richard Falk. Grace Mojtabai was helpful in a conversation at the very beginning of my work (and of course I mined her book, *Blessed Assurance*, closely). I also had good conversations about my work and fundamentalism in general with Karen McCarthy Brown, Randall Balmer (and his *Mine Eyes Have Seen the Glory*), and Philip Greven (and his *Spare the Child*). Catherine Keller of Drew University heard much of this book in our extended conversations on the apocalyptic, and she read it all carefully in many drafts. Her learned disquisitions seeped into my mind in ways that my occasional footnotes to her work could only begin to acknowledge. As someone who really knows the Bible and theology, she also saved me much embarrassment. Esther Menaker read the final manuscript, even on her vacation, and made some helpful comments. For a couple of years I was a consultant to The Fundamentalism Project at the University of Chicago run by Martin Marty, whose comments and work I found helpful. I had interesting conversations with the members of the Christian group headed by Nancy Ammerman, especially with Susan Harding and David Stoll. In the larger meetings, I learned much from Sam Heilman, my colleague in City University, and profited much from the graduate course we co-taught on "Jewish and Christian Fundamentalism."

Roger Williamson provided me an unusually helpful forum to talk about my ideas at the "Life and Peace Institute" in Uppsala, Sweden, for three years running, albeit always in the deepest, darkest of Swedish winters. Perhaps one should talk about the end of the world in a place where the sun never shines except to illuminate the horizon briefly between late morning coffee break and early afternoon tea. Roger also provided many useful bibliographic suggestions, saved me from serious errors, and improved the overall manuscript with his careful reading. He also introduced me to many Swedish friends whose research interest coincided with my own, especially Owe Gustafsson and Sigbert Axelson of Uppsala University.

Peter Parrish first steered me toward the apocalyptic aspects of the Civil War many years ago, and Donald Capps gave me good advice about the sermons after Lincoln's death. Harold Holzer sponsored a presentation on Lincoln and the American apocalyptic at the Lincoln Group of New York, and read and commented on part of what is chapter 8. I also presented an earlier version of that paper at a Lincoln conference organized by William Pedersen at the State University of Louisiana in Shreveport in the fall of 1992. Other Lincoln scholars helped as well: Cullom Davis, Mark Johnson, and Tom Schwartz.

Many (perhaps too many) groups bore up listening to me on fundamentalism over the years. I am particularly grateful to colleagues at my own Center on Violence and Human Survival at John Jay Col-

ACKNOWLEDGMENTS lege for tolerating more presentations of my work than I can remember. Harvey Cox, Daniel Ellsberg, and Rabbi Marshall Meyer (who also later read and commented on chapter 9) all made helpful comments on a preliminary presentation of my research. My friends gathered at the Open Center in New York City in the early summer of 1993 to listen to and encourage me at a time when my spirits were flagging. I thank the students in my courses over the years who gave more than they knew as I rambled on.

I was lucky to get the ideal editor for this book in Lauren Bryant. She knew exactly how to mix the stick and the carrot in the early stages, and then read what I wrote with intelligence and perception, including drafts of chapters and two versions of the final manuscript. She filled nearly every page of text with marginal comments and crossed out all my best lines in ways that vastly improved the final version.

My agent, Charlotte Sheedy, turned my offbeat idea of studying fundamentalists into a publishing enterprise that ended up as pages between the covers of an actual book. Her unflagging confidence in me is warmly appreciated.

My first-born, Michael, taught me more about fundamentalism than he may realize, and engaged me in many valuable conversations about the themes in this book. My middle son, Matthew, read early drafts of the manuscript, participated in several seminars in which I presented material, and joined me in an invaluable dialogue about endism over the years. It encouraged me that he got it all from the start. Christopher, my youngest boy with whom friends say I am fused at the hip and to whom this book is dedicated, lived through the writing of it as no one else in our cozy apartment. In time he, too, will read it and learn then what I was doing all those early mornings at the computer.

Last but not least I thank my wife, Cathy, who has lived with fundamentalists in our marriage almost as long as we have been together. She tolerated my absences at churches on Sundays and far too many Bible study meetings during the week, not to mention my endless conversation on the topic for a good seven years. She bore up well, however, and provided encouragement at dark moments. In this kind of work on the end of the world, off-center support was often the most helpful. Once, at a crucial juncture in my writing, I described the dilemma and said that I was in a high state of anxiety. "Eat," she said, and laughed. I gained a little weight and solved the problem.

Index

THE STARLESS SEA

ALSO BY ERIN MORGENSTERN

The Night Circus

ERIN MORGENSTERN

THE

STARLESS

SEA

DOUBLEDAY
CANADA

Doubleday Canada and colophon are registered trademarks of
Penguin Random House Canada Limited

Library and Archives Canada Cataloguing in Publication

Title: The starless sea / Erin Morgenstern.
Names: Morgenstern, Erin, author.
Identifiers: Canadiana (print) 20190077824 | Canadiana (ebook)
20190077832 | ISBN 9780385686228
(hardcover) | ISBN 9780385686235 (EPUB)
Classification: LCC PS3613.O745 S73 2019 | DDC 813/.6—dc23

This book is a work of fiction. Names, characters, places and
incidents are products of the author's imagination or are used
fictitiously. Any resemblance to actual events or locales or
persons, living or dead, is entirely coincidental.

Book design: Pei Loi Koay
Case images: (bee) Vikulichka, KatarinaF, (key) sabri deniz kizil,
(sword) akarin chatariyawich; all Shutterstock
Jacket and endpaper art: Dan Funderburgh @ Début Art
Jacket design: John Fontana
Printed and bound in the USA

Published in Canada by Doubleday Canada,
a division of Penguin Random House Canada Limited

www.penguinrandomhouse.ca

10 9 8 7 6 5 4 3 2 1

THE
STARLESS
SEA

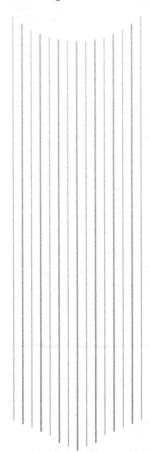

BOOK I

SWEET

SORROWS

SWEET SORROWS

Once, very long ago...

There is a pirate in the basement.

(The pirate is a metaphor but also still a person.)

(The basement could rightly be considered a dungeon.)

The pirate was placed here for numerous acts of a piratey nature considered criminal enough for punishment by those non-pirates who decide such things.

Someone said to throw away the key, but the key rests on a tarnished ring on a hook that hangs on the wall nearby.

(Close enough to see from behind the bars. Freedom kept in sight but out of reach, left as a reminder to the prisoner. No one remembers that now on the key side of the bars. The careful psychological design forgotten, distilled into habit and convenience.)

(The pirate realizes this but withholds comment.)

The guard sits in a chair by the door and reads crime serials on faded paper, wishing he were an idealized, fictional version of himself. Wondering if the difference between pirates and thieves is a matter of boats and hats.

After a time he is replaced by another guard. The pirate cannot discern the precise schedule, as the basement-dungeon has no clocks to mark the time and the sound of the waves on the shore beyond the stone walls muffles the morning chimes, the evening merriment.

This guard is shorter and does not read. He wishes to be no one but himself, he lacks the imagination to conjure alter egos, even the imagination to empathize with the man behind the bars, the only other soul in the room beyond the mice. He pays elaborate amounts of attention to his shoes when he is not asleep. (He is usually asleep.)

Approximately three hours after the short guard replaces the reading guard, a girl comes.

The girl brings a plate of bread and a bowl of water and sets them outside the pirate's cell with hands shaking so badly that half the water spills. Then she turns and scampers up the stairs.

The second night (the pirate guesses it is night) the pirate stands as close to the bars as he can and stares and the girl drops the bread nearly out of reach and spills the bowl of water almost entirely.

The third night the pirate stays in the shadows of the back corner and manages to keep most of his water.

The fourth night a different girl comes.

This girl does not wake the guard. Her feet fall more softly on the stones and any sound they make is stolen away by the waves or by the mice.

This girl stares into the shadows at the barely visible pirate, gives a little disappointed sigh, and places the bread and bowl by the bars. Then she waits.

The pirate remains in the shadows.

After several minutes of silence punctuated by the guard's snoring, the girl turns away and leaves.

When the pirate retrieves his meal he finds the water has been mixed with wine.

The next night, the fifth night if it is night at all, the pirate waits by the bars for the girl to descend on her silent feet.

Her steps halt only briefly when she sees him.

The pirate stares and the girl stares back.

He holds out a hand for his bowl and his bread but the girl places them on the ground instead, her eyes never leaving his, not allowing so much as the hem of her gown to drift into his reach. Bold yet coy. She gives him a hint of a bow as she returns to her feet, a gentle nod of her head, a movement that reminds him of the beginning of the dance.

(Even a pirate can recognize the beginning of a dance.)

The next night the pirate stays back from the bars, a polite distance that could be closed in a single step, and the girl comes a breath closer.

Another night and the dance continues. A step closer. A step back. A movement to the side. The next night he holds out his hand again to accept what she offers and this time she responds and his fingers brush against the back of her hand.

The girl begins to linger, staying longer each night, though if the guard stirs to the point of waking she departs without a backward glance.

She brings two bowls of wine and they drink together in companionable silence. The guard has stopped snoring, his sleep deep and restful. The pirate suspects the girl has something to do with that. Bold and coy and clever.

Some nights she brings more than bread. Oranges and plums secreted in the pockets of her gown. Pieces of candied ginger wrapped in paper laced with stories.

Some nights she stays until moments before the changing of the guards.

(The daytime guard has begun leaving his crime serials within reach of the cell's walls, ostensibly by accident.)

The shorter guard paces tonight. He clears his throat as though he might say something but says nothing. He settles himself in his chair and falls into an anxious sleep.

The pirate waits for the girl.

She arrives empty-handed.

Tonight is the last night. The night before the gallows. (The gallows are also a metaphor, albeit an obvious one.) The pirate knows that there will not be another night, will not be another changing of the guard after the next one. The girl knows the exact number of hours.

They do not speak of it.

They have never spoken.

The pirate twists a lock of the girl's hair between his fingers.

The girl leans into the bars, her cheek resting on cold iron, as close as she can be while she remains a world away.

Close enough to kiss.

"Tell me a story," she says.

The pirate obliges her.

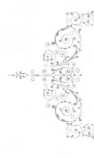

SWEET SORROWS

There are three paths. This is one of them.

Far beneath the surface of the earth, hidden from the sun and the moon, upon the shores of the Starless Sea, there is a labyrinthine collection of tunnels and rooms filled with stories. Stories written in books and sealed in jars and painted on walls. Odes inscribed onto skin and pressed into rose petals. Tales laid in tiles upon the floors, bits of plot worn away by passing feet. Legends carved in crystal and hung from chandeliers. Stories catalogued and cared for and revered. Old stories preserved while new stories spring up around them.

The place is sprawling yet intimate. It is difficult to measure its breadth. Halls fold into rooms or galleries and stairs twist downward or upward to alcoves or arcades. Everywhere there are doors leading to new spaces and new stories and new secrets to be discovered and everywhere there are books.

It is a sanctuary for storytellers and storykeepers and storylovers. They eat and sleep and dream surrounded by chronicles and histories and myths. Some stay for hours or days before returning to the world above but others remain for weeks or years, living in shared or private chambers and spending their hours reading or studying or writing, discussing and creating with their fellow residents or working in solitude.

Of those who remain, a few choose to devote themselves to this space, to this temple of stories.

There are three paths. This is one of them.

This is the path of the acolytes.

Those who wish to choose this path must spend a full cycle of the moon in isolated contemplation before they commit. The contemplation is thought to be silent, but of those who allow themselves to be locked away in the stone-walled room, some will realize that no one can hear them. They can talk or yell or scream and it violates no rules. The contemplation is only thought to be silent by those who have never been inside the room.

Once the contemplation has ended they have the opportunity to leave their path. To choose another path or no path at all.

Those who spend their time in silence often choose to leave both the path and the space. They return to the surface. They squint at the sun. Sometimes they remember a world below that they once intended to devote themselves to but the memory is hazy, like a place from a dream.

More often it is those who scream and cry and wail, those who talk to themselves for hours, who are ready when the time comes to proceed with their initiation.

Tonight, as the moon is new and the door is unlocked, it reveals a young woman who has spent most of her time singing. She is shy and not in the habit of singing, but on her first night of contemplation she realized almost by accident that no one could hear her. She laughed, partly at herself and partly at the oddity of having voluntarily jailed herself in the most luxurious of cells with its feather bed and silken sheets. The laugh echoed around the stone room like ripples of water.

She clasped her hand over her mouth and waited for someone to come but no one did. She tried to recall if anyone had told her explicitly not to speak.

She said "Hello?" and only the echoes returned her greeting.

It took a few days before she was brave enough to sing. She had never liked her singing voice but in her captivity free of embarrassment and expectation she sang, softly at first but then brightly and boldly. The voice that the echo returned to her ears was surprisingly pleasant.

She sang all the songs she knew. She made up her own. In moments when she could not think of words to sing she created nonsense languages for lyrics with sounds she found pleasing.

It surprised her how quickly the time passed.

Now the door opens.

The acolyte who enters holds a ring of brass keys. He offers his other palm to her. On it sits a small disk of metal with a raised carving of a bee.

Accepting the bee is the next step in becoming an acolyte. This is her final chance to refuse.

She takes the bee from the acolyte's palm. He bows and gestures for her to follow him.

The young woman who is to be an acolyte turns the warm metal disk over in her fingers as they walk through narrow candlelit tunnels lined with bookshelves and open caverns filled with mismatched chairs and tables, stacked high with books and dotted with statues. She pets a statue of a fox as they pass by, a popular habit that has worn its carved fur smooth between its ears.

An older man leafing through a volume glances up as they pass and recognizing the procession he places two fingers to his lips and inclines his head at her.

At her, not at the acolyte she follows. A gesture of respect for a position she does not yet officially hold. She bows her head to hide her smile. They continue down gilded stairways and through curving tunnels she has never traversed before. She slows to look at the paintings hung between the shelves of books, images of trees and girls and ghosts.

The acolyte stops at a door marked with a golden bee. He chooses a key from his ring and unlocks it.

Here begins the initiation.

It is a secret ceremony. The details are known only to those who undergo it and those who perform it. It has been performed in the same fashion always, as long as anyone can remember.

As the door with the golden bee is opened and the threshold crossed the acolyte gives up her name. Whatever name this young woman was called before she will never be addressed by it again, it stays in her past. Someday she may have a new name, but for the moment she is nameless.

The room is small and round and high-ceilinged, a miniature version of her contemplation cell. It holds a plain wooden chair on one side and a waist-high pillar of stone topped with a bowl of fire. The fire provides the only light.

The elder acolyte gestures for the young woman to sit in the wooden chair. She does. She faces the fire, watching the flames dance until a piece of black silk is tied over her eyes.

The ceremony continues unseen.

The metal bee is taken from her hand. There is a pause followed by the sound of metal instruments clinking and then the sensation of a finger on her chest, pressing into a spot on her breastbone. The pressure releases and then it is replaced by a sharp, searing pain.

(She will realize afterward that the metal bee has been heated in the fire, its winged impression burned into her chest.)

The surprise of it unnerves her. She has prepared herself for what she knows of the rest of the ceremony, but this is unexpected. She realizes she has never seen the bare chest of another acolyte.

When moments before she was ready, now she is shaken and unsure.

But she does not say *Stop.* She does not say *No.*

She has made her decision, though she could not have known everything that decision would entail.

In the darkness, fingers part her lips and a drop of honey is placed on her tongue.

This is to ensure that the last taste is sweet.

In truth the last taste that remains in an acolyte's mouth is more than honey: the sweetness swept up in blood and metal and burning flesh.

Were an acolyte able to describe it, afterward, they might clarify that the last taste they experience is one of honey and smoke.

It is not entirely sweet.

They recall it each time they extinguish the flame atop a beeswax candle.

A reminder of their devotion.

But they cannot speak of it.

They surrender their tongues willingly. They offer up their ability to speak to better serve the voices of others.

They take an unspoken vow to no longer tell their own stories in reverence to the ones that came before and to the ones that shall follow.

In this honey-tinged pain the young woman in the chair thinks she might scream but she does not. In the darkness the fire seems to consume the entire room and she can see shapes in the flames even though her eyes are covered.

The bee on her chest flutters.

Once her tongue has been taken and burned and turned to ash, once the ceremony is complete and her servitude as an acolyte officially begins, once her voice has been muted, then her ears awaken.

Then the stories begin to come.

SWEET SORROWS
To deceive the eye.

The boy is the son of the fortune-teller. He has reached an age that brings an uncertainty as to whether this is something to be proud of, or even a detail to be divulged, but it remains true.

He walks home from school toward an apartment situated above a shop strewn with crystal balls and tarot cards, incense and statues of animal-headed deities and dried sage. (The scent of sage permeates everything, from his bedsheets to his shoelaces.)

Today, as he does every school day, the boy takes a shortcut through an alleyway that loops behind the store, a narrow passage between tall brick walls that are often covered with graffiti and then whitewashed and then graffitied again.

Today, instead of the creatively spelled tags and bubble-lettered profanities, there is a single piece of artwork on the otherwise white bricks.

It is a door.

The boy stops. He adjusts his spectacles to focus his eyes better, to be certain he is seeing what his sometimes unreliable vision suggests he is seeing.

The haziness around the edges sharpens, and it is still a door. Larger and fancier and more impressive than he'd thought at first fuzzy glance.

He is uncertain what to make of it.

Its incongruousness demands his attention.

The door is situated far back in the alley, in a shadowed section hidden from the sun, but the colors are still rich, some of the pigments metallic. More delicate than most of the graffiti the boy has seen. Painted in a style he knows has a fancy French name, something about fooling the eye, though he cannot recall the term here and now.

The door is carved—no, painted—with sharp-cut geometric patterns that wind around its edges creating depth where there is only flatness. In the center, at the level where a peephole might be and stylized with lines that match the rest of the painted carving, is a bee. Beneath the bee is a key. Beneath the key is a sword.

A golden, seemingly three-dimensional doorknob shimmers despite the lack of light. A keyhole is painted beneath, so dark it looks to be a void awaiting a key rather than a few strokes of black paint.

The door is strange and pretty and something that the boy does not have words for and does not know if there are words for, even fancy French expressions.

Somewhere in the street an unseen dog barks but it sounds distant and abstract. The sun moves behind a cloud and the alley feels longer and deeper and darker, the door itself brighter.

Tentatively, the boy reaches out to touch the door.

The part of him that still believes in magic expects it to be warm despite the chill in the air. Expects the image to have fundamentally changed the brick. Makes his heart beat faster even as his hand slows down because the part of him that thinks the other part is being childish prepares for disappointment.

His fingertips meet the door below the sword and they come to rest on smooth paint covering cool brick, a slight unevenness to the surface betraying the texture below.

It is just a wall. Just a wall with a pretty picture on it.

But still.

Still there is the sensation tugging at him that this is more than what it appears to be.

He presses his palm against the painted brick. The false wood of the door is a brown barely a shade or two off from his own skin tone, as though it has been mixed to match him.

Behind the door is somewhere else. Not the room behind the wall. Something more. He knows this. He feels it in his toes.

This is what his mother would call a moment with meaning. A moment that changes the moments that follow.

The son of the fortune-teller knows only that the door feels important in a way he cannot quite explain, even to himself.

A boy at the beginning of a story has no way of knowing that the story has begun.

He traces the painted lines of the key with his fingertips, marveling at how much the key, like the sword and the bee and the doorknob, looks as though it should be three-dimensional.

The boy wonders who painted it and what it means, if it means anything. If not the door at least the symbols. If it is a sign and not a door, or if it is both at once.

In this significant moment, if the boy turns the painted knob and opens the impossible door, everything will change.

But he does not.

Instead, he puts his hands in his pockets.

Part of him decides he is being childish and that he is too old to expect real life to be like books. Another part of him decides that if he does not try he cannot be disappointed and he can go on believing that the door could open even if it is just pretend.

He stands with his hands in his pockets and considers the door for a moment more before walking away.

The following day his curiosity gets the better of him and he returns to find that the door has been painted over. The brick wall whitewashed to the point where he cannot even discern where, precisely, the door had been.

And so the son of the fortune-teller does not find his way to the Starless Sea.

Not yet.

There is a book on a shelf in a university library.

This is not unusual, but it is not where this particular book should be.

The book is mis-shelved in the fiction section, even though the majority of it is true and the rest is true enough. The fiction section of this library is not as well traversed as other areas, its rows dimly lit and often dusty.

The book was donated, part of a collection left to the university per the previous owner's last will and testament. These books were added to the library, classified by the Dewey Decimal System, given stickers with barcodes inside their covers so they could be scanned at the checkout desk and sent off in different directions.

This particular book was scanned only once to be added to the catalogue. It does not have an author named within its pages, so it was entered in the system as "Unknown" and started off amongst the U-initialed authors but has meandered through the alphabet as other books move around it. Sometimes it is taken down and considered and replaced again. Its binding has been cracked a handful of times, and once a professor even perused the first few pages and intended to come back to it but forgot about it instead.

No one has read this book in its entirety, not since it has been in this library.

Some (the forgetful professor included) have thought, fleetingly, that this book does not belong here. That perhaps it should be in the special collection, a room that requires students to have written permission to visit and where librarians hover while they look at rare books and no one is allowed to check anything out. There are no barcodes on those books. Many require gloves for handling.

But this book remains in the regular collection. In immobile, hypothetical circulation.

The book's cover is a deep burgundy cloth that has aged and faded from rich to dull. There were once gilded letters impressed upon it but the gold is gone now and the letters have worn away to glyphlike dents. The top corner is permanently bent from where a heavier volume sat atop it in a box during a stretch in a storage facility from 1984 to 1993.

Today is a January day during what the students refer to as J-term, when classes have not yet started but they are already welcomed back on campus, and there are lectures and student-led symposiums and theatrical productions in rehearsal. A post-holiday warm-up before the regular routines begin again.

Zachary Ezra Rawlins is on campus to read. He feels mildly guilty about this fact, as he should be spending his precious winter hours playing (and replaying, and analyzing) video games in preparation for his thesis. But he spends so much time in front of screens he has a near-compulsive need to let his eyeballs rest on paper. He reminds himself that there is plenty of subject overlap, though he has found subject overlap between video games and just about anything.

Reading a novel, he supposes, is like playing a game where all the choices have been made for you ahead of time by someone who is much better at this particular game. (Though he sometimes wishes choose-your-own-adventure novels would come back into fashion.)

He has been reading (or rereading) a great many children's books as well, because the stories seem more story-like, though he is mildly concerned this might be a symptom of an impending quarter-life crisis. (He half expects this quarter-life crisis to show up like clockwork on his twenty-fifth birthday, which is only two months away.)

The librarians took him to be a literature major until one of them struck up a conversation and he felt obliged to confess he was actually one of those Emerging Media Studies people. He missed the secret identity as soon as it was gone, a guise he hadn't even realized he enjoyed wearing. He supposes he looks like a lit major, with his square-framed glasses and cable-knit sweaters. Zachary still has not entirely adjusted to New England winters, especially not one like this with its never-ceasing snow. He shields his southern-raised body with heavy layers of wool, wrapped in scarves and warmed with thermoses full of hot cocoa that he sometimes spikes with bourbon.

There are two weeks left in January and Zachary has exhausted most of his to-read list of childhood classics, at least the ones in this library's collection, so he has moved on to books he has been meaning to read and others chosen at random after testing the first few pages.

It has become his morning ritual, making his choices in the book-dampened library quiet of the stacks and then returning to his dorm to read the day away. In the skylighted atrium, he shakes the snow from his boots on the rug by the entrance and drops *The Catcher in the Rye* and *The Shadow of the Wind* into the returns box, wondering if halfway through the second year of a master's degree program is too late to be unsure about one's major. Then he reminds himself that he likes Emerging Media and if he'd spent five and a half years studying literature he would probably be growing weary of it by now, too. A reading major, that's what he wants. No response papers, no exams, no analysis, just the reading.

The fiction section, two floors below and down a hallway lined with framed lithographs of the campus in its youth, is, unsurprisingly, empty. Zachary's footsteps echo as he walks through the stacks. This section of the building is older, a contrast to the bright atrium at the entrance, the ceilings lower and the books stacked all the way up, the light falling in dim confined rectangles from bulbs that have a tendency to burn out no matter how often they are changed. If he ever has the money after graduating Zachary thinks he might make a very specific donation to fix the electrical wiring in this part of the library. Light enough to read by brought to you by Z. Rawlins, Class of 2015. You're welcome.

He seeks out the W section, having recently become enamored of Sarah Waters, and though the catalogue listed several titles, *The Little Stranger* is the only one on the shelf so he is saved decision-making. Zachary then searches for what he thinks of as mystery books, titles he does not recognize or authors he has never heard of. He starts by looking for books with blank spines.

Reaching to a higher shelf that a shorter student might have needed a stepladder to access, he pulls down a cloth-covered, wine-colored volume. Both spine and cover are blank, so Zachary opens the book to the title page.

Sweet Sorrows

He turns the page to see if there is another that lists the author but it moves directly into the text. He flips to the back and there are no acknowledgments or author's notes, just a barcode sticker attached to the inside of the back cover. He returns to the beginning and finds no copyright, no dates, no information about printing numbers.

It is clearly quite old and Zachary does not know much about the history of publishing or bookbinding, if such information is possibly not included in books of a certain age. He finds the lack of author perplexing. Perhaps a page has gone missing, or it was misprinted. He flips through the text and notices that there are pages missing, vacancies and torn edges scattered throughout though none where the front matter should be.

Zachary reads the first page, and then another and another.

Then the lightbulb above his head that has been illuminating the U–Z section blinks and darkens.

Zachary reluctantly closes the book and places it on top of *The Little Stranger*. He tucks both books securely under his arm and returns to the light of the atrium.

The student librarian at the front desk, her hair up in a bun skewered by a ballpoint pen, encounters some difficulty with the mysterious volume. It scans improperly first, and then as some other book entirely.

"I think it has the wrong barcode," she says. She taps at her keyboard, squinting at the monitor. "Do you recognize this one?" she asks, handing the book to the other librarian at the desk, a middle-aged man in a covetable green sweater. He flips through the front pages, frowning.

"No author, that's a new one. Where was it shelved?"

"In fiction, somewhere in the Ws," Zachary answers.

"Check under Anonymous, maybe," the green-sweatered librarian suggests, handing back the book and turning his attention to another patron.

The other librarian taps the keyboard again and shakes her head. "Still can't find it," she tells Zachary. "So weird."

"If it's a problem . . ." Zachary starts, though he trails off, hoping that she'll just let him take it. He feels oddly possessive about the book already.

"Not a problem, I'll mark it down in your file," she says. She types something into the computer and scans the barcode again. She pushes the authorless book and *The Little Stranger* across the desk toward him along with his student ID. "Happy reading!" she says cheerfully before turning back to the book she had been reading when Zachary approached the desk. Something by Raymond Chandler, but he cannot see the title. The librarians always seem more enthusiastic during J-term, when they can spend more time with books and less with frazzled students and irate faculty.

During the frigid walk back to his dorm Zachary is preoccupied by both the book itself, itching to continue reading, and wondering why it was not in the library system. He has encountered minor problems with such things before, having checked out a great number of books. Sometimes the scanner will not be able to read a barcode but then the librarian can type the number in manually. He wonders how they managed in the time before the scanner, with cards in catalogues and little pockets with signatures in the backs of books. It would be nice to sign his name rather than being a number in a system.

Zachary's dorm is a brick building tucked amongst the crumbling cluster of graduate residences and covered in dead, snow-dusted ivy. He climbs the many stairs to his fourth-floor room, tucked into the eaves of the building, with slanted walls and drafty windows. He has covered most of it with blankets and has a contraband space heater for the winter. Tapestries sent from his mother drape the walls and make the room admittedly cozier, partially because he cannot seem to get the sage smell out no matter how many times he washes them. The MFA candidate next door calls it a cave, though it is more like a den, if dens had Magritte posters and four different gaming systems.

His flat-screen TV stares out from the wall, black and mirrorlike. He should throw a tapestry over it.

Zachary puts his books on his desk and his boots and coat in the closet before heading down the hall to the kitchenette to make a cup of cocoa. Waiting for the electric kettle to boil he wishes he had brought the wine-colored book with him, but he is trying to make a point of not having his nose constantly in a book. It is an attempt to appear friendlier that he's not certain is working yet.

Back in his den with the cocoa he settles into the beanbag chair bequeathed to him by a departing student the year before. It is a garish neon green in its natural state, but Zachary draped it with a tapestry that was too heavy to hang on the wall, camouflaging it in shades of brown and grey and violet. He aims the space heater at his legs and opens *Sweet Sorrows* back to the page the unreliable library lightbulb had stranded him on and begins to read.

After a few pages the story shifts, and Zachary cannot tell if it is a novel or a short-story collection or perhaps a story within a story. He wonders if it will return and loop back to the previous part. Then it changes again.

Zachary Ezra Rawlins's hands begin to shake.

Because while the first part of the book is a somewhat romantic bit about a pirate, and the second involves a ceremony with an acolyte in a strange underground library, the third part is something else entirely.

The third part is about him.

The boy is the son of the fortune-teller.

A coincidence, he thinks, but as he continues reading the details are too perfect to be fiction. Sage may permeate the shoelaces of many sons of fortune-tellers but he doubts that they also took shortcuts through alleyways on their routes home from school.

When he reaches the part about the door he puts the book down.

He feels light-headed. He stands up, worried he might pass out and thinking he might open the window and instead he kicks over his forgotten mug of cocoa.

Automatically, Zachary walks down the hall to the kitchenette to get paper towels. He mops up the cocoa and goes back to the kitchenette to throw away the sopping towels. He rinses his mug in the sink. The mug has a chip he is not certain was there before. Laughter echoes up the stairwell, far away and hollow.

Zachary returns to his room and confronts the book again, staring at it as it rests nonchalantly on the beanbag chair.

He locks his door, something he rarely does.

He picks up the book and inspects it more thoroughly than he had before. The top corner of the cover is dented, the cloth starting to fray. Tiny flecks of gold dot the spine.

Zachary takes a deep breath and opens the book again. He turns to the page where he left off and forces himself to read the words as they unfold precisely the way he expects them to.

His memory fills in the details left off the page: the way the whitewash reached halfway up the wall and then the bricks turned red again, the dumpsters at the other end of the alley, the weight of his schoolbook-stuffed backpack on his shoulder.

He has remembered that day a thousand times but this time it is different. This time his memory is guided along by the words on the page and it is clear and vibrant. As though the moment only just happened and is not more than a decade in the past.

He can picture the door perfectly. The precision of the paint. The trompe l'oeil effect he couldn't name at the time. The bee with its delicate gold stripes. The sword pointed upright toward the key.

But as Zachary continues reading there is more than what his memory contains.

He had thought there could be no stranger feeling than stumbling across a book that narrates a long-ago incident from his own life that was never relayed to anyone, never spoken about or written down but nevertheless is unfolding in typeset prose, but he was wrong.

It is stranger still to have that narration confirm long-held suspicions that in that moment, in that alleyway facing that door he was given something extraordinary and he let the opportunity slip from his fingers.

A boy at the beginning of a story has no way of knowing that the story has begun.

Zachary reaches the end of the page and turns it, expecting his story to continue but it does not. The narrative shifts entirely again, to something about a dollhouse. He flips through the rest of the book, scanning the pages for mentions of the son of the fortune-teller or painted doors but finds nothing.

He goes back and rereads the pages about the boy. About him. About the place he did not find behind the door, whatever a Starless Sea is supposed to be. His hands have stopped shaking but he is lightheaded and hot, he remembers now that he never opened the window but he cannot stop reading. He pushes his eyeglasses farther up the bridge of his nose so he can focus better.

He doesn't understand. Not only how someone could have captured the scene in such detail but how it is here in a book that looks much older than he is. He rubs the paper between his fingers and it feels heavy and rough, yellowing to near brown around the edges.

Could someone have predicted him, down to his shoelaces? Does that mean the rest of it could be true? That somewhere there are tongueless acolytes in a subterranean library? It doesn't seem fair to him to be the solitary real person in a collection of fictional characters, though he supposes the pirate and the girl could be real. Still, the very idea is so ludicrous that he laughs at himself.

He wonders if he is losing his mind and then decides that if he is able to wonder about it he probably isn't, which isn't particularly comforting.

He looks down at the last two words on the page.

Not yet.

Those two words swim through a thousand questions flooding his mind.

Then one of those questions floats to the surface of his thoughts, prompted by the repeated bee motif and his remembered door.

Is *this* book from *that* place?

He inspects the book again, pausing at the barcode stuck to the back cover.

Zachary looks closer, and sees that the sticker is obscuring something written or printed there. A spot of black ink peeks out from the bottom of the sticker.

He feels mildly guilty about prying it off. The barcode was faulty, anyway, and likely needs to be replaced. Not that he has any intention of returning the book, not now. He peels the sticker off slowly and carefully, trying to remove it in one piece and attempting not to rip the paper below it. It comes off easily and he sticks it to the edge of his desk before turning back to what is written below it.

There are no words, only a string of symbols that have been stamped or otherwise inscribed onto the back cover, faded and smudged but easily identifiable.

The exposed dot of ink is the hilt of a sword.

Above it is a key.

Above the key is a bee.

Zachary Ezra Rawlins stares at the miniature versions of the same symbols he once contemplated in an alleyway behind his mother's store and wonders how, exactly, he is supposed to continue a story he didn't know he was in.

SWEET SORROWS
Invented life.

It began as a dollhouse.

A miniature habitat carefully constructed from wood and glue and paint. Meticulously crafted to re-create a full-size dwelling in the most exquisite level of detail. When it was built it was gifted to and played with by children, illustrating daily happenings in simplified exaggerations.

There are dolls. A family with a mother and father and son and daughter and small dog. They wear delicate cloth replicas of suits and dresses. The dog has real fur.

There is a kitchen and a parlor and a sunroom. Bedrooms and stairs and an attic. Each room is filled with furniture and decorated with miniature paintings and minuscule vases of flowers. The wallpaper is printed with intricate patterns. The tiny books can be removed from the shelves.

It has a roof with wooden shingles each no bigger than a fingernail. Diminutive doors that close and latch. The house opens with a lock and key and expands, though most often it is kept closed. The doll life inside visible only through the windows.

The dollhouse sits in a room in this Harbor on the Starless Sea. The history of it is missing. The children who once played with it long grown and gone. The tale of how it came to be placed in an obscure room in an obscure place is forgotten.

It is not remarkable.

What is remarkable is what has evolved around it.

What is a single house, after all, with nothing surrounding it? Without a yard for the dog. Without a complaining neighbor across the street, without a street to have neighbors on at all?

Without trees and horses and stores. Without a harbor. A boat. A city across the sea.

All this has built up around it. One child's invented world has become another's, and another's, and so on until it is everyone's world. Embellished and expanded with metal and paper and glue. Gears and found objects and clay. More houses have been constructed. More dolls have been added. Stacks of books arranged by color serve as landscape. Folded-paper birds fly overhead. Hot air balloons descend from above.

There are mountains and villages and cities, castles and dragons and floating ballrooms. Farms with barns and fluffy cotton sheep. A working clock of a reincarnated watch keeps time atop a tower. There is a park with a lake and ducks. A beach with a lighthouse.

The world cascades around the room. There are paths for visitors to walk on, to access the corners. There is the outline of what was once a desk beneath the buildings. There are shelves on the walls that are now distant countries across an ocean with carefully rippled blue paper waves.

It began as a dollhouse. Over time, it has become more than that.

A dolltown. A dollworld. A dolluniverse.

Constantly expanding.

Almost everyone who finds the room feels compelled to add to it. To leave the contents of their pockets repurposed as a wall or tree or temple. A thimble becomes a trash can. Used matchsticks create a fence. Loose buttons transform into wheels or apples or stars.

They add houses made from broken books or rainstorms conjured from glass glitter. They move a figure or a landmark. They escort the tiny sheep from one pasture to another. They reorient the mountains.

Some visitors play in the room for hours, creating stories and narratives. Others look around, adjust a crooked tree or door, and depart. Or they simply move the ducks around the lake and are satisfied with that.

Anyone who enters the room affects it. Leaves an impression upon it even if it is unintentional. Quietly opening the door lets a soft draft rustle over the objects inside. A tree might topple. A doll might lose its hat. An entire building might crumble.

An ill-placed step might crush the hardware store. A sleeve could catch on the top of a castle, sending a princess tumbling to the ground below. It is a fragile place.

Any damage is usually temporary. Someone will come along and provide repairs. Restore a fallen princess to her battlement. Rebuild the hardware store with sticks and cardboard. Create new stories upon the old ones.

The original house in the center changes in subtler ways. The furniture moves from room to room. The walls are painted or papered over. The mother and father dolls spend time separately in other structures with other dolls. The daughter and son leave and return and leave again. The dog chases cars and sheep and dares to bark at the dragon.

Around them, the world grows ever larger.

It sometimes takes the dolls quite a while to adapt.

ZACHARY EZRA RAWLINS sits on the floor of his closet with the door closed, surrounded by a forest of hanging shirts and coats, his back up against where the door to Narnia would be if his closet were a wardrobe, having something of an existential crisis.

He has read *Sweet Sorrows* in its entirety and read it again and thought perhaps he should not read it a third time but read it a third time anyway because he could not sleep.

He still cannot sleep.

Now it is three a.m. and Zachary is in the back of his closet, a version of his favorite reading spot when he was a child. A comfort he has not returned to in years and never in this closet, which is ill-suited for such sitting.

He sat in his childhood closet after he found the door, he remembers that now. It was a better closet for sitting. A deeper one, with pillows he had dragged in to make it more comfortable. That one didn't have a door to Narnia, either, he knows because he checked.

Only the singular section of *Sweet Sorrows* is about him, though there are pages missing. The text comes back to the pirate and the girl again but the rest is disjointed, it feels incomplete. Much of it revolves around an underground library. No, not a library, a book-centric fantasia that Zachary missed his invitation to because he didn't open a painted door when he was eleven.

Apparently he went around looking for the wrong imaginary entryways.

The wine-colored book rests at the foot of the bed. Zachary will not admit to himself that he is hiding from it, in the closet where it cannot see him.

A whole book and he has no idea even after reading it three times how he should proceed.

The rest of the book doesn't feel as tangible as those few pages near the beginning. Zachary has always had a complicated view of magic because of his mother, but while he can grasp herbalism and divination the things in the book are very much beyond his definition of real. *Magic* magic.

But if those few pages about him are real, the rest could be . . .

Zachary puts his head between his knees and tries to keep his breathing steady.

He keeps wondering who wrote it. Who saw him in that alleyway with the door and why they wrote it down. The opening pages imply that the first stories are nested: the pirate telling the story about the acolyte, the acolyte seeing the story about the boy. Him.

But if he's in a story within a story who is telling it? Someone must have typeset it and bound it in a book.

Someone somewhere knows this story.

He wonders if someone somewhere knows he's sitting on the floor of his closet.

Zachary crawls out into his room, his legs stiff. It is near dawn, the light outside his window a lighter shade of dark. He decides to take a walk. He leaves the book on the bed. His fingers start twitching immediately, wanting to take it with him so he can read it again. He wraps his scarf around his neck. Reading a book four times in one day is perfectly normal behavior. He buttons his wool coat. Having a physical response to a lack of book is not unusual. He tugs his knit hat down over his ears. Everyone spends nights on the floor of their closet during grad school. He pulls on his boots. Finding an incident from your childhood in an authorless mystery book is an everyday occurrence. He slips his hands into his gloves. Happens to everyone.

He puts the book in the pocket of his coat.

Zachary trudges through newly fallen snow without a destination in mind. He passes the library and continues toward a hilly stretch of campus near the undergraduate dorms. He could adjust his route to pass his old dorm but he does not, he always finds it strange to look at a window he used to look out from the other side. He works his way through the crisp unbroken snow, crushing the pristine surface under his boots.

He usually enjoys the winter and the snow and the cold even when he can't feel his toes. There's a wonder to it, left over from reading about snow in books before he got to experience it for himself. His first snow was a laughter-filled night spent in the field outside his mother's farmhouse, making snowballs with his bare hands and constantly losing his footing in shoes he discovered after the fact were not waterproof. Inside their cashmere-lined gloves, his hands tingle thinking about it.

He is always surprised how quiet the snow is, until it melts.

"Rawlins!" a voice calls from behind him and Zachary turns. A bundled figure with a striped hat waves a brightly mittened hand at him and he watches the mismatched color move over a field of white as it trudges up the hill through the snow, sometimes hopping in the foot holes he has left. When the figure is a few yards away he recognizes Kat, one of the few undergrads from his department who has moved from acquaintance to almost-friend, mostly because she took it upon herself to get to know everyone and he has been Kat-approved. She runs a video-game-themed cooking blog and tends to try out her often delicious experiments on the rest of them. *Skyrim*-inspired sweet rolls and classic *BioShock* cream-filled cakes and maraschino truffle odes to *Pac-Man* cherries. Zachary suspects she doesn't sleep and she has a tendency to appear out of thin air to suggest cocktails or dancing or some other excuse to coerce him out of his room, and while Zachary has never articulated the fact that he is grateful to have someone like her in his otherwise highly introverted lifestyle he is pretty sure she already knows.

"Hey, Kat," Zachary says when she reaches him, hoping he won't appear as off-kilter as he feels. "What brings you out so early?"

Kat sighs and rolls her eyes. The sigh drifts away as a cloud in the frigid air.

"God-awful early is the only hour I can get lab time for as-of-yet unofficial projects, how 'bout you?" Kat shifts her bag on her shoulder and nearly loses her balance, Zachary puts a hand out to steady her but she recovers on her own.

"Couldn't sleep," Zachary answers, which is true enough. "Are you still working on that scent-based project?"

"I am!" Kat's cheeks betray the smile hidden by her scarf. "I think it's the key to immersive experience, virtual reality isn't all that real if it doesn't smell like anything. I can't figure out how to get it to work for in-home use yet but my site-specific stuff is going well. I'm probably going to need beta testers in the spring if you'd be willing."

"If spring ever shows up, I'm game." Kat's projects are legendary throughout the department, elaborate interactive installations, and always memorable regardless of how successful she deems them. They make Zachary's work feel overly cerebral and sedentary by comparison, especially since so much of his own work is analyzing work already done by others.

"Excellent!" Kat says. "I'll put you on my list. And I'm glad I ran into you, are you busy tonight?"

"Not really," Zachary says, having not thought about the fact that the day would go on, that the campus would continue in its routines and he is the only one who has had his universe turned askew.

"Could you help me run my J-term class?" Kat asks. "Seven to eight thirty or so?"

"Your Harry Potter knitting class? I'm not a very good knitter."

"No, that's on Tuesdays, this one is a salon-style discussion called Innovation in Storytelling and this week's topic is gaming. I'm trying to have a guest co-moderator for each class and Noriko was supposed to do this one but she bailed on me to go skiing. It'll be super chill, no lecturing or anything you need to prepare, just babbling about gaming in a relaxed yet intellectual setting. I know that's your jam, Rawlins. Please?"

The impulse to say no that Zachary has for pretty much anything that involves talking to people arises automatically, but as Kat bounces on her heels to keep warm and he considers the proposal, it sounds like a good way to get out of his head and away from the book for a little while. This is what Kat does, after all. It is good to have a Kat.

"Sure, why not," he says. Kat whoops. The whoop echoes over the snow-covered lawn, prompting a pair of disgruntled crows to abandon their perch in a nearby tree.

"You're awesome," Kat says. "I'll knit you a Ravenclaw scarf as a thank-you."

"How did you know—"

"Please, you're so obviously Ravenclaw. See you tonight, we meet in the lounge in Scott Hall, the one in the back on the right. I'll text you details when my hands thaw. You're the best. I'd hug you but I think I'd fall down."

"Sentiment appreciated," Zachary assures her and he considers, here in the snow, asking if Kat has ever heard of something called the Starless Sea, because if anyone would have heard of a possibly fairy-tale, possibly mythical location it would be Kat, but articulating it aloud would make it too real and instead he watches as she trudges off toward the science quad where the Emerging Media Center is housed, though he realizes she might very well be headed to the chemistry labs instead.

Zachary stands alone in the snow, overlooking the slowly waking campus.

Yesterday it felt like it always does, like almost not quite home. Today he feels like an impostor. He breathes in deeply, the pine-scented air filling his lungs.

Two black dots mar the pale blue of the cloudless sky, the crows that took flight moments ago in the process of disappearing into the distance.

Zachary Ezra Rawlins commences the long walk back to his room.

Once he has kicked off his boots and peeled off his winter layers, Zachary takes out the book. He turns it over in his hands and then puts it down on his desk. It doesn't look like anything special, like it contains an entire world, though the same could be said of any book.

Zachary pulls his curtains shut and is half asleep before they settle over the window, blocking out the sun-brightened snowscape and the figure watching him from across the street in the shadow of an unruly spruce.

Zachary wakes hours later when his phone chirps a text alert at him, the vibration rattling it enough that it falls off the desk and onto the floor, landing softly on a discarded sock.

7pm scott hall first floor lounge—from the front entrance go past the stairs & turn right down the hall, it's behind the french doors & looks like the postapocalyptic version of a room where fancy ladies have tea. i'll be there early. you're the best. <3 k.

The clock on the phone informs him that it is already 5:50 and Scott Hall is clear across campus. Zachary yawns and drags himself out of bed and down the hall to take a shower.

Standing in the steam, he thinks he dreamed the book but the relief that this thought brings slowly dissipates and he remembers the truth.

He scrubs his skin near raw with the homemade almond oil and sugar mixture his mother gifts him every winter, this year's batch is scented with vetiver to promote emotional calm. Maybe he can scrub off that boy standing in that alleyway. Maybe the real Zachary is under there somewhere.

Every seven years each cell in your body has changed, he reminds himself. He is not that boy anymore. He is twice removed from that boy.

Zachary spends so long in the shower that he has to rush to get ready, grabbing a protein bar when he realizes he hasn't eaten all day. He tosses a notebook in his satchel and his hand hovers over *Sweet Sorrows* before grabbing *The Little Stranger* instead.

He is halfway out the door when he doubles back to put *Sweet Sorrows* in his bag as well.

As he walks toward Scott Hall his damp hair freezes in curls that brush crunchily against his neck. The snow is crisscrossed with so many boot tracks that there is hardly an untouched patch on campus. Zachary passes a lopsided snowman wearing a real red scarf. A line of busts of former college presidents is mostly obscured in snow, stray marble eyes and ears peeking out from beneath the flakes.

Kat's directions prove helpful once he arrives at Scott Hall, one of the residences he's never been in before. He passes the stairs and a small empty study room before finding the hallway and following it for some time until he reaches a half-open pair of French doors.

He's not sure he has the right room. A girl sits knitting in an armchair while a couple of other students rearrange some of the postapocalyptic-looking tea-party furniture, velvet chairs and settees worn thin and wounded by time, a few repaired with duct tape.

"Yay, you found us!" Kat's voice comes from behind him and he turns to find her holding a tray with a teapot and several stacked tea-cups. She looks smaller with her coat and striped hat removed, her buzzed-short hair a fuzzy shadow covering her head.

"I didn't realize you were serious about the tea," Zachary says, helping her move the tray to a coffee table in the middle of the room.

"I don't jest about tea. I have Earl Grey and peppermint and some sort of immunity-boosting thing with ginger. And I made cookies."

By the time the tea and the multiple trays of cookies are arranged the class has filtered in, about a dozen students, though it feels like more with all the coats and scarves flung over the backs of chairs and couches. Zachary settles into an ancient armchair by the window that Kat directs him to with a cup of Earl Grey and an oversize chocolate chip cookie.

"Hi everyone," Kat says, pulling the attention in the room away from baked goods and chatter. "Thanks for coming. I think we have some newbies who missed last week, so how about we do quick intros around the room, starting with our guest moderator." Kat turns and looks at Zachary expectantly.

"Okay . . . um . . . I'm Zachary," he manages between chews before swallowing the rest of his cookie. "I'm a second-year Emerging Media grad student, I mostly study video-game design with a focus on psychology and gender issues."

And I found a book in the library yesterday that someone wrote my childhood into, how's that for innovative storytelling? he thinks but does not say aloud.

The introductions continue and Zachary retains identifying details and areas of interest better than names. Several are theater majors, including a girl with impressive multicolored dreadlocks and a blond boy with his feet propped up on a guitar case. The girl with cat-eye glasses who looks vaguely familiar is an English major, as is the girl who continues to knit but barely glances down at her work. The rest are mostly Emerging Media undergrads, some of them he recognizes (the guy in the blue hoodie, the girl with the tattooed vines peeking out of the cuffs of her sweater, ponytail guy) but no one he knows as well as Kat.

"And I'm Kat Hawkins, senior Emerging Media and theater double major and I mostly spend my time trying to turn games into theater and theater into games. And also baking. Tonight we're going to discuss video games specifically, I know we have a lot of gamers here but if you're not please ask if you need terminology clarification or anything like that."

"How are we defining 'gamer'?" the guy in the blue hoodie asks with enough of an edge in his voice that Kat's bright expression darkens almost imperceptibly.

"I follow the Gertrude Stein definition: a gamer is a gamer is a gamer," Zachary jumps in, adjusting his glasses and hating himself for the pretentiousness but hating the guy who needs to define everything a little bit more.

"As far as how we're defining 'game' in this context," Kat continues, "let's keep along the lines of narrative games, role-playing games aka RPGs, etcetera. Everything should come back to story."

Kat prompts Zachary into sharing some of his standard primers on game narrative, character agency, choices, and consequences, points he's made in so many papers and projects that it's a pleasant change to relate them to a group that hasn't heard them all a thousand times before.

Kat jumps in here and there and it doesn't take long for the discussion to take off organically, questions becoming debates and points volleying between sips of tea and cookie crumbs.

The conversation veers into immersive theater which was last week's topic and then back to video games, from the collaborative nature of massive multiplayer back to single-player narratives and virtual reality with a brief stopover on tabletop games.

Eventually the question of why a player plays a story-based game and what makes it compelling comes up to be examined and dismantled.

"Isn't that what anyone wants, though?" the girl with the cat-eye glasses asks in response. "To be able to make your own choices and decisions but to have it be part of a story? You want that narrative there to trust in, even if you want to maintain your own free will."

"You want to decide where to go and what to do and which door to open but you still want to win the game," ponytail guy adds.

"Even if winning the game is just ending the story."

"Especially if a game allows for multiple possible endings," Zachary says, touching on the subject of a paper he'd written two years previously. "Wanting to co-write the story, not dictate it yourself, so it's collaborative."

"It'll work in games better than anything," one of the Emerging Media guys muses. "And maybe avant-garde theater," he adds when one of the theater majors starts to object.

"Choose Your Own Adventure digital novels?" the knitting English major throws out.

"No, commit to being a full-blown game if you're going to go through all the decision-making option trees, all the if-thens," the girl with the vine tattoos argues, talking with her hands so the vines help emphasize her points. "Proper text stories are preexisting narratives to fall into, games unfold as you go. If I get to choose what's going to happen in a story I want to be a mage. Or at least have a fancy gun."

"We're veering off topic," Kat says. "Sort of. What makes a story compelling? Any story. In basic terms."

"Change."

"Mystery."

"High stakes."

"Character growth."

"Romance," the guy in the blue hoodie chimes in. "What? It's true," he adds when several raised eyebrows turn in his direction. "Sexual tension, is that better? Also true."

"Obstacles to overcome."

"Surprises."

"Meaning."

"But who decides what the meaning is?" Zachary wonders aloud.

"The reader. The player. The audience. That's what you bring to it, even if you don't make the choices along the way, you decide what it means to you." The knitting girl pauses to catch a slipped stitch and then continues. "A game or a book that has meaning to me might be boring to you, or vice versa. Stories are personal, you relate or you don't."

"Like I said, everyone wants to be part of a story."

"Everyone *is* a part of a story, what they want is to be part of something worth recording. It's that fear of mortality, 'I Was Here and I Mattered' mind-set."

Zachary's thoughts begin to wander. He feels old, not certain if he was ever so enthusiastic as an underclassman and wondering if he seemed as young to the grad students then as this group seems to him now. He thinks back to the book in his bag, turning over ideas about what it is to be in a story, wondering why he has spent so much of his time propelling narratives forward and trying to figure out how to do the same with this one.

"Isn't it easier to have words on a page and leave everything up to the imagination?" another of the English majors asks, a girl in a fuzzy red sweater.

"The words on the page are never easy," the girl in the cat-eye glasses points out and several people nod.

"Simpler, then." Red-sweater girl holds up a pen. "I can create a whole world with this, it may not be innovative but it's effective."

"It is until you run out of ink," someone retorts.

Someone else points out that it's nine already and more than one person jumps up, apologizes, and rushes off. The rest of them continue to chat in fractured groups and pairs and a couple of the Emerging Media students hover over Zachary, inquiring about class recommendations and professors as they put the room more or less back in order.

"That was so great, thank you," Kat says once she's gotten his attention again. "I owe you one, and I'm going to get started on your scarf this weekend, I promise you'll have it while it's still cold enough to wear it."

"You don't have to but thanks, Kat. I had a good time."

"Me too. And oh, Elena's waiting in the hall. She wanted to catch you before you left but didn't want to interrupt while you were talking to people."

"Oh, okay," Zachary says, trying to remember which one was Elena.

Kat gives him another hug and whispers in his ear, "She's not trying to pick you up, I forewarned her that you are orientationally unavailable."

"Thanks, Kat," Zachary says, trying not to roll his eyes and knowing she probably used that exact phrase instead of simply saying that he's gay because Kat hates labels.

Elena turns out to be the one in the cat-eye glasses, leaning against the wall and reading a Raymond Chandler novel Zachary can now identify as *The Long Goodbye* and he realizes why she looks familiar. He probably would have placed her if her hair had been in a bun.

"Hey," Zachary says and she looks up from her book with a dazed expression he's used to wearing himself, the disorientation of being pulled out of one world and back into another.

"Hi," Elena says, coming out of the fiction fog and tucking the Chandler in her bag. "I don't know if you remember me from the library yesterday. You checked out that weird book that wouldn't scan."

"I remember," Zachary says. "I haven't read it yet," he adds, not sure why the lie is necessary.

"Well after you left I got curious," Elena says. "The library's awfully quiet and I've been on a mystery kick so I decided to do some investigating."

"Really?" Zachary asks, suddenly interested when before he had been lying in nervous apprehension. "Did you find anything?"

"Not a lot, the system's so barcode-happy that if the computer doesn't recognize it it's hard to dig up a file, but I remembered that the book looked kind of old so I went down to the card archives, back from when everything was stored in those fabulous wooden catalogues, to see if it was there and it wasn't but I did manage to decipher how it was coded, there's a couple of digits in the barcode that indicate when it was added to the system, so I cross-referenced those."

"That's some impressive librarian detective work."

"Ha, thank you. Unfortunately, the only thing it turned up was that it was part of a private collection, some guy died and a foundation distributed his library to a bunch of different schools. I updated the files and wrote down the name, so if you want to find any of the other books someone should be able to print out a list for you. I'm working most mornings until classes start up again if you're interested." Elena digs around in her bag and pulls out a folded scrap of lined notebook paper. "Some of them should be in the rare book room and not in circulation, but whatever. I gave it a catalogue entry so it should scan fine whenever you return it."

"Thanks," Zachary says as he takes the paper from her. *Item acquired,* a voice in his head remarks. "I'd like that, I'll stop by sometime soon."

"Cool," Elena says. "And thanks for coming tonight, that was a great discussion. See you around."

She's gone before he can say goodbye.

Zachary unfolds the paper. There are two lines of text, written in remarkably neat handwriting.

From the private collection of J. S. Keating, donated in 1993.
A gift from the Keating Foundation.

SWEET SORROWS

There are three paths. This is one of them.

Paper is fragile, even when bound with string in cloth or leather. The majority of the stories within the Harbor on the Starless Sea are captured on paper. In books or on scrolls or folded into paper birds and suspended from ceilings.

There are stories that are more fragile still: For every tale carved in rock there are more inscribed on autumn leaves or woven into spiderwebs.

There are stories wrapped in silk so their pages do not fall to dust and stories that have already succumbed, fragments collected and kept in urns.

They are fragile things. Less sturdy than their cousins who are told aloud and learned by heart.

And there are always those who would watch Alexandria burn.

There always have been. There always will be.

So there are always guardians.

Many have given their lives in service. Many more have had their lives taken by time before they could lose them in other fashions.

It is rare for a guardian not to remain a guardian always.

To be a guardian is to be trusted. To be trusted, all must be tested.

Guardian testing is a long and arduous process.

One cannot volunteer to be a guardian. Guardians are chosen.

Potential guardians are identified and watched. Scrutinized. Their every move, every choice, and every action is marked by unseen judges. The judges do nothing but observe for months, sometimes years, before they issue their first tests.

The potential guardian will not be aware that they are being tested. It is critical to steep the tests in ignorance to result in uncorrupted responses. Many tests will never be recognized as tests, even in hindsight.

Candidates for guardianship who are dismissed at these early stages will never know that they were ever considered. They will go about their lives and find other paths.

Most candidates are dismissed before the sixth test.

Many do not make it past the twelfth.

The rhythms of the first test are always the same, whether it occurs within a Harbor or without.

In a large public library a small boy browses books, biding time before he is meant to meet up with his sister. He stands on his toes to reach volumes shelved above his head. He has long since abandoned the children's section but is not yet tall enough to reach all of the other shelves.

A woman with dark eyes and a green scarf—not a librarian, as far as he can tell—hands him the book he had been reaching for and he shyly nods his thanks. She asks if he will do her a favor in return, and when he agrees she requests that he keep an eye on a book for her, pointing out a thin volume bound in brown leather sitting on a nearby table.

The small boy agrees and the woman leaves. Minutes pass. The boy continues browsing shelves, always keeping the small brown book in sight.

Several more minutes pass. The boy considers looking around for the woman. He checks his watch. Soon he will have to leave himself.

Then a woman walks by without acknowledging him and picks up the book.

This woman has dark eyes and wears a green scarf. She looks quite similar to the first woman but she is not the same person. When she turns to walk away with the book, the boy seizes up with mild panic and confusion.

He asks her to stop. The woman turns, her face a question mark.

The boy stammers that the book belongs to someone else.

The new woman smiles and points out the fact that they are in a library and the books belong to everyone.

The boy almost lets her leave. Now he is not even certain it is a different woman, as this woman is nearly identical. He is going to be late if he waits much longer. It would be easier to let the book go.

But the boy protests again. He explains in too many words that he had been asked to watch it for someone.

Eventually the woman relents and hands the book to the small flustered boy.

He holds the hard-won object to his chest.

He is unaware that he has been tested but he is proud of himself nonetheless.

Two minutes later, the first woman returns. This time he recognizes her. Her eyes are lighter, the pattern on the green scarf is distinct, golden hoops climb up her right ear and not her left.

The woman thanks him for his service when he hands her the thin brown book. She reaches into her bag and pulls out a wrapped piece of candy and puts a finger to her lips. He tucks it into his pocket, understanding such things are not permitted in the library.

The woman thanks him again and departs with the book.

The boy will not be approached directly for another seven years.

Many of the initial tests are similar, watching for care and respect and attention to detail. Observing how they react to everyday stress or extraordinary emergencies. Weighing how they respond to a disappointment or a lost cat. Some are asked to burn or otherwise destroy a book. (To destroy the book, no matter how distasteful or offensive or badly written, is to fail the test.)

A single failure results in dismissal.

After the twelfth test, the potential guardians will be made aware that they are being considered. Those who were not born below are brought to the Harbor and housed in rooms no resident ever sees. They study and are tested again in different ways. Tests of psychological strength and willpower. Tests of improvisation and imagination.

This process occurs over the course of three years. Many are dismissed. Others quit somewhere along the way. Some, but not all, will figure out that perseverance is more important now than performance.

If they make it to the three-year mark, they are given an egg.

They are released from their training and studying.

Now they need only return with the same egg, unbroken, six months later.

The egg stage is the undoing of many a potential guardian.

Of those who depart with their eggs, perhaps half return.

The potential guardian and their unbroken egg are brought to an elder guardian. The elder guardian gestures for the egg and the potential guardian holds it aloft on their palm.

The elder guardian reaches out but instead of taking the offering closes the potential guardian's fingers around the egg.

The elder guardian then presses down, forcing the potential guardian to shatter the egg.

All that remains in the potential guardian's hands is cracked eggshell and dust. A fine golden powder that will never completely fade from their palm, it will shimmer even decades later.

The elder guardian says nothing of fragility or responsibility. The words do not need to be spoken. All is understood.

The elder guardian nods their approval, and the potential guardian has reached the end of their training and the beginning of their initiation.

A potential guardian, once they have passed the egg test, is given a tour.

It commences in familiar rooms of the Harbor, starting at the clock in the Heart with its swooping pendulum and moving outward through the main halls, the residents wings and reading rooms and down into the wine cellar and the ballroom with its imposing fireplace, taller than even the tallest of the guardians.

Then they are shown rooms never seen by anyone but the guardians themselves. Hidden rooms and locked rooms and forgotten rooms. They go deeper than any resident, any acolyte. They light their own candles. They see what no one else sees. They see what has come before.

They may not ask questions. They may simply observe.

They walk the shores of the Starless Sea.

When the tour reaches its end the potential guardian is brought to a small room with a burning fire and a single chair. The guardian is seated and asked a single question.

Would you give your life for this?

And they answer, yes or no.

Those who answer yes remain in the chair.

They are blindfolded, their hands are bound behind their back. Their robes or shirts are adjusted to expose their chests.

An unseen artist with a needle and a pot of ink pierces their skin, over and over again.

A sword, perhaps three or four inches in length, is tattooed on each guardian.

Each sword is unique. It has been designed for this guardian and no other. Some are simple, others intricate and ornamented, depicted in elaborate detail in black or sepia or gold.

Should a potential guardian answer in the negative, the sword that has been designed for them will be catalogued and never inscribed on skin.

Few say no, here, after all they have seen. Very few.

Those who do are also blindfolded, their hands bound behind their backs.

A long, sharp needle is inserted quickly, piercing the heart.

It is a relatively painless death.

Here in this room it is too late to choose another path, not after what they have seen. They are allowed to choose not to be a guardian, but here, this is the only alternative.

Guardians are not identifiable. They wear no robes, no uniforms. Their assignments are rotated. Most stay within the Harbor but several roam the surface, unnoticed and unseen. A trace of golden dust upon a palm means nothing to those who do not understand its significance. The sword tattoo is easily concealed.

They may not seem to be in servitude to anything, but they are.

They know what they serve.

What they protect.

They understand what they are and that is all that matters.

They understand that what it is to be a guardian is to be prepared to die, always.

To be a guardian is to wear death on your chest.

ZACHARY EZRA RAWLINS is standing in the hall and staring at the scrap of notebook paper when Kat comes out of the lounge wrapped in her winter layers again.

"Hey, you're still here!" she remarks.

Zachary folds the piece of paper and puts it in his pocket.

"Has anyone ever told you that you have stellar observational skills?" he asks, and Kat punches him in the arm. "I deserved that."

"Lexi and I are going to the Gryphon for a drink if you want to come," Kat says, gesturing over her shoulder at the theater major with the dreadlocks who is pulling her coat on.

"Sure," Zachary says, since the operating hours of the library prevent him from investigating the clue in his pocket further and the Laughing Gryphon serves an excellent sidecar.

The three of them make their way through the snow away from campus and downtown to the short strip of bars and restaurants glowing against the night sky, the trees lining the sidewalk wearing coats of ice around their branches.

They continue some of the conversation from earlier, which segues into Kat and Lexi recapping the discussion from the previous class for Zachary, and they are describing site-specific theater for him when they reach the bar.

"I don't know, I'm not big on audience participation," Zachary says as they settle into a corner table. He has forgotten how much he likes this bar, with its dark wood and bare Edison bulbs illuminating the space from mismatched antique fixtures.

"I *hate* audience participation," Lexi assures him. "This is more self-directed stuff, where you go where you want to go and decide what to watch."

"Then how do you make sure any given audience member sees the whole narrative?"

"You can't guarantee it but if you provide enough to see hopefully they can piece it together for themselves."

They order cocktails and half the appetizer section of the menu and Lexi describes her thesis project to Zachary, a piece that involves, among other things, deciphering and following clues to different locations to find fragments of the performance.

"Can you believe she's not a gamer?" Kat asks.

"That is legitimately surprising," Zachary says and Lexi laughs.

"I never got into it," she explains. "And besides, you have to admit it's a little intimidating to outsiders."

"Fair point," Zachary says. "But the theater stuff you do sounds like it's not that far off."

"She needs gateway games," Kat says, and between cocktail sips and bacon-wrapped dates and balls of fried goat cheese dipped in lavender honey they assemble a list of games that Lexi might like, though she is incredulous when they point out that some of them could take up to a hundred hours to play through thoroughly.

"That's insane," she says, sipping at her whiskey sour. "Do you guys not sleep?"

"Sleep is for the weak," Kat responds, writing more game titles down on a napkin.

Somewhere behind them a tray of drinks crashes and they wince in unison.

"I hope that wasn't our next round," Lexi says, peering over Zachary's shoulder at the fallen tray and the embarrassed waitress.

"You get to live in a game," Zachary points out as they return to their conversation, to a topic he knows he's discussed with Kat before. "For so much longer than a book or a movie or a play. You know how you have real-life time versus story time, how stories leave out the boring bits and condense so much? A long-form RPG has some substance to it, leaves time to wander the desert or have a conversation or hang out in a pub. It might not be the closest thing to real life but pacing-wise it's closer than a movie or a TV show or a novel." The thought, combined with recent events and the alcohol, makes him a little dizzy and he excuses himself to go to the men's room.

Once there, though, the Victorian-printed wallpaper repeating into infinity in the mirror does nothing to help the dizziness. He takes off his glasses and places them by the side of the sink and splashes cold water on his face.

He stares at his blurry, damp reflection.

The old-school jazz playing at a comfortable volume outside is amplified in this tiny space and Zachary feels uncomfortably as though he is falling through time.

The blurry man in the mirror stares back at him, looking as confused as he feels.

Zachary dries his face with paper towels and composes himself as best he can. Once he puts his glasses on the details look too sharp, the brass of the doorknob, the illuminated bottles lining the bar, as he walks back to the table.

"Some guy was totally checking you out," Kat tells him when he sits down. "Over—oh, wait, he's gone." She scans the rest of the bar and frowns. "He was over there a minute ago, by himself in the corner."

"You're sweet to make up phantom paramours for me," Zachary says, taking a sip of the second sidecar that arrived in his absence.

"He was there!" Kat protests. "I'm not making him up, am I, Lexi?"

"There was a guy in the corner," Lexi confirms. "But I have no idea if he was checking you out or not. I thought he was reading."

"Sad face," Kat says, sweeping her frown around the room once more but then she changes the subject, and eventually Zachary manages to lose himself in the conversation as the snow starts to fall again outside.

They slip and slide back to campus, parting ways in the glow of a streetlamp when Zachary turns down the curving street that leads to the graduate dorms. He smiles as he listens to their chatter fading in the distance. Snowflakes catch in his hair and on his glasses and he feels like he is being watched and he looks over his shoulder at the streetlight but there is only snow and trees and a reddish haze in the sky.

Back in his room Zachary returns to *Sweet Sorrows* in his cocktail haze and starts reading again from the beginning, but sleep creeps up and steals him away after two pages and the book falls closed on his chest.

In the morning it is the first thing he sees and without thinking about it too much he puts the book in his bag, pulls on his coat and boots, and heads to the library.

"Is Elena here?" he asks the gentleman at the circulation desk.

"She's at the reserve desk, around the corner to the left."

Zachary thanks the gentleman librarian and continues through the atrium and around the corner to a counter with a computer where Elena sits, her hair back in its bun and her nose in a different Raymond Chandler novel this time, *Playback*.

"Can I help you?" she asks without looking up, but when she does she adds, "Oh, hi! Didn't expect to see you so soon."

"I got curious about the library mystery," Zachary says, which is true enough. "How's that one?" he asks, pointing at the Chandler. "I haven't read it."

"So far so good, but I don't like to commit to an opinion until the end of a book because you never know what might happen. I'm reading all his novels in publication order, *The Big Sleep* is my favorite. Did you want that list?"

"Yeah, that'd be great," Zachary says, pleased that he's managing to sound fairly casual.

Elena types something into the computer, waits, and types something else.

"Looks like everything else has proper author names, so much for mysteries, but there's some fiction and nonfiction. I'd help you find them but I'm stuck on the desk until eleven." She clicks again and the ancient printer next to the desk whirs to life. "As far as I can tell there were more books in the original donation, it's possible that they were too fragile for circulation or damaged. These twelve are what's out there, maybe the one you have is a second volume of something?" She hands Zachary the printed list of titles and authors and call numbers.

Her hypothesis is a good one and not something Zachary had considered. It would make sense. He looks over the titles but nothing jumps out as particularly meaningful or intriguing.

"You are an excellent library detective," he says. "Thank you for this."

"You're welcome," Elena says, picking up her Chandler again.

"Thank you for livening up my workday. Let me know if you have trouble finding anything."

Zachary starts in the familiar fiction section. He peruses the shelves under the unreliable lightbulbs, picking out the five fiction titles on the list in alphabetical order.

Appropriately, the first is a Sherlock Holmes novel. The second is *This Side of Paradise*. He's never heard of the next two, but they appear to be regular volumes, with proper copyright pages. The last is *Les Indes noires* by Jules Verne, in the original French and therefore misshelved. All appear to be regular, if old, editions. None of them seem to have anything in common with *Sweet Sorrows*.

Zachary tucks the pile of books under his arm and heads toward nonfiction. This part proves more difficult as he checks and rechecks call numbers and backtracks. Slowly he procures the other seven books, his enthusiasm waning as none of them resemble *Sweet Sorrows*. Most of them are astronomy- or cartography-related.

His last option brings him back near fiction to the myths. Bulfinch's *The Age of Fable, or Beauties of Mythology*. It looks new, as though it has never been read, despite bearing a date of 1899.

Zachary places the blue volume with its gilded detailing on his stack of books. The bust of Ares on the cover looks contemplative, his eyes downcast as though he shares Zachary's disappointment at not finding a clear companion for *Sweet Sorrows*.

He heads back upstairs to the almost empty reading rooms (a librarian with a cart organizing books, a student in a striped sweater typing at a laptop, a man who looks like he's probably a professor actually reading a Donna Tartt novel) and heads to the far corner of the room, spreading his books out on one of the larger tables.

Zachary methodically inspects each volume. He peers at endpapers and turns every page, looking for clues. He refrains from removing barcode stickers but none of them seem to be covering anything of importance, and he's not sure what another bee or key or sword would tell him, anyway.

After seven books with not so much as a dog-eared page, Zachary's eyes are strained. He needs a break and probably caffeine. He takes a notebook from his bag and writes a note he suspects will be unnecessary: *Back in 15 minutes, please do not reshelve.* He wonders if reshelve is actually a word and decides he doesn't care.

Zachary leaves the library and walks down to the corner café where he orders a double espresso and a lemon muffin. He finishes both and heads back to the library, passing a *Calvin and Hobbes*–worthy army of tiny snowmen he hadn't noticed before.

He returns to the reading room, even quieter now with only the librarian organizing her cart. Zachary takes off his coat and resumes his careful perusal of each book. The ninth volume he checks, the Fitzgerald, has occasional passages underlined in pencil but nothing obtuse, just the really good lines. The next two are unmarked and judging by the state of their spines, don't even appear to have been read.

Zachary reaches for the final volume and his hand lands on empty table. He looks back to the stack of books, thinking that he may have miscounted. But there are eleven books in that pile. He counts them again to be certain.

It takes him a moment to realize which is missing.

The Age of Fable, or Beauties of Mythology has vanished. The contemplative bust of Ares is nowhere to be seen. Zachary checks under the table and chairs, on nearby tables and on the closest bookshelves, but it is gone.

He walks back to the other side of the room where the librarian is shelving books.

"Did you happen to notice anyone take any books from that table over there while I was gone?" he asks.

The librarian looks and shakes her head.

"No," she says. "But I wasn't paying much attention either. A couple of people came in and out."

"Thanks," Zachary says and walks back to the table, sinking low into his chair.

Someone must have picked up the book and wandered off with it. Not that it matters, since eleven books told him nothing, the chances of the twelfth being a revelation were slim.

Though the chances of one of them vanishing into thin air probably weren't all that high, either.

Zachary takes the Sherlock Holmes and the Fitzgerald to check out and leaves the rest of the volumes on the table to be reshelved, which should be a word if it's not.

"No luck," he tells Elena as he passes the reserve desk.

"Bummer," she says. "If I encounter any other library mysteries I'll let you know."

"I'd appreciate that," Zachary says. "Hey, is it possible to find out if someone checked a book out in the last hour or so?"

"It is if you know the title. I'll meet you at the circulation desk and check for you. No one's come by all morning for reserves, if they do now they can wait five minutes."

"Thanks," Zachary says and heads out to the atrium while Elena ducks through a door into a librarian-exclusive passageway. She reappears behind the circulation desk before he even reaches it.

"Which book?" she asks, flexing her fingers over the keyboard.

"*The Age of Fable, or Beauties of Mythology,*" Zachary says. "Bulfinch."

"That's on the list, isn't it?" Elena says. "Could you not find it?"

"I did but I think someone picked it up while I wasn't looking," Zachary says, tired of book-related falsifications.

"This says we have two copies and neither one is checked out," Elena says, looking at the screen. "Oh, but one of those is an e-book. Anything that's out and about here should be shelved again by tomorrow morning. I can check those out for you, too."

"Thanks," Zachary says, handing her the books and his ID. He somehow doubts the book will be returning to its shelf anytime soon. "For everything, I mean. I appreciate it."

"Anytime," Elena says, handing his books back to him.

"And read some Hammett, please," Zachary adds. "Chandler's great but Hammett's better. He was an actual detective."

Elena laughs and one of the other librarians shushes her. Zachary gives her a wave as he leaves, relishing the librarian-on-librarian shushing.

Outside in the snow everything is crystal clear and too bright. Zachary heads back to his dorm, turning over in his mind the possibilities of what might have happened to the vanished book and not settling on anything.

He is relieved that he kept *Sweet Sorrows* in his bag today.

As he walks he thinks of something he hasn't tried yet and feels rather stupid about it. When he gets back to his room he drops his bag on the floor and heads straight for his computer.

He googles "Sweet Sorrows" first even though he expects what he gets: pages upon pages of Shakespeare quotes and bands and articles about sugar consumption. He searches for bees and keys and swords. The results are a mix of Arthurian legends and lists of items from *Resident Evil*. He attempts various combinations and finds a bee and a key on the coat of arms of a fictional magic school. He notes the name of the book and the author, curious as to whether or not the symbology is coincidental.

At several points in *Sweet Sorrows* the place is referred to as the Harbor on the Starless Sea, but a search for "Starless Sea" turns up little more than a Dungeon Crawl Classic that sounds appropriate but unrelated and Google suggests that perhaps he meant *Sunless* Sea either in reference to an upcoming video game or as a line from Samuel Taylor Coleridge's Kubla Khan poem.

Zachary sighs. He tries image searches and scrolls through page after page of cartoons and skeletons and dungeon masters and then something catches his eye.

He clicks the image to enlarge it.

The black-and-white photograph looks candid and not posed, maybe even cropped from a larger image. A woman in a mask, her head turned away from the camera, leaning in to listen to the man standing next to her who is also masked and wearing a tuxedo. There are several indistinguishable people around them, it looks like it might have been taken at a party.

Around the woman's neck is a series of three layered chains with a charm hanging from each one.

Zachary clicks the image again to view it full-size.

Hanging from the top chain is a bee.

Below it is a key.

Below the key is a sword.

Zachary clicks again to view the page the image came from, a post on a pinboard site asking if anyone knows where to buy the necklace.

But beneath that there is a source link for the photo.

Zachary clicks the link with a hand over his mouth and finds himself staring at a photo gallery.

Algonquin Hotel Annual Literary Masquerade, 2014.

Another click informs him that this year's event is three days away.

SWEET SORROWS

A knock upon the memory of a door.

There is a door in a forest that was not always a forest.

The door is no longer a door, not entirely. The structure that held it collapsed some time ago and the door fell along with it and now lies on the ground rather than standing upright.

The wood that composed it has rotted. Its hinges have rusted. Someone took its doorknob away.

The door remembers the time when it was complete. When there was a house with a roof and walls and other doors and people inside. There are leaves and birds and trees now but no people. Not for years and years.

So the girl comes as a surprise.

She is a small girl, too small to be wandering in the woods alone. But she is not lost.

A girl lost in the woods is a different sort of creature than a girl who walks purposefully through the trees even though she does not know her way.

This girl in the woods is not lost. She is exploring.

This girl is not scared. She is not unnerved by the darkness of the clawing shadows cast by the trees in the late-afternoon sun. She is not bothered by the thorns and branches that tug at her clothes and scratch at her skin.

She is young enough to carry fear with her without letting it into her heart. Without being scared. She wears her fear lightly, like a veil, aware that there are dangers but letting the crackling aware-ness hover around her. It does not sink in, it buzzes in excitement like a swarm of invisible bees.

The girl has been told many times not to wander too far into these woods. Warned not to play in them at all and she resents her explorations being dismissed as "play."

Today she has gone so far into the woods that she wonders if she has started going out of them again toward the other side. She is not concerned about finding her way back. She remembers spaces, they stick in her mind even when they are expansive ones filled with trees and rocks. Once she closed her eyes and spun around to prove to herself that she could pick the right direction when she opened them again and she was only wrong by a little bit and a little bit wrong is mostly right.

Today she finds rocks that might once have been a wall, clustered in a line. Those that are piled on each other do not reach very high, even in the highest places it would be easy to climb over them, but the girl picks a medium-high spot to tackle instead.

On the other side of the wall there are clinging vines that snake over the ground, making it difficult to walk so the girl explores closer to the wall instead. It is a more interesting spot than others she has found in the woods. Were the girl older she might recognize that there was once a structure here but she is not old enough to put the pieces of crumbling rock together in her mind and assemble them into a long-forgotten building. The hinge of the door stays buried beneath years of leaves near her left shoe. A candlestick hides between rocks and the shadows fall in such a way that even this intrepid explorer does not discover it.

It is getting dark, though enough of the now golden sun remains to light her way home if she climbs back over the wall and retraces her steps, but she does not. She is distracted by something on the ground.

Away from the wall there is another line of stones, set in an almost-circle. A most-of-an-oval shape. A fallen archway that might once have contained a door.

The girl picks up a stick and uses it to dig around the leaves in the middle of the arch of stones. The leaves crumble and break and reveal something round and metal.

She pushes more of the leaves out of the way with the stick and uncovers a curling ring about the size of her hand, which might once have been brass but has tarnished in mossy patterns of green and brown.

One side is attached to another piece of metal that remains buried.

The girl has only ever seen pictures of door knockers but she thinks this might be one even though most of the ones she has seen have lions biting the metal rings and this ring does not, unless the lion is hiding in the dirt.

She has always wanted to use a door knocker to knock upon a door and this one is on the ground and not in a picture.

This one she can reach.

She wraps her fingers around it, not caring how dirty they become in the process, and lifts it up. It is heavy.

She lets the knocker drop again. The result is a satisfying clang of metal on metal that echoes through the trees.

The door is delighted to be knocked upon after so long.

And the door—though it is mere pieces of what it once was—remembers where it used to lead. It remembers how to open.

So now, when a small explorer knocks, the remains of this door to the Starless Sea let her in.

The earth crumbles beneath her, pulling her into the ground feetfirst in a cascade of dirt and rocks and leaves.

The girl is too surprised to scream.

She is not afraid. She does not understand what is happening so her fear only buzzes excitedly around her as she falls.

When she lands she is all curiosity and scraped elbows and dirt-covered eyelashes. The lion-less door knocker rests bent and broken by her side.

The door is destroyed in the fall, too damaged to remember what it once was.

A tangle of vines and dirt obscures any evidence of what has occurred.

ZACHARY EZRA RAWLINS sits on a train bound for Manhattan, staring out the window at the frozen tundra of New England, and begins, not for the first time today, to question his life choices.

It is too conveniently timed a coincidence not to pursue, even for a tenuous, jewelry-based connection. He spent a day getting himself organized, procuring a rather expensive ticket to the party and an even more expensive hotel room across the street from the Algonquin which was completely booked. The ticket details included the dress code: formal, literary costumes encouraged, masks required.

Far too much time was wasted worrying over where to find a mask until he thought to text Kat. She had six of them, several involving feathers, but the one packed in his duffel bag with his carefully rolled suit is of the Zorro variety, black silk and surprisingly comfortable. ("I was the man in black from *The Princess Bride* for Halloween last year," Kat explained. "That's literary! Do you want my poufy black shirt, too?")

Zachary wonders if he should have left yesterday, as there is only one train per day and this one is supposed to get him to New York with a couple of hours to spare, but it is stopping frequently due to the weather.

He takes off his watch and shoves it in his pocket after glancing at it four times in the space of three minutes.

He is not sure why he is so anxious.

He is not entirely certain what he is going to do when he gets to the party.

He doesn't even really know what the woman in the photograph looks like. There's no way of knowing whether she will be there this year.

But it's the only bread crumb he has to follow.

Zachary takes his phone out of his coat and pulls up the copy of the photo he has saved and stares at it again even though he has already committed it to memory down to the disembodied hand in the corner holding a glass of sparkling wine.

The woman in the photo has her head turned to the side and her profile is mostly mask, but her body is facing the camera, the layered necklace with its golden bee and key and sword as clear and bright as stars against her black gown. The gown is slinky, the woman wearing it curvy and either tall or wearing very high heels, everything below her knees is obscured by a potted palm conspiring with her dress to pull her into the shadows. Her hair above the mask is dark and swept up in one of those styles that looks effortless but probably involves a great deal of construction. She could be twenty or forty or anywhere in between. For that matter the photo looks as though it could have been taken that many years ago, everything within the frame looks timeless.

The man at the woman's side wears a tuxedo, his arm is raised in a way that suggests his hand is resting on her arm but her shoulder conceals the rest of his sleeve. The ribbon of a mask is visible against his slightly greying hair but his face is completely obscured by her own. A sliver of neck and ear reveal that his complexion is much deeper than hers but little else. Zachary turns the phone in his hand trying to get a look at the man's face, momentarily oblivious to the futility of the action.

The train slows to a halt.

Zachary looks around. The train car is less than half full. Mostly solo passengers, each having claimed their own pair of seats. A group of four at the other end of the car is chatting, sometimes loudly, and Zachary regrets not bringing his headphones. The girl across from him has huge ones, between the headphones and her hoodie she's almost completely obscured, facing the window and probably asleep.

A static-punctuated announcement comes over the speaker, a variation on the one that has been relayed three times before. Stopped due to ice on the tracks. Waiting for it to be cleared. We apologize for the delay and will be moving again as soon as possible etcetera etcetera.

"Excuse me," a voice says. Zachary looks up. The middle-aged woman sitting in front of him has turned around over the high back of her seat to face him. "Do you happen to have a pen?" she asks. She wears several looping layers of colorful beaded necklaces and they jingle as she talks.

"I think so," Zachary says. He rummages around in his satchel and comes up first with a mechanical pencil but then tries again and finds one of the gel rollers that seem to procreate at the bottom of his bag. "Here you go," he says, handing it to the woman.

"Thank you, I'll just be a minute," the woman says and she jingles back out of sight behind her seat.

The train begins to move and travels enough that the snow and trees outside the windows are replaced by different snow and different trees before it slows to a stop again.

Zachary takes *The Little Stranger* out of his bag and starts to read, trying to forget where he is and who he is and what he's doing for a little while.

The announcement that they have reached Manhattan comes as a surprise, pulling Zachary from his reading.

The other occupants are already gathering their luggage. The girl with the headphones is gone.

"Thank you for this," the woman in front of him says as he slings his satchel over his shoulder and picks up his duffel bag. She gives him back his pen. "You're a lifesaver."

"You're welcome," Zachary says, putting the pen back in his bag. He falls into line with the passengers impatiently making their way off the train.

Exiting onto the street from Penn Station is overwhelming and disorienting, but Zachary has always found Manhattan to be disorienting and overwhelming in general. So much energy and people and stuff in such a small footprint. There is less snow here, clumped in gutters in miniature mountains of grey ice.

He reaches Forty-Fourth Street with two hours left before the party. The Algonquin appears quiet but it is difficult to tell from the outside. He nearly misses the entrance to his own hotel across the street and then wanders through a sunken lobby lounge and past a glass-walled fireplace before locating the front desk. He checks in without incident, flinching as he hands over his credit card even though he has more than enough to cover the total from years upon years of large birthday checks sent in lieu of visits from his father. The desk clerk promises to send a clothes steamer up to his room so he can attempt to undo whatever damage his bag has unleashed on his suit.

The windowless upstairs hallways are submarine-like. His room is more mirrored than any hotel room he has ever stayed in before. Floor-to-ceiling mirrors across from the bed and on both walls in the bathroom make the small space seem larger but they also make him feel as though he's not alone.

The steamer arrives, dropped off by a bellhop who he forgets to tip but it's too early to prep his suit so Zachary distracts himself with the gigantic round bathtub, even though the mirror-bathtub Zacharys are disturbing. Bathtub opportunities are few and far between. His dorm has a less-than-private row of showers and the claw-foot tub at his mother's Hudson River Valley farmhouse always looks appealing but refuses to keep water warm for longer than seven minutes at a time. There is, strangely, a single taper candle in the bathroom complete with a box of matches, which is an interesting touch. Zachary lights it and the one flame becomes many within the mirrors.

Somewhere mid-bath he admits to himself that if this excursion proves unsuccessful he will give up on the entire endeavor. Return *Sweet Sorrows* to the library and try to forget about it and turn his attention back to his thesis. Maybe visit his mom on his way back to school for an aura cleansing and a bottle of wine.

Maybe his story began and ended that day in that alleyway. Maybe his story is about missed opportunities that cannot be recaptured.

He closes his eyes, blocking out the mirror Zacharys.

He sees those two words again in their serifed typeface.

Not yet.

He wonders why he believes it because someone wrote it down in a book. Why he believes anything at all and where to draw mental lines, where to stop suspending his disbelief. Does he believe that the boy in the book is him? Well, yes. Does he believe painted doors on walls can open as though they were real and lead to other places entirely?

He sighs and sinks below the surface, remaining under until he has to return for oxygen-related reasons.

Zachary gets out of the tub before the water has cooled, a decadent bathtub miracle. The fluffy hotel robe makes him think he should stay in fancy hotels more often and then he remembers how much this single night cost him and decides to enjoy it while he can and avoid the minibar.

A muffled ding from his bag signals a text message: a photo from Kat of a half-finished blue-and-bronze-striped scarf with accompanying text that reads *almost done!*

He texts back *Looks great! Thanks again, see you soon* and starts steaming his suit. It doesn't take much time though his shirt proves to be a bigger problem and he gives up after a few passes, figuring he'll leave his jacket or his vest on for the entire evening so the back of the shirt can remain unpresentable.

Mirror Zachary looks downright dashing and regular Zachary wonders if the lighting and the mirrors are in an attractiveness conspiracy with each other. He forgets what he looks like without his glasses, he so rarely wears his contact lenses.

It's not a specifically literary costume, but even without the mask he feels like a character in his black suit with its near-invisible pinstripes. He bought the suit two years ago and hasn't worn it much but it's well-tailored and fits properly. It looks better now, paired with a charcoal shirt instead of the white one he's worn it with before.

He leaves his hat and gloves and scarf, considering he's only going across the street, and keeps his mask in his pocket along with a printout of his ticket even though it implied he could give his name at the door. He brings his wallet but leaves his phone, not wanting to take his everyday world along.

Zachary takes *Sweet Sorrows* from his bag and puts it in the pocket of his coat and then switches it to the inside pocket of his suit jacket where it is just small enough to fit. Perhaps the book will act like some sort of beacon and draw whatever or whoever it is he's looking for to him.

He believes in books, he thinks as he leaves the room. That much he knows for sure.

SWEET SORROWS

Those who seek and those who find.

There is a door in the back of a teahouse. A pile of crates blocks it and the common thought amongst the staff is that the door leads to a disused closet that is likely occupied by mice. Late one night a new assistant attempting to make herself useful will open it to see if the crates will fit inside and she will discover that it is not a storage closet at all.

There is a door at the bottom of a star-covered sea, resting in the ruins of a sunken city. On one dark-as-night day a diver armed with portable breath and light will find this door and open it and slip into a pocket of air along with a number of very confused fish.

There is a door in a desert, covered in sand. Its worn stone surface loses its detail in sandstorms as the time passes. Eventually it will be excavated and relocated to a museum without ever being opened.

There are numerous doors in varying locations. In bustling cities and remote forests. On islands and on mountaintops and in meadows. Some are built into buildings: libraries or museums or private residences, hidden in basements or attics or displayed like artwork in front parlors. Others stand freely without the assistance of supplemental architecture. Some are used with hinge-loosening frequency and others remain undiscovered and unopened and more have simply been forgotten, but all of them lead to the same location.

(How this is accomplished is a matter of much debate and no one has of yet discovered a satisfying answer. There is much disagreement on this and related subjects, including the precise location of the space. Some will argue passionately for one continent or another but such arguments often result in impasses or admissions that perhaps the space itself moves, the stone and the sea and the books shifting beneath the surface of the earth.)

Each door will lead to a Harbor on the Starless Sea, if someone dares to open it.

Little distinguishes them from regular doors. Some are simple. Others are elaborately decorated. Most have doorknobs waiting to be turned though others have handles to be pulled.

These doors will sing. Silent siren songs for those who seek what lies behind them.

For those who feel homesick for a place they've never been to.

Those who seek even if they do not know what (or where) it is that they are seeking.

Those who seek will find.

Their doors have been waiting for them.

But what happens next will vary.

Sometimes, someone finds a door and opens it and peers inside only to close it again.

Others when faced with a door will leave it undisturbed, even if their curiosity is piqued. They think they need permission. They believe the door awaits someone else, even if it is in fact waiting for them.

Some will find a door and open it and pass through to see where it leads.

Once there they wander through the stone halls, finding things to look at and things to touch and things to read. They find stories tucked in hidden corners and laid out on tables, as though they had been there always, waiting for their reader to arrive.

Each visitor will find something or someplace or someone that catches their fancy. A book or a conversation or a comfortable chair in a well-curated alcove. Someone will bring them a drink.

They will lose track of time.

Occasionally a visitor will become overwhelmed, disoriented, and dazed by all there is to explore, the space closing around their lungs and their heart and their thoughts, and they will find their way back before much time has passed, back to the familiar surface

THE STARLESS SEA   63

and the familiar stars and the familiar air, and most will forget that such a place exists, much less that they set foot in it themselves. It will fade like a dream. They will not open their door again. They may forget there was a door at all.

But such reactions are rare.

Most who find the space have sought it, even if they never knew that this place was what they had been seeking.

And they will choose to stay awhile.

Hours or days or weeks. Some will leave and return, keeping the place as an escape, a retreat, a sanctuary. Living lives both above and below.

A few have built their residences on the surface around their doors, keeping them close and protected and preventing others from utilizing them.

Others, once they have passed through their respective door, wish never to return to whatever it was that they left. The lives they left behind become the dreams, waiting not to be returned to but to be forgotten.

These people stay and take up residency and these are the ones who begin to shape what the space will become while they inhabit it.

They live and they work. They consume art and stories and create new art and new stories to add to the shelves and the walls. They find friends and lovers. They put on performances and play games and weave community out of camaraderie.

They throw elaborate festivals and parties. Occasional visitors return for such events, swelling the general population, enlivening even the quieter halls. Music and merriment ring through the ballrooms and the far corners. Bare feet are dipped in the Starless Sea by those who descend to its shores, emboldened by giddiness and wine.

Even those who keep to their private chambers and their books emerge from their solitude on such occasions, and some are persuaded to join the revelry while others content themselves with observation.

Time will pass unmeasured in dancing and delights and then

those who choose to leave will begin to find their way to the egress, to be taken back to their respective doors.

They will say their goodbyes to the ones who remain.

The ones who have found their haven in this Harbor.

They have sought and they have found and here they choose to remain, whether they choose a path of dedication or simply a permanent residency.

They live and they work and they play and they love and if they ever miss the world above they rarely admit it.

This is their world, starless and sacred.

They think it impervious. Impenetrable and eternal.

Yet all things change in time.

ZACHARY EZRA RAWLINS arrives at the Algonquin approximately four minutes after he leaves his hotel room. It would have taken even less time if he hadn't had to wait first for the elevator and then for a cab to pass by on the street.

The party is not quite in full swing but already lively. A line of people waiting to check in crowds the lobby. The hotel is a more classic style than the one Zachary is staying in and feels particularly old-fashioned with the formally dressed crowd, rich dark wood, and potted palms artfully but dimly lit.

Zachary puts on his mask while he waits in line. A woman in a black dress hands out white masks to guests who have not brought their own and Zachary is glad that he did, the white ones are plastic and do not look particularly comfortable, though the effect of them scattered around the room is striking.

He gives his name to the woman at the desk. She does not ask to see his ticket and he tucks it in the pocket of his suit jacket. He checks his coat. He is given a paper wristband that looks like the spine of a book, printed with the date instead of a title. He is informed about the bar (open, tips appreciated) and then he is set free and does not know what to do with himself.

Zachary wanders the party like a ghost, grateful for the mask that allows him to hide in plain sight.

In some respects it is like any number of dressy parties, with chatter and clinking glasses and music that bubbles up from beneath the conversations, carrying the rhythm of everything along with it. Party-goers draped over armchairs and milling in corners in one room, a fairly well-occupied dance floor in another where the music takes over the conversation and insists upon being heard. A party scene from a movie, though a movie that can't quite settle on issues of time period or hem length. There is an undertone of awkwardness that Zachary recalls from weddings with a majority of unacquainted guests, and in his experience it fades as the evening and the alcohol progress.

In other respects, this particular party is unlike anything he's ever experienced. The bar off the main room is lit entirely in blue. There are not a great number of obvious literary costumes, but there are scarlet letters and dictionary-page fairy wings and an Edgar Allan Poe with a fake raven on his shoulder. A picture-perfect Daisy Buchanan sips a martini at the bar. A woman in a little black dress has Emily Dickinson poems printed on her stockings. A man in a suit has a towel draped over his shoulder. A number of people could easily fit into works by Austen or Dickens.

Someone in the corner is dressed as a highly recognizable author or, Zachary thinks as he gets a closer look, it might actually be that highly recognizable author and Zachary has a panicked realization that some of the people who write the books on his bookshelves are actual people who go to parties.

His favorite costume is worn by a woman in a long white gown and a simple gold crown, a reference he can't quite place until she turns around and the gown's draped back includes a pointed pair of ears hanging from a hood and a tail trailing along with the train. He remembers dressing as Max from *Where the Wild Things Are* himself when he was five, though his costume was nowhere near as elegant.

Zachary looks for golden necklaces but finds none with bees or keys or swords. The only key he spots is rigged to appear as though it is disappearing into the back of someone's neck, but that key he recognizes as a clever comic-book reference.

He finds himself wishing the proper people to talk to would light up or have hovering indicator arrows over their heads or dialogue options to choose from. He doesn't always wish that real life were more like video games, but in certain situations it would be helpful. Go here. Talk to this person. Feel like you're making progress even though you don't know what it is you're trying to do, exactly.

He is increasingly distracted by the details when he should be focusing on jewelry. He orders one of the literary cocktail creations at the bar, a Drowning Ophelia made with gin and lemon and fennel syrup, served with a spring of rosemary and a napkin with an appropriate *Hamlet* quote printed on it. Other guests sip Hemingway Daiquiris and Vespers garnished with complicated curls of lemon. Flutes of sparkling wine are served with ribbons that read "Drink Me" wrapped around their stems.

Bowls on tables are filled with escaped typewriter keys. Candles illuminate glass holders wrapped in book pages. One hallway is festooned with writing implements (fountain pens, pencils, quills) hanging from the ceiling at various heights.

A woman in a beaded gown and matching mask sits in a corner at a typewriter, tapping out tiny stories on scraps of paper and giving them to guests that pass by. The one she hands to Zachary reads like a long-form fortune cookie:

He wanders alone but safe in his loneliness.
Confused but comforted by his confusion.
A blanket of bewilderment to hide himself under.

He hasn't managed to escape attention, even pretending to be the ghost at the feast. He wonders if the masks make people braver, more likely to strike up conversations with the hint of anonymity. Other wandering ghosts approach with remarks about the drinks and the atmosphere. Sharing typewriter stories is a popular conversation starter and he gets to read a few different tales, including one about a stargazing hedgehog and another about a house built over a stream with the sound of the water echoing through the rooms. He overhears someone mention that there are people doing private storytelling sessions in other rooms but speaks to no one who has yet been on the receiving end of one. He gets confirmation that yes, it is indeed that famous author across the room and by the way there's another one just over there that he hadn't even noticed.

In the blue-tinged bar he finds himself conversing about cocktails with a man in a suit wearing one of the house-provided masks and a Hello, My Name Is tag with "Godot" written on it stuck to his lapel.

Zachary notes the name of a Godot-recommended bourbon on the back of his printed-out ticket.

"Excuse me," a lady in an oddly childlike pale blue dress and white knee socks says and then Zachary realizes that she's talking to him. "Have you seen the cat around here by any chance?" she asks.

"The cat?" Zachary guesses her to be a brunette Alice of the Wonderland variety until she is joined by another lady in an identical ensemble and then it is obvious, if slightly disconcerting, that they are the twins from *The Shining*.

"The hotel has a resident cat," the first twin explains. "We've been looking for her all night but so far no luck."

"Help us look?" her doppelgänger asks and Zachary agrees even though it sounds like a potentially ominous invitation given their appearance.

They decide to split up to cover more ground and Zachary wanders back near the dance floor, pausing to listen to the jazz band, trying to place the familiar-sounding piece of music.

He peers into the shadows behind the band even though he thinks it unlikely that a cat would hang around with all the noise.

Someone taps him on the shoulder.

The woman dressed as Max, taller than he expected with her crown, stands behind him.

"Would you like to dance?" she asks.

Say something suave, a voice in Zachary's head commands.

"Sure," is what his mouth comes up with, and the voice inside his head throws up its arms in disappointment, but the king of the wild things doesn't seem to mind.

The details of her costume are even more impressive up close. Her gold mask matches her crown, both cut from leather in simple shapes and treated with a rich metallic finish. Beneath the mask her eyes are lined with gold and even her eyelashes sparkle with the same golden glitter sprinkled throughout her upswept dark hair that Zachary now suspects might be a wig. White buttons lining the front of her gown are practically invisible against the fabric, secured with gold thread.

Her perfume is even perfectly suited to the costume, an earthy blend that somehow smells like dirt and sugar at the same time.

After a minute of silent not quite awkward dancing, once Zachary has remembered how to lead and found the rhythm of the song (some jazz standard he recognizes but couldn't name), he decides he should probably say something, and after mentally grasping for ideas he settles on the first thing he thought when he saw her earlier.

"Your Max costume is far superior to my Max costume," he says. "I'm relieved I didn't wear mine, it would have been embarrassing."

The woman smiles, the type of knowing almost smirk Zachary associates with classic film stars.

"You wouldn't believe how many people have asked who I'm supposed to be," she says, with a clear hint of disappointment.

"They should read more," Zachary responds, echoing her tone.

"You are yourself with a mask on, aren't you?" the woman asks, dropping her voice.

"More or less," Zachary answers.

The king of the wild things who might possibly be wearing a wig smiles at him. A real smile this time.

"More, I think," she says after considering him. "What brings you here this evening, beyond fondness for literature and cocktails? You seem like you're looking for someone."

"Sort of," Zachary admits. He'd almost forgotten. "But I don't think they're here."

He pulls her into a turn mostly to avoid bumping into another couple but the flutter of her gown makes the move look so impressive that several people nearby pause to watch them.

"That's a shame," the woman says. "They have deprived themselves of a lovely party and lovely company, I think."

"Also I was looking for the cat," Zachary adds. The woman's smile brightens.

"Ah, I saw Matilda earlier in the evening but I don't know where she went off to. It is sometimes more effective to let her find you, in my experience." She pauses but then adds, in a wistful whisper: "How lovely to be a hotel cat. We should all be so lucky."

"What brings you here tonight?" Zachary asks her. The music has changed and he loses his footing momentarily and thankfully recovers without stepping on her feet.

But before the woman can answer, something beyond Zachary's right shoulder catches her eye. She stiffens, a shift he can feel more than see, and he thinks perhaps this is a woman who is good at wearing many different kinds of masks.

"Excuse me for a moment," she says. She rests a hand on Zachary's lapel and someone to the side snaps a photograph. The woman starts to turn away but then stops and bows at Zachary first, or something between a curtsey and a bow that seems at once formal and silly, especially since she is the one with the crown. Zachary returns the gesture as best he can and as she disappears into the crowd someone nearby applauds, as if they were part of a performance.

The photographer comes up and asks him for their names. Zachary decides to request that they simply be listed as guests if the photos are posted anywhere and the photographer reluctantly agrees.

Zachary wanders the lobby again, more slowly due to the tighter crowd, a growing disappointment tugging at him. He looks again for jewelry, for bees or keys or swords. For a sign. He should have worn them himself, or drawn them on his hand or found a bee-patterned pocket square. He does not know why he ever thought he could find a single stranger in a room filled with them.

Zachary looks for anyone he has talked to already, thinking perhaps he could inquire nonchalantly about . . . he's not sure what anymore. He can't even find his Max in the crowd. He encounters a particularly dense knot of partygoers (one in impressive green silk pajamas holding a rose in a glass cloche) and ducks behind a column, moving closer to the wall to get around them, but as he does someone in the crowd grabs his hand and pulls him through a doorway.

The door closes behind them, muffling the party chatter and cutting off the light.

Someone else is in the darkness with him, the hand that pulled him in has released him but someone is standing close by. Taller, maybe. Breathing softly. Smelling of lemon and leather and something that Zachary can't identify but finds extremely appealing.

Then a voice whispers in his ear.

"Once, very long ago, Time fell in love with Fate."

A male voice. The tone deep but the cadence light, a storyteller voice. Zachary freezes, waiting. Listening.

"This, as you might imagine, proved problematic," the voice continues. "Their romance disrupted the flow of time. It tangled the strings of fortune into knots."

A hand on his back pushes him gently forward and Zachary takes a tentative step into the darkness, and then another. The storyteller continues, the volume of his voice now loud enough to fill the space.

"The stars watched from the heavens nervously, worrying what might occur. What might happen to the days and nights were Time to suffer a broken heart? What catastrophes might result if the same fate awaited Fate itself?"

They continue walking down a dark hall.

"The stars conspired and separated the two. For a while they breathed easier in the heavens. Time continued to flow as it always had, or perhaps imperceptibly slower. Fate wove together the paths that were meant to intertwine, though perhaps a string was missed here and there."

Now a turn, as Zachary is guided in a different direction through the darkness. In the pause he can hear the band and the party, the sound muffled and distant.

"But eventually," the storyteller continues, "Fate and Time found each other again."

A firm hand on Zachary's shoulder halts their movement. The storyteller leans closer.

"In the heavens, the stars sighed, twinkling and fretting. They asked the moon her advice. The moon in turn called upon the parliament of owls to decide how best to proceed."

Somewhere in the darkness the sound of wings beating, close and heavy, moving the air around them.

"The parliament of owls convened and discussed the matter amongst themselves night after night. They argued and debated while the world slept around them, and the world continued to turn, unaware that such important matters were under discussion while it slumbered."

In the darkness a hand guides Zachary's own to a doorknob. Zachary turns it and the door opens. In front of him he thinks he sees a sliver of a crescent moon and then it vanishes.

"The parliament of owls came to the logical conclusion that if the problem was in the combination, one of the elements should be removed. They chose to keep the one they felt more important."

A hand pushes Zachary forward. A door closes behind him. He wonders if he has been left alone but then the story continues, the voice moving around him in the darkness.

"The parliament of owls told their decision to the stars and the stars agreed. The moon did not, but on this night she was dark and could not offer her opinion."

Here Zachary remembers, vividly, the moon disappearing in front of his eyes a moment before as the story continues.

"So it was decided, and Fate was pulled apart. Ripped into pieces by beaks and claws. Fate's screams echoed through the deepest corners and the highest heavens but no one dared to intervene save for a small brave mouse who snuck into the fray, creeping unnoticed through the blood and bone and feathers, and took Fate's heart and kept it safe."

Now a mouselike movement scurries up Zachary's arm and over his shoulder. He shivers. The movement stops over his heart and the weight of a hand rests there a moment before lifting again. A long pause follows.

"When the furor died down there was nothing else left of Fate."

A gloved hand settles over Zachary's eyes, the darkness grows warmer and darker, the voice closer now.

"The owl who consumed Fate's eyes gained great sight, greater sight than any that had been granted to a mortal creature before. The parliament crowned him the Owl King."

The hand remains over Zachary's eyes but another rests briefly on the top of his head, a momentary weight.

"In the heavens the stars sparkled with relief but the moon was full of sorrow."

Another pause here. A long one, and in the silence Zachary can hear his breathing along with the storyteller's. The hand does not leave his eyes. The scent of leather mingles with lemon and tobacco and sweat. He is beginning to get nervous when the story continues.

"And so Time goes on as it should and events that were once fated to happen are left instead to chance, and Chance never falls in love with anything for long."

The storyteller guides Zachary to the right, moving him forward again.

"But the world is strange and endings are not truly endings no matter how the stars might wish it so."

Here they stop.

"Occasionally Fate can pull itself together again."

The sound of a door opening in front of him, and Zachary is guided forward again.

"And Time is always waiting," the voice whispers, a warm breath against Zachary's neck.

The hand that had been covering Zachary's eyes lifts and a door clicks shut behind him. Blinking against the light, his heart pounding in his ears, he looks around to find himself back in the hotel lobby, in a corner half hidden by a potted palm.

The door behind him is locked.

Something hits his ankle and he looks down to find a fluffy grey-and-white cat rubbing its head against his leg.

He reaches down to pet it and only then does Zachary realize that his hands are shaking. The cat does not appear to mind. She stays with him for a moment and then walks off into the shadows.

Zachary heads back to the bar, still deep in story daze. He tries to remember if he has heard this particular tale before but he cannot despite the fact that it feels familiar, like a myth he read somewhere and subsequently forgot. The bartender mixes him another Drowning Ophelia but apologizes as they've run out of the fennel syrup. He has substituted honey and added a prosecco float. It's better with the honey.

Zachary looks around for the woman dressed as Max but he cannot find her.

He sits at the bar, feeling like a failure and yet overwhelmed by all that has happened as he attempts to catalogue the entire evening. *Drank rosemary for remembrance. Looked for a cat. Danced with the king of the wild things. Excellent-smelling man told me a story in the dark. Cat found me.*

He tries to remember the name of the bourbon that Godot had mentioned earlier and pulls his ticket from his jacket pocket.

As he does, a rectangle of paper the size of a business card falls from his pocket and flutters to the floor.

Zachary picks it up, trying to recall if anyone he had spoken to had given him a card.

But it is not a business card. It contains two lines of handwritten text.

Patience & Fortitude
1 a.m. Bring a flower.

Zachary checks his watch: 12:42.
He turns the card over.
On the back is a bee.

SWEET SORROWS
There are three paths. This is one of them.

As long as there have been bees, there have been keepers.

They say that there was one keeper in the beginning but as the stories multiplied there was a need for more.

The keepers were here before the acolytes, before the guardians.

Before the keepers there were the bees and the stories. Buzzing and humming.

There were keepers before there were keys.

A fact usually forgotten, as they are so synonymous with keys.

It is also a forgotten fact that once there was a single key. A long, thin key made of iron, its bow dipped in gold.

Many copies of it, but a solitary master. The copies worn on chains around each keeper's neck. Falling so often against their chests that many wore the impression of the key imbedded in their flesh, metal wearing against skin.

This is the origin of a tradition. No one remembers this now. A mark on a chest arising as an idea because of a mark on a chest. Obvious until it is forgotten.

The role of the keepers has changed over time, more than any of the other paths. Acolytes light their candles. Guardians move unseen and alert.

Keepers once kept only their bees and their stories.

As the space grew larger they kept rooms, dividing stories by type or by length or by unknown whim. Carving shelves for books into rock or building racks of metal or cabinets of glass and tables for the larger volumes. Chairs and pillows for reading and lamps to read by. Adding more rooms as they were needed, round rooms with fires at the center for telling stories aloud. Cavernous rooms with excellent acoustics for performing stories in dance or song. Rooms to repair books, rooms to write books, empty rooms to be used for whatever purposes might arise.

The keepers made doors for the rooms and keys to open them or keep them closed. The same key for every door, at first.

More doors led to more keys. At one time a keeper could identify every door, every room, every book, now they could not. So they acquired individual sections. Wings. Levels. One keeper might not ever meet all the other keepers. They move in circles around each other, sometimes intersecting, sometimes not.

They burned their keys into their chests so that they might be known as keepers at all times. To be reminded that they have a responsibility even if their key (or keys) hang on a hook on a wall and not around their necks.

How one becomes a keeper has also changed.

In the beginning they were chosen and raised as keepers. Born in the Harbor or brought there as infants too young to remember the sky even as a dream. Taught from a tiny age about the books and the bees and given wooden toy keys to play with.

After a time it was decided that the path, like the one of the acolytes, should be voluntary. Unlike the acolytes, the volunteers are put through a training period. If they wish to volunteer after the first training period, they enter a second. After the second, the remainder go through a third.

This is the third period of training.

The potential keeper must pick a story. Any story they please. A fairy tale or a myth or an anecdote about a late night and too many bottles of wine, as long as it is not a story of their own.

(Many who believe at first that they wish to be keepers in truth are poets.)

They study their story for a year.

They must learn it by memory. By more than memory, they must learn it by heart. Not so that they can simply recite the words but so that they feel them, the shape of the story as it changes and lifts and falls and rushes or meanders toward its climax. So that they can recall and relate the story as intimately as if they have lived it themselves and as objectively as if they have played every role within.

After the year of study they are brought to a round room with a single door. Two plain wooden chairs wait in the center, facing each other.

Candles dot the curved wall like stars, glowing from sconces set at irregular heights.

Every bit of the wall that is not occupied by a candle or voided by the door is covered in keys. They stretch from the floor over the wall and continue unseen past the highest candles into the shadows above. Long brass keys and short silver ones, keys with complicated teeth and keys with elaborate decorative heads. Many are ancient and tarnished but as a collection they shimmer and sparkle in the candlelight.

There is a copy here of every key in the Harbor. If one is needed another is made to take its place so that none are ever lost.

The only key that does not have a twin hanging in this room is the key that opens the door in its wall.

It is a distracting room. It is meant to be.

The potential keeper is brought to the room and asked to sit.

(Most choose the chair facing the door. Those who choose to face away from the door almost always perform better.)

They are left alone for anywhere from a few minutes to an hour.

Then someone enters the room and sits in the chair opposite them.

And then they tell their story.

They may tell their story however they wish. They may not leave the room and they may not bring anything but themselves into it. No props, no paper to read from.

They do not have to remain in their chair, though their singular audience must.

Some will sit and recite, allowing their voice to do the work.

More animated storytelling can involve anything from standing on the chair to pacing the room.

A potential keeper once stood, walked around to the back of her audience's chair, leaned in, and whispered the entire story into their ear.

One sang his story, a long, involved tale that moved from sweet and soft and melodic to howling pain and back again.

Another, using her own chair for assistance, extinguished each candle as her story progressed, finishing the terrifying tale in darkness.

When the story is complete the audience departs.

The potential keeper remains alone in the room for anywhere from a few minutes to an hour.

A keeper will come to them then. Some will be thanked for their work and their service and dismissed.

For the rest, the keeper will ask the potential keeper to choose a key from the wall. Any key they please.

The keys are not labeled. The choice is made by feel, by instinct, or by fancy.

The key is accepted and the potential keeper returns to their seat. They are blindfolded.

Their chosen key is taken and heated in flame and then it is pressed into the new keeper's chest. Creating a scarred impression approximately where it might have lain if they had worn it on a chain around their neck.

In the darkness the keeper will see themselves inside the room their chosen key unlocks. And as the sharpness of the pain fades they will begin to see all the rooms. All the doors. All the keys. All the things they keep.

Those who are made keepers are not made keepers because they are organized, because they are mechanically minded or devoted or deemed more worthy than others. Devotion is for acolytes. Worthiness for guardians. Keepers must have spirit and keep it aloft.

They are made keepers because they understand why we are here.

Why it matters.

Because they understand the stories.

They feel the buzzing of the bees in their veins.

But that was before.

Now there is only one.

ZACHARY EZRA RAWLINS checks his watch three times while he waits to retrieve his coat from the coat check. He reads the note again. *Patience & Fortitude. 1 a.m. Bring a flower.*

He is ninety-four percent certain that Patience and Fortitude are the names of the lions outside the New York Public Library, only a few blocks away. The six percent uncertainty is not enough to be worth considering alternate possibilities and the minutes insist on ticking by at a much quicker pace than they seemed to be earlier.

"Thank you," he says to the girl who brings him his coat, too enthusiastically judging by the look on her face which is readable even with her mask obscuring part of it, but Zachary is already halfway to the door.

He pauses, remembering the note's single instruction, and pulls a flower from an arrangement near the door as surreptitiously as he can manage. It is a paper flower, its petals cut from book pages, but it is, technically, a flower. It will have to do.

He takes off his mask before he goes outside, shoving it into the pocket of his coat. His face feels strange without it.

The air outside hits him like a frozen wall and then something harder hits, knocking Zachary to the ground.

"Oh, I'm so sorry!" a voice above him says. Zachary looks up, blinking, his eyes stinging from the cold and his post-cocktail vision insisting that he is being addressed by a very polite polar bear.

As he blinks more the polar bear loses some but not all of its fuzziness, transforming into a white-haired woman in an equally white fur coat offering him a white-gloved hand.

Zachary accepts and lets the polar-bear woman help him to his feet.

"You poor dear," she says, brushing dirt off his coat, the white gloves fluttering over his shoulders and his lapels and somehow remaining clean themselves. The woman gives him a red lipstick frown. "Are you all right? I wasn't even looking where I was walking, silly me."

"I'm fine," Zachary says, ice clinging to his trousers and a dull ache in his shoulder. "Are you all right?" he asks, even though neither the woman nor her coat seem to have a hair out of place, and both now appear more silver than white.

"I am uninjured and unobservant as well," the woman says, her gloves fluttering again. "I've not had a man fall at my feet in some time regardless of the circumstances, my dear, so thank you for that."

"You're welcome," Zachary says, his smile automatic as the pain in his shoulder recedes. He almost asks the woman if she has been at the party but he is too concerned about the minutes ticking by. "Have a lovely evening," he says, leaving her in the pool of light under the hotel awning and continuing down the street.

He checks his watch again as he turns at the corner onto Fifth Avenue. He has a few minutes left.

As he closes the distance between himself and the library, listening to the cabs rushing over the damp pavement, his autopilot starts to falter. His hands are freezing. He looks down at the now somewhat squashed paper flower in his hand. He gives it a closer inspection to see if he can guess what book the petals are made from but the text is in Italian.

Zachary's pace slows as he approaches the library steps. Despite the late hour there are a handful of people milling around. A cluster of black coats laughs and chatters as they wait for the light to change to cross the street. A couple kisses against a low stone wall. The stairs themselves are empty and the library is closed but the lions remain at their posts.

Zachary passes one lion he assumes is Fortitude and stops near the center of the steps, halfway between the lions. He looks at his watch: 1:02 a.m.

Did he miss his meeting, if it even is a meeting, or does he have to wait?

Should have brought a book, he thinks as he always does while waiting somewhere without one before he remembers and reaches into his jacket.

But *Sweet Sorrows* is no longer in his pocket.

Zachary looks through all of his pockets to be certain but the book is gone.

"Looking for this?" someone asks from behind him.

Standing on the library stairs a few steps above him there is a man wearing a peacoat, the collar turned up around a heavy wool scarf. His dark hair is greying at the temples, framing a face that would be called handsome if the word *rugged* or *unconventionally* were attached to it. He wears black dress pants and shiny shoes but Zachary cannot remember seeing him at the party.

In one of his black-gloved hands he holds *Sweet Sorrows*.

"You took that from me," Zachary says.

"No, someone else took it from you and I took it from them," the man explains, walking down the stairs and stopping next to Zachary. "You're welcome."

The hairs on the back of Zachary's neck recognize the voice before the rest of him does. This man is his storyteller.

"There are people following you who want this book," the man continues. "They currently believe they have this book. What we have now is a window of time where they will not follow you, a window that will close in approximately half an hour when they realize that this has gone missing. Again. Come with me."

The man puts *Sweet Sorrows* in his coat and starts walking, passing by Patience and turning south. He doesn't look back. Zachary hesitates and then follows.

"Who are you?" Zachary asks when he catches up with the man at the street corner.

"You can call me Dorian," the man says.

"Is that your name?"

"Does it matter?"

They cross the street in silence.

"So what's the flower for?" Zachary asks, holding up the paper-petaled blossom between fingers near-numb from the cold.

"I wanted to see if you'd follow instructions," Dorian answers.

"Passable, though that's not an actual flower. At least you're good at improvising."

Dorian takes the flower from Zachary, gives it a little twirl, and tucks it in a buttonhole on his coat.

Zachary shoves his freezing hands into his pockets.

"You haven't even asked who I am," he notes, confused as to how someone can be so intriguing and yet annoying at the same time.

"You are Zachary Ezra Rawlins. Zachary, never Zack. Born March eleventh, nineteen ninety, in New Orleans, Louisiana. Relocated to upstate New York in two thousand four with your mother shortly after your parents divorced. You've been attending university in Vermont for the last five-and-a-half years, currently working on a thesis on gender and narrative in modern gaming. You have a very high GPA. You're an introvert with minor anxiety issues, there are several people you are friendly with but no truly close friends. You've been in two serious romantic relationships and both ended badly. Earlier this week you checked a book out of a library and subsequently the book in question was indexed in a computer system making it traceable and since then the book, and you along with it, have been followed. You aren't that difficult to follow but additionally they're mapping your phone and they planted a tracking device on you that you fortunately left at your hotel. You like well-crafted cocktails and fair-trade cocoa and you probably should have worn a scarf. I know who you are."

"You forgot I'm a Pisces," Zachary says through gritted teeth.

"I thought that was implied with the inclusion of your birth date," Dorian says with a small shrug. "I'm a Taurus, if we get through this I should ask your mother to do my chart."

"What do you know about my mother?" Zachary asks, exasperated. He rushes to keep up with Dorian's pace and each intersection they reach brings a fresh blast of freezing air that cuts through his coat. He has stopped checking street signs but believes they are moving southeast.

"Madame Love Rawlins, spiritual adviser," Dorian says as they turn again. "Only lived in Haiti until she was four but affects the accent sometimes because the customers tend to like it. Specializes in psychometry and dabbles in tarot and tea leaves. You lived above her store in New Orleans. That's where the door that you didn't open was, right?"

Zachary wonders how he could possibly know about the door but then the simple answer dawns on him.

"You've read the book."

"I skimmed the first few chapters, if you can call them chapters. I wondered why you seemed so attached to it, now I understand. They must not know that you're in it, otherwise they would be much more interested in you and they're very book-focused at the moment."

"Who are they?" Zachary asks as they turn down a wider street that he recognizes as Park Avenue.

"A bunch of cranky bastards who think they're doing the right thing when *right* in this case is subjective," Dorian says, bristling in such a fashion that Zachary guesses the crankiness might be personal and probably goes both ways. "I can give you the history lesson but not now, we don't have time."

"Where are we going, then?"

"We are going to their U.S. headquarters which is fortunately a few blocks from here," Dorian explains.

"Wait, we're going to *them*?" Zachary asks. "I don't—"

"Most of *them* will not be there, which will be to our advantage. When we get there, you are going to give them this."

Dorian reaches into his bag and hands Zachary a book, a different book. Thick and blue and familiar with a drawing embossed in gold on the cover. A bust of Ares.

Zachary turns the book to read the spine even though he knows what it will say. *The Age of Fable, or Beauties of Mythology.* The library sticker on the spine has been peeled off.

"You took this from the library," Zachary says, the statement sounding more painfully obvious once he speaks it aloud. "You were there."

"Correct, ten points to Ravenclaw. Though it wasn't very clever of you to gather up all those books only to leave them unsupervised because you wanted a muffin."

"It was a quality muffin," Zachary defensively snaps in response and to his surprise Dorian laughs, a pleasant, low laugh that makes him feel a little less cold.

"A quality muffin is just a cupcake without frosting," Dorian remarks before he continues. "You are going to bring this book to them."

"Won't they know this isn't the book they want?" Zachary opens the back cover and finds its barcode is missing as well, the initials JSK written on the paper where it had been.

"The people who have been following you would," Dorian says. "But they've been distracted. Those they left to babysit their collection will be the low-ranking sort, not high enough to be privy to details about which book it is exactly that anyone is looking for. You will give them this one, you will retrieve another for me, and I will give this back to you."

He holds up *Sweet Sorrows* again and Zachary thinks a second too late that he could grab it and run. His hands are too cold to take out of his pockets. This man, whatever his actual name is, could probably outrun him, too.

"Does all this book-juggling serve a purpose?" Zachary asks.

Dorian slides *Sweet Sorrows* back into his coat.

"You help me with this book-juggling, as you call it, and I will get you there."

Zachary doesn't need him to clarify where "there" is but he also doesn't know what to say. A blinking neon light catches the snow in the gutter in front of them, shifting it from grey to red to grey again.

"It's real," Zachary says, not quite a question.

"Of course it's real," Dorian says. "You know that. You feel it down to your toes or you wouldn't be here."

"Is it—" Zachary starts but then he cannot finish the question. *Is it the way it is in the book?* He aches to know but he also suspects real places are never properly captured in words. There is always more.

"You will not get there without my help," Dorian continues as they pause at a red-handed crosswalk despite the lack of traffic. "Not unless you have an arrangement with Mirabel that I am unaware of."

"Who's Mirabel?" Zachary asks as they begin to walk again.

Dorian stops in the middle of the street and turns to Zachary and stares at him, a questioning stare topped by skeptical eyebrows.

"What?" Zachary asks after the pause goes on long enough to make him uncomfortable, glancing both ways for taxis.

"You don't . . ." Dorian starts but then stops again. The skeptical eyebrows lower into an expression that looks more like concern but then he turns and keeps walking. "We don't have time for this, we're almost there. I'm going to need you to listen very carefully and follow instructions."

"No improvising?" Zachary asks, a little more sharply than he intended to.

"Not unless you have no other options. No lending pens to anyone, either, if you were wondering about the tracking device. You are going to tell whoever answers the door that you have a drop-off for the archive. Show them the book but do not let it out of your hands. If they do not allow you entry immediately say that Alex sent you."

"Who's Alex?"

"Not a who, Alex is a code. You are going to wear this and make certain that they see it but do not draw attention to it, it's an older style than they wear currently but it's the best I could do."

Dorian hands him a piece of metal on a long chain. A silver sword.

"You will be led through a hall and up a flight of stairs to another hall with several locked doors. A room will be unlocked for you. At approximately this time the doorbell will ring. Your escort will need to attend to it. Assure your escort that you can handle the book drop yourself and you will see yourself out the back, this is customary and will not seem odd. Your escort will depart."

"How can you be sure?" Zachary asks, pulling the chain over his head as they make another turn. The streets around them are more residential, dotted with trees and occasional corner stores and restaurants.

"They are quite strict about their protocols but some are more strict than others," Dorian says, his pace quickening as they continue. "Always answer the door is one of the stricter ones and it will take priority. Now, the room will have books on shelves and in glass cases. You are concerned with the cases. In one of the cases there will be a book bound in brown leather, with faded gilding around the page edges. You will know which one it is. You will swap your Bulfinch's mythology for that book. Place that book in your coat while in that room, there are cameras in the halls. Best keep your head down in general but I don't think anyone monitoring will recognize you based on your photo."

"They have a photo of me?" Zachary asks.

"They have a yearbook photo that looks nothing like you, don't worry about it. Return the way you came, down the stairs but when you reach the main hall go around to the back of the stairs. From there you can go down to the basement and out the back door. That door leads to the garden and there's a gate at the back, go out the gate and turn right. Proceed to the end of the alley and back to the street. I'll be waiting across the street, when I see you I'll start walking. Follow me for six blocks and if you are certain no one has followed you, catch up with me. This is it," Dorian says, stopping at a partially shadowed corner. "Halfway down the block on the left, grey building, black door, number 213. Do you have any questions?"

"Yes I have questions," Zachary says, louder than he means to. "Who the hell are you, anyway? Where did you come from? Why can't you do this yourself? What's so important about this particular book and who are these people really and what did the mouse do with Fate's heart? Who is Mirabel and at what point during all this covert activity am I allowed to go back to my hotel to get my face windows? Eyeglasses. Spectacles."

Dorian sighs and turns toward Zachary, his face half in light and half in shadow and Zachary realizes now that he is younger than he looks, the greying hair and the frequently furrowed eyebrows making him read older.

"Forgive my impatience," Dorian says, dropping his voice and stepping closer. His eyes glance briefly down the street and then back to Zachary. "You and I have a common destination and before I can go there I need that book. I cannot do this myself because they know me and if I set foot in that building I will never come out of it again. I am asking you for your help because I believe that you might be willing to help me. Please. I will beg you if I must."

For the first time Dorian's voice takes on the quality it had in the darkness back at the party, the storyteller cadence that turns the street corner into a sacred place.

Dorian holds his gaze, and for a moment the feeling in his chest Zachary had thought to be nervousness is something else entirely but then it turns back into nervousness. He feels too warm.

Zachary doesn't know what to say so he nods and turns, leaving Dorian in the shadows, his heart pounding in his ears, his feet drawing him down a deserted street lined with brownstone buildings illuminated by pools of light from streetlamps and persistent strings of twinkling holiday lights looped through trees.

What are you doing? a voice in his head asks and he doesn't have a good answer for it. Doesn't know what or why or even where, exactly, because he forgot to check the street sign on the corner. He could keep walking, hail a cab, return to his hotel. But he wants his book back. And he wants to know what happens next.

A quest has been set in front of him and he is going to see it through.

Some buildings do not have visible numbers so Zachary cannot keep count but it doesn't take long to reach the one he is looking for. It is a different sort of building than the ones that surround it, the facade a grey stone instead of brown, the windows covered with ornate black bars. He would have taken it for an embassy if it had a flag, or a college club. Something about it is too cold for it to seem like a private residence.

He glances back down the street before he climbs the steps but if Dorian is waiting there Zachary cannot see him. Zachary goes over his instructions in his head as he approaches the door, worried he is going to forget something.

The doorway is lit by a single bulb in an elaborate sconce that hangs over a metal plaque. Zachary leans in to read it.

Collector's Club

No hours of operation, no other information at all. The glass above the door is frosted but the lights are on inside. The door is black with gold numbers: 213. Definitely the right one.

Zachary takes a deep breath and presses the doorbell.

SWEET SORROWS
Lost cities of honey and bone.

In the depths there is a man lost in time.

He has opened the wrong doors. Chosen the wrong paths.

Wandered farther than he should have.

He is looking for someone. Something. Someone. He does not remember who the someone is, does not have the ability, here in the depths where time is fragile, to grasp the thoughts and memories and hold on to them, to sort through them to recall more than glimpses.

Sometimes he stops and in the stopping the memory grows clear enough for him to see her face, or pieces of it. But the clarity motivates him to continue and then the pieces fall apart again and he walks on not knowing for whom or what it is he walks.

He only knows he has not reached it yet.

Reached her yet.

Who? He looks toward the sky that is hidden from him by rock and earth and stories. No one answers his question. There is a dripping he mistakes for water, but no other sound. Then the question is forgotten again.

He walks down crumbling stairs and trips over tangled roots. He has long since passed by the last of the rooms with their doors and their locks, the places where the stories are content to remain on their shelves.

He has untangled himself from vines blossoming with story-filled flowers. He has traversed piles of abandoned teacups with text baked into their crackled glaze. He has walked through puddles of ink and left footprints that formed stories in his wake that he did not turn around to read.

Now he travels through tunnels with no light at their ends, feeling his way along unseen walls until he finds himself someplace somewhere sometime else.

He passes over broken bridges and under crumbling towers.

He walks over bones he mistakes for dust and nothingness he mistakes for bones.

His once-fine shoes are worn. He abandoned his coat some time ago.

He does not remember the coat with its multitude of buttons. The coat, if coats could remember such things, would remember him but by the time they are reunited the coat will belong to someone else.

On clear days memories focus in his mind in scattered words and images. His name. The night sky. A room with red velvet drapery. A door. His father. Books, hundreds and thousands of books. A single book in her hand. Her eyes. Her hair. The tips of her fingers.

But most of the memories are stories. Pieces of them. Blind wanderers and star-crossed lovers, grand adventures and hidden treasures. Mad kings and cryptic witches.

The things he has seen and heard with his own eyes and ears mix with tales he has read or heard with his own eyes and ears. They are inseparable down here.

There are not many clear days. Clear nights.

There is no way to tell the difference here in the depths.

Night or day. Fact or fiction. Real or imagined.

Sometimes he feels he has lost his own story. Fallen out of its pages and landed here, in between, but he remains in his story. He cannot leave it no matter how he tries.

The man lost in time walks along the shore of the sea and does not look up to see the lack of stars. He wanders through empty cities of honey and bone, down streets that once rang with music and laughter. He lingers in abandoned temples, lighting candles for forgotten gods and running his fingers over the fossils of unaccepted offerings. He sleeps in beds that no one has dreamed upon in centuries and his own sleep is deep, his dreams as unfathomable as his waking hours.

At first the bees watched him. Followed him while he walked and hovered while he slept. They thought he might be someone else.

He is just a boy. A man. Something in between.

Now the bees ignore him. They go about their own business. They decided that one man out of his depth is no cause for alarm but even the bees are wrong from time to time.

ZACHARY EZRA RAWLINS waits in the cold for so long that he rings
the bell of the Collector's Club a second time with a nearly frozen
finger. He's only sure he managed to ring it at all because he can hear
a low chime from within the building.

After the second chime he hears someone moving behind the door.
The click of multiple locks being undone.

The door opens a few inches, a metal chain keeping it latched
but from the opening a short young woman looks up at him. She is
younger than Zachary but not so much so that she would be considered a girl and reminds him of someone or maybe she has one of
those faces. The look she gives him is a mix of wariness and boredom.
Apparently even strange covert organizations have interns that get
stuck with the lousy shifts.

"May I help you?" she asks.

"I, uh, I'm dropping this off for the archive," Zachary says. He
pulls *The Age of Fable, or Beauties of Mythology* partway out of his coat
pocket. The woman peers at it but does not ask to see it. She asks for
something else.

"Your name?"

This is a question Zachary has not anticipated.

"Does it matter?" he asks, in the best impression of Dorian he can
manage. He shifts his coat in what he hopes is a nonchalant way, making sure the silver sword is visible.

The woman frowns.

"You may leave the item with me," she says. "I will see that it is—"

"Alex sent me," Zachary interrupts.

The woman's expression shifts. The boredom seeps out of it and
the wariness takes over.

"Just a minute," she says. The door closes entirely and Zachary starts to panic but then realizes that she is unlatching the chain. The door opens again almost immediately.

The woman ushers him into a small foyer lined with frosted glass that prevents him from seeing what lies beyond it. Another door waits on the opposite wall, also composed mostly of frosted glass. The double entryway seems more about obfuscation than security.

The woman locks and chains the front door and then hurriedly moves to unlock the frosted-glass door. She wears a long blue dress that looks simple and old-fashioned, like a robe, with a high neckline and large pockets on either side. Around her neck is a silver chain with a sword, a different design than the one that Zachary wears, thinner and shorter, but similar.

"This way," she says, pushing the frosted-glass door open.

Should I pretend I've been here before or not? That would have been a good question to ask Dorian. Zachary guesses the answer would have been yes, considering he's supposed to know where the back door is, but it makes that more difficult not to stare.

The hallway is bright and high-ceilinged with white walls, lit by a line of crystal chandeliers running from the foyer to the stairs at the back. A deep blue carpet covers the stairs and flows down into the hall like a waterfall, catching the irregular light that makes it appear even more liquid.

But what Zachary cannot help but stare at are the doorless doorknobs hanging on either side of the hall.

Suspended from white ribbons at varying heights there are brass doorknobs and crystal doorknobs and carved-ivory doorknobs. Some seem to have rusted to the point of staining the length of ribbon to which they cling. Others have gathered greyish-green patinas. Some hang near the ceiling far above Zachary's head and others skim the floor. Some are broken. Some are attached to escutcheons and others are only knobs or handles. All of them are missing their doors.

Each doorknob has a tag, a string attaching a rectangular piece of paper that reminds Zachary of the type of tag placed on the toes of corpses in mortuaries. He slows his pace so he can take a closer look. He catches city names and numbers he thinks might be latitudes and longitudes. Along the bottom of each tag is a date.

As they walk through the hall the air around them shifts over the ribbons causing the doorknobs to sway gently, knocking into their neighbors with a sorrowful hollow ringing sound.

There are hundreds of them. Maybe thousands.

Zachary and his escort ascend the waterfall of stairs in silence, the doorknobs echoing behind them.

The stairs turn and loop in both directions but the woman goes up the set on the right. A larger chandelier hangs in the center of the looping stairs, lightbulbs obscured behind droplets of crystal.

Both sides of the stairs lead to the same hall on an upper floor, this one with a lower ceiling and no ribbon-strung doorknobs. This hallway has its own doors, each painted a matte black in stark contrast with the white walls surrounding them. Each door is numbered, a brass numeral in the center. As they walk down the hall the numbers are all low but do not appear to be sequential. They pass a door marked with a six and another with a two and then eleven.

They stop at a door near the end of the hall by the large barred window Zachary could see from the street, this one marked with an eight. The woman pulls a small ring of keys from her pocket and unlocks the door.

A loud chime strikes from below them. The woman's hand pauses over the doorknob and Zachary can see the conflict playing out on her face, to go or to stay.

The chime strikes again.

"I can take care of this," Zachary says, holding up the book for good measure. "I'll see myself out the back. No worries."

Too casual, he thinks to himself but his escort bites her lip and then nods.

"Thank you, sir," she says, returning her keys to her pocket. "Have a pleasant evening."

She takes off down the hall at a much brisker pace than before as the chime rings a third time.

Zachary watches until she reaches the stairs and then he opens the door.

The room inside is darker than the hallway, the lights arranged in a fashion he has occasionally seen in museums: the contents lit at carefully chosen angles. The bookshelves that line the wall are lit from within, books and objects glowing, including what appears to be an actual human hand floating in a glass jar, palm facing outward as though in greeting. Two long glass display cases run the length of the room, lit from the inside so the books appear to float. Heavy curtains hang over the windows.

It does not take Zachary long to find the book he has been sent for, there are ten books in one case and eight in the other, and only one is bound in brown leather. The light around it catches the formerly gilded edges of the pages, the pieces around the corners that have held on to their gold more tightly shimmering. It is one of the smaller volumes, thankfully, easily pocket-size. Others are larger and some appear quite heavy.

Zachary inspects the case, trying to recall if any of his instructions included how to open it. He cannot find any hinges or latches.

"Puzzle box," Zachary mutters to himself.

He looks closer. The glass is set in panels, each book in its own transparent box even though the boxes are connected one to another. There are nearly invisible seams separating one from the next. The brown book sits in a section near one end, second from the last on the left. He checks it from both sides and then crawls under the table to see if it opens from beneath but finds nothing. The table has a heavy base made of some kind of metal.

Zachary stands and stares at the case. The lights are wired, so the wires must go somewhere, but none are visible on the outside. If the wires run through the table, maybe the entire thing is electric.

He searches the perimeter of the room for switches. The one next to the door turns on a chandelier he didn't even notice in the shadows above. It's simpler than those in the hall and doesn't add much light.

The wall with the windows has complicated latches but nothing else. Zachary pulls open one set of curtains and finds a window that overlooks the brick wall of the building next door.

He pulls back the other curtains and finds not a window but a wall with a line of switches on it.

"Ha!" he says aloud.

There are eight switches in something that resembles a fuse box, and none of them are labeled. Zachary switches the first one and the lights on one of the bookcases go out, the suspended hand vanishing. He turns it back on and skips down to the eighth switch, guessing that the top six are the shelves.

The lights switch off in one case, not the one he's attempting to open, the other one, and there is a clanking noise. He goes to inspect the case and finds that the glass has remained in place but the base has sunk down about a foot lower, allowing access to the books.

Zachary hurries back to the switches and turns the eighth switch back on as he turns the seventh one off. The clanking doubles as the tables move.

The brown leather book is now accessible and Zachary takes it from its spot in the case. He inspects it as he walks back to the switches. It reminds him of *Sweet Sorrows,* the quality of the leather and the fact that it has nothing printed on the outside, no visible title or author. He opens the cover and the pages are illuminated with beautiful borders and illustrations but the text is in Arabic. He closes it again and puts it in the inside pocket of his suit jacket.

Zachary toggles switch number seven back on.

But the lights remain off, the case remains lowered. The clanking noise is replaced by the screech of metal on metal.

Zachary switches it off again. Then he remembers.

He takes *The Age of Fable, or Beauties of Mythology* from his coat and places it in the spot where the brown leather volume had been and tries the switch again.

This time it clanks happily and the lights pop back on as the case slides closed, locking the books inside.

Zachary glances at his watch, realizing that he has no idea how long he has been in the room. He straightens the curtains and puts the book in his coat. He turns off the chandelier and steps quietly back into the hall.

He closes the door as softly as he can. His escort is nowhere to be seen but he hears a voice from the floor below as he makes his way toward the stairs.

When he is halfway down the stairs on the landing, about to turn down toward the main hall, the voice raises and he can hear it better.

"No, you don't understand, he's here *now*," the escort who is no longer escorting him says.

A pause. Zachary slows his steps, peering around the turn in the stairs as the voice continues, sounding more and more anxious. There is an open door on the side of the hall close to the stairs that he had not noticed before.

"I think he knows more than we'd anticipated . . . I don't know if he has the book, I thought . . . I'm sorry. I didn't . . . I am listening, sir. Under any circumstances, understood."

From the pauses Zachary guesses she's on a phone. He creeps down the stairs as quickly and quietly as he can, careful not to start the doorknobs swaying on their ribbons as he reaches the hallway. From here he can see into the room where the young woman is standing with her back toward him, speaking into the receiver of an old-fashioned black rotary telephone that sits on a dark wood desk. Next to the phone is a ball of yarn and half a scarf looped on knitting needles and then Zachary realizes why the woman looked familiar.

She was in Kat's class. The supposed English major who knit the entire time.

Zachary ducks around the back of the stairs as stealthily as he can manage and stops out of sight. The voice has paused but he hasn't heard the phone receiver replaced in its cradle. He continues along the side of the stairs unseen until he comes to a door. He opens it carefully and quietly, uncovering a narrow flight of much less ornate stairs leading to the floor below.

Zachary closes the door gently behind him and creeps down the stairs slowly, hoping with each footfall that they won't creak. Halfway down he thinks he hears the phone being hung up, and then a sound that might be someone heading up the stairs above.

These stairs end in an unlit room full of boxes but light filters through a pair of frosted-glass doors that Zachary guesses is his exit. There doesn't appear to be another one, but he looks just in case.

The doors have several latches but all of them are easily undone, and it takes less time than Zachary expects to get back outside in the cold. A light snow has begun to fall, bright flakes catch in the wind and circle around him, many of them never finding their way to the ground.

A short flight of stairs leads down to a garden that is mostly ice and rocks with a fence of black iron bars that match the ones on the windows. The gate is at the back, the alleyway behind it. Zachary walks toward it, slower than he would prefer, but his dress shoes are not well-suited to the slippery stone.

A siren wails in the distance. A car horn joins it.

Zachary brushes a layer of ice from the latch on the gate, beginning to breathe a little easier.

"Leaving so soon?" a voice behind him asks.

Zachary turns, his hand on the gate.

Standing on the stairs in front of the open glass doors is the polar-bear woman, still in her fur coat, looking both more and less like a bear as she smiles at him.

Zachary says nothing, but can't bring himself to move.

"Stay and have a cup of tea," the woman says, casual and gracious, seemingly ignoring the fact that they are standing in the snow as he is in the midst of escaping into the night with stolen literature.

"I really must be going," Zachary says, choking back the nervous laugh that threatens to accompany the statement.

"Mister Rawlins," the woman says, descending a single step toward him but then stopping again, "I assure you that you are in over your head. Whatever you think is going on here, whatever side you have been coerced to think you are on, you are mistaken. You have stumbled into something you have no business meddling with. Please come inside out of the cold, we shall have a cup of tea and a polite discussion and then you may be on your way. I shall pay for your return train to Vermont as a gesture of goodwill. You will go back to your studies and we will all pretend none of this ever happened."

Zachary's thoughts bubble over with questions and debates. Who should he trust, what should he do, how did he manage to go from near-clueless to deeply embroiled in whatever this is in a single evening. He has no real reason to trust Dorian more than he trusts this woman. He doesn't have enough answers to go with all of his questions.

But he has an answer, one that makes this decision in this moment in the snow an easy one.

No way is he going to go home and play pretend. Not now.

"I respectfully decline," Zachary says. He pulls the gate open and it screeches, sending pieces of ice falling over his shoulders. He doesn't look back at the woman on the stairs, he runs down the alleyway as fast as his impractical footwear will allow.

There is another gate at the end of the alley, and as he fusses with the latch he spots Dorian across the street, leaning against a building and reading by the light from the still-open bar on the corner, deeply absorbed in *Sweet Sorrows* and frowning at it in a way that Zachary finds familiar.

Zachary ignores both his instructions and the streetlight, hurrying across the empty street.

"I thought I told you—" Dorian starts, but Zachary doesn't let him finish.

"I just declined an invitation to late-night intimidation tea from a lady in a fur coat and I'm guessing you know who she is. She certainly knew who I was so I don't think any of this is as covert as you would like it to be."

Dorian puts the book back in his coat and mutters something in a language Zachary doesn't recognize but he guesses the meaning is probably profane and turns toward the street with his hand raised. It takes Zachary a moment to realize that he's hailing a cab.

Dorian ushers Zachary into the cab before he can ask where it is they're going but directs the driver to Central Park West and Seventy-Seventh. Then he sighs and puts his head in his hands.

Zachary turns and looks behind them as they pull away from the curb. The younger woman is standing on the street corner, a dark coat pulled over her robe. He cannot tell if she has seen them or not from this distance.

"Did you get the book?" Dorian asks him.

"Yes I did," Zachary says. "But before I give it to you, you're going to tell me why I did that."

"You did that because I asked you nicely," Dorian says and it doesn't annoy Zachary as much as he expects it to. "And because it belongs to me, not to them, as much as a book belongs to anyone. I got your book back for you, you got mine back for me."

Zachary watches Dorian as he stares out the window at the snow. He looks tired. Weary-tired and maybe a little sad. The paper flower is still tucked in the lapel of his coat. Zachary decides not to pry any further about the book for now.

"Where are we going?" he asks.

"We need to get to the door."

"There's a door? Here?"

"There should be if Mirabel held up her part of the bargain and wasn't stopped in the process," Dorian explains. "But we need to get there before they do."

"Why?" Zachary asks. "Are they trying to get there, too?"

"Not that I'm aware of," Dorian says. "But they don't want us going there, they don't want anyone going there anymore. Do you know how simple it is to destroy a door made of paint?"

"How simple?"

"As simple as throwing more paint on it, and they always have paint."

Zachary looks out the window at the buildings passing by and the snowflakes starting to stick to signs and trees. He glimpses the Empire State Building, bright and white against the sky, and he realizes that he has no idea what time it is and doesn't care enough to check his watch.

The TV screen in the cab chatters away about headlines and movies and Zachary reaches over to mute it, unconcerned about anything else going on in the world, real or fictional.

"I don't suppose we have time to stop and get my bag," he says, already knowing the answer. His contact lenses are beginning to war with his eyeballs.

"I'll make certain you are reunited with your belongings as soon as possible," Dorian says. "I know you have a lot of questions, I will do my best to answer them once we're safe."

"Are we not safe now?" Zachary asks.

"Frankly, I'm impressed that you made it out of there," Dorian says. "You must have caught them at least partially by surprise. Otherwise they wouldn't have let you go."

"Under any circumstances," Zachary mutters to himself, recalling the overheard phone call. They hadn't planned on letting him go. There probably wasn't tea, either. "They knew who I was the whole time," he tells Dorian. "The one who answered the door was in Vermont pretending to be a student, it took me a while to recognize her."

Dorian frowns but says nothing.

They sit in silence as the cab speeds up streets.

"Is Mirabel the one who paints the doors?" Zachary asks. It seems relevant enough to ask.

"Yes," Dorian says. He does not elaborate. Zachary glances over at him but he is staring out the window, one of his knees bouncing restlessly.

"Why did you think I knew her?"

Dorian turns and looks at him.

"Because you danced with her at the party," he says.

Zachary tries to recall his conversation with the woman dressed as the king of the wild things but it is fragmented and hazy in his mind.

He is about to ask Dorian how he knows her but the cab slows to a stop.

"At the corner here is fine, thank you," Dorian says to the driver, handing him cash and refusing change. Zachary stands on the sidewalk, attempting to orient himself. They've stopped next to Central Park, near one of the gates pulled closed for the night, and across from a large building he recognizes.

"Are we going to the museum?" he asks.

"No," Dorian says. He watches the cab drive off and then turns and jumps the wall into the park. "Hurry up," he says to Zachary.

"Isn't the park closed?" Zachary asks, but Dorian is already walking ahead, disappearing into the shadows of the snow-covered branches.

Zachary awkwardly climbs over the icy wall, almost losing his footing on the other side but regains his composure at the expense of getting his hands covered in dirt and ice.

He follows Dorian into the park, looping around deserted paths and leaving tracks in unblemished snow. Between the trees he can make out something that looks like a castle. It is easy to forget that they are in the middle of the city.

They pass a sign declaring part of the frosted foliage the Shakespeare Garden, and then they cross a small bridge over part of the frozen pond and after that Dorian slows and stops.

"It appears the night is moving in our favor," Dorian says. "We got here first." He gestures at an archway of rock, half hidden in the shadows.

The door painted on the rough stones is simple, less ornate than the one that Zachary remembers. It has no decorations, only a gleaming doorknob of brass paint and matching hinges around a plain door that looks like wood. The rock is too uneven for it to fool anyone's eye. At the top there are letters that look carved, something Zachary can't distinguish that might be Greek.

"Cute," Dorian says to himself, reading the text over the door.

"What does it say?" Zachary asks.

"Know Thyself," Dorian says. "Mirabel is fond of embellishment, I'm amazed she had the time in this weather."

"That's half the Rawlins family motto," Zachary says.

"What's the other half?"

"And Learn to Suffer."

"Maybe you should look into changing that part," Dorian says. "Would you like to do the honors?" he adds, gesturing at the door.

Zachary reaches toward the doorknob, not certain he truly believes this isn't all some elaborate prank, part of him expecting to be laughed at, but his hand closes over cold metal, round and three-dimensional. It turns easily and the door swings inward, revealing an open space much larger than it should possibly be. Zachary freezes, staring.

Then he hears something—someone—behind them, a rustling in the trees.

"Go," Dorian says and pushes him, a sharp shove between his shoulder blades and Zachary stumbles forward through the door. At the same second something wet hits him, splashing over his back and up his neck, dripping down his arm.

Zachary looks down at his arm, expecting blood but instead he finds it covered in shimmering paint, droplets falling from his fingers like molten gold.

And Dorian is gone.

Behind him, what had been an open door moments before is now a wall of solid rock. Zachary bangs his hands against it, leaving metallic smudges of gold paint on smooth, dark stone.

"Dorian!" he calls but the only response is his own voice echoing around him.

When the echo fades the quiet is heavy. No rustling trees, no distant cars rushing over damp pavement.

Zachary calls out again but the echo sounds halfhearted, knowing that somehow no one can hear him, not here. Wherever *here* is.

He turns from the gold-smudged wall and looks around. He stands on a stretch of rock in a space that looks like a cave. A spiral stair is carved into the round space leading downward and somewhere below something is casting a soft, warm light upward, like firelight but steadier.

Zachary moves away from the space where the door had been and walks slowly down the stairs, leaving a trail of gold paint along the stone.

At the bottom of the stairs, seamlessly fitted into the solid rock, is a pair of golden doors flanked with hanging lanterns suspended from chains that is undoubtedly an elevator. It is covered in elaborate patterns including a bee, a key, and a sword aligned along the center seam.

Zachary puts out his hand to touch it, half expecting it to be a clever illusion like the painted doors but the elevator is cool and metal, the designs embossed and clearly defined beneath his fingertips.

This is a significant moment, he thinks, hearing the words in his head in his mother's voice. A moment with meaning. A moment that changes the moments that follow.

It feels like the elevator is watching him. To see what he will do.

Sweet Sorrows never mentioned an elevator.

He wonders what else *Sweet Sorrows* never mentioned.

He wonders what has happened to Dorian.

On the side, beneath one of the lanterns, is a single unmarked hexagonal button surrounded by gold filigree and set into the rock like a jewel.

Zachary presses it and it comes alight with a soft glow.

A loud, low rumble starts from somewhere below, growing louder and stronger. Zachary takes a step backward. The lanterns shudder on their chains.

Abruptly, the noise stops.

The button light extinguishes itself.

A soft chime sounds from behind the doors.

Then the bee and the key and the sword split down the center as the elevator opens.

SWEET SORROWS
. . . Time fell in love with Fate.

The pirate tells the girl not the single story she requested but many stories. Stories that fold into other stories and wander into snippets of lost myths and forgotten tales and yet to be told wonderments that turn back around again into each other until they return to two people facing each other through iron bars, a storyteller and a story listener with no more whispered words left between them.

The post-story silence is heavy and long.

"Thank you," the girl says softly.

The pirate accepts her thanks with a silent nod.

It is almost dawn.

The pirate untangles his fingers from the girl's hair. The girl steps back from the bars.

She places a hand over her chest and gives the pirate a low, graceful bow.

The pirate mirrors the gesture, the bowed head, the hand near his heart, the formal acknowledgment that their dance has ended.

He pauses before he lifts his head, holding on to the moment as long as he can.

When he raises his eyes the girl has already turned from him and walked silently to the opposite wall.

Her hand hovers above the key. She does not look over at the guard or back at the pirate. This is her decision and she needs no outside assistance in making it.

The girl slips the key from its hook. She is careful not to let it rattle against its ring or clatter against the stone.

She walks back across the room with the key in her hand.

The click as the key unlocks the cell, even the creak of the door does not wake the guard.

There are no words exchanged as the girl gifts the pirate his freedom and he accepts it. As they ascend the dark stairs, nothing is spoken about what might happen next. What will occur once they reach the door at the top. What uncharted seas wait for them beyond it.

Just before they reach the door the pirate pulls the girl back to him and catches her lips with his. No bars between them now, twined together on a darkened stair with only fate and time to complicate matters.

This is where we leave them—a girl and her pirate, a pirate and his savior—in a kiss in the darkness before a door opens.

But this is not where their story ends.

This is only where it changes.

New Orleans, Louisiana, fourteen years ago

It is almost dawn. A greyish haze pushes the darkness from night to not quite day but there is light from the street pouring into the alley, more than enough light to paint by.

She is accustomed to low-light painting.

The air is colder than she had expected and her fingerless gloves are better for brush-holding than warmth. She pulls the sleeves of her sweatshirt farther down her wrists, leaving traces of paint, but the cuffs were already well paint-smudged, in various shades and finishes.

She adds another line of shadow down the faux-wood panels, giving them more definition. The bulk of the work is done, has been done since the night was still night and not even considering becoming dawn, and she could leave it as it is but she does not want to. She's proud of this one, this is good work and she wants to make it better.

She switches brushes, pulling a thinner one from the fan of painting tools sticking out from her ponytail, thick black hair streaked with blue that disappears in this particular light. She rummages quietly in the backpack by her feet and changes her paints from shadow grey to metallic gold.

The details are her favorite part: A shadow added here and a highlight there and suddenly a flat image gains dimension.

The gold paint on its tiny brush leaves gilded marks over the hilt of the sword, the teeth of the key, the stripes on the bee. They glitter in the darkness, replacing the fading stars.

Once she is pleased with the doorknob she switches brushes again, finishing touches now.

She always saves the keyhole for last.

Maybe it feels like something close to a signature, a keyhole on a door that has no key. A detail that is there because it should be, not out of any necessity of engineering. Something to make it feel complete.

"That's very pretty," a voice says behind her and the girl jumps, the paintbrush tumbling from her fingers and landing by her feet, pausing to smear her shoelaces with keyhole-dark black on its way down.

She turns and a woman is standing behind her.

She could run but she's not certain which direction to run in. The streets look different in the almost-light.

She forgets how to say hello in this particular language and is not certain if she should say *hello* or *thank you* so she says nothing.

The woman is considering the door and not the girl. She wears a fluffy robe the color of an under-ripe peach and holds a mug that says *Real Witch* on it. Her hair is tied up in a rainbow-printed scarf. She has a lot of earrings. There are tattoos on her wrists: a sunshine and a line of moons. She's shorter than the girl but seems bigger, takes up more room in the alley despite being a smaller person. The girl shrinks farther into her hooded sweatshirt.

"You're not supposed to paint on there, you know," the woman says. She takes a sip from her mug.

The girl nods.

"Someone's going to come and paint over it."

The girl looks at the door and then back at the woman and shrugs.

"Come have a cup of coffee," the woman says and turns and walks down the alley and around the corner without waiting for an answer.

The girl hesitates, but then she sticks her paintbrush in her ponytail with the rest and collects her bag and follows.

Around the corner is a store. A neon sign in the shape of an upraised palm with an eye in the middle rests unlit in the center of the large window, surrounded by velvet curtains obscuring the inside. The woman stands in the doorway, holding the door open for the girl.

A bell chimes as it closes behind them. The inside of the store is not like any store the girl has seen before, filled with candles and mismatched furniture. Bundles of dried sage tied with colorful strings hang from the ceiling, surrounded by twinkling lights on strings and paper lanterns. On a table there is a crystal ball and a pack of clove cigarettes. A statue of an ibis-headed god peers over the girl's shoulder as she tries to find a place to stand out of the way.

"Sit," the woman says, waving her at a velvet couch covered in scarves. The girl knocks into a fringed lampshade on her way toward the couch, the fringe continuing to dance after she is seated, holding her bag in her lap.

The woman returns with two mugs, the new one emblazoned with a five-point star inside a circle.

"Thank you," the girl says quietly as she takes the mug. It is warm in her cold hands.

"You *can* speak," the woman says, settling herself into an ancient Chesterfield chair that sighs and creaks as she sits. "What's your name?"

The girl says nothing. She sips the too-hot coffee.

"Do you need someplace to stay?" the woman asks.

The girl shakes her head.

"You sure about that?"

The girl nods this time.

"I didn't mean to startle you out there," the woman continues. "Have to be a little wary of teenagers outside at odd hours." She takes a sip of her coffee. "Your door is very nice. Sometimes they paint not so nice things on that wall, because people say a witch lives here."

The girl frowns and then points at the woman, who laughs.

"What gave it away?" she asks and though the question does

not sound serious the girl points at the coffee mug anyway. *Real Witch.*

The woman laughs harder and the girl smiles. Making a witch laugh feels like a lucky sort of thing.

"Not trying to hide it, obviously," the woman says, chuckling. "But some of those kids talk a lot of nonsense about curses and devils and some of the more easily swayed ones believe it. Someone threw a rock through the window not that long ago."

The girl looks over at the window, covered by the velvet curtains, then down at her hands. She is not certain she understands people sometimes. There is paint underneath her fingernails.

"Mostly I read," the woman continues, "like a book about a person, only I read it through an object they've handled. I've read car keys and wedding rings. I read one of my son's video-game controllers once, he didn't appreciate that but I read him all the time anyway, he's written all over the floors and the wallpaper and the laundry. I could probably read your paintbrushes."

The girl's hand flies up to the fan of brushes in her hair protectively.

"Only if you want to know, honeychild."

The girl's expression changes at the endearment, she translates it a number of times in her head and thinks that this woman must be a witch to know such things, but she says nothing.

The girl puts her mug down on the table and stands up. She looks toward the door, holding her bag.

"Time to go already?" the woman remarks but does not protest. She puts down her own coffee and walks the girl to the door. "If you need anything you come back here, anytime. Okay?"

The girl looks as though she might say something but doesn't. Instead she glances at the sign on the door, a hand-painted piece of wood on a ribbon that says *Spiritual Adviser,* with little stars painted around the edges.

"Maybe you can paint me a new sign next time," the woman adds. "And here, take these." Impulsively she plucks a pack of cards from a shelf, high enough to discourage shoplifters, and hands them to the girl. She reads cards only rarely herself but she enjoys giving them as unexpected gifts when the moment feels right, as this moment does. "They're cards with stories on them," she explains as the girl looks curiously at the cards in her hand. "You shuffle the pictures and they tell you the story."

The girl smiles, first at the woman and then down at the cards which she holds gently, like a small living thing. She turns to walk away but stops suddenly after a few steps and turns back before the door has closed behind her.

"Thank you," the girl says again, not much louder than before.

"You're welcome," the woman says to the girl, and as the sun rises the witch's path takes her back into the store and the girl's path takes her somewhere else. The bell above the door chimes over their parting.

Inside, the witch picks up the girl's mug, its star facing toward her palm. She doesn't have to read it but she's curious and mildly concerned with the girl's well-being, out on the streets alone.

The images come quick and clear, clearer than what is typical for an object held for only a few minutes. More pictures, more people, more places, and more things than should fit in a single girl. Then the witch sees herself. Sees the cardboard moving boxes and the hurricane on the television and the white farmhouse surrounded by trees.

The empty mug falls to the floor, knocking into a table leg but it does not break.

Madame Love Rawlins walks outside, the bell above the door chiming again. She looks first down the quiet street and then around the corner down the alley toward the painted door, not yet dry.

But the girl herself has vanished.

BOOK II

FORTUNES

AND

FABLES

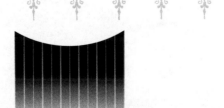

FORTUNES AND FABLES:

THE STAR MERCHANT

Once there was a merchant who traveled far and wide, selling stars.

This merchant sold all manner of stars. Fallen stars and lost stars and vials of stardust. Delicate pieces of stars strung on fine chains to be worn around necks and spectacular specimens fit to display under glass. Fragments of stars were procured to be given as gifts for lovers. Stardust was purchased to sprinkle at sacred sites or to bake into cakes for spells.

The stars in the merchant's inventory were carried from place to place in a large sack embroidered with constellations.

The prices for the merchant's wares were high but often negotiable. Stars could be acquired in exchange for coins or favors or secrets, saved by wishful dreamers in hopes that the star merchant might cross their path.

Occasionally the star merchant traded stars for accommodations or transport while traveling from place to place. Stars were traded for nights spent in inns with company or without.

One dark night on the road the star merchant stopped at a tavern to while away the time before the sun returned. The merchant sat by the fire drinking wine and struck up a conversation with a traveler who was also staying the night at the tavern, though their paths would take them in different directions come morning.

"To Seeking," the star merchant said as their wine was refilled.

"To Finding," came the traditional response. "What is it that you sell?" the traveler asked, tilting a cup toward the constellation-covered sack. This was a topic they had not yet discussed.

"Stars," the star merchant answered. "Would you care to

peruse? I shall offer you a discount for being good company. I might even show you the pieces I keep in reserve for distinguished customers."

"I do not care for stars," the traveler said.

The merchant laughed. "Everyone wants the stars. Everyone wishes to grasp that which exists out of reach. To hold the extraordinary in their hands and keep the remarkable in their pockets."

There was a pause here, filled by the crackling of the fire.

"Let me tell you a story," the traveler said, after the pause.

"Of course," the star merchant said, gesturing for their wine to be replenished once again.

"Once, very long ago," the traveler began, "Time fell in love with Fate. Passionately, deeply in love. The stars watched them from the heavens, worrying that the flow of time would be disrupted or the strings of fortune tangled into knots."

The fire hissed and popped anxiously, punctuating the traveler's words.

"The stars conspired and separated the two. Afterward they breathed easier. Time continued to flow as it always had, Fate wove together the paths that were meant to intertwine, and eventually Fate and Time found each other again—"

"Of course they did," the star merchant interrupted. "Fate always gets what Fate wants."

"Yet the stars would not accept defeat," the traveler continued. "They pestered the moon with concerns and complaints until she agreed to call upon the parliament of owls."

Here the star merchant frowned. The parliament of owls was an old myth, invoked as a curse in the land where the merchant had lived as a child, far from this place. Falter on your path and the parliament of owls will come for you. The merchant listened carefully as the tale continued.

"The parliament of owls concluded that one of the elements should be removed. They chose to keep the one they felt more important. The stars rejoiced as Fate was pulled apart. Ripped into pieces by beaks and talons."

"Did no one try to stop them?" the star merchant asked.

"The moon would have, certainly, had she been there. They chose a night with no moon for the sacrifice. No one dared intervene save for a mouse who took Fate's heart and kept it safe," the traveler said, then paused to take a sip of wine. "The owls did not notice the mouse as they feasted. The owl who consumed Fate's eyes gained great sight and was crowned the Owl King."

There was a sound then, outside in the night, that might have been wind or might have been wings.

The traveler waited for the sound to cease before resuming the story.

"The stars rested, smugly, in their heavens. They watched as Time passed in broken-hearted despair and eventually they questioned all that they once thought indisputable truth. They saw the crown of the Owl King passed one to another like a blessing or a curse, as no mortal creature should have such sight. They twinkle in their uncertainty, still, even now as we sit here below them."

The traveler paused to finish the last of the wine, the story ended.

"As I said, I do not care for stars. Stars are made of spite and regret."

The star merchant said nothing. The constellation-covered bag rested heavily by the fire.

The traveler thanked the star merchant for the wine and for the company and the merchant returned the sentiments. Before retiring the traveler leaned in and whispered in the merchant's ear.

"Occasionally, Fate pulls itself together again and Time is always waiting."

The traveler left the star merchant alone, sitting and drinking and watching the fire.

In the morning when the stars had fled under the watchful eye of the sun the star merchant inquired whether the traveler had departed, if there might be time to bid a proper farewell.

The star merchant was politely informed that there had been no other guests.

ZACHARY EZRA RAWLINS sits on a velvet bench in the fanciest elevator he has ever occupied wondering if it is not an elevator at all but rather a stationary room rigged to feel like an elevator because he has been sitting in it for what feels like a very, very long time.

He wonders if it's possible to have sudden-onset claustrophobia and his contact lenses are reminding him why he rarely wears his contact lenses. The probably-elevator hums and occasionally makes a shuddering movement accompanied by a scraping sound, so it is likely moving and his stomach feels as though he is falling at a polite rate in a gilded cage, or maybe he is more drunk than he thinks he is. Delayed-reaction cocktailing.

The chandelier hanging above him shakes and shimmers, throwing fragmented light over the slightly baroque interior, gold walls and maroon velvet mostly worn of their respective shine and fuzziness. The bee/key/sword motif is repeated on the interior doors but there is nothing else adorning anything, no numerical information, no floor indicator, not even a button. Apparently there is one place to go and they haven't reached it yet. The paint along his back and arm has started to dry, metallic flakes of it clinging to his coat and hair, itching along his neck, and stuck underneath his fingernails.

Zachary feels too awake yet extremely tired. Everything buzzes, from his head to his toes, and he can't tell if it's the elevator or the alcohol or something else. He stands and paces, as much as he can pace in an elevator, no more than two steps in any given direction.

Maybe it's the fact that you finally walked through a painted door and didn't end up where you expected to, the voice in his head suggests.

Did I know what I expected? Zachary asks himself.

He pauses his pacing and faces the elevator doors. He reaches out to touch them, his hand falling on the key motif. It vibrates beneath his fingers.

For a moment he feels like an eleven-year-old boy in an alleyway, the door beneath his fingers paint instead of metal but reverberating and the jazz music from the party is stuck in his head, looping, layering a dancing spin over everything and suddenly it feels like the elevator is moving much, much faster.

Abruptly, it stops. The chandelier jumps in surprise, sending down a shower of twinkling light as the doors open.

Zachary's suspicions that he wasn't actually traveling anywhere were unfounded, as the room he is looking out toward is not the cave-like space he started in. This is a luminous room with a curved paneled ceiling. It reminds him of the atrium from the university library but smaller, with honey-colored marble walls, opaque and varied in tone, but translucent and glowing, covering everything except for the stone floor and the elevator and another door on the other side of the room. He suspects he actually is as far underground as the length and speed of the elevator ride suggested, even though the voice in his head keeps insisting that such things are impossible. It is too quiet. There is a heaviness in the air, the feel of weight above him.

Zachary steps out of the elevator and the doors close behind him. The clanking sound resumes, the elevator returning to somewhere else. Above its doors is a half-moon indicator with no numbers, only a gold arrow moving slowly upward.

Zachary walks to the door on the other side of the room. It's a large door with a golden doorknob that reminds him of his original painted door, only bigger, as though it has grown along with him, and this one is not painted but real carved wood, its gilded embellishments fading in places but the bee and the key and the sword remain distinct.

Zachary takes a breath and reaches for the doorknob. It is warm and solid and when he tries to turn it, it does not budge. He tries again, but the door is locked.

"Seriously?" he says aloud. He sighs and takes a step back. The door has a keyhole and, feeling silly about it, Zachary bends down to look through it. There is a room beyond, that much is obvious, but other than an irregular movement to the light, he cannot discern anything else.

Zachary sits on the floor, which is polished stone and not very comfortable. He can tell from this angle that the stone is worn down in the center of the doorway. Many people have walked here before him.

Wake up, the voice in his head says. *You're usually good at this sort of thing.*

Zachary stands, leaving flakes of gold paint behind him, and goes to inspect the rest of the room.

There is a button near the elevator, half concealed in marble and whatever brassy metal the marble panels are connected with. Zachary pushes the button, not expecting a result, and gets precisely that. The button remains unlit, the elevator silent.

He tries the other doorless walls next and finds them more cooperative.

In the middle of the first wall is an alcove set at window height. It vanishes from view even a few steps away, lost in the glow of the marble. Inside, there is a bowl-like depression, a basin, as though it is a wall fountain with no water, the sides curving inward to a flat spot on the bottom.

In the center sits a small black bag.

Zachary picks up the bag. It has a familiar weight in his hand. The lifting of the bag reveals a single word carved into the stone beneath it.

Roll

"You have got to be kidding," Zachary says as he turns the contents of the bag onto his palm.

Six dice of the classic six-sided variety, carved from dark stone. Each side has a symbol rather than numbers or dots, engraved and accented with gold. He turns one over so he can identify all of the symbols. The bee and the key and the sword are familiar but there are more. A crown. A heart. A feather.

Zachary puts the bag to the side and gives the dice a thorough shake before letting them tumble into the stone basin. When they settle, all of the symbols are the same. Six hearts.

He barely has time to read them before the bottom falls out of the basin and the dice and the bag disappear.

Zachary doesn't bother checking the door before walking to the opposite wall and he is unsurprised to find a matching alcove.

A tiny stemmed glass rests inside, the type for sipping cordials or liqueurs, with a matching glass lid on top like some of his fancier teacups.

Zachary picks up the glass. Again, a single word is carved underneath.

Drink

The glass contains a small measure of honey-colored liquid, not much more than a sip.

Zachary removes the lid from the glass and sets it down next to the carved instruction. He sniffs the liquid. It has a honey sweetness but it also smells of orange blossom and vanilla and spice.

Zachary recalls innumerable fairy-tale warnings against eating or drinking in underworlds and at the same time realizes he is incredibly thirsty.

He suspects this is the only way forward.

He downs the drink in a single shot and replaces the empty glass on the stone. It tastes of everything he smelled in it and more—apricot and clove and cream—and it has a very, very strong kick of alcohol.

He loses his equilibrium enough to reconsider the relative stupidity of the whole idea but as quickly as the glass falls into its own abyss, it passes. His head, which had been pounding and swimming and sleepy before, feels clearer.

Zachary returns to the door and when he turns the knob it moves, the lock clicking open for him, allowing him through.

The room beyond the door looks like a cathedral, its sweeping high ceilings intricately tiled and buttressed, if *buttressed* is a word. There are six large columns, also tiled in patterns though some tiles are missing here and there, mostly near the bases, leaving bare stone visible beneath. The floor is covered with tiles worn down to the stone beneath, more so near Zachary's feet and in a loop around the perimeter of the round space, with heavier wear near the other entrances. There are five entrances not counting the door he has stepped through. Four are archways, leading off in different directions into darkened halls, but directly opposite a large wooden door rests slightly ajar, a soft light beyond.

There are chandeliers, some hanging at irregular, chandelier-inappropriate heights, and others resting on the floor in illuminated piles of metal and crystal, their tiny bulbs dimmed or extinguished entirely.

A larger light above is not a chandelier at all but a cluster of glowing globes hung amongst brass hoops and bars. Craning his neck Zachary can see hands at the end of the bars, human hands cast in gold and pointing outward, the tile above them laid out in a pattern of numbers and stars. In the center, the midpoint of the room, a chain drops from the ceiling, terminating in a pendulum that hangs inches above the floor, slowly swaying in a tight rotation.

Zachary thinks the entire contraption might be a model of the universe or maybe a clock of some sort but he has no idea how to read it.

"Hello?" he calls. From one of the darkened halls there is a creaking sound, like a door opening, but nothing follows. Zachary walks the perimeter of the room, peering down hallways filled with books filed on long curving shelves and stacked on floors. Down one hall he spots a glowing pair of eyes staring back at him but he blinks and the eyes are gone.

Zachary turns his attention back to the maybe-universe, maybe-clock to inspect it from a different angle. One of the smaller bars is moving in time with the pendulum, and as he attempts to discern if any of the globe shapes have moons there is a voice behind him.

"May I be of assistance, sir?"

Zachary turns so quickly he hurts his neck and flinches and is unable to tell whether the man who is regarding him with mild concern is reacting to the action or his presence or both.

Someone else is in this place. This place is actually here.

This is all happening.

Zachary dissolves into instant, near-hysterical laughter. A bubbling giggle that he attempts to stifle and fails. The man's expression switches from mild concern to moderate.

This man gives an immediate impression of agedness, probably because of his stark white hair, worn long and styled in impressive braids. But Zachary blinks and stares and as his contact lenses reluctantly focus he can tell the man is maybe pushing fifty, or at least not as old as the hair implies. It's also dotted with pearls strung along the braids, camouflaged when their sheen isn't caught in the light. His eyebrows and eyelashes are dark, black like his eyes. His skin looks darker in contrast with his hair but is a mid-toned brown. He wears wire-rimmed glasses balanced on an equine nose and reminds Zachary a little bit of his seventh-grade math teacher but with much cooler hair and a deep red, gold-embroidered robe tied with a number of looping cords. On one hand he wears several rings. One ring looks like an owl.

"May I be of assistance, sir?" the man repeats, but Zachary can't stop laughing. He opens his mouth to say something, anything, but nothing will come. His knees forget how to work and he slumps to the floor in a pile of wool coat and gold paint, finding himself at eye level with a ginger cat who peers around the edges of the man's robes and stares at him with amber eyes and this somehow makes the whole situation even crazier and he has never laughed himself into a panic attack before but hey, there's a first time for everything.

The man and the cat wait patiently, as though hysterical paint-covered visitors are commonplace.

"I . . ." Zachary starts and then realizes he has absolutely no idea where to begin. The tile beneath him is cold. He slowly gets to his feet, half expecting the man to offer him a hand when he does a particularly clumsy job of it but the man's hands stay by his sides, though the cat takes a step forward, sniffing at Zachary's shoes.

"It is perfectly all right if you need a moment," the man says, "but I'm afraid you will have to leave. We are closed."

"We're what?" Zachary asks, regaining his balance, but as he does the man's scrutinizing gaze settles on a spot near the third button on Zachary's open coat.

"You are not supposed to be here," the man says, looking at the silver sword that hangs around Zachary's neck.

"Oh . . ." Zachary starts. "Oh, no . . . this isn't mine," he tries to clarify but the man is already ushering him back toward the door and the elevator. "Someone gave this to me for . . . disguise purposes? I'm not a . . . whoever they are."

"They don't simply give those away," the man responds coolly.

Zachary doesn't know how to reply and now they're back at the door again. He's gathered that Dorian is a probably former member of the organization collecting rogue doorknobs to decorate their Manhattan town house but can't be certain if the sword is Dorian's own or a copy or what. He was not prepared for jewelry-based accusations in underground cathedrals currently closed for business or renovations. He was not prepared for anything that has happened this evening except maybe the cab ride.

"He called himself Dorian, he asked me to help him, I think he's in trouble, I don't know who the sword people are," Zachary explains in a rush but even as he says the words they feel almost like a lie. Guardians don't seem to work the way that *Sweet Sorrows* suggested, though he's fairly certain that's what they are.

The man says nothing and having walked Zachary politely yet forcibly back to the elevator he stops and gestures at the hexagonal button next to it with his ring-covered hand.

"I wish you and your friend the best in overcoming your current difficulties but I must insist," he says. He indicates the button again.

Zachary pushes the button, hoping the elevator will continue to be slow in order to buy him time to explain or understand what is going on but the button does nothing. It doesn't light up, it doesn't make a sound. The elevator doors remain shut.

The man frowns, first at the elevator and then at Zachary's coat. No, at the paint on his coat.

"The door you entered through, was it painted?" he asks.

"Yes?" Zachary answers.

"I gather from the state of your overcoat that door is no longer operational. Is that so?"

"It sort of disappeared," Zachary says, not believing it himself even though he was there.

The man closes his eyes and sighs.

"I warned her this would be problematic," he says to himself and then he asks, "What did you roll?" before Zachary can ask who he means.

"Pardon?"

"Your dice," the man clarifies, with another elegant gesture indicating the wall behind him. "What did you roll?"

"Oh . . . uh . . . all hearts," Zachary says, recalling the dice tumbling into the darkness and feeling light-headed. He wonders again what it means and if maybe all of anything is a bad thing to roll.

The man stares at him, scrutinizing his face more thoroughly than he had before with a quizzical expression that looks like recognition, and though it seems like he is about to ask something else he does not. Instead he says, "If you would be so kind as to come with me."

He turns and walks back through the door. Zachary follows at his heels, feeling like he has accomplished something. At least he doesn't have to leave as soon as he's arrived.

Particularly considering he's not certain where he is, exactly. It is not what he expected, this sweeping space with its crumpled chandeliers and dusty piles of books. There are more tiles, for a start. It is grander and older and quieter and darker and more intimate than he imagined it would be when he got here and he realizes now how certain he had been that he would get here somehow because *Sweet Sorrows* implied as much.

Not yet, he thinks, looking up at the universe spinning above him with its hands pointing in alternating directions, wondering what it is that he is meant to do now that he is here.

"I know why you are here," the man says as they pass the swinging pendulum, as though he can hear Zachary's thoughts.

"You do?"

"You are here because you wish to sail the Starless Sea and breathe the haunted air."

Zachary's feet halt beneath him at the comforting trueness of the statement combined with the confusion of not understanding what it means.

"Is this the Starless Sea?" he asks, following again as the man heads to the far side of the grand hall.

"No, this is only a Harbor," comes the answer. "And, as I have already mentioned, it is closed."

"Maybe you should put up a sign," Zachary says before he can bite his tongue and the statement earns him a more withering glance than any of his math teachers could ever have managed and he mumbles an apology.

Zachary follows the man and the ginger cat who has rejoined the procession into what he can only think of as an office, though it is unlike any office he has ever seen before. The walls are all but hidden behind bookshelves and filing cabinets and card catalogues with their rows of tiny drawers and labels. The floor is covered in tile similar to the ones outside, a worn path evident from the door to the desk. A green glass lamp glows near the desk and strings of paper lanterns loop around the tops of the bookshelves. A phonograph softly plays something classical and scratched. A fireplace occupies most of the wall opposite the door, the fire burning low in its hearth covered in a silken screen so the flickering light appears russet-colored. An old-fashioned twig broom leans against the wall nearby. A sword, a large, real sword, hangs above a mantel that contains several books, an antler, another cat (live but asleep), and several glass jars of varying sizes filled with keys.

The man settles himself behind a large desk covered in papers and notebooks and bottles of ink and appears much more at ease though Zachary remains nervous. Nervous and oddly more intoxicated than he felt earlier.

"Now then," the man says as the ginger cat sits on the corner of the desk and yawns, its amber eyes trained on Zachary. "Where was your door?"

"Central Park," Zachary says. His tongue feels heavy in his mouth and it's becoming difficult to form words. "It was destroyed by those . . . club people? I think the fur coat polar-bear lady is their leader? She threatened me with tea. And the guy who said his name was Dorian might be in trouble? He had me take this from their headquarters, he didn't say why."

Zachary removes the book from his coat and holds it out. The man takes it, frowning. He opens it and flips through a few pages and watching upside-down Zachary thinks the Arabic text looks like English but his eyes are likely playing tricks on him because his contact lenses are itching and he wonders if maybe he's allergic to cats and the man closes the book again before he can be certain.

"This belongs down here, so thank you for that," the man says, handing it back. "You may keep it for your friend if you like."

Zachary looks down at the brown leather book.

"Shouldn't someone . . ." he says, almost to himself, "I don't know, rescue him?"

"Someone should, I'm sure," the man responds. "You will not be able to depart without an escort so you will have to wait for Mirabel to return. I can arrange quarters for you in the meantime, you look as though you could use some rest. I simply require some additional information before we proceed. Name?"

"Uh . . . Zachary. Zachary Ezra Rawlins," Zachary provides obediently instead of asking one of the numerous questions he has himself.

"A pleasure to make your acquaintance, Mister Rawlins," the man says, writing Zachary's name in one of the ledgers on the desk. He checks the time on a pocket watch and adds that to the ledger as well. "They call me the Keeper. You said your temporary entrance was in Central Park, I assume you were referring to the one in Manhattan, in New York, in the United States of America?"

"Yeah, that Central Park."

"Very good," the Keeper says, noting something else in the ledger. He marks another document that might be a map and then gets up from the desk and walks over to one of the chests of tiny drawers behind him. He removes something from one of the drawers and turns and hands it to Zachary: a round gold locket on a long chain. On one side there is a bee. On the other there is a heart.

"If you need to find your way back to this spot—most call it the Heart—this will point your way."

Zachary opens the locket to reveal a compass with a single mark where north would be, its needle spinning erratically.

"Will you be needing to know the location of Mecca?" the Keeper asks.

"Oh, no, thanks, though. I'm agnostopagan."

The Keeper cocks his head questioningly.

"Spiritual but not religious," Zachary clarifies. He doesn't say what he is thinking, which is that his church is held-breath story listening and late-night-concert ear-ringing rapture and perfect-boss fight-button pressing. That his religion is buried in the silence of freshly fallen snow, in a carefully crafted cocktail, in between the pages of a book somewhere after the beginning but before the ending.

He wonders what, exactly, was in that thing he drank earlier.

The Keeper nods and turns his attention to the cabinets, opening another drawer and removing something and closing it again.

"If you would come with me, Mister Rawlins," the Keeper says, exiting the room. Zachary looks at the cat but the cat, disinterested, closes its eyes and does not follow.

The Keeper closes the office door and leads Zachary down one of the book-filled halls. This space feels more underground, like a tunnel, lit with occasional candles and lanterns, with a low rounded ceiling and turns that do not follow any obvious pattern. Zachary is thankful for his compass after the third turn through a maze of doors and books, one hall branching off into others, opening up into larger chambers, and funneling into the tunnel-like hall again. Books are packed onto shelves that curve with the rock or piled on tables and chests and chairs like a literary-centric antique store. They pass a marble bust wearing a silk top hat and another sleeping cat on an upholstered armchair tucked into an alcove. Zachary keeps expecting to encounter other people but there isn't anyone. Maybe everyone is asleep and the Keeper is on the night shift. It must be very late by now.

They stop at a door flanked by bookshelves peppered with small glowing lanterns. The Keeper unlocks the door and gestures for Zachary to enter.

"I apologize for the state—" the Keeper stops and frowns, looking in at a room that requires no apologies.

The room is . . . well, the room is the most glorious hotel room Zachary could imagine, except in a cave. There is a great deal of velvet, most of it dark green, fitted over chairs and hanging in curtains over a four-poster bed that has been turned down in anticipation of its guest's arrival. There is a large desk and multiple reading nooks. The walls and floor are stone that peeks out from between bookshelves and framed art and mismatched rugs. It is beyond cozy. A fire burns in the fireplace. The lamps by the bed are lit, as though the room had been expecting him.

"I hope this will be to your liking," the Keeper says, though a hint of the frown remains.

"This is awesome," Zachary replies.

"The washroom is through the door at the rear," the Keeper says, gesturing toward the back of the room. "The Kitchen may be accessed via the panel near the fireplace. The light level in the hall will be raised in the morning. Please do not feed the cats. This is your key." The Keeper hands Zachary a key on another long chain. "If there is anything you require please do not hesitate to ask, you know where to find me." He takes a pen and a small rectangular piece of paper from his robes and inscribes something. "Good night, Mister Rawlins. I hope you enjoy your stay." He places the rectangle of paper in a small plaque by the door, gives Zachary a short bow, and disappears back down the hall.

Zachary watches him go and then turns to look at the paper in the plaque. In calligraphic script on ivory paper placed in a brass plaque it reads:

Z. Rawlins

Zachary closes the door, wondering how many names have occupied that spot before and how long it has been since the last one. After a few seconds of hesitation he locks the door.

He rests his head against the door and sighs.

This can't be real.

Then what is it? the voice in his head asks and he doesn't have an answer.

He shrugs off his paint-stained coat and drapes it over a chair. He makes his way to the washroom, barely taking the time to register the black-and-white tiles and the claw-foot tub before washing his hands and removing his contact lenses, watching his reflection slip out of focus in the mirror above the sink. He tosses his contacts into a bin and briefly wonders what he is going to do without corrective lenses but he has more pressing concerns.

He returns to the blur of velvet and firelight in the main room, kicking off his shoes as he walks, managing to remove his suit jacket and vest before he reaches the bed but he is asleep before he can deal with additional buttons, linen sheets and lamb's-wool pillows swallowing him like a cloud and he welcomes it, his last thoughts before sleeping a fleeting mix of reflections on the evening that has finally ended, questions and worries about everything from his sanity to how to get paint out of his hair and then it is gone, the last wisp of thought wondering how you go to sleep if you're already dreaming.

Once there was a man who collected keys. Old keys and new keys and broken keys. Lost keys and stolen keys and skeleton keys.

He carried them in his pockets and wore them on chains that clattered as he walked around the town.

Everyone in the town knew the key collector.

Some people thought his habit strange but the key collector was a friendly sort and had a thoughtful air and a quick smile.

If someone lost a key or broke a key they could ask the key collector and he would usually have a replacement that would suit their needs. It was often faster than having a new key made.

The key collector kept the most common shapes and sizes of keys always at hand, in case someone was in need of a key for a door or a cupboard or a chest.

The key collector was not possessive about his keys. He gave them away when they were needed.

(Though often people would have a new key made anyway and return the one they had borrowed.)

People gave him found keys or spare keys as gifts to add to his collection. When they traveled they would find keys to bring back with them, keys with unfamiliar shapes and strange teeth.

(They called the man himself the key collector but a great many people aided with the collecting.)

Eventually the key collector had too many keys to carry and began displaying them around his house. He hung them in the windows on ribbons like curtains and arranged them on bookshelves and framed them on walls. The most delicate ones he kept under glass or in boxes meant for jewels. Others were piled together with similar keys, kept in buckets or baskets.

After many years the entire house was filled near to bursting with keys. They hung on the outside as well, over the doors and the windows and draped from the eaves of the roof.

The key collector's house was easily spotted from the road.

One day there was a knock upon his door.

The key collector opened the door to find a pretty woman in a long cloak on his doorstep. He had never seen her before, nor had he seen embroidery of the sort that trimmed her cloak: star-shaped flowers in gold thread on dark cloth, too fine for travel though she must have traveled far. He did not see a horse or a carriage and supposed she might have left them at the inn for no one passed through this town without staying at the inn and it was not far.

"I have been told you collect keys," the woman said to the key collector.

"I do," said the key collector, though this was obvious. There were keys hanging above the doorway where they stood, keys on the walls behind him, keys in jars and bowls and vases on the tables.

"I am looking for something that has been locked away. I wonder if one of your keys might unlock it."

"You are welcome to look," the key collector said and invited the woman inside.

He considered asking the woman what manner of key she sought so he might help her look but he knew how difficult it was to describe a key. To find a key you had to understand the lock.

So the key collector let the woman search the house. He showed her every room, every cabinet and bookshelf lined with keys. The kitchen with its teacups and wineglasses filled with keys, save for the few that were used more frequently, empty and waiting for wine or for tea.

The key collector offered the woman a cup of tea but she politely refused. He left her to her searching and sat in the front parlor where she could find him if she needed and he read a book.

After many hours the woman returned to the key collector.

"It is not here," she said. "Thank you for letting me look."

"There are more keys in the back garden," the key collector said, and led the woman outside.

The garden was festooned with keys, strung from ribbons in a rainbow of colors. Keys tied with bows hung from trees and bouquets of keys displayed in glazed pots and vases. Birdcages with keys hung on the tiny swings inside with no birds to be seen. Keys set into the paving stones along the garden paths. A bubbling fountain contained piles of keys beneath the water, sunken like wishes.

The light was fading so the key collector lit the lanterns.

"It is lovely here," the woman said. She began to look through the garden keys, keys held by statues and keys wound around topiaries. She stopped in front of a tree that was just starting to blossom, reaching out to a key, one of many hanging from red ribbons.

"Will that key suit your lock?" the key collector asked.

"More than that," the woman answered. "This is my key. I lost it a very long time ago. I'm glad it found its way to you."

"I am glad to return it," the key collector said. He reached up to untie the ribbon for her, leaving it hanging from the key in her hand.

"I must find a way to repay you," the woman said to the key collector.

"No need for that," the key collector told her. "It is my pleasure to help reunite you with your locked-away thing."

"Oh," the woman said. "It is not a thing. It is a place."

She held the key out in front of her at a height above her waist where a keyhole might have been if there was a door and part of the key vanished. The woman turned the key and an invisible door unlocked in the middle of the key collector's garden. The woman pushed the door open.

The key and its ribbon remained hanging in midair.

The key collector looked through the door into a golden room with high arched windows. Dozens of candles stood on tables laid for a great feast. He heard music playing and laughter coming from out of sight. Through the windows he could see waterfalls and mountains, a sky brightly lit by two moons and countless stars reflected in a shimmering sea.

The woman walked through the door, her long cloak trailing over the golden tiles.

The key collector stood in his garden, staring.

The woman took the key on its ribbon from its lock.

She turned back to the key collector. She raised a hand in invitation, beckoning him forward.

The key collector followed.

The door closed behind him.

No one ever saw him again.

ZACHARY EZRA RAWLINS wakes up long ago and far away, or at least that's what it feels like.

Disoriented and woozy, his mind a second behind his body, like pulling himself through crystal-clear mud. As though he's still drunk but doing it wrong.

The only other time he felt similar was a night he would prefer to forget that involved too much chardonnay and he associates the feeling with that, a bright, crystalline white-wine sensation: tingling and sharp and a touch oaky. Getting up not remembering that he has fallen down.

He rubs his eyes, looking around at the blur of the room, confused because it is too large and remembering he is in a hotel and as the events of the night before find their way through the haze the room congeals in his blurry vision and he remembers that he is not in a hotel at all and he starts to panic.

Breathe, the voice in his head says and he listens, thankfully, and tries to keep his focus on inhale and exhale and repeat.

Zachary closes his eyes but reality seeps in through his other senses. The room smells of a formerly crackling fire and sandalwood and something dark and deep and unidentifiable. There is a far-off chiming noise that must have woken him. The bed and the pillows are marshmallow soft. His curiosity wages a silent war with his anxiety making it more difficult to breathe, but as he forces his lungs into taking slow, steady breaths, curiosity wins and he opens his eyes.

The room is brighter now, light comes through panels of amber glass set into the stone above the door, filtering in from the hall. It's a light he associates more with late afternoon than morning. There is more *stuff* in the room than he remembers, even without his glasses he can make out the Victrola by the armchairs, the dripping candles on the mantel. The painting of a ship at sea hanging over the fireplace.

Zachary rubs his eyes but the room remains the same. Not knowing what else to do, he pulls himself reluctantly from the marshmallow bed and begins an approximation of his morning routine.

He finds his discarded clothes in the bathroom, stiff with paint and dirt, and wonders if this place has laundry services. For some reason laundry concerns drag him back to the reality of the situation, dreams or hallucinations probably don't involve such mundane problems. He tries to recall a single dream that ever involved thinking "I might need new socks" and fails.

The bathroom is also full of more stuff than he remembered: a mirrored cabinet contains a toothbrush and toothpaste in a metal tube and several neatly labeled jars of creams and oils, one of them an aftershave that smells of cinnamon and bourbon.

There is a separate shower next to the tub and Zachary does his best to wash the gold paint out of his hair, to scrape the last of it from his skin. There are soaps in fancy dishes and all of them smell woodsy or resiny, as though everything has been tailored to his scent preferences.

Wrapped in a towel Zachary inspects the rest of the room, looking for something to wear that is not his sweaty, paint-stained suit.

A wardrobe looms over one wall next to a non-matching dresser. Not only is there something to wear, there are options. The drawers are filled with sweaters and socks and underwear, the wardrobe hung with shirts and trousers. Everything looks handmade, natural fibers and no tags. He puts on a pair of brown linen pants and a collarless moss green shirt with polished wood buttons. He takes out a grey cable-knit sweater that reminds him of one of his own favorites. In the bottom of the wardrobe there are several pairs of shoes and of course they fit, which bothers him more than the clothing since most of it is loose-fitting and adjustable, everything fits but that could be explained away by him being on the slim side of standard but the shoes are scary. He slides on a pair of brown suede shoes that could have been tailor-made (cobbler-made?) for him.

Maybe they have elves who measure feet and make shoes while you sleep, the voice in his head suggests.

I thought you were the practical voice of reason, head voice, Zachary thinks back, but receives no response.

Zachary puts the room key and his compass and, after a moment's hesitation, Dorian's sword back around his neck. He tries to push the worry about what has occurred up there while he has been down here to the back of his mind. He distracts himself by looking around the room, even though he can't see it all that well. Up close things are clear enough, but it means exploring a few steps at a time, taking in the space in small gulps.

He takes a book from one of the shelves, recalling a story that was probably a *Twilight Zone* episode: so much to read and no eyeglasses.

He flips the book open to a random page anyway and the printed words are crisp and clear.

Zachary looks up. The bed, the paintings on the walls, the fireplace, everything has the distinct fuzziness his ophthalmological cocktail of nearsightedness and astigmatism casts on the world. He looks back at the book in his hands.

It's a volume of poetry. Dickinson, he thinks. Perfectly legible, the type sharp even though the font is small, down to the pinprick periods and minuscule commas.

He puts the book down and picks up another. It's the same, perfectly readable. He replaces it on the shelf. He goes to the desk where the brown leather book he procured from the Collector's Club for Dorian rests. He attempts to see if whatever trick this is will focus the illustrations and the Arabic as well but when he opens the book to the title page not only are the curling illuminations clear, the title is in English.

Fortunes and Fables

it reads, clearly, obviously, in a fancy script but definitely in English. He wonders if it is printed in different languages and he didn't notice before but as he flips through the pages each one shows the same familiar alphabet.

Zachary puts the book down, light-headed again. He can't remember when he last ate. Was it at the party? Was that only the night before? He remembers the Keeper mentioning something about the Kitchen near the fireplace.

By the still-fuzzy fireplace (though he can tell from this distance that the ship in the painting above is captained and crewed by rabbits in an otherwise realistic seascape) is a panel set into the wall, like a cabinet door fitted into the stone, with a small button next to it.

Zachary opens the door to find a space that could be a dumbwaiter, with a small thick book and a box inside, a folded note card perched on top. Zachary picks up the card.

Greetings, Mr. Rawlins. Welcome.

We hope you enjoy your stay.

Should you require or desire refreshment of any sort, please do not hesitate to use our service system. It is designed to be as convenient as possible.

· *Inscribe your request upon a card. The book contains a selection of offerings but please do not let its listings dictate your choices, we will be happy to prepare anything you wish if it is within our means.*

· *Place your request card in the dumbwaiter. Close the door and press the button to send your request to the Kitchen.*

· *Your refreshment will be prepared and sent to you. A chime will indicate its arrival.*

· *Please return any unneeded or unused dishes, etcetera, via the same method when you are finished.*

· *Additional access is available throughout the Harbor in designated areas for use when you are not in your chamber.*

If you have any questions feel free to include them with your requests and we shall do our best to answer them.

Thank you, and again, we hope you will enjoy your stay.

—The Kitchen

Inside the box there are a number of similar note cards and a fountain pen. Zachary flips through the book which contains the longest

menu he has ever seen: chapters and lists of food and beverages organized and cross-referenced by style, taste, texture, temperature, and
regional cuisines by continent.

He closes the book and picks up a card and after some consideration he writes down *Hello* and *thanks for the welcome* and requests
coffee with cream and sugar and a muffin or a croissant, whatever
they might have. He puts the card in the dumbwaiter and closes the
door and presses the button. The button lights up and there is a soft
mechanical noise, a miniature version of the elevator hum.

Zachary turns his attention back to the room and the books but a
minute later there is a chime from the wall. As he opens the door he
wonders if he did something incorrectly or if perhaps they are out of
both muffins and croissants but inside he finds a silver tray containing a steaming pot of coffee, an empty mug, a bowl of sugar cubes and
a tiny pitcher of (warmed) cream accompanied by a basket of warm
pastries (three muffins of varying flavors, croissants of the butter and
au chocolat variety, as well as a folded pastry that appears to involve
apples and goat cheese). There is also a chilled bottle of sparkling
water and a glass and a folded cloth napkin with a single yellow flower
tucked inside.

Another card informs him that the lemon poppy seed muffin is
gluten-free and if he has any dietary restrictions to please let them
know. Also if he would like jam or honey.

Zachary stares at the pastry basket as he pours his coffee, adding a
drop of cream and a single sugar cube. The coffee is a stronger blend
than he is used to but smooth and excellent and so is everything he
tries from the pastry basket of wonderment. Even the water is particularly nice, though he has always thought that sparkling water feels
fancier because of the bubbles.

What *is* this place?

Zachary takes his pastries (which, though delicious, are blurry) and
his coffee back to the desk, trying to clear his head with the aid of caffeine and carbohydrates. He opens Dorian's book again. He turns the
pages slowly. There are old-fashioned illustrations, lovely full-color
pages sprinkled throughout, and the titles make it seem like a book
of fairy tales. He reads a few lines of one called "The Girl and the

Feather" before turning back to the beginning, but as he does a key falls from the space beneath the spine of the book and clatters onto the desk.

The key is long and thin, a skeleton key with a rounded head and small simple teeth. It is sticky, as though it had been glued into the spine of the book, behind the pages and underneath the leather.

Zachary wonders if it was the book or the key that Dorian was after. Or both.

He opens the book again and reads the first story, which includes within it a version of the same tale Dorian told him in the dark at the party. It does not, to his disappointment, elaborate as to what the mouse did with Fate's heart. Reading the story brings back more complicated emotions than Zachary knows how to deal with this early in the morning so he closes the book and strings the key on the chain along with his room key and then pulls on the grey turtleneck sweater. It is such a heavy knit that the keys and the compass and the sword are camouflaged beneath the cables and it keeps them from clattering. He expects the sweater to smell like cedar but instead it smells faintly of pancakes.

On a whim he writes a note to the Kitchen and asks about laundry.

Do please send us anything that needs cleaning, Mr. Rawlins

comes the quick response.

Zachary piles his paint-splattered suit in the dumbwaiter as neatly as he can and sends it down.

A few seconds later the bell chimes, and at this point Zachary wouldn't be surprised if his clothes were somehow clean already but instead he finds the forgotten contents of his pockets returned: his hotel key and his wallet and two pieces of paper, one the note from Dorian and the other a printed ticket with a scribbled word that was once a bourbon and is now a smudge. Zachary leaves everything on the mantel, beneath the bunny pirates.

He finds a messenger bag, an old military-type bag in a faded olive green with a number of buckles. He puts *Fortunes and Fables* inside along with a muffin carefully wrapped in his napkin and then, after half making the rumpled bed, leaves the room, locking the door behind him, and attempts to find his way back to the entrance. The Heart, the Keeper had called it.

He makes three turns before he resorts to consulting his compass. The halls look different, brighter than before, the light changed. There are lamps tucked between books, strings of bulbs hanging from the ceilings. Lights that look like gas lamps at intersections. There are stairs but he doesn't remember stairs so he doesn't take any of them. He passes through a large open room with long tables and green glass lamps that looks very library-like except for the fact that the entire floor is sunken into a reflecting pool, with paths left raised and dry to traverse the space or to reach the table islands. He passes a cat staring intently into the water and follows its gaze to a single orange koi swimming under the cat's watchful eye.

This place is not what Zachary had pictured while reading *Sweet Sorrows*.

It is bigger, for a start. He can never see terribly far in one direction at any time but it feels like it goes on forever. He can't even think how to describe it. It's like an art museum and an overflowing library were relocated into a subway system.

More than anything it reminds Zachary of his university campus: the long stretches of walkways connecting different areas, the endless bookshelves, and something he can't put his finger on, a feeling more than an architectural feature. A studiousness underlying a place of learning and stories and secrets.

Though he appears to be the only student. Or the only one who isn't a cat.

After the reflecting-pool reading room and a hall full of books that all have blue covers Zachary takes a turn that leads him back to the tiled cathedral-esque entrance with its universe clock. The chandeliers are brighter, though some are slumped on the floor. They are suspended (or not) by long stringlike cords and chains, in blues and reds and greens. He hadn't noticed that before. The tiles look more colorful but chipped and faded, parts seem like murals but there are not enough pieces left in place to make out any of the subjects. The pendulum sways in the middle of the room. The door to the elevator is closed but the door to the Keeper's office is open, widely now, the ginger cat visible on an armchair, staring at him.

"Good morning, Mister Rawlins," the Keeper says without looking up from his desk before Zachary can knock on the open door. "I hope you slept well."

"I did, thank you," Zachary replies. He has too many questions but he has to start somewhere. "Where is everyone?"

"You are the only guest at the moment," the Keeper answers but continues to write.

"But aren't there . . . residents?"

"Not currently, no. Is there anything else you need?"

The Keeper hasn't moved his eyes from his notebook so Zachary tries the most specific question he has.

"This is kind of random but do you happen to have spare eyeglasses around here somewhere?"

The Keeper looks up, putting down his pen.

"I am so sorry," he says, getting up and crossing the room to reach one of the many-drawered cabinets. "I do wish you would have inquired last night, I should have something that will suit. Near-sighted or far?"

"Near with astigmatism in both eyes but a strong nearsighted should help."

The Keeper opens a few different drawers and then hands Zachary a small box containing several pairs of eyeglasses, mostly wire-rimmed but a few with thicker frames and a single pair of horn-rimmed.

"Hopefully one of these should suffice," the Keeper says. He returns to the desk and his writing while Zachary tries on different pairs of glasses, abandoning the first for being too tight but several fit fine and are surprisingly close to his prescription. He settles on a pair in a coppery color with rectangular lenses.

"These will be great, thank you," he says, handing the box back to the Keeper.

"You are welcome to keep them for the duration of your stay. May I assist you with anything else this morning?"

"Is . . . is Mirabel back yet?" Zachary asks.

Again the Keeper's face falters into something that could be mild annoyance but it passes so quickly Zachary can't be sure. He guesses that the Keeper and Mirabel might not be on the best of terms.

"Not yet," the Keeper says, his tone betraying nothing. "You are welcome to explore at your leisure while you wait. I ask that any locked doors remain locked. I will . . . inform her of your presence when she arrives."

"Thanks."

"Have a pleasant day, Mister Rawlins."

Zachary takes his cue to leave and returns to the hall, noticing the details now that he has corrective lenses to assist him. It looks a breath away from being a crumbling ruin. Held together by spinning planets and ticking clocks and wishful thinking and string.

Part of him wants to interrogate the Keeper but most of him prefers to tread lightly given their interaction last night. Maybe Mirabel will be more forthcoming about . . . well, anything. Whenever she turns up. He remembers the masked king of the wild things and can't picture her here.

Zachary picks a different hall to wander down, this one has shelves carved into the stone, books piled in irregular cubbies along with teacups and bottles and stray crayons. This hall has paintings as well, a number of them possibly done by the same artist who painted the seafaring rabbits in his room, highly realistic but with whimsical details. A portrait of a young man in a coat with a great many buttons but the buttons are all tiny clocks, from the collar to the cuffs, each reading different times. Another is a bare forest by moonlight but a single tree is alive with golden leaves. A third is a still life of fruit and wine but the apples are carved into birdcages, tiny red birds inside.

Zachary tries a few doors that don't have name tags but most are locked.

He wonders where the dollhouse is, if it is real.

Almost as soon as he thinks it he spots a doll on a shelf.

A single rounded wooden doll painted like a woman wrapped in a robe of stars. Her eyes are closed but her simple painted mouth is curled up in a smile, a few strokes of slivered-moon paint creating an entire expression of expectant calm. An expression like the closing of the eyes before blowing out the candles on a birthday cake. The doll is carved in a style that reminds him at first of his mother's kokeshi collection, but then he finds a well-disguised seam around its rounded waist and realizes it is more like a Russian *matryoshka*. He carefully turns the doll and separates the top half from the lower.

Within the lady in her robe of stars is an owl.

Within the owl is another woman, this one wearing gold, her eyes open.

Within the golden woman is a cat, its eyes the same shade of gold as the woman who came before.

Within the cat is a little girl with long curly hair and a sky-blue dress, her eyes open but looking off to the side, more interested in something else beyond the person looking at her.

The tiniest doll is a bee, actual-size.

Something moves at the end of the hall where the stone is draped with red velvet curtains—something bigger than a cat—but when Zachary looks there is nothing. He joins all of the dolls' halves together separately and leaves them standing in a row along the shelf, rather than letting them remain trapped all in one person, and then continues on.

There are so many candles that the scent of beeswax permeates everything, soft and sweet mingling with paper and leather and stone with a hint of smoke. *Who lights all of these if there's no one else here?* Zachary wonders as he passes a candelabra holding more than a dozen smoldering tapers, wax dripping down over the stone that has clearly been dripped on by many, many candles before.

One door opens into a round room with intricately carved walls. A single lamp sits on the floor and as Zachary walks around it the light catches different parts of the carvings, revealing images and text but he cannot read the whole story.

Zachary walks until the hall opens into a garden, with a soaring ceiling like the marble near the elevator, casting a sunlight-like glow over books abandoned on benches and fountains and piled near statues. He passes a statue of a fox and another that looks like a precarious stack of snowballs. In the center of the room is a partially enclosed space that reminds him of a teahouse. Inside are benches and a life-size statue of a woman seated in a stone chair. Her gown falls around the chair in realistically carved rippling cloth, and everywhere, in her lap, on her arms, tucked into the creases of her gown and the curls in her hair there are bees. The bees are carved from a different color of stone than their mistress, a warmer hue, and appear to be individual pieces. Zachary picks one up and then replaces it. The woman looks down, her hands in her lap with the palms facing up as though she should be reading a book.

By the statue's feet, surrounded by bees and resting like an offering, is a glass half filled with dark liquid.

"I knew I was going to miss it," someone says behind him.

Zachary turns. If he hadn't recognized her voice he would not have guessed this could be the same woman from the party. Her hair without the dark wig is thick and wavy and dyed in various shades of pink beginning in pomegranate at the roots and fading to ballet-slipper at her shoulders. There are traces of gold glitter around her dark eyes. She's older than he had thought, he'd guessed a few years older than him but it might be more. She wears jeans and tall black boots with long laces and a cream-colored sweater that looks as though it spent as little time as possible in the transition from sheep to clothing and yet the whole ensemble has an air of effortless elegance to it. Several chains draped around her neck hold a number of keys and a locket like Zachary's compass and something that looks like a bird skull cast in silver. She somehow, even without the tail, still seems like Max.

"Miss what?" Zachary asks.

"Every year around this time someone leaves her a glass of wine," the pink-haired lady answers, pointing at the glass by the statue's feet. "I've never seen who does it, and not for lack of trying. Another year a mystery."

"You're Mirabel."

"My reputation precedes me," Mirabel says. "I have always wanted to say that. We never had proper introductions, did we? You're Zachary Ezra Rawlins and I am going to call you Ezra, because I like it."

"If you call me Ezra I'm going to call you Max."

"Deal," she agrees with that movie-star smile. "I retrieved your stuff from your hotel, Ezra. Left it in the office when I came to find you so there's probably a cat sitting on it now keeping it safe. Also I checked you out of the aforementioned hotel and I owe you a dance since we were interrupted. How are you and what's-his-name settling in?"

"Dorian?"

"He told you his name is *Dorian*? How Oscar Wilde indulgent of him, I thought he was bad enough with his drama eyebrows and his sulking. He said I should call him Mister *Smith,* he must like you better."

"Well whatever his name is, he's not here," Zachary says. "Those people have him."

Mirabel's smile vanishes. The instant concern doubles the worry that Zachary has been trying to force to the back of his mind.

"Who has him?" she asks, though Zachary can tell she already knows.

"The people with the paint and the robes, the Collector's Club, whoever they are. *These* people," he adds, pulling the silver sword from underneath his sweater, cursing when it gets tangled and realizing he is more upset than he would care to admit.

Mirabel says nothing but she frowns and looks past Zachary at the statue of the woman with her bees and lack of book.

"Is he already dead?" Zachary asks, though he doesn't want to hear the answer.

"If he's not, it's for one reason," Mirabel says, her attention on the statue.

"Which is?"

"They're using him as bait." Mirabel walks over to the statue and picks up the glass of mystery wine. She contemplates it for a moment and then lifts it to her lips and downs the whole thing. She puts the empty glass back and turns to Zachary.

"Shall we go and rescue him, Ezra?"

Once there was a princess who refused to marry the prince she was meant to marry. Her family disowned her and she left her kingdom, trading her jewelry and the length of her hair for passage to the next kingdom, and then the next, and then the land beyond that which had no king and there she stayed.

She was skilled at sewing so she set up a shop in a town that had no seamstress. No one knew she had been a princess, but it was the kind of place that did not ask questions about what you were before.

"Did this land ever have a king?" the princess asked one of her best customers, an old woman who had lived there for many years but could no longer see well enough to do her own mending.

"Oh yes," the old woman said. "It still does."

"It does?" This surprised the princess for she had not heard such a thing before.

"The Owl King," the old woman said. "He lives on the mountain beyond the lake. He sees the future."

The princess knew the old woman was joking with her, for there was nothing on the mountain beyond the lake except for trees and snow and wolves. This Owl King must be a children's bedtime story, like the Rider on the Night Wind or the Starless Sea. She asked no further questions about the former monarchy.

After several years the princess became quite close with the blacksmith, and some time after that they were married. On one late night she told him that she had been a princess, about the castle she grew up in, the tiny dogs who slept on silk embroidered pillows, and the shrew-faced prince from the neighboring kingdom she had refused to marry.

Her blacksmith laughed and did not believe her. He told her that she should have been a bard and not a seamstress and kissed the curve between her waist and her hip but ever after that he called her Princess.

They had a child, a girl with huge eyes and a screaming cry. The midwife said she was the loudest baby she had ever heard. The girl was born on a night with no moon which was bad luck.

One week later the blacksmith died.

The princess worried then as she never had before about bad luck and curses and about the baby's future. She asked the old woman for advice and the old woman suggested she take the child to the Owl King, who could see such things. If she were a bad-luck child, he would know what to do.

The princess thought this silly but as the child grew older she would scream at nothing or stare for long hours with her large eyes at empty space.

"Princess!" the girl said to her mother one day when she was beginning to learn words. "Princess!" she repeated, patting her mother on the knee with a small hand.

"Who taught you that word?" the princess asked.

"Daddy," answered her daughter.

So the princess took the girl to see the Owl King.

She took a wagon to the base of the mountain beyond the lake and climbed the old path from there despite the wagon driver's protests. The climb was long but the day was bright, the wolves asleep, or perhaps the wolves were a thing that people talked about and not a thing that was. The princess stopped occasionally to rest and the girl would play in the snow. Sometimes the path was difficult to see but it was marked with stacked stones and faded banners that might once have been gold.

After a time the princess and her daughter came to a clearing, all but hidden in a canopy of tall trees.

The structure in the clearing might once have been a castle but was now a ruin, its turrets broken save for a single tower, and its crumbling walls covered in vines.

The lanterns by the door were lit.

Inside, the castle looked quite like the one the princess had lived in once upon a time only dustier and darker. Tapestries with gryphons and flowers and bees hung from the walls.

"Stay here," the princess told the girl, placing her on a dusty carpet surrounded by furniture that might once have been grand and impressive.

While her mother looked upstairs the small girl amused herself by making up stories about the tapestries and talking to the ghosts, for the castle was filled with ghosts and they had not seen a child in some time and crowded around her.

Then something gold caught the girl's eye. She toddled over to the shiny object and the ghosts watched as she picked up the single shed feather and marveled that so small a girl could wield such a magical talisman but the girl did not know what the word *wield* meant or the word *talisman* so she ignored the ghosts and first tried to eat the feather but then she put it in her pocket after deciding it was not good for eating.

As this was occurring, the princess found a room with a door marked with a crown.

She opened the door into the still-standing tower. Here she found a room mostly in shadow, the light filtering in from high above, leaving a soft bright spot in the center of the stone floor. The princess walked into the room, stopping in the light.

"What do you wish?" a voice came from the darkness, from all around.

"I wish to know my daughter's future," the princess asked, thinking it was not truly an answer to the question because she wished so many other wishes, but it was what brought her here, so it is what she asked.

"Let me see the girl," the voice said.

The princess went and fetched the girl who cried when taken from her newfound ghost friends but laughed and clapped as they followed in a crowd up the stairs.

The princess carried the girl into the tower room.

"Alone," the voice said from the darkness.

The princess hesitated but then placed the girl in the light and went back to the hall, waiting nervously, surrounded by ghosts she could not see, even as they patted her on the shoulder and told her not to fret.

Inside the tower room the small girl looked at the darkness and the darkness looked back.

From the shadows where the girl was staring came a tall figure with the body of a man and the head of an owl. Large round eyes stared down at the girl.

"Hello," said the girl.

"Hello," said the Owl King.

After some time the door opened and the princess went back inside to find the girl sitting alone in the pool of light.

"This child has no future," the darkness said.

The princess frowned at the girl, trying to decide what answer she had wanted that was not this one. She wished, for the first time, that she had not left her kingdom at all and that she had made her choices differently.

Perhaps she could leave the girl here in this castle and tell the town that the wolves took her. She could pack her things and move away and start again.

"Make me a promise," the darkness said to the princess.

"Anything," the princess answered and immediately regretted it.

"Bring her back when she is grown."

The princess sighed and nodded and took the protesting child away from the castle, back down the mountain and to their small house.

In the years that followed the princess would sometimes think of her promise and sometimes forget it and sometimes wonder if it had all been a dream. Her daughter was not a bad-luck child after all, she rarely screamed once she was old enough to walk and no longer stared at empty nothingness and seemed luckier than most.

(The girl had a mark like a scar between her waist and her hip that resembled a feather but her mother could not recall where it came from or how long it had been there.)

On the days when the princess thought the memory of the castle and the promise was real she told herself that someday she would go back up the mountain and take the girl and if there was nothing there it would be a nice hike and if there was a castle she would figure out what to do when the time came.

Before the girl was grown the princess fell ill and died.

Not long after that, her daughter disappeared. No one in the town was surprised.

"She was always a wild one," the women who lived long enough to be old women would say.

The world is not now as it was then but they continue to tell stories about the castle on the mountain in that town near the lake.

In one such tale a girl finds her way back to a castle she half remembers and thought she dreamed. She finds it empty.

In another version a girl finds her way back to a castle she half remembers that she thought was a dream. She knocks at the door.

It swings open for her, held wide in greeting by ghosts she can no longer see.

The door closes behind her and she is never heard from again.

In the most rarely told story a girl finds her way back to a castle she half remembers as if from a dream, a place she was promised to return to though she herself was not the promise-maker.

The lanterns are lit for her arrival.

The door opens before she can knock.

She climbs a familiar stair that she knows was not a dream at all. She walks down a hall she has traversed once before.

The door marked with the crown is open. The girl steps inside.

"You have returned," the darkness says.

The girl says nothing. This part of what was not a dream at all has haunted her most, more than the ghosts. This room. This voice.

But she is not afraid.

From the darkness the owl-headed man appears. He is not as tall as she remembers.

"Hello," the girl says.

"Hello," the Owl King replies.

They stare at each other in silence for a time. The ghosts watch from the hall, wondering what might happen, marveling at the feather in her heart that the girl cannot see though she feels it fluttering.

"Stay three nights in this place," the Owl King says to the girl who is no longer a girl.

"Then will you let me go?" the girl asks, though it is not what she means, at all.

"Then you will no longer desire to leave," the Owl King says, and everyone knows the Owl King speaks only truth.

The girl spends one night, and then another. By the end of the second night she can see the ghosts again. By the third she has no desire to leave, for who would leave their home once they had found it?

She is there, still.

ZACHARY EZRA RAWLINS follows Mirabel down passageways taking sharp turns between halls that he had not noticed before and through doors he had not realized were in fact doors. He slows as they pass over a glass floor, staring down at another hallway full of books below their feet but then hurries to keep up. They arrive back in the Heart in half the time that Zachary expected and Mirabel walks not to the elevator as he had anticipated but over to one of the slumped chandeliers where there hangs a faded grey leather jacket and a black messenger bag.

"Do I need a coat?" Zachary asks as Mirabel puts on her jacket, wondering if he should retrieve his paint-covered one from his room and realizing he forgot to send it down to the Kitchen to be cleaned.

To his left there is a *meow* and Zachary turns to see the ginger cat sitting in the doorway of the Keeper's office. Beyond it, the Keeper sits at his desk, writing, though despite the continuing motion of his pen against paper he is watching them intently over the top of his spectacles. Zachary almost lifts a hand to wave but decides not to.

"Oh," Mirabel says, ignoring both the cat and the Keeper and considering Zachary's linen pants and turtleneck sweater. "Probably, let's find you one. You should leave your bag." Zachary puts his bag down while Mirabel takes a quick turn down the hall nearest the elevator and opens a door to reveal a gigantic mess of a closet, piled with coats and hats and typewriters, boxes of pencils and pens and odd pieces of broken statuary. She grabs a hunter green wool coat with brown elbow patches plucked from the chaos like a perfect-condition vintage-store treasure and hands it to Zachary, nimbly stepping over a crumbling bust on the floor, a lone plaster eye staring forlornly at her boots. "This should fit," she says, and of course it does.

Zachary follows Mirabel through the door to the glowing antechamber. She presses the button for the elevator and it lights up obediently. The arrow shifts its attention downward.

"Did you drink it?" Mirabel asks as they wait.

"Did I what now?"

She points to the wall where the small glass of liquid had been, opposite the dice.

"Did you drink it?" she repeats.

"Oh . . . yeah, yeah I did."

"Good," Mirabel says.

"Did I have another option?"

"You could pour it out or move the glass to the other side of the room or any number of things. But no one's ever stayed who didn't drink it."

The elevator dings and the doors slide open.

"What did you do with it?" Zachary asks. Mirabel sits on one of the velvet benches and he takes a seat opposite. He's pretty sure it's the same elevator but he's also pretty sure he dripped paint all over it and the velvet benches are worn but spotless.

"Me?" Mirabel says. "Nothing."

"You left it there?"

"No, I never did any of it. The dice or the *drink me* bit. The entrance exam."

"How'd you manage that?" Zachary asks.

"I was born down here."

"Really?"

"No, not really. I hatched from a golden egg that a Norwegian forest cat sat on for eighteen moons. That cat still hates me." She pauses for a second before adding, "Yes, *really*."

"Sorry," Zachary says. "This is all . . . this is a lot."

"No, I'm sorry," Mirabel says. "I'd say I'm sorry you got dropped into the middle of this but truthfully I'm grateful for the company." She pulls a cigarette case from her bag and opens it, offering it to Zachary and before he can clarify that he doesn't smoke he sees that the case is filled with small round candies, each one a different color. "Would you like a story? It might make you feel better and they'll only work while we're on the elevator."

"You're kidding," Zachary says. He takes a pale pink disk that looks like it might be peppermint.

Mirabel smiles at him. She puts the case away without taking one herself.

Zachary puts the candy on his tongue. He was right, peppermint. No, steel. Cold steel.

The story unfolds in his head more than in his ears and there are words but there aren't, pictures and sensations and tastes that change and progress from the initial mint and metal through blood and sugar and summer air. Then it's gone.

"What was that?" Zachary says.

"That was a story," Mirabel says. "You can try to tell it to me but I know they're hard to translate."

"It was . . ." Zachary pauses, trying to wrap his head around the brief, strange experience that did indeed leave a story in his head, like a half-remembered fairy tale. "There was a knight, like the shining-armor type. Many people loved him but he never loved any of them in return and he felt badly about all the hearts he broke so he carved a heart on his skin for each broken one. Rows and rows of scarred hearts on his arms and his legs and across his chest. Then he met someone he wasn't expecting and . . . I . . . I don't remember what happened after that."

"Knights who break hearts and hearts that break knights," Mirabel says.

"Do you know it?" Zachary asks.

"No, each one's different. They have similar elements, though. All stories do, no matter what form they take. Something was, and then something changed. Change is what a story is, after all."

"Where did those come from?"

"I found a jar full of them years ago. I like to keep them on hand, like always having a book with you, and I do that, too."

Zachary looks at this pink-haired mystery woman, with the knight and his hearts lingering on his tongue.

"What is this?" he asks. Meaning all of it, everything, and trusting she will understand.

"I will never have a satisfying answer to that question, Ezra," she says and the smile that accompanies the sentiment is a sad one. "This is the rabbit hole. Do you want to know the secret to surviving once you've gone down the rabbit hole?"

Zachary nods and Mirabel leans forward. Her eyes are ringed with gold.

"Be a rabbit," she whispers.

Zachary stares at her and somewhere in the staring he realizes he feels a little bit calmer.

"You painted my door in New Orleans," he says. "When I was a kid."

"I did. I thought you were going to open it, too. It's a litmus test: If you believe enough to try to open a painted door you're more likely to believe in wherever it leads."

The elevator jolts to a stop.

"That was fast," Zachary remarks. If his concept of time is not utterly failing him, his own descent had taken three times as long, at least. Maybe his candy story took more time to dissolve than he'd thought.

"I told it we were in a hurry," Mirabel says.

The elevator opens in what looks to be the same stone column staircase with its suspended lanterns that Zachary remembers from before.

"Question," he says.

"You're going to have a lot of those," Mirabel says as they climb the stairs. "You might want to start writing them down."

"Where are we now, exactly?"

"We are in between," Mirabel says. "We're not in New York yet, if that's what you mean. But we're also not *there* anymore, either. It's an extension of the elevator, way back in the day there were stairs and you kept walking and walking. Or you fell. Or there was just a door. I don't know, there aren't many records. Sometimes there aren't stairs here but the elevator has been around for a while. Like a tesseract except for space instead of time. Or are tesseracts for both? I don't remember, I'm ashamed of myself."

They stop at a door at the top of the stairs, set into the rock. A simple wooden door, nothing fancy, no symbols. Mirabel takes one of the keys from around her neck and unlocks it.

"I hope they didn't put a bookcase in front of it again," she says as she pushes it open a few inches and then stops, peering out the opening before pushing it open farther. "Quick," she says to Zachary, pulling him through and closing the door behind them.

Zachary glances back and there is no door, just a wall.

"Look for it," Mirabel says and then Zachary can make out the lines, pencil lines on the wall thin as paint cracks forming the door, a subtle shading that could be a smudge forming a handle above a mark that is more clearly a keyhole.

"This is a door?" he asks.

"This is an incognito door for emergencies. I don't expect anyone to find it but I keep it locked anyway. I'm surprised they haven't but I'm here a lot, they probably think it's for different book-related reasons. Book places tend to be more receptive to doors, I think it's because of the high concentration of stories all in one place."

Zachary looks around. The slice of bare wall is tucked between tall wooden bookshelves stuffed full of books, some of them labeled with red signs that look familiar but he's not sure why. Mirabel beckons him forward and as they move from the stacks out to a larger space with tables of books and another covered with vinyl records and more signs, past a few people browsing quietly, he realizes why the space is familiar.

"Are we at the Strand?" he asks as they walk up a wide flight of stairs.

"What gave you that idea?" Mirabel asks. "Was it that big red sign that says 'Strand' and 'Eighteen Miles of Books'? That quantification feels inaccurate, I bet there's more than that."

Zachary does recognize the more crowded main floor of the enormous bookstore with its tables of new arrivals and best sellers and staff picks (he has always been fond of staff picks) and tote bags, lots of tote bags. It strikes him that it feels ever so slightly like the book-filled space somewhere below it, but on a smaller scale. The way a stray scent might feel like a remembered taste while not grasping the experience entirely.

They navigate their way past tables and shoppers and the long line by the cashiers but soon they are out on the sidewalk in a blisteringly cold wind and Zachary very much wants to go back inside because the books are there and also because linen pants were not designed for January snow and slush.

"It shouldn't be too long to walk," Mirabel says. "Sorry it's so poetry today."

"So *what?*" Zachary asks, not certain he heard her correctly.

"Poetry," Mirabel repeats. "The weather. It's like a poem. Where each word is more than one thing at once and everything's a metaphor. The meaning condensed into rhythm and sound and the spaces between sentences. It's all intense and sharp, like the cold and the wind."

"You could just say it's cold out."

"I *could.*"

The light falling over the streets is low, late afternoon. They dodge pedestrians on their way up Broadway and by Union Square before taking a right and then Zachary loses his familiar Manhattan landmarks, the map of the city in his mind dissolving into gridded blocks that disappear into nothingness and river. Mirabel is better at dodging pedestrians than he is.

"We have a stop to make first," she says, pausing in front of a building and opening a glass door, holding it open to allow a couple in layers upon layers of coats and scarves to exit.

"Are you serious?" Zachary says, looking up at the ubiquitous green mermaid sign. "We're stopping for *coffee?*"

"Caffeine is an important weapon in my arsenal," Mirabel replies as they go inside and join the end of the short line. "What would you like?"

Zachary sighs.

"I'm buying," Mirabel prods. She pokes him in the arm. He doesn't remember when she put on knit fingerless gloves and his own freezing extremities have glove envy.

"Tall skim milk matcha green tea latte," Zachary says, annoyed that warm beverages actually seem like a good idea given the weather with its cold poetry.

"Got it," Mirabel replies with a thoughtful nod like she's sizing him up via Starbucks order. He's not sure what matcha and foam say about him.

Everything seems normal, standing in line for coffee, the floor damp with melted slush. The glass case filled with neatly labeled baked goods. People sitting in corners staring at laptops.

It's *too* normal. It's disconcerting and making him dizzy and maybe once you go to wonderland you're supposed to stay there because nothing will ever be the same in the real world, in the other world, afterward. Afterworld. He wonders if the maybe-students, maybe-writers typing on their computers would believe him if he told them there was an underground trove of books and stories beneath their feet. They wouldn't. He wouldn't. He's not sure he does. The only thing keeping him from writing the whole thing off as an extraordinary hallucination is the pink-haired lady next to him. He stares at the back of Mirabel's head as she investigates a shelf full of travel mugs. Her ears are pierced multiple times with silver hoops. There's a scar behind her ear, a line maybe an inch long. Her roots are starting to show near her scalp, a dark brown probably close to the color of the wig she wore at the party and he wonders if she went dressed as herself. He tries to remember if he saw her talk to anyone else. If she interacted with anyone but him.

He couldn't have made up this much detail on a person. Imaginary ladies can't order coffee at Starbucks, probably.

It is a relief when the girl behind the register looks directly at Mirabel and asks what she would like.

"A grande honey stardust, no whip," Mirabel says and though Zachary thinks maybe he heard her wrong the cashier girl punches the order onto her screen without question. "And a tall skim milk matcha green tea latte."

"Name?"

"Zelda," Mirabel says.

The girl gives her a total and Mirabel pays in cash, dropping her change into the tip jar. Zachary follows her to the other end of the counter.

"What was that you ordered?" he asks.

"Information," Mirabel responds but does not elaborate. "Not enough people take advantage of the secret menu, have you ever noticed that?"

"I go to independent coffee shops that write self-deprecating menus on chalkboards."

"Yet you had a very specific Starbucks order at the ready."

"Zelda," the barista calls out, placing two cups on the counter.

"Is that *Zelda* for Princess or Fitzgerald?" Zachary asks as Mirabel picks them up.

"Little bit of both," she says, handing him the smaller cup. "C'mon, let's brave the poetry again."

Outside the light is dwindling, the air colder. Zachary clings to his cup and takes a sip of too-hot green foam.

"What did you really order?" he asks as Mirabel starts walking.

"It's basically an Earl Grey tea with soy milk and honey and vanilla," Mirabel says, holding up her cup. "But this is why I ordered it." She lifts it higher so Zachary can see the six-digit number written in Sharpie on the bottom of the cup: *721909*.

"What does that mean?" he asks.

"You'll see."

The light is fading by the time they reach the next block, leaving a sunset glow.

"How do you know Dorian?" Zachary asks, trying to sort through his questions and thinking maybe he should get a notebook or something to keep them in, they fly in and out of his head so fast. He takes another sip of his quickly cooling latte.

"He tried to kill me once," Mirabel says.

"He what?" Zachary asks, as Mirabel stops in the middle of the sidewalk.

"Here we go," she says.

Zachary hadn't even recognized the tree-lined street. The building with its Collector's Club sign looks normal and friendly and maybe a little ominous but that's more to do with the lack of people on this particular block.

"Are you done with that?" Mirabel asks, gesturing at his cup. Zachary takes a last sip and hands it to her. She nestles both empty cups into a pile of snow by the stairs.

"There's another place that's also called the Collector's Club not far from here," she remarks as they approach the door.

"There is?" Zachary asks, regretting not asking if Mirabel has a plan of some sort.

"That one is for stamp collectors," she says.

She turns the handle on the door and to Zachary's surprise it opens. The small antechamber is dark, save for a red light on the wall next to a small screen. An alarm system.

Mirabel punches 7-2-1-9-0-9 into the alarm keypad.

The light turns green.

Mirabel opens the second door.

The foyer is dim, only a purplish light filters through the tall windows, making the ribbons with their doorknobs appear a pale blue. There are more of them than Zachary remembered.

He wants to ask Mirabel how she managed to order the alarm code at Starbucks and also what precisely she meant by *tried to kill me once* but thinks silence might be better. Then Mirabel pulls one of the doorknob ribbons, tearing it from wherever it was hooked to the ceiling high above, and it falls in a clattering sound of doorknobs hitting other doorknobs, a cacophony of low tones like bells.

So much for silence.

"You could have rung the doorbell," Zachary observes.

"They wouldn't have let us in if I did that," Mirabel responds. She picks up a doorknob—a coppery one with a greenish patina—and glances at its tag. Zachary reads it upside down: *Tofino, British Columbia, Canada, 8.7.05.* "And they only set the alarm when no one's on duty." They walk farther down the hall and she runs her fingers along the ribbons like the strings of a harp. "Can you imagine all the doors?" she asks.

"No," Zachary answers honestly. There are too many. He reads more tags as they pass: *Mumbai, India, 2.12.13. Helsinki, Finland, 9.2.10. Tunis, Tunisia, 1.4.01.*

"Most of them were lost before they were closed, if you know what I mean," Mirabel says. "Forgotten and locked away. Time did as much damage as they did, they're tying up loose ends."

"This is all of them?"

"They have similar buildings in Cairo and Tokyo, though I don't think there's any order to which remains end up where. These are decorative, there are more in boxes. All the bits that can't be burned."

She sounds so sad that Zachary doesn't know what to say. They start to climb the stairs in silence. The last of the light sneaks in through the windows above them.

"How do you even know he's here?" Zachary asks, suddenly wondering if this is a rescue mission or if Mirabel has other reasons for being in this space under cover of darkness. The emptiness is starting to feel conspicuous. Too convenient.

"Are you concerned that this might be a trap, Ezra?" Mirabel asks as they turn onto the landing.

"Are you, *Max*?" he retorts.

"I'm sure we're much too clever for that," Mirabel says but then she stops in her tracks as they near the top of the stairs.

Zachary follows her eyes upward to something ahead of them in the second-floor hallway, a shadow in the fading light. A shadow that is quite clearly Dorian's body, suspended from the ceiling and displayed like the doorknobs below, tied and tangled in a net of pale ribbons.

FORTUNES AND FABLES:

THE INN AT THE EDGE OF THE WORLD

An innkeeper kept an inn at a particularly inhospitable cross-roads. There was a village up the mountain some ways away, and cities in other directions, most of which had better routes for traveling toward or away from them, particularly in the winter, but the innkeeper kept his lanterns lit for travelers throughout the year. In summers the inn would be close to bustling and covered in flowering vines but in this part of the land the winters were long.

The innkeeper was a widower and he had no children so he now spent most of his time in the inn alone. He would occasionally venture to the village for supplies or a drink at the tavern but as time passed he did so less frequently because every time he would visit someone well-meaning would suggest this available woman or that available man or several combinations of eligible village dwellers at once and the innkeeper would finish his drink and thank his friends and head back down the mountain to his inn alone.

There came a winter with storms stronger than any seen in years. No travelers braved the roads. The innkeeper tried to keep his lanterns lit though the wind extinguished them often and he made certain there was always a fire burning in the main hearth so the smoke would be visible if the wind did not steal that away as well.

The nights were long and the storms were fierce. The snows consumed the mountain roads. The innkeeper could not travel to the village but he was well supplied. He made soups and stews. He sat by the fire and read books he had been meaning to read.

He kept the rooms of the inn prepared for travelers who did not come. He drank whiskeys and wine. He read more books. After time and storms passed and stayed he kept only a few of the rooms readied, the ones closest to the fire. He sometimes slept in a chair by the fire himself instead of retreating to his room, something he would never dream of doing when there were guests. But there were no guests, just the wind and the cold, and the inn began to feel more like a house and it occurred to the innkeeper that it felt emptier as a house than as an inn but he did not dwell on that thought.

One night when the innkeeper had fallen asleep in his chair by the fire, a cup of wine beside him and a book open on his lap, there came a knock at the door.

At first the now woken innkeeper thought it was the wind, as the wind had spent much of the winter knocking at the doors and the windows and the roof, but the knocking came again, too steady to be the wind.

The innkeeper opened the door, a feat that took longer than usual as the ice insisted on keeping it shut. When it relented the wind entered first, bringing a gust of snow along with it, and after the snow came the traveler.

The innkeeper saw only a hooded cloak before he set his attention to closing the door again, fighting with the wind which had other ideas. He made a remark about the weather but the wind covered his voice with its indignant howling, enraged at not being allowed inside.

When the door was closed and latched and barred for good measure the innkeeper turned to greet the traveler properly.

He did not know, looking at the woman who stood in front of him, what he had expected from someone brave or foolish enough to traverse these roads in this weather but it was not this. Not a woman pale as moonlight with eyes as dark as her night-black cloak, her lips blue from the cold. The innkeeper stared at her, all of his standard greetings and affable remarks for new arrivals vanished from his mind.

The woman began to say something—perhaps a greeting of her own, perhaps a comment on the weather, perhaps a wish or a warning—but whatever she meant to say was lost in a stammer and without a word the innkeeper rushed her to the fireside to warm her.

He settled the traveler into his chair, taking her wet cloak, relieved to see she wore another cloak layered beneath, one as white as the snow she escaped from. He brought her a cup of warm tea and stoked the fire while the wind howled outside.

Slowly the woman's shivering began to ease. She drank her tea and stared at the flames and before the innkeeper could ask her any of his many questions she was asleep.

The innkeeper stood and stared at her. She looked like a ghost, as pale as her cloak. Twice he checked to be certain she was breathing.

He wondered if he was asleep and dreaming, but his hands were chilled from opening the door, a small cut stinging where one of the latches had bit into a finger. He was not asleep, though this was as strange as any dream.

As the woman slept the innkeeper troubled himself with preparing the closest room though it was already prepared. He lit the fire in its smaller hearth and added an extra layer to the bed. He put a pot of soup on to simmer and bread to warm so that the woman might have something to eat if she wished when she woke. He considered carrying her to the room but it was warmer by the fire so he laid another blanket over her instead.

Then, for lack of anything left to occupy himself with, the innkeeper stood and stared at her again. She was not terribly young, strands of silver ran through her hair. She wore no rings or circlets to indicate that she was married or otherwise promised to anyone or anything but herself. Her lips had regained their color and the innkeeper found his gaze returning there so often that he went to pour himself another cup of wine to keep his thoughts from distracting him further. (It did not work.) After a time he fell asleep in the other chair nearest the fire.

When the innkeeper woke it was still dark, though he could not tell if it was night or day blanketed by snow and storms. The fire continued to burn but the chair next to him was empty.

"I did not want to wake you," a voice said behind him. He

turned to find the woman standing there, no longer quite so moonlight pale, taller than he remembered, with an accent to her speech that he could not place though he had heard accents from many lands in his time.

"I'm sorry," he said, apologizing both for falling asleep and for failing to live up to his usual high standard of innkeeping. "Your room is . . ." he began, turning toward the door to the room but he saw that her cloak was already draped by the fire, the bag he had left by her chair at the end of the bed.

"I found it, thank you. Truthfully I did not think anyone would be here, there were no lanterns and I could not see the firelight from the road."

The innkeeper had a general rule about not prying into the matters of his guests but he could not help himself.

"What were you doing out in such weather?" he asked.

The woman smiled at him, an apology of a smile and he knew from the smile that she was not a foolish traveler, though he could have guessed as much from the fact that she arrived at all.

"I am meant to meet someone here, at this inn, at this cross-roads," she said. "It was arranged long ago, I do not think the storms were anticipated."

"There are no other travelers here," the innkeeper told her. The woman frowned but it was fleeting, gone in an instant.

"May I stay until they arrive?" she asked. "I can pay for the room."

"I would advise staying in any case, given the storms," the inn-keeper said, and the wind howled on its cue. "No payment will be necessary."

The woman frowned and this frown lasted longer this time but then she nodded.

As the innkeeper began to ask for her name the wind blew the shuttered windows open, sending more snow swirling through the large open hall and annoying the fire. The woman helped him shutter them again. The innkeeper glanced out into the rag-ing darkness and wondered how anyone had managed to travel through it.

After the windows were shut and the fire returned to its pre-vious strength the innkeeper brought soup and warm bread and wine as well. They sat and ate together by the fire and talked of books and the woman asked questions about the inn (how long had it been there, how long had he been the innkeeper, how many rooms were there, and how many bats in the walls) but the innkeeper, already regretting his previous behavior, asked the woman nothing of herself and she volunteered very little.

They talked long after the bread and the soup were gone and another bottle of wine opened. The wind calmed, listening.

The innkeeper felt then that there was no world outside, no wind and no storm and no night and no day. There was simply this room and this fire and this woman and he did not mind.

After an immeasurable amount of time the woman suggested, hesitantly, that she should perhaps sleep in a bed rather than a chair and the innkeeper bid her a good night though he did not know if it was night or day and the darkness outside refused to comment on the matter.

The woman smiled at him and closed the door to her room and in that moment on the other side of the door the innkeeper felt truly lonely for the first time in this space.

He sat by the fire in thought for some time, holding an open book he did not read, and then he retired to his own room across the hall and slept in a dreamless sleep.

The next day (if it was a day) passed in a pleasant manner. The traveling woman helped the innkeeper bake more bread and taught him how to make a type of little bun he had never seen before, shaped into crescents. Through clouds of flour they told stories. Myths and fairy tales and old legends. The innkeeper told the woman the story of how the wind travels up and down the mountain searching for something it has lost, that the howling is it mourning its loss and crying for its return, so the stories go.

"What did it lose?" the woman asked.

The innkeeper shrugged.

"The stories are different," he told her. "In some it lost the lake that once sat in the valley where a river runs now. In others it lost a person whom it loved, and howls because a mortal cannot love the wind the way that the wind loves it in return. In the common version it has lost only its way, because the placement of the mountains and the valley is unusual, the wind gets confused and lost and howls because of it."

"Which one do you think is true?" the woman asked and the innkeeper stopped to consider the question.

"I think it is the wind, howling as the wind will always howl with mountains and valleys to howl through, and I think people like to tell stories to explain such things."

"To explain to children that there is nothing to fear in the sound, only sadness."

"I suppose."

"Why then do you think the stories continue to be told once the children are grown?" the woman asked and the innkeeper did not have a satisfying answer to that question, so he asked her another.

"Do you have stories they tell to explain such things where you are from?" he asked, and again he did not ask where that was. He still could not place her accent and could not think of anyone he had met who put the same lilting emphasis on the local tongue.

"They sometimes tell a story about the moon when it is gone from the sky."

"They tell those here, too," the innkeeper said and the woman smiled.

"Do they say where the sun goes when it too is missing?" she asked and the innkeeper shook his head.

"Where I am from they tell a story about it," the woman said, her attention on the work in front of her, the steady movement of her hands through the flour. "They say that every hundred years— some versions say every five hundred, or every thousand—the sun disappears from the daytime sky at the same time the moon vanishes from the night. They say their absence is coordinated so that they may meet in a secret location, unseen by the stars, to discuss the state of the world and compare what each has seen over the past hundred or five hundred or thousand years. They meet and talk and part again, returning to their respective places in the sky until their next meeting."

It reminded the innkeeper of another, similar story and so he asked a question he regretted as soon as it fell from his lips.

"Are they lovers?" he asked and the woman's cheeks flushed. He was about to apologize when she continued.

"In some versions they are," she said. "Though I suspect if the story were true they would have too much to discuss to have time for such things."

The innkeeper laughed and the woman looked up at him in surprise but then she laughed as well and they continued to tell their stories and bake their bread and the wind wound its way around the inn, listening to their tales and forgetting for a time what it was that it had lost.

Three days passed. The storms raged on. The innkeeper and the woman continued to pass the time in comfort, in stories, in meals, and in cups filled and refilled with wine.

On the fourth day there was a knock upon the door. The innkeeper went to open it. The woman remained seated by the fire.

The wind was calmer then and only a small amount of snow entered alongside this second traveler. The snowflakes melted as soon as the door was closed.

The innkeeper's comment about the weather died on his lips as he turned toward this new traveler.

This traveler's cloak was a worn color that must once have been gold. It still shone in places. This traveler was a woman with dark skin and light eyes. Her hair was kept shorter than any fashion the innkeeper had seen but it too was near gold in color. She did not seem to feel the cold.

"I am to meet another traveler here," this woman said. Her voice was like honey, deep and sweet.

The innkeeper nodded and gestured toward the fire at the opposite end of the hall.

"Thank you," this woman said. The innkeeper helped her remove the cloak from her shoulders, the snow melted and dripping from it, and he took it from her to hang to dry. She, too, wore another layered cloak, sensible for the weather, this one faded and gold.

The woman walked to the fireplace and sat in the other chair. The innkeeper was too far away to hear them but there seemed to be no greeting, the conversation immediate.

The conversation went on for some time. After an hour had passed the innkeeper put together a plate of bread and dried fruit and cheese and brought it to the women, along with a bottle of wine and two cups. They ceased their conversation as he approached.

"Thank you," the first woman said as he placed the food and the wine on the table near the chairs. She rested her hand on his for a moment. She had not touched him so before and he could not speak so he merely nodded before he left them to their conversation. The other woman smiled and the innkeeper could not tell what she was smiling at.

He let them talk. They did not move from their chairs. The wind outside was quiet.

The innkeeper sat at the far end of the hall, close enough for either woman to beckon if he was needed but far enough that he could not hear a single word spoken between them. He arranged another plate for himself but only picked at it, save for the crescent-shaped roll that melted on his tongue. He tried to read but could not manage more than a page at a time. Hours must have passed. The light outside had not changed.

The innkeeper fell asleep, or he thought perhaps he did. He blinked and outside was darkness. The sound that woke him was the second woman rising from her chair.

She kissed the other woman on the cheek and walked back across the hall.

"I thank you for your hospitality," she said to the innkeeper when she reached him.

"Will you not be staying?" he asked.

"No, I must be going," the woman said. The innkeeper fetched her golden cloak, bone-dry and warm in his hands. He draped it over her shoulders and helped her fasten its clasps and she smiled at him again, a warm, pleasant smile.

She looked as though she might say something to him then, perhaps a warning or a wish, but instead she said nothing and smiled once more as he opened the door and she walked out into the darkness.

The innkeeper watched until he could no longer see her (which was not long) and then he closed and latched the door. The wind began to howl again.

The innkeeper walked over to the fire, to the dark-haired woman sitting by it, only then realizing that he did not know her name.

"I will have to leave in the morning," she said without looking up at him. "I would like to pay you for the room."

"You could stay," the innkeeper said. He rested his hand on the side of her chair. She looked down at his fingers and again placed her hand upon his.

"I wish that were so," she said quietly.

The innkeeper raised her hand to his lips.

"Stay with me." He breathed his request across her palm. "Be with me."

"I will have to leave in the morning," the woman repeated. A single tear slid down her cheek.

"In this weather who can tell when it is morning?" the innkeeper asked and the woman smiled.

She rose from her chair by the fire and took the innkeeper by the hand into her room and into her bed and the wind howled around the inn, crying for love found and mourning for love lost.

For no mortal can love the moon. Not for long.

ZACHARY EZRA RAWLINS is fairly certain someone hit him on the back of the head though he mostly remembers the front of his head hitting the stairs and that's where the pain is most noticeable as he regains consciousness. He is also fairly certain he heard Mirabel say something about someone breathing though now he's not sure who she was talking about.

He's not completely certain about anything other than the fact that his head hurts, a lot.

And he is most definitely tied to a chair.

It's a nice chair, a high-backed one with arms that Zachary's own arms are currently fastened to with cords that are themselves quite high-quality: black cord wrapped in several loops from his wrists to his elbows. His legs are bound, too, but he can't see them under the table.

The table is a long dark-wood dining table, situated in a dimly lit room that he assumes is somewhere in the Collector's Club given the height of the ceiling and the moldings but this room is darker, only the table is lit. Little pot lights in the ceiling cast uniform puddles of light from one end of the table to the other where there is an empty chair upholstered in navy blue velvet that probably looks like the one he is currently tied to because it feels like the type of room where the chairs would match.

Through his headache he can hear soft classical music playing. Vivaldi, maybe. He can't tell where the speakers are. Or if there are no speakers and it is wafting in from outside the room. Or maybe the Vivaldi is in his imagination, a hallucinatory musical complication from a mild head injury. He doesn't remember what happened, or how he ended up at this blue velvet dinner party for one with no dinner.

"I see you've joined us again, Mister Rawlins." The voice comes from all around the room. Speakers. And cameras.

Zachary searches his throbbing head for something to say, trying to keep his face from betraying how nervous he is.

"I was led to believe there would be tea."

There is no response. Zachary stares at the empty chair. He can hear the Vivaldi but nothing else. Manhattan shouldn't be this quiet on principle. He wonders where Mirabel is, if she's in a different room tied to a different chair. He wonders if Dorian is somehow alive, which seems unlikely, and he finds he doesn't want to consider that. He realizes he is starving, or thirsty, or both, what time is it, anyway? It's a stupid thing to realize and the newly realized hunger gnaws at him, like an itch, competing with his throbbing head for his attention. A curl of hair falls in his face and he tries to flip it back into place with creative head gestures but it remains, caught on the edge of his replacement glasses. He wonders if Kat has finished his Ravenclaw scarf yet and if he'll ever see Kat again and how long it will take before anyone on campus thinks to worry about him. A week? Two? More? Kat will think he decided to stay in New York for a while, no one else will notice until classes start back up again. Perils of being a quasi-hermit. There are probably bathtubs full of lye somewhere in this building.

He is having a heated argument with the voice inside his head about whether or not his mother will *know* if he dies because maternal intuition and also *fortune-teller* when the door behind him opens.

The girl from the other night, the one who'd pretended to be a mild-mannered knitting co-ed in Kat's class, enters with a silver tray and places it on the table. She doesn't say anything, she doesn't even look at him, and then leaves the same way she came.

Zachary looks at the tray, unable to reach it, his hands bound to the chair.

On the tray is a teapot. A low, squat iron pot sitting atop a warmer with a single lit candle, with two empty handleless ceramic cups sitting next to it.

The door on the other end of the room opens and Zachary is unsurprised to see the polar-bear lady though she has shed her coat. Now she wears a white suit and the whole ensemble is very David

Bowie–esque despite her silver hair and olive complexion. She even has different-colored eyes: one dark brown and one disconcertingly pale blue. Her hair is tied up in a chignon, her red lipstick perfect and vaguely menacing in a retro way. The suit has a tie that is tied in a neater knot than Zachary has ever been able to manage and that detail annoys him more than anything else.

"Good evening, Mister Rawlins," she says, stopping when she reaches his side. He half expects her to tell him not to get up. She gives him a smile, a pleasant sort of smile that might have put him at ease were he not so far beyond ease at this point. "We have not been properly introduced. My name is Allegra Cavallo."

She reaches over and picks up the teapot. She fills both cups with steaming green tea and replaces the pot on its warmer.

"You are right-handed, yes?" she asks.

"Yes?" Zachary answers.

Allegra takes a small knife from her jacket. She runs the tip of the knife over the cords on his left arm.

"If you try to untie your other hand or otherwise escape, you will lose this hand." She presses the tip of the knife into the back of his left wrist, not quite enough to draw blood. "Do you understand?"

"Yes."

She slips the knife between the cords and the chair and releases his arm in two swift cuts, the cord falling in curling pieces to the floor.

Allegra replaces the knife in her pocket and takes one of the teacups. She walks the length of the table and sits in the chair at the other end.

Zachary doesn't move.

"You must be thirsty," Allegra says. "The tea is not poisoned, if you were expecting such passive tactics. You will note I filled my cup from the same pot." She takes a pointed sip of her tea. "It's organic," she adds.

Zachary picks up his cup with his left hand, his shoulder protesting as he does so, adding to the injury list. He takes a sip of the tea. A grassy green tea, almost but not quite bitter. On his tongue there is a knight with a broken heart. Broken hearts. His head hurts. Heart hurts. Something. He puts the teacup down.

Allegra watches him with studied interest from the other end of the table, the way one watches a tiger in a zoo or possibly the way the tiger watches the tourists.

"You don't like me, do you, Mister Rawlins?" she asks.

"You tied me to a chair."

"I had you tied, I didn't do it myself. I also gave you tea. Does one action negate the other?"

Zachary doesn't answer. After a pause she continues.

"I made a bad first impression, I fear. Knocking you down in the snow. First impressions are so important. You had superior meet-cutes with the others, no wonder you like them both better. You've cast me as a villain."

"You tied me to a chair," Zachary repeats.

"Did you enjoy my party?" Allegra asks.

"What?"

"At the Algonquin. You didn't pay much attention to the fine print. It was thrown by a charitable foundation that I run. It promotes literacy for underprivileged children around the world, sets up libraries, provides grants for new writers. We also work on improving prison libraries. The party is an annual fund-raiser. There are always unexpected guests, it's practically traditional."

Zachary sips his tea silently. He recalls the party having something to do with a literary charity.

"So you close one library to open others?" he asks as he puts his cup down.

"That place is not a library," Allegra says sharply. "Not in any sense of the word. It is not some underground level of Alexandria if you were drawing incorrect conclusions. It is older than that. There are no concepts that grasp it entirely, not in any language. People get so caught up in the naming of things."

"You take away the doors."

"I protect things, Mister Rawlins."

"What's the point of a library-museum if no one gets to read the books?"

"Preservation," Allegra says. "You think I want to hide it, don't you? I am protecting it. From . . . from a world that is too much for it. Can you imagine what could happen if it were to become common knowledge? That such a place exists, accessible from nearly anywhere. That some place *magical,* for lack of a better term, waits beneath our feet? What might happen once there are blog posts and hashtags and tourists? But we are getting ahead of ourselves. You stole something from me, Mister Rawlins."

Zachary says nothing. It is more statement of fact than accusation so he does not protest.

"Do you know why he wanted that volume in particular?" she asks. "The book he had you lie your way into this building to procure? Likely not, he was never the type to divulge more information than necessary."

Zachary shakes his head.

"Or perhaps he did not want to admit his own sentimentality," Allegra continues. "When one of our order is initiated they are given the first book they ever protected, in their first test, as a gift. Most do not remember the specifics but he did, remembered the book, that is. Several years ago we adjusted this practice to keep the books here or in one of our other offices. Pity he won't get it back after going through all that trouble."

"You're guardians," Zachary says, and Allegra's eyes widen. He hopes he put the right kind of emphasis on the word so she cannot tell if it was just an observation and not a connection.

"We've had a great many names over the years," Allegra says and Zachary manages not to sigh his relief. "Do you know what it is that we do?"

"Guard?"

"You are cheeky, Mister Rawlins. You probably think it is charming. More likely you use humor as a defense mechanism because you are more insecure than you want others to think."

"So you're guardians but you don't . . . guard?"

"What do you care about?" Allegra asks. "Your books and your games, am I correct? Your stories."

Zachary shrugs his shoulders in what he hopes is a noncommittal way.

Allegra puts down her teacup and rises from her chair. She moves away from the table and into the shadows on the side of the room. From the sound Zachary guesses that she might be unlocking a cabinet but he can't see. The noise repeats and then stops and Allegra steps back into the light around the table, the lamps grasping again at her white suit to the point where it nearly glows.

She reaches a hand out and places something on the table, just out of Zachary's reach. He cannot tell what it is until her hand moves away.

It is an egg.

"I will tell you a secret, Mister Rawlins. I agree with you."

Zachary says nothing, having not actually stated that he agrees with anything she's said and not entirely certain if he does or not.

"A story is like an egg, a universe contained in its chosen medium. The spark of something new and different but fully formed and fragile. In need of protection. You want to protect it, too, but there's more to it than that. You want to be inside it, I can see it in your eyes. I used to seek out people like you, I am practiced at spotting the desire for it. You want to be in the story, not observing it from the outside. You want to be under its shell. The only way to do that is to break it. But if it breaks, it is gone."

Allegra reaches a hand out to the egg and lets it hover over the shell, putting it in shadow. She could crush it easily. There is a silver signet ring on her index finger. Zachary wonders what's inside this particular egg, exactly, but Allegra's hand does not move. "We prevent the egg from breaking," she continues.

"I'm not sure I'm following the metaphors anymore," Zachary says, his gaze lingering on the egg on the table. Allegra pulls her hand back and the egg is in the light again. Zachary thinks he can see a hairline crack along its side but that might be his imagination.

"I am attempting to explain something to you, Mister Rawlins," Allegra says, wandering back into the shadows around the table. "It may be some time before you understand it fully. There was a point in history when there were guards and guides within that space that you have briefly visited but that time has passed. There were failures in the system. We have a new one now. I would respectfully request that you abide by the new order."

"What does that mean?" Zachary asks and before the question is finished Allegra yanks his head backward by his hair and he can feel the tip of the knife pressing behind his right ear.

"You had another book," Allegra says, calm and quiet. "A book you found in the library at your school. Where is it?" She voices the inquiry with a pointed lightness, the same tone with which she might ask if he would prefer honey with his tea. The candle under the teapot flickers and gutters and dies.

"I don't know," Zachary says, trying not to move his head but the rising panic is tempered with confusion. Dorian had *Sweet Sorrows.* They may not have searched him well enough to get the keys out from under his giant sweater but they certainly would have found the book on Dorian. Or on his body. Zachary swallows, the taste of green tea broken heart dry in his throat. He focuses his eyes on the egg on the table. *This can't be happening,* he thinks, but the knife pressing against his skin insists that it is.

"Did you leave it down there?" Allegra asks. "I need to know."

"I told you, I don't know. I had it but I . . . I lost it."

"A pity. Though I suppose that means there's nothing keeping you here. You could go back to Vermont."

"I could," Zachary says. Going home is suddenly more appealing since walking away is better than not walking out of this building at all, which is beginning to feel like a distinct possibility. "I could also tell no one about this . . . or that place that defies nomenclature . . . or that any of this ever happened. Maybe I made it all up. I drink a lot."

Overkill, the voice in his head warns, and immediately regrets its choice of phrasing. The knife presses back into the skin by his ear. He can't tell if it's blood or sweat dripping down his neck.

"I know you won't, Mister Rawlins. I could cut off your hand to ensure you that I am serious about this. Have you ever noticed how many stories include lost or mutilated hands? You'd be in interesting company. But I believe we can come to an agreement without getting messy, do you agree?"

Zachary nods, recalling the hand in the glass jar and wondering if its former owner also once occupied this chair. The knife moves away.

Allegra steps aside but remains hovering by his shoulder.

"You are going to tell me everything you remember about that book. You are going to write down every detail you can recall, from its contents to its binding and after you are finished I will put you on a train to Vermont and you will never set foot on this island called Manhattan again. You will speak to no one about the Harbor, about this building or this conversation, about anyone you have met or about that book. Because I'm afraid if you do, if you write or tweet or so much as drunkenly whisper the phrase *Starless Sea* in a darkened pub I will be forced to make a phone call to the operative that I've stationed within sniper distance of your mother's farmhouse."

"The what?" Zachary manages to ask despite the desert dryness of his throat.

"You heard me," Allegra says. "It's a lovely house. Such a nice garden with the trellis, it must be beautiful in the spring. It would be a pity to break one of those stained-glass windows."

She holds something out in front of him. A phone displaying a photograph of a house covered in snow. His mother's house. The nondenominational holiday lights are still up on the porch.

"I thought you might need more encouragement," Allegra says, putting the phone away and walking back to the other end of the table. "Some pressure on something you value. You haven't had enough time to value the other two yet regardless of how smitten you might be. I guessed your mother would be a better pressure point than your father what with his new and improved family. We'd have to take out the whole house in that case. Gas explosion, maybe."

"You wouldn't . . ." Zachary starts but stops. He has no idea what this woman would or wouldn't do.

"Casualties have come before," she says, mildly. "More will follow. This is important. It is more important than my life and more important than yours. You and I are footnotes, no one will miss us if we are not included in this story. We exist outside the egg, we always have." She gives him a smile that doesn't reach her mismatched eyes and lifts her teacup.

"That egg is filled with gold," Zachary says, looking at it again. What he had taken for a crack was a stray hair caught on the lens of his glasses.

"What did you say?" Allegra asks, teacup pausing mid-lift, but then the lights go out.

FORTUNES AND FABLES:

THE THREE SWORDS

The sword was the greatest the smith had ever made after years of making the most exquisite swords in all the land. He had not spent an inordinate amount of time on its crafting, he had not used the finest of materials, but still this sword was a weapon of a caliber that exceeded his expectations.

It was not made for a particular customer and the smith found himself at a loss as he tried to decide what to do with it. He could keep it for himself but he was better at crafting swords than at using them. He was reluctant to sell it, though he knew it would fetch a good price.

The sword smith did what he always did when he felt indecisive, he paid a visit to the local seer.

There were many seers in neighboring lands who were blind and saw in ways that others could not though they could not use their eyes.

The local seer was merely nearsighted.

The local seer was often found at the tavern, at a secluded table in the back of the room, and he would tell the futures of objects or people if he was bought a drink.

(He was better at seeing the futures of objects than the futures of people.)

The sword smith and the seer had been great friends for years. Sometimes he would ask the seer to read swords.

He went to the tavern and brought the new sword. He bought the seer a drink.

"To Seeking," the seer said, lifting his cup.

"To Finding," the sword smith replied, lifting his drink in return.

They talked of current events and politics and the weather before the smith showed him the sword.

The seer looked at the sword for a long time. He asked the smith for another drink and the smith obliged.

The seer finished his second drink and then handed the sword back.

"This sword will kill the king," the seer told the smith.

"What does that mean?" the smith asked.

The seer shrugged.

"It will kill the king," he repeated. He said no more about it.

The smith put the sword away and they discussed other matters for the rest of the night.

The next day the sword smith tried to decide what to do with the sword, knowing that the seer was rarely wrong.

Being responsible for the weapon that killed the king did not sit well with the sword smith, though he had previously made many swords that had killed many people.

He thought he should destroy it but he could not bring himself to destroy so fine a sword.

After much thought and consideration he crafted two additional swords, identical and indistinguishable from the first. Even the sword smith himself could not tell them apart.

As he worked he received many offers from customers who wished to purchase them but he refused.

Instead the sword smith gave one sword to each of his three children, not knowing who would receive the one that would kill the king, and he gave it no more thought because none of his children would do such a thing, and if any of the swords fell into other hands the matter was left to fate and time and Fate and Time can kill as many kings as they please, and will eventually kill them all.

The sword smith told no one what the seer had said, lived all his days and kept his secret until his days were gone.

The youngest son took his sword and went adventuring. He was not a terribly good adventurer and he found himself distracted visiting unfamiliar villages and meeting new people and eating interesting food. His sword rarely left its scabbard. In one village he met a man he fancied greatly and this man had a fondness for rings. So the youngest son took his disused sword to a smith and had it melted down, and then hired a jeweler to craft rings from the metal. He gave the man one ring each year for every year they spent together. There were a great many rings.

The eldest son stayed at home for years and used his sword for dueling. He was good at dueling and made quite a lot of money. With his savings he decided to take a sea voyage and he took his sword with him, hoping he might learn as he traveled and improve his skills. He studied with the crew of the ship and would practice on the deck when the winds were calm but one day he was disarmed too close to the rail. His sword fell into the sea and sank to the bottom, impaling itself into coral and sand. It is there still.

The middle child, the only daughter, kept her sword in a glass case in her library. She claimed it was decorative, a memory of her father who had been a great sword smith, and that she never used it. This was not true. She often took it from its resting place when she was alone, late at night, and practiced with it. Her brother had taught her some dueling but she had never used this particular sword for duels. She kept it polished, she knew every inch, every scratch. Her fingers itched for it when it was not nearby. The feel of it in her hand was so familiar that she carried the sword with her into her dreams.

One night she fell asleep in her chair by the fire in the library. Though the sword rested in its case on the shelf nearby she held it in her hand when she began to dream.

In her dream she walked through a forest. The branches of the trees were heavy with cherry blossoms, hung with lanterns, and stacked with books.

As she walked she felt many eyes watching her but she could not see anyone. Blossoms floated around her like snow.

She reached a spot where a large tree had been cut down to a stump. The stump was surrounded by candles and piled with books and atop the books there was a beehive, honey dripping from it and falling over the books and the stump of the tree though there were no bees to be seen.

There was only a large owl, perched atop the beehive. A white-and-brown owl wearing a golden crown. Its feathers ruffled as the sword smith's daughter approached.

"You have come to kill me," the Owl King said.

"I have?" the sword smith's daughter asked.

"They find a way to kill me, always. They have found me here, even in dreams."

"Who?" the sword smith's daughter asked, but the Owl King did not answer her question.

"A new king will come to take my place. Go ahead. It is your purpose."

The sword smith's daughter had no wish to kill the owl but it seemed she was meant to. She did not understand but this was a dream and such things make sense in dreams.

The daughter of the sword smith cut off the Owl King's head. One swift, well-practiced swing sliced through feather and bone.

The owl's crown fell from its severed head, clattering to the ground near her feet.

The sword smith's daughter reached down to retrieve the crown but it disintegrated beneath her fingers leaving naught but golden dust.

Then she woke, still in the chair by the fire in her library.

On the shelf where the sword had been there was a white-and-brown owl perched on the empty case.

The owl remained with her for the rest of her days.

ZACHARY EZRA RAWLINS sits frozen in the darkness. He can hear the Vivaldi though he cannot remember if it had been playing the entire time under the conversation and the tea. There is a scraping sound that is likely Allegra pushing her chair back. Zachary keeps waiting for his eyes to adjust but they don't, the darkness is thick and solid like something pulled over his eyes.

That sound was definitely the click of a door opening and he guesses Allegra has abandoned him, leaving him stuck tied to his chair but another sound follows, something hitting the other end of the table hard enough that it reverberates all the way down to the other side, and the sound of something falling to the floor and a tea-cup breaking.

Then footsteps, coming closer.

Zachary tries to hold his breath and fails.

The footsteps stop next to his chair and someone whispers in his ear.

"You didn't think I'd let her talk you to death, did you, Ezra?"

"What is going—" Zachary starts to ask but Mirabel shushes him, whispering.

"They might be recording. I got the lights but the audio and the cameras are a different system. Rescue mission proceeding more or less as planned, thank you for being distracting." A movement against his arms breaks the cords on his wrist and Mirabel pulls the chair back so she can free his feet.

She must have good night vision, in the darkness she takes his hand and he knows his palm is sweaty but he doesn't care. He squeezes her hand and she squeezes back and if there are sides to whatever all of this is he feels pretty good about siding with the king of the wild things.

In the hall streetlight sneaks in through the windows, just enough to see by.

Mirabel leads him down the stairs and around to the basement stairs and Zachary is mildly relieved to know where he is going even though he can't see all that well. Shadows upon shadows with an occasional glimpse of purple-pink from Mirabel's hair. But when they reach the basement they don't exit to the ice-covered garden, Mirabel leads him in the opposite direction, deeper into the house.

"Where—" he starts but Mirabel shushes him again. They turn down a hallway, losing the light from the garden and falling back into darkness and then somewhere in the darkness Mirabel opens a door.

At first Zachary thinks maybe it is one of *her* doors, but as his eyes adjust he can tell they are still in the Collector's Club. The room is smaller than the ones upstairs and windowless, lit by an old-fashioned lantern set on a pile of cardboard boxes and the light flickers over walls covered in framed paintings, like a disused miniature gallery.

Dorian is slumped on the floor near the boxes, unconscious but obviously breathing and Zachary feels something in his heart unclench that he didn't realize had been clenched in the first place and he is mildly annoyed by the implication of that but then he is distracted by the other door.

In the center of the room stands a door in its frame with no wall surrounding it. It is fastened to the floor somehow but there is open space above and to each side, more cardboard boxes visible behind it against the far wall.

"I knew they had one," Mirabel says. "I could feel it in the back of my head but I couldn't find it since I didn't know where it was. I don't know where they took it from, it's not one of the old New York doors."

The door looks ancient, with nails set in studded patterns along the edges, a heavy round knocker clenched in the jaws of a tiger and a curving handle rather than a doorknob. A door more suited for a castle. The frame doesn't match, the finish shinier. An old door set in a new frame.

"Will it work?" Zachary asks.

"One way to find out."

Mirabel pulls the door open and instead of the far wall and the cardboard boxes there is a cavern lined with lanterns. This in between has no stairs; the elevator door waits opposite, farther away than should be possible.

Zachary steps around to the back of the door. From behind it is a standing frame. He can see Mirabel through it, but when he comes back to the front there is the cavern and the elevator again, clear as day.

"Magic," he mutters under his breath.

"Ezra, I'm going to ask you to believe in a lot of impossible things but I'd appreciate it if you would refrain from using the m-word."

"Sure," Zachary says, thinking that the m-word doesn't explain everything that's happening right now anyway.

"Help me with him, would you?" Mirabel asks, moving toward Dorian. "He's heavy."

Together they lift Dorian, each taking an arm. Zachary has played this game with many an overly intoxicated companion but this is different, the sheer dead weight of a completely unconscious rather tall man. He still smells good. Mirabel has the superior upper-body strength but together they manage to keep Dorian upright, his scuffed wingtip shoes dragging along the floor.

Zachary glances at one of the paintings on the wall and recognizes the space depicted within it. Shelves of books lining a tunnel-like hall, a woman in a long gown walking away from the viewer, holding a lantern much like the one currently sitting nearby on a cardboard box.

The painting next to it is also a depiction of a familiar underground not-library: a slice of curving hallway, figures disrupting the light from around the bend and casting shadows over the books but remaining out of sight. The one below is similar, a nook with an empty armchair and a single lamp, darkness flecked with gold.

Then they pass through the door and Zachary's view of the paintings is replaced by a wall of stone.

They carry Dorian across the cavern to the elevator.

Behind them there is a noise and Zachary belatedly thinks he should have closed the door. There are footsteps. Something falling. A faraway door slam. Then comes the chime of the elevator's arrival and safety feels like worn velvet and brass.

It's easier to settle Dorian on the floor than the benches. The elevator doors remain open, waiting.

Mirabel looks back the way they came, through the still-open door into the Collector's Club.

"Do you trust me, Ezra?" she asks.

"Yes," Zachary answers without taking the time to consider the question.

"Someday I'm going to remind you that you said that," Mirabel says. She reaches into her bag and pulls out a small metal object and it takes Zachary a moment to realize it's a handgun. The small fancy sort that a femme fatale might tuck into a garter belt in a different sort of story.

Mirabel lifts the gun and points it back through the open door and shoots the lantern where it sits on its stack of cardboard boxes.

Zachary watches as the lantern explodes in a shower of glass and oil and the flames catch and grow, feasting on cardboard and wallpaper and paintings and then his view is obscured by the elevator doors as they close and then they are descending.

Once there was a woman who sculpted stories.

She sculpted them from all manner of things. At first she worked with snow or smoke or clouds, because their tales were temporary, fleeting. Gone in moments, visible and readable only to those who happened to be present in the time between carving and disintegrating, but the sculptor preferred this. It left no time to fuss over details or imperfections. The stories did not remain to be questioned and criticized and second-guessed, by herself or by others. They were, and then they were not. Many were never read before they ceased to exist, but the story sculptor remembered them.

Passionate love stories that were manipulated into the vacancies between raindrops and vanished with the end of the storm.

Tragedies intricately poured from bottles of wine and sipped thoughtfully with melancholy and fine cheeses.

Fairy tales shaped from sand and seashells on shorelines slowly swept away by softly lapping waves.

The sculptor gained recognition and drew crowds for her stories, attended like theatrical performances as they were carved and then melted or crumbled or drifted away on the breeze. She worked with light and shadow and ice and fire and once sculpted a story out of single strands of hair, one plucked from each member of her audience and then woven together.

People begged her to sculpt with more permanence. Museums requested exhibitions that might last more than minutes or hours.

The sculptor conceded, gradually.

She sculpted stories out of wax and set them over warm coals so they would melt and drip and fade.

She organized willing participants into arrangements of tangled limbs and twined bodies that would last as long as their living pieces could manage, the story changing from each angle viewed and then changing more as the models fatigued, hands slipping over thighs in unsubtle plot twists.

She knit myths from wool small enough to keep in pockets though when read with too much frequency they would unravel and tangle.

She trained bees to build honeycombs on intricate frames forming entire cities with sweet inhabitants and bitter dramas.

She sculpted stories with carefully cultivated trees, stories that continued to grow and unfold long after they were abandoned to control their own narratives.

Still people begged for stories they could keep.

The sculptor experimented. She constructed metal lanterns with tiny hand cranks that could be turned to project tales on walls when a candle was placed within them. She studied with a clockmaker for a time and built serials that could be carried like pocket watches and wound, though eventually their springs would wear out.

She found she no longer minded that the stories would linger. That some enjoyed them and others did not but that is the nature of a story. Not all stories speak to all listeners, but all listeners can find a story that does, somewhere, sometime. In one form or another.

Only when she was much older did the sculptor consent to work with stone.

At first it proved difficult but eventually she learned to speak with the stone, to manipulate it and discern the tales it wished to tell and to sculpt it as easily as she once sculpted rain and grass and clouds.

She carved visions in marble, with moving pieces and lifelike features. Puzzle boxes and unsolvable riddles, multiple possible endings left unfound and unseen. Pieces that would stand steadfastly and pieces in constant motion that would wear themselves to ruin.

She carved her dreams and her desires and her fears and her nightmares and let them mingle.

Museums clamored for her exhibits but she preferred to show her work in libraries or in bookstores, on mountains and on beaches.

She would rarely attend these showings and when she did she did so anonymously, lost amongst the crowd, but some would know her and quietly acknowledge her presence with a nod or a lifted glass. A few would speak with her about subjects other than the stories on display, or tell her their own stories or remark on the weather.

At one such exhibit a man remained to speak with the sculptor after the crowds departed, a man who seemed more like a mouse, quiet and nervous, a world unto himself pulled tight and secretive, his words soft and delicate.

"Would you hide something in a story for me?" the mouselike man asked the sculptor. "There are . . . there are those who seek what I must conceal and would turn the universe inside out to find it."

This was a dangerous request, and the sculptor asked for three nights to consider her answer.

The first night she did not think on the matter, concerning herself with her work and her rest and the small things that brought her happiness: the honey in her tea, the stars in the night sky, the linen sheets on her bed.

The second night she asked the sea, since the sea has hidden many things in its depths, but the sea was silent.

The third night she did not sleep, constructing a story in her head that could hide anything, no matter what it might be, deeper than anything had been hidden before, even in the depths of the sea.

After three nights the mouselike man returned.

"I will do what you request," the sculptor told him, "but I do not wish to know what it is you desire to hide. I will provide a box for it. Will it fit in a box?"

The man nodded and thanked the sculptor.

"Do not thank me yet," she said. "It will take a year to finish. Come back then with your treasure."

The man frowned but then nodded.

"It is not a treasure in the traditional sense," he said, and kissed the sculptor on her hand knowing he would never be able to pay for such a service, and he left her to her work.

The sculptor toiled for her year. She refused all other requests and commissions. She created not one story but many. Stories within stories. Puzzles and wrong turns and false endings, in stone and in wax and in smoke. She crafted locks and destroyed their keys. She wove narratives of what would happen, what might happen, what had already happened, and what could never happen and blurred them all together.

She combined her work with permanence and stone with the work she had created when she was young, blended elements that would withstand the test of time with those that might vanish as soon as they were completed.

When the year was up the man returned.

The sculptor handed him an elaborately carved and decorated box.

The man placed the precious object that he needed to hide inside. The sculptor did not show him how to close it, or how it might open again. Only she knew that.

"Thank you," the man said and he kissed the sculptor on her lips this time as payment—the most he could give—and she took the kiss in exchange and thought it fair.

The sculptor did not hear anything of the man after he departed. The story remained in place.

Many years later those who sought what had been hidden found the sculptor.

When they realized what she had done they cut off her hands.

a now forgotten city, a very, very long time ago

The pirate (who remains a metaphor yet also a person and sometimes has difficulty embodying both at once) stands on the shore, watching the ships that sail the Starless Sea near this Harbor.

He allows his mind to picture himself and the girl at his side aboard one of these ships, sailing farther into the distance and further into the future, away from this Harbor and toward a new one. He imagines it so clearly that he almost believes it will happen. He can see himself, away from this place, free from its rules and constraints, bound to nothing but her.

He can almost see the stars.

He pulls the girl close to keep her warm. He kisses her shoulder, pretending he will have her for a lifetime when in truth they have only minutes left together.

The time the pirate sees in his mind is not in the city now. It is not soon.

The ships are far from the shore. The bells behind them are already ringing in alarm.

The pirate knows, though he does not wish to admit it even to himself, that they have so far yet to go.

The girl (who is also a metaphor, an ever-changing one that only sometimes takes the form of a girl) knows this as well, she knows it better than he does but they do not discuss such things.

This is not the first time they have stood together on these shores. It will not be the last.

This is a story they will live over and over again, together and apart.

The cage that contains them both is a large one that does not have a key.

Not yet.

The girl pulls the pirate away from the glow of the Starless Sea and into the shadows, to make the most of what moments remain between them before time and fate intervene.

To give him more of her to remember.

After they are found, when the girl meets her death with open eyes and her lover's screams echoing in her ears, before the starless darkness claims her once again, she can see the oceans of time that rest between this point and their freedom, clear and wide.

And she sees a way to cross them.

BOOK III

THE

BALLAD OF

SIMON

AND

ELEANOR

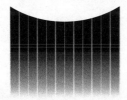

The Ballad of Simon and Eleanor

the naming of things, part I

The small girl stares with wide brown eyes at each person who comes to observe her. A dark cloud of frizzy hair surrounds her head, stray leaves hiding within it. She holds a door knocker the way a smaller child might handle a rattle or a toy. Tightly. Protectively.

She has been placed in an armchair in one of the galleries, as though she is herself a piece of art. Her feet do not touch the ground. Her head has been examined and some concern has been raised over injury, though she is not bleeding. A bruise blooms near her temple, a greenish hue spreading over light brown skin. It does not seem to bother her. She is given a plate of tiny cakes and eats them in small, serious bites.

She is asked her name. She appears not to understand the question. There is some debate over how translations might work for someone so young (few recall the last time there was a child in this place) but she understands other inquiries: She nods when asked if she is thirsty or hungry. She smiles when someone brings her an old stuffed toy, a rabbit with thinning fur and floppy ears. Only when the rabbit is presented does she relinquish the door knocker, clutching the bunny with equal intensity.

She does not recall her name, her age, anything about her family. When asked how she got there she holds up the door knocker with a pitying look in her large eyes, as the answer is terribly obvious and the people peering down at her are not very observant.

Everything about her is analyzed, from the make of her shoes to her accent as they begin to coerce single words or phrases, but she speaks rarely and all anyone can agree on is that there are hints of

Australia or possibly New Zealand, though some insist the slight accent on her English is South African. There are a number of old doors left uncatalogued in each country. The girl does not give reliable geographical information. She remembers people and fairies and dragons with equal clarity. Large buildings and small buildings and forests and fields. She describes bodies of water of indiscernible size that could be lakes or oceans or bathtubs. Nothing to point clearly toward her origin.

Throughout the investigations it remains an unspoken truth that she cannot easily be returned to wherever she has fallen from if her door no longer exists.

There is talk of sending her back through another door, but no one in the dwindling population of residents volunteers for such a mission, and the girl appears happy enough. Does not complain. Does not ask to go home. Does not cry for her parents, wherever they might be.

She is given a room where everything is too big for her. Clothes that fit reasonably well are found and one of the knitting groups provides her with sweaters and socks spun from colorful yarn. Her shoes are cleaned and remain her only pair until she outgrows them, the rubber soles worn through to holes then patched and worn through again.

They call her *the girl* or *the child* or *the foundling,* though the more semantic-minded residents point out that she was not abandoned, not as far as anyone knows, so the term *foundling* is inaccurate.

Eventually she is called Eleanor, and some say afterward she was named for the queen of Aquitaine, and others claim the choice was inspired by Jane Austen, and still others say she once responded to the request for her name with "Ellie" or "Allira" or something like that. (In truth the person who suggested the name plucked it from a novel by Shirley Jackson but neglected to clarify due to the unfortunate fate of that other, fictional Eleanor.)

"Does she have a name yet?" the Keeper asks, not looking up from his desk, his pen continuing to move across the page.

"They've taken to calling her Eleanor," the painter informs him.

The Keeper puts down his pen and sighs.

"Eleanor," he repeats, putting the emphasis on the latter sylla-bles, turning the name into another sigh. He picks up his pen and resumes his writing, all without so much as a glance at the painter.

The painter does not pry. She thinks perhaps the name has a par-ticular meaning to him. She has only known him a short amount of time. She decides to stay uninvolved in the matter, herself.

This Harbor upon the Starless Sea absorbs the girl who fell through the remains of a door the way the forest floor consumed the door: She becomes part of the scenery. Sometimes noticed. Mostly ignored. Left to her own devices.

No one takes responsibility. Everyone assumes someone else will do it, and so no one does. They are all preoccupied with their own work, their own intimate dramas. They observe and question and even participate but not for long. Not for more than moments, here and there, scattered through a childhood like fallen leaves.

On that first day, in the chair but before the bunny, Eleanor answers only a single question aloud when asked what she was doing out on her own.

"Exploring," she says.

She thinks she is doing a very good job of it.

ZACHARY EZRA RAWLINS finds himself in an elevator with a pink-haired lady with a gun who he's pretty sure has just committed arson on top of the already committed crimes of the day and an unconscious man who might be an attempted murderer and his throbbing head cannot decide if he needs a nap or a drink or why, exactly, he feels more comfortable now in present elevator company than he had before.

"What the . . . ?" Zachary starts and then can't figure out the rest of the words so he finishes the question aimed at Mirabel with hand gestures indicating both the gun in her hand and the elevator door.

"It'll render that door useless, hopefully it will take her a while to locate another one. Don't look at me like that."

"You're pointing a gun at me."

"Oh, I'm sorry!" Mirabel says, looking down at her hand and then placing the gun in her bag. "It's a single-bullet antique, one-and-done. You're bleeding."

She looks behind Zachary's ear and takes a handkerchief printed with clocks from her pocket. She pulls it away more bloodied than he had expected.

"It's not that bad," she tells him. "Just keep this on it. We'll get it cleaned up later. It might scar, but then we'd be twins." She lifts her hair to show him the scar behind her ear, which he had noticed earlier, and he doesn't need to ask how she got it.

"What is going on here?" Zachary asks.

"That's a complicated question, Ezra," Mirabel says. "You're very tense. I take it teatime was not particularly pleasant."

"Allegra threatened my mother," Zachary says. He has a feeling that Mirabel is trying to distract him. To keep him calm.

"She does that," Mirabel says.

"She meant it, didn't she?"

"Yes she did. But that threat was attached to telling anyone about our destination, wasn't it?"

Zachary nods.

"She has her priorities. Maybe stay down here for a few days, I can do some reconnaissance. Allegra won't do anything unless she feels she has no choice. She's had opportunities to get rid of all three of us and we're alive and kicking. Mostly," she adds, looking down at Dorian.

"But she actually kills people?" Zachary asks.

"She hires people to do the wet work. Case in point." She nudges Dorian's leg with the toe of her boot.

"Are you serious?" Zachary asks.

"Do you need another story?" Mirabel asks, reaching for her bag.

"No, I do not need another story," Zachary answers, but as he says it the taste of the knight and his broken hearts comes back to his tongue and he remembers more details: the patterned engraving on the knight's armor, the summer evening field blooming with jasmine. It is muddled in his mind like a memory or a dream captured in sugar. It calms him, unexpectedly.

Zachary sits back on the faded velvet bench and leans his head against the elevator wall. He can feel it vibrating. The chandelier above is moving and it makes him dizzy so he closes his eyes.

"Then tell me a story," Mirabel says, and it pulls him out of the sleepy dizziness. "Why don't you begin at your beginning and tell me how we got here. You can skip the childhood prequel part, I know that one already."

Zachary sighs.

"I found this book," he says, tracing everything backward and landing squarely on *Sweet Sorrows*. "In the library."

"What book?" Mirabel asks.

Zachary hesitates but then describes the events that led from the book finding to the party. A short sketch of the preceding days and he is annoyed at how little time it takes to relay and how it doesn't sound like all that much when distilled into individual events.

"What happened to the book?" Mirabel asks when he's finished.

"I thought he had it," Zachary says, looking down at Dorian. He looks asleep rather than unconscious now, his head resting on the edge of the velvet bench.

Mirabel goes through Dorian's pockets, turning up a set of keys, a ballpoint pen, a slim leather wallet containing a large amount of cash, and a New York Public Library card in the name of David Smith along with a few business cards with other names and professions and several blank cards marked with the image of a bee. No credit cards, no ID. No book.

Mirabel takes a few bills from Dorian's wallet and puts the rest of his things back in his pockets.

"What's that for?" Zachary asks.

"After all we went through to rescue him he's paying for our coffee. Wait, we both had tea, didn't we? Either way, it's on him."

"What do you think they did to him?"

"I think they interrogated him and I think they didn't get the answers they wanted and then they drugged him and strung him up for dramatic impact and waited for us to show up. I can help once we get him inside."

On cue the elevator stops and the doors open, revealing the antechamber. Zachary tries to pinpoint the feeling the arrival has and can only think that if the apartment above his mother's store in New Orleans still existed seeing it again might feel like this, but he cannot tell if it is nostalgia or disorientation. He tries not to think about it too much, it is hurting his head.

Zachary and Mirabel lift Dorian using the same system of careful awkward weight balancing as before. Dorian is no help at all with the forward motion. Zachary hears the elevator close and head off to wherever it lives when not occupied by unconscious men and pink-haired ladies and confused tourists.

Mirabel reaches out for the doorknob, shifting more of Dorian's weight over to Zachary. The doorknob doesn't turn.

"Dammit," Mirabel says. She closes her eyes and tilts her head, like she's listening to something.

"What's the matter?" Zachary asks, expecting one of the many keys around her neck might solve the problem.

"He's never been here before," she says, nodding at Dorian. "He's new."

"He is?" Zachary asks, surprised, but Mirabel continues.

"He has to do the entrance exam."

"With the dice and the drinking?" Zachary asks. "How is he supposed to do that?"

"He isn't," Mirabel says. "We're going to proxy for him."

"We're going to . . ." Zachary lets the question trail off, understanding what she means before he finishes asking.

"I'll do one, you do the other?" Mirabel asks.

"Sure, I guess," Zachary agrees. He leaves Mirabel holding Dorian mostly upright and turns back to the two alcoves. He picks the side with the dice, partly because he has more experience with dice than with mystery liquid and partly because he's not sure he wants to drink more mystery liquid and it doesn't feel right to spill it.

"Concentrate on doing it for him and not yourself," Mirabel says when he reaches the little alcove with its dice reset to roll again.

Zachary reaches for the dice and misses, grasping the air next to them instead. He must be more exhausted than he'd thought. He tries again and takes the dice in his hand and rolls them around in his fingers. He doesn't know much about Dorian, doesn't even know his real name, but he closes his eyes and conjures the man in his mind, a combination of walking in the streets in the cold and the paper flower in his lapel and the scent of lemon and tobacco in the dark in the hotel and the breath against his neck and he lets the dice tumble from his palm.

He opens his eyes. The wobbling dice are hazy in his vision but then they focus.

One key. One bee. One sword. One crown. One heart. One feather.

The dice settle and stop and before the last one ceases to move the bottom falls out of the alcove and they disappear into the darkness.

"What did he get?" Mirabel asks. "Wait, let me guess: swords and . . . keys, maybe."

"One of each," Zachary says. "I think, unless there are more than six things."

"Huh," Mirabel says in a tone that Zachary can't decipher as she lets him take hold of Dorian again who suddenly feels much more *there* with the memory of the storytelling fresh in his mind and that faint lemon scent. It's warmer down here than Zachary remembers. He realizes he lost his borrowed coat somewhere.

On the other side of the room Mirabel picks up the covered glass and looks at it carefully before uncovering it and drinking it. She shudders and replaces the glass in the alcove.

"What did it taste like when you drank it?" she asks Zachary as she takes Dorian's other arm again.

"Um . . . honey spice vanilla orange blossom," Zachary says, recalling the liqueur-like flavor, though the list of notes does not do it justice. "With a kick," he adds. "Why?"

"That one tasted like wine and salt and smoke," Mirabel says. "But he would have drunk it. Let's see if it worked."

This time the door opens.

Zachary's relief is temporary, realizing how far they have to go as they enter the giant hall.

"Now we get him checked in," Mirabel says. "Then you and I are having a real drink, we've earned it."

The walk to the Keeper's office attracts the attention of a few curious cats who peer out from behind stacks of books and chandeliers to watch their progress.

"Wait here," Mirabel says, shifting all of Dorian's weight to Zachary's shoulder and again it is surprisingly heavy and more *something* than Zachary would care to admit. "Straight flush, right?"

"I don't think that term applies to dice."

Mirabel shrugs and heads into the Keeper's office. Zachary can't make out most of the conversation, only words and phrases that make it clear it is more argument than conversation, and then the door swings open and the Keeper marches in his direction.

The Keeper doesn't even glance at Zachary, focusing his attention on Dorian, pulling his head up and brushing the thick salt-and-pepper hair back from his temples and staring at him, a much more thorough visual exam than Zachary received himself.

"You rolled his dice for him?" the Keeper asks Zachary.

"Yes?"

"You rolled for him, specifically, you did not simply let them fall?"

"Well, yeah?" Zachary answers. "Was that okay?" he asks, half to the Keeper and half to Mirabel who has followed him out of the office with Zachary's bags slung over her shoulder and a compass and a key dangling from chains in her hand.

"It is . . . unusual," the Keeper says but does not elaborate, and seemingly finished with his perusal of Dorian he releases him, Dorian's head settling on Zachary's shoulder. Without another word the Keeper turns and walks past Mirabel, and goes back into his office and closes the door. They exchange a pointed look as they pass each other but Zachary only sees Mirabel's side and her expression doesn't give away enough for him to interpret.

"What was that about?" Zachary asks as Mirabel helps him with Dorian again, after adding his satchel to the bag collection.

"I'm not sure," Mirabel answers but doesn't meet his eyes. "Rule-bending combined with a low-probability roll, maybe. Let's get him to his room. Don't trip over cats."

They make their way down halls that Zachary hasn't seen before (one is painted copper, another has books hanging from loops of rope) and some too narrow to walk three abreast so they have to pass through sideways. Everything looks bigger and stranger than Zachary remembers, more looming shadows and more places and books to get lost in. Hallways appear to be moving, trailing off in different directions like snakes and Zachary keeps his eyes trained on the floor in front of them to steady himself.

They come to a hall strewn with café tables and chairs, all black, piled with books with gilded edges. One table has a cat: a small silver tabby with folded ears and yellow eyes who regards them curiously. The floor is tiled in black and gold in a pattern like vines. Some of the tiled vines climb the walls, covering the stone up to the curving ceiling. Mirabel pulls out a key and opens a door between the vines. Beyond it there is a room quite like Zachary's but in blues, the furniture mostly lacquered and black. Not quite art deco blended with the sort of room that looks like it would smell like cigars and kind of does come to think of it. The tiles on the floor are checkered where they're not covered by navy rugs. The lit fireplace is small and arched. A number of filament bulbs hang unshaded from cords suspended from the ceiling, dimly glowing.

Zachary and Mirabel put Dorian on the bed, a pillow-covered pile of navy with a fanned headboard, and Zachary's dizziness returns, along with the realization of how much his arms hurt. From the look on Mirabel's face as she massages her shoulder she likely feels the same.

"We need to have a rule about unconsciousness around here," she says. "Or maybe we need wheelbarrows." She goes to a panel near the fireplace. Zachary can guess what it is though this one is a thinner, sleeker door than his own dumbwaiter. "Take off his shoes and coat, would you?" Mirabel asks as she writes on a piece of paper.

Zachary removes Dorian's scuffed wingtips revealing bright purple socks with individually knit toes and then carefully untangles him from his coat, noticing the paper flower, partially crushed, in the lapel. As Zachary puts the coat down on a chair he tries to uncrush the flower, realizing that he can read it though he remembers that the words had been in Italian.

Do not be afraid; our fate cannot be taken from us; it is a gift.

He starts to ask Mirabel about translations without using the m-word but as the text swims from English to Italian and back again the dizziness intensifies. He looks up and the room is undulating, like he's underwater and not just underground. He loses his balance, putting a hand out to the wall to steady himself and missing.

Mirabel turns at the sound of the falling lamp.

"You didn't drink anything while you were tied up, did you?" she asks.

Zachary tries to answer her but crashes to the floor instead.

The Ballad of Simon and Eleanor
a girl is not a rabbit, a rabbit is not a girl

The girl in the bunny mask wanders the hallways of the Harbor. She opens doors and crawls under desks and stands stock-still in the middle of rooms, staring blankly ahead sometimes for long stretches of time.

She startles those who stumble upon her, though such occasions are rare.

The mask is a lovely thing, antique and likely Venetian though no one recalls its origin. A fading pink nose surrounded by realistic whiskers and gold filigree. The ears stretch above the girl's head, making her appear taller than she is, a soft pink-gold blush inside giving the impression of listening, catching every sound that breaks the silence resting like a blanket over this place in this time.

She is accustomed to it now, this place. She knows to walk softly and lightly so her footsteps do not echo, a skill she learned from the cats though she cannot make her steps cat-silent no matter how hard she tries.

She wears trousers that are too short and a sweater that is too big. She carries a knapsack that once belonged to a long-dead soldier who never would have imagined his bag ending up on the narrow shoulders of a girl in the guise of a rabbit as she explores subterranean rooms that she has been expressly forbidden to enter.

In the bag there is a canteen of water, a carefully wrapped parcel of biscuits, a telescope with a scratched lens, a mostly blank notebook, several pens, and a number of paper stars carefully folded from notebook pages filled with nightmares.

She drops the stars in the far corners, leaving her fears behind bookshelves and tucked into vases. Scattering them in hidden constellations.

(She does this with books as well, removing the pages she does not care for and sending them off into the shadows where they belong.)

(The cats play with the stars, batting bad dreams or uncomfortable prose from one hiding place to another, changing the patterns of the stars.)

The girl forgets the dreams once she lets them go, adding to the long list of things she does not remember: What time she is meant to go to bed. Where she puts books she starts but does not finish. The time before she came to this place. Mostly.

Of the before time she remembers the woods with the trees and the birds. She recalls being submerged in bathtub water and staring up at a flat white ceiling, different from the ceilings here.

It is like remembering a different girl. A girl in a book she read and not a girl she was herself.

Now she is a different thing with a different name in a different place.

Bunny Eleanor is different from regular Eleanor.

Regular Eleanor wakes up late at night and forgets where she is. Forgets the difference between things that have happened and things that she read in books and things she thinks maybe happened but maybe did not. Regular Eleanor sometimes sleeps in her bathtub instead of her bed.

The girl prefers being a bunny. She rarely removes her mask.

She opens doors she has been told not to open and discovers rooms with walls that tell stories and rooms with pillows for naps embroidered with bedtime stories and rooms with cats and the room with the owls she found once and never again and one door she has not managed to open yet in the burned place.

The burned place she found because someone put shelves in front of it tall enough to keep big people out but not small bunny girls and she crawled under and through.

The room contained burned books and black dust and something that might once have been a cat but was not anymore.

And the door.

A plain door with a shiny brass feather set into the center, above the girl's head.

The door was the only thing in the room not covered in black dust.

The girl thought maybe the door was hidden behind a wall that burned away with the rest of the room. She wonders why anyone would hide a door behind a wall.

The door refused to open.

When Eleanor gave up due to frustration and hunger and walked back to her room the painter found her, covered in soot, and put her in a bath but did not know what she had been up to because the fire was before the painter's time.

Now Eleanor keeps going back to look at the door.

She sits and stares at it.

She tries whispering through the keyhole but never receives a response.

She nibbles on biscuits in the darkness. She doesn't have to remove her bunny mask because it doesn't cover her mouth, one of many reasons why the bunny mask is the best mask.

She rests her head on the floor, which makes her sneeze, but then she can see the tiniest sliver of light.

A shadow passes by the door and disappears again. Like when the cats pass by her room at night.

Eleanor presses her ear against the door but hears nothing. Not even a cat.

Eleanor takes a notebook and a pen from her bag.

She considers what to write and then inscribes a simple message. She decides to leave it unsigned but then changes her mind and draws a small bunny face in the corner. The ears are not as even as she would like but it is identifiable as a bunny which is the important part.

She rips the page from the notebook and folds it, pressing along the creases so it stays flat.

She slips the paper under the door. It stops halfway. She gives it an extra push and it passes into the room beyond.

Eleanor waits, but nothing happens and the nothing happening becomes quickly boring so she leaves.

Eleanor is in another room, giving a biscuit to a cat, the note half forgotten, when the door opens. A rectangle of light spills into the soot-covered space.

The door remains open for a moment, and then it slowly closes.

ZACHARY EZRA RAWLINS half wakes underwater with the taste of honey in his mouth. It makes him cough.

"What did you drink?" he hears Mirabel's voice from far away but when he blinks she is inches from his face, staring at him, blurry, her hair a backlit halo of pink. His glasses are gone. "What did you drink?" blurry underwater Mirabel repeats. Zachary wonders if mermaids have pink hair.

"She gave me tea," he says, each word slow like the honey. "Intimidatey tea."

"And you *drank* it?" Mirabel asks incredulously as Zachary thinks maybe he nods. "You need more of this."

She puts something to his lips that might be a bowl and is definitely filled with honey. Honey and maybe cinnamon and clove. It's just liquid enough to drink and tastes like cough-medicine Christmas. *Always winter never nondenominational seasonal holidays,* Zachary Narnia-thinks and coughs again but then Princess Bubblegum—no, Mirabel—forces him to drink more of it.

"I can't believe you were that stupid," she says.

"She drank it first," Zachary protests, the words almost at a normal pace. "She poured both cups."

"And she chose which cup you got, right?" Mirabel says and Zachary nods. "The poison was in the cup, not the tea. Did you drink the whole cup?"

"I don't think so," Zachary says. The room is getting clearer. His glasses weren't missing after all, they're on his face. The underwater feeling fades. He's sitting in an armchair in Dorian's art deco room. Dorian is asleep on the bed. "How long was I . . ." he starts to ask but can't find the word to complete the question, even though he knows it is a little word. Oou. Tout.

"A few minutes," Mirabel answers. "You should have more of that."

Out. That's the word. Sneaky little word. Zachary sips the liquid again. He can't remember if he likes honey or not.

Behind him the dumbwaiter chimes and Mirabel goes to check it. She removes a tray filled with vials and bowls and a towel and a box of matches.

"Light this and put it on the nightstand, please," Mirabel instructs him, handing him the matches and a cone of incense with a ceramic burner. Zachary realizes it's a test as soon as he tries to light the match, his coordination failing him. It takes three attempts.

Zachary holds the lit match to the incense, reminded of all the times he performed the same action for his mother. He concentrates on holding his hand steady, more difficult than it should be, and lets the incense catch before softly blowing the flame down to a smoking ember, the scent rich and immediate but unfamiliar. Sweet but minty.

"What is it?" Zachary asks as he places it on the nightstand, curls of smoke wafting over the bed. His hands feel less shaky but he sits back down and takes another sip of the honey mixture. He thinks he does like honey.

"No idea," Mirabel says. She puts some liquid on the small towel and places it on Dorian's forehead. "The Kitchen has its house remedies, they tend to be effective. You know about the Kitchen, right?"

"We've met."

"They don't usually include the incense unless it's serious," Mirabel says, frowning at the curling smoke and looking back at Dorian. "Maybe it's for both of you."

"Why would Allegra poison me?" Zachary asks.

"Two possibilities," Mirabel says. "One, she was going to knock you out and send you back to Vermont so you'd wake up with mild amnesia and if you remembered anything you would think it was a dream."

"Two?"

"She was trying to kill you."

"Great," Zachary says. "And this is an antidote?"

"I have never encountered a poison it couldn't counteract. You're feeling better already, aren't you?"

"Just a little blurry," Zachary says. "You said he tried to kill you once."

"It didn't work," Mirabel says and before Zachary can ask her to elaborate there is a knock at the open door.

Zachary expects it to be the Keeper but there's a young woman at the threshold looking concerned. This girl is about his age, bright-eyed and short with dark hair tamed into braids that frame her face but left wild in the back. She wears an ivory-colored version of the Keeper's robe but simpler, except for the intricate white-on-white embroidery around the cuffs and hem and collar. She looks question-ingly at Zachary and then turns to Mirabel and raises her left hand, holding her palm sideways and then turning it flat, palm up. Zachary knows without asking for a translation that she's inquiring as to what is going on.

"We've been having adventures, Rhyme," Mirabel says and the girl frowns. "There was a daring rescue and bondage and tea and a fire and two-thirds of us got poisoned. Also this is Zachary, Zachary this is Rhyme."

Zachary puts two fingers to his lips and inclines his head in greeting automatically, knowing this girl must be an acolyte and remembering the gesture from *Sweet Sorrows*. As soon as he does it he feels stupid for assuming but Rhyme's eyes light up and the frown vanishes. She places a hand over her breastbone and inclines her head in return.

"Well you two are going to get along just fine," Mirabel observes, shooting a curious glance at Zachary before returning her attention to Dorian. She raises a hand to coerce the smoke from the incense closer, curls of it following the motions of her fingers and drifting along her arm. "You and Rhyme have something in common," Mira-bel says to Zachary. "Rhyme found a painted door when she was a youngster, only she opened hers. That was what, eight years ago?"

Rhyme shakes her head and holds up all of her fingers.

"You're making me feel old," Mirabel says.

"You didn't go home?" Zachary asks and immediately regrets the question as the light fades from Rhyme's face. Mirabel interrupts before he can apologize.

"Is everything all right, Rhyme?" she asks.

Rhyme gestures again and this one Zachary can't interpret. A fluttering of fingers that moves from one hand to the other. Whatever it means, Mirabel seems to understand.

"Yes, I have it," she says. She turns to Zachary. "Please excuse us for a moment, Ezra," she says. "If he's not awake by the time the incense goes out light another one, would you? I'll be back."

"Sure," he says. Mirabel follows Rhyme out of the room, retrieving her bag from a chair as she goes. Zachary tries to remember if the bag looked like it had something large and heavy in it earlier, because it certainly does now. Mirabel and the bag are gone before he can get a better look at it.

Alone with Dorian, Zachary occupies himself with watching the curling smoke float around the room. It swirls over the pillows and drifts up to the ceiling. He tries to perform the same elegant conjuring gesture that Mirabel used to urge the smoke in the right direction but it curls up his arm instead, wrapping around his head and his shoulder. His shoulder doesn't hurt anymore but he can't remember when it stopped.

He leans over Dorian to adjust the cloth on his forehead. The top two buttons on Dorian's shirt are undone, Mirabel must have done that, maybe to make it easier for him to breathe. Zachary's gaze moves back and forth from the curling smoke to Dorian's open collar and then his curiosity gets the better of him.

It feels like an intrusion, though it is a single button's worth of trespassing. Still, Zachary hesitates as he undoes the button, wondering what Dorian might make of "I was looking for your sword" as an excuse.

The lack of a sword emblazoned on Dorian's chest comes as both a surprise and a disappointment. Zachary had been wondering what it looked like more than whether or not it was there at all. The extra button's worth of revelation has exposed a few more inches of well-muscled chest covered in a fair amount of hair and several bruises but no ink, nothing marking him as a guardian. Maybe that tradition is no longer upheld, replaced by silver swords like the one beneath his sweater. How much of *Sweet Sorrows* is fact and how much is fiction and how much has simply changed with time?

Zachary re-buttons the extra button, noticing as he does that while there is no sword there is a hint of ink higher, around Dorian's shoulders. The edge of a tattoo covering his back and neck, but he can only make out branch-like shapes in the light.

He wonders about the line between keeping an eye on someone who is unconscious and watching someone sleep and decides maybe he should read. The Kitchen would probably make him a drink, but he's not thirsty, or hungry, though he thinks he should be.

Zachary gets up from his chair, relieved that the action doesn't revive the blurry underwater feeling, and finds his bags where Mirabel left them near the door and realizes that he's finally been reunited with his duffel. He takes out his phone, its battery unsurprisingly dead, though he doubts it would have a signal down here anyway. He puts it away and retrieves the brown leather book of fairy tales from the satchel.

Zachary returns to the chair by the bed and reads. He is partway through a story about an innkeeper in a snow-covered inn that is so absorbing he can almost hear the wind when he notices the incense has burned out.

He puts the book down on the nightstand and lights another cone of incense. The smoke wafts over the book as it catches.

"At least you have your book back even though I don't have mine," Zachary remarks aloud. He thinks perhaps he will have a drink, maybe a glass of water to get the honey taste out of his mouth, and goes to inscribe a request for the Kitchen. His hand is on the pen when he hears Dorian's voice behind him, sleepy but clear.

"I put your book in your coat."

The Ballad of Simon and Eleanor

time-crossed is not the same as star-crossed

Simon is an only child, his name inherited from an older brother who died at birth. He is a replacement. He sometimes wonders if he is living someone else's life, wearing someone else's shoes and someone else's name.

Simon lives with his uncle (his dead mother's brother) and his aunt, constantly reminded that he is not their son. The specter of his mother hangs over him. His uncle only mentions her when drinking (also the only time he will call Simon a bastard) but he drinks often. Jocelyn Keating is invoked as everything from a trollop to a witch. Simon doesn't remember enough of his mother to know if she was a witch or not. He once dared to suggest he might not be a bastard, as no one is certain of his parentage and his mother was with whatever man might be his father long enough for there to be two Simons so they might have secretly been married but that got a wineglass thrown at his head (badly aimed). His uncle did not recall the exchange afterward. A maid cleared away the broken glass.

On Simon's eighteenth birthday he is presented with an envelope. Its wax seal has an impression of an owl and the paper is yellowed with age. The front reads:

For Simon Jonathan Keating on the occasion of the eighteenth anniversary of his birth

It had been kept in some bank box somewhere, his uncle explains. Delivered that morning.

"It's not my birthday," Simon observes.

"We were never certain of your birth date," his uncle states with a matter-of-fact dullness. "Apparently it is today. Many happy returns."

He leaves Simon alone with the envelope.

It is heavy. There is more than a letter inside. Simon breaks the seal, surprised that his uncle did not already open it himself.

He hopes that his mother has written him a message, speaking to him across time.

It is not a letter.

The paper has no salutation, no signature. Only an address. Somewhere in the country.

And there is a key.

Simon turns the paper over and finds two additional words on the reverse.

memorize & burn

He reads the address again. He looks at the key. He rereads the front of the envelope.

Someone has given him a country house. Or a barn. Or a locked box in a field.

Simon reads the address a third time, then a fourth. He closes his eyes and repeats it to himself and checks that he is correct, reads it one more time for good measure and drops the paper into the fireplace.

"What was in that envelope?" his uncle asks, too casually, at dinner.

"Just a key," Simon answers.

"A key?"

"A key. A keepsake, I suppose."

"*Harrumph,*" his uncle grumbles into his wineglass.

"I might pay a visit to my school friends in the country next weekend," Simon remarks mildly and his aunt comments on the weather and his uncle *harrumphs* again and one anxious week later Simon is on a train with the key in his pocket, staring out the window and repeating the address to himself.

At the station he asks for directions and is pointed down a winding road, past empty fields.

He does not see the stone cottage until he is on its doorstep. It is concealed behind ivy and brambles, a garden left to its own devices that has nearly consumed the building it surrounds. A low stone wall separates it from the road, the gate rusted shut.

Simon climbs over the wall, thorns tugging at his trousers. He pulls down a curtain of ivy in order to access the cottage door.

He tries the key in the lock. It turns easily but getting inside is another matter. He pushes and shoves and clears more ivy vines before convincing it to open at last.

Simon sneezes as he enters the cottage. Each step kicks up more dust as he walks and it floats through the low sunlight, among leaf-shaped shadows creeping over the floors.

One of the more persistent tendrils of ivy has found its way through a window crack and curled around a table leg. Simon opens the window, allowing fresher air and brighter light inside.

Teacups are stacked in an open cupboard. A kettle hangs by the fireplace. The furniture (a table and chairs, two armchairs by the fire, and a tarnished brass bed) is covered in books and papers.

Simon opens a book and finds his mother's name inscribed inside the cover. *Jocelyn Simone Keating.* He never knew her middle name. He understands where his name originates. He is not certain he likes this cottage, but apparently it is his now to like or dislike as he pleases.

Simon opens another window as wide as the ivy permits. He finds a broom in a corner and sweeps, attempting to banish as much dust as he can as the light fades.

He does not have a plan, which now feels foolish.

Simon had thought that someone might be here. His mother, perhaps. Surprise, not dead. Witches can be hard to kill if he remembers his stories correctly. It could pass for a witch's cottage. A studious witch with a fondness for tea.

The sweeping would be easier if he swept out the back door, so he unlatches and opens it and finds himself looking not at the field behind the house but down a spiraling stone stair.

Simon looks out the ivy-covered window to the right of the door and into the fading sunlight.

He looks back through the door. The space is wider than the wall, easily overlapping the window.

At the bottom of the stairs there is a light.

Broom in hand, Simon descends until he reaches two glowing lanterns flanking an iron grate, like a cage set into the rock.

Simon opens the cage and steps inside. There is a brass lever. He pulls it.

The door slides shut. Simon glances up at a lantern suspended from the ceiling and the cage sinks.

Simon stands bewildered with his broom as they descend and then the cage shudders to a stop. The door opens.

Simon steps into a glowing chamber. There are two pedestals and a large door.

Both pedestals have cups set upon them. Both cups have instructions.

Simon drinks the contents of one, the taste like blueberries and cloves and night air.

The dice in the other he rolls upon the pedestal, watching as they settle and then both pedestals sink into the stone.

The door opens into a large hexagonal room with a pendulum hanging from the center. It glows with dancing light from a number of lamps flanking halls that twist out of sight.

Everywhere there are books.

"May I be of assistance, sir?"

Simon turns to find a man with long white hair standing in a doorway. Somewhere farther off he can hear laughter and faint music.

"What is this place?" Simon asks.

The man looks at Simon and glances down at the broom in his hand.

"If you would come with me, sir," the man says, beckoning him forward.

"Is this a library?" Simon asks, looking around at the books.

"After a fashion."

Simon follows the man into a room with a desk stacked with papers and books. Tiny drawers with metal pulls and handwritten plaques line the walls. A cat on the desk looks up as he approaches.

"First visits can be disorienting," the man says, opening a ledger. He dips a quill in ink. "What door did you enter through?"

"Door?"

The man nods.

"It . . . it was in a cottage not far from Oxford. Someone left me the key."

The man had started writing in the ledger but now stops and looks up.

"Are you Jocelyn Keating's son?" he asks.

"Yes," Simon answers, a little too enthusiastically. "Did you know her?"

"I was acquainted with her, yes," the man answers. "I am sorry for your loss," he adds.

"Was she a witch?" Simon asks, looking at the cat on the desk.

"If she was she did not confide such information in me," the man responds. "Your full name, Mister Keating?"

"Simon Jonathan Keating."

The man inscribes it in the ledger.

"You may call me the Keeper," the man says. "What did you roll?"

"Pardon?"

"Your dice, in the antechamber."

"Oh, they were all little crowns," Simon explains, recalling the dice on the pedestal. He had tried to see the other pictures but only made out a heart and feather.

"All of them?" the Keeper asks.

Simon nods.

The Keeper frowns and marks the ledger, the quill scratching along the paper. The cat on the desk lifts a paw to bat at it.

The Keeper puts down the quill to the cat's chagrin and walks to a cabinet on the other side of the room.

"Initial visits are best kept short, though you are welcome back at any time." The Keeper hands Simon a chain with a locket on the end. "This will point you to the entrance if you lose your way. The elevator will return you to your cottage."

Simon looks at the compass in his hand. The needle spins in the center. *My cottage,* he thinks.

"Thank you," he says.

"Do please let me know if I can be of any assistance."

"May I leave this here?" Simon holds up the broom.

"Of course, Mister Keating," the Keeper says, gesturing at the wall by the door. Simon leans the broom against it.

The Keeper returns to his desk. The cat yawns.

Simon walks out of the office and watches the pendulum.

He wonders if he is asleep and dreaming.

He takes a book from a stack near the wall and puts it down again. He wanders down a hallway lined with curving shelves so the books surround him at all angles, like a tunnel. He cannot tell how the ones above his head manage not to fall.

He tries opening doors. Some are locked but many open, revealing rooms filled with more books, chairs and desks and tables with bottles of ink and bottles of wine and bottles of brandy. The sheer volume of books intimidates him. He does not know how one would choose what to read.

He hears more people than he sees, footsteps and whispers close but unseen. He spots a figure in a white robe lighting candles and a woman so absorbed in the book she is reading that she does not look up as he passes.

He walks through a hall filled with paintings, all images of impossible buildings. Floating castles. Mansions melded together with ships. Cities carved into cliffs. The books around them all seem to be volumes on architecture. A corridor leads him to an amphitheater where actors appear to be rehearsing Shakespeare. He recognizes it as *King Lear,* though the parts have been reversed so there are three sons with a tremendous old woman as their mother descending into madness. Simon watches for some time before wandering on.

There is music playing somewhere, a pianoforte. He follows the sound but cannot locate its source.

Then a door catches his eye. A wardrobe overflowing with books has been placed partially in front of it, leaving it half hidden or half found.

The door wears a brass image of a heart aflame.

The doorknob turns easily when Simon tries it.

A long wooden table occupies the center of the room, strewn with papers and books and bottles of ink but in a way that invites new work rather than suggesting work interrupted. Pillows are strewn about on the floor and over a chaise longue. On the chaise longue there is also a black cat. It stands and stretches and jumps down, leaving through the door that Simon has opened.

"You are quite welcome," he calls after the cat but the cat says nothing and Simon returns his attention to the now catless room.

Along the walls there are five other doors. Each one is marked with a different symbol. Simon closes his door behind him and finds an identical heart on its opposite side. The other doors have a key, a crown, a sword, a bee, and a feather.

Between the doors there are columns, and thin bookshelves suspended from the ceiling like swings, the books stacked flat on their sides. Simon cannot fathom how one might reach the highest shelves until he realizes they are strung on pulleys, able to be raised or lowered.

There are lamps over each door, burning brightly save for the door with the key, which is completely extinguished, and the door with the feather, which has been dimmed.

A piece of paper slides out from under the door with the feather.

Simon picks it up. There is soot on the outside, which blackens his fingers. The words on the paper are written in wobbling, child-like penmanship.

Hello.
Is there someone behind this door
or are you a cat?

There is a drawing of a rabbit beneath.

Simon turns the doorknob. It sticks. He inspects the lock and finds a latch which he turns and then tries again. This time the door submits.

It opens into a dark room with bare walls. No one is there. He looks around the back of the door but sees only darkness.

Confused, Simon closes the door again.

He turns the note over.

He takes a quill from the table, dips it in an inkwell, and writes a response.

I am not a cat.

He folds the paper and slides it under the door. He waits. He opens the door again.

The note is gone.

Simon closes the door.

He turns his attention to a bookcase.

Behind him, the door swings open. Simon cries out in surprise.

In the doorway there is a young woman with brown hair piled in curls and braids around silver filigree bunny ears. She wears a strange knit shirt and a scandalously short skirt over blue trousers and tall boots. Her eyes are bright and wild.

"Who are you?" this girl who has materialized out of nothingness asks. The note is clutched in her hand.

"Simon," he says. "Who are you?"

The girl considers this question longer, tilting her head, the bunny ears lilting toward the door with the sword.

"Lenore," Eleanor answers, which is a touch of a lie. She read it in a poem once and thought it prettier than Eleanor, despite the similarity. Besides, no one ever asks her name so this seems a good opportunity to try out a new one.

"Where did you come from?" Simon asks.

"The burned place," she says, as though that is sufficient explanation. "Did you write this?" She holds out the note.

Simon nods.

"When?"

"Moments ago. Was that from you, the message on the other side?" he asks, though he thinks the handwriting looks too juvenile for this to be true, he wonders about the rabbit ears.

Eleanor turns over the note and looks at the awkward letters, the loopy rabbit.

"I wrote this eight years ago," she says.

"Why would you slip such an old note under the door just now?"

"I put it under the door right after I wrote it. I don't understand."

She frowns and closes the door with the feather on it. She walks to the other side of the room. Somewhere in the interim Simon notices that she is quite pretty, despite the eccentricities of her wardrobe. Her eyes are dark, almost black, her skin a light brown, and there is a hint of something foreign to her features. She seems as unlike the girls his aunt sometimes parades by him as it is possible to be. He tries to imagine what she would look like in a gown, and then what she would look like without a gown, and then he coughs, flustered.

She looks at each of the doors in turn.

"I don't understand," she says to herself. She turns and looks at Simon again. No, stares at him, scrutinizing him from his hair to his boots. "Are there any bees in here?" she asks him. She starts looking behind the bookshelves and under the pillows.

"Not that I have seen," Simon tells her, reflexively looking under the table. "There was a cat, earlier, but it departed."

"How did you get here?" she asks him, catching his eyes from beneath the other side of the table. "Down here, I mean, the place not the room."

"Through a door, in a cottage—"

"You have a door?" Eleanor asks. She sits on the floor amongst the chairs, cross-legged, looking at him expectantly.

"It is not mine, precisely," Simon clarifies. Though he supposes it is, if the cottage is his. A strange inheritance. He sits as well, pushing a chair out of the way, so they are facing each other in a forest of chair legs with a table canopy.

"I thought most of the doors were gone," Eleanor confides.

Simon tells her about his mother, about the envelope and the key and the cottage. She listens intently and he adds as much detail as he can think to. The wax seal on the envelope. The ivy on the cottage. She wears a curious expression as he describes the cage-like elevator but does not interrupt.

"Your mother was here?" Eleanor asks when he has brought the story through the door and into the room in which they now sit.

"Apparently." Simon thinks this might be better than a letter, to have spaces she occupied and books she read.

"What did she look like?" Eleanor asks.

"I don't remember," Simon answers, and suddenly wishes to change the subject. "I have never met a girl who wears trousers before," he says, hoping she does not take offense.

"I can't climb things in a dress," Eleanor explains, as though stating a simple fact.

"Climbing is not for girls."

"Anything is for girls."

Her expression is so serious it makes him consider the statement. It runs counter to everything his uncle says about girls but he thinks perhaps his uncle does not know as much about girls as he lets on, and his aunt has very particular ideas about what constitutes *ladylike*.

He wonders if he has stumbled upon a place where girls do not play games, where there are not unspoken rules to follow. No expectations. No chaperones. He wonders if his mother was like that. Wonders what makes a woman a witch.

They continue volleying questions and answers back and forth, sometimes so many at once it is like juggling to answer one and then another and more in between. Simon tells her things he has never told anyone. He confides fears and exposes worries, thoughts falling from his lips that he dared not speak aloud but it is different here, with her.

She tells him about the place. About the books and the rooms and the cats. She has a tiny jar of honey in her bag and she lets him taste it. He expects sweetness but it is more than that, rich and golden and smoky.

Simon is lost for words, licking honey from his fingers, thinking thoughts he cannot express and is certain would be inappropriate if he could.

Eleanor does not know what to make of this boy with his frilly shirt and buttoned jacket. Is he a boy or a man? She is not sure how to tell the difference. He pronounces his *r*'s strangely. She is not certain if he is handsome, she has little reference for such things, but she likes his face. There is an openness in it. She wonders if he has no secrets. He has brown eyes but his hair is blond, she has read so many books where blond hair goes with blue eyes that she finds it incongruous. His face is so much more than hair and eye color, she wonders why books do not describe the curves of noses or the length of eyelashes. She studies the shape of his lips. Perhaps a face is too complicated to capture in words.

Eleanor reaches out and touches his hair. He looks so surprised that she pulls her hand back.

"I'm sorry," she says.

"It's all right." Simon reaches out and takes her hand in his. His fingers are warm and honey-sticky. Her heart is beating too fast. She tries to remember books with boys in frilly shirts to guess at how she is meant to behave. All she can remember is dancing, which seems inappropriate, and embroidery, which she does not know how to do. She probably shouldn't be staring but he is staring back so she does not stop.

They continue to talk, sitting hand in hand. Eleanor traces tiny circles in his palm with her fingertips as they discuss the Harbor, the hallways, the rooms, the cats.

The books.

"Do you have a particular favorite?" Simon asks.

Eleanor considers this. It is not a question she has ever been asked, but a book comes to mind.

"I do. I . . . I do. It's . . ." Eleanor pauses. "Would you like to read it?" she asks instead of trying to explain it. Books are always better when read rather than explained.

"I would, very much so," Simon answers.

"I can get it and you can read it and then we could talk about it. If you like it. Or if you don't, I would want to know why, exactly. It's in my room, would you come with me?"

"Of course."

Eleanor opens the door with the feather on it.

"I'm sorry it's so dark," she says. She takes a metal rod from her bag and presses something that makes it glow brightly, steady and white. She shines it into the darkness and Simon can see the crumbling remains of the room, the burned books. There is a scent like smoke.

Eleanor steps out of one room and into the other.

Simon follows and walks directly into a wall. When the stars behind his eyes from the impact clear he looks out at the darkness he had seen before, the burned room and the girl both gone.

Simon pushes against the darkness but it is solid.

He knocks upon it, as though the darkness were a door.

"Lenore?" he calls.

She will come back, he tells himself. She will fetch the book and return. If he cannot follow, he can wait.

He closes the door and rubs his forehead.

He turns his attention to the bookshelves. He recognizes volumes by Keats and Dante but the other names are unfamiliar. His thoughts keep returning to the girl.

He runs his fingers over the velvet pillows piled on the chaise longue.

The door with the feather opens and Eleanor enters, a book in her hand. She has changed her clothing, she wears a dark blue shirt that drapes over her shoulders with a long pink scarf looped around her neck.

When her eyes meet his, she starts, the door swinging shut behind her. She stares at him, wide-eyed.

"What happened?" Simon asks.

"How long was I gone?" she asks.

"A moment?" Simon had not thought to measure the time, distracted by his thoughts. "No more than ten minutes, surely."

Eleanor drops the book and it falls, fluttering open and then closing again on the ground near her feet. Her hands fly to her face and cover her mouth and Simon, at a loss for what to do, retrieves the book, looking curiously at its gilded cover.

"Whatever is the matter?" he asks. He resists the urge to flip through the pages though the temptation is there.

"Six months," Eleanor says. Simon does not understand. He raises an eyebrow and Eleanor scowls in frustration. "Six months," she repeats, louder this time. "Six months this room has been empty every time I've opened that door and today here you are again."

Simon laughs, despite her seriousness.

"That's absurd," he says.

"It's true."

"It's nonsense," Simon declares. "You're playing at something. One does not simply disappear for moments and claim to be vanished for months on end. Here, I'll show you."

Simon turns to the door with the heart and steps into the hallway, book in hand.

"Come and see," he says, turning back to the room, but it is empty. "Lenore?"

Simon steps into the room but there is no one. He looks at the book in his hands. He closes the door and opens it again.

He could not have imagined a girl.

Besides, if there was no girl, where did the book come from?

He turns it over in his hands.

He reads because the reading soothes his nerves.

He waits for the door to open again, but it does not.

ZACHARY EZRA RAWLINS finds *Sweet Sorrows* exactly where Dorian said it would be, inside the pocket of his paint-splattered coat, thrown over the back of a chair in his room where he had left it after he arrived.

He didn't even notice. The book is small enough to be slipped into the pocket of a coat without its wearer noticing, especially if said wearer were cold and confused and intoxicated. Zachary feels he should remember. The missed intimacy annoys him.

It's the first chance he's had to check, returning to his room after who knows how many hours watching Dorian though he didn't say another word while Zachary sat and read his book of fairy tales, growing more confused by mentions of the Starless Sea and what seemed like several different Owl Kings. Rhyme relieved him from his watch but he couldn't follow her explanation of where Mirabel had gone and he now thinks he should have asked her to write it down and wonders if that's allowed.

His own room feels comfortable and familiar, the fire burning merrily again. He thinks maybe the bed has been made but it's so fluffy it's difficult to tell. The Kitchen has sent back his clothes, including his suit, folded and spotless.

He sends his forgotten coat down to see if they can help with that and decides he should probably eat something.

Moments later the bell dings and he finds the Kitchen has taken his request for "all the dumplings" literally but the assortment proves as delicious as it is intimidatingly vast. Single dumplings in countless varieties are presented on individual covered dishes, some accompanied by dipping sauces. Each ceramic cover has a painted scene:

a figure going on a journey, the same simple figure repeated on each piece surrounded by a different environment. A forest full of birds. A mountaintop. A nighttime city.

Zachary cannot manage to visit even half of the dumpling destinations so he leaves the rest covered, hoping they will maintain their respective temperatures.

He starts a collection of the blue glass sparkling water bottles along a shelf. Maybe he can find candles to put in them. He's not opposed to making himself comfortable. He's already comfortable. The kind of comfortable that involves occasionally lying on the bathroom tile and reminding oneself to breathe.

With his bag back he has his own clothes again but they are not as nice as the clothing from the room. Even comparing his regular glasses against the borrowed ones gives a slight advantage to the newer pair, so Zachary continues wearing them as well.

He finds an electrical outlet by one of the lamps and plugs in his phone, though the effort feels futile.

He sits by the fire and pages through *Sweet Sorrows* again, relieved to be reunited with it. There are more missing pages than he remembers. Maybe he should show the book to Mirabel. He pauses at the bit about the son of the fortune-teller. *Not yet.* Well, he's here now. He's made it to the Harbor even if he hasn't found the Starless Sea. Now what?

Maybe he could trace the book backward. Where was it before? He remembers his long-ago library clue. From the library of . . . somebody. He closes his eyes and tries to picture the piece of paper Elena gave him after Kat's class, donated by . . . something foundation . . . dammit. There was a J, he thinks. Maybe.

Keating. The name comes back to him but he can't remember the initials. He can't believe he forgot to bring the piece of paper along.

One thing is certain: He's not going to find his next move here unless his next move is a nap.

Zachary tucks *Sweet Sorrows* in his bag, sends his dishes back to the Kitchen and asks for an apple (it sends a silver bowl filled with yellow apples touched with spots of soft blushing pink), and sets off into the wilds of the Harbor again.

He tries not to use his compass but he has no idea what direction he's moving in at any given time. He finds a room filled with tables and armchairs, some set in individual alcoves around the room and a large empty space with more chairs and a cascading fountain in the middle.

In the bottom of the fountain there are coins, some he recognizes and others are unfamiliar, piles of wishes resting under softly bubbling water. He thinks of the fountain full of keys and the key collector from Dorian's book and wonders what happened to him.

No one ever saw him again.

He wonders if anyone is wondering what happened to *him* yet. Probably not.

Beyond the fountain is a hall with a lower ceiling, its entrance obscured by a bookshelf and an armchair. He has to move the chair to proceed. The hall is dimly lit with closed doors and as Zachary walks he realizes what is strange about it. It is not the relative lack of books or cats, rather that the doors along the hall have no doorknobs, no handles. Only locks. He pauses at one and pushes but it doesn't budge. A closer inspection of the wood around the door reveals streaks of black char along the edges. There's a hint of smoke in the air, like a long-extinguished fire. There's a spot on the door where the doorknob had been, a vacancy that has been plugged with a piece of newer, unburned wood. Something moves in the shadows at the other end of the hall again, too big to be a cat, but when he looks there's nothing there.

Zachary walks back the way he came, toward the fountain, and chooses a different hall. It is more brightly lit but "brightly" is a comparative term here. Most of the space has light enough to read by and little more.

He wanders aimlessly, avoiding going back to check on Dorian and mildly annoyed that so much of his mind is occupied by thinking about it (*him*).

He passes a painting of a candle and he could swear it flickers as he goes by so he investigates and it is not a painting at all but a frame hung on the wall around a shelf, a candle in a silver candlestick set inside and flickering. He wonders who lit it.

A meow behind him interrupts his wondering. Zachary turns to find a Persian cat staring at him, its squished face contorted in a skeptical glare.

"What's your problem?" he asks the cat.

"Meooorwrrrorr," the cat says in a hybrid meow-growl implying that it has so many problems it does not even know where to begin.

"I hear you," Zachary says. He looks back at the candle, dancing in its frame.

He blows it out.

Immediately, the picture frame shudders and moves downward. The whole wall is moving, from the picture frame down, sinking into the floor. It stops when the bottom of the frame reaches the tiled ground, the extinguished candle halting at cat-eye level.

In the vacancy where the frame had been is a rectangular hole in the wall. Zachary looks down at the cat who is more interested in the candle, batting at a curl of smoke.

The opening is large enough for Zachary to step through but there's not enough light. Most of the light here comes from a fringed lamp on a table across the hall. Zachary pulls the lamp as close to the newfound hole in the wall as its cord will allow, wondering how the electricity works down here and what happens if it goes out.

The lamp consents to coming close to the opening but not all the way in. Zachary rests it on the floor and leans it—the fringe delighting the cat—so it tilts toward the opening. He steps over the not-painting and inside.

His shoes crunch on things on the floor that are known only to the darkness and Zachary thinks maybe it's better that way. The lamp is doing an admirable job of illuminating but it takes his eyes awhile to adjust. He pushes his borrowed glasses up closer to the bridge of his nose.

He realizes that the room is not getting brighter because everything within it is burned. What he'd guessed to be dust is ash, settled over the remains of what was, and Zachary recognizes precisely what was, before, some indeterminable amount of time before he arrived.

The desk in the center of the room and the dollhouse atop it have been burned into blackness and rubble.

The dollhouse has collapsed onto itself, the roof caving into the space below. Its inhabitants and surroundings have been incinerated and left to memories. The entire room is filled with charred paper and objects burned beyond recognition.

Zachary reaches up to touch a single star suspended on a somehow intact string from the ceiling and it falls to the floor, lost amongst the shadows.

"Even tiny empires fall," Zachary says, partly to himself and partly to the cat who peers over the top of the picture frame from the hall.

In response, the cat drops out of sight.

Zachary's shoes crunch over burned wood and broken bits of a world that was. He walks toward the dollhouse. The hinge that once opened the house like a door is intact and he unlatches it, the hinge breaking with the movement and the facade falling onto the table, leaving the interior exposed.

It is not as thoroughly destroyed as the rest of the room but it is burned and blackened. Bedrooms are indistinguishable from living rooms or the kitchen. The attic has fallen into the floor below and taken most of the roof along with it.

Zachary spots something in one of the burned rooms. He reaches in and lifts it from the ruins.

A single doll. He wipes the soot from it with his sweater and holds it up to the light. It's a girl doll, maybe the daughter of the original doll family, painted and porcelain. Cracked, but not broken.

Zachary leaves her standing upright in the ashes of the house.

He'd wanted to see it as it was. The house and the town and the city across the sea. The multitude of additions and overlapping narratives. He'd wanted to add something to it, maybe. To make his own mark on the story. He hadn't realized how much he'd wanted to until faced with the reality that he cannot. He can't decide if he's sad or angry or disappointed.

Time passes. Things change.

He looks around the room, the larger room that now houses a single girl standing in the ashes of her world. There are strings where stars or planets may once have hung from the ceiling, little wisps like spiderwebs. He can see now that there is more that has survived whatever conflagration consumed the room. A shipwreck in one corner that was once an ocean, a length of train track along the side of the table, a grandfather clock falling from the window of the main house, and a deer, black from its hooves to its tiny antlers but intact, watching him from a shelf with glassy pinprick eyes.

The walls are covered with former wallpaper curled up in strips like birch bark. Next to the shelf with the deer is a door with no doorknob and he wonders if it is the same one he passed by earlier.

The room suddenly feels more like a tomb, the scent of burned paper and smoke stronger.

In the hall the lamp falls, either of its own volition or aided by the cat. The bulb breaks with a soft cracking noise and takes the light with it, leaving Zachary alone in the dark with the charred remains of a miniature universe.

He closes his eyes and counts backward from ten.

Something inside him expects to open his eyes and find himself back in Vermont but he is exactly where he was ten seconds earlier, and now he can see a little bit of light, guiding him.

He climbs out of the opening in the wall, careful not to trip on the broken lamp. He replaces it on the table and does his best to push the pieces of broken glass out of the way.

There are a few votive candles tucked into bookshelves and he uses one to relight the taper in its frame. The frame moves back up into place as soon as the candle is lit, the wall closing away the remains of the doll universe again.

"Meow," the Persian cat says, suddenly at his feet.

"Hey," Zachary says to the cat. "I'm going to go this way." He points down the hall to the left, a decision he makes as he vocalizes it. "You can come if you want, if not, no big deal. You do you."

The cat stares up at him and twitches its tail.

The hall to the left is short and dim and opens into a room surrounded by columns composed of marble statues, figures nakedly supporting the ceiling in twisting combinations of twos and threes, though the statues seem more focused on one another than on their architectural function.

The ceiling is gilded and set with dozens of tiny lights, casting a warm glow over the frozen marble orgy beneath it.

Zachary glances over his shoulder and the cat is following him but when he looks it stops and licks a paw nonchalantly as though it is not following him at all and just happens to be heading in the same direction.

Zachary continues down another hall leading away from the columned room with two more statues beyond. One statue peers into the room and the other turns away, covering its marble eyes.

The cat finds something and bats it around, watching it skitter across the floor. The object loses its appeal quickly, though, and the cat gives it a final bat and continues on its way. Zachary goes to see what the object is and finds an origami star with one bent corner. He puts it in his pocket.

Eventually Zachary finds himself at the Heart, more or less by accident. The door to the Keeper's office is open but the Keeper doesn't look up until Zachary knocks on the open door.

"Hello, Mister Rawlins," he says. "How are you feeling?"

"Better, thank you," Zachary answers.

"And your friend?"

"He's asleep but he seems okay. And . . . I broke a lamp, in one of the halls. I can clean it up if you have a broom or something." His eyes fall on an old-fashioned twig broom standing in a corner.

"That will not be necessary," the Keeper says. "I shall have it taken care of. Which hallway?"

"Back that way and around," Zachary says, indicating the way he came from. "Near a picture frame with a real candle in it."

"I see," the Keeper says, writing something down. His tone is just odd enough that Zachary decides to pry, thinking that maybe he's too polite as a general rule.

"What happened to the dollhouse room?" he asks.

"There was a fire," the Keeper replies without looking up, seemingly unsurprised that Zachary had found it.

"I'd gathered that," Zachary says. "What caused it?"

"An accumulation of unforeseen circumstances," the Keeper says. "An accident," he adds when Zachary does not immediately respond.

"I cannot describe the details of the event because I did not witness it myself. Is there anything else I might help you with?"

"Where is everyone?" Zachary asks, the annoyance obvious in his voice but the Keeper does not look up from his writing.

"You and I are here, your friend is in his room, Rhyme is likely watching him or attending to her duties, and I do not know Mirabel's current location, she keeps her own counsel."

"That's it?" Zachary asks. "There's five of us and . . . cats?"

"That is correct, Mister Rawlins," the Keeper says. "Would you like a number for the cats? It might not be accurate, they are difficult to count."

"No, that's okay," Zachary says. "But where . . . where'd everyone go?"

The Keeper pauses and looks up at him. He looks older, or sadder, Zachary can't tell which. Maybe both.

"If you are referring to our former residents, some left. Some died. Some returned to the places that they came from and others sought out new places and I hope that they found them. You are already acquainted with those of us who remain."

"Why do *you* remain?" Zachary asks.

"I remain because it is my job, Mister Rawlins. My calling, my duty, my raison d'être. Why are you here?"

Because a book said I was supposed to be, Zachary thinks. *Because I'm worried about going back because of crazy ladies in fur coats who keep hands in jars. Because I haven't figured out the puzzle yet even though I don't know what the puzzle is.*

Because I feel more alive down here than I did up there.

"I'm here to sail the Starless Sea and breathe the haunted air," he says and the echoed statement earns a smile from the Keeper. He looks younger when he smiles.

"I wish you the best of luck with that," he says. "Is there anything else I might help you with?"

"The former residents, was one of them named Keating?" Zachary asks.

The Keeper's expression shifts now to something that Zachary can't read.

"There have been multiple bearers of that name within these halls."

"Did . . . did any of them have a library?" Zachary asks. "Upstairs?"

"Not that I am aware of."

"When were they here?"

"Very long ago, Mister Rawlins. Before your time."

"Oh," Zachary says. He tries to think of other questions and doesn't know what to ask. *Sweet Sorrows* is in his bag and he could show it to the Keeper but something makes him hesitate. He's tired, suddenly, and as a candle gutters on the Keeper's desk the smoke sends his thoughts back to the dollhouse and the destruction of the universe and he thinks maybe he should go lie down or something.

"Are you feeling all right?" the Keeper asks.

"I'm okay," Zachary says and it tastes like a lie. "Thank you."

He winds his way through halls that seem darker and emptier. The underground feeling presses on him. So much stone between here and the sky. So much heaviness hanging above his head.

His room feels like a pocket of safety as he reaches it, and as soon as he crosses the threshold he steps on something that has been slipped under his door.

He moves his shoe. Beneath it is a folded piece of paper.

Zachary reaches down and picks it up. There's a Z on the outside, the fancy sort crossed with a line in the middle. Apparently it's meant for him.

There are four lines of text inside, in handwriting he doesn't recognize. It doesn't seem like a letter or a note. He thinks it might be a fragment of a poem or a story.

Or a puzzle.

The Queen of the Bees has been waiting for you
Tales hidden within to be told
Bring her a key that has never been forged
And another made only of gold

The Ballad of Simon and Eleanor
book borrowing

Simon knows it has been hours. He is tired and hungry and recalls that he'd packed food for this purpose and left his bag in the cottage and brought a broom instead which now seems impractical. He doesn't believe Lenore's claim that so much time had passed but she has not returned and now he is half asleep and her book is quite strange and he is not certain he likes any of this.

He wonders about his mother, that she hid such a place in a cottage in the country.

Reluctantly he follows his compass back to the entrance hall.

He tries to open the door but it is locked.

He tries again, giving the handle an extra push.

"You cannot take that with you," a voice says behind him. He turns to find the Keeper standing in his doorway, beyond the swinging pendulum. It takes Simon a moment to realize the Keeper refers to the gold-edged book in his hand.

"I wanted to read it," Simon explains, though it seems obvious. What else would he want to do with a book? Though it is not quite true. He wants to do more than read it. He wants to study it. He wants to savor it. He wants to use it as a window to see inside another person. He wants to take the book into his home, into his life, into his bed because he cannot do the same with the girl who gave it to him.

There must be a formal book-lending process here, he thinks.

"I would like to borrow this book, if I may," he says.

"You must leave something in its place," the Keeper tells him.

Simon furrows his brow and then points at the broom still resting by the office door.

"Will that do?"

The Keeper considers the broom and nods.

He goes to the desk and inscribes Simon's name on a piece of paper and ties it to the broom. The cat on the desk yawns and Simon yawns in response.

"The title of the volume?" the Keeper asks.

Simon looks down at the book, even though he knows the answer.

"*Sweet Sorrows,*" he replies. "It doesn't have an author listed here."

The Keeper looks up at him.

"May I see that?" he asks.

Simon hands him the book.

The Keeper looks it over, studying its binding and endpapers.

"Where did you find this?" he asks.

"Lenore gave it to me," Simon answers. He assumes he does not need to tell the Keeper who Lenore is, as she is rather memorable. "She said it is her favorite."

The expression on the Keeper's face is strange as he hands the book to Simon.

"Thank you," he says, relieved to have it back.

"Your compass," the Keeper responds with an open palm, and Simon stares blankly for a second before taking the golden chain from his neck. He almost asks if something is wrong, or about Lenore, or any of his many questions, but none of them will consent to being articulated.

"Good night," he says instead and the Keeper nods and this time when Simon tries to leave the door opens for him without protest.

He falls asleep standing up in the cage as it ascends, jolted back to half awake when it stops.

The lantern-lit stone room looks the same as before. The door leading back into the cottage is still open.

Moonlight shines through the cottage windows. Simon cannot guess what time it might be. It is cold and he is too tired to light a fire but grateful for his coat.

He collapses on the bed without clearing the books from it, *Sweet Sorrows* clutched in one hand.

It falls to the floor as he sleeps.

Simon wakes disoriented with book-shaped bruises along his back. He does not remember where he is or how he got here. The morning light peeks in through the gaps in the ivy. A still-open window squeaks on its hinges as the wind tugs at it.

The memory of the key and the cottage and the train seeps back into his cloudy thoughts. He must have fallen asleep. He had the strangest dream.

He tries the door at the back of the cottage but it sticks, probably held shut by the brambles outside.

He builds a fire in the hearth.

He doesn't know what to do with this space and these books, these things that his mother presumably left for him.

He finds a long, low trunk behind the bed. The lock is rusted shut but so are the hinges and a good kick with the heel of his boot manages to break them both. Inside there are faded papers and more books. One of the documents is the deed to the cottage made out in his name and including a great deal of the surrounding land. He looks through the rest for some missive from his mother, annoyed that she would have anticipated his eighteenth birthday and his finding this place without addressing him personally, and he finds most of the other papers inscrutable: snippets of notes and papers that seem like fairy tales, long rambling things about reincarnation and keys and fate. The only letter is not one from his mother but one written to her, a rather ardent missive signed from someone named Asim. The thought crosses Simon's mind that this might well be from his father.

He wonders, suddenly, if his mother knew she was going to die. If she was preparing this in anticipation of her absence. It is not a thought he has entertained before and he does not like it.

He has an inheritance. A dusty, book-filled, ivy-infested one. It is something to call his own.

He wonders if he could live here. If he would want to. Perhaps with carpets and better chairs and a proper bed.

He sorts through books and stacks myths and fables on one side of the table, histories and geographies on the other, and leaves volumes he cannot differentiate in the middle. There are books of maps and books written in languages he cannot read. Several are marked with annotations and symbols: crowns and swords and drawings of owls.

He finds a small volume by the bed that is not as dusty as the others and when he recognizes it he drops it again. It falls onto the pile of books, barely distinguishable from the rest.

It was not a dream.

If the book was not a dream, the girl is not a dream.

Simon goes to the back door and pushes it. Shoves it. Throws all his weight into his shoulder to force it open and this time it relents.

Here now is the stair again. The lanterns at the bottom.

The metal cage waiting for him.

The descent is maddeningly slow.

There are no pedestals in the antechamber this time. The door allows him entrance without question.

The Keeper's office is closed and Simon hears the door open as he heads down a corridor but he does not look behind him.

It is difficult to locate the door with the heart again without his compass. He takes wrong turns and doubles back again and again. He climbs stairs made of books.

Finally he finds a familiar turn, and then the shadowed nook and the door with its burning heart.

The room beyond it is empty.

He tries the door with the feather but it insists on opening into nothingness. He closes the door again.

She could return at any moment.

She might never return.

Simon paces around the table. When he tires of pacing he sits on the chaise longue, first angling it so he can face the door. He wonders how long that cat had waited in this room for someone to open a door to release it and how it was left inside in the first place.

He tires of sitting and goes back to pacing.

He picks up a quill from the table and considers writing a letter and slipping it under the door.

He wonders what to write that would be of any use. He thinks he understands now why his mother did not leave him any letters. He cannot even tell Lenore what time or day he was here waiting as he does not have available measurements for time. He realizes how difficult it is to determine the passage of time without sunlight.

He puts the quill down.

He wonders how long is an appropriate time to wait for a girl who may or may not have been a dream. Wonders if he could have dreamed a girl in a real place or if the place is a dream and then his head hurts so he thinks perhaps he should find something to read instead of continuing to think.

He regrets leaving *Sweet Sorrows* in the cottage. He looks through the books on their shelves. Many are unfamiliar and strange. A heavy volume with footnotes and a raven on its cover pulls his attention more than the others, and he finds himself so drawn into its tale of two magicians in England that he loses track of time.

Then the door with the feather opens, and she is here.

Simon puts the book down. He does not wait for her to say anything. He cannot wait, he is too afraid that she will vanish again and never reappear. He closes the distance between them as quickly as he can and then he kisses her desperately, hungrily, and after a moment she kisses him back in equal measure.

Kissing, Eleanor thinks, is not done any justice in books.

They peel off each other's clothes in layers. He curses at the strange clasps and fasteners on her garments while she laughs at the sheer number of buttons on his.

He leaves her bunny ears on.

It is easier to be in love in a room with closed doors. To have the whole world in one room. In one person. The universe condensed and intensified and burning, bright and alive and electric.

But doors cannot stay closed forever.

ZACHARY EZRA RAWLINS stands in front of a statue of a woman covered in bees wondering if it takes a crown to make a queen.

This is the only identity he can think of for the Queen of the Bees from his newfound quest (*Is this a side quest or a main quest?* the voice in his head ponders) but he doesn't know how to give her keys. He searched the marble statue for keyholes and found nothing but cracks, not that he has keys to give. He's stuck on the never-been-forged part and he's not sure where to find a gold key. Maybe he should sort through all the jars in the Keeper's office, or find the room with the keys from *Sweet Sorrows* and he realizes the keys in the jars might be those same keys, put into storage.

He has inspected every bee, investigated the entire marble chair the woman sits upon, and found nothing. Maybe there's another woman somewhere who rules the bees. The bees aren't even part of the statue, they're carved from a different stone in a warmer appropriate honey color and they're movable. They all might belong somewhere else. Some of them have moved since the first time Zachary saw this statue.

Zachary places a single bee on each of the woman's open palms and leaves her alone to think whatever thoughts statues think when they are alone underground and covered with bees.

He chooses a new-to-him hall, pausing at a contraption that looks like a large old-fashioned gumball machine filled with metallic orbs of various shades. Zachary turns the ornate handle and the machine dispenses a copper sphere. It is heavier than it looks and once Zachary figures out how to open it he finds a tiny scroll tucked inside that unfurls like ticker tape with a surprisingly long tale written upon it about lost loves and castles and crossed destinies.

Zachary tucks the empty copper ball and the now tangled story in his bag and continues along the hall until he reaches a large staircase that leads down to an expansive space. A massive ballroom, utterly empty. Zachary tries to imagine how many people it would take to fill it with dancers and revelry. It is taller than the Heart, its soaring ceilings disappearing into shadows that could be mistaken for night sky. Fireplaces line the walls, one of them lit and the rest of the light comes from lanterns hanging from chains strung along the walls. He wonders if Rhyme lights them in case someone passes through the room, or in case someone wants to dance, or if they light themselves, in giddy flaming anticipation.

As he walks across the ballroom, Zachary feels more acutely that he has missed something. He has arrived too late, the party is over. If he had opened that painted door so long ago would he already have been too late then? Probably.

There is a door on the far wall, past the fireplaces and beyond a stretch of dark open archways. Zachary opens the door and finds someone else in the midst of the post-party emptiness.

Mirabel is curled up amongst racks filled with bottles, up in a window-like nook on a wall with no window in a wine cellar with more than enough wine for all the parties that are not occurring in the ballroom. She wears a long-sleeved black dress that could probably be described as slinky if it wasn't so voluminous. It obscures her legs and the stacks of wine below her and part of the floor. She has a glass of sparkling wine in one hand and her nose is buried in a book and as Zachary gets closer he can read the cover: *A Wrinkle in Time*.

"I was annoyed about not remembering the tesseract technicalities," Mirabel says without looking up or clarifying any specifics regarding space or time. "You may be interested in knowing that the damage due to an electrical fire in the basement of a private club in Manhattan was extensive but controlled and did not spread to neighboring buildings. They might not even have to tear it down."

She rests her book on a nearby wine bottle, open to keep her page marked, and looks down at him.

"The building was, reportedly, unoccupied at the time," she continues. "I'd like to know where Allegra is before I take you back up, if that's all right with you."

Zachary thinks it likely doesn't matter whether or not it is all right with him, and again finds himself in no great hurry to return to the surface.

"Who's the Queen of the Bees?" he asks.

Mirabel looks at him quizzically enough for him to be certain that she didn't write the note, but then she shrugs her shoulders and points behind him.

Zachary turns. There are long wooden tables with benches tucked amongst the racks of wine, and other window-like nooks in the stone walls, the largest of which holds the massive painting that Mirabel is pointing at.

It is a portrait of a woman in a low-cut, wine-red gown holding a pomegranate in one hand and a sword in the other. The background is a textured darkness with the light coming from the figure herself. It reminds Zachary of a Rembrandt painting, the way she glows within the shadows. The woman's face is entirely obscured by a swarm of bees. A few of the bees have wandered downward to investigate the pomegranate.

"Who is she?" Zachary asks.

"Your guess is as good as mine," Mirabel says. "It has rather heavy Persephone overtones."

"Queen of the Underworld," Zachary says, staring at the painting, trying to figure out how to give it keys and failing. He wishes the pomegranate had a keyhole painted into it, that would be whimsical and appropriate.

"You're well-read, Ezra," Mirabel remarks, sliding down from her perch.

"I'm well-mythed," Zachary corrects. "When I was a kid I thought Hecate and Isis and all the orishas were friends of my mom's, like, actual people. I suppose in a way they were. Still are. Whatever."

Mirabel lifts an open bottle of champagne from an ice bucket on one of the tables. She holds it up and offers it to Zachary.

"I'm more of a cocktail guy," he says, though he is also of the opinion that sparkling wine is an anytime beverage and appreciates Mirabel's style.

"What's your poison?" she asks as she refills her glass. "I owe you a drink, and a dance, and other things, I'm sure."

"Sidecar, no sugar," Zachary replies, distracted by the deck of cards sitting next to the champagne.

Mirabel slinks over to the wall on the other side of the painting, her gown following behind. She taps a part of the wall that opens, revealing a hidden dumbwaiter.

Zachary returns his attention to the cards.

"Are these yours?" he asks.

"I shuffle them compulsively more than I read them," she says. "I'm surprised there aren't more down here, they're basically stories in pieces that can be rearranged."

Zachary flips a card, expecting a familiar tarot archetype but the image on the card is a strange one: a black-and-white anatomical sketch surrounded by a swirl of watercolor blood.

The Lung

The title is appropriate for the illustration: a single lung, not a pair. The watercolor blood looks like it is moving, swirling into the lung and out again.

Zachary puts the card back on top of the pile.

A chime sounds from the door on the wall, startling him.

"Does your mother read cards?" Mirabel asks as she hands him a chilled coupe glass, its rim distinctly un-sugared.

"Sometimes," Zachary says. "People tend to expect it so she'll lay out some cards when she reads but she mostly holds objects and gets impressions from them. It's called psychometry."

"She measures souls."

"I guess so, if you're into direct translations." Zachary takes a sip of his sidecar. It is quite possibly the most perfect sidecar that he has ever tasted and he wonders how perfection can be so disconcerting.

"The Kitchen is an excellent mixologist," Mirabel says in reply to his litany of facial expressions. "As I was saying, we should lay low. Pun not entirely intended. Don't tell me you can't find anything to occupy yourself with, or anyone for that matter." Mirabel continues before Zachary can protest the statement, "To think if you'd picked up a different library book you wouldn't be here right now. I'm sorry you lost it."

"Oh," Zachary says, "I had it the whole time. Dorian had put it in my coat." He takes *Sweet Sorrows* from his bag and hands it to Mirabel. "Do you know where it came from?"

"It could be one of the books from the Archive," she says, flipping through the pages. "I'm not certain, only acolytes are allowed in the Archive. Rhyme would know more but she probably won't tell you, she takes her vows seriously."

"Who wrote it?" Zachary asks. "Why am I in it?"

"If it is from the Archive it was written down here. I've heard that the records kept in the Archive aren't exactly chronological. Someone must have removed it and brought it topside. That might be why Allegra was looking for it, she likes keeping things locked up."

"Is that what she's doing, trying to keep it locked up?"

"She thinks locking it away will keep it safe."

"Safe from what?" Zachary asks.

Mirabel shrugs. "People? Progress? Time? I don't know. She might have succeeded if it wasn't for me. There were only real doors once upon a time and she'd closed so many before I figured out that I could paint new ones and now she tries to close those, too. Close it away and keep it from harm."

"She talked a lot about eggs and keeping them from breaking."

"If an egg breaks it becomes more than it was," Mirabel says, after considering the matter. "And what is an egg, if not something waiting to be broken?"

"I think the egg was a metaphor."

"Can't make an omelet without breaking a few metaphors," Mirabel says. She closes *Sweet Sorrows* and hands it back to Zachary. "If it does belong in the Archive I don't think Rhyme would mind if you kept it, as long as it stays down here."

As she turns to refill her wineglass Zachary notices an addition to the numerous chains around her neck.

A layered series of chains with a gold sword much like the one around his own neck, accompanied by a key and a bee.

"Is that necklace gold?" Zachary asks, pointing. Mirabel looks at him curiously and then glances down at the key.

"I think so. It's gold-plated, at least."

"Did you wear it to the party last year?"

"I did, you reminded me with your origin story in the elevator. I'm glad it was useful. Useful jewelry is the best kind of jewelry."

"Can . . . can I borrow the key?"

"You don't have enough jewelry already?" Mirabel says, looking at his compass and his keys and Dorian's sword hanging like a talisman.

"Look who's talking."

Mirabel narrows her eyes and sips her wine but then she reaches behind her neck to undo the clasp. She untangles the chain with the key from the rest of her neckwear and hands it to him.

"Don't melt it down," she says, letting it drop into his open palm.

"Of course not. I'll bring it back."

Zachary puts the necklace in his bag.

"What are you up to, Ezra?" Mirabel asks and he almost tells her but something stops him.

"I'm not sure yet," he says. "I'll let you know if I find out."

"Please do," Mirabel says with a curious smile.

Zachary picks up her glass of wine from the table and takes a sip of it. It tastes like winter sun and melting snow, bubbles bright and sharp and bursting.

There is a story here for each bubble in each bottle, in every glass in every sip.

And when the wine is gone the stories will remain.

Zachary isn't certain if the voice is the normal voice in his head or another voice entirely, if maybe Mirabel's wine is made of stories like her weird tin filled with not-mints.

He isn't certain about anything.

He isn't even certain that he minds not being certain about anything.

He downs the rest of his sidecar to wash the story voices away and when it settles there is a question on his tongue instead.

"Max, where's the sea?"

"The what?"

"The *sea*. The Starless Sea, the body of water on which this place is a Harbor."

"Oh," Mirabel says, frowning into her fizzing glass. Zachary waits for her to tell him that the Starless Sea is a bedtime story for children or that the Starless Sea is a state of mind or that there is no Starless Sea at all and there never was but she doesn't. She stands and says, "This way." She plucks the champagne bottle from the table and walks out of the wine cellar and into the ballroom.

Zachary follows, leaving his empty glass next to a deck of cards that would tell him the whole story if he laid them out in the proper order.

Mirabel leads him through the shadowed arches near the door to the wine cellar that are so dark Zachary had not noticed the stairs beyond them. He cannot see more than an arm's length in front of him as they descend. He stays two stairs behind Mirabel in order not to step on the hem of her gown and even in that two-stair distance she practically vanishes into the shadows.

"How far down is it?" he starts to ask but the darkness takes the word *How* and volleys it back to him: *How how how how how.*

The darkness, he understands now, is very, very large.

The stairs terminate at a long low wall carved into the rock, short columns rising from the raw stone floor.

Zachary glances back up the stairs where six archways of light stare out into the dark.

"So you wish to see the sea," Mirabel singsongs, looking out over the wall into the darkness, and Zachary cannot tell if she is talking to him or to herself or to the darkness that he assumes is a cave. The cave answers: *See see sea sea sea.*

"Where is it?" Zachary asks.

Mirabel steps closer to the stone wall and looks over. Zachary stands next to her and looks down.

The light from the ballroom catches an expanse of raw stone before the rock tapers off into nothingness and shadow. Zachary can just make out his silhouette on the stone alongside Mirabel's but the light doesn't reach anything resembling water or waves.

"How far down is it?"

In response to this question Mirabel takes the champagne bottle and tosses it into the darkness. Zachary waits for it to crash against the rock or splash into the sea he doesn't believe is there but it does neither. He keeps waiting. And waiting.

Mirabel sips her wine.

After a time that would be more appropriately measured in minutes than seconds there is the softest sound far, far below, so far that Zachary cannot tell if the sound is breaking glass or not. The echo picks it up halfheartedly and carries it partway back as though the effort is too great to bring such a small sound so far.

"The Starless Sea," Mirabel says, gesturing with her glass both at the abyss below and the darkness above, devoid of stars.

Zachary stares out into the nothingness, not knowing what to say.

"These used to be the beaches," Mirabel tells him. "People would dance in the surf during the parties."

"What happened?"

"It receded."

"Is . . . is that why people left or did it recede because people left?"

"Neither. Both. You could try to point out a single moment that started the exodus but I think it was just time. The old doors were crumbling long before Allegra and company started tearing them down and displaying doorknobs like hunting trophies. Places change. People change."

She takes another sip of her wine and Zachary wonders if she's thinking of someone in particular but he doesn't ask.

"It's not what it was," Mirabel continues. "Please don't feel bad about missing the heyday, the heyday was over and the tide was out long before I was born."

"But the book—" Zachary begins not knowing quite what he's going to say and then Mirabel cuts him off.

"A book is an interpretation," she says. "You want a place to be like it was in the book but it's not a place in a book it's just words. The place in your imagination is where you want to go and that place is imaginary. This is real," she places her hand on the wall in front of them. The stone is cracked near her fingers, a fissure running down the side and disappearing into a column. "You could write endless pages but the words will never be the place. Besides, that's what it was. Not what it is."

"It could be that again, couldn't it?" Zachary asks. "If we fixed the doors, people would come."

"I appreciate that *we*, Ezra," Mirabel says. "But I've been doing this for years. People come but they don't stay. The only one who ever stayed is Rhyme."

"The Keeper said all of the old residents left or died."

"Or disappeared."

"Disappeared?" Zachary repeats and the cavern around them echoes his echo, breaking the word into fragments and picking its favorite: *Appear, appear, appear.*

"Do me a favor, Ezra," Mirabel says. "Don't wander too far down."

She turns and kisses him on the cheek and walks up the stairs.

Zachary takes one last look into the darkness and then follows her.

He knows their conversation is over before he reaches the top, but she gives him a little parting tip of her empty glass when he walks past and continues across the expansive ballroom.

He can feel her watching as he goes and he doesn't turn around. He does a little pirouette in the middle of the empty dance floor and he hears her laugh as he continues on.

Everything feels okay, suddenly, even in the ballroom emptiness and the crackling of one fire that should be a dozen.

Maybe everything is burning, has burned, will burn.

Maybe he shouldn't drink things down here, as a general rule.

Maybe, he thinks as he ascends the stairs at the far end of the ball-room, there are more mysteries and more puzzles down here than he can ever hope to solve.

As Zachary reaches the top of the stairs a shadow passes by the end of the hall and he can tell by the hair that it's Rhyme. He tries to catch up but she manages to stay ahead of him.

He watches as she dims some lamps and ignores others.

Curious both in general and about where Rhyme goes when she's not floating through the halls lighting candles, Zachary continues to follow her from a good distance.

He follows her down a hall filled with delicate carvings and large statues as she lights candles held out toward her by marble hands.

Rhyme stops abruptly and Zachary steps back into a shadowed alcove, tucked behind a life-size statue of a satyr and a nymph frozen in an impressively acrobatic embrace. He can see Rhyme through a window of thigh and arm. She's stopped in front of a carved stone wall. She reaches up and presses something against it and the wall slides open.

Rhyme steps inside and the wall slides back into place behind her, like the wall behind the candle painting.

Zachary goes to look at the wall but he can't see the door now that it is closed. The carved pattern in the stone is all vines and flowers and bees.

Bees.

Most of the carving is raised but the bees are intaglioed, highly detailed bee-shaped vacancies in the stone.

He tries to remember where Rhyme had pressed the door and finds a single bee.

She must have had a bee to place in it. Like a key.

Maybe this is the acolyte-access-only Archive Mirabel mentioned.

The wall moves again and Zachary ducks behind the statue.

Rhyme comes out from the wall and touches the door again. She does have something in her hand, something small and metallic that Zachary guesses is bee-shaped.

In her other hand is a book.

Rhyme waits for the door to close and then she turns around. She looks over at the statue of the nymph and the satyr and she holds up the book. She puts it down on one of the tables.

Rhyme looks at the statue again, pointedly, then walks away.

Zachary goes to pick up the book. He can't decide if this turn of events makes him better or worse at following people.

This book is small and gilded. It looks like *Sweet Sorrows* but bound in dark blue. There are no markings on the cover or the back or any indication as to which is which.

The text inside is handwritten. Zachary thinks at first that it might be a diary but then the first page has a title.

The Ballad of Simon and Eleanor

The Ballad of Simon and Eleanor
a short lecture on the nature of time

They cannot stay in this room forever. They know that, but they do not discuss it, distracted by tangled naked limbs and untangling and finding new ways to tangle them again. They find a bottle of wine tucked behind a stack of books but there is no door to the Kitchen here and eventually one of them will have to leave.

The practical worries tug at the buoyancy Simon feels but he pushes them back in his mind as long as he can. He presses his face into Eleanor's neck and focuses on her, on her skin, the way she smells, the way she laughs, the way she feels beneath him and above him.

They lose track of relative time.

But untracked time leads to problems of hydration and starvation.

"What if we could leave together through one of the other doors?" Eleanor suggests as she pulls on her strangely striped stockings, looking around at the bee and the key and the sword and the crown.

The bee door refuses to budge. The sword door doesn't have a knob, something Simon had not noticed before. The crown door opens onto a pile of solid stone, the hall beyond it has collapsed. A few stray pebbles roll into the room before Simon closes the door again.

Which leaves only the door with the key.

It is locked but Eleanor uses the metal pieces on her necklace to coerce it open.

Beyond it is a curving hall filled with bookshelves.

"Do you recognize it?" Simon asks.

"I'd have to look around more," Eleanor says. "A lot of the halls look the same."

She puts a hand out and nothing stops its passage forward.

"You try," she suggests and Simon repeats the gesture. Again, nothing prevents his hand from moving from room to hall.

They look at each other. There is nothing else to do. There are no other options.

Simon offers his hand and Eleanor links her fingers in his.

Together they step into the hall.

Eleanor's fingers vanish within Simon's own like mist.

The door swings shut behind him with a slam.

"Lenore?" Simon calls but he knows she is gone. He tries the door, a matching key inlayed on this side, and finds it is locked. He knocks but receives no response.

His mind races with options and settles on nothing satisfactory. He decides to try to find his own door, his door with the heart, because that door is unlocked.

Simon traverses mazelike halls and sees nothing familiar for some time. He finds a table laid out with fruit and cheese and biscuits and stops to eat as much as he can and stuffs several biscuits and a plum into the pockets of his coat.

Soon he finds himself back in the Heart.

He knows how to reach the heart-marked door from here and rushes there only to find that its doorknob has been removed. A plug of wood occupies the vacancy its removal has left. The keyhole is similarly filled.

Simon goes back to the Heart.

The door to the Keeper's office is closed but opens as soon as Simon knocks.

"How may I be of assistance, Mister Keating?" the Keeper asks.

"I need to get into a room," Simon explains. He sounds out of breath, as though he has been running. Perhaps he was, he does not remember.

"There are a great many rooms here," the Keeper says. "I must request that you be more specific."

Simon explains the location of the door, describes the flaming heart upon it.

"Ah," the Keeper says. "That door. Access to that room is not permitted. My apologies."

"That door wasn't locked before," Simon protests. "I need to get back to Lenore."

"Who?" the Keeper asks, and now Simon senses that the Keeper understands perfectly well what is going on. He has mentioned Lenore before, when he took *Sweet Sorrows* home. He doubts the Keeper's memory is so poor.

"Lenore," Simon repeats. "She lives down here, she is my height, she has dark hair and brown skin and she wears silver rabbit ears. You must know who I mean. There is no one like her, not any-where."

"We have no resident by that name," the Keeper says, coolly. "I'm afraid you must be confused, young man."

"I am not confused," Simon insists, his voice louder than he intended. A cat on a chair in the corner wakes from its nap and glares at him before stretching and jumping down and exiting the office.

The Keeper's glare is worse than the cat's.

"Mister Keating, what do you know about time?" he asks.

"Pardon?"

The Keeper adjusts his spectacles and continues.

"I will assume what you know of time is based on how it works above, where it is measurable and relatively uniform. Here, in this office and the places nearest to the anchor in the center of the Heart, time works much the same as it does up there. There are . . . places . . . farther and deeper from this location that are less reli-able."

"What does that mean?" Simon asks.

"It means if you encountered someone whom I have no record of it is because they have not been here yet," the Keeper explains. "In time," he adds, to clarify.

"That's absurd."

"The absurdity of the matter does not make it less true."

"Let me back in that room, please, sir," Simon pleads. He does not know what to make of all this talk of time, he wishes only to return to Lenore. "I am begging you."

"I cannot. I am sorry, Mister Keating, but I cannot. That door has been closed."

"Unlock it, then."

"You misunderstand me," the Keeper says. "It has not been *locked,* it has been *closed.* It will no longer open, not for any key. It was a necessary precaution."

"Then how do I find her again?" Simon asks.

"You may wait," the Keeper suggests. "It may be a period beyond waiting, I cannot say."

Simon says nothing. The Keeper sits at his desk and straightens a pile of books. He brushes a layer of blotting powder from his open ledger.

"You may not believe me, Mister Keating, but I understand how you feel," the Keeper says.

Simon continues to protest and argue with the Keeper but it is the most infuriating type of argument as nothing he says, nothing he does, including kicking chairs and throwing books, has any effect on the Keeper's impervious calm.

"Nothing can be done," the Keeper says, repeatedly. He looks as though he dearly wants a cup of tea but does not want to leave Simon to his own devices. "It must have been a rift in time that you stumbled upon. Such things are volatile and must be sealed."

"I was going into the future?" Simon asks, trying to understand. A clandestine underground library is one thing, traveling through time is another.

"Possibly," the Keeper answers. "More likely you were both passing through a space that had loosened itself from the bounds of time. A place where time did not exist."

"I don't understand."

The Keeper sighs.

"Think of time as a river," he says, drawing a line in the air with his finger. He wears several rings and they glint in the light. "The river flows in one direction. If there is an inlet along that river the water within it does not flow the same way as the rest of the river. The inlet does not follow the same rules. You found an inlet. Sometime, months or perhaps years from now, this girl you speak of finds the same inlet. You both stepped out of the river of time and into another space. A space in which neither of you belonged."

"Are there other spaces like that? Other inlets, down here?"

"Your line of thinking is not wise. Not in the least."

"So there is a way to find her, it is *possible*."

"I suggest you go home, Mister Keating," the Keeper says. "Whatever you are seeking here you will not find it."

Simon scowls. He looks around at the office, at the wooden drawers with their brass handles and the leather chairs with their fancy pillows. There are several compasses on chains in a dish on the desk. His broom, his mother's broom, rests against the wall by the door. On one pillow a cat is curled up as though it is asleep but it has one eye half open and fixed on him.

"I appreciate the advice, sir," Simon tells the Keeper. "But I will not be taking it."

Simon takes one of the compasses from the dish on the desk and turns on his heel, walking briskly but not running, walking deeper into the depths toward the Starless Sea and looking back only once to be certain that the Keeper has not followed him. There is nothing behind him but books and shadows.

Simon consults the compass and continues on, despite the needle insistently pointing him in the opposite direction. He keeps the Heart behind him as he heads out into the unknown.

Out where time is less reliable.

ZACHARY EZRA RAWLINS sits on a faded leather sofa far below the surface of the earth, at a time that might be very late at night, next to a crackling fireplace, reading.

The book that Rhyme left for him is entirely handwritten. Zachary has only managed a few pages so far. It's slow, reading a handwritten book. Additionally, he's not certain what language it is written in. If he unfocuses his eyes the letters jumble into something he doesn't recognize as a language, which is headache-inducing and frustrating. He puts the book down and moves a lamp so he can see better.

He tries to sort through how this book connects to everything else. He's certain that the girl who is also a rabbit is the same one that fell through the memory of a door in *Sweet Sorrows,* and the narrative has just moved out of the Harbor on the Starless Sea to introduce a Keating.

Zachary yawns. If he's going to read the whole book he's going to need caffeine.

His normal Kitchen-writing pen has wandered off likely due to cat interference so he looks for another one. There are usually a few on the mantel beneath the bunny pirates. He moves a candle and a paper star and something falls to the ground.

He reaches to pick up the plastic hotel keycard and his hand freezes, midair.

Took you long enough, the voice in his head remarks.

Zachary hesitates, deciding between all the mysteries in need of investigation.

He puts the key in his pocket and leaves the room.

The halls are dim, it must be later than he'd thought. He takes a wrong turn, trying to remember how to reach his destination.

He finds himself in a familiar tiled hall. He stops at a door that practically disappears into the darkness. He stands indecisively in front of it. There is a line of light visible underneath.

Zachary knocks on Dorian's door once and then again and is about to leave when the door swings open.

Dorian looks at him—no, through him—eyes wide yet tired and Zachary thinks maybe he was asleep but then realizes that he's fully dressed but badly buttoned and barefoot and there's a glass of scotch in his hand.

"'You have come to kill me,'" Dorian says.

"I—what?" Zachary answers but Dorian continues without pausing, narrating.

"... the Owl King said. 'I have?' the sword smith's daughter asked."

"Are you really, really drunk right now?" Zachary asks, looking past Dorian at the nearly empty decanter on the desk.

"'They find a way to kill me, always. They have found me here, even in dreams.'" Dorian turns back to the room on the word *here,* the scotch in his glass following a half-second behind and splashing out the side.

"You *are* really, really drunk right now."

Zachary follows as Dorian continues telling the story, partly to him and partly to the room in general. *Fortunes and Fables* sits open on the desk next to the scotch. Zachary glances at it and sees that it is open to the story about the three swords, the illustration of an owl atop a pile of books on a tree stump covered in candles, the illustrator having ignored the part about the beehive.

"'A new king will come to take my place,'" Dorian says behind him. "'Go ahead, it is your purpose.'"

He holds out the glass and Zachary takes the opportunity to remove it from his hand, placing it on the desk out of harm's way.

Zachary had secretly wanted another story time with Dorian but this is not what he'd had in mind. He stands and watches and listens, through the decapitation of the owl and the disintegrating crown and despite the peculiarities of the telling and the state of the storyteller it feels real, realer now than when he read the same words on the page. Like it all actually happened once upon a time.

"Then she woke, still in the chair by the fire in her library."

Dorian punctuates the sentence by collapsing into his own chair by the fire. His head lolls against the back of the armchair and his eyes close and stay closed.

Zachary moves to check on him but as soon as he reaches the chair Dorian leans forward and continues as though the story had not paused at all.

"On the shelf where the sword had been there was a white-and-brown owl perched on the empty case." Dorian points to a bookshelf behind Zachary and Zachary turns, expecting to see the owl and he does. Amongst the books there is a small painting of an owl with a golden crown hovering above its head.

"The owl remained with her for the rest of her days," Dorian whispers into Zachary's ear before he slumps back into the chair.

Even this intoxicated he's a very good storyteller.

"Who is the Owl King, really?" Zachary asks after the post-story silence.

"Shhh," Dorian replies, lifting a hand to Zachary's mouth to shush him. "We can't know that yet. When we know it will mean we're at the end of the story."

His fingers hang on Zachary's lips for a moment before his hand falls, a moment that tastes of scotch and sweat and turning pages.

Dorian's head rests on the tall back of the armchair and late-night drunken story time is over.

Zachary takes his cue to leave, pausing at the desk to pick up the almost empty glass of scotch. He drinks what remains, partly so Dorian won't finish it himself if he wakes since he's probably had enough but mostly because Zachary wants to taste what Dorian has been tasting. Smooth and smoky and a little bit melancholy.

Zachary closes the door as softly as he can, leaving Dorian mostly asleep and possibly dreaming in his chair by the fire in his personal corner of this not quite library, wishing there was a cat around to keep a watchful eye.

Zachary isn't sure where he's going even though his destination is set in his mind, or at least it had been when he'd left his room originally, how long ago was that? Story time has confused his sense of actual time. Maybe he wanted company.

When he reaches the Heart it is darker than he's seen it before, only a few bulbs on the various chandeliers are lit.

The door to the Keeper's office rests ajar. A slice of light falls into the darkened Heart.

Zachary can hear the voices from inside and it strikes him that he has never overheard a conversation in this place before, or thought that anyone could hear his own conversations for that matter, despite the endless corners and hallways and perfectly placed locations for eavesdropping.

He moves closer because it is the direction he was headed anyway, wondering if unintentional eavesdropping counts as eavesdropping.

"This isn't going to work." The Keeper's voice is low and something is different about it. It has lost the formal edge that it has carried in all of Zachary's conversations with him.

"You don't know that," Mirabel's voice replies.

"Do you know differently?" the Keeper asks her.

"He has the book," Mirabel says in response and the Keeper says something else but Zachary cannot hear the reply.

Zachary steps closer to the office, hidden in the shadows, actively listening now. He can see only a sliver of the office, a fragment of shelves and parts of books, the corner of the desk, the tail of the ginger cat. Shadows interrupt the light from the lamps, moving parts of the space from dark to light to dark again. He can make out the Keeper's voice again.

"You should not have gone there," he says. "You should not have gotten Allegra involved—"

"Allegra was already involved," Mirabel interrupts. "Allegra's been involved ever since she started closing off doors and possibilities along with them. We're so close—"

"All the more reason not to provoke her."

"There wasn't another way. We needed him, we needed *that*"— Zachary can see part of Mirabel's arm move as she indicates something across the room but he cannot see what—"and the book has been returned. You've given up, haven't you?"

The pause goes on so long that Zachary wonders if the office has another door that Mirabel might have left through but then the Keeper's voice breaks the silence, his tone changed, his voice lower.

"I don't want to lose you again."

Surprised, Zachary moves and his sliver of visible room fragment shifts.

The curve of Mirabel's back as she sits on the corner of the desk, facing away from him. The Keeper standing, his hand reaching out and sliding over her neck and shoulder, slipping the sleeve of her dress down as he moves closer, brushing his lips against the newly bared skin.

"Maybe this time will be different," Mirabel says softly.

The ginger cat meows in the direction of the door and Zachary turns away and walks quickly down the closest hall, continuing until he's certain no one has followed, wondering at how easy it is to miss things even when they're happening right in front of you.

He turns and looks over his shoulder and there in the middle of the hallway is his squish-faced Persian friend.

"Do you want to keep me company?" Zachary asks and the request sounds sad. Part of him wants to go back to his own bed and part of him wants to go curl up in a chair next to Dorian and another part of him doesn't know what he wants.

The Persian cat stretches and approaches and stops by Zachary's feet. It looks up at him expectantly.

"Okay then," Zachary says and with the cat by his side he winds his way through halls and rooms filled with other people's stories until they reach the garden filled with sculptures.

"I think I figured it out," Zachary tells the cat. The cat does not reply, preoccupied with the inspection of a statue of a fox about its own size frozen mid-leap, its multiple tails sweeping down along the ground.

Zachary turns his attention to a different statue.

He stands in front of the seated woman with her multitude of bees and wonders who sculpted her. Wonders how many corners of this place her bees have wandered off to, placed in pockets or assisted in their journeys by cats.

He wonders if anyone ever looked at her and thought she wanted something other than a book in her open palms.

Wonders if she ever had a crown.

Wonders who left her that glass of wine.

Zachary places the golden key from Mirabel's necklace in the statue's right hand.

He puts his plastic hotel key card in her left hand.

Nothing happens.

Zachary sighs.

He is about to ask the cat if it is hungry and is questioning how firm the "don't feed the cats" rule might be when the buzzing starts.

It comes from within the statue. A buzzing, humming sound.

The woman's stone fingers begin to move, curling closed over the keys. A single bee tumbles from her arm and onto the floor.

There is a scraping sound, followed by a heavy mechanical thunk.

But the statue, keys clasped in her hands, does not move again.

Zachary reaches out and touches her hand. It is closed around the key as though it had been carved that way.

Nothing else has changed, but there was the noise.

Zachary walks around the statue.

The back of the stone chair has slid down into the floor.

The statue is hollow.

There's a staircase below her.

At the bottom of the stairs there is a light.

Zachary looks back at the cat sitting beneath the feet of the hovering marble fox, curled in a multitude of tails. The only tail that twitches is the cat's.

The cat meows at him.

Maybe all moments have meaning.

Somewhere.

Zachary Ezra Rawlins steps inside the Queen of the Bees and descends farther into the depths.

Eleanor does not know what to do with the baby.

The baby cries and eats and cries some more and sometimes sleeps. The order or duration of these activities has no logical progression.

She expected the Keeper to be more helpful but he is not. He does not like the baby. He refers to it as *the child* and not by name, though Eleanor herself is at fault for that because she has not yet given the baby a name.

(Eleanor used to be *the child* herself. She does not know when that stopped or what she is now if she is something else.)

The baby does not require a name. There are no other babies to confuse it with. It is the only one. It is special. Unique. It is *the baby*. Sometimes *the child,* but it is very much a baby.

Before the baby was born Eleanor read all the books she could find about babies but books did not prepare her for the actual baby. Books do not scream and wail and fuss and stare.

She asks the Keeper questions but he does not answer them. He keeps the door to his office closed. She asks the painter and the poets and they help for hours at a time, the painter more than the poets, allowing her to slip into too-short dreamless sleeps but eventually it is always her and it, alone together.

She writes notes to the Kitchen.

She is not certain the Kitchen will reply. She sometimes wrote it tiny notes when she was younger, it would not always respond. If she wrote *Hello,* it would write *Hello* in return and it would answer questions, but once Eleanor asked who it was down there cooking and preparing and fixing things but that note went unanswered.

She sends her first baby-related inquiry with trepidation, relieved when the light turns on.

The Kitchen provides excellent responses to her questions. Detailed lists of things to try. Politely worded encouragements and suggestions.

The Kitchen sends up bottles of warm milk for the baby and cupcakes for Eleanor.

The Kitchen suggests she read to the baby and Eleanor feels stupid for not trying that before. She misses *Sweet Sorrows* and regrets giving it away. She feels sorry for pulling pages out, all the bits she didn't like when she first read it. She wonders if she would like those parts better now if she could read them again but they are lost, folded into stars and thrown in dark corners like her old nightmares. She tries to remember why it was she did not like them. There was the part about the stag in the snow that made her heart hurt, and the bit about the rising sea and someone lost an eye but she does not recall who. She thinks now it is silly to be upset by the fates of characters who do not exist to the point of ripping out pages and hiding them away but it made sense to her at the time. This place made more sense when she was a rabbit, sneaking through the darkness like she owned it, like the world was hers. She can't remember when that changed.

Perhaps she herself is a page that was torn from a story and folded into a star and thrown in the shadows to be forgotten.

Perhaps she should not steal books from hidden archives only to rip out their pages and then give them away, but it is too late to change any of that now and a beloved book is still beloved even if it was stolen to begin with and imperfect and then lost.

Eleanor remembers most of *Sweet Sorrows* well enough to repeat parts of it to the baby, the stories about the pirate, the dollhouse, the bit about the girl who fell through a door that seems so familiar she sometimes thinks she lived it, though she read it so many times it almost feels as though she did.

The Kitchen sends a stuffed rabbit with soft brown fur and floppy ears.

The baby likes the bunny more than it likes most things.

Between the bunny and the reading Eleanor manages to find some calm, even if it is often temporary.

She misses Simon. She is done crying, though she spent plenty of nights and days sobbing once she had been convinced there was no getting back into the room and that even if she did she would never see Simon again.

She knows she will never see him again because the Keeper told her as much. She will never see him again because *he* never saw her again. The Keeper knows because he was there. Has always been here. He mumbled something about time and waved her away.

Eleanor thinks the Keeper understands the past better than he understands the future.

She never felt she belonged here and now she feels it doubly so.

She looks for Simon in the baby's face but finds only hints of him. The baby has her dark hair though it is pale when not screaming. She wanted so badly for the baby to have Simon's blondish hair but none of the books suggest that a baby's hair color changes from black to something else after a certain time. Eye color might, but right now they stay squeezed shut so much Eleanor isn't certain what color they are.

She should give it a name.

It feels like too much responsibility, to give someone else a name.

"What should I name it?" she writes to the Kitchen.

When the light comes on and Eleanor opens the door there is not a tray or a card but a scrap of paper that looks as though it was torn from a book with a single word written on it.

Mirabel

Vermont, two weeks ago

The bar is dimly lit with vintage bulbs that cast a candle-like glow over its glassware and its occupants. Additional light filters in from the windows despite the late hour, the streetlamps illuminating the snow to day-like brightness.

A man whose name is not Dorian sits alone at a table in a corner, his back to the wall. The wall sports a pair of deer antlers, a taxidermied pheasant, and a portrait of a young man hung as a traitor in a war no one living now remembers. The still-living man in front of the painting faces out toward the rest of the bar in a way that suggests he is watching the entire space and not one other table in particular.

One person in particular.

The drink he is nursing was suggested by the waitress when he requested something scotch-forward and he forgets its clever name but there is maple involved.

He has an open book but he is not reading (he has already read it). It merely allows him to keep his gaze focused in the direction of a table of three across the way, the view only partially obscured by the occasional patron lingering near the bar, which is topped by a massive piece of marble that looks as though it was rescued from a much older building.

Two young women (one he has seen already, in the morning in the snow) and a marginally older man. He had questioned the nature of the relationship earlier but the more he follows and the more he watches, the more he sees and the more he wants to know.

The two women are the couple, if he is reading body language and eye contact correctly. He catches a hand placed on a thigh that confirms his suspicions and he is pleased with himself despite the fact that he has done this before, many times, in many bars, and he is long past the point of being proud of a well-developed skill. He is good at this. Has always been good at this, reading people like books from across dimly lit rooms.

The women he can read. The one with the very short hair talks quickly, emphasizes her points with her hands, looks around at the rest of the bar frequently. The other woman is more subdued, comfortable and relaxed, she's slipped her feet from her boots under the table and Dorian is momentarily envious. She's at home in this space, with these people, though she listens in a particularly attentive way. She knows the other two but not as well as she would like to.

Then there's the man.

He's facing almost away, the light catching his profile when he lifts his cocktail glass, his expression lost entirely when he turns, a shadow of snow-damp curls.

Dorian had expected a boy. A student. A handful of collegiate clichés. This is a man. A young man, but a man. An intriguing man. A man who studies video games of all things.

Looking at him now Dorian can't see it. He cannot read the handful of facts on the man in front of him. He had thought *social anxiety* and *hermit* earlier but that's not what he's looking at. The shyness is a minor discomfort that vanished halfway through the first round of drinks. He listens more than he talks but when he does talk there is nothing awkward about his manner. He occasionally pushes his glasses up the bridge of his nose and appears to be drinking a sidecar though he must have asked for it to be served without a sugared rim.

A man he can't read. It is as vexing as having a book he cannot touch. An all too familiar frustration.

"How's the book?"

Dorian looks up to find the waitress at his shoulder, refilling his water. She probably swooped by to check the level of his drink: half full or half empty, depending on optimism. He glances at the book in his hands. *The Secret History.* He has quietly longed for relationships with the type of intensity of those within its pages, regardless of the bacchanalian murderousness, but never found it and has now reached an age where he expects he never will. He has read the book seven times already but he does not tell the waitress that.

"It's very good," he says.

"I started that bird one but I couldn't get into it."

"This one's better," Dorian assures her, coolly enough to shut down the flirtation. Some but not all of the warmth fades from her smile.

"Good to know," she says. "Let me know if I can get you anything."

Dorian nods and returns his attention to just above the top of his book. He thinks the group he is looking at does not have the same level of camaraderie as the characters in his hand but there's something there. Like each of them individually is capable of the intensity if not the murder but this is not the right grouping. Not quite. He watches their table, watches the hand gestures and the arriving food, and watches something make all three of them laugh and he smiles despite himself and then hides his smile in his drink.

Every few minutes he performs a cursory perusal of the room. Pretty good crowd, probably because there are only a handful of bars in this town. He glances at the Tenniel illustration of a gryphon over the bar and wonders if anyone ever names bars after the Mock Turtle.

Below the sign, amongst a knot of other patrons, a girl who looks a touch familiar lifts her arm in a gesture meant to attract the bartender's attention but as her arm moves over a tray of glasses waiting to be delivered to a table Dorian sees the purpose of the motion. The almost invisible trail of powder that settles into the sidecar with no sugar below and dissolves into the liquid.

The girl leaves without getting the bartender's attention at all, slipping first into an anonymous cluster of drinkers and then out the door. Don't stay to watch. He knows that one. He used to break that particular rule occasionally, to be certain. These newer recruits don't take the time to see the nuances around the guidelines. Certainty is worth bending rules for.

He could let it go.

He has performed similar actions himself, many times. And worse. He thinks of the last time—the *last* time—and his hands start to shake. For a moment he is in a different city in a dark hotel room and everything he thought he knew is wrong and his world tilts and then he collects himself again. He puts down his book.

He wonders if the powder in this particular glass is the low-grade amnesia version or the serious stuff. Either would be undetectable, leave its recipient woozy in an hour or two, followed by passing out and waking up terribly hungover or not waking up at all.

Dorian rises from his chair as a waitress picks up the tray and by the time he reaches it he has decided both that it probably is the serious stuff and that it doesn't matter.

It is simple to knock into the waitress, to send the tray and its contents crashing to the floor, simple to apologize for fabricated clumsiness, to offer to assist and be waved away, to return to his table as though that was always his destination and not his point of origin.

How did everything lead to this? One book, one man. Years of mystery and tedium and now things insist on happening all at once.

He's too interested already. He knows that.

Why did he have to be interesting?

The unexpectedly interesting young man gets up from his table, leaving the two women chatting. He turns and walks to the back of the bar, something in his face changes as soon as he's out of sight of the table. Not a drunkenness but a dreaminess, a not quite there, lost in thought fog, maybe with a bit of worry thrown in. Curiouser and curiouser.

Dorian glances back at the table and one of the women is looking right at him. She breaks eye contact immediately and continues talking, writing something down on a cocktail napkin. But she saw him. Watched him watching.

Time to go.

He puts his book away and slides more than enough cash for his single cocktail and a good tip under his empty glass. He's outside in the snow avoiding the puddles of light from the streetlamps by the time Zachary Ezra Rawlins returns to his table.

Dorian can see the table from here, a hazy shadow through a frosted pane of glass but distinct from the other shadows moving through the space.

He knows better than this. He shouldn't be here. He should have walked away a year ago, after a different night in a different city when nothing went according to plan.

How many dramas are unfolding around us right at this very moment?

Again his hands start to shake and he shoves them in the pockets of his coat.

Something broke then but he's here now. He doesn't know where else to go. What else to do.

He could leave. He could run. Keep running. Continue hiding. He could forget all this. This book, his book, the Starless Sea, all of it.

He could.

But he won't.

As Dorian stands in the snow with shaking, near-frozen fingers and scotch-warmed thoughts, watching Zachary through the glass, he isn't thinking about everything that's inevitably about to happen.

He's thinking, *Let me tell you a story.*

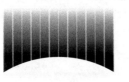

BOOK IV

WRITTEN

IN

THE

STARS

a paper star folded from a page removed from a book

There is a stag in the snow.

Blink and he will vanish.

Was he a stag at all or was he something else?

Was he a sentiment hanging unspoken or a path not taken or a closed door left unopened?

Or was he a deer, glimpsed amongst the trees and then gone, disturbing not a single branch in his departure?

The stag is a shot left untaken. An opportunity lost.

Stolen like a kiss.

In these new forgetful times with their changed ways sometimes the stag will pause a moment longer.

He waits though once he never waited, would never dream to wait or wait to dream.

He waits now.

For someone to take the shot. For someone to pierce his heart.

To know he is remembered.

ZACHARY EZRA RAWLINS descends a narrow staircase beneath a statue, a Persian cat following at his heels. The stairs below his feet are ragged and irregular, one crumbles as he steps on it and he slips down three more, reaching out to the sides to catch his balance.

Behind him the cat mews and gracefully navigates its way over the remains of the broken stair, stopping again when it reaches him.

"Show-off," Zachary says to the cat. The cat says nothing.

Show-off, a voice repeats from somewhere below. An echo, Zachary thinks. A clear, delayed echo. That's all.

He almost believes it, too, but the cat's ears fold back and it hisses at the shadows and Zachary goes back to not knowing what to believe.

He descends the remaining stairs carefully, relieved when the cat continues with him.

On a ledge at the bottom is a lamp, the handled kind that might once have contained a genie but is currently occupied only by burning oil. Strings and pulleys surround it along with a mechanism that looks like a flint near the flame. It must have been lit automatically when the door opened.

The lamp is the only light in the space so Zachary picks it up by its curved handle. As he lifts it, a golden disk beneath raises and the strings and pulleys move. Muffled clanking comes from within the walls and then there is a spark in the shadows. Another lamp lit at the far end of a dark hall, a bright spot like a firefly guiding the way forward.

Zachary walks down the hall with the lamp, the cat following.

Halfway down the hall the light catches on a key on a ring hanging from a hook on the wall.

Zachary reaches out and takes the key.

"Meoowrrr," the cat remarks, in approval or dissent or indifference.

Zachary brings the key and the lamp farther down the hall and the cat and the darkness follow.

Near the end of the hall is an alcove with a lamp that matches the one in his hand.

Beyond the lamp is an arched door of smooth stone, unmarked save for a keyhole.

Zachary slides the key on its ring into the keyhole and it clicks and turns. Zachary pushes on the stone and opens the door.

His lamp and the one on the wall flicker.

The cat hisses at the space beyond the door and bolts back down the hallway.

Zachary listens as the cat flies back up the stairs, hears the crumbling stone of the broken steps crumbling further, and then nothing.

He takes a deep breath and steps into the room.

It smells like dirt and sugar, like Mirabel's perfume.

The lamplight falls on pieces of stone columns and carved walls.

In front of him is a pedestal, a podium, with a golden disk on it.

Zachary places the lamp on the disk and it lowers with the weight. A clanking sound follows.

Around the room lamps hanging from the columns spark to life. A few remain unlit, their lanterns missing or perhaps just out of oil.

Beyond the columns the room is lined with long horizontal alcoves. Zachary wonders why the space seems familiar, and then he sees a single skeletal hand at the edge of one of the shadowed spaces.

It is a crypt.

For a moment Zachary wants to flee, to follow the cat up the stairs. But he doesn't.

Someone wanted him to see this.

Someone—or something—thinks he should be here.

Zachary closes his eyes and collects himself and then he investigates the room.

He starts with its occupants.

At first he thinks they might be mummified but as he moves closer he can see that the strips of cloth wrapped loosely around the bodies are covered in text. Most have dried and decayed along with their wearers but some of them are legible.

sings to herself when she thinks no one is listening
reads the same books over and over again until each page is intimately
 familiar
walks barefoot through the halls, quiet as a cat
laughs so easy and so often as though the whole universe delights him

They're wrapped in memories. Memories of who they were when they were alive.

Zachary reads what he can without disturbing them. The unraveling sentences and the sentiments that catch the light.

he did not wish to be here any longer

one strip of text reads, wrapped around a wrist that is now no more than bone, and Zachary wonders if it means what he thinks it likely means.

In one alcove there is an urn. It has no memories with it.

The others are empty.

Zachary turns his attention to the rest of the room. Some of the columns have carved indentations, sloped surfaces like podiums beneath their lamps.

One podium holds a book. It looks extremely old. It has no cover, only loosely bound pages.

Zachary picks up the book as carefully as he can.

The parchment breaks to pieces in his hands, crumbling into fragments over the podium.

Zachary sighs and the sigh carries more of the fragments from the podium to the stone at his feet.

He tries not to feel too badly about it. Maybe the book, like the people around it, was already gone.

He looks down at the former book fallen around his feet and attempts to read but there are only bits and pieces.

He makes out a single word.

Hello

Zachary blinks and glances at another fragment of paper.

Son, it reads.

He reaches for another piece, large enough to pick up.

of the fortune-

The paper turns to dust in his fingers but the words remain burned into his eyes.

Zachary looks at another broken piece of ancient paper, though he knows what it will say before he reads it.

tell

er

Zachary closes his eyes, listening for the *this is not happening* voice in his head but the voice in his head remains silent. The voice knows that this is happening and so does he.

Zachary opens his eyes. He bends down and sifts through the broken book on the ground, focusing on the first fragment with text that he finds and then another and another.

there are three
things lost
in time

Zachary continues to search as the book continues to deteriorate. The only pieces he can discern are single words.

sword
book
man

The words vanish almost as soon as they are found until only two remain in the dust.

find
man

Zachary searches through the pile of crumbling paper for additional clarification but the bibliomancy session is over. This book that is no longer book-shaped has nothing more to say.

Zachary brushes the dust of prophetic paper from his hands. Find man. He thinks about the man lost in time from *Sweet Sorrows*. He has no idea how to go about finding someone who has been lost in time at the behest of the ghosts of former books. He stares at corpses who do not bother staring back at him, their staring days long past.

Zachary takes the lamp from its pedestal and the rest of the lights extinguish themselves.

He walks out the door pausing to pull the key from its lock.

The door swings shut.

The hallway outside feels longer.

Zachary hangs the key on its hook and replaces the lamp on its shelf. It sinks into place and the light at the other end of the hall vanishes.

Zachary glances down the hallway. It disappears into darkness but the farthest reach of the lamplight finds a shape in the shadows, someone standing in the center of the hall, staring at him.

Zachary blinks and the figure is gone.

He runs up the crumbling stairs, not daring to look back and nearly tripping over the Persian cat who has been patiently waiting for him at the top.

Nightmare number 113:

I am sitting in a very big chair and I cannot get out of it. My arms are tied to the chair arms but my hands are gone. There are people without faces standing around me feeding me pieces of paper that have all the things I am supposed to be written on them but they never ask me what I am.

ZACHARY EZRA RAWLINS is halfway to the elevator, halfway to returning to Vermont and his university and his thesis and his normal, halfway to forgetting any of this ever happened, and hey, maybe he'll take the cat with him and someday he'll convince himself that the whole underground library wonderland was an elaborate fantasy backstory about where the cat came from that he told himself so many times he started to believe it when the cat was only ever a squish-faced stray who followed him home, wherever home is.

Then he remembers the door he entered through last time in the basement of the Collector's Club was burned and likely rendered useless.

So halfway to the elevator with the cat still following, Zachary turns and heads back to his room instead.

In the center of his door is a Post-it Note. The paper is a muted blue rather than the traditional yellow.

In small, neat letters it reads: *All you need to know has been given to you.*

Zachary takes the note from the door. He reads it four times and turns it over, finding nothing on the reverse. He reads it again not believing its statement as he enters the room, the fireplace crackling and waiting for him.

The cat follows him inside. Zachary locks the door behind the cat.

He sticks the Post-it Note to the frame of the bunny pirate painting.

He looks down at his wrists.

He did not wish to be here any longer.

He tries to remember the last time he talked to someone who

wasn't a cat. Was drunken-Dorian story time a few hours ago? Did that even happen? He doesn't know anymore.

Maybe he is tired. What's the difference between tired and sleepy? He puts on pajamas and sits in front of the fireplace. The Persian cat curls up at the foot of the bed, quietly making him feel a little better. All this comfort shouldn't feel so uncomfortable.

Zachary stares at the flames, remembering the shadowed figure in the hallway, staring at him in a space filled with nothing but corpses.

Maybe your mind is playing tricks on you, the voice in his head suggests.

"I thought you were my mind," Zachary says aloud and on the bed the cat stirs and stretches and settles again.

The voice in his head does not respond.

Zachary suddenly desperately wants someone to talk to but also doesn't want to leave the room. He thinks of texting Kat because Kat is usually up at all hours though he doesn't know what he would write. *Hey K, stuck in an underground library dungeon, how's the snow?*

He finds his phone and it has a partial charge, not as high as it should be given the length of time its been plugged in but enough to turn it on.

The picture from the party at the Algonquin he had saved is still there and now it is obvious that the masked woman in the photograph is Mirabel, and even more clear to him that the man speaking with her is Dorian. He wonders what they were whispering about a year ago and can't decide whether or not he wants to know.

There are no missed calls and three text messages. A photo of his finished scarf from Kat, a reminder from his mother that Mercury is going into retrograde soon, and a four-word message from an unknown number:

Tread carefully, Mr. Rawlins.

Zachary turns his phone off. There isn't any service down here anyway.

He goes to the desk and picks up a pen and inscribes two words on a card.

Hello, Kitchen.

He places it in the dumbwaiter and sends it on its way and he has almost convinced himself that the Kitchen and the story-covered corpses and the place itself and Mirabel and Dorian and the room he's standing in and his pajamas are all figments of his imagination when the bell dings.

Hello, Mr. Rawlins, how may we help you?

Zachary thinks for a long time before he inscribes a reply.

Is this real?

He writes. It sounds too vague but he sends it anyway.

The dumbwaiter dings a moment later and inside along with another card there is a mug with a curl of steam rising from it and a plate covered with a silver dome.

Zachary reads the note.

Of course it is real, Mr. Rawlins. We hope you feel better soon.

The mug is filled with warm coconut milk with turmeric and black pepper and honey.

Beneath the silver dome there are six small, perfectly frosted cupcakes.

Thank you, Kitchen.

Zachary writes.

He takes his mug and his cupcakes and sits in front of the fire again.

The cat stretches and comes to sit with him, sniffing at the cupcakes and licking frosting from his fingertips.

Zachary doesn't remember falling asleep. He wakes curled up in front of the dying fire on a pile of pillows, the Persian cat nestled into his arm. He doesn't know what time it is. What is time, anyway?

"What is time, anyway?" Zachary asks the cat.

The cat yawns.

The dumbwaiter dings, the light on the wall glowing, and Zachary can't remember it dinging on its own before.

Good morning, Mr. Rawlins.

The note inside reads.

We hope you slept well.

There is a pot of coffee and a rolled omelet and two toasted slices of sourdough bread and a ceramic jar of butter drizzled with honey and dusted with salt and a basket filled with mandarin oranges.

Zachary starts to write a thank-you but inscribes a different sentiment instead.

I love you, Kitchen.

He doesn't expect a reply but there is another chime.

Thank you, Mr. Rawlins. We are quite fond of you as well.

Zachary eats his breakfast (he shares the omelet with the cat, for-getting the rule about feeding the cats and having already broken it with buttercream frosting the night before) and thinks, his head clearer than it had been.

"If you were a man lost in time where would you be?" Zachary asks the cat.

The cat stares at him.

All you need to know has been given to you.

"Oh, right," Zachary says as the realization dawns. He sorts through the books near the fireplace to find the one that Rhyme gave him and flips to the page where he left off. He takes the book to the desk and moves a lamp so he can see better and the cat sits in his lap, purring. Zachary peels and eats a mandarin orange in small segments of sun-shine as he reads.

He reads and frowns and reads more and then he turns a page and there is nothing else. The rest of the pages are blank. The story, his-tory, whatever it is, stops mid-book.

Zachary remembers the man lost in time wandering cities of honey and bone in *Sweet Sorrows* and the mention of the Starless Sea in *Fortunes and Fables* and wonders if all of these stories are somehow the same story. Wonders where Simon could be now and how to go about finding him. Wonders about the burned place and the broom in the Keeper's office. Wonders what, precisely, happens to the son of the fortune-teller.

On the corner of the desk is an origami star that he had pocketed. He picks it up and looks closer. There is writing on it.

Zachary unfolds the star. It stretches out into a long strip of paper. It contains words so tiny they seem whispered:

Nightmare number 83: I am walking in a dark dark place and something big and slithery is slithering in the dark so close I could reach and touch it but if I touch the slithery thing it will know I am here and it will eat me very slowly.

Zachary lets the nightmare flutter onto the desk and picks up the book again. He turns to the last written page and rereads it, pausing at the final word in the unfinished book.

Zachary gently removes the cat from his lap. He puts the cat on the floor and the book in his bag along with a cigarette lighter so he doesn't end up stuck in the dark again and he slips on his shoes. He pulls a maroon sweater on over his pajamas and goes to look for Mirabel.

Once in a long while an acolyte chooses to give up something other than their tongue as they take their vows.

Such acolytes are rare. One will not remember the last exception that came before. They will not serve long enough to meet the one who follows.

The painter has lost her way.

She thinks (she is wrong) that choosing this path (a path, any path) will bring her closer to this place she once loved, this place that has changed around her as time changes all things.

She wishes to rekindle flames long extinguished.

To find something she has lost that she cannot name but feels the absence of within her like a hunger.

The painter makes her decision without telling anyone. Only her single student notices her absence but thinks little of it having learned long ago that sometimes people disappear like rabbits into hats and sometimes they return and other times they do not.

The acolytes allow for this rare concession, as their numbers are dwindling.

The painter spends her time in solitude and contemplation categorizing losses and regrets trying to determine if there was ever anything she could have done to prevent any of them or if they simply passed through her life and out again like waves upon a shore.

She thinks if she has an idea for a new painting at any point during her time locked away she will refuse this path and return to her paints and let the bees find someone else to serve them.

But there are no new ideas. Only old ones, turned over and over again in her mind. Only the safe and the familiar, things she has captured and recaptured in brushstrokes so many times that she finds nothing but emptiness within them.

She considers trying to write but has always felt more comfortable with images than with words.

When the door opens long before the painter expects it to she accepts her bee without hesitation.

The acolyte and the painter walk down empty halls toward an unmarked door. Only a single cat notices them in this moment and though the cat recognizes this mistake for what it is he does not interfere. It is not the way of cats to interfere with fate.

The painter expects to sacrifice both eyes but only one is taken.

One will be more than enough.

As the images flood the painter's sight, as she is bombarded by so many pictures unfolding in such detail that she cannot separate one from the other, cannot dream of capturing even fractions of them in oils on canvas even as her fingers itch for her brushes, she realizes this path was not meant for her.

But it is too late now to choose another.

ZACHARY EZRA RAWLINS walks the halls of the Harbor, realizing that he doesn't actually know where Mirabel's room is, he had not thought to ask. He loops down through the cavernous ballroom to where he last saw her but the wine cellar is unoccupied. The painting of the lady with her bee-covered face looms over the racks of wine and before Zachary leaves again he picks an interesting-looking bottle to put in his bag, an unnamed red marked with a lantern and crossed keys.

Zachary takes a different flight of stairs up from the ballroom and doesn't know where he is. He has wandered from familiar to un- again.

He pauses, trying to get his bearings, by a reading nook lined with books with a single armchair and a small table formed from a broken column. There's a teacup on it, with a lit candle burning where the tea should be.

Between the bookshelves is a small brass plate with a button, like an old-fashioned light switch. Zachary presses it.

The bookshelf slides back, opening into a hidden room.

It would take an eternity to find all the secrets here, the voice in his head observes. *To solve a fraction of the mysteries.* Zachary doesn't argue with it.

The room beyond looks like something from an old manor house, or a period-piece murder mystery. Dark wood panels and green glass lamps. Leather sofas and overlapping Oriental rugs and walls covered in bookshelves, one of which has opened to allow Zachary inside. In between the shelves there are framed paintings lit with gallery lights and a proper door, open and leading out to a hall.

An enormous painting is displayed on the wall opposite. A nighttime forest scene, a crescent moon visible between the branches, but within the forest there is an immense birdcage, so large that on the perch inside where a bird might be there is a man, turned away from the viewer, sitting forlornly in his prison.

The trees surrounding the cage are covered with keys and stars, hanging by ribbons from branches and tucked into nests and fallen onto the ground below. It makes Zachary think of his bunny pirates. It might have been painted by the same artist. The wine-cellar bee lady might have been, too, for that matter.

Dorian stands in front of the painting, staring at it. He wears a long felted wool coat, midnight blue and collarless and perfectly tailored to fit him with polished buttons that might be wood or bone shaped like stars so he matches the painting. The coat has coordinating trousers but he's barefoot.

He turns as the bookshelf closes behind Zachary.

"You're here," Dorian says, and it sounds more like an observation about the place in general than Zachary appearing out of a bookshelf in particular.

"Yes, I am."

"I thought I'd dreamed you."

Zachary has no idea how to respond to that comment and is relieved when Dorian turns his attention back to the painting. He probably thinks that drunken story time was also a dream and maybe that's for the best. Zachary walks over and stands next to Dorian and side by side they observe the man in his cage.

"I feel like I've seen this before," Dorian remarks.

"It reminds me of the key collector's garden, from your book," Zachary says and Dorian turns to him, surprised. "I read it. I'm sorry." The apology is automatic though he's not actually sorry.

"Don't be," Dorian says. He turns back to the painting.

"How are you feeling?" Zachary asks.

"Like I'm losing my mind, but in a slow, achingly beautiful sort of way."

"Yeah, I get that. So *better*, then."

Dorian smiles and Zachary wonders how you can miss someone's smile when you've only seen it once before.

"Yes, *better*. Thank you."

"You're not wearing shoes."

"I hate shoes."

"Hate is a strong emotion for footwear," Zachary observes.

"Most of my emotions are strong," Dorian responds and again Zachary doesn't know how to reply and Dorian saves him from having to.

Dorian takes a step toward Zachary, suddenly and unexpectedly close, and reaches out his hand, placing it on Zachary's chest above his heart. It takes Zachary a moment to realize what he's doing: confirming his solidity. He wonders how easy it is to feel a heartbeat through a sweater.

"You're really here," Dorian says quietly. "We're both really *here*."

Zachary doesn't know what to say so he just nods as they stare at each other. There is a warmness to the brown of Dorian's eyes that he had not been able to see before. There is a scar above his left eyebrow. There are so many pieces to a person. So many small stories and so few opportunities to read them. *I would like to look at you* seems like such an awkward request.

Zachary watches Dorian's eyes move across his skin in a similar fashion, wondering how many of their thoughts are shared ones.

Dorian looks down at his hand and sighs.

"Are you wearing pajamas?" he asks.

"Yes," Zachary says, realizing that he is indeed still wearing his blue-striped pajamas and then he starts to laugh at the absurdity of it all and after a brief hesitation Dorian joins him.

Something changes in the laughter, something is lost and something else is found and though Zachary does not have words for what has happened, there is an ease between them that wasn't there before.

"What were you doing in the bookshelf?" Dorian asks.

"I was trying to figure out what to do next," Zachary says. "I was looking for Mirabel but I couldn't find her and then I got lost so I started looking for something familiar and I found you."

"Am I familiar?" Dorian says and Zachary wants to say *Yes, yes you are the most familiar and I don't understand how* but that is too much truth right now so instead he says, "If you were a man lost in time where would you be?"

"Don't you mean *when* would I be?"

"That, too," Zachary says, smiling despite the realization that the whole locating-a-man-lost-in-time quest might be far more difficult than he'd thought. He looks back at the painting.

"How are *you* feeling?" Dorian asks him in response to whatever grumpy frustration his face is betraying.

"Like I've lost my mind already and post-mind life is one puzzle after another." Zachary looks at the man in the cage. The cage looks real, the lock heavy and looped through the bars on a chain. It looks real enough to touch. To fool the eye.

For a moment he feels like that boy he was again, standing in front of a painted door he won't dare to open. What's the difference between a door and a cage? Between *not yet* and *too late*?

"What kind of puzzles?" Dorian asks.

"Ever since I got here it's been all notes and clues and mysteries. First there was the Queen of the Bees but she just led me to a hidden crypt filled with memory-wrapped dead people where my cat abandoned me and a book told me there were three things lost in time. Please don't look at me like that."

"A book told you?"

"It fell apart in little instructional pieces but I don't know what it means and I was surrounded by corpses so I didn't particularly want to stick around to figure it out and the book was gone anyway. Also there was a ghost in the hall after that. I think. Maybe."

"Are you certain you didn't imag—"

Zachary cuts him off before he can say the word.

"You think I'm making it up?" Zachary asks. "We're in an underground library, you've seen painted doors open on solid walls, and you think I'm *imagining* bibliomancy and maybe-ghosts?"

"I don't know," Dorian says. "I don't know what to believe right now."

The two of them stare at each other in a silence laced with multiple types of tension until Zachary can't take it any longer.

"Sit," he says, pointing at one of the leather sofas. There is a reading lamp with a green glass shade poised over it. He expects Dorian to argue but he doesn't, he sits as directed and says nothing, compliant, though his expression betrays his annoyance. "Finish reading this," Zachary says, taking *Sweet Sorrows* from his bag and handing it to Dorian. "When you're done, read this one." He puts *The Ballad of Simon and Eleanor* on a table nearby. "Do you have your book with you?"

Dorian takes *Fortunes and Fables* from the pocket of his coat. "You won't be able to read . . ." He pauses as Zachary takes the book from him. "You said you already read it."

"I did," Zachary says. "I thought rereading might be helpful. What is it?" he asks, watching the question forming on Dorian's face.

"To the best of my knowledge you only speak English and French."

"I wouldn't call what I can do in French *speaking*," Zachary clarifies, trying to gauge how mad he is and finding the anger has dissipated. He sits on the other sofa and carefully opens *Fortunes and Fables*. "The books translate themselves down here. I think speech does, too, but I've only been speaking to people in English or hand gestures. Come to think of it the Keeper probably doesn't speak to me in English, that was presumptuous."

"How is that possible?" Dorian asks.

"How is any of this possible? I don't even understand the physics of the bookshelves."

"I asked you that in Mandarin."

"You speak Mandarin?"

"I speak a lot of languages," Dorian says and Zachary pays close attention to his lips. They don't quite match the words that reach his ears, like when the book translations blur before they settle again. Zachary wonders if he even would have noticed the difference if he wasn't looking for it.

"Did you say that in Mandarin, too?" he asks.

"I said that in Urdu."

"You *do* speak a lot of languages."

Dorian sighs and looks down at the book in his hands and then at the man in the cage on the wall and then back at Zachary.

"You look like you want to leave," Zachary says and Dorian's expression immediately shifts to one of surprise.

"I don't have anywhere to go," he says, and he holds Zachary's gaze for a moment before turning his attention to *Sweet Sorrows*.

Zachary is midway through *Fortunes and Fables* wondering if there is more than one Owl King when Dorian suddenly looks up at him.

"This . . . this boy in the library, with the woman in the green scarf. This is me," he says.

"You are having a much calmer reaction to being in the book than I did."

"How . . ." Dorian starts and trails off, still reading. A minute later he adds, "It's only that part at the beginning, I never did any of these other tests."

"But you were a guardian."

"No, I was a member in high standing of the Collector's Club," Dorian corrects without looking up from the page. "Though I would gather that the club is an evolution of this. There are . . . similarities." Dorian looks up from the book and around the room, at the bookshelves and the painting and the door out to the hall. A cat passes by without so much as glancing inside. "Allegra always said we had to wait until it was safe and secured. She told me that for years and I believed her. 'Safe and secured' was a constantly moving goal. Always more doors to close and more problematic individuals to eliminate. Always *soon* and never *now*."

"Is that what the whole Collector's Club believes?"

"That if they do what Allegra tells them for long enough they will earn their place in paradise which is—as Borges supposed—a kind of library? Yes, they do believe that."

"That sounds like a cult," Zachary observes.

To his surprise Dorian laughs.

"It does indeed," he admits.

"Did you believe all that?" Zachary asks.

Dorian considers the question before he responds.

"Yes I did. I believed. Steadfastly. I accepted a lot of things on faith and there came a night that made me question everything and I ran away. I disappeared. That did not go over well. They froze my cards under all my aliases, made some versions of me no longer exist and put others on watch lists and no-fly lists and all sorts of lists. But I had a great deal of cash and I was in Manhattan. It's easy to stay lost in Manhattan. I could walk around midtown in a suit with a briefcase and I'd vanish into the crowd though I was usually going to the library."

"What changed your mind?" Zachary asks.

"Not what. *Who.* Mirabel changed my mind," Dorian says and before Zachary can inquire further Dorian returns his attention back to the book, the conversation pointedly and clearly halted.

They read in silence for some time. Zachary sneaks occasional glances at Dorian, trying to guess where he is in the book based on eyebrow reaction.

Eventually Dorian closes *Sweet Sorrows* and puts it down on the table. He frowns and holds out a hand and Zachary gives him *The Ballad of Simon and Eleanor* without a word and they return to reading.

Zachary is lost in a fairy tale (wondering what kind of box the story sculptor hid what he's guessing was Fate's heart inside) when Dorian closes the book.

Slowly they attempt to sort through a thousand questions. For every connection they make between one book and another there are more that don't fit. Some stories seem completely separate and distant and others feel explicitly connected to the story they have found themselves in together now.

"There was . . ." Dorian starts but then pauses and when he continues he addresses the man on the wall instead of the man sitting across from him. "There was an organization that was referred to as the Keating Foundation. Never publicly, it was an in-house term. I never knew its origin, no one was ever named Keating but it can't be a coincidence."

"The library had this marked as a gift from the Keating Foundation," Zachary says, holding up *Sweet Sorrows.* "How were they related to the Collector's Club?"

"They worked in opposition. They were. . . . targets to be eliminated." Dorian pauses. He stands and paces the room and Zachary has a sudden sense of the cage in the painting not being restricted to the wall.

"What did your crypt book tell you again?" Dorian asks, pausing to pick up *The Ballad of Simon and Eleanor* and flipping through it while he paces.

"There are three things lost in time. A book, a sword, and a man. *Sweet Sorrows* must be the book, since Eleanor gave it to Simon and then it spent, what, a hundred years on the surface? The instructions said 'find man' and not 'find man and sword' so maybe the sword has already been returned, too. There's a sword in the Keeper's office, hanging all conspicuous in plain sight."

"Simon's the man lost in time," Dorian says.

"He must be. The man lost in time from *Sweet Sorrows* even has the coat with the buttons."

Dorian picks up *Sweet Sorrows,* flipping back and forth between both books.

"Who do you think is the pirate?" he asks.

"I think the pirate is a metaphor."

"A metaphor for what?"

"I don't know," Zachary says. He sighs and looks back at the man in his painted cage surrounded by so many keys.

"Who is the painter?" Dorian asks at the same time that the voice in Zachary's head poses the same question.

"I don't know," Zachary says. "I've seen a bunch that are probably by the same artist. There's one with bunny pirates in my room."

"May I see it?"

"Sure."

Zachary puts *Sweet Sorrows* and *The Ballad of Simon and Eleanor* in his bag and Dorian replaces *Fortunes and Fables* in his pocket and they set off down the hall, one that Zachary sort of recognizes, a tunnel-shaped one where the bookshelves curve with each turn.

"How much have you seen?" Zachary asks as they walk, watching Dorian slow and stare at their surroundings.

"Just a few rooms," he responds, looking down past his bare feet. The floor in this hall is glass, revealing a room below filled with movable panel screens with stories printed on them, though from this perspective it is a story about a cat in a maze. "The only people I've seen are you and that fluffy-haired angel girl in the white robes who doesn't speak."

"That's Rhyme," Zachary says. "She's an acolyte."

"Does she have a tongue?"

"I didn't ask, I figured it would be rude."

Dorian pauses at an ornate telescope resting next to an armchair. It is aimed at a window set into the stone wall next to it. He undoes the latch and opens the window. The view beyond it is mostly darkness with a soft light in the distance.

Dorian returns to the telescope and looks out the window through it. Zachary watches as a smile tugs at the corner of his lips. After a moment he steps aside and gestures for Zachary to look.

Once Zachary's eyes have adjusted to eyeglasses-plus-telescope-lenses he can see into the distance, through a cavernous space. There are windows into other rooms, in some other part of the Harbor, carved into a wall of jagged rock that descends into the shadows, but on the expanse of illuminated stone there rests the remains of a large ship. Its hull is cracked in two, its sea stolen from beneath it. A tattered flag hangs limply from its mast. Piles of books are stacked on the sloping deck.

"Were there sirens here, do you think?" Dorian asks, his voice very close to Zachary's ear. "Singing sailors to shipwreck?"

Zachary closes his eyes, trying to imagine this ship on a sea.

He turns from the telescope, expecting Dorian to be next to him but Dorian has already moved farther down the hall.

"Can I ask you a question?" Zachary says when he catches up with him.

"Of course."

"Why did you help me, back in New York?" It is something Zachary has not been able to figure out, thinking that there must be more to it than simply getting his own book back.

"Because I wanted to," Dorian says. "I've spent a great deal of my life doing what other people wanted for me and not what I wanted myself and I'm trying to change. Impulse decisions. No shoes. It's refreshing in a terrifying sort of way."

A few turns and a hall filled with stained-glass stories later they reach Zachary's door. Zachary goes to open it but it is locked. He had forgotten that he locked it and retrieves his keys from beneath his sweater.

"You're still wearing it," Dorian remarks, looking at the silver sword and Zachary doesn't know how to respond to that beyond the terribly obvious affirmation that yes he is still wearing it and rarely takes it off but as he opens the door he is immediately distracted by the indignant howling of the Persian cat that he has accidentally locked inside.

"Oh, I'm sorry," Zachary says to the cat. The cat says nothing, only weaves its way through his legs before heading off down the hallway.

"How long was he in here?" Dorian asks.

"A couple of hours?" Zachary guesses.

"Well at least he was comfortable," Dorian says, looking around the room. He turns his attention to the painting over the mantel. It looks like a classic tall-ship seascape, with ominous clouds and choppy waves, completely realistic save for the leporine pirates. "Do you think it's a coincidence?" he asks. "A girl who pretends to be a rabbit who knows a painter, and then the paintings with the rabbits?"

"You think the painter painted them for Eleanor."

"I think it's a possibility," Dorian says. "I think there is a story here."

"I think there are a lot of stories here," Zachary says. He puts his bag down and the bottle of wine clanks against the stone. Zachary takes it out and brushes dust from the lantern and the keys on it, wondering who bottled it and how long it had been in the cellar, waiting for someone to open it. Why not now?

Zachary looks at the corked bottle and frowns.

"Don't judge me," he says to Dorian as he picks up a pen from the desk and uses it to push the cork all the way into the bottle, a trick he used many, many times as an undergraduate lacking proper bar tools.

"We could have found a corkscrew somewhere," Dorian remarks as he observes the inelegant process.

"You used to be mildly impressed by my improvisational skills," Zachary responds, holding up the successfully opened bottle.

Dorian laughs as Zachary takes a swig of the wine. It probably would benefit from decanting and maybe glasses but it is rich and lush and bright. Luminous, somehow, like the lantern on it. It doesn't whisper verses or stories around his tongue and into his head, thankfully, but it tastes older than stories. It tastes like myth.

Zachary offers the bottle up to Dorian and he takes it, letting his fingers rest over Zachary's as he does so.

"You went back for me, didn't you?" Dorian asks suddenly. "I'm sorry I didn't mention it earlier, everything's still cloudy."

"It was mostly Mirabel," Zachary says. "I sidekicked and then I got tied to a chair and poisoned." It all feels distant now, even though it was so recent. "I got better," he adds.

"Thank you," Dorian says. "You didn't have to do that. You owed me nothing and I . . . thank you. I thought I might not wake up at all and instead I woke up here."

"You're welcome," Zachary says, though he feels he should say more.

"How long ago was that?" Dorian asks. "Four days? Five? A week? It feels longer."

Zachary looks at him wordlessly, without a proper answer. He thinks it might be a week, or a lifetime, or a moment. He thinks *I feel like I have known you forever* but he doesn't say it and so they only hold each other's gaze, not needing to say anything.

"Where did you get this?" Dorian asks after he takes a sip from the bottle.

"In the wine cellar. It's at the far end of the ballroom, past where the Starless Sea used to be."

Dorian looks at him with that thousand-questions expression in his eyes but instead of asking any of them he takes another swig of wine and hands the bottle back to Zachary.

"It must have been something extraordinary, back in its time," he says.

"Why do you think people came here?" Zachary says, taking another myth-tinged sip before handing the bottle to Dorian, unable to tell if the rush in his head and his pulse is from the wine or the way Dorian's fingers move over his.

"I think people came here for the same reason we came here," Dorian says. "In search of something. Even if we didn't know what it was. Something more. Something to wonder at. Someplace to belong. We're here to wander through other people's stories, searching for our own. To Seeking," Dorian says, tilting the bottle toward Zachary.

"To Finding," Zachary responds, repeating the gesture once Dorian hands him the bottle.

"I do like that you've read my book," Dorian says. "Thank you again for helping me get it back."

"You're welcome."

"Strange, isn't it? To love a book. When the words on the pages become so precious that they feel like part of your own history because they are. It's nice to finally have someone read stories I know so intimately. Which was your favorite?"

Zachary considers the question while also considering the particular use of the word *intimately*. He thinks over the stories, snippets of images coming back to him as he lets himself consider them simply as stories instead of trying to break them apart searching for their secrets. He looks at the bottle in his hands, the keys and the lantern, thinking of seers in taverns and shared bottles in snow-covered inns.

"I don't know. I liked the one with the swords. So many of them were kind of sad. I think the innkeeper and the moon were my favorite, but I wanted . . ." Zachary stops, not certain what he wanted from it. *More,* maybe. He hands the bottle back to Dorian.

"You wanted a happier ending?"

"No . . . not necessarily happier. I wanted more story. I wanted to know what happened afterward, I wanted the moon to figure out a way to come back even if she couldn't stay. All those stories are like that, they feel like pieces of bigger stories. Like there's more that happens beyond the pages."

Dorian nods, thoughtfully. "Is that a wardrobe?" he asks, gesturing at the piece of furniture on the other side of the room.

"Yes," Zachary says, distracted into stating the obvious.

"Have you checked it?"

"For what?" Zachary asks but realizes as Dorian's disbelieving eyebrow rises. "Oh. Oh, no, I haven't."

It is, he thinks, the only proper wardrobe he has ever had and after the considerable amount of time he has spent sitting in closets literally and figuratively he cannot believe he has not yet checked this one for a door to Narnia.

Dorian hands the bottle of wine to Zachary and walks over to the wardrobe.

"I have never been particularly fond of Narnia myself," Dorian says as he runs his fingers over the carved wooden doors. "Too much direct allegory for my tastes. Though it does have a certain romance to it. The snow. The gentlemanly satyr."

He opens the doors and smiles, though Zachary cannot tell what it is he's smiling at.

He reaches out an arm and parts the hanging rows of linen and cashmere, slowly, carefully. Drawing the motion out rather than reaching immediately to touch the back of the wardrobe. Taking his time.

He doesn't even need words to tell a story, a voice somewhere in Zachary's head observes and he suddenly desperately wishes that he was currently occupying the sweater that Dorian has his hand on and he is so distracted by this thought that it takes him a moment to realize that Dorian has stepped into the wardrobe and vanished.

 *a paper star that has been so mangled by circumstance
and time that its shape is only vaguely recognizable as a star*

A man momentarily found in time storms down a hall, finding
his way out of time again.

A fallen candelabra is not an unusual thing. The acolytes
anticipate them, they have a way of knowing when a flame might
tumble. There are methods for avoiding accidents.

Acolytes cannot predict the actions of a man who has been
lost in time. They cannot know where or when he will appear.
They are not there when and where he does.

There are not as many acolytes as there once were and they are
all, at this moment, tending to other matters.

The fire creeps at first and then catches, pulling books from
their shelves in curling paper and reducing candles to pools of
molten wax.

It tears through the halls, moving like the sea over everything
in its path.

It finds the room with the dollhouse and it claims it for its
own, an entire universe lost in flame.

The dolls see only brightness and then nothing.

ZACHARY EZRA RAWLINS stares into a wardrobe that contains only a great deal of sweaters and linen shirts and trousers and questions his sanity again.

"Dorian?" he says. He must be hiding in the shadows, curled up beneath hanging garments the way Zachary has sat so many times himself, in a world alone, compact and forgotten.

Zachary reaches a hand through sweaters and shirts, wondering why he would accept shadows as shadows in a place where so much is more than what it seems and where his fingers should touch solid wood they touch nothing instead.

He laughs but it catches in his throat. He steps into the wardrobe, reaching farther and there is emptiness where the back should be, beyond where the wall would have met his fingers.

He takes one step and then another, cashmere brushing against his back. The light from his room fades quickly. He puts a hand out to his side and hits slightly curving solid stone. A tunnel, maybe.

Zachary walks forward. He reaches into the darkness in front of him and a hand grabs his.

"Let's see where this goes, shall we?" Dorian whispers in his ear.

Zachary grasps Dorian's hand and thus entwined they proceed through the tunnel as it turns, leading them into another room.

This room is lit by a single candle, placed in front of a mirror so its flame is doubled.

"I don't think this is Narnia," Dorian says.

Zachary lets his eyes adjust to the light. Dorian is correct, it is not Narnia. It is a room filled with doors.

Each door is carved with images. Zachary walks toward the closest one, losing his grip on Dorian's hand in the process and regretting it but too curious.

On the door there is a girl holding a lantern aloft against a dark sky teeming with winged creatures, screaming and clawing and hissing at her.

"Let's not open that one," Zachary says.

"Agreed," Dorian says, looking over his shoulder.

They move from door to door. Here is a carved city spiked with curving towers. There an island under a moonlit sky.

One door depicts a figure behind bars reaching out to another in a separate cage and it reminds Zachary of the pirate in the basement. He goes to open it but Dorian pulls his attention to another.

This door holds a carved celebration. Dozens of faceless figures dancing under banners and lanterns. One banner has a string of moons engraved upon it, a full moon surrounded by waxing and waning crescents.

Dorian opens the door. The space beyond is dark. He steps inside.

Zachary follows but as soon as he enters Dorian is gone.

"Dorian?" Zachary says, turning back to the room with its multitude of doors but that too has vanished.

He turns again and he is standing in a well-lit hallway lined with books.

A pair of women in long gowns brush by, clearly more interested in each other than him, laughing as they pass.

"Hello?" Zachary calls after them but they do not turn.

He looks behind him. There is no door, only books. Tall shelves messily stacked and piled, a well-used collection, some sitting open. A few shelves down there is a handsome young man with ginger hair so bright it borders on a proper red browsing through one of the volumes.

"Excuse me," Zachary says but the man does not look up from his book. Zachary puts a hand out to touch him on the shoulder and the fabric feels strange beneath his fingers, there but not there. The idea of touching a man's shoulder in a suit jacket and not the actual feeling. The touch version of a movie that has not been dubbed properly. Zachary pulls his hand back in surprise.

The ginger-haired man looks up, not quite at him.

"Are you here for the party?" he asks.

"What party?" Zachary responds but before the man can answer they are interrupted.

"Winston!" a male voice calls from around the next bend in the hallway, in the direction that the girls in gowns had been heading. The ginger-haired man puts down his book and gives Zachary a little bow before going to follow the voice.

"I think I saw a ghost," Zachary hears him remark casually to his companion before they disappear down the hall.

Zachary looks at his hands. They look the same as usual. He picks up the book the man had replaced on the shelf and it feels solid but not quite solid in his hands, like his brain is telling him he's holding a book without there actually being a book there.

But there is a book there. He opens it and to his surprise he recognizes the fragments of poetry on the page. Sappho.

someone will remember us
I say
even in another time

Zachary closes the book and puts it back on the shelf, the weight of it not quite transferring at the same time as the action but he finds himself anticipating the tactile discrepancies already.

Laughter bubbles from another hall. Music plays in the distance. Zachary is undoubtedly within his familiar Harbor on the Starless Sea but everything is vibrant and alive. There are so many people.

He walks by something he thinks is a golden statue of a naked woman until she moves and he realizes the gold is meticulously painted onto an actual naked woman. She reaches out and touches his arm as he passes, leaving streaks of golden powder on his sleeve.

As he continues few others acknowledge him but people seem to know he is there. They move out of the way as he passes. The frequency of people increases as he walks and then he realizes where they are going.

Another turn brings him to the wide stair that leads down to the ballroom. The stairs are festooned with lanterns and garlands of paper dipped in gold. Confetti cascades in gilded waves over the stone steps. It clings to the hems of gowns and cuffs of trousers, drifting and swirling as the crowd descends.

Zachary follows, swept up in the tide of partygoers. The ballroom they enter is both familiar and completely unexpected.

The space he knows as hollow and empty is teeming with people. All of the chandeliers are lit, casting dancing light over the hall. The ceiling is littered with metallic balloons. Long glimmering ribbons hang from them and as Zachary gets closer he sees they are weighted with pearls. Everything is undulating, shimmering, and golden. It smells like honey and incense, musk and sweat and wine.

Virtual reality isn't all that real if it doesn't smell like anything, a voice remarks in his head.

The curtains of balloons are mazelike, the enormous space divided and fragmented by almost transparent walls. One space becomes many: improvised rooms, alcoves, small vignettes of chairs, carpets in rich jewel tones covering the stone floor, and tables draped in silks of darkest night-sky blue dotted with stars, covered in brass bowls and vases, piled with wine and fruit and cheese.

Beside him is a woman with her hair tied up in a scarf wearing acolyte robes holding a large bowl filled with golden liquid. As he watches, guests dip their hands into the bowl, removing them again covered in shimmering gold. It drips down arms and on sleeves and Zachary spies golden fingerprints behind ears and down the backs of necks, suggestive traces over necklines and below waists.

Closer to the center of the ballroom the ribbon curtains open, allowing the room to expand into its full scope. A dance floor occupies most of the space, stretching out to the archways on the far side.

Zachary moves around the edge. Dancers twirl so close that gowns brush against his legs. He reaches the looming fireplace and finds it covered in candles, piled in the hearth and lined along the mantel, dripping wax into pools on the stone. In between the candles there are bottles filled with gold sand and water containing small white fish with fanned tails glowing like flames in the light. Above the flames and the fish there are painted sigils. A full moon flanked by crescents, waxing and waning.

A motion near Zachary's hand draws his attention and when he looks down he finds that someone has pressed a folded piece of paper into his palm. He glances at the partygoers around him but they are all absorbed in their own world.

He unfolds the paper. It is covered in handwritten text scrawled in gold ink.

The moon had never asked a boon of Death or Time but there was something that she wished, that she wanted, that she desired more than she had ever desired anything before.

A place had become precious to her, and a person within it more so.

The moon returned to this place as often as she could, in stolen moments of borrowed time.

She had found an impossible love.

She resolved to find a way to keep it.

Zachary looks up at the sea of people surrounding him, dancing and drinking and laughing. He cannot see Dorian anywhere but he must have written this so he must be nearby. Zachary refolds the paper and tucks the fragment of story in his pocket and continues through the ballroom.

Beyond the fireplace there are tables covered in bottles. A woman wearing a suit stands behind them, pouring and mixing liquids and handing them out to passersby in delicate glasses. Zachary watches as she works, combining liquids that smoke and foam and change color from clear to gold to red to black to clear again.

He hears the mixologist wish someone a blessed lunar new year as she hands them a coupe glass covered in a layer of gold leaf that would have to be broken in order for the drink to be consumed. Zachary walks on before the surface is disturbed.

In a quiet corner a man pours sand on the floor in tones of black and grey and gold and ivory in intricate patterns, mandala-like circles depicting dancing figures and balloons and a large fire, with an outer circle of cats and a far outer circle of bees. He carves the details into the sand with the edge of a feather. Zachary moves closer to get a better view but as soon as it is complete the man brushes it all away and begins again.

Nearby, a woman dressed in ribbons and nothing else lounges on a settee. The ribbons have poems on them, circling her throat and her waist and curling down between her legs. She has many admirers reading her but she reminds Zachary too much of the bodies in the crypt and he starts to turn away when one of the lines of text catches his eye.

First the moon went to speak with Death.

Zachary moves closer to read the story as it continues down the woman's arm and around her wrist.

She asked if Death might spare a single soul.
   Death would have granted the moon any wish within her power for Death is nothing if not generous. This was a simple gift, easily given.

The ribbon ends there, curling around the woman's ring finger. Zachary reads other ribbons but there is nothing more about the moon.

Zachary walks on to find another part of the ballroom with hundreds of books suspended from the ceiling, spines flung open and hovering. He reaches up to touch one of the books just above his head and its pages flutter in response. The entire flock of books rearranges itself, changing formation like geese.

He thinks he sees Dorian on the other side of the dance floor and tries to make his way in that direction. He moves with the crowd. There are so many people. No one does more than glance at him though he feels less like a ghost, the space and the people around him seeming more solid. He almost feels the fingers that graze his.

"There you are," a voice says next to him but it is not Dorian, it is the ginger-haired young man from before. He has lost his jacket and his arms are covered in gold down to his fingertips. Zachary thinks he has misheard and the man is addressing someone else but he is looking directly at him. "When are you?" the man asks.

"What?" Zachary asks, still not certain the man is talking to him.

"You're not now," the ginger-haired man remarks, lifting a golden hand to Zachary's face and gently brushing his cheek with his fingers and Zachary feels it, really feels it this time, and he is so surprised he cannot answer. The ginger-haired man moves to draw him onto the dance floor but the crowd shifts around them, pulling them apart and then the man is gone again.

Zachary tries to find the edge of the room, away from the crowd. He'd thought the musicians were behind him but now the flute is in front of him and there are drums somewhere to his left. The lights are lower, maybe the balloons are sinking, the space getting smaller as he moves toward the periphery. He passes a golden dress abandoned on an armchair, shed like a snakeskin.

When Zachary reaches the wall he finds it covered in text, written in brushstrokes of gold on the dark stone. The words are difficult to read, the metallic pigment catching too much or too little of the light. Zachary follows the story as it unfolds along the wall.

> *The moon spoke with Time.*
> *(They had not spoken in a great while.)*
> *The moon asked Time to leave a space and a soul untouched.*
> *Time made the moon wait for an answer. When she received it there was a condition.*
> *Time agreed to help the moon only if the moon in turn aided Time in finding a way to hold on to Fate.*
> *The moon made this promise, though she did not yet know how to unbreak that which had been broken.*
> *And so Time consented to keep a place hidden away, far from the stars.*
> *Now in this space the days and nights pass differently. Strangely, slowly. Languid and luscious.*

Here the words on the wall cease. Zachary looks out at the party, watching balloons drift past the chandeliers and dancers spinning and a girl nearby painting lines of prose onto another girl's bare skin in gold paint likely borrowed previously to inscribe the wall. A man passes by with a tray full of small cakes, frosted with poems. Someone hands Zachary a glass of wine and then it is gone and he does not recall where it went.

Zachary scans the crowd, searching for Dorian, wondering if somehow he's managed to get himself lost in time that is currently passing strangely and slowly and how he should go about getting unlost and then his gaze falls on a man across the room, also leaning against the wall, a man with elaborate pale braids that have been dipped in gold but otherwise the Keeper looks exactly the same. Not a day younger or older. He is watching someone in the crowd but Zachary cannot see who. He looks for clues as to what year this might be but the fashions are so varied it is difficult to guess. Twenties? Thirties? He wonders if the Keeper would be able to see him, wonders how old the Keeper is, anyway, and who he is staring at so intently.

He tries to follow the direction of the Keeper's stare, walking through an archway that leads to a stairway covered in candles and lanterns that cast shimmering, shifting golden light over the waves that stretch out into darkness.

Zachary stops and stares at the glimmering surf of the Starless Sea. He takes a step toward it and then another and then someone pulls him back. An arm reaches around his chest and a hand closes over his eyes, calming the swirling movement and dimming the golden firelight.

A voice he would know anywhere whispers in his ear.

"And so the moon found a way to keep her love."

Dorian leads him backward, onto the dance floor. Zachary can feel the sea of revelers around them even though he cannot see them, truly feel them with no delays of sensation though at the moment his senses are completely attuned to the voice in his ear and the breath against his neck, letting Dorian take him and the story wherever he wishes to go.

"An inn that once sat at one crossroads now rests at another," Dorian continues, "somewhere deeper and darker where few will ever find it, by the shores of the Starless Sea."

Dorian removes his hand from Zachary's eyes and turns him now, almost a spin, so they stand face-to-face, dancing in the center of the crowd. Dorian's hair is streaked with gold that trails down his neck and over the shoulder of his coat.

"It is there, still," he says and pauses for so long that Zachary thinks perhaps the story has concluded but then he leans closer. "This is where the moon goes when she cannot be seen in the sky," Dorian slowly breathes each word against Zachary's lips.

Zachary moves to close the fraction of distance left between them but before he can there is a cracking noise like thunder. The floor beneath their feet shakes. Dorian loses his balance and Zachary grabs his arm to steady him, to prevent him from crashing into any of the other dancers but there are no other dancers. There is no one. No balloons, no party, no ballroom.

They stand together in an empty room with a carved door that has fallen from its hinges, the celebration depicted upon it frozen and broken.

Before Zachary can ask what happened another explosion follows the first, sending a shower of rock over their heads.

The Starless Sea is rising.

The owls watch as the tides shift, slowly at first.

They fly over waves that break upon long-abandoned shores.

They call out warnings and exaltations.

The time has come. They have waited so long.

They screech and celebrate until the sea is so high that they too must seek shelter.

The Starless Sea continues to rise.

Now it floods the Harbor, pulling the books from their shelves and claiming the Heart for itself.

The end has come.

Here now is the Owl King bringing the future on his wings.

ZACHARY EZRA RAWLINS tumbles through a curtain of cashmere and linen, pulling down sweaters and shirts as he and Dorian crash back through the wardrobe, the tunnel behind them collapsing, sending up a cloud of dust.

In Zachary's chamber most of the books have toppled from their shelves. The abandoned bottle of wine has fallen, spilling its contents over the side of the desk. The bunny pirates are shipwrecked on the floor by the fireplace.

Another tremor brings the wardrobe crashing down and Zachary runs for the door with Dorian at his heels. Zachary grabs his bag and slings it over his shoulder.

Zachary heads for the Heart, not knowing where else to go, wondering where exactly one is supposed to go during an earthquake when one is underneath the earth.

The tremors cease but the damage is evident. They trip over fallen shelves and furniture, pausing to free a tabby cat from under a collapsed table. The tabby flees without thanking them.

"I didn't think she'd actually do it," Dorian says, watching the cat jump over a fallen candelabra pooling beeswax on the stone before disappearing into the shadows.

"Do what?" Zachary asks but then there is a crash ahead of them and they continue on, in the opposite direction from the cat, which Zachary silently notes as a bad sign.

Just before they reach the Heart, where someone is shouting but Zachary cannot make out the words because of a clanking metallic noise, Dorian pulls him back and puts his arm out against the wall, blocking Zachary's path forward.

"I need you to know something," Dorian says. From the Heart there is another crashing sound and Zachary looks off in the direction it came from but Dorian reaches up and turns Zachary's face to his own, tangling his fingers in Zachary's hair.

So quietly Zachary can barely hear him against the continuing clamor, Dorian says, "I need you to know that what I feel for you is real. Because I think you feel the same. I have lost a lot of things and I don't want to lose this, too."

"What?" Zachary asks, not certain he's heard correctly and wanting way more information about what kind of feelings he's referring to and also curious as to why, exactly, Dorian has chosen a particularly inopportune time to have this conversation but it turns out it is not a conversation at all, because Dorian holds his gaze for only a moment more before releasing him and walking away.

Zachary remains against the wall, dazed. More books tumble from shelves nearby as the floor trembles again.

"What is happening right now?" he asks aloud and no one, not even the voice in his head, has an answer.

Zachary adjusts his bag on his shoulder and follows Dorian.

As they reach the Heart the cause of the clanking sound is clear: The clockwork universe has collapsed, its pendulum swinging freely and tangling around large loops of metal, something above futilely attempting to move them and they rise and fall at irregular intervals, hammering against the floor, smashing already cracked tiles into dust. The golden hands are intact but one now tilts toward the cracking tile below and the other points accusingly at the pile of rock where the door to the elevator used to be.

The shouting grows louder, coming from the Keeper's office. Dorian stares up at the collapsing clockwork and Zachary realizes Dorian never got to see the Heart the way it was and everything unfolding around them feels acutely unfair and upsetting and for a moment—just a moment—he wishes they had never come here.

The Keeper's voice is the first one that becomes distinguishable.

"I did not *allow* anything," he says—no, yells—at someone Zachary cannot see. "I understand—"

"You don't understand," a voice interrupts and Zachary recognizes it more because Dorian freezes beside him than he actually recalls what Allegra sounds like. "I understand because I have seen where this will lead and I will not let it happen," Allegra says and then she appears in the office doorway in her fur coat, facing them with her red lipstick twisted into a grimace. The Keeper follows her, his robes covered in dust.

"I see you are still alive, Mister Rawlins," Allegra remarks calmly, casually, as though she were not yelling a moment before, as though they are not standing amongst broken, clanking metal and fluttering pages liberated from their bindings. "I know someone who would be pleased about that."

"What?" Zachary says even though he means *who* and the question is muffled by the din behind him and Allegra doesn't answer.

For a second her eyes flick back and forth between him and Dorian, the one blue eye brighter than Zachary remembered, and he has an impression of being looked at, being truly seen for the first time, and then it is gone.

"You don't even know," she says and Zachary cannot tell if she's speaking to him or to Dorian. "You have no idea why you're here." Or both, Zachary thinks, as she turns her attention squarely on Dorian. "You and I have unfinished business."

"I have nothing to say to you," Dorian tells her. The universe punctuates his statement with a clanging thud on the tiled floor.

"What makes you think I want to *talk*?" Allegra asks. She walks toward Dorian and only when they are almost face-to-face does Zachary see the gun in her hand, partially obscured by the fur cuff of her coat.

The Keeper reacts before Zachary can process what's happening. He grabs Allegra's wrist and pulls her arm back, taking the revolver from her hand but not before she pulls the trigger. The bullet travels upward instead of where it had been aimed, directly at Dorian's heart.

The shot ricochets off one of the golden hands hanging above them, sending it swinging, twisting backward, and smashing into the gears.

The bullet comes to rest in the tiled wall, in the center of a mural that was once a depiction of a prison cell with a girl on one side of the bars and a pirate on the other but it has cracked and faded and the damage added by the small piece of metal is indistinguishable from the damage done by time.

Above, the mechanism swinging the planets strikes down again and this time the tiled floor succumbs to its pressure, cracking the stone below the tiles in a fissure that opens not into another book-filled hall as Zachary expects but into a cave, a gaping cavern of rock that stretches farther down, much, much farther down into shadows and darkness.

You forget that we are underground, the voice in his head remarks. *You forget what that means,* it continues and Zachary is no longer certain the voice is in his head after all.

The pendulum breaks free from the tangled metal and plummets.

Zachary listens for it to hit the bottom, remembering Mirabel's champagne bottle, but hears nothing.

The fissure moves from crack to rift to chasm quickly, pulling stone and tiles and planets and broken chandeliers and books with it, approaching the spot where they stand like a wave.

Zachary takes a step back, into the office doorway. The Keeper puts a hand on his arm to steady him and it feels like everything that follows happens slowly though in truth it takes only a moment.

Allegra slips, the floor crumbling beneath her heels as the edge of the opening finds her feet and she reaches out for something, anything, to grasp as she falls.

Her fingers settle on the midnight blue wool of Dorian's star-buttoned coat and she pulls both the coat and the man within it backward and they tumble together into the chasm.

For a split second as they fall Zachary's eyes meet Dorian's and he remembers what Dorian said minutes, seconds, moments before.

I don't want to lose this.

Then Dorian is gone and the Keeper is holding Zachary back from the edge as he screams into the darkness below.

a paper star that has been unfolded and refolded
into a tiny unicorn but the unicorn remembers the time
when it was a star and an earlier time when it was part of
a book and sometimes the unicorn dreams of the time before
it was a book when it was a tree and the time even longer
before that when it was a different sort of star

The son of the fortune-teller walks through the snow.

He carries a sword that was crafted by the finest of sword smiths, long before he was born.

(The sword's sisters are both lost, one destroyed in fire in order to become something new and the other sunken in the seas and forgotten.)

The sword now rests in a scabbard once worn by an adventurer who perished in an attempt to protect one she loved. Both her sword and her love were lost along with the rest of her story.

(For a time songs were sung about this adventurer, but little truth remained within the verses.)

So clothed in history and myth the son of the fortune-teller looks toward a light in the distance.

He thinks he is almost there but he has so far to go.

en route to (and in) Sardinia, Italy, twenty years ago

It is a Tuesday when the painter packs her bags and leaves, intending never to return. No one remembers afterward that it was a Tuesday, and few remember the departure at all. It is one of many that occur in the years surrounding that Tuesday. They begin to blend together long before anyone dares use the word *exodus*.

The painter herself is only vaguely aware of the day or the month or the year. For her this day is marked by its meaning and not its details, the culmination of months (years) of watching and painting and trying to understand and now that she understands she can no longer simply watch and paint.

No one looks up as she passes by in her coat with her bag. She makes a single stop at a particular door where she leaves her paints and brushes. She puts the case down quietly. She does not knock upon the door. A small grey cat watches.

"Make sure that she gets that," the painter says to the cat and the cat obediently sits on the case in a protective yet nap-like manner.

The painter will regret this action later, but it is not one of the things she has foreseen.

The painter takes a winding route to the Heart. She knows shorter ones, she would know them blindfolded. She could find her way around this space by touch or scent or something deeper that guides her feet. She takes final walks through favored rooms. She straightens skewed picture frames and neatens piles of books. She finds a box of matches laid out next to a candelabra and puts the matches in her pocket. She takes a last turn through the whispering hallway and it tells her a story about two sisters on separate quests and a lost ring and a found love and it does not resolve itself completely but whispered hallway stories rarely do.

When the painter reaches the Heart she can see the Keeper at his desk in his office but his attention remains on his writing. She considers asking him to find an appropriate place to hang the painting she has left in her studio, recently completed, but she does not. She knows someone will find it and hang it. She can see it already, on a wall surrounded by books.

She does not know who the figures in the painting are, though she has seen them many times in fractured images and half-formed visions. There is a part of her that hopes they do not exist, and another part that knows they do or they will. They are there in the story of the place, for now.

The painter glances up at the gently shifting clockwork universe. Through one eye she sees it shimmering and perfect, each piece moving as it should. Through the other eye it is burning and broken.

A golden hand points her toward the exit.

If she is going to change the story, this is where she starts.

(The Keeper will look up at the sound of the door as it closes behind her but he will not realize who has departed until much later.)

The painter passes the spot in the antechamber where she rolled her dice when she first arrived. All swords and crowns.

She sees more swords and crowns now. A golden crown in a crowded room. An old sword on a dark shore wet with blood. She has the urge to return to her paints but she cannot paint all of the things that she sees. She could never paint all of them. She has tried. There is not enough time and not enough paint.

The painter presses the button for the elevator and it opens immediately, as though it has been waiting for her. She lets it take her away.

Already her eye with its sight is clouding. The pictures are fading. It is a great relief and it is terrifying.

By the time the elevator deposits her in a familiar cave lit by a single lantern, there is only haze. The images and events and faces that have haunted her for years are gone.

Now she can barely see the door outlined in the rock in front of her.

She has never seen herself leave. She once swore she would never leave. She made a vow yet here she is, breaking it beyond repair. The achieving of this impossible thing emboldens her.

If she can change this part of the story she can change more of it.

She can change the fate of this place.

She turns the doorknob and pushes.

The door opens onto a beach, a stretch of moonlit sand. The door is wooden, and if it was painted once the sand and the wind have conspired to wear the wood bare. It is hidden in a cliffside, obscured by rock. It has been mistaken for driftwood by everyone who has glimpsed it for years, ever since the last time the painter was here, before she was ever called the painter, when she was just Allegra, a then young woman who found a door and went through it and didn't come back. Until now.

Allegra looks up and down the empty beach. There is too much sky. The repetitive beating of the waves along the shore is the only sound. The scent is overwhelming, the salt and the sea and the air crashing into her in an aggressive assault of nostalgia and regret.

She closes the door behind her, letting her hand rest on the weather-worn surface, smooth and soft and cool.

Allegra drops her bag on the sand. The fur coat follows, the night air heavy and too warm for fur.

She takes a step back. She lifts the heel of her boot and kicks. A solid kick, enough to crack the old wood.

She kicks it again.

When she can do no more damage with her boots she finds a rock to smash against it, the wood cracking and splintering, slicing her hands, fragments stinging beneath her skin.

Eventually it is a pile of wood and not a door. Nothing behind it but solid rock.

Only the doorknob remains, fallen into the sand, grasping ragged bits of wood that were once a door and before that were a tree and are no longer either.

Allegra takes the matches from her coat and ignites the former door and watches it burn.

If she can prevent anyone from entering she can prevent the things that she has seen from happening. The object within the jar in her bag (an object she saw and painted before she understood what it was and long before it became an object within a jar) will be insurance. Without doors she can prevent the return of the book and everything that would follow.

She knows how many doors there are.

She knows that any door can be closed.

Allegra turns the doorknob over in her hands. She considers throwing it into the sea but places it in her bag with the jar instead, wanting to hold on to any part of the place that she can.

Then Allegra Cavallo sinks to her knees on an empty beach by a star-covered sea and sobs.

BOOK V

THE

OWL

KING

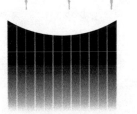

ZACHARY EZRA RAWLINS is being dragged backward, away from the rift that has torn open the Heart of this Harbor and into the Keeper's office where the floor has remained intact, his feet slipping on the broken tiles.

"Sit," the Keeper says, forcing Zachary into the chair behind the desk. Zachary tries to stand again but the Keeper holds him down. "Breathe," the Keeper advises but Zachary can't remember how. "*Breathe,*" the Keeper repeats and Zachary takes one slow, gasping breath after another. He doesn't understand how the Keeper is so calm. He doesn't understand anything that's happening right now but he keeps breathing and once his breath is steady the Keeper lets him go and he remains in the chair.

The Keeper takes a bottle from a bookshelf. He fills a glass with clear liquid and places it in front of Zachary.

"Drink this," he says, leaving the bottle and walking away. He doesn't add "it will make you feel better" and Zachary doesn't believe, not right now in this chair, that he will ever feel better but he drinks it anyway and coughs.

It doesn't make him feel better.

It makes everything sharper and clearer and worse.

Zachary puts the glass down next to the Keeper's notebook and tries to focus on something, anything that isn't the last awful moments replaying themselves over and over in his head. He looks at the open notebook and reads, one page and then another.

"These are love letters," he says, to himself in surprise as much as to the Keeper who does not respond.

Zachary keeps reading. Some are poems and others are prose but every line is passionate and explicit and clearly written to or about Mirabel.

He glances up at the Keeper who stands in the doorway, looking out at a chasm into which the universe has fallen save for a single star that dangles defiantly from the ceiling.

The Keeper hits the doorframe so hard that it cracks and Zachary realizes the apparent calm is barely contained rage.

He watches as the Keeper sighs and places his hand against the frame. The crack repairs itself, slowly mending until only a line remains.

The stones in the Heart begin to rumble and shift. Broken rock moves over the void in the floor, rebuilding the surface piece by piece.

The Keeper returns to the desk and picks up the bottle.

"Mirabel was in the antechamber," the Keeper says, answering the question Zachary had not dared ask as he pours a glass for himself. "I will not be able to retrieve her body or what is left of it until the wreckage is cleared. The repairs will take some time."

Zachary tries to say something, anything, but he cannot and instead he puts his head down on the desk, trying to understand.

Why only the two of them are here in a room filled with loss and books. Why everything that was crumbling before is broken now and why only the floor seems to be repairable. Where the ginger cat has gone.

"Where's Rhyme?" Zachary asks when he finds his voice again.

"Likely somewhere safe," the Keeper says. "She must have heard this coming. I think she tried to warn me but I did not understand at the time."

Zachary doesn't ask the Keeper to refill his glass but he does it anyway.

Zachary reaches for the glass but his hand closes over an object next to it, a single die, an older one than the dice from the entrance exam but with the same symbols carved into its sides. He picks it up instead.

He rolls it onto the desk.

It lands, as he expects it to, on the single carved heart.

Knights who break hearts and hearts that break knights.

"What do hearts mean?" Zachary asks.

"Historically the dice have been rolled to see what kismet has to say about a new arrival to this place," the Keeper says. "For a time the results were used to gauge potential for paths. Hearts were for poets, those who wore their hearts open and aflame. Long before that they were used by storytellers and rolled to nudge a story toward romance or tragedy or mystery. Their purpose has changed over time but there were bees before there were acolytes and swords before there were guardians and all of those symbols were here before they were ever carved upon dice."

"There are more than three paths, then."

"Each of us has our own path, Mister Rawlins. Symbols are for interpretation, not definition."

Zachary thinks through bees and keys and doors and books and elevators, reviewing the path that brought him to this room and this chair. The more he traces moments back the more he thinks maybe it was all too late even before it started.

"You tried to save him," Zachary says to the Keeper. "When Allegra was going to shoot Dorian you stopped her."

"I did not wish you to suffer as I suffer, Mister Rawlins. I thought I might prevent the moment we have found ourselves in now. I am sorry I was not successful. I have felt what you are feeling myriad times. It does not get any easier. It simply becomes familiar."

"You've lost her before," Zachary says. He is beginning to understand even if he is not yet certain that he believes.

"Many, many times," the Keeper confirms. "I lose her, through circumstance or Death or my own stupidity and years pass and she returns again. This time she was convinced something had changed, she never told me why."

"But . . ." Zachary starts and then stops, distracted by the memory of Dorian's voice in his ear.

(*Occasionally Fate can pull itself together again and Time is always waiting.*)

"The person you knew as Mirabel," the Keeper continues, "no, I'm sorry, you called her Max, didn't you? She has lived in different vessels over the centuries. Sometimes she remembers and others . . . The incarnation before this one was named Sivía. She was soaking wet when she came out of the elevator, you reminded me of her when you first arrived dripping with paint. It must have been raining near Reykjavík that night, I never asked. I didn't recognize her at first. I rarely do and I wonder after how I could be so blind, every time. And it always ends in loss. Sivía believed that could change as well."

He pauses, staring into his glass. Zachary waits a moment before asking, "What happened to her?"

"She died," the Keeper answers. "There was a fire. It was the first such incident in this space and there she was, right in the center of it. I gathered what I could to bring to the crypt but it was difficult to separate what was once a woman from pieces of former books and cats. Afterward I thought perhaps she had been the last. After the fire everything did change. Slowly at first, but then the doors closed one after another until I was certain she could not return even if she wished to, and then one day I looked up and she was already here."

"How long have *you* been here?" Zachary asks, staring at the man in front of him, thinking about metaphorical pirates in basement cages and Time and Fate and burned places, remembering how the Keeper looked from across the gilded ballroom. He looks exactly the same now. There are more pearls in his hair.

"I have always been here," the Keeper answers. He puts his glass down on the desk. He picks up the die and holds it in his palm. "I was here before there was a here to be in." He rolls the die on the desk and does not watch it fall. "Come, I would like to show you something."

The Keeper stands and walks toward the back of the office, to a door Zachary hadn't noticed, tucked between two tall bookshelves.

Zachary looks down at the desk.

Faceup on the die is a single key but Zachary doesn't know what it is meant to lock or unlock. He gets to his feet, finding his legs more steady than he expects. He glances out at the Heart where the floor is still slowly reassembling its broken pieces. He follows the Keeper, pausing at a bookshelf that contains a familiar-looking jar with a hand floating inside, waving hello or goodbye or some other sentiment in his direction. He recalls the heavy object in Mirabel's bag after they escaped the Collector's Club and wonders briefly who the hand belonged to before it was jarred and then he moves into the room beyond the office.

The Keeper lights a lamp, illuminating a chamber smaller than Zachary's, or maybe so filled with books and art that it seems smaller. The bed in the corner is also covered in books. Books are stacked two rows deep on shelves and piled on all available surfaces and most of the floor. Zachary looks around for the ginger cat but does not find it.

He pauses at a shelf occupied by notebooks identical to the one on the desk. They have names along their spines. *Lin, Grace, Asha, Étienne*. Many names have more than one notebook. Several *Sivía*s are followed by rows of echoing *Mirabel*s.

Zachary turns to the Keeper who is lighting the other lamps to ask about them but the question dies on his lips.

Beyond the Keeper there is a large painting on the wall.

Zachary's first thought is that it's a mirror, because he is in it, but as he moves closer the Zachary in the painting remains motionless, though he is rendered with such realistic detail it looks like he should be breathing.

It is a life-size portrait. The painting Zachary stands toe-to-toe with the actual one, in the same suede shoes, the same blue pajama pants that somehow manage to look elegant and classical in oil paint. But the painting Zachary is shirtless, holding a sword in one hand, hanging lightly by his side, and a feather in the other, held aloft.

Dorian stands behind him. Leaning in toward painting Zachary and whispering in his ear. One of Dorian's arms is wrapped around him, palm tilted upward and covered in honeybees that dance on his fingertips and swarm up his wrist. Dorian's other hand, held out to the side, is draped in chains with dozens of keys dangling from them.

Above their heads floats a golden crown. Beyond it is a vast night sky filled with stars.

It is all achingly realistic, except for the fact that this Zachary's chest is cracked open, his heart exposed, the star-filled sky visible behind it. Or maybe it's Dorian's heart. Maybe it's both. Either way it is anatomically correct down to its arteries and aorta but painted in metallic gold and covered in flames, glowing like a lantern, casting perfectly painted flecks of light over the bees and the keys and the sword and both of their faces.

"What is this?" Zachary asks the Keeper.

"This is the last piece Allegra painted here," the Keeper answers.

"Allegra's the painter." Zachary remembers the basement room filled with paintings of the Harbor in the Collector's Club. "When did she paint this?"

"Twenty years ago."

"How is that possible?"

"I would think the child of a fortune-teller would not need to ask."

"But . . ." Zachary stops, his head more drowning than swimming. "My mom doesn't . . ." He stops again. Maybe his mother does see this clearly but doesn't paint. He's never asked.

This is stranger than reading about himself in *Sweet Sorrows.* Maybe because he can only assume that he is the boy in the book when he is absolutely, unquestionably the man in the painting.

"You knew who we were," he says, looking again at the painting version of Dorian, remembering the way the Keeper had scrutinized him when they brought him down.

"I knew your faces," the Keeper says. "I have looked at that painting every day for years. I knew you might arrive someday but I did not know if someday was months or decades or centuries away."

"You would have been here even if it was centuries, right?" Zachary asks.

"I may only depart when this place is gone, Mister Rawlins," he says. "May we both outlive it."

"What happens now?"

"I wish I could say. I do not know."

Zachary looks back at the painting, at the bees and the sword and the keys and the golden heart, his gaze first avoiding and then inevitably finding its way back to Dorian.

"He tried to kill me once," Zachary says, remembering Mirabel on a snow-covered sidewalk a lifetime ago and what she'd said later when he'd asked about it.

It didn't work.

"I'm afraid I don't follow," the Keeper says.

"I think something changed," Zachary says, trying to tie his bubbling thoughts together.

There is a sound in the doorway and the Keeper looks up. His eyes widen. A wordless gasp escapes his lips and his ring-covered hand rises to cover it.

Zachary turns, expecting what he sees but Mirabel is still a surprise, standing in the doorway covered in dust and holding the ginger cat in her arms.

"Change is what a story is, Ezra," Mirabel says. "I thought I already told you that."

DORIAN IS FALLING.

He has been falling for some time, long past the duration suitable for any calculable distance.

He has lost sight of Allegra. She was a weight on his coat and then a blur of white and then gone in a shower of stone and tile and gilded metal. A passing ring that might have been lost by a planet hit his shoulder with such force he is certain it is broken but after that there was only darkness and rushing air and now he is alone and somehow still falling.

Dorian doesn't recall exactly what happened. He remembers the floor cracking and then there was no floor, only crashing chaos.

He remembers the look on Zachary's face which was likely mirrored on his own. A mixture of surprise and confusion and horror. Then it was gone, in an instant. Less.

Dorian thinks this would all feel stranger were it not an almost familiar feeling, as he has been falling for more than a year now and it only just became literal.

Or maybe he has always been falling.

He does not know which direction is up any longer. The free-fall is dizzying and his chest feels as though it might burst if he does not remember how to breathe but breathing feels so complicated. *Must be getting somewhere near the center of the earth,* he Alice-thinks.

Then there is light in a direction that is likely below. It is dim but approaching at a faster rate than he thought possible.

Thoughts clutter his mind, too many to focus on one, as though they are all vying to be final. He thinks that if he is about to die he should have begun collecting his final thoughts earlier. He thinks about Zachary and regrets a lot of things he didn't say and didn't do. Books he didn't read. Stories he didn't tell. Decisions he didn't make.

He thinks about the night with Mirabel that changed everything but he's not certain he regrets that, even now.

He thought he would have figured out what he believes before it all came to an end but he has not.

The light below grows closer. He is falling through a cavern. Its floor is glowing. Dorian's thoughts become flashes. Images and sensations. Crowded sidewalks and yellow taxis. Books that felt truer than people. Hotel rooms and airports and the Rose Room at the New York Public Library. Standing in the snow looking at his future through the window of a bar. An owl wearing a crown. A gilded ballroom. An almost kiss.

The last thought that crosses Dorian's mind before he reaches the illuminated ground below, as he tries to move so that he might hit it bare-feet-first, the thought that wins its place as the final thought of a long, thoughtful fall is: *Maybe the Starless Sea isn't just a children's bedtime story.*

Maybe, *maybe* beneath him there will be water.

But as the fall reaches its end and Dorian crashes into the Starless Sea he realizes no, it is not water.

It is honey.

ZACHARY EZRA RAWLINS stares at Mirabel as she stands impossibly in the doorway. She is covered in dust, powdered stone that blankets her clothes and her hair. Her jacket has a rip along one sleeve. Blood blooms red over her knuckles and in a line down her neck but she seems otherwise unharmed.

Mirabel puts the ginger cat down. It rubs against her legs and then walks back to its preferred chair.

The Keeper murmurs something under his breath and then he walks toward her, navigating his way through the piles of books without taking his eyes off of Mirabel.

Watching them look at each other Zachary feels suddenly that he is trespassing in someone else's love story.

When the Keeper reaches Mirabel he pulls her into such a passionate embrace that Zachary turns away but turning away puts him face-to-face with the painting again and so he closes his eyes instead. For a moment he can feel, sharply and strongly, within the air in his lungs, precisely what it is to lose and find and lose again, over and over and over.

"We don't have time for this."

Zachary opens his eyes at the sound of Mirabel's voice to see her turn and walk back through the door to the office. The Keeper follows.

Zachary hesitates but then follows them. He hovers in the doorway, watching Mirabel kick the desk chair toward the fireplace. One of the jars on the mantel topples, scattering its keys.

"You didn't think I had a plan," Mirabel says, climbing up on the chair. "There has always been a plan, people have worked on this plan for centuries. There have simply been some . . . complications in its execution. Are you coming, Ezra?" she asks without looking at Zachary.

"Am I what?" Zachary says at the same time that the Keeper asks "Where are you going?" and the questions overlap into *What are you?* which Zachary thinks is also a very good question.

"We have to rescue Ezra's boyfriend because apparently that's what we do," Mirabel says to the Keeper. She yanks the sword from its display over the fireplace. Another container of keys shatters and spills.

"Mirabel—" the Keeper starts to protest but she lifts the sword and points it at him. It is obvious from the way she holds it that she knows how to use it.

"Stop, please," she says. A warning and a wish. "I love you but I will not sit here and *wait* for this story to change. I am going to make it change." She holds his gaze over the length of the sword and after a long wordless conversation she lowers the sword and hands it to Zachary. "Take this."

"'It's dangerous to go alone,'" Zachary quotes in response as he takes it, even though the completed quote is out of order, addressing it partly to her and partly to himself and partly to the sword in his hand. It is a thin, double-edged straight sword that looks like it belongs in a museum though he supposes that's where it's been, in a way. The hilt has elaborate scrollwork and the leather on the grip is worn and Zachary can tell that it has been held many times before by many other hands. It's still sharp.

It is the same sword he is holding in the painting, though the painting version has been polished. It is heavier than it looks.

"I need something else to wear," Mirabel says, climbing down from the chair and brushing dust off her sleeves, frowning at the torn one. "Give me a minute and meet me at the elevator, Ezra."

She doesn't wait for Zachary to respond before she leaves. She doesn't say another word to the Keeper.

The Keeper stares out the door after Mirabel even though she's moved out of sight. Zachary watches him watching the space where she had been.

"You're the pirate," Zachary says. All of the stories are the same story. "In the basement. From the book." The Keeper turns to look at him. "Mirabel's the girl who rescued you."

"That was a very long time ago," the Keeper says. "In an older Harbor. And *pirate* is not a proper translation. *Rogue* might be closer. They used to call me the Harbormaster until they decided Harbors should not have masters."

"What happened?" Zachary asks. He has been wondering ever since he read *Sweet Sorrows* for the first time. *This is not where their story ends.* Clearly.

"We did not make it far. They executed her in my place. They drowned her in the Starless Sea. They made me watch."

The Keeper reaches out and rests a ring-covered hand on Zachary's forehead and the touch is that of someone—something—much more ancient than Zachary could possibly have imagined. The sensation moves like waves from his head down to his toes, rippling and buzzing over his skin.

"May the gods bless and keep you, Mister Rawlins," the Keeper says after he takes his hand away.

Zachary nods and takes his bag and the sword and walks out of the office.

He avoids the parts of the floor that are still diligently repairing themselves, keeping to the edge of the Heart, not looking back, not looking down, only looking ahead at the broken door that leads to the elevator.

Mirabel stands in the middle of the antechamber, shaking out her tangled hair, the pinks returning to more vibrant hues. She's wiped most of the dust from her face and changed into the same fuzzy sweater she was wearing the first time Zachary met her dressed as herself.

"He blessed you, didn't he?" she asks.

"Yes," Zachary answers. He can still feel the buzzing against his skin.

"That should help," Mirabel says. "We're going to need all the help we can get."

"What happened?" Zachary asks, looking around at the chaos. The glowing amber walls are cracked, some of them shattered completely. The elevator is smoking.

Mirabel looks down at the rubble and pushes something with the toe of her boot. The dice at her feet roll but do not settle. They fall into a crack in the floor and disappear.

"Allegra got desperate enough to try to close the door from the other side," she explains. "Do you like this place, Ezra?"

"Yes," Zachary answers, confused, but even as he says the word he realizes he does not mean this place now the way it is with its empty halls and broken universe. He means the place it was before, when it was alive. He means a crowded ballroom. A multitude of seekers looking for things they do not have names for and finding them in stories written and unwritten and in each other.

"Not as much as Allegra does," Mirabel says. "My mother vanished from this place when I was five and after she disappeared Allegra raised me. She taught me to paint. She left when I was fourteen and commenced her attempts to seal all of this away. When I started painting doors hoping to let someone, anyone in again she tried to have me killed, many times, because she saw me as a danger."

She pauses and Zachary doesn't know what to say. His head is still reeling with too many stories and too many complicated feelings.

There is a moment here. A moment when Zachary could say that he's sorry because he is, but the sentiment feels too small, or he could take her hand and say nothing and let the gesture speak for him but her hand is too far away.

So Zachary does nothing and then the moment is gone.

"We have to go now, we have things to do," Mirabel says. "What is it your mom calls points like these? Moments with meaning? I met her once, she gave me coffee."

"You what?" Zachary asks but Mirabel doesn't answer, she walks to the elevator. The doors part for her. The elevator sits several inches below the floor and moves an inch lower as Mirabel steps into it.

"You did say you trusted me, Ezra," she says, watching him hesitate.

"I did," Zachary admits as he steps carefully into the elevator next to her, the floor unsteady beneath his feet, the sword heavy in his hand. The buzzing feeling has ceased. He feels oddly calm. He can handle being a sidekick for whatever comes next. "Where are we going, Max?" he asks.

"We're going down," Mirabel says. She takes a step back and then lifts her boot and kicks the side of the elevator, hard.

The elevator shakes and sinks a few more inches and then the calm drops out of Zachary's stomach as they abruptly plummet downward.

DORIAN SINKS INTO a sea of honey, a slow-moving current pulling him downward. It is too thick to swim through, pulling at his clothes and weighing him down. Drowning him in sweetness.

This is not even in the top one hundred ways he expected to die. Not even close.

He cannot see the surface but he reaches out, stretching his fingers as far in the direction he believes is up as he can manage but he cannot feel if there is air around them, if he is anywhere near the surface.

What a stupid, poetic way to die, he thinks, and then someone grabs ahold of his hand.

He is pulled from the sea and over something that feels like a wall, and someone settles him onto a smooth, hard surface that does not feel steady.

Dorian tries to articulate his gratitude but he opens his mouth and chokes on sticky sweetness.

"Stay down," a voice says near his ear, the words muffled and far away. He still can't open his eyes but the owner of the voice pushes him down, his back against a wall. Every breath is a sugary gasp and the surface he is on is moving. The sounds beyond his clogged ears are irregular and screeching. Something hits his shoulder, grasping and clawlike. He covers his head with his arms but that makes it too difficult to breathe. He wipes at his face and removes some but not all of the honey and his breath loosens. There is something above him, hovering.

The surface he sits on tilts suddenly and he slips sideways. When it settles the screeching noise has subsided. Dorian coughs and someone puts a piece of cloth in his hand. He wipes his face with it, enough to open his eyes and start to put together what, exactly, he is looking at.

He is on a boat. A ship. No, a boat. A boat with aspirations of being a ship, with dozens of tiny lanterns strung along its multitude of dark sails. Maybe it is a proper ship. Someone is helping him remove his honey-soaked coat.

"They're gone for now, but they'll be back," a voice says, clearer now. Dorian turns to get a better look at his rescuer as she shakes his star-buttoned coat over the rail of the ship, letting the drops of honey return to the sea.

Her hair is a complicated tangle of dark waves and braids tied back in a scrap of red silk. Her skin is light brown with a distinctive pattern of freckles over the bridge of her nose. Her eyes are dark and ringed with lines of black and shimmering gold that look more war paint than makeup. She wears strips of brown leather tied like a vest over what might once have been a sweater but it is now more a looping neckline and cuffs strung together by loose stitches and stray yarn, leaving most of her shoulders and the tops of her arms exposed, a large scar visible as it curves around her left tricep. Beneath the vest her skirt is voluminous and tied up in fluffy loops like a parachute, pale and almost colorless, a cloud over her dark boots.

She hangs the coat over the rail to continue its dripping unaided, making certain it is secure enough that it won't fall.

"Who's gone?" Dorian starts to ask but only gets out the *who* before choking on honey again. The woman hands him a flask and when he puts it to his lips the water is better than anything he has ever tasted.

The woman looks at him in a pitying way and hands him another towel.

"Thank you," he says, trading the flask for the cloth, the thanks sticky-sweet on his lips.

"The owls are gone," the woman says. "They came to investigate the commotion. They like to know when things change."

She walks away across the deck, leaving Dorian to collect himself. Strings of glowing lanterns loop around and up the mast, over sails the color of red wine. The lights continue along the railing like fireflies, going to a higher level by the bow, where there is a carved figurehead of a rabbit, its ears running back along the sides of the ship.

Dorian takes long, deep breaths. Each one less sweet than the last. So, not dead yet. His shoulder doesn't hurt anymore. He looks down at his bare chest and arms, certain he should have some residual injuries, some scrapes and scratches at least, but there is nothing.

Well, not quite nothing.

On his chest, over his breastbone, is a tattoo of a sword. A scimitar-style sword with a curved blade. Its hilt is impossibly gold, metallic ink shimmering beneath his skin.

Breathing is suddenly difficult again and Dorian pulls himself to his feet. He steadies himself against the rail and looks out at the Starless Sea. Pieces of the model universe sink slowly into the honey. A single golden hand points desperately upward, disappearing as he watches. The cavern extends into the shadows, the sea softly glowing. In the distance shadows are moving, fluttering like wings.

The honey drips from his hair and his trousers, pooling around his bare feet. He steps out of it, the deck warm beneath his toes.

He walks toward the bow of the ship, following where the woman he assumes is its captain has gone.

He finds her sitting beside something covered in silk that matches the sails laid out on the deck.

"Oh," he says when he realizes what it is.

It is difficult for him to process everything he feels, looking at Allegra's body.

"Did you know her?" the captain asks.

"Yes," Dorian answers. He does not add that he has known this woman for half of his life, that she was the closest thing to a mother he ever had, that he loved her and hated her in equal measure, that moments ago he would have killed her with his own hands and yet standing here now he feels a loss the depths of which he cannot explain. He feels untethered. He feels lost. He feels free.

"What was her name?" the captain asks.

"Her name was Allegra," Dorian says, realizing now that he doesn't know if it was her real name.

"We called her the painter," the captain says. "Her hair was different then," she adds, gently touching one of Allegra's silver locks.

"You knew her?"

"She let me play with her paints sometimes when I was a rabbit. I was never very good."

"When you were what?"

"I used to be a rabbit. I'm not anymore. I don't need to be. It's never too late to change what you are, it took me a long time to figure that out."

"What's your name?" Dorian asks, though he knows already. There cannot be many former rabbits in such places.

The captain frowns at him. It is clearly not a question she has been asked in some time and she pauses, considering it.

"They used to call me Eleanor, up there," she says. "It's not my name."

Dorian stares at her. She's not old enough to be Mirabel's mother. Not nearly, she might even be younger than Mirabel. But she looks like her, the eyes and the shape of her face. He wonders how time works down here.

"What's your name?" Eleanor asks.

"Dorian," he says. It feels truer than any other name he's used. He's starting to like it.

Eleanor looks at him and nods, then she turns back to Allegra.

Allegra's eyes are closed. A long gash of a wound covers part of her head, cutting across her neck, though there isn't much blood. Most of her body is covered in honey, sticking to the silk, her fur coat lost somewhere in the sea. It strikes Dorian how lucky he was to survive the fall. He wonders if he believes in luck. The neck of Allegra's blouse has come undone enough that Dorian looks for the sword tattooed on her chest, but there is no sword. There is only a delicate scar in the shape of a bee.

Eleanor kisses Allegra on the forehead and then pulls the silk cloth up to cover her face.

She stands and looks at Dorian.

"I can take you there, if that's where you're going," Eleanor says, pointing at him. "I know where it is."

"Take me where?" Dorian asks.

"The place on your back."

Dorian puts a hand up to his shoulder, touching the topmost edge of the very elaborate, very real tattoo that covers his back. The branches of a tree, the canopy of a forest of cherry blossoms, star-sparkling with lanterns and lights though all of that is background for the centerpiece: a tree stump covered in books dripping with honey under a beehive with an owl sitting atop it, wearing a crown.

ZACHARY EZRA RAWLINS is dancing. The ballroom is crowded, the music too loud, but there is an ease here, a constant perfect movement. His dance partners keep changing, all of them masked.

Everything is shimmering and gold and beautiful.

"Ezra," he hears Mirabel's voice, too soft and distant with her face so close. "Ezra come back to me," she says.

He doesn't want to go back. The party just started. The secrets are here. The answers are here. He will understand everything after one more dance, please, one more.

A gust of wind separates him from his current partner and he cannot grab ahold of another. Gold-covered fingers slip through his. The music falters.

The party fades, blown away with a breath, and in front of his eyes Mirabel comes into almost-focus, her face inches from his. He blinks at her, trying to remember where they are but then he realizes he has absolutely no idea where they are right now.

"What happened?" Zachary asks. The world is blurry and spinning, as though he is still dancing though he can tell now that in reality he is lying on a hard floor.

"You were unconscious," Mirabel says. "It was probably the impact, knocking the wind out of you. We didn't have the most graceful of landings." She indicates a pile of metal nearby. The remains of the elevator. "Here," she adds, "I took these off for ease of respiratory assistance but they did remain intact."

She hands him his eyeglasses.

Zachary sits up and puts them on.

The elevator has collapsed in such a way that Zachary is astonished that they—well, that *he*—survived the fall. Maybe the Keeper's blessing helped and the gods were looking out, because there is no elevator shaft above it, only a large open cavern.

Mirabel helps Zachary get to his feet.

They are in a courtyard surrounded by six large freestanding stone arches, most of them broken but the ones still standing have symbols carved into their keystones. Zachary can only make out a key and a crown but he can guess the rest. Beyond the arches is a ruin that was once a city.

The only word that comes to mind as Zachary looks at the structures surrounding them is *ancient* but it is a nonspecific ancient, like an architectural fever dream in stone and ivory and gold. Columns and obelisks and pagoda-like roofs. Everything shimmers, as though the whole city and the cavern that contains it has been covered in a layer of crystal. Mosaics stretch across walls and are laid into the ground beneath his feet, though most of the ground is covered in books. Piles of them, heaped and strewn over the space, abandoned by whoever had once been here to read them.

The cavern is massive, enclosing the city easily. On the far walls there are cliffs, carved with stairways and roads and towers lit up like lighthouses. Though they are only isolated beacons, everything glows. It all feels too big to be underground. Too vast and too complex and too forgotten.

A fire burns next to the elevator in a structure that looks like a fountain but is flowing with flame, dripping bowls of it draped like crystals over a chandelier, though only some of them are lit. There are similar fountains around the courtyard but the rest are dark.

Zachary picks up a book and it is solid and heavy in his hands, its pages sealed together with something sticky that turns out to be honey.

"Lost cities of honey and bone," he remarks.

"Technically it's a Harbor, though most Harbors are city-like," Mirabel clarifies as Zachary returns the unreadable tome to its resting spot. "I remember this courtyard, it was the Heart of this Harbor. They would hang lanterns from the arches during the parties."

"You remember this?" Zachary asks, looking out over the empty city. No one has been in this place for a very long time.

"I remembered a thousand lifetimes before I could talk," Mirabel says. "Some have faded with time and most of them seem more like half-forgotten dreams but I recognize places I've been before when I'm in them. I suppose it's like being haunted by your own ghost."

Zachary watches her as she stares out over the broken buildings. He tries to decide if she looks more or less real here than she did waiting in line for coffee in the middle of Manhattan but he cannot. She looks the same, only bruised and dust-covered and tired. The firelight plays with her hair, pulling it through tones of red and violet and refusing to let it settle on a single color.

"What happened here?" Zachary asks, trying to wrap his thoughts around everything, part of his mind still swirling in a golden ball-room. He prods another book with his toe. It refuses to open, its pages sealed shut.

"The tides came up," Mirabel says. "That's how it goes, historically. One Harbor sinks and a new one opens somewhere higher. They change themselves to suit the sea. It never receded before but I suppose even a sea can feel neglected. No one was paying attention anymore so it wandered back to the depths where it came from. Look, you can see where the canals were, there." She points at a spot where bridges cross over a stretch of nothing.

"But . . . where's the sea now?" Zachary asks, wondering how far down the nothing goes.

"It must be farther down. It's lower than I thought it would be. This is one of the lowest Harbors. I don't know what we'll find if we have to go deeper."

Zachary looks at the book-covered remains of a once-sunken city. He tries to imagine it filled with people and for a moment he can picture it—the streets teeming with people, the lights stretching out into the distance—and then it is a lifeless ruin again.

He was never at the beginning of this story. This story is much, much older than he is.

"I lived three lifetimes in this Harbor," Mirabel says. "In the first I died when I was nine. All I wanted was to go to the parties to see the dancing but my parents told me I had to wait until I was ten and then I never got to be ten, not in that life. The following lifetime I reached seventy-eight and I did more than my share of dancing but I was always going to be mortal until I was conceived outside of time. People who believed in the old myths tried to construct a place for that to happen. They attempted it in Harbor after Harbor. They passed down theories and advice to their successors. They toiled down here and on the surface and they had a lot of names over the years even as their numbers dwindled. Most recently they were named after my grandmother."

"The Keating Foundation," Zachary guesses. Mirabel nods.

"Most of them died before I could thank them. And in all that time no one ever considered what would happen afterward. No one thought about consequences or repercussions."

Mirabel picks up the sword from where it rests on the ground. She gives it a practiced twirl. In her hands it appears featherlight. She continues to spin it as she speaks.

"I—well, a previous me—smuggled this out of a museum concealed down the back of a very uncomfortable gown. It was before metal detectors and guards don't check down the backs of ladies' gowns as a general rule. Thank you for returning the book, it had been lost for a very long time."

"Is that what we're doing here?" Zachary asks. "Returning lost things?"

"I told you, we're rescuing your boyfriend. Again."

"Why do I feel like that's not—wait," Zachary says. "You'd seen the painting."

"Of course I had. I've spent a lot of time in a bed that faces it. It's one of Allegra's best. I did a charcoal study of it once but I could never get your face right."

"That's why you wanted us both down here. Because we're in the painting."

"Well . . ." Mirabel starts but then she gives him a half shrug that suggests he might be correct.

"That's not fate, that's . . . art history," Zachary protests.

"Who said anything about fate?" Mirabel says but she smiles as she says it, the glamorous old-movie-star smile that looks frightening in the firelight.

"Aren't you . . ." Zachary pauses because *Aren't you Fate?* sounds like too absurd a question to ask even when casually discussing past lives and despite the fact that he already almost believes that the woman in front of him is somehow, crazily, Fate. He stares at her. She looks like a regular person. Or maybe she's like her painted doors: an imitation so precise as to fool the eye. The shifting firelight falls on different pieces of her, allowing the rest to disappear into shadow. She looks at him with dark, unblinking eyes and smudged mascara and he doesn't know what to think anymore. Or what to ask.

"What are you?" Zachary settles on and immediately wishes he hadn't.

Mirabel's smile vanishes. She takes a step toward him, standing too close. Something changes in her face, as though she were wearing an invisible mask that has been removed, a personality conjured from pink hair and snark as false as a tail and a crown from a faraway party. Zachary tries to remember if he has ever felt the same nameless ancient presence from her that he felt with the Keeper and somehow he knows it was always there and that the vanished smile is older than the oldest of movie stars. She leans in close enough to kiss him and her voice is low and calm when she speaks.

"I'm a lot of things, Ezra. But I am not the reason you didn't open that door."

"What?" Zachary asks even though he is certain he already knows what she means.

"It is your own damned fault that you didn't open that door when you were however old, no one else's," Mirabel tells him. "Not mine and not whoever painted over it, either. Yours. You decided not to open it. So don't stand there and invent mythology that allows you to blame me for your problems. I have my own."

"We're not here to find Dorian, we're here to find Simon, aren't we?" Zachary asks. "He's the last thing lost in time."

"You're here because I need you to do something that I can't," Mirabel corrects him. She shoves the sword at him, hilt upward, forcing him to take it. It's even heavier than he remembers. "And you're here because you followed me, you didn't have to."

"I didn't *have* to?"

"No, you didn't," Mirabel says. "You want to think that you did or that you were *supposed* to but you always had a choice. You don't like choosing, do you? You don't do anything until someone or something else says that you can. You didn't even decide to come here until a book gave you permission. You'd be sitting in the Keeper's office wallowing if I hadn't dragged you out of there."

"I would not—" Zachary protests, infuriated by the sentiments and the truths behind them but Mirabel interrupts.

"Shut up," she says, holding up a hand and looking off behind him.

"Don't tell me to—" Zachary starts but then he turns to see what she is looking at and stops.

A shadow like a storm cloud is moving in their direction, accompanied by a sound like wind. The flames on the fire fountain waver.

The cloud grows larger and louder and Zachary realizes what he is looking at.

The sound is not wind but wings.

Zachary Ezra Rawlins has seen an owl that wasn't of the taxidermy variety only once before, not far from his mother's farmhouse, on a spring evening just before dusk, perched by the side of the road on a telephone wire. He had slowed as he drove by because there were no other cars and because he wanted to make sure that it was, in fact, an owl and not some other bird of prey and the owl had stared at him with undeniably owl-y eyes and Zachary had stared back until another car came by behind him and he continued driving and the owl remained, staring after him.

Now there are many, many owls staring at him with dozens and dozens of eyes and they are getting closer. A shadow made of wings and claws, descending on them. Owls swooping down from above and soaring through streets, disturbing the bones and the dust.

The fire falters in the changing air, sputtering and dimming, darkening the shadows so the cloud of owls consumes first one street and then another as it moves closer.

Zachary feels Mirabel put a hand on his arm but he cannot look away from the dozens—no, hundreds—of eyes staring down at them.

"Ezra," Mirabel says, squeezing his arm. "Run."

For a second Zachary stands frozen but then something in his brain manages to react to Mirabel's voice and follow her instruction, grabbing his bag from the ground and bolting in the opposite direction, away from the darkness and the eyes.

Zachary runs through the archways and toward the buildings and down the first street he reaches, tripping over books and faltering, trying to hold on to both his bag and the sword. He can hear Mirabel behind him, her boots hitting the ground a fraction of a second after his own, but he doesn't dare look back.

When the street splits he hesitates but Mirabel's hand on his back nudges him to the left and Zachary runs down another street, another dark path where he cannot see more than two steps in front of him.

He takes another turn and the echo on his footsteps has vanished. He glances back and Mirabel is gone.

Zachary freezes, torn between retracing his steps to find Mirabel and continuing forward.

Then the shadows around him move. Deep hollows of windows and doorways on either side of him are filled with wings and eyes.

Zachary stumbles backward, falling, dropping the sword. The stone path beneath him scrapes his palms as he tries to steady himself.

The owls are above him, he cannot see how many in the shadows. One grabs at his hand, claws biting into his skin.

Zachary retrieves the sword and swings it blindly, its blade catching on claws and feathers, cleaving into blood and bone. The screeching that follows is deafening but the owls back away long enough for Zachary to get on his feet, slipping on blood-splattered stone.

He runs as fast as he can, not looking back. He has no sense of direction in this labyrinthine city so he settles for following his ears, moving away from the sound of wings.

He takes turn after turn. This alley turns onto a road that takes him across a bridge, the nothingness beneath it deep with something golden far below but Zachary does not pause to look. He reaches the other side and there is no road, no path, only a gap followed by the remains of a staircase that commences above his head and continues upward, missing the rest of its steps.

Zachary turns back and the city seems empty but then the owls appear, one and then another and another until they are an indistinguishable mass of wings and eyes and talons.

There are more of them than he'd thought possible, moving so quickly that he cannot imagine they could ever be outrun. Why they even dared to try.

Zachary looks at the stairs above him. They seem solid, carved into the rock. They're not that high. The gap in front of them is not that wide. He could reach them. He tosses the sword onto the lowest step and it stays there, steady.

Zachary takes a breath and leaps upward, one hand finding its grip on the stone stair and the other settling on the sword and then the sword slips, taking his grip with it.

And so the sword pulls Zachary Ezra Rawlins away from this broken stairway in a forgotten city and instead sends him sliding down into the darkness below.

DORIAN HAS NOT spent much of his life covered in honey so he had never before realized how it can get absolutely everywhere and insist on staying there. He fills another bucket with cold water from the barrels stored in the ship's hull and pours it over his head, shivering as it cascades against his skin.

If he thought he was dreaming such shocking cold might wake him up, but Dorian knows he isn't dreaming. Knows it down to his toes.

After he removes as much honey as he can he puts his clothes back on, leaving his star-buttoned coat hanging open. *Fortunes and Fables* rests in the inside pocket, having somehow survived its travels unharmed and un-honeyed.

Dorian runs a hand through his still-sticky, greying hair, feeling too old for all of these marvels and wondering when he went from young and faithful and obedient to confused and adrift and middle-aged but he knows exactly when it was because that moment haunts him, still.

Dorian returns to the deck. The boat has sailed into a different system of caverns now, the stone threaded with crystal that looks like quartz or citrine. The stalactites have been carved with patterns: vines and stars and diamonds. The whole space is lit by the lights from the boat and the soft luminescence of the sea.

As the ship drifts along he can see through to other caverns, glimpses of connected spaces. Stairways and tall crumbling arches. Broken statues and elaborate sculptures. Underground ruins gently illuminated by honey. In the distance a waterfall (honeyfall) foams and spills over the rocks. There is a world beneath the world beneath the world. Or at least there used to be.

Eleanor is on the quarterdeck, adjusting a series of instruments that Dorian doesn't recognize but navigating such a vessel likely takes some creativity. One looks like a string of hourglasses. Another a compass shaped like a globe, indicating up and down as well as the standard directions.

"Better?" she asks, glancing up at his wet hair as he approaches.

"Much, thank you," Dorian answers. "May I ask you a question?"

"You may, but I might not have an answer, or if I have an answer it might not be the right one or a good one. Questions and answers don't always fit together like puzzle pieces."

"I didn't have this, up there," Dorian says, indicating the sword tattooed on his chest.

"That's not a question."

"How do I have it now?"

"Did you *think* that you did?" Eleanor asks. "Those things can get confused down here. You probably believed it should be there so now it's there. You must be a good storyteller, usually it takes a while. But you did spend a fair amount of time in the sea, that will do it, too."

"It was only an idea," Dorian says, remembering how he felt reading Zachary's book, reading about what guardians once were, trying to guess what his sword would have looked like if he were a real guardian and not a poor imitation of one.

"It's a story you told yourself," Eleanor says. "The sea heard you telling it so now it's there. That's how it works. It usually has to be personal, a story you wear against your skin, but I can manage it with the ship now. It took a lot of practice."

"You willed this ship into existence?"

"I found parts of it and told myself the story of the rest of it and eventually they were the same, the found parts and the story parts. It can steer itself but I have to tell it where to go and nudge it back in the right direction sometimes. I can change the sails but they like being this color. Do you like them?"

Dorian looks up at the deep red sails and for a moment they brighten and then settle back into burgundy.

"I do like them," Dorian says.

"Thank you. Did you have the tattoo on your back up there?"

"Yes."

"Did it hurt?"

"Very much," Dorian says, recalling session after session spent in a tattoo parlor that smelled of coffee and Nag Champa incense and played classic rock at volumes high enough to cover the buzzing of needles. He had copied the single-page illustration on a photocopier years earlier to hang on a wall, never thinking that he would lose the book and during the time when it was all he had left of *Fortunes and Fables* he wanted it closer than the wall, where no one could take it from him.

"It's important to you, isn't it?" Eleanor asks.

"Yes, it is."

"Important things hurt sometimes."

Dorian smiles at the statement, despite the truth of it or because of it.

"It'll take us a while to get there," Eleanor says, adjusting the compass globe and looping a rope over the ship's wheel.

"I don't think I understand where we're going," Dorian admits.

"Oh," Eleanor says. "I can show you."

She checks the compass again and then leads him down to the captain's cabin. There is a long table in the center covered in beeswax candles. Leather armchairs are tucked into the corners next to a potbellied stove with a pipe that leads up and out through the deck. Along the back there are multicolored stained-glass windows. Ropes and ribbons and a large hammock covered in blankets hang from the beams in the ceiling. A stuffed bunny with an eye patch and a sword sits on a shelf, along with various other objects. An antlered skull. Clay mugs filled with pens and pencils, jars of ink and paintbrushes. Strings of feathers hang along the walls, drifting as the air changes around them.

Eleanor walks to the far end of the table. In between the candles there is a pile of paper, all different textures and sizes and shapes. Some of it is transparent. Most pieces have lines and annotations.

"It's hard to map a place that changes," she explains. "The map has to change along with it."

She picks up one corner of the pile of paper on the table and attaches it to a hook hung from a rope on the ceiling. She does the same with the other corners and turns a pulley on the wall and the map pieces lift up, attached to each other with ribbons and string. It rises in layers, fluffing up like a multitiered paper cake. The topmost levels are filled with books, Dorian finds the ballroom and then the Heart (a small red jewel of a heart hangs there along with the remains of a watch) and a tall empty space below, cutting through multiple layers. Below there are caverns and roads and tunnels. Looking closer he can see paper cutouts of tall statues, stray buildings, and trees. Gold silk snakes in and out of the lower layers, a tiny boat pinned onto one near the center. The silk trails all the way down to the surface of the table where it pools in waves surrounded by paper castles and towers.

"This is the sea?" Dorian asks, touching the golden silk.

"*Sea* is easier to say than 'complicated series of rivers and lakes,' isn't it?" Eleanor answers. "It's all connected but there are different pockets. We're in one of the higher ones. It goes down here," she points to the lower levels that are not as detailed as the rest of the map. "But it's not safe down there if you're not an owl, it changes too much. This is only what I've seen for myself."

"How far does it go?" Dorian asks.

Eleanor shrugs. "I haven't found out yet," she says. "We're here," she touches a minuscule boat on one of the golden waves in the center. "We'll follow along here and turn here," she indicates two swirls of silk that move upward, "and then I can leave you here." She points at a series of paper trees.

"How do I get back here?" Dorian asks, pointing up to the Heart.

Eleanor considers the map and then moves to the other side of the table. She gestures toward the opposite side of the forest.

"If you come out here and then go this way," she points to a path that leads up from the trees, "you should be able to find the inn." Here there is a building with a tiny lantern. "From the inn you should be able to change roads to get up here." She brings him around the corner of the map and shows him the paths closest to the Harbor. "Once you're there your compass should work again and that always points you back here." She indicates the Heart.

Dorian looks at the chain around his neck that holds the key to his room and the locket-size compass. He opens it and a small amount of honey drips out but the needle spins wildly, unable to find its way.

"Is that what this does?" he asks. No one had explained it to him before.

"It won't be the same when you get back," Eleanor says. "Sometimes you can't go back to the same old place, you have to go to the new ones."

"I'm not trying to get back to the place," Dorian says. "I'm trying to get back to a person." Admitting it aloud feels like an affirmation.

"People change, too, you know."

"I do know," Dorian says, nodding. He doesn't want to think about it. He had always wanted to be in the place but he didn't understand until he was finally there that the place was merely a way to get to the person and now he has lost them both.

"You might have been gone for a long time already," Eleanor says. "Time is different down here. It passes slower. Sometimes it doesn't stop to pass at all and it just skips around."

"Are we lost in time?"

"You might be. I'm not *lost.*"

"What are you doing down here?" Dorian asks. Eleanor considers the question, looking at the layers of map.

"For a while I was looking for a person but I didn't find them and after that I was looking for myself. Now that I've found me I'm back to exploring, which is what I was doing in the first place before I was doing anything else and I think I was supposed to be exploring all along. Does that sound silly?"

"That sounds like a great adventure."

Eleanor smiles to herself. She and Mirabel have the same smile. Dorian wonders what happened to Simon, now that he understands how much space and time there is to be lost in down here. He tries not to think about how much time might have passed above already as Eleanor collapses the map, folding the Heart down into the Starless Sea.

"We're near a good place for the goodbye," she says. "If you're ready."

Dorian nods and together they return to the deck. They have traveled into another cavern, this one carved with massive alcoves, each alcove containing a towering statue of a person. There are six of them, each holding an object though many of them are broken and all of them are covered in crystallized honey.

"What is this place?" Dorian asks as they walk toward the bow.

"Part of one of the old Harbors," Eleanor answers. "The sea level was higher the last time I passed through. I should update my map. I thought she'd like it here. She told me once that people who died down here were supposed to be returned to the Starless Sea because the sea is where the stories come from and all endings are beginnings. Then I asked her what happens to people who are born down here and she said she didn't know. If all endings are beginnings, are all beginnings also endings?"

"Maybe," Dorian says. He looks down at Allegra's body, draped in silk and tied with ropes to a wooden door.

"It was all I had that was the right size," Eleanor explains.

"It's appropriate," Dorian assures her.

Together they lift the door and lower it over the rail and down to the surface of the Starless Sea. The edges dip into the honey but the door stays afloat.

Once the door has moved a distance from the ship Eleanor stands up on the rail and tosses one of the paper lanterns onto the door. It lands over Allegra's feet and tips, the candle inside catching first on its paper shell and then on the silk, working its way over the ropes.

The door and its occupant, both aflame, drift farther from the ship.

Dorian and Eleanor stand side by side at the rail, watching.

"Do you want to say something nice?" Eleanor asks.

Dorian stares at the burning corpse of the woman who took his name and his life and made him a thousand promises that were never kept. The woman who found him when he was young and lost and alone and gave him a purpose and set him on a path that has proved to be more surprising and strange than he was led to believe. A woman he had trusted beyond all others until a year ago and a woman who would have shot him in the heart very recently had time and fate not intervened.

"No, I don't want to say anything," he tells Eleanor and she turns and looks at him thoughtfully, but then she nods and returns her attention starboard, considering the now distant flames for a long time before she speaks.

"Thank you for seeing me when other people looked through me like I was a ghost," Eleanor says and an unexpected sob catches in Dorian's throat.

Eleanor puts a hand over Dorian's on the rail and they stay like that in silence, watching long after the flame fades out of sight and the ship continues to steer itself to its destination.

The burning door illuminates the faces of the ancient statues as it passes.

They are only stone likenesses of those who dwelt in this space long before but they recognize one of their own and pay their silent respects as Allegra Cavallo is returned to the Starless Sea.

ZACHARY EZRA RAWLINS stares upward toward a dim light that shines (not brightly) at a distance he had already thought of as deep from a spot very, very far below it.

What's the opposite of a fear of heights? Fear of depths?

There is a cliff, a shadow that stretches up to the dim light from the city. He can sort of see the bridge. There's only the barest amount of light where he's landed, like warm-toned moonlight.

He does not remember landing, only slipping and continuing to slip and then having already landed.

He has landed on a pile of rocks. His leg hurts but nothing seems broken, not even his indestructible glasses.

Zachary reaches out to pull himself up and his fingers close over a hand.

He yanks his arm back.

He reaches out again, tentatively and the hand is still there, frozen, extending out from the pile of rocks that is not a pile of rocks at all. Next to the hand is a leg and a round shape like half a head. As Zachary pulls himself up he rests his hand on a disembodied hip.

He stands in a sea of broken statues.

An arm nearby is holding an unlit torch, a real one from the looks of it, not one carved from stone. Zachary moves slowly toward it and takes it from the statue's hand.

He puts the sword down by his feet and fumbles around in his bag for the cigarette lighter, grateful to past Zachary for including it in the inventory.

It takes a few tries but he manages to light the torch. It gives him light enough to navigate, though he doesn't know which way to go.

He lets gravity dictate his way forward, following the sloping surface in whichever direction is easiest to step. The statues shift beneath his feet. He uses the sword to balance himself.

It is difficult to manage both sword and torch over the uneven surface but he dares not leave either behind. He needs the torch for light and the sword feels . . . important. The broken statues shift, creating miniature avalanches of body parts. He drops the sword and puts his hand out to steady himself and he hits something softer than stone.

The skull beneath his fingers is not carved from ivory or marble. It is bone, clinging to the last of the flesh that once surrounded it. Zachary's fingers tangle in what is left of its hair. He pulls his hand back quickly, stray hairs chasing after his fingers.

Zachary rests the torch in the awaiting hand of a nearby statue so he can get a closer look that he's not certain he wants.

The corpse that is almost a skeleton is concealed amongst the broken statues. Had Zachary been walking a few paces to either side he never would have noticed it, though now he can smell the decay.

This body is not wrapped in memories. It wears scraps of disintegrating clothing. Whoever it once contained is gone, and they have taken their stories with them, leaving their bones and their boots and a leather scabbard wrapped around their torso, fit for a sword it does not contain.

Zachary pauses, torn between the obvious usefulness of the scabbard and the amount of corpse contact it will take to obtain it, and after an internal debate he holds his breath and clumsily unhooks the belt from its former owner, collapsing bones and rot and unidentifiable liquids in the process.

He has a sudden thought that this is what will become of him down here and he pushes it from his mind as forcefully as he can, focusing on the bits of leather and metal.

When he frees the scabbard and its leather straps it does fit the sword, not perfectly but well enough that he will not have to carry it. It takes him a minute to figure out how to wear it over his sweater but eventually the sword stays in place on his back.

"Thank you," Zachary says to the corpse.

The corpse says nothing, silently grateful to be of assistance.

Zachary keeps moving, stumbling over statues. It is easier now. He switches the torch from one hand to the other to rest his arm.

The pieces of broken statues grow smaller, eventually there is only gravel beneath his feet. The expanse of marble resolves into something that might be a path.

The path turns into a tunnel.

Zachary thinks the torch might be getting dimmer.

He does not know how long he has been walking. He wonders if it is still January, if somewhere far above it is still snowing.

He can hear only his footsteps, his breath, his heartbeat, and the crackling flame of the torch that is definitely getting dimmer which is disappointing because he had hoped it would be a magic endless-light torch and not a regular extinguishable one.

There is a sound nearby that he is not causing. A movement along the ground.

The sound continues, growing louder. Something large is moving nearby. Behind him and now beside him.

Zachary turns and looks up as the torchlight illuminates a single large, dark eye surrounded by light fur. The eye stares at him placidly and then blinks.

Zachary reaches out and touches softest fur. He can feel each breath beneath his hand, the thunder of a massive heartbeat, and then the creature blinks again and turns away, allowing the torchlight to catch the length of its long ears and the fluff of its tail before it disappears.

Zachary stares into the darkness after the giant white rabbit.

Did this all begin with a book?

Or is it older than that? Is everything that brought him here now much, much older?

He tries to pinpoint the moments, tries to sort out their meanings.

There are no meanings. Not anymore.

The voice is like a whisper made of wind.

"What?" Zachary asks aloud.

"*What?*" his echo answers him over and over and over.

You are too late. It is foolish to continue.

Zachary reaches back and pulls the sword from its scabbard, holding it out against the darkness.

You are already dead, you know.

Zachary pauses and listens though he does not want to.

You took a walk too early in the morning and collapsed from fatigue and stress and then hypothermia followed but your body has been buried in snow. No one will find you until spring melts it away. There is so much snow. Your friends think you are missing when in truth you are beneath their feet.

"That's not true," Zachary says. He does not sound as certain as he would like to.

You're right, it isn't. You have no friends. And all of this is a fabrication. Your brain's feeble attempt to preserve itself. Telling itself a story with love and adventure and mystery. All of those things you wanted in your life that you were too busy playing your games and reading your books to go out and find. Your wasted life is ending, that is why you are here.

"Shut up," Zachary says to the darkness. He intended to shout it but his words are weak, not even strong enough to echo.

You know this is true. You believe it because it is more believable than this nonsense. You are pretending. You have imagined these people and these places. You tell yourself a fairy tale because you are too afraid of the truth.

The torchlight is fading. Cold like snow creeps over his skin.

Let go. You will never find your way out. There is no way out. You are at the end now. Game over.

Zachary forces himself to keep walking. He can no longer see where the path goes. He concentrates on one step and then another. He shivers.

Give up. Giving up is easier. Giving up will be warmer.

The torch goes out.

You don't have to be afraid of dying because you are already dead.

Zachary tries to move forward but he cannot see.

You are dead. You perished. There is no extra life. You had your chance. You played your game. You lost.

Zachary falls to his knees. He had thought he had a sword, why would he have a sword? That's so stupid.

It is stupid. It's nonsense. It is time you stopped fantasizing about swords and time travel and men who don't lie to you and owl royalty and the Starless Sea. None of those things exist. You made them up. All of this is in your head. You can stop walking. There is nowhere to go. You're tired of walking.

He is tired of walking. Tired of trying. He doesn't even know what he wants, what it is that he's looking for.

You don't know what you want. You never did and you never will. It is over and done with. You have reached the end.

There is a hand on Zachary's arm. He thinks there is a hand on his arm. Maybe.

"Don't listen," a different voice says near his ear. He doesn't recognize the voice or its accent. Maybe British or Irish or Scottish or something. He is bad at accent identification like he is bad at everything else. "It lies," this voice continues. "Don't listen."

Zachary doesn't know which voice to believe even though British-Irish-Scottish accents tend to sound official and important and the other voice didn't have an accent but maybe there aren't any voices at all maybe he should rest awhile. He tries to lie down but someone pulls at his arm.

"We cannot stay here," one of the voices insists. The British one.

You imagined help for yourself, you are so desperate to believe. That's pathetic.

The hand releases his arm. There was never a hand there, there was nothing.

A light flares, a sudden brightness sweeping over the space. For a second there is a tunnel and a path and huge wooden doors in the distance and then darkness again.

You are a small, sad, unimportant man. None of this matters. Nothing you can do will have any impact on anything. You have already been forgotten. Stay here. Rest.

"Get up," the other voice says and the hand is there again, dragging Zachary forward.

Zachary pulls himself awkwardly to his feet. The sword in his hand hits his leg.

He does have a sword.

No.

The voice in the darkness changes. Before it was calm. Now it is angry.

No, the darkness repeats as Zachary tries to move and someone—*something*—grabs ahold of his ankles, wrapping around his legs and trying to pull him down again.

"This way," the other voice says, more urgently now, leading him forward. Zachary follows, each step meeting with increased resistance from the ground. He tries to run but he can barely walk.

He tightens his grip on the hilt of the sword. He focuses on the hand on his arm and not the other things that are sliding up his legs and around his neck though they feel just as real.

He is not alone. This is happening.

He has a sword and he is in a cavern beneath a lost city somewhere in the vicinity of the Starless Sea and he has lost track of Fate and he cannot see but he still believes, dammit.

His feet move faster now, one step and then another and another, though the thing in the darkness follows, keeping pace as they continue down a path that ends at something that feels like a wall.

"Wait," the voice that is not the darkness says and the hand leaves Zachary's arm, replaced by something that is not a hand, heavy and cold and curling around his shoulder.

In front of him there is a sliver of light from an open door.

The darkness makes a horrible sound that is not a scream but that is the closest word Zachary has for the screeching terror in his head and around it.

It is so loud that Zachary stumbles and the darkness grabs at him, tearing at his shoes, curling around his legs, pulling him back. He loses his balance and falls, sliding backward, trying to hold on to the sword.

Someone reaches an arm around his chest and pulls him toward the light and the door. Zachary cannot tell if the man or the darkness is stronger but with one arm he holds tight to his rescuer and with the other he stabs at the darkness with his sword.

The darkness hisses at him.

You don't even know why you are here, it calls as Zachary is pulled into the light, the voices in his ears and in his head. *They are using you—*

The doors close, muffling the voices, but they continue to shudder and shake, something on the other side trying to get in.

"Help me with this," the man says as he pushes against the doors, attempting to keep them closed. Zachary blinks, his eyes adjusting, but he can see the large wooden bar the man is struggling with and he gets to his feet, taking the other end of the heavy bar and sliding it into the metal braces set along the doors.

The bar slips into place, securing the doors shut.

Zachary leans his forehead against the doors and tries to steady his breathing. The doors are massive and carved and feel more real and solid beneath his skin with every passing second. He is alive. He is here. This is happening.

Zachary sighs and looks up and around at the space that he has entered, and then at the man standing next to him.

This space is a temple. The doors are one set of four that lead to an open atrium. It continues up and up and up in tiers surrounded by wooden stairs and balconies. Fires burn in hanging bowls, their moving light accentuated by the candles placed on every surface in lieu of offerings, dripping wax on carved altars and on the shoulders and open palms of statues. Long banners of book pages strung from thread are draped over the balconies like flags, fluttering and freed from their bindings.

Within this sanctuary of light, Zachary Ezra Rawlins and Simon Jonathan Keating stare at each other in bewildered silence.

IT WAS EASIER than he anticipated, identifying her amongst the masked guests at the party. Initiating a conversation. Escalating it. Inviting her up to his hotel room, booked under a fictional name.

He expected her to be more wary.

He expected a lot of things from this evening that have not come to pass.

Getting to this point was so easy that it nags at him, louder now that they are away from the party chatter and the music. This was too easy. Too easy to identify her with the bee and key and sword draped obviously and gaudily around her neck. Too easy to get her talking. Too easy to bring her upstairs, to a location without witnesses save for the city outside the window too filled with its own concerns to notice or care.

It was all too easy and the ease of it bothers him.

But it is also now too late.

Now she stands by the window though there is not much of a view. Part of the hotel across the street, a corner of night sky with no visible stars.

"Do you ever think about how many stories are out there?" she asks, placing a finger on the glass. "How many dramas are unfolding around us right at this very moment? I wonder how long a book you would need to record them. You'd probably need an entire library to hold a single evening in Manhattan. An hour. A minute."

He thinks then that she knows why he is here and that's why it was so easy and he can't afford to hesitate any longer.

There is a part of him that wants to remain in the charade, continue playing this part and wearing this mask.

He finds he wants to keep talking with her. He is distracted by her question, thinking of all the other people in this city, all the stories filling this street, this block, this hotel. This room.

But he has a job to do.

He takes his weapon from his pocket as he approaches her.

She turns and looks at him, wearing an expression he cannot read. She lifts her hand and rests her palm against the side of his face.

He can tell where her heart is before he strikes. He doesn't even have to look away from her eyes, the motion is so well-practiced it is almost automatic, a skill so honed he doesn't have to think about it though here and now the not thinking bothers him.

Then it is done, one of his hands pressed against the neckline of her gown and the other against her back to keep her from falling or pulling away. From a distance, viewed through the window, it would appear romantic, the long thin needle piercing her heart a detail lost in an embrace.

He waits for her breath to catch, for her heart to stop.

It does not.

Her heart continues to beat. He can feel it beneath his fingers, stubborn and insistent.

She continues to look up at him, though the expression in her eyes has changed and now he understands. Before she had been weighing him. Now he has been weighed and left wanting and her disappointment is as obvious and evident as the blood running down her back and through his fingers and the still-beating heart beneath his hand.

She sighs.

She leans forward, leans into him, pressing her drumming heart against his fingers and her breath, her skin, all of her is so impossibly alive in his arms that he is terrified.

She reaches up, casual and calm, and removes his mask. She lets it fall to the ground as she stares in his eyes.

"I am so very tired of the romance of the dead girl," she says. "Aren't you?"

Dorian wakes with a start.

He is in an armchair in the captain's quarters of a pirate ship upon a sea of honey. He tries to convince his mind that the Manhattan hotel room was the dream.

"Did you have a nightmare?" Eleanor asks from across the room.

She is adjusting her maps. "I used to have nightmares and I would write them down and fold them up into stars and throw them away to be rid of them. Sometimes it worked."

"I will never be rid of this one," Dorian tells her.

"Sometimes they stay," Eleanor says, nodding. She makes a change to the gold silk and collapses the maps again. "We're almost there," she says, and she goes out to the deck.

Dorian spends another breath in a remembered hotel room before he follows her. He takes the knapsack she has given him containing a few potentially useful items, including a flask full of water though Eleanor claims he spent enough time in the honey that he shouldn't be hungry or thirsty for a while. There is a pocketknife and a length of rope and a box of matches.

She somehow found a pair of boots that fit him, tall and cuffed and quite piratey. They are almost comfortable. Along with his star-buttoned coat he looks like he walked out of a fairy tale. Maybe he did.

He goes out to the deck and freezes in his boots at the sight in front of him.

A dense forest of cherry trees in full bloom fills the cavern, all the way up to the edge of the river. Twisting tree roots disappear below the surface of the honey while stray blossoms fall and float downstream.

"It's pretty, isn't it?" Eleanor says.

"It's beautiful," Dorian agrees, though the single word cannot capture the way the sight of this long-beloved place is tearing at his heart.

"I won't be able to stop long with this current," Eleanor explains. "Are you ready to go?"

"I think so," Dorian says.

"When you find the inn tell the innkeeper I said hello, please," Eleanor says.

"I shall," Dorian tells her. And because he knows he might not have another chance he adds: "I know your daughter."

"You know Mirabel?" Eleanor asks.

"Yes."

"She's not my daughter."

"She's not?"

"Only because she's not a person," Eleanor clarifies. "She's something else dressed up like a person, the way the Keeper is. You know that, don't you?"

"I do," Dorian admits, though he would not have been able to explain it so simply. The dream that was all memory replays in his mind again, following through the rest of that night they spent together in a hotel bar as his world fractured and fell apart and Mirabel caught the pieces in the bottom of a martini glass. He wonders sometimes what might have happened, what he might have done, had she not stayed with him.

"I think it's probably hard to be not a person when you're stuck inside a person," Eleanor muses. "She always seemed very mad about everything. What is she like now?"

Dorian doesn't know how to answer the question. He feels a heartbeat in his fingers that is not there. For a moment, remembering, conjuring the idea of the person who is not a person, he feels again the way he felt that night, and underneath all the terror and confusion and wonder there is a perfect calm.

"I don't think she's mad anymore," he tells Eleanor. Though even as he says it he thinks perhaps that calm is more akin to the calm within a storm.

Eleanor tilts her head, considering, and then she nods, seemingly pleased.

Dorian wishes he could give Eleanor something for her kindness, in payment for the transportation. For saving his life, something that seems to run in the family.

He has but one thing to give and he realizes now it was the fact that the book was not being read that bothered him more than the fact that it was not in his possession. Besides, he carries it with him always, in ink on his back and constantly unfolding in his head.

Dorian takes *Fortunes and Fables* from the pocket of his coat.

"I'd like you to have this," he says, handing it to Eleanor.

"It's important to you," she says. A statement and not a question.

"Yes."

Eleanor turns the book over in her hands, frowning at it.

"I gave a book that was important to me to someone a long time ago," she says. "I never got it back. I'm going to get this back to you someday, is that all right?"

"As long as you read it first," Dorian says.

"I will, I promise," Eleanor says. "I hope you find your person."

"Thank you, my captain," Dorian says. "I wish you a great many future adventures." He bows at her and she laughs and here and now they separate to further their respective stories.

Dorian's disembarking is a complicated feat of ropes and a carefully managed jump and then he is standing on the shore watching the ship become smaller and smaller as it continues down the coast.

From here he can read the text carved into its side:

To Seek & to Find

The ship becomes a glowing light in the distance and then it is gone and Dorian is alone.

He turns to face the forest.

They are larger cherry trees than he has ever seen, looming and gnarled, branches twisting in all directions, some high enough to skim the rock walls of the cavern high above and others low enough to touch, all weighted with thousands of pink blossoms. Roots and trunks grow through solid stone ground that cracks open around them.

Paper lanterns are strung from branches, some from impossible heights, dotting the canopy like stars. They sway though there is no breeze.

As Dorian walks into the forest there are occasional stumps between the trees. Some are covered in burning candles, dripping over the sides and onto the ground. Others are stacked with books and Dorian reaches to pick one up only to find that the books themselves are solid wood, part of the former tree, carved and painted.

Blossoms drift down around him. A trail has been cleared and defined by markers on the trees, flat stones set into their roots with single candles burning on them. Dorian follows this path, quickly losing sight of the Starless Sea. He can no longer hear the sound of the waves against the shore.

A single petal flutters and falls on his hand and dissolves like a snowflake on his skin.

As Dorian walks on the blossoms continue to fall, a few petals at a time, but then they begin to accumulate, drifting over the path.

He cannot pinpoint the moment when they turn from cherry blossoms to snow.

His boots leave prints as he walks farther. There are fewer lights marking the path. The blossom snow falls heavier, taking the candle flames away. It is colder now, each blossom that strikes Dorian's exposed skin feels like ice.

The darkness comes quick and heavy. Dorian cannot see.

He takes one step forward and then another, his boots sinking deep into the snow.

There is a sound. At first he thinks it is wind but it is steadier, like breathing. There is something moving beside him, then in front of him. He cannot see anything, the darkness is absolute.

He stops. Carefully he feels his way into his knapsack, his hands closing over the box of matches.

Blindly, Dorian attempts to light a match. The first falls from his shivering fingers. He takes a breath and steadies himself and tries another.

The match catches, casting a single trembling flame's worth of light.

A man stands in the snow in front of Dorian. Taller than him, thinner but with broader shoulders. Atop the broad shoulders is the head of an owl, staring down at him with large, round eyes.

The owl head tilts, considering him.

The large round eyes blink.

The flame reaches the end of the match. The light flickers and fades.

The darkness envelops Dorian again.

ZACHARY EZRA RAWLINS has pictured many a character from a book never dreaming he would end up face-to-face with one of them, and even though he knew that Simon Keating was an actual person and not a book character he'd had a character pictured in his head anyway who was not at all the person he is currently looking at.

This man is older than the eighteen-year-old that Zachary had imagined, though what is age for someone lost in time? He looks thirtyish, with dark eyes and long dirty-blond hair pulled back into a ponytail with several feathers tied into it. A ruffled shirt that might once have been white is now grey but his waistcoat has fared better, missing several buttons that have been replaced by knotted strings. He wears a strip of leather looped twice around his waist like a doubled belt, from it hang several items, including a knife and a coil of rope. More strips of leather and cloth are wrapped around his knees and elbows and his right hand.

His left hand is missing, cut off above the wrist. The end of this arm is also wrapped and protected, and both the skin visible above it and part of his neck have clearly been very badly burned at some point in the past.

"Can you still hear them?" Simon asks.

Zachary shakes his head, as much to get the memory of the voices out as to answer the question. He dropped his torch at some point though now he doesn't remember if he actually had a torch at all. He tries to remember and recalls statues and darkness and a giant bunny.

He looks up at effigies who for centuries stared out at festivals and worshippers and then at emptiness and after the emptiness their sight was claimed by the honeyed sea and when the tides receded and the light returned they stared first at a single man and now at two.

"They told you lies," Simon assures Zachary, nodding back at the door. "It is fortunate that I heard you."

"Thank you," Zachary says.

"Move through this," Simon advises him. "Let it move through you and then let it go."

Simon turns away, leaving Zachary to collect himself. He is shaking but starting to calm, trying to take in everything in front of him and around him and above him.

There are dozens of giant statues. Some figures have animal heads and others have lost their heads entirely. They are posed throughout the space in a way that looks so organic that Zachary would not be surprised if they moved, or perhaps they are moving, very, very slowly.

Hung between the outstretched limbs and crowns and antlers there are ropes and ribbons and threads tying the statues to the balconies and the doors and strung with book pages and keys and feathers and bones. A long sequence of brass moons hangs down the center of the atrium. Some of the ropes are strung on gears and pulleys.

Two of the statues are so large that the balconies are built around them, one on either side. They face each other, over all the other dramas unfolding in stone and on paper and in person.

The nearest one has such detail in its form and likeness that Zachary recognizes the Keeper even though part of his face is obscured by fluttering paper and the curve of a crescent moon. His hands are held out in a familiar-looking gesture, raised as though he is expecting a very large book to be placed in his open palms but instead there are red ribbons, long strips of blood-colored silk, draped across his fingers and around his wrists and then stretching outward, binding him to the balconies and the doors and to the other statue that he faces.

The figure opposite doesn't look like Mirabel but it's clearly meant to be her, or someone she used to be. Red ribbons are tied around her wrists and looped around her neck, trailing down to the ground and pooling around her feet like blood. *Hey, Max,* Zachary thinks, and the statue turns its head ever so slightly to stare at him with empty stone eyes.

"Are you injured?" Simon asks as Zachary stumbles backward, catching his balance on an altar behind him. Its surface is soft beneath his hand, the stone covered in layers upon layers of dripped wax. Zachary shakes his head in response to the question, though he isn't certain. He can still feel the heaviness of the darkness in his lungs and in his shoes. Maybe he should sit down. He tries to remember how. The ribbons fluttering nearby have words written on them that Zachary cannot read, prayers or pleas or myths. Wishes or warnings.

"I'm . . ." Zachary starts but he does not know how to complete the statement. He does not know what he is. Not right now.

"Which one are you?" Simon asks, scrutinizing him. "The heart or the feather? You carry the sword but you do not wear the stars. This is confusing. You should not be here. You were meant to be somewhere else."

Zachary opens his mouth to ask what Simon is talking about, exactly, but instead he says the only thing that his thoughts keep returning to: "I saw a bunny."

"You saw . . ." Simon looks at him quizzically and Zachary is unsure he spoke properly, his thoughts feel so separate from his body.

"A bunny," he repeats, slowly enough that the word sounds wrong again. "A big one. Like an elephant only . . . bunny."

"The celestial hare is not a *bunny*," Simon corrects him before turning his attention to the ropes and gears above their heads. "If you saw the hare that means the moon is here," he says. "It is later than I had thought. The Owl King is coming."

"Wait . . ." Zachary starts, grounding himself unsteadily with a question he has asked before. "Who is the Owl King?"

"The crown passes from one to another," Simon answers, preoccupied with adjusting ropes with well-practiced single-handed motions. "The crown passes from story to story. There have been many owl kings with their crowns and their claws."

"Who's the Owl King now?" Zachary asks.

"The Owl King is not a who. Not always. Not in this story. You confuse what was with what is." Simon sighs, pausing his tinkering and returning his attention to Zachary. He explains haltingly, searching for the right words. "The Owl King is a . . . phenomenon. The future crashing into the present like a wave. Its wings beat in the spaces between choices and before decisions, heralding change . . . change of the long-awaited sort, the change foretold by prophecies and warned of by omens, written in the stars."

"Who are the stars?" It is a question Zachary has thought before but not yet asked aloud, though he remains confused as to whether the Owl King is a person or a bird or a type of weather.

Simon stares at him and blinks.

"We are the stars," he answers, as though it is the most obvious of facts afloat in a sea of metaphors and misdirections. "We are all stardust and stories."

Simon turns away and unties a rope from one of the hooks near the wall. He tugs it and far above the gears and pulleys swing into motion. A crescent shape turns in on itself and disappears. "This is not right," he says, pulling a different rope that shifts the fluttering pages. "Doors are closing, taking possibilities with them. The story is recorded even when she is unsure of how it goes and now someone else follows after her, reading. Looking for the ending."

"What?" Zachary asks though maybe he means *who* and he can't remember the difference.

"The story," Simon repeats as though it answers the question instead of creating new ones. "I was in the story and then wandered outside of it and I found this place where I could listen instead of being read. Everything whispers the story here, the sea and the bees whisper and I listen and I try to find the shape of it all. Where it has been and where it is going. New stories wrap themselves around the old ones. The ancient stories that flames whisper to moths. This one wears thin in the places it has been told and retold. There are holes to fall into. I have tried to record it and I have failed."

Simon gestures up at the statues, at the ribbons and ropes and papers and keys.

"This is . . ." Zachary begins.

"This is the story," Simon finishes his thought for him. "If you remain down here long enough you will hear it buzzing. I capture as much as I can. It eases the sound."

Zachary looks closer. Within the ribbons and ropes and gears and keys there is more, shifting and glimmering and changing in the fire-light:

A sword and a crown surrounded by a swarm of paper bees.

A ship without a sea. A library. A city. A fire. A chasm filled with bones and dreams. A figure in a fur coat on a beach. A shape like a cloud or a small blue car. A cherry tree with book-page blossoms.

The keys and the ribbons shift and the images within them grow clearer, too clear to be woven from paper and thread.

Vines climb through windows to curl around a ginger cat asleep in the Keeper's office. Two women sit on a picnic table beneath the stars, drinking and talking. Behind them a boy stands in front of a painted door that will never open.

Zachary looks from another angle and for a moment the entire ephemeral structure appears to be an enormous owl encompassing the room and then in a fluttering of pages it fragments into bits of story again. The changed viewpoint brings both more and less. Fig-ures that were entwined are now separate. Somewhere it is snowing. There is an inn at a crossroads and someone is walking toward it.

There is a door in the moon.

"The story is changing." Simon's voice comes as a surprise beside him, Zachary is so absorbed in the shifting images, though when he looks again there is only a tangle of paper and metal and cloth. "It moves too quickly. Events are overlapping."

"I thought time wasn't . . ." Zachary starts but stops again, unsure of what time wasn't or won't be or is. "I thought time was different here."

"We proceed at different rates but we are all moving into the future," Simon tells him. "She was holding it in like a breath and now she is gone. I did not think that would happen."

"Who?" Zachary asks but Simon does not answer, switching more ropes with his one hand.

"The egg is cracking," he says. "Has cracked. Will crack."

Above them a series of keys fall, clattering against one another like chimes.

"Soon the dragon will come to eat the world." Simon turns back to Zachary. "You should not be here. The story followed you here. This is where they want you to be."

"Who?" Zachary asks again and this time it seems like Simon hears the question. He leans in and whispers, as though he fears someone else might hear.

"They are gods with lost myths, writing themselves new ones. Can you hear the buzzing yet?"

At his words the air changes. A curling breeze moves through the room, sending book pages and ribbons fluttering and extinguishing a number of candles. Simon moves quickly to relight them as the space sinks into shadow.

Zachary takes a few steps to stay out of Simon's way and backs into a statue of a helmeted warrior mounted on a gryphon, frozen mid-pounce on an unseen enemy, sword drawn and wings spread.

Perched on the statue's sword is a small owl, staring down at him.

Zachary jumps back in surprise and reaches to draw his own sword but he has left it on the ground some distance away. The owl continues to stare. It is very small, mostly fluff and eyes. There is an object clutched in its talons.

"Why would you fear that which guides you?" Simon asks calmly without turning to look at him, preoccupied with candle lighting. The room grows brighter. "The owls have only ever propelled the story forward. It is their purpose. This one has been waiting for someone to arrive. I should have known." He moves off, muttering to himself.

The small owl drops the object it carries at Zachary's feet.

Zachary looks down.

On the stone by his shoe is a folded-paper star.

The owl flies upward and perches on a balcony rail, continuing to stare down at Zachary. When Zachary does nothing the owl gives an impatient hoot of encouragement.

Zachary picks up the paper star. There is text printed on it. It looks familiar. He wonders how far the cats batted it through hallways before it fell all the way down here to wherever the owl fetched it from. Before it found its way to here and now.

Zachary unfolds the star and reads.

The son of the fortune-teller stands before six doorways,

ZACHARY EZRA RAWLINS looks down at words he has been long-ing to read, near delirious to have finally found another sentence that starts with the son of the fortune-teller in a familiar serifed typeface on a piece of paper removed from a book before being turned into a star and then gifted to him by a small owl and then he stops.

The owl hoots at him from the balcony.

He is not ready. He doesn't want to know.

Not yet.

He folds the page back into a star and puts it in his pocket without reading more than the first few words.

Three things lost in time. All right here. *Sweet Sorrows* in his bag, the sword at his feet, and Simon across the room.

Zachary feels something should happen now that all of them are together but nothing has. Not here, at least. Maybe they're all still lost and now he's just lost along with them.

Find man.

Found him. Now what?

Zachary turns his attention back to Simon who is still lighting candles on altars and staircases. The ground is covered in beeswax. Stretches of it look like honeycomb, though any perfect hexagons have been undone by footsteps and time.

As the light increases Zachary can see the other layers that have been built over this temple. An alcove for offerings now holds a pile of blankets. There are stacks of jars placed on the floor, removed from a less wax-covered place and brought here. This is where the man lost in time has been, hidden away for weeks or months or centuries.

Zachary walks over to Simon, following in his steps as he lights his candles.

"You are words on paper," Simon whispers, to himself or to Zachary or to the words above them clinging to their respective papers. "Be careful what stories you tell yourself."

"What do you mean?" Zachary asks, recalling the voices in the dark and wondering if they were such a story. Simon starts at the sound of his voice, turning toward him in surprise.

"Hello," Simon greets him anew. "Are you here to read? I believed once that I was here to read and not be read but the story has changed."

"Changed how?" Zachary says. Simon looks at him blankly. "How has the story changed?" he clarifies, gesturing upward at the pages and the statues, worried by Simon's behavior and even more concerned about the way everything keeps repeating and becoming more confusing when it should be getting clearer.

"It is broken," Simon answers, without elaborating as to how one goes about breaking a story. Perhaps it is like breaking a promise. "Its edges are sharp."

"How do I fix it?" Zachary asks.

"There is no fixing. There is only moving forward in the brokenness. Look, there," Simon indicates something within the story that Zachary cannot see. "You with your beloved and your blade. The tides will rise. There is a cat looking for you."

"A cat?" Zachary looks up at the owl and if owls could shrug the owl would shrug but they cannot, not distinctly, and so the owl ruffles its feathers instead.

"So many symbols when at the end and in the beginning there are only ever bees," Simon remarks.

Zachary sighs and picks up the sword. So many symbols. *Symbols are for interpretation, not definition,* he reminds himself. The sword feels lighter now, or perhaps he is growing accustomed to the weight of it. He puts it back in the scabbard.

"I have to find Mirabel," he tells Simon.

Simon stares at him blankly.

"*Her,*" Zachary says, pointing up at the statue. "Your . . ." he stops himself, worried that if Simon doesn't already know Mirabel is his daughter that the revelation might be too much so he starts again. "Mirabel . . . Fate, whoever she is. This incarnation has pink hair and she's usually up in the higher Harbor. I don't know if you can see her in the story but she's my friend and she's down here somewhere and I have to find her."

Zachary thinks that now he has more than one person to find but does not want to get into that. Doesn't want to think about it. About him. Even though the name that is probably not his real name repeats like a mantra in the back of his mind. *Dorian Dorian Dorian.*

"She is not your friend," Simon says, disrupting Zachary's thoughts, disrupting his entire being. "The mistress of the house of books. If she left you, she meant to do so."

"What?" Zachary says but Simon continues on, pacing around statues and pulling at more ropes and ribbons, the pages and objects strung above swirling into a storm. The owl cries from the balcony and flies down, perching on Zachary's shoulder.

"You should not have brought the story here," Simon admonishes Zachary. "I stay away from where the story is, I am not supposed to be in it any longer. When I tried to return before, it brought only pain."

Simon looks at the empty space where his left hand should be.

"Once I went back into the story and it ended in flames," he says. "The last time I moved closer a woman with one sky-bright eye took my hand and warned me never to return."

"Allegra." Zachary remembers the hand in the jar. Maybe it was insurance, to keep part of Simon lost forever, or just her standard intimidation technique carried out beyond intimidating.

"She is gone now."

"Wait, gone-gone or lost gone?" Zachary asks, but Simon does not clarify.

"You should come with me," he says. "We must leave before the sea claims us for its own."

"Does that say I go with you?" Zachary asks, pointing up at the ribbons and gears and keys, using his right arm so as not to jostle the owl on his left shoulder. Following instructions woven into a giant moving story sculpture doesn't seem much better than taking them from book pages.

He isn't about to go back into the darkness but there is more than one way to go from here.

Simon stares up at the story, gazing at it like he is searching for a particular star in a vast sky.

"I do not know which one you are," he says to Zachary.

"I'm Zachary. I'm the son of the fortune-teller. I need to know what to do next, Simon, please," Zachary says. Simon turns and looks at him quizzically. No, not quizzically. Blankly.

"Who is Simon?" he asks, returning his attention to the gears and the statues, as though the answer to his question is there in the starless expanse and not within himself.

"Oh," Zachary says. "*Oh.*"

This is what it is to be a man lost in time. To have lost one's self to the ages. To see but in the seeing to not remember, not even one's own name.

Not without being reminded.

"Here," Zachary says, fumbling around in his bag. "You should have this."

He holds out *The Ballad of Simon and Eleanor.*

Simon stares at the book, hesitating, as though a story still neatly fitted in its binding is an unusual object to encounter, but then he accepts the offering.

"We are words on paper," he says softly, turning the book over in his hands. "We are coming to the end."

"Reading it might help you remember," Zachary suggests.

Simon opens the book and quickly closes it again.

"We do not have time for this. I am going up, it will be safer to be higher once it starts." Simon moves to one of the other looming doors and pulls it open. The path beyond is lit but he returns to take a torch from the hand of a statue anyway. "Will you come with me?" he asks, turning back to Zachary.

The owl digs its tiny talons into Zachary's shoulder and Zachary cannot tell if the gesture is meant to encourage or discourage.

Zachary looks up at the story he has found himself in with the moon missing at its center. He looks at the statues of Mirabel and the Keeper and at many other figures that he does not have names for that must have played their roles in this tale at some point or another. He wonders how many people have passed through this space before, how many people breathed in this air that smells of smoke and honey and if any of them felt the way he feels now: unsure and afraid and unable to know which decision is the right one, if there is a right decision at all.

Zachary turns back to Simon.

The only answer he has is a question of his own.

"Which way is the Starless Sea?"

DORIAN STANDS IN the darkness in the snow, shivering due to more than the cold.

He has dropped his matches.

He can see nothing and he can still see the owl eyes looking at him. He did not know it was possible to feel so naked when fully dressed in the dark.

Dorian takes a breath and closes his eyes and holds out his empty trembling hand, palm up. An offering. An introduction.

He waits, listening to the steady breathing sound. He keeps his hand extended.

A hand takes his in the darkness. Long fingers curl over his, gripping him gently but firmly.

The hand leads him onward.

They walk for some time, Dorian taking each snow-slowed step one after another, following where the owl-headed man leads, trusting that this is the way forward. The darkness seems endless.

Then there is a light.

It is so soft that Dorian thinks he might be imagining it, but as he walks on the light grows brighter.

The steady sound of breathing near him stops, taken by the wind.

The fingers clutched in his vanish. One moment there is a hand holding his and then nothing.

Dorian tries to articulate his gratitude but his lips refuse to form words in the cold. He thinks it, as loudly as he can, and hopes that someone will hear.

He walks toward the light. As he gets closer he can tell there are two.

Lanterns glowing on either side of a door.

He cannot see the rest of the building but there is a door knocker in the shape of a crescent moon in the center of the night-blue door. Dorian lifts it with a nearly frozen hand and knocks.

The wind pushes him inside as the door opens.

The space Dorian enters is the antithesis of what he has left, warm brightness erasing the dark cold. A large open hall filled with firelight and books, dark wood beams and windows covered in frost. It smells of spiced wine and baking bread. It is comforting in a way that defies words. It feels like a hug, if a hug were a place.

"Welcome, traveler," a deep voice says.

Behind him a heavyset man with an impressive beard bolts the door against the wind. If the place were a person it would be this man, comfort made flesh, and it is all Dorian can do not to sink into his arms and sigh.

He attempts to return the greeting and finds he is too cold to speak.

"Terrible weather for traveling," the innkeeper remarks and whisks Dorian over to an enormous stone fireplace that covers almost the entire far wall of the grand hall.

The innkeeper settles Dorian into a chair and takes his knapsack from him, placing it on the floor within sight. He looks like he might try to take Dorian's coat but thinks better of it and settles on removing his snow-covered boots and leaving them to dry by the fire. The innkeeper disappears, returning with a blanket that he lays over Dorian's lap and a contraption filled with glowing coals that he places under the chair. He drapes a warmed cloth around Dorian's neck like a scarf and hands him a steaming cup.

"Thank you," Dorian manages to say, taking the cup with shivering hands. He takes a sip and cannot taste the liquid but it is warming and that is all that matters.

"We'll have you thawed soon, not to worry," the innkeeper says, and it is true, the warmth of the drink and fire and the place soak into Dorian. The chill begins to lift.

Dorian listens to the wind howl, wondering what it is howling about, wondering if it is a warning or a wish. The flames dance merrily in the fireplace.

It is strange, Dorian thinks, to sit in a place you imagined a thousand times. To have it be all that you thought it might be and more. More details. More sensations. It is stranger still that this place is filled with things he never imagined, as though the inn has been pulled from his mind and embellished by another unseen storyteller.

He is becoming accustomed to strangeness.

The innkeeper brings another cup and another warmed cloth to replace the first.

Dorian unbuttons the stars on his coat to better keep the warmth close to his skin.

The innkeeper glances down and notices the sword on Dorian's chest and steps back in surprise.

"Oh," he says. "It's you." His eyes flick back to Dorian's and then back to the sword. "I have something for you."

"What?" Dorian asks.

"My wife left something for me to give to you," the innkeeper says. "She gave me instructions in case you arrived during one of her absences."

"How do you know it's meant for me?" Dorian asks, each word heavy on his tongue, still defrosting.

"She told me someday a man would arrive bearing a sword and dressed in the stars. She gave me something and asked me to keep it locked away until you got here, and now here you are. She mentioned you might not know you were looking for it."

"I don't understand," Dorian says and the innkeeper laughs.

"I don't always understand, either," he says. "But I believe. I admit I did think you would have an actual sword and not a picture of one."

The innkeeper pulls a chain from beneath his shirt. A key hangs from it.

He moves one of the stones from the hearth in front of the fire, revealing a well-hidden compartment with an elaborate lock. He opens it with the key and reaches inside.

The innkeeper takes out a square box. He blows a layer of dust and ash from it and polishes it with a cloth taken from his pocket before he hands it to Dorian.

Dorian accepts the box, bewildered.

The box is beautiful, carved in bone with gold inlayed into elaborate designs. Crossed keys cover the top surrounded by stars. The sides are decorated with bees and swords and feathers and a single golden crown.

"How long have you had this?" Dorian asks the innkeeper.

The innkeeper smiles.

"A very long time. Please don't ask me to attempt to calculate it. I no longer keep any clocks."

Dorian looks down at the box. It is heavy and solid in his hands.

"You said your wife gave this to you to give to me," Dorian says and the innkeeper nods. Dorian runs his fingers over a sequence of golden moons along the edge of the box. Full and then waning and then vanished and then returned, waxing and then full again. He wonders if there is any difference between story and reality down here. "Is your wife the moon?"

"The moon is a rock in the sky," the innkeeper says, chuckling. "My wife is my wife. I'm sorry she's not here right now, she would have liked to meet you."

"I would have liked that, too," Dorian says. He looks back at the box in his hands.

There does not seem to be a lid. The gold motifs repeat and encircle every side and he cannot find a hinge or a seam. The moon waxes and wanes along its edges, over and over again. Dorian trails his chilled fingertips over each one, wondering how long it will be before the moon is new and dark and the innkeeper's wife is here again and then he pauses.

One of the full moons on what he assumes is the top of the box has an indentation, a six-sided impression concealed in its roundness, something he can feel more than see.

It is not a keyhole, but something could fit there.

He wishes Zachary were here with him, because Zachary might be better at such puzzles and for a multitude of other reasons.

What's missing? he thinks, looking over the box. There are owls and cats hidden in the negative space between the gold designs. There are stars and shapes that could be doors. Dorian thinks over all of his stories. What isn't here that should be?

It strikes him, sudden and simple.

"Do you have a mouse?" he asks the innkeeper.

The innkeeper looks at him quizzically for a moment and then he laughs.

"Can you come with me?" he asks.

Dorian, substantially warmer than he was when he arrived, nods and gets to his feet, placing the box on a table next to the chair.

The innkeeper leads him across the hall.

"This inn was once somewhere else," the innkeeper explains. "Little has changed within its walls but I once mentioned to my wife that I sometimes miss the mice. They used to chew through sacks of flour and secret seeds away in my teacups, it was infuriating but I was accustomed to it and I found I missed them once they were gone. So she brings them to me."

He stops at a cabinet tucked in between a pair of bookshelves and opens its door.

The shelves inside are covered with silver mice, some dancing and others sleeping or nibbling on minuscule pieces of golden cheese. One wields a small golden sword. A tiny knight.

Dorian reaches into the cabinet and picks up the mouse with the sword. It stands on a six-sided base.

"May I?" he asks the innkeeper.

"Of course," the innkeeper replies.

Dorian brings the mouse knight back to the chair by the fireplace and places it into the indentation in the moon on the box. It fits perfectly.

He turns the mouse and the hidden lid clicks loose.

"Ha!" the innkeeper exclaims delightedly.

Dorian places the silver mouse with its sword down next to the box. He lifts the lid.

Inside is a beating human heart.

ZACHARY EZRA RAWLINS, when he was very young, would play with crystals from his mother's expansive collection: staring into them, holding them up to lights and gazing at inclusions and cracks and wounds fractured and healed by time, imagining worlds within the stones, entire kingdoms and universes held in his palms.

The spaces he envisioned then are nothing compared to the crystalline caverns he walks through now, with a torch held aloft to light his way and an owl perched on his shoulder, digging its talons into his sweater.

When he hesitates at intersections the owl flies ahead, scouting. It reports back with indiscernible signals relayed through blinks or ruffling of feathers or hoots and Zachary pretends to understand even though he does not and thus together they continue forward. Simon warned him that the sea was a far distance but failed to mention that the path was this dark and winding.

Now this man who is not quite lost in time and his feathered companion come to a campfire, well-built and burning, waiting for them. Next to the fire is a large cloth tent that appears to have sheltered many previous travelers in spaces with more weather. The inside is bright and inviting.

The tent is massive, tall enough for Zachary to stand up and walk around in. There are pillows and blankets that seem stolen from other places and other times and arranged here to provide respite for the passing weary traveler, too much color for such a monochrome space. There is even a post outside waiting for his torch to rest in, and something else hanging below it.

A coat. A very old coat with a great many buttons.

Zachary discards his travel-damaged sweater and carefully puts on Simon's long-lost coat. The buttons are emblazoned with a crest, though in the light he cannot make out more than a smattering of stars.

The coat is warmer than his sweater. It is loose in the shoulders but Zachary does not care. He hangs his sweater on the post.

As Zachary buttons his new ancient coat the owl resettles itself on his shoulder and together they go to investigate the tent.

Inside the tent is a table set with a modest feast.

A bowl stacked with fruit: apples and grapes and figs and pomegranates. A round, crusty loaf of bread. A roasted Cornish game hen.

There are bottles of wine and bottles of mystery. Tarnished silver cups waiting to be filled. Jars of marmalade and honeycomb. A small object carefully wrapped in paper that turns out to be a dead mouse.

"I think this is for you," Zachary says but the owl has already swooped down to claim its treat. It looks up at him with the tail dangling from its beak.

On the other side of the tent is a table covered with inedible objects, neatly laid out on a gold-embroidered cloth.

A penknife. A cigarette lighter. A grappling hook. A ball of twine. A set of twin daggers. A tightly rolled wool blanket. An empty flask. A small metal lantern punched with star-shaped holes. A pair of leather gloves. A coiled length of rope. A rolled piece of parchment that looks like a map. A wooden bow and a quiver of arrows. A magnifying glass.

Some, but not all, of it will fit in his bag.

"Inventory management," Zachary mutters to himself.

In the center of the table of supplies there is a folded note. Zachary picks it up and flips it open.

when you're ready
choose a door

Zachary looks around the tent. There are no doors, only the flaps he entered through, tied open with cords.

He takes the torch from its resting place and walks out into the cavern, following the path beyond the tent.

Here the path stops abruptly at a crystalline wall.

In the wall where the path should continue there are doors.

One door is marked with a bee. Another with a key. And a sword and a crown and a heart and a feather though the doors are not in the order he has become accustomed to. The crown is at the end. The bee is in the center next to the heart.

The son of the fortune-teller stands before six doorways, not knowing which one to choose.

Zachary sighs and returns to the tent. He puts down the torch and picks up a thankfully already open bottle of wine and pours himself a cup. He has been given a place to pause before he proceeds and he is going to take it, despite its resemblance to similar virtual respites he has taken before. Nothing like too many health potions placed just before a door to signify something dangerous to come.

He considers the table filled with objects trying to decide what to take and pauses to catalogue what he already has:

One sword with scabbard.

One small owl companion currently tearing apart a silk cushion with its talons.

A chain around his neck with a compass, its needle currently spinning in circles. Two keys: his room key and the narrow key that had fallen out of *Fortunes and Fables* that he somehow never managed to ask Dorian about, and a small silver sword. Zachary moves on to examining the contents of his bag to think about someone, something, *anything* else.

There is *Sweet Sorrows,* comforting in its familiarity. A cigarette lighter. A fountain pen he doesn't remember putting in the bag at all, and a very squished gluten-free lemon poppy seed muffin wrapped in a cloth napkin.

Zachary discards the muffin on the table with the rest of the food. He pulls apart the Cornish game hen that is somehow still hot. Why didn't Mirabel stick around if she was here so recently? Maybe he has found himself in a pocket outside of time where food stays perpetually warm. He puts more of it on a silver plate and pulls a cushion closer to the fire and sits. The owl hops over and perches nearby.

Zachary looks at the choices set before him, chewing thoughtfully on the wing of a roasted hen, wondering idly if it is rude to eat a bird in the presence of another bird and then remembering a story Kat told him once about witnessing a seagull murder a pigeon and coming to the conclusion that it probably isn't.

He drinks his wine while he weighs his options and his future and his past and his story. How far he's come. The unknowable distance left to go.

Zachary takes the folded-paper star from his pocket. He turns it over in his hand, letting it dance over his fingers.

He hasn't read it.

Not yet.

The owl hoots at him.

The son of the fortune-teller tosses the paper star with his future inscribed upon it into the campfire.

The flames consume it, charring and curling the paper until it is no longer a star, the words it once contained lost and gone forever.

Zachary stands and picks up the rolled parchment from the inventory table. It is a map, a roughly drawn one containing a circle of trees and two squares that might be buildings. A path is marked moving from the building to a spot in the surrounding forest. It doesn't seem helpful.

Zachary puts it back and instead takes the penknife, the cigarette lighter to have a spare, the rope, and the gloves and puts them in his bag. After considering the rest of the objects he takes the twine as well.

"Are you ready?" he asks his owl.

The owl responds by flying out past the campfire and into the shadows.

Zachary takes the torch and follows it to the wall of doors.

The doors are large and carved from a darker stone than the crystal surrounding them. The symbols on them are painted in gold.

There are so many doors.

Zachary is sick of doors.

He takes his torch and explores the shadows, away from the doors and the tent, among jagged crystal and forgotten architecture. He carries the light into places long unfamiliar with illumination that accept it like a half-remembered dream.

Eventually he finds what he is looking for.

On the wall there is the faintest trace of a line. An arm's reach away there is another.

Someone has scratched the idea of a door upon the face of the cavern.

Zachary brings the torch closer. The crystal drinks in the light, enough for him to see the shape of the etched doorknob.

The son of the fortune-teller stands in front of another door drawn on another wall.

A man this far into a story has his path to follow. There were many paths, once, in a time that is past, lost many miles and pages ago. Now there is only one path for Zachary Ezra Rawlins to choose.

The path that leads to the end.

Hudson River Valley, New York, two years from now

The car looks older than it is, painted and repainted in less than professional manners, currently sky blue and wearing a number of bumper stickers (a rainbow flag, an equal sign, a fish with legs, the word *Resist*). It approaches the winding drive tentatively, unsure if it has found the right address as its GPS has been confusing its driver, unable to locate satellites and losing signals and being the target of a great many creative profanities.

The car pulls up to the house and stops. It waits, observing the white farmhouse and the barn behind it wearing a rich indigo shade rather than the more traditional red.

The driver's door opens and a young woman steps out. She wears a bright orange trench coat, too heavy for the almost summer weather. Her hair is cut pixie short and bleached a colorless shade that has not fully committed to being blond. She removes her round sunglasses and looks around, not entirely certain she has reached her destination.

The sky is car-matching blue, dotted by puffy clouds. Flowers bloom along the drive and the front walkway, splotches of yellow and pink marking the path from the car to the porch that is festooned with chimes and prisms dangling from strings, casting rainbows over the monochrome house.

The front door is open but the screen door is closed and latched. A sign hangs next to the door, a fading, hand-painted sign with stars and letters formed from steam rising in curls

from a tiny coffee cup: *Spiritual Adviser.* There is no doorbell.
The young woman knocks on the doorframe.

"Hello?" she calls. "Hello? Mrs. Rawlins? It's Kat Hawkins,
you said I could come by today?"

Kat takes a step back and looks around. It must be the right
house. There can't be many Spiritual Adviser farms. She looks
out toward the barn and spots a rabbit's tail as it hops away
through the flowers. She is wondering if she should try around
the back when the door opens.

"Hello, Miss Kitty Kat," the woman at the door says. Kat
has pictured Zachary's mother a number of times but never
properly conjured the person standing in the doorway: a small
curvy woman in overalls, her hair an inordinate amount of
tight curls tied up in a paisley scarf. Her face is wrinkled yet
young and round with large eyes lined with glittering green
eyeliner. A tattoo of a sun is partially visible on one forearm,
a triple moon on the other.

She swoops Kat into a bigger hug than she expected from
such a small person.

"It's nice to finally meet you, Mrs. Rawlins," Kat says but
Madame Love Rawlins shakes her head.

"That's Ms., and not to you, honeychild," she corrects.
"You call me Love or Madame or Momma or whatever else
you please."

"I brought cookies," Kat says, holding up a box and
Madame Love Rawlins laughs and leads her into the house.
The front hall is lined with art and photographs and Kat
pauses at a photo of a young boy with dark curls wearing a
serious expression and too-big eyeglasses. The following
rooms are painted in Technicolor and stuffed with mismatched
furniture. Crystals of every color are arranged in patterns on
tables and walls. They pass under a sign that reads *as above,
so below* and through a beaded curtain into a kitchen with
an antique stove and a sleeping borzoi who is introduced as
Horatio.

Madame Love Rawlins settles Kat at the kitchen table with

a cup of coffee and transfers the honeybee-shaped lemon cookies from their box to a floral-patterned china plate.

"Aren't you . . ." Kat stops, not certain whether the question is appropriate or not but since she's already started she might as well say it. "Aren't you worried?"

Madame Love Rawlins takes a sip of her coffee and looks at Kat over the rim of her mug. It is a pointed look, a look that means more than the words that she says after. Kat can read it. It's a warning. Apparently it's still not safe to talk about, not really. Kat wonders if anyone told Madame Love Rawlins that it was all over and if it sounded like a lie when she heard it, too.

"Whatever happens will happen whether I worry about it or not," Madame Love Rawlins says once she puts her mug down again. "It will happen whether or not you worry about it, too."

Kat does worry, though. Of course she worries. She wears her worry like a coat she never takes off. She worries about Zachary and she worries about other things that clearly cannot be discussed even here, tucked away in the hills amongst the trees surrounded by protection spells and crystals and an inattentive guard dog. Kat picks up a honeybee cookie from the plate and looks at it, wondering if Madame Love Rawlins knows about the bees as she chews on a honey-lemon wing. Then she tells her something she has not yet admitted to anyone.

"I wrote a game for him," Kat says. "For my thesis. You know how sometimes authors say they write a book for a single reader? It was like I wrote a game for a single player. A lot of people have played it now but I don't think anyone *gets* it, not like he would." She takes a sip of her coffee. "I started writing it like a choose-your-own-adventure thing in a notebook, all these mini-myths and stories within stories with multiple endings. Then I turned it into a text game, so it's more complicated and has more options, that's where it is now but the company that hired me wants me to maybe develop it further, do a full-blown version of it."

Kat stops, gazing into the depths of her coffee cup and thinking about choices and movement and fate.

"You don't think he's ever going to get to play it," Madame Love Rawlins says.

Kat shrugs.

"He'll want to play it when he comes back."

"I was going to ask how you know he'll be back but then I remembered what your job is," Kat says, and Madame Love Rawlins laughs.

"I don't *know*," she says. "I feel. It's not the same. I could be wrong, but we'll have to wait and see. Last time I talked to Zachary I could tell he was going somewhere to clear his head. It's been longer than I thought it would be." She looks out the window, thoughtful, for so long Kat wonders if she's forgotten that she has company, but then she continues. "A long time ago I had my cards read by a very good reader. I didn't think much of it at first, I was young and more concerned with the immediate future than the long-term, but as time went on I realized she was spot-on. Everything she told me that day has come to pass except one thing, and I have no reason to believe there would be one thing she was wrong about when she was right about everything else."

"What was the thing?" Kat asks.

"She said I'd have two sons. I had Zachary and for years afterward I thought maybe she was just bad at math, or maybe he was twins for a moment before he was born and then not, but then I figured it out and I should have figured it out sooner. I know he'll be back because I haven't met my son-in-law yet."

Kat grins. The sentiment makes her happy, so matter-of-fact and simple, so accepting when everything with her own parents is a constant struggle. But she's not sure she believes it. It would be nice to believe.

Madame Love Rawlins asks about her plans and Kat tells her about the job she's accepted in Canada, how she's going to drive to Toronto to visit friends for a few days before continuing on. The friends are a fiction invented to sound less like the truth of exploring an unfamiliar city solo but Madame Love Rawlins withholds comment. Kat mentions virtual reality and once she

gets to the subject of scent Madame Love Rawlins brings out her
collection of hand-blended perfume oils and they sniff bottles
while discussing memory and aromatherapy.

They unload Zachary's belongings from the sky-blue car
together, taking several trips up to one of the spare bedrooms.

Alone in the room after the last trip, Kat takes a folded
striped scarf from her bag. In the time since she knit this
particular scarf her feelings have changed regarding the sorting
of personalities into overly simplified, color-coded house
categories but she is still fond of stripes. Next to the scarf she
leaves a key-chain flash drive with <3 *k*. written on it in metallic-
silver Sharpie.

Kat takes a bright teal notebook from her bag. She puts it
down on the desk but then picks it up again. She looks back
toward the stairs, listening to Madame Love Rawlins move from
room to room, the rain-like sound of the beaded curtain.

Kat puts the notebook back in her bag. She is not ready to
part with it. Not yet.

Downstairs on the porch Madame Love Rawlins gives Kat a
vial of citrusy oil (for mental clarity) and another hug.

Kat turns to leave but Madame Love Rawlins takes Kat's face
in her hands and looks her in the eyes.

"Be brave," she says. "Be bold. Be loud. Never change for
anyone but yourself. Any soul worth their star-stuff will take the
whole package as is and however it grows. Don't waste your time
on anyone who doesn't believe you when you tell them how you
feel. On that Tuesday in September when you think you have
no one to talk to you call me, okay? I'll be waiting by the phone.
And drive the speed limit around Buffalo."

Kat nods and Madame Love Rawlins stands on tiptoe to
kiss her on her forehead and Kat tries very hard not to cry
and succeeds until she is informed that she is welcome for
Thanksgiving or Canadian Thanksgiving and whatever her
winter holidays of choice are because there is always, always a
winter solstice party.

"You think you don't have a house to go home to but you do
now, understand?"

Kat can't stop the few tears that manage to escape but she coughs and inhales the bright spring air and nods wordlessly and she feels different than she did when she arrived. For a moment as she walks back to her car Kat believes, truly believes that this woman sees more than most, sees far and sees deep and if she believes Zachary is alive then Kat believes that, too.

Kat puts her sunglasses on and starts the car.

Madame Love Rawlins waves from the front porch as the car drives away. She goes back inside, kissing her fingertips and pressing them against the photo of the curly-haired boy before returning to the kitchen to pour herself another cup of coffee. The borzoi yawns.

The sky-blue car heads out the winding drive and into its future.

BOOK VI

THE

SECRET DIARY

OF

KATRINA

HAWKINS

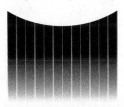

excerpt from the Secret Diary of Katrina Hawkins

Okay, we're going to do this longhand because I don't trust the Internet anymore.

Not that I ever trusted the Internet.

But this has gotten weird.

Not that it wasn't weird before.

But whatever.

I'm going to put all the stuff I've learned so far in here so I don't lose it again. I took my notes off my laptop, I deleted the files but I'll transcribe them here before I shred the printed copies.

They wiped my phone somehow, so those notes are lost and gone and probably partially forgotten. I'll try to re-create what I remember here, in as close to chronological order as I can.

I got a burner phone for emergencies.

I want to keep as much as I can all in one portable place that I can have with me at all times.

Just you and me now, notebook.

I hope I can read my handwriting later.

I hope wherever this all leads it's worth it.

Whenever that happens.

Funny thing: When grown-ass people up and vanish and there's no obvious evidence of foul play no one goes all full-blown detective step-retracing or anything.

So I did.

Partially because I was annoyed at how "people disappear all the time" it got and partially because I think I saw Z more than anyone those last few days.

The police wanted to know why Z was in NYC and I knew it was that costume party (I told the police that, they said they'd look into it but I don't know if they did, they looked at me like I was making things up when I said Z borrowed my mask) but it all seemed last-minute and unplanned so I tried to do some extra step-retracing from the couple of days before.

He seemed . . . I don't know. Like himself but more extreme. Like he was more and less there. I keep thinking of that conversation we had out in the snow when I asked him to co-teach and how it felt . . . something. He was distracted by something and I meant to ask him what but then when we went out after that Lexi was there the whole time and I know he doesn't know L well enough for that sort of convo and then he was gone.

The police don't like "he seemed distracted" when you don't know what it was that was distracting.

It sounds so empty. Isn't everyone distracted, like, all the time?

They also didn't like that my answer to "What were you texting him about?" was "The Harry Potter scarf I knit for him."

"Aren't you a little old for that?" one of them asked me in that *you are far too old for that you entitled millennial overgrown child* tone.

I shrugged.

I hate that I shrugged.

"How well do you know him?" they asked me, over lukewarm police-station tea in an environmentally unfriendly disposable cup with the teabag in it, trying to be more than leaf-flavored water and failing.

How well does anyone know anyone? We had a handful of overlapping classes and all the game people know each other more or less. We hung out sometimes at bars or by the crappy coffee machine in the media building lounge. We talked about games and cocktails and books and being only children and not minding being only children even though people seemed to think we should.

I wanted to tell them that I knew Z well enough to ask him for a favor and to return it. I knew which cocktails on a bar menu he would order and how if there wasn't anything interesting he'd get a sidecar. I knew we had similar views on how games can be so much more than just shooting things, that games can be anything, including shooting things. Sometimes he would go dancing with me on Tuesday nights because we both liked it better when the clubs weren't so crowded and I knew he was a really good dancer but he had to have at least two drinks before you could get him out on the floor. I knew he read a lot of novels and he was a feminist and if I saw him around campus before 8 a.m. it was probably because he hadn't slept yet. I knew I felt like we were right at that place where you go from being regular friends to help-you-move-dead-bodies friends but we weren't quite there yet, like we needed to do one more side quest together and earn a few more mutual approval points and then it would be something a little more comfortable, but we hadn't figured out our friendship dynamic entirely.

"We were friends," I told them and it sounded wrong and right.

They asked me if he was seeing anyone and I said I didn't think so and then they seemed like they didn't believe me about the friends thing anymore, because a friend would know. I almost told them I knew he had a lousy breakup with that MIT guy (he had a noun name, Bell or Bay or something) but I didn't, because it was ages ago and I'm pretty sure it was mostly because of long-distance issues and it didn't seem super relevant.

They asked if I thought he would have done something—like jumped-off-a-bridge something—and I said I didn't think so, but I also think most of us are two steps away from jumping off something most of the time and you never know if the next day is going to push you in one direction or another.

They asked me for my number but they never called.

I called and left messages a couple of times to see if they'd found out anything.

No one ever called me back.

THE SON OF THE FORTUNE-TELLER stands in a snow-covered field. More snow is lightly falling around him, clinging to his eyeglasses and hair. Surrounding the field there are trees, holding a dusting of flakes in their branches. The night sky is clouded but softly glowing as it hides the stars and the moon.

Zachary turns and there is a door behind him, a rectangle standing freely in the middle of the field, opening into a crystal cavern. Firelight flickers far beyond it, reaching out toward the snow, but the torch that was in Zachary's hand a moment ago has vanished along with his owl.

The air in his lungs is crisp and bright and difficult to breathe.

Everything feels too much. Too wide and too open. Too cold and too strange.

In the distance there is a light and as Zachary walks toward it through the lightly falling snow it becomes many small lights strung along the facade of a very familiar building. A plume of smoke curls up from the chimney, winding its way through the snow and toward the stars.

He was just here. Was it only weeks ago? Maybe. Maybe not. It looks the same, year after year.

Zachary Ezra Rawlins walks past the indigo barn that looks black in the light and up the snow-covered stairs of his mother's farmhouse. He stands on the back porch, cold and confused. There is a sword strapped to his back in an ancient leather scabbard. He is wearing an antique coat that has been lost in time and found again.

He can't believe Mirabel sent him home.

But he's here. He can feel the snow on his skin, the worn boards beneath his feet. There are twinkling lights strung around the railing and hung from the eaves. The porch is strewn with holly branches wrapped in silver ribbons and bowls left out for the faeries.

Beneath the scent of the snow there is the fire burning in the fireplace and cinnamon from the cookies that have likely just emerged from the oven.

The lights are on inside. The house is filled with people. Laughter. The clinking of glasses. Music that is unmistakably Vince Guaraldi.

The windows are frosted over. The party is a haze of light and color broken into rectangles.

Zachary looks out over the barn and the gardens. Cars are parked all along the driveway, some he recognizes and others he doesn't.

At the edge of the woods beyond the barn there is a stag, staring at him through the snow.

"There you are," a voice says behind him and Zachary goes warm and cold at the same time. "I've been looking for you."

The stag disappears into the woods. Zachary turns toward the voice.

Dorian stands behind him on the porch. His hair has been cut shorter. He looks less tired. He's wearing a sweater patterned with reindeer and snowflakes that manages to be both ironically festive and incredibly flattering. On his feet are striped wool socks and no shoes.

There is a glass of scotch with star-shaped ice cubes in his hand.

"What happened to your sweater?" Dorian asks him. "I thought keeping them on even after the winner of the ugly sweater contest was crowned was a rule?"

Zachary stares at him mutely. His brain cannot comprehend the appearance of this familiar person in this very separate, equally familiar context.

"Are you feeling all right?" Dorian asks.

"How are you here?" Zachary asks when he finds his voice.

"I was invited," Dorian answers. "The invitation has arrived addressed to both of us for several years now, you know that."

Zachary looks back toward the door in the field and he cannot see it through the snow. It seems as though it was never there. As if all of it was a dream. An adventure he imagined for himself.

He wonders if he's dreaming now but he doesn't remember falling asleep.

"Where did we meet?" Zachary asks the man standing beside him. Dorian looks askance at the question but after a short pause he indulges him.

"In Manhattan. At a party at the Algonquin Hotel. We took a walk in the snow afterward and ended up at one of those dimly lit speakeasy-style bars where we talked until dawn and then I walked you back to your hotel like a gentleman. Is this a test?"

"When was that?"

"Almost four years ago. Do you want to go back? We can do an anniversary thing if you'd like."

"What . . . what do you do for a living?"

Dorian's expression turns briefly from skeptical to concerned but then he replies, "Last time I checked I was a book editor, though now I'm regretting admitting that because if you'd forgotten I might have been able to trick you into finally showing me the project you've been toying with that you're not sure if it's a book or a game, the one with the pirate. Have I passed the test yet? It's cold out here."

"This can't be real." Zachary reaches for the porch rail, too afraid to touch the person beside him. The rail is solid beneath his fingers, the snow melting against his skin, gently numbing.

Everything here feels gently numbing.

"Did you drink too much of that punch Kat made? She did hang a warning sign on it, that's why I stuck to this." Dorian lifts the glass in his hand.

"What happened to Mirabel?" Zachary asks.

"Who's Mirabel?" Dorian takes a sip of his scotch.

"I don't know," Zachary says and it's true. He doesn't know. Not entirely. Maybe he made her up. Conjured her from myth and hair dye. She would be here if she were real, his mom would like her.

The concern returns to Dorian's face, mostly in the eyebrows.

"Are you having another episode?" he asks.

"Am I *what*?"

Dorian looks down into his glass and takes a too-long pause before he says anything. When he does every word is calm, his tone even and well-practiced.

"In the past you've had some difficulty separating fantasy from reality," he says. "Sometimes you have episodes where you don't remember things, or you remember other things that never happened. You haven't had one in a while. I'd thought your new meds were helping but maybe—"

"I don't have episodes," Zachary protests but he can barely get the statement out. It's getting harder to breathe, every breath is confusion and ice. His hands are shaking.

"It's always worse in the winter," Dorian says. "We'll get through it."

"I—" Zachary starts but cannot finish. He cannot steady himself. The ground no longer feels solid beneath his feet. He is having some difficulty separating reality from fantasy. "I don't—"

"Come back inside, love." Dorian leans in to kiss him. The gesture is casual, comfortable. As though he has done this a thousand times before.

"This is a story," Zachary whispers against Dorian's lips before they reach his own. "This is a story that I'm telling myself."

He raises a still-trembling hand to Dorian's lips and pushes him gently away. He feels real. Real and solid and comfortable and familiar. This would be easier if he didn't feel so real.

The chatter and the music from the house fade, as though someone or something has turned down the background volume.

"Are you wearing pajamas?" the idea of Dorian asks.

Zachary looks up at the sky again. The clouds have parted. The snow has stopped.

The moon looks down at him.

"You're not supposed to be here right now," Zachary calls up to the moon. "I'm not supposed to be here right now," he says to himself.

Zachary turns back to this idea of Dorian dressed up as his date to his mother's annual winter solstice extravaganza that delights him almost as much as it scares him and says, "I'm afraid I must be going."

"What are you talking about?" Dorian asks.

"I'd like to be here," Zachary says, and he means it. "Or maybe in a different version of here. And I think I might be in love with you but this isn't actually happening right now so I have to leave."

Zachary turns and walks back the way he came.

"*Might* be?" Dorian calls after him.

Zachary resists the urge to look back. That's not really Dorian, he reminds himself.

He keeps walking, even though part of him wants to stay. He continues through the moonlit snow, moving away from the house even though it feels like moving backward. Maybe it was a test. Go backward to go forward.

He walks toward the door in the field but as he gets closer he can see there is no door. Not anymore.

There is only snow. Drifts of it that continue into the woods.

Zachary remembers the map he opted not to include in his inventory. Two buildings surrounded by woods. But he cannot see the farmhouse anymore, he only knows the direction it should be in, if it is there at all. He tries to remember which way the arrow pointed on the map, which part of the woods it indicated, or even where the stag had been, but he cannot and he decides he doesn't care.

If this is a story he is telling himself, he can tell himself to go forward.

Away from here.

He looks up into a star-filled sky. The moon stares down at him.

Zachary stares back.

"We're not supposed to be here," Zachary yells up at the moon again.

The moon says nothing.

She only watches.

Waiting to see what happens next.

excerpt from the Secret Diary of Katrina Hawkins

I gave the IT department a sob story about my missing friend and nonexistent e-mail I "accidentally" deleted and I had to resort to actual tears but they checked Z's university e-mail for me, since the police didn't bother. Nothing after the day he disappeared but, like, nothing before that either. Nothing in January at all, which is super weird. I was positive I played e-mail tag with him over something or other the first week and I forwarded him my J-term class schedule so he'd have it.

I checked my own e-mail and there's nothing from Z at all, not for months, and I *know* there should be.

I checked his room. I waited until no one was on his floor. His lock was easy to pick, all the interior locks on campus are crap.

His laptop was there and I booted it up but someone had reset it to factory default settings. It wasn't even password-protected. His files are gone, his games are gone, that excellent *Blade Runner* wallpaper he had, poof. Standard-issue hi-def naturescape.

That doesn't seem normal.

I looked for library books but didn't find any, maybe he took them to NY. He always had a pile of library books.

The one weird-ish thing I found was a little piece of paper under the bed. It was under a sock so it was easy to miss (Z must have done his laundry like every other day, even the floor clothes were clean) but it matched the notepad on the desk.

It was covered in random scribbles, like he was taking notes while doing something else. Most of it is illegible but there's a drawing in the middle. Well, three drawings.

A bee, a key, and a sword.

In a line down the middle.

They're in a rectangle that looks like it might be a door or it might be a rectangle, Z's not the greatest artist. The bee looks more like a fly but it has stripes so I'm guessing it's supposed to be a bee.

It seemed like it might be important so I pocketed it.

Then I stole his PS4.

Bet they weren't smart enough to wipe that.

Z was apparently not clever enough to leave clues hidden in game saves on his PS4. Or he didn't have the time or forethought or what-not but still. Disappointed detective face.

Nothing on PSN or anything.

Maybe he had his own secret notebook somewhere. He probably has it if he did.

I feel like fictional mysteries have more clues than this. Or, like, clues that actually lead to more clues. I wanted a trail and what I have is miscellaneous weird stuff that is not trail-shaped.

I don't know what I was expecting to find, maybe someone he'd messaged and told about his plans or something. If he had a plan. Maybe he didn't.

I found the charity that threw the party that Z went to—I'm working on the assumption that he *did* go to the party, I know he checked into the hotel because the police checked on that, so they're not completely useless—but this charity is weird.

They give/raise tons of money for all these literary things and a lot of them sound cool but when I tried to trace them to a source or even a person—a CEO or anything—it loops around again, one charity is part of another and that's listed as a subsidiary of one of the others but they're Möbius strip charities that never end on a person. It sounds like a money-laundering front but I called a few places and they all confirmed receiving donations but couldn't give me any other info.

So I kept digging. I found a bunch of addresses and tried a few phone numbers. One left me in recorded-message purgatory and another was disconnected.

The closest address that was buried in a subpage of a subpage on one of the websites (one of the ones that wasn't search-engineable, BTW, so buried that it seemed like it wasn't supposed to be findable) was in Manhattan.

I looked it up.

It burned down like, two days after that party.

That can't be a coincidence.

I'm in Manhattan.

I took pictures of that building, it's all blocked off. The shell of the building looks okay except the windows are toast and there's a lot of smoke damage. It's kind of a shame, it's a pretty building.

It has a sign that says Collector's Club. A lady came out of one of the buildings across the street to walk her dog and I asked about it, she said it was an electrical fire and complained about electrical systems in old buildings while her pug (Balthazar) investigated my boots. I asked what kind of club it was and she said she thought it was one of those private-member clubs but wasn't sure what type. Said she saw people going in and out but not very often. Said they got a lot of deliveries, but then seemed like she thought she shouldn't have said that which makes sense because it is a spying-on-the-neighbors-out-the-window thing to say. Either that or she decided I was weird for asking so many (two!) questions about a burned building but she and her pug took off. Maybe she thought I was an arsonist in training.

I looked up "Collector's Club" but it's too generic to be helpful. There's a club for stamp collectors with the same name that's only a few blocks away. Nothing online connects that name with that address, not that I can tell.

I scoped out the alley behind the building and all its access points and managed to walk through it without looking lost. I kept my hood up and kept walking because there were cameras back there but I got a good long glance at the back of the building. It wasn't as deep as the rest on the block, with a fence and a snow-piled garden that looked pristine even though the back of the building had the same broken windows and the back doors were boarded up.

The gate was a fancy iron thing and where the two gate halves came together in the middle of all the decorative swirls was a sword.

I don't think that's a coincidence, either.

I'm not sure I believe in coincidences anymore.

I took a long walk afterward. I meandered down from midtown and ended up at the Strand. I weirdly kept thinking that I'd run into Z there. Like he'd lost track of time browsing through the stacks and hadn't realized how many days had gone by already.

I was in that musty-smelling basement level for a long time and I kept feeling like someone was watching me, or that something was close by that I was missing. This is dumb but I felt like the right book was there, somewhere, and if I closed my eyes and reached out to a shelf it would be there, right beneath my fingers.

I tried it a couple of times but it didn't work.

All the books were just books.

I went to Lantern's Keep and after being a cocktail geek at my waiter (he asked if I was a bartender so I had to admit I just drink a lot) I used the not-my-hotel WiFi to do a dark net deep-dive and found this conspiracy-theory site that actually had some level-headed people on it (they debunked most of the stuff people posted about on their message board within, like, twenty minutes).

I registered with a fake e-mail and joined and posted this:

Looking for info:
Bee
Key
Sword

I forgot to screen cap, bad me. But I got three replies within ten minutes, one calling me a troll, one that was just seven question marks, and the third was a shrug emoji.

Five minutes later the post was removed and I had two messages in my board inbox.

The first was from one of the admins and just said "Don't."

I replied and said it wasn't spam, just a question.

The admin replied again and said: "I know. Don't. You don't want to get into that."

The second message, from an account with no posts and an alphanumeric nonsense username was this:

Crown
Heart
Feather

The Owl King is coming.

THE SON OF THE FORTUNE-TELLER walks through the snow, talking to the moon.

He asks her to show him which way to go or to give him a sign or to let him know, somehow, that everything will be fine even if it is a lie but the moon says nothing and Zachary trudges on, the snow clinging to the legs of his pajamas and falling into his shoes.

He complains that she should be doing something instead of just glowing there and then apologizes, for who is he to question the actions or inactions of the moon?

The woods do not seem to be getting any closer no matter how far he walks. He should have reached them by now.

Zachary knows, despite the presence of the stars and the moon, that he is still far below the surface of the earth. He can feel the heaviness looming above him.

After what seems like a very long time with no progress he pauses to sort through his bag for anything that might be useful. His fingers close around a book and he stops searching.

He takes out *Sweet Sorrows*. He doesn't open it, he only holds it for a moment and then places it in the pocket of his coat, to keep it closer.

The bag free of all of its books suddenly feels heavy. The remainder of its contents seem unnecessary.

None of these objects are going to help him. Not here.

Zachary drops the bag on the ground, abandoning it to the snow.

He loops his fingers through the chains around his neck, with their key and sword and a compass currently incapable of pointing him in any direction.

He holds on to them as he continues walking. Lighter now with only his book and his sword to carry.

He wishes Dorian were actually here. He wishes it almost more than he wishes he knew what to do next.

"If Dorian is down here somewhere I want to see him," Zachary says to the moon. "Right now."

The moon does not reply.

(She has not replied to any of his requests.)

As Zachary walks his thoughts keep returning to the place he left behind and the imaginary party within it and the way it felt to see this story he has found himself in seep into his normal life and fill the empty spaces.

There are footsteps approaching. Someone running, the sound muffled by the snow. Zachary freezes. A hand grabs his arm.

Zachary rounds on the person behind him, pulling the sword from the scabbard to keep this new delusion at bay.

"Zachary, it's me," Dorian says, holding his hands up defensively. He looks just as Zachary remembers, from the longer hair to the star-buttoned coat, except moonlit and covered in snow.

"Where does the moon go when she's not in the sky?" Zachary asks without lowering the sword and he knows from the smile that he gets in response that this is not a fantasy, this is the real person. Here but not here. Standing with him in the moonlit snow and also somewhere else but actually Dorian. He knows it down to his nearly frozen toes.

"An inn that once rested at one crossroads that is now down here with the rest of whatever this is," Dorian says, waving a hand around at the snow and the stars. "I'm there now. I think I might be asleep. I was looking out the window at the snow thinking about you and then I saw you and then I was out here. I don't recall leaving the building."

Zachary lowers the sword.

"I thought I'd lost you," he says.

Dorian takes his arm again, pulling him closer, leaning his forehead against Zachary's. He feels warm yet cold and real yet not real, all at once.

This person is a place Zachary could lose himself in, and never wish to be found.

It starts to snow again.

"You're down here too now, aren't you?" Dorian asks. "The world beneath the world beneath the world?"

"I took the elevator with Max—Mirabel, I mean—after you fell. I'm farther down than that now, somewhere past a lost city of honey and bone. I went through a door. I should stop doing that. I lost my owl."

"Do you think you could find the inn from where you are?"

"I don't know," Zachary says. "I must be getting close to the Starless Sea. You and I might not even be in the same time anymore. If . . . if anything happens—"

"Don't you dare," Dorian interrupts him. "Don't you dare make this goodbye. I am going to find you. We are going to find each other and we are going to figure this out together. You may be by yourself but you are not alone."

"*It's dangerous to go alone,*" Zachary says, almost automatically and at least partly to stop the tears that are stinging his eyes along with the snow. He replaces the sword in its scabbard and removes it from his back. "Take this," he says, offering the sword to Dorian. It feels like the thing to do. Dorian probably knows how to use it.

Dorian accepts the sword and starts to say something else but then he vanishes, quicker than a blink. He is there and then he is not. There aren't even footprints left in the snow. No indication that he was ever there.

Except the sword is gone. Along with the moon who has vanished behind the clouds.

The snow is lighter now, the flakes almost floating. Snow-globe snow.

Zachary reaches out just to be certain there is nothing to touch. The snow wraps around his outstretched hand and slips under the cuff of his inherited coat.

Dorian was here, he thinks to himself in an affirmation. *He's down here somewhere and he's alive and I am not alone.*

Zachary takes a deep breath. The air is not so cold anymore.

There is a soft noise nearby. Zachary turns and here is the stag, staring at him. Close enough to see its breath clouding in the air.

The stag's antlers are gold and covered with candles, twisting and burning like a crown of flame and wax.

Zachary stares at the stag and the stag stares back, its eyes like dark glass.

For a moment neither of them moves.

Then the stag turns and walks toward the trees.

Zachary follows.

They reach the edge of the woods sooner than he expects. Moon-light or starlight or imaginary artificial light filters in through the trees though most of the space stays in shadow. The snow looks more blue than white and the trees themselves are gold. Zachary pauses to inspect the trunk of one more closely and finds its bark covered in delicate gold leaf.

Zachary follows the stag through the trees as closely as he can though sometimes it is no more than a light guiding him onward. He loses sight of the field quickly, consumed by this gilded forest that is both deep and dark.

The trees grow larger and taller. The ground feels uneven and Zach-ary brushes the snow away with his shoe to find it is not earth but keys, piles of them shifting beneath his feet.

The stag guides Zachary to a clearing. The trees here part, reveal-ing a stretch of star-filled sky above. The moon is gone and when Zachary returns his attention to the ground the stag has abandoned him as well.

The trees surrounding the clearing are draped with ribbons. Black and white and gold, wound around branches and trunks and tangled in the snow.

The ribbons are strung with keys.

Small keys and long keys and large heavy keys. Ornate keys and plain keys and broken keys. They rest in piles in boughs and swing freely from branches, their ribbons crossing and tangling, binding them to one another.

In the center of the clearing is a figure seated in a chair, facing away from him. Looking off into the woods. It is difficult to see in the light but Zachary catches the barest hint of pink.

"Max," Zachary calls but she does not turn. He moves toward her but the snow slows his progress, allowing only single steps at a time. It seems like an eternity before he reaches her.

"*Max*," he calls again but still the figure in the chair does not turn. She does not even move as he gets closer. The hope he had not realized he was clinging to so tightly dissolves beneath his fingers along with her shoulder as he reaches to touch her.

The figure in the chair is carved from snow and ice.

As her gown cascades around the chair the ripples in the fabric become waves, and within the waves there are ships and sailors and sea monsters and then the sea within her gown is lost in the drifting snow.

Her face is empty and icy but it is not merely a resemblance like the statues from before, this is as precise a likeness as could be captured in frozen water, as though it has been molded from the flesh-and-blood version. It is Mirabel down to its snow-flecked eyelashes, perfect save for the now broken shoulder.

Within her chest there is a light. It glows red underneath the snow, creating the soft illusion of pink that he had seen from afar.

Her hands rest in her lap. He expects them to be held out and waiting for a book like the statue of the Queen of the Bees but instead they hold a length of torn ribbon, like the ribbons in the trees, only if this one once had a key strung on it the key has been removed.

Zachary can see now that she is not looking out into the trees. She is looking at the other chair in front of her.

This chair is empty.

It is as though she has been here, always, waiting for him.

The keys hanging from the trees sway and clatter against one another, chiming like bells.

Zachary sits down in the chair.

He looks at the figure facing him.

He listens to the keys as they dance on their ribbons, striking against one another around them.

He closes his eyes.

He takes a deep breath. The air is cool and crisp and star-bright.

Zachary opens his eyes again and looks at the figure of Mirabel in front of him. Frozen and waiting, her gown weighed down by old tales and former lifetimes.

He can almost hear her voice.

Tell me a story, she says.

It is what she has been waiting for.

Zachary obliges her.

DORIAN WAKES IN an unfamiliar room. He can still feel the snow against his skin and the sword in his hand but no snow could survive here in this warmth and his fingers are clutched around the blankets piled on the bed and nothing more.

Outside the inn the wind howls, confused by this turn of events.

(The wind does not like to be confused. Confusion ruins its sense of direction and direction is everything to the wind.)

Dorian pulls on his boots and his coat and abandons the comfort of his room. As he fastens the star-shaped buttons the carved bone against his fingertips feels no more or less real than the sword had felt in his hand moments before, or the memory of Zachary's chilled skin against his.

The lanterns in the main hall have been dimmed but the fire still burns in the expansive stone fireplace. Candles increase the spread of the light over the tables and chairs.

"Did the wind wake you?" the innkeeper asks, rising from one of the chairs by the fire, an open book in his hand. "I can get you something to help you sleep if you'd like."

"No, thank you," Dorian says, staring at this man who has been plucked from his head, in a hall he has longed to visit a thousand times. If Dorian could conjure a place to forget where he had come from or where he was going it would be this.

"I have to leave," he says to the innkeeper.

Dorian goes to the door of the inn and opens it. He expects the snow and the forest but he looks instead at a shadowed, snowless cavern. In the distance there is a shape like a mountain that could be a castle. It is very, very far away.

"Close it," the innkeeper says behind him. "Please."

Dorian hesitates but then he closes the door.

"The inn can only send you where you are meant to go," the inn-keeper tells him. "But *that,*" he points at the door, "is a depth where only the owls dare to fly, waiting for their king. You cannot go there unprepared."

He crosses back to the fire and Dorian follows him.

"What do I need?" Dorian asks.

Before the innkeeper can answer the door opens, its hinges flung wide. The wind enters first, bringing a gust of snow along with it, and after the snow comes a traveler wearing a long hooded cloak the color of the night sky embroidered with constellations in silver thread. Even after the traveler pulls back her hood snowflakes continue to cling to her dark hair and remain sparkling over her skin.

The door slams itself shut behind her.

The moon goes directly to Dorian, taking a long parcel wrapped in midnight-blue silk from her cloak as she approaches.

"This is yours," she says as she hands it to him, forgoing the unnec-essary introductions. "Are you ready? There is not much time."

Dorian knows what the parcel contains before he unwraps the silk, the weight of it familiar in his hand though he has held it only once before in a dream.

(If the sword could sigh with relief as it is taken from its scabbard it would, for it has been lost and found so many times before and it knows this time will be the last.)

"We cannot send him out there," the innkeeper says to his wife. "It's . . ." He cannot bring himself to articulate what it is and danger beyond articulation is worse than anything Dorian can imagine.

"It is where he wishes to go," the moon insists.

"I'll find Zachary there, won't I?" Dorian asks.

The moon nods.

"Then that is where I'm going."

(There is a pause here, filled only by the wind and the crackling of the fire and the hum of the story impatient to continue, purring like a cat.)

"I'll get his bag," the innkeeper says, leaving Dorian alone with the moon.

"This inn is a tethered space," she tells him. "It remains the same no matter how the tides change. Once you leave here you will be untethered again and you will not be able to trust anything you encounter. There are things in the shadows, whether they were god or mortal or story once, they are something else now. They will tailor themselves to suit you so they might pull you from your path."

"To suit me?"

"To frighten or confuse or seduce. They will use your thoughts to ensnare you. We exist at the edges here, of what you might call story or myth. It can be difficult to navigate. Hold tightly to what you believe."

"What if I don't know what I believe?" Dorian asks.

The moon looks at him with night-dark eyes and for a moment it seems as though she might give him something, perhaps a warning or a wish, but instead she takes Dorian's hand in hers and lifts it to her lips and then she lets him go. The gesture is simple and profound and within it he finds the answer to his question.

The innkeeper returns with Dorian's bag. It is heavier now, Dorian can feel the weight of the heart-filled box that has been placed inside. He should probably return the heart to Fate but he decides to concern himself with finishing one story at time.

Dorian opens the door of the inn, revealing the same dark vista as before. It looks more like a castle than a mountain now. There might even be a light in one of the windows, but it is too far away to be certain.

"May the gods bless and keep you," the innkeeper says. He places the lightest of kisses on Dorian's lips.

Armed with a sword and a heart, Dorian steps into the unknown and leaves the inn behind.

The wind howls after him as he leaves in fear of what is to come, but a mortal cannot understand the wishes of the wind no matter how loud it cries and so these final warnings go unheeded.

I feel like I've heard of the Owl King before but I don't know where.

I asked Elena what she'd wanted to talk to Z about after class that night and she said he'd been in the library checking out some weird book that wasn't in the system and then he came back after to track down other books from the same donation, total library-detective mode (her words) but she didn't know why and he hadn't said. She did mention a couple of the books (including the first one) were still missing, so maybe he has them.

She gave me the name she gave him from the book donation. J. S. Keating, so I did some digging. A lot of digging.

Jocelyn Simone Keating, born 1812. Not a lot on her, no marriage records or subsequent kids or anything. Sounds like she was disowned. Other Keatings: brother, married, no kids, just a "ward" without a name recorded dead as a teen. Brother's wife died, he remarried, wife number two died and later the brother died ancient and alone I guess. There were two other Keating cousins who didn't make it out of their twenties. Then that's, like, the end of the Keatings, or at least that branch since it's a common enough name.

No death record for Jocelyn. Not that I can find.

But the books were donated in her name, like, less than thirty years ago? Elena let me dig through the library files when her supervisor was on his lunch break and I found the full record, though it wasn't digital at the time because they were still transferring and it's a low-res scan of a handwritten paper and half of it is illegible.

But there's something about a foundation and instructions for donations and how does a lady leave her library to a bunch of different universities in different countries when some of them didn't even exist when she died? I mean, seriously, even if she lived to be a hundred this school was founded, like . . . longhand math, boo . . . something like forty or fifty years after that?

Elena helped me find some of the other donated books and some of them are, like, way too modern to belong to a lady in 18whatever. There's Jazz Age stuff in there. Maybe it wasn't *her* library, maybe it was a library named after her? Or it's just the foundation and the name is a carry-over from something earlier. I can't find info about the Keating Foundation anywhere, it's like it's not a thing.

One of those books had that bee drawing in it again. Bee-key-sword in faded ink along the back cover underneath the barcode sticker.

This is all so weird. And not, like, good weird. I love a good weird.

I shut down my Twitch account because someone keeps spamming my chat with bee emotes.

I got a text on my phone from Unknown that says *Stop snooping, Miss Hawkins.*

I didn't reply.

All my texts to or from Z are gone.

THE SON OF THE FORTUNE-TELLER sits in a chair surrounded by keys in the middle of a starlit forest talking to a woman made of snow and ice.

At first he does not know what to say.

He does not think of himself as a storyteller. He never has.

He thinks of all the tales he grew up feasting on, myths and fairy tales and cartoons.

He remembers *Sweet Sorrows* and its test for keepers, the storytelling surrounded by keys and how they could tell any story but their own, but he does not have a story.

He has nothing practiced. Nothing prepared. But the request is so open-ended.

Tell me a story.

The request comes with no specifications or requirements.

So Zachary begins to speak, haltingly at first but gradually becoming more comfortable, as though he is talking to an old friend in a dimly lit bar over well-crafted cocktails instead of sitting in a snow-covered fairy-tale wood addressing a silent effigy.

He starts with an eleven-year-old boy finding a painted door in an alleyway. He describes the door in great detail, down to its painted keyhole. He tells her how the boy did not open it. How afterward he wished that he had and how at odd moments over the following years he would think about it, how the door haunted him and how it haunts him, still.

He tells her about moving from place to place to place and never feeling like he ever belonged in any of them, how wherever he was he would almost always rather be someplace else, preferably somewhere fictional.

He tells her how he worries that none of it means anything. That none of it is important. That who he is, or who he thinks he is, is just a collection of references to other people's art and he is so focused on story and meaning and structure that he wants his world to have all of it neatly laid out and it never, ever does and he fears it never will.

He tells her things he has never told anyone.

About the man who broke his heart in such a long, drawn out process that he couldn't discern hurt from love and how whenever he tries to sort out how he feels now long after the end of it the feeling is just a void.

He tells her how the university library became a touchstone for him after that, how when he felt himself falling he would go and find a new book and fall into it instead and be someone somewhere else for a while. He describes the library down to its unreliable lightbulbs and finding *Sweet Sorrows* and how that moment unexpectedly changed all the moments that followed.

He reads *Sweet Sorrows* to her, relying on memory when the starlight is not enough to illuminate the words. He tells her Dorian's fairy tales about castles and swords and owls, about lost hearts and lost keys and the moon.

He tells her how he always felt like he was searching for something, always thinking about that unopened door and how disappointed he felt once he went through another painted door and that feeling still didn't go away but how for just a moment in a gilded ballroom preserved in time it did. He found what he had been seeking, a person not a place, a particular person in this particular place, and then the moment and the place and the person were gone.

He recounts everything that followed, from the elevator crash to the voices in the darkness to finding Simon in his sanctuary attempting to record the story and out through the snow and past the phantasmagoric holiday party and into the woods with the stag until he brings his story into the clearing that they currently inhabit, describing it down to the details of the ships carved into her gown.

Then, with nothing left to tell that he has carried with him, Zachary makes things up.

He wonders aloud where one of the frozen ships in her gown is heading and as he speaks the ship moves, sailing out over the icy waves, away from Mirabel and across the snow.

The forest changes around it, the trees fading as the ship sails through them but Zachary remains in his chair and the ice version of Mirabel stays with him, listening, as he finds his way forward, slow and stumbling when the words won't come but he waits and he does not chase it, he follows the ship and the story where they wish to go.

As the ship sails the snow melts around it, waves swirling and crashing against its hull.

He pictures himself on this ship as it crosses the sea. Dorian is there and so is his lost owl companion. He adds his Persian cat for good measure.

Zachary imagines a place where the ship is going, not to take its inhabitants home but to bring them somewhere undiscovered. He sails the ship and the story to places it has not yet traveled.

Through time and fate and past the moon and the sun and the stars.

Somewhere there is a door, marked with a crown and a heart and a feather, that has not been opened.

He can see it right in front of him, shimmering in the shadows. Someone holds a key that will open it. Beyond the door there is another Harbor on the Starless Sea, alive with books and boats and waves washing against stories of what was and what will be.

Zachary follows the stories and the ship as far as he can and then he brings them back. To right here and right now. To this snow-covered moment that is once again surrounded by a forest covered in keys.

Here he stops.

The ship anchors itself back in the frozen gown with its monsters.

Zachary sits with Mirabel, together in the post-story silence.

He has no idea how much time has passed, if any time has passed at all.

After the silence he stands and walks over to his audience. He takes a small bow, leaning in toward her.

"Where does it end, Max?" he whispers in her ear.

Her head turns swiftly toward him, staring at him with blank ice eyes.

Zachary freezes, too surprised to move as she lifts her hand and reaches not for him but for the key dangling from his neck.

She takes the long thin key that was hidden in *Fortunes and Fables,* separating it from the compass and the sword and holds it on her palm. A layer of frost forms over the key.

She rises from her chair, pulling Zachary upright with the motion. Her gown crumbles, sending the ships and the sailors and the sea monsters within its tides down into their icy graves.

Then she pushes her palm and the key upon it against Zachary's chest, between the open buttons of his coat.

Her hand is so cold that it burns, pressing the white-hot metal into his skin.

With her other hand she reaches out and pulls him closer, winding her icy fingers through his hair and drawing his lips to hers.

Everything is too hot and too cold and Zachary's entire world is an imagined kiss in brightest darkness that tastes like honey and snow and flame.

There is a tightness in his chest that grows and burns and he can no longer tell where the ice ends and he begins and just when he thinks he can tolerate no more it shatters and stops.

Zachary opens his eyes and tries to catch his breath.

The ice likeness of Mirabel is gone.

The key is missing, leaving the sword and compass abandoned on the chain. The burned impression of the key is marked on Zachary's chest and will remain there always.

The rest of the keys have vanished as well, along with their trees.

Zachary is no longer in the woods.

He stands now in a snow-covered alleyway that never, if it still existed in its true form, would contain such snow.

There is a new figure carved from ice with him now. A smaller one, bespectacled and curly-haired, wearing a hooded sweatshirt and carrying a backpack, facing a brick wall that is not ice but genuine brick, most of it whitewashed and pale, blending in with the snow.

Upon the wall there is an intricately painted door.

The colors are rich, some of the pigments metallic. In the center, at the level where a peephole might be and stylized with lines that match the rest of the painted carving, there is a bee.

Beneath the bee there is a key. Beneath the key there is a sword.

Zachary reaches out to touch the door, his fingertips meeting the door between the bee and the key, and they come to rest on smooth paint covering cool brick, a slight unevenness to the surface betraying the texture below.

It is a wall. A wall with a pretty picture on it.

A picture so perfect as to fool the eye.

Zachary turns back to the ghost of his younger self but the figure is gone. The snow is gone. He is alone in an alleyway standing in front of a painted door.

The light has changed. A predawn glow chases away the stars.

Zachary reaches for the painted doorknob and his hand closes over cold metal, round and three-dimensional.

He opens the door and steps through it.

And so the son of the fortune-teller finds his way to the Starless Sea.

DORIAN NAVIGATES THE DEPTHS with Fate's heart in its box carefully wrapped and contained in a pack strapped to his back and a sword that is much more ancient than him but not nearly as ancient as the things staring at him from the shadows and all of them are still sharp.

A sword does not forget how to find its mark when it is held by a hand that knows how to use it.

Its blade and the sleeves of Dorian's star-buttoned coat are covered in blood.

There are . . . *things* that have followed him since he left the inn and more that have joined them as he walks on.

Things that want his life and his flesh and his dreams.

Things that would crawl under his skin and wear him like a coat.

They have not had a mortal come so close to tempt them in countless years.

They change their shapes around him. They use his own stories against him.

It is not what Dorian had expected, even with the moon's warnings.

It all feels too real.

One moment he is in a cavern, his gaze trained on a distant light, and the next he is walking on a city street. He can feel the sunlight on his skin and smell the exhaust from the passing cars.

He trusts nothing that he sees.

Dorian continues down a crowded city sidewalk in what would pass for midtown Manhattan if it were not looked at too closely. He dodges pedestrians with practiced skill.

Businessmen and tourists and small children turn and stare as he passes.

Dorian avoids making eye contact with anyone or anything but then he reaches a familiar landmark flanked by two large cats.

He never realized before just how big Patience and Fortitude are. The two larger-than-life-size lions track him with glossy black eyes that do not belong to them.

Dorian pauses in front of the library stairs, tightening his grip on his sword, wondering if stone lions will bleed the way everything else this place puts in his way has bled.

He braces himself, waiting for the lions to pounce, but instead something grabs him from behind, wrapping around his neck and pulling him into the street.

It slams Dorian into the side of a taxi, the screeching of horns throwing off his equilibrium, but he maintains his grip on his sword and when he recovers his balance he swings and the sword meets its target, swift and certain.

The thing that he cuts down looks first like a briefcase-wielding businessman and then like an amorphous, many limbed shadow, and then a small child, screaming, and then nothing.

The street and the taxis and the library and the lions fade along with it, leaving Dorian alone in an expansive cavern.

Above him the starless darkness is so vast that he could almost believe it is sky.

There is a castle in the distance. A light glows in the window of its highest tower. Dorian can see it and the softly glowing shore it rests above. He keeps his sights set on it, as the castle does not shift and change the way the rest of the world down here does and he uses it like a lighthouse to guide his way.

Blood that is not his own pools in his boots, seeping in through each footstep.

Beneath his feet the ground changes, shifting from stone to wood. Then it begins to tilt, swaying over waves that are not really there.

He is on a ship. Sailing over open ocean beneath a bright night sky.

Standing on the deck in front of him there is a figure in a fur coat that appears to be Allegra but he knows it is not Allegra.

They are trying to disarm him.

Dorian tightens his grip on the sword.

excerpt from the Secret Diary of Katrina Hawkins

They're watching me now. Literally right now as I'm writing this.

I'm at the Noodle Bar and while I was in line to order my ramen this random guy behind me starts chatting me up, like, asked about my "a well-read woman is a dangerous creature" t-shirt and if I've tried some other ramen place nearby and then while I was ordering he dropped something in my bag, I don't know if it's a bug or something, I'm waiting until he leaves and then I'll dump everything out and check. The guy is currently sitting on the other side of the restaurant at what's probably a "respectable" distance. He has his nose in a book, I recognize the cover but can't see the title. Some new-release front-table thing. But he's not reading. He has it opened to somewhere near the end but the dust jacket's like, too pristine for mostly finished reading and it's that type of jacket that totally gets fingerprints on it, especially if you read and eat at the same time.

I might be getting too good at this.

But he's hardly looking at the book and barely eating his noodles. He sucks at subtlety. He's watching me write. Eyeing up my journal like he's trying to figure out how he's going to snag it when I'm not looking.

I'm always looking now.

You will pry this *Adventure Time* notebook from my cold dead hands, ya ding-dong.

It kind of reminds me of that guy who was watching Z at the Gryphon that night but this guy is younger and not as silver-fox-in-training cute.

(Tried to track *that* guy down, too, awhile ago. Asked
the waitresses and the bartenders but only one waitress
remembered him—said she tried to flirt with him and he shot
her down but was nice about it—but she hadn't seen him before
or since.)

This guy has now figured out that I am not leaving before he
does. No way. I will find some back-door-through-the-kitchen
spy-movie-escape-route nonsense if he tries to out-sit me.

Later now. I won the ramen-place standoff, the guy eventually left,
super slow and reluctant like he wanted to linger over the remains of
his noodle bowl.

Never turned more than two pages of that book in over half an
hour.

I took a long looping route in the wrong direction when I left
and now I've stopped in the park to dump out my bag.

There's a tiny little button transmitter, like, watch-battery size
and kinda sticky, so it stayed on the inside of the bag even after
I dumped it and I never would have found it if I hadn't noticed
him drop it in there. I don't know if it's a GPS or a microphone
or what.

This is all really weird.

Home now.

I bought an extra chain for my door and a motion detector on
my way home.

Then I baked cinnamon sour cream cookies and mixed myself
a clover club since I had the eggs out already and started a
comfort replay of *Dark Souls* and now I feel a little better about
life and myself and existence.

Every time the screen says *You Died* I feel better.

You Died.

You Died and the world keeps going.

You Died and it wasn't so bad, was it? Have a cookie.

. . .

I just sat and cried for half an hour but I kind of feel better.

I think Z's dead. There, I said it. I wrote it down, anyway.

I think at some point I stopped looking for *him* and started looking for *why* and now the why is messing with me.

I stuck that possibly-tracking-device thing on a cat in the park.

THE SON OF THE FORTUNE-TELLER walks through a door and into a wide open cavern, far, far below the surface of the earth. Below the harbors, below the cities, below the books.

(The single book he carries is the first to be brought so deep. The stories here have never been bound in such a fashion, they are left loose and wild.)

Zachary wonders if he has been in this cavern the entire time, walking through it while he saw what looked and felt like snow and trees and starlight. If he has now traveled through his stories and come out the other side.

Something hits his ankle, soft yet insistent, and he looks down to find the familiar, squished face of his Persian cat.

"Hey," he says. "How'd you get down here?"

The cat does not reply.

"I heard you were looking for me."

The cat neither confirms nor denies this statement.

Zachary glances behind him, unsurprised to find the door he stepped through has vanished. There is a cliff where it had been, a tall cliff that might have a structure atop it, it is difficult to tell from this angle.

The cat pushes its head against Zachary's leg again, nudging him in the other direction.

This way there is stone expanse that terminates in a ridge. There is a glow beyond it.

He can hear the waves.

"Are you coming?" Zachary asks the cat.

The cat does not reply, but it also does not move. It sits and calmly licks a paw.

Zachary takes a few steps forward, moving closer to the ridge. The cat does not follow.

"You're not coming?"

The cat stares at him.

"Fine," Zachary says, though it is not what he means. "You can talk, can't you?" he asks.

"No," says the cat. It bows its head and turns, walking off into the shadows, leaving Zachary staring dumbly after it.

He watches until he can no longer see the cat, which is not long, and then he walks toward the ridge. When he is high enough to see what waits beyond it he realizes where he is.

Zachary Ezra Rawlins stands on the shore of the Starless Sea.

The sea glows, like candlelight behind amber. An ocean caught in perpetual sunset.

Zachary takes a deep breath expecting sea-salt sharpness but the air here is rich and sweet.

He walks down to the edge, watching the waves coat the rocks as they approach and retreat. Listening to the sound they make: a gentle, lulling hum.

Zachary takes off his shoes. He places them out of reach of the waves and steps into the gently rolling surf and laughs as the sea clings to his toes.

He reaches down and runs a hand over the surface of the honeyed sea. He lifts a finger to his lips and tentatively licks it. He has been given sweetness when he expected salt. He is not certain he would want to swim in this sea, even though it is delicious.

He would think it impossible had he not succumbed to believing impossible things much earlier.

What happens now? he thinks but almost immediately the question leaves his mind. It doesn't matter. Not right now. Not here in the depths where time is fragile.

For right now this is his entire world. Starless and sacred.

In front of him the Starless Sea stretches into the distance. There is the ghost of a city across the sea, empty and dark.

There is an object on the ground by his feet, where the sea touches the shore. Zachary picks it up.

A broken champagne bottle. It looks as though it has been here for years. The label has worn away. Its broken edges are jagged and sharp and dripping with honey.

Zachary looks up at the cavernous darkness. The structure looming above him almost looks like a castle.

Beyond it, Zachary can see the layers and the levels spiraling up. Shadows that are deeper than others. Spaces that curve and move outward, speckled with lights that are not stars.

He marvels for a moment at how far he has come, turning the broken bottle over in his hands and picturing the stairs and the ballroom so very high above.

He hears footsteps approaching. Appropriate, he thinks, to have found Fate again now that he's finally reached the Starless Sea. Now that *not yet* is just now.

"Hi, Max," Zachary greets her. "I found your—"

There is a strange swift motion as he turns. For a moment his vision is a shadowed blur and when it focuses, it is not Mirabel standing in front of him.

It is Dorian.

Zachary tries to say Dorian's name but he can't and Dorian stares at him in eyebrow-raised shock and Zachary can't breathe and he's never met anyone who literally took his breath away before and maybe he is actually in love but wait, he seriously can't breathe right now. He feels light-headed. The glow from the sea is fading. The broken champagne bottle falls from his fingers and shatters.

Zachary Ezra Rawlins glances down at his chest where Dorian's hand is wrapped around the hilt of the sword and just as he begins to understand what is happening everything goes black.

excerpt from the Secret Diary of Katrina Hawkins

I was at the Gryphon sitting in a booth in the back so I wasn't in anyone's line of sight drinking and reading and this older woman in a white fur coat sat herself down across from me like I'd been waiting for her. She had one blue eye and one brown eye and a crystal-clear martini in her hand with two (matching) olives in it. The glass was still frosty, she must have just picked it up at the bar.

"You're a difficult woman to locate, Miss Hawkins," she said with a fake pleasant smile that looked almost real.

"I'm not," I said. "It's not that big a city. There are, like, two bars that I go to. You probably have my class schedule, too, right? Don't really need the tracking devices."

She stopped smiling. Definitely one of *them* but now I've earned the big guns, this lady's a pro. No obvious spying from across the room this time.

She didn't say anything so I asked, "What did that used to be?"—nodding at the gigantic fur coat. She wasn't going for inconspicuous at all and I kind of admired that.

"It's faux," she said, which was disappointing. "How's the book?" She tipped her martini at my copy of *The Kick-Ass Writer.*

"It's for class," I said, which is true. The chattiness threw me off. I didn't think any of these people were actually going to talk to me, ever.

"You miss him, don't you?" She directed this remark at my drink. Sidecar. I'd ordered it because I couldn't think of anything else, I just wanted to sit somewhere that wasn't my apartment. I forgot to tell them to hold the sugar and it was making the stem of the glass sticky.

"Do you know where he is?" I asked.

She didn't say anything but she had this weird look in her eye—the brown one, I thought the blue one was a cloudy-cataract situation. I couldn't tell what the look was, I know it sounds like it should have been an *aha you DO know where he is* moment but it wasn't. She looked at me and sipped her martini and when she put it back down she said, "You must be sad about your breakup."

I haven't told anyone that Lexi and I broke up. L got all mad at me when I started trying to figure out what happened to Z and said he probably just took off and said I was just mad that he didn't tell me and then I accused her of setting up the bee-key-sword thing as one of her theatrical scavenger hunts and then she called me a "waste of her time" which seemed overly harsh and I'm not sure I am sad. I feel okay about it. I'm not sure I want to be in a relationship right now anyway. Things change. Things are changing particularly fast right now, like a week ago everything was different. It's still snowing, though. That hasn't changed.

"Not really," I said.

"But you don't have anyone anymore," the lady said. "Not *really.*"

I was pissed because she was kind of right but I wasn't about to tell her that. I have my notebook and my projects and I was sitting there alone with my drink because there was no one else I wanted to be drinking with. I don't have people. She said it in a way that kind of implied she knew my family isn't all that fond of me either.

I didn't say anything.

"You're on your own. Wouldn't you prefer to belong somewhere?"

"I belong here," I said. I didn't understand what she was getting at.

"For how long?" the lady asked. "You'll stay for a two-year graduate program because you don't know what else to do and then you'll have to leave. Wouldn't you like to be a part of something bigger than you are?"

"I'm not religious," I told her.

"It is not a religious organization," she said.

"What is it, then?"

"I'm afraid I can't tell you that. Not unless you agree to join us."

"Is this a cult or something?"

"Or something."

"I'm going to need more information," I told her, and I took a sip of my sidecar because it seemed like something to do but it made my fingers sticky. Sugar on cocktail rims is stupid. "Or is this an 'I know too much already' situation?"

"You do, but I'm not particularly concerned about that. If you were to tell anyone what you know, or what you think you know, no one would believe you."

"Because it's too weird?"

"Because you're a woman," she said. "That makes you easier to write off as crazy. *Hysterical.* If you were a man it might be an issue."

I didn't say anything. I was waiting for my more information. She stared at me for a long time. Definitely not a natural blue on the eye.

"I like you, Miss Hawkins," she said. "You're tenacious and I admire tenacity when it is not misplaced. Currently yours is misplaced but I think I might make good use of it. You're clever and determined and passionate and those are all qualities I look for. And you're a storyteller."

"What does that have to do with anything?"

"It means you have an affinity for our area of interest."

"Literary charity, right? I didn't think literary charities had this much of a secret-society vibe."

"The charitable organization is a front and you knew that," the lady said. "Do you believe in magic, Miss Hawkins?"

"In an Arthur C. Clarke sufficiently-advanced-technology-is-indistinguishable-from-magic type magic or actual magic-magic?"

"Do you believe in the mystical, the fantastical, the improbable, or the impossible? Do you believe that things others dismiss as dreams and imagination actually exist? Do you believe in fairy tales?"

I think my stomach fell into my feet because I have literally always been the kid who believes in fairy tales but I didn't know what to do because I wasn't a kid, I was a twenty-something in a cocktail bar who never feels old enough to drink so I said, "I don't know."

"You do," the lady said, sipping her martini again. "You just don't know how to admit it."

I probably made a face at her but I don't remember.

I asked what she wanted from me.

"I want you to leave this place with me and not return. You will leave your life and your name behind. You will aid me in protecting a place most people would not believe exists. You will have a purpose. And someday I will take you to that place."

"I'm not really a *someday* baby, sorry."

"Aren't you? Hiding in your academic temples avoiding the real world."

That, I thought, was a pretty low blow even if it was accurate but at that point she was pissing me off so I said, "Dude, if you have some fairy-tale place to be in why are you in the back of a bar talking to me?"

She gave me this weird look and I don't know if it was because I called her *dude* or if it was something else and she stopped and thought about that more than most of the things I'd said, but then she just took a business card out of her pocket and slid it across the table at me.

It said *Collector's Club*.

There was a phone number on it.

And a little sword at the bottom.

True confession: I was kind of tempted. I mean, how often does some old lady offer you a fairy-tale law-enforcement job like she's the wonderland police? But something felt off and I

like my name and the fact that she dodged the question about
Z rubbed me the wrong way.

"Did Zachary accept your job offer or is he the one who
burned down your clubhouse?" I asked, figuring it would be one
or the other. From the look on her face it was the latter. The fake
smile was back.

"I can tell you a great many things that you would like to know,
but first you would have to agree to my terms. There is nothing
for you here. Aren't you curious?"

I was. I was super-duper curious. I was beyond curious. I
thought about telling her I'd think about it if she let me talk to
Z or if she could prove he was alive but I didn't get the sense she
was the bargaining type. If I didn't follow her now I was never
going to see this lady again.

"I don't think so," I told her. She looked legit disappointed and
then composed herself again.

"Is there anything I can say that might change your mind?" she
asked.

"What happened to your eye?" I asked, even though I knew
whatever she said wasn't going to change anything.

The smile I got for that question was real.

"Once upon a time I sacrificed an eye in exchange for the
ability to see," she said. "I'm sure you know magic requires
sacrifices. For years I could see the whole story. It doesn't work
anymore, not here, because I made a decision and it left me with
hazy versions of the now. Sometimes I miss the clarity, but again,
sacrifices."

I almost believed her. I stared at her and that cloudy blue
eye stared back at me and caught the light from one of those
vintage bulbs above us and it wasn't a cataract at all, it was
a swirling stormy sky, clear as anything. A crack of lightning
flashed across it.

I downed the rest of my sidecar, grabbed my book and my bag
and my coat with my stupid, sticky hands, and stood up, and
lifted the book to my forehead, and saluted her.

I left the business card on the table.

And I got the heck out of there.

"I'm disappointed, Miss Hawkins," she said as I walked away. I didn't turn around and I couldn't quite hear what she said next but I knew what it was.

"We'll be keeping an eye on you."

THE SON OF THE FORTUNE-TELLER is dead.

His world is an impossibly quiet darkness, empty and formless.

Somewhere in the formless darkness there is a voice.

Hello, Mister Rawlins.

The voice sounds very, very far away.

Hello hello hello.

Zachary cannot feel anything, not even the ground beneath his feet. Not even his feet, for that matter. There is only nothingness and a very faraway voice and nothing else.

Then it changes.

It is like waking and not remembering falling asleep but it is not gradual, his consciousness returns suddenly and shockingly, his existence suspended in surprise.

He is back in his body. Or a version of his body. He is lying on the ground wearing pajama pants and no shoes and a coat he still thinks of as Simon's though both the coat and this death-worn version of it know they belong to the one who wears them.

On his chest is the mark of a freshly burned key but no wound, no blood.

He also has no heartbeat.

But the thing that convinces him beyond any doubt that he is truly dead is the fact that his glasses are gone and still, everything before his eyes is clear.

Zachary's ideas about any possible afterlife have always varied, from nothingness to reincarnation to self-created infinite universes, but always came back to the futility of guessing and assuming he would find out when he died.

Now he is dead and lying on a shore much like the one he died upon, only different, but he is too angry to notice the differences just yet.

He tries to recall what happened and the memory is painfully clear.

He had Dorian back. Right there in front of him. Just for a moment he'd found what he'd been seeking but then the story didn't go the way it was supposed to.

He thought he'd finally (*finally*) get that kiss and more than that and he replays those last moments over in his head wishing he'd known they were the last moments and even if he had known he doesn't know now what he would have done, if he would have had time to react.

It was definitely Dorian, there on the shore of the Starless Sea. Maybe Dorian didn't think it was him. He hadn't thought Dorian was himself at first either, back in the snow. He'd raised the same sword then but this time Dorian did, in fact, know how to use it.

It feels as though all of the pieces were put in place to lead to this moment and he put half of them there himself.

He is mad at himself for so many things he did and didn't do and how much time he wasted waiting for his life to begin and now it is over and then he has another thought and is suddenly, distinctly livid at someone else.

Zachary pulls himself to his feet and screams at Fate but Fate does not answer.

Fate does not live here.

Nothing lives here.

You're here because I need you to do something that I can't.

That's what Mirabel had said, post–elevator crash and pre–everything else.

She needed him to die.

She knew.

She knew the entire time that this would happen.

Zachary tries to scream again but he doesn't have the heart.

He sighs instead.

This isn't fair. He'd barely gotten started. He was supposed to be in the middle of his story, not at the end or in whatever post-death epilogue this is.

He hasn't even done anything. Accomplished anything. Has he? He doesn't know. He located a man lost in time or maybe he became one. He made his way to the Starless Sea. He found what he sought and he lost it again, all in a single breath.

He tries to decide if he's changed since this all started because isn't that the point and he feels different than he did but he can't weigh feeling different versus having changed from inside himself with no heartbeat, standing on a shore with no shoes.

A shore.

Zachary looks out at the sea. This is not the shore he stood on before, moments (was it moments?) before. It resembles it, including the cliffs behind him, but there are differences.

On this shore there is a boat.

A small rowboat, its oars neatly placed against its seat, half in the sea and half on the shore.

Waiting for him.

The sea surrounding it is blue. A bright, unnatural blue.

Zachary dips a toe into the blue and it flutters.

It is confetti. Paper confetti in varying shades of blue and green and purple, with white along the edges for the surf. As it stretches farther out from the shore there are streamers mixed in with it, long curls of paper pretending to be waves.

Zachary looks up at the looming structure on the cliff behind him that is undoubtedly a castle, though it is constructed from painted cardboard. He can tell from here that it is only a facade, two walls with windows lacking structure and dimension. The idea of a castle painted and propped up to fool the eye from a greater distance than this.

Beyond the castle there are stars: giant folded-paper stars hanging from strings that vanish into darkness. Shooting stars suspended mid-shoot and planets at various heights with and without rings. An entire universe.

Zachary turns and looks out over the paper water.

There is a city across the sea.

This city is aglow with twinkling lights.

The storm of emotions he has been tumbling through ceases, replaced by an unexpected calm.

Zachary looks down at the boat. He picks up an oar. It is lightweight but solid in his hand.

He pushes the boat out onto the paper sea and it stays afloat. It sends the confetti water shifting and swirling.

Zachary looks across the sea at the city again.

Apparently he isn't finished with his quest.

Not yet.

Fate isn't done with him, even in death.

Zachary Ezra Rawlins steps into the boat and starts to row.

excerpt from the Secret Diary of Katrina Hawkins

Hi notebook, it's been awhile.

Everything got sort of quiet. I didn't know what to do after the lady in the bar and I got all paranoid for ages even about writing anything down or talking about anything so I put my head down and worked and time passed and nothing happened and now it's summer.

Well, one thing did happen and I didn't write it down at the time.

Someone gave me a key. It was in my campus mailbox. It's a heavy brass key but the top of it is shaped like a feather, so it looks like a quill pen that ends in key teeth instead of a nib. It had a tag tied to it with string, like an old-fashioned package tag, and it said *For Kat when the Time comes* on it. I figured it was an invite to somebody's thesis project but nothing ever followed up on it. I still have it. I put it on my key chain (the feather loops around at the top). I left the tag on. Guess I'm still waiting for the Time to come.

I thought the bar lady would come back. Like it was the Refusal of the Call but I'm not on that kind of Hero's Journey, I guess. It felt like the right decision at the time but you know, you wonder. What might have happened next?

That's what I started working on, even though it was unplanned. I wasn't working, at all, for a while there and I didn't know what I wanted to do, I didn't know what I wanted at all so I kept thinking about what is it that I want and kept coming back to telling stories in game form. I got to thinking all of this might be a halfway decent game if it were a game. Part spy movie, part fairy tale, part choose your own adventure. Epic branching story that doesn't stick to a single genre or one set path and turns into different stories but it's all the same story. I'm trying to play with the things you can do in a game that you can't do in a book. Trying to capture more story. A book is made of paper but a story is a tree.

You meet someone in a bar. You follow them or you don't.

You open a door. Or you don't.

Either way the point is: What happens next?

It's taking an absurd amount of notebooks full of possibilities but it's getting somewhere.

What happened next in *Real Life*™ is that I found Jocelyn Keating. Sort of.

I found Simone Keating.

Months ago I'd asked my friend Preeti in London to do some library detective work on the Keating Foundation for me if she could but then I didn't hear anything so I'd figured she didn't find anything but yesterday she texted me that she found some things and do I still want them.

She probably thinks I'm nuts because I gave her a brand-new e-mail address and had her text me the second she sent everything so I could print it all immediately and then delete the e-mail. I told her to delete it after she sent it, too. Hopefully that's enough. Told you: paranoid.

Apparently back in the day there was this British library society that wasn't an "official" library society. Mostly people who weren't allowed in the standard societies. Lots of ladies, but not all.

They seem kind of badass, in a nerdy way.

It looks like it was an underground society, so there aren't a lot of records.

But some private library in London had a couple of files, someone had found them and tried to find more information to see if there was enough for an article or a book or something but nothing substantial ever came out of it.

So there's, like, no proper record that it was an official

group but there are fragments of notebooks and a couple
of photographs. Faded sepia images with people in amazing
hats and ascots and all that taken in front of these beautiful
bookshelves, the kind in cages where everything looks precious
and fancy and possibly-disguising-secret-passages-y.

The notebook pieces aren't all that legible, and I'm reading,
like, printouts of scans, but this is what I can make out:

> *. . . catalogued doors in three additional cities. A. has not yet reported
> back from Edo. Awaiting response. Missed contact with . . .*
>
> *. . . suspects we are between incarnations. We exercise patience as our
> predecessors have before us and as we fear many of our successors will
> continue to. We shall do what we can to progress what has been put in
> motion.*
>
> *. . . spent more time below. The room is complete and believed to be
> functional. All now rests on faith. There has been discussion of scattering
> the archives for safety, J. has moved many of the papers to the cottage . . .*

That's it. The rest is too faded to read or just partial numbers.
I don't know what it means. This would be easier if secret
societies weren't so secretive. There's something else that's
all fragments about six doors and a place in some other place
existing "out of time" and "the final incarnation" and I don't
know, it's a little Gozer worshippy.

Then there are the photographs.

One photo has a blond lady sitting at a desk, not looking at
the camera. Head down, hair swept up, reading a book. She's
wearing a necklace that might be heart-shaped, I can't tell. Can't
tell how old she is, either.

The back says *Simone K.* There's a date but it's so faded I can
barely make out the 1 and the 8 that might be followed by a 6 or
a 5, I can't tell. Preeti said they didn't have any other labels but
guessed they might be 1860s. The journal pieces can't be much
later than that or they would have called it Tokyo instead of Edo.

There's a group shot, too. Thirteen people in front of the
bookshelves, some standing and others sitting, all kind of

looking like they'd rather be reading. It's super blurry. I know people had to stand still for an absurdly long time for old-school photos but this looks like a particularly restless bunch. One of the ladies is smoking a pipe. Nobody's in focus, plus the photo has water damage along the top and one side.

But one of the names handwritten on the back says *J. S. Keating.* Well, you can read the *J* and the *S* and it's either a *K* or an *H* and an *ing.*

If the names are in order she's the blond lady standing second from the right, turned to say something or listen to the guy at the end who's almost vanished with the water damage. Can't make out his whole name on the back but it starts with an *A.* The lady is the same one from the Simone photo.

Below the list of names it says: *meeting of the owls.*

THE SON OF THE FORTUNE-TELLER rows a boat across an ocean made of paper.

The structure on the shore behind him looks like a proper castle now. A light glows in an upper window. The shadow of a dragon curls around the highest tower.

The oars dip into confetti and streamers, stirring them up in aquatic shimmers of blue and green though there is no sky here to reflect such colors.

Zachary looks at the space where the sky should be, wondering if somewhere up there someone is making changes to this universe.

Moving a small boat across an ocean. It must seem like nothing from such a distance. A tiny motion in a much larger tableau.

It feels a lot bigger from down here in the center of the ocean.

It takes a lot longer than he expects to reach the city across the sea.

There are many lights along the skyline but Zachary rows toward the brightest one.

As he gets closer he can see that it is a lighthouse.

As he gets closer still he can tell the lighthouse has been imagined from a wine bottle with a candle burning in its neck.

It is the opposite of the castle and its dragon, watching the shape of the city settle into buildings and towers surrounded by painted mountains and then resolve further into the objects they have been constructed from.

The paper confetti around the boat ushers him onto the shore.

Zachary pulls the boat up on the beach so the sea cannot take it away again.

This shore is covered in sand, each grain enormous. But there is only a dusting of it. Beneath it there is a solid surface. Zachary brushes the sand away from a section of it near the boat and uncovers the polished mahogany of the desk this part of the world rests upon, its varnish scratched by sand and time.

He walks from the beach onto green paper grass. He knows now where he is, even if he does not understand why he is here. He walks farther into the doll universe he had longed to see, though he never imagined viewing it from this perspective.

Along the beach there are cliffs and caves and treasure chests and much more to explore but Zachary knows where he is going. He walks inland, the paper grass crunching beneath his bare feet.

He walks past a toppled ruin of a temple and a snow-covered inn, the paper snowflakes scattered over the green of the grass.

He crosses a bridge made of keys and a meadow filled with paper book-page flowers. He does not stop to read them.

Some parts of the world reveal their pieces for what they are: paper and buttons and wine bottles. Others are perfect imitations in miniature.

From far away they look like what they are meant to represent but as Zachary gets closer the textures are wrong. The artificiality bleeds through.

A farmhouse is surrounded by balls of cotton pretending to be sheep.

Above him folded-paper birds flutter on strings. Hanging, not flying.

As Zachary continues walking the buildings grow more frequent. He loops through streets as the space becomes a city filled with tall cardboard buildings lined with unevenly spaced windows. He walks past a hotel and through an alleyway lined with lanterns and banners, decorated for a festival that is not occurring.

The city becomes a smaller town. Zachary walks down a main street lined with buildings. Stores and restaurants and cocktail bars. A post office and a tavern and a library.

Some of the buildings have toppled. Others have been reconstructed with tape and glue. Embellished and expanded and empty, even the ones that have figures posed within them, staring blankly out of windows or into wineglasses.

This is the idea of a world without anything breathing life into it.

The pieces without the story.

It's not real.

The emptiness in Zachary's chest aches for something real.

He walks past a lone doll in a tailored suit with too-big stitches resting facedown in the middle of the street.

Zachary tries to lift it but the porcelain cracks, breaking the doll's arm, so he leaves it where it lies and continues on.

At the top of a hill, overlooking the town, there is a house.

It has a large front porch and a multitude of windows clouded over in amber. On its roof is a widow's walk that would provide a view of the sea. Someone could have seen him coming from there, but the balcony is currently unoccupied.

It looks more real than the rest of the world.

The world that has been constructed around it with paper and glue and found objects.

He can see the hinges on the side of the dollhouse. The lock keeping its facade in place.

The lanterns on either side of the door are lit.

Zachary walks up the steps of the dollhouse to the front porch.

There is a humming sound. A buzz.

The door is open.

He has been expected.

A sign hanging above the door reads:

know thyself and learn to suffer

The buzzing grows louder. It multiplies and changes and chatters and then resolves itself into words.

Hellohellohellohellohellohello.

Hello Mister Rawlins you are here at last hellohello.

Hello.

excerpt from the Secret Diary of Katrina Hawkins

It's been more than a while this time, notebook. I reread because I didn't remember where I left off.

It's weird, not being able to remember your own thoughts even when you wrote them down. Sometimes it's like Kat from Before is just someone I passed on the street.

I never found out anything else about Jocelyn Keating, I still haven't remembered where I've heard of the Owl King before, I still don't know what that key is for, I occasionally see someone watching me at the library and freak out about it, which is so much fun.

I have trouble sleeping.

And Z's still missing.

It's been more than a year.

I played a lot of phone tag with Z's mom and I have all his stuff now, pulled out of university storage and sitting in boxes in my apartment. I keep telling his mom I can bring them to her but she insists I wait until after I graduate next May. Who am I to argue with a fortune-teller? Besides, Z has excellent taste in books so now I'm stocked up on reading material.

I don't really talk to people anymore, I know I should but it's hard. I was seeing this guy who bartends at the Adjective Noun for a while and he was nice but I kind of let it fizzle. I didn't return a text once and never heard from him again and now he's always generic bartender pleasant to me when I go in there and it's weird, like I imagined the whole thing and it didn't actually happen.

It's like the photograph. I didn't write about that here, but a few months ago I found a photograph online from that masquerade charity party. It was a gallery of images and one of them was a woman in a long white gown wearing a crown with a guy in a suit and it looked like they had either just stopped dancing or they were about to start. They looked like they knew each other. Neither of them were looking at the camera. She had her hand over his heart.

I didn't recognize the woman but the guy was Z. There was lens flare and she was in sharper focus, but it was totally him. He was wearing my mask.

The photo didn't have a caption.

When I tried to load a larger image to save the file it gave me a Page Not Found error and I went over and over the galleries again and it was gone.

I can see it, in my head. But lately I'm never sure I didn't imagine it. I saw what I wanted to see or something like that.

I deleted all of my social media not long after that. I shut down my blog. I stopped baking, too, except for failed experiments in gluten-free puff pastry.

I've tried to keep myself busy, though.

My Notebooks of Endless Possibilities turned into my grad thesis and possibly more than that so I came to Manhattan for a meeting (still here, back to Vermont tomorrow) and the second day I was here I got a text from an unknown number.

Hello, Kat. Northeast corner of Union Square, 1 p.m.

Beneath it was a bee emoji, a key emoji, and a sword emoji.

I went, because of course I did.

The farmers' market was set up in Union Square so the place was a zoo and it took me a while to find somewhere to stand and I didn't know what I was supposed to be looking for so I assumed someone was looking for me. Sure, following anonymous text instructions was sketchy but the middle of a crowded street corner seemed safe enough and, fine, whatever. I was curious.

I was there for about three minutes when my phone buzzed again with another text.

Look up.

I looked up. It took me a minute but then I spotted the girl standing in an upper window of the ginormous Barnes and Noble, looking down at me, holding up one hand like she was going to wave but she wasn't waving. She had a phone in her other hand that she started typing on once she saw me see her.

I recognized her. She'd come to my classes a few times around when Z disappeared but then I didn't see her after that January. She was a knitter. She'd helped perfect my golden stitch pattern. We'd had a cool conversation about overlapping narratives, too, and how no single story is ever the whole story. Sarah something.

She was there, *then,* and I hadn't ever thought of her. Not once.

The pay phone next to me started ringing. Seriously. I didn't even think those worked, I had them categorized in my mind as nostalgic street-art objects.

Another text buzzed my phone. *Answer it.* I looked up again. She had two phones, one was up to her ear and she was texting on the other. Figures. Never enough phones.

People around me were starting to look at me funny, I was standing too close to the phone for anyone else to get it.

So I picked it up.

"I'm guessing your name isn't Sarah," I said once I had the receiver at my ear.

"It's not," she said. Her voice came through the phone a second after her lips moved up in the window. She paused for a long time but she stayed on her phone. We just stood there looking at each other. She had this weird sad almost smile.

"Is there something you wanted to tell me?" I asked when I couldn't take the silence anymore.

"She asked you to join us and you said no, didn't she?"

I didn't have to ask who or what she was talking about.

"I decided to keep my options open," I said.

"You were smart."

She sounded bitter. I waited for her to say something else. Someone in one of the farmers' market tents was selling Manhattan rooftop honey and I got distracted wondering about city bees versus country bees and worrying over whether or not Manhattan bees have enough flowers.

"I wanted to belong to something, you know?" not-Sarah said but she didn't wait for me to answer. "Something important. I wanted to do something that had purpose to it, something . . . something special. Upper management dismantled the whole organization. We all got dismissed. No one knows what happened. I don't know what to do now."

I said, "Sounds like that sucks for you," which was kinda mean even though it did actually sound like it kinda sucked. She took it pretty well.

"I know this has been hard for you," she said. "I didn't want you to be on edge all the time. I wanted to let you know that no one's watching you anymore."

"You were."

She shrugged.

"What happened to the place you were supposed to be protecting?" I asked.

"I don't know. I've never been there. Maybe it's gone. I don't even know if it exists."

"Why don't you look for it?" I asked her.

"Because I signed an agreement that stated if I did they could terminate me, literally. I was assured that clause was intact when they paid me off and gave me a new identity. They'd kill me if they knew I was talking to you now."

"Seriously?" I asked, because really now.

"All of it is serious," she said. "They talked about eliminating you but decided it was too risky in case it resulted in more people looking into the Rawlins case."

"Where's Zachary?" I asked and then I kind of wished I hadn't in case she was going to confirm that he was dead because no matter what I think I've gotten accustomed to that tiny piece of hope that sits in the middle of the not knowing.

"I don't know," she said, quickly, more panicky. She looked over her shoulder. "I . . . I don't know. I do know it's all over now. I thought you should know."

I think she wanted me to say thank you. I didn't.

I said, "Who's the Owl King?"

And she hung up on me.

She turned from the window and walked away into the bookstore.

I knew I wouldn't be able to find her. Really easy to disappear in a five-floor bookstore in the middle of Manhattan.

I texted the number again but it said Delivery Failure.

I don't know how to start looking for a place that maybe doesn't even exist.

THE SON OF THE FORTUNE-TELLER stands in the doorway of a life-size dollhouse filled with larger-than-life-size honeycomb and occupied by bees the size of cats. Bees crawl down the stairs and across the windows and the ceiling, over armchairs and sofas and chandeliers.

All around Zachary the bees are buzzing, elated by his arrival.

Hello hello Mister Rawlins thank you for visiting no one has visited us in such a long long time we have been waiting.

"Hello?" Zachary answers, not meaning it to sound quite so much like a question but it is a question, he is nothing but questions as he enters the dollhouse. His feet sink into the honey that coats the floor as he steps into the entrance hall.

Hello Mister Rawlins hellohellohello.

The giant bees move this way and that over the honeycomb-encased rooms, traveling up and down the stairs, flitting from room to room, going about their business whatever their business might be.

"How . . . how do you know my name?" Zachary asks.

It has been told to us many times Mister Zachary Ezra Rawlins sir.

"What is this?" he asks. He walks farther into the house, each step slow and sticky.

This is a dollhouse a house for dolls a house to keep the story in it doesn't all fit in the house most stories don't most stories are bigger this one is very big.

"Why am I here?"

You are here because you are dead so now you are here in between places also because you are the key she said she would send us a key when it was time to end a key to lock the story away when it was finished and here you are.

Zachary looks down at the key-shaped scar on his chest.

"Who told you that?" he asks, though he knows.

The story sculptor, comes the buzzing answer, not the one that Zachary expected. *The one who sculpts the story sometimes she is in the story sometimes she is not sometimes she is pieces sometimes she is a person she told us you were coming very long ago we have waited for you a long long time Mister Rawlins.*

"For me?"

Yes Mister Rawlins you have brought the story here thank you thank you the story has not been here in a very long time we cannot lock away a Harbor story that has wandered so far away from us we usually go up up up and this time we came down down down we came down here to wait and now we are here together with the story would you like a cup of tea?

"No, thank you," Zachary says. He peers at a grandfather clock dripping with honey in the front hall, its decorative face depicting an owl and a cat in a small boat, its hands paused in wax a minute before midnight. "How do I get out of here?" he asks.

There is no out there is only in.

"Well then what happens next?"

There is no next not here this is the end do you not know what end means?

"I know what end means," Zachary says. The calm he felt before is gone, replaced by a humming buzzing agitation and he cannot tell if it is coming from the bees themselves or from somewhere else.

Are you all right Mister Rawlins what is the matter you should be happy you like this story you like us you are our key you are our friend you love us you said you did.

"I did not."

You did you did we gave you cupcakes.

Zachary remembers writing his eternal devotion in fountain pen on paper sent down a dumbwaiter that feels long ago and far away.

"You're the Kitchen," he says, realizing that he has already had several conversations with bees before though they seem to be more articulate in writing.

In that place we are the Kitchen but here we are ourselves.

"You're bees."

We like bees. Would you care for a refreshment we can turn honey into any-

thing anything anything you can imagine we are very good at it we have had a lot of practice we can give you the idea of a cupcake and it would taste very real exactly like real cake only smaller. Would you like a cupcake?

"No."

Would you like two cupcakes?

"No," Zachary repeats, louder.

We know we know you would like a cocktail and a cupcake yes yes that would be better.

Before Zachary can reply a bee nudges him over to a small table upon which now sits a frosted coupe glass filled with lemon-bright liquid and a small cupcake decorated with a much smaller bee.

Out of curiosity Zachary picks up the glass and takes a tiny sip, expecting it to taste like honey and it does but it also tastes familiarly of gin and lemon. A bee's knees. Of course.

Zachary returns the glass to the table.

He sighs and walks farther into the house. Some of the bees follow him, muttering something about cake. Most of the furniture is honey-covered but some of it remains untouched. His bare feet sink into honey-drenched carpets as he walks.

Beyond the front hall there is a parlor and a study and a library.

On a table in the library there is a dollhouse. A different dollhouse than the Victorian structure Zachary currently occupies, a miniature building composed of tiny bricks and many windows. It looks like a school or maybe a library of the public sort. Zachary peers in one of the windows and there are no dolls and no furniture but there are pictures painted on the walls inside.

A pool of honey surrounds the building like a moat.

"Is this supposed to be the Starless Sea?" Zachary asks the bees.

That is the next story this one is ending now the key has come to lock it up and fold it and put it away to be read or told or to stay where it is tucked away we do not know what will happen after it ends but we are glad to have company we do not always have company for endings.

"I don't understand."

You are the key you have brought the end it is time to lock it up and say goodbye good night farewell we have been waiting for you a very long time Mister Rawlins we did not know you would be the key we cannot always see keys for what they are when we meet them sometimes they are surprises hello surprise.

Zachary continues walking through the house, into a formal dining room set for a nonexistent dinner party. There is a cake on the sideboard with a single slice missing though the cakeless void has been filled with beeswax.

He wanders through a butler's pantry that leads to the kitchen. This is a space meant for living that is currently occupied only by bees and a solitary dead man.

At the back of the house is a sunroom, its sprawling windows clouded with honey. Here he finds a single doll. A girl doll, painted and porcelain. Cracked but not broken. She sits in a chair, her legs not quite bent properly, staring out a window as though she is waiting for someone to arrive, someone sneaking in through the back garden.

There is a book in her hand. Zachary takes it from her but it is not a real book. It is a piece of wood made to resemble a book. It cannot open.

Zachary looks out the honey-covered window. He wipes it as clear as he can with the palm of his hand and looks out over the garden, over the city and the paper sea. So many stories within the story and here he is at the end of them all.

"This story can't end yet," Zachary says to the bees.

Why Mister Rawlins why not it is time for the end now the story is over the key is here it is time.

"Fate still owes me a dance."

An indiscernible buzzing follows the statement before it settles into words.

Oh oh oh hrmmm we do not know why she did that we do not always understand her ways would you like to speak with her Mister Rawlins sir we can build you a place to speak to the story sculptor a place in the story where you can talk to her and she can talk to you we cannot talk to her ourselves because she is not dead right now but we can build a place for talking or dancing we are good at building places for the story there is not a lot of time left it won't last very long but we could do that if you would like would you like that?

"Yes, I would like that, please," Zachary says. He continues to stare out the window at the world as he waits, with an unfinished idea of a book in his hands.

The bees begin to build the story of a space within this space. A new room inside the dollhouse.

They hum as they work.

I remembered where I'd heard of the Owl King before.

I don't know why it took me so long.

I was at this party a couple of years ago, maybe a few months before Z disappeared. I don't remember. I think it was summer. It must have been summer because I remember humidity and mosquitoes and that nighttime heat haze. One of those house parties at a friend of a friend's and I wouldn't have been able to pick the house or the friend's friend out of a lineup afterward, because all the houses look blue-grey-brown in the light and on certain streets they all look the same, one blending into another, and sometimes the friends of friends do, too.

This house had those cool string lights out back. The hardcore ones with proper lightbulbs that look like they're on loan from some French café.

I was getting some air or something, I don't remember why I was outside. I remember being in the yard looking up at the sky and trying to remember my constellations even though I can only ever pick out Orion.

I was alone out there. Maybe it was too humid or there were too many bugs or it was late enough that there weren't that many people left and everyone was inside. I was sitting on a picnic table that was too big for the size of the yard, just kind of staring up at the universe.

Then this girl—no, woman. Lady. Whatever. This lady came out and offered me a drink. I figured she was a grad student or an assistant professor or somebody's roommate or something but I couldn't guess her age. Older than me. Not by a lot.

It's funny how that works. How for so long a single year of difference matters and then after a certain point a year is nothing.

She gave me an opaque plastic cup identical to the one I'd abandoned inside but with better bourbon in it, on the rocks.

I accepted because mysterious ladies offering bourbon under the stars is very much my aesthetic.

She sat next to me and told me that we were the people that the narrative would have followed out from the party if we were in a movie or a novel or something. We were where the story was, the story you could follow like a string, not all the overlapping party stories in the house, tangled up with too many dramas soaked in cheap alcohol and stuffed into not enough rooms.

I remember we talked about stories, and how they work and how they don't and how life can seem so slow and weird when you expect it to be more like a story, with all the boring bits and everyday stuff edited out. The sort of stuff Z and I used to talk about.

We talked about fairy tales and she told me one I'd never heard before even though I know a lot of fairy tales.

It was about a hidden kingdom. Like a sanctuary place and no one knew where it was exactly but you found it when you needed it. It called out in dreams or sang siren songs and then you found a magic door or a portal or whatever. Not always but sometimes. You had to believe or need it or just be lucky, I guess.

It made me think of Rivendell, someplace quiet and away to finish writing a book in, but this hidden kingdom was underground and had a seaport, if I'm remembering it right. It probably did because it was on something called the Starless Sea and I know I'm not misremembering that part because it was definitely underground, thus the no stars. Unless that whole part was a metaphor. Whatever.

I remember the space more than the story that went with it but I think the story part had to do with this hidden kingdom being a temporary space. And how it was meant to end and vanish because vanishing fairy kingdoms are a thing, and the place had a beginning and a middle and was moving toward an end but then it got stuck. I think maybe it started over a bunch of times, too, but I don't remember.

And some parts of the story got trapped outside of the story space and other bits lost their way. Someone was trying to keep the story from ending, I think.

But the story wanted an ending.

Endings are what give stories meaning.

I don't know if I believe that. I think the whole story has meaning but I also think to have a whole story-shaped story it needs some sort of resolution. Not even a resolution, some appropriate place to leave it. A goodbye.

I think the best stories feel like they're still going, somewhere, out in story space.

I remember wondering if this story was an analogy about people who stay in places or relationships or whatever situations longer than they should because they're afraid of letting go or moving on or the unknown, or how people hold on to things because they miss what the thing was even if that isn't what that same thing is now.

Or maybe that's what I got out of it and someone else hearing the same story would see something different.

But anyway, this hidden kingdom was kept alive in that magical fairy-tale way and in the same way that it would sing to people who needed to find it for sanctuary purposes it started whispering for someone to come and destroy it. The space found its own loopholes and worked its own spells, so it could have an ending.

"Did it work?" I remember asking, because she stopped the story there.

"Not yet," she said. "But it will, someday."

We talked about something else after that but there was more to the story. It had, like, a whole cast of characters and felt like a proper fairy tale. There was a knight, maybe? I think he was sad? Or there were two of them, and one of them had a broken heart.

And some Persephone-esque lady who kept leaving and coming back and there was a king and I remembered before that it was a bird king but I'd forgotten what kind of bird and now I swear it was an owl. Maybe. Probably.

But I forget what it means, what it meant in the story.

It's weird, I can remember so much of it now. I remember the lights and the stars and the opaque plastic cup in my hand and the melting ice watering down my bourbon and that pot-mixed-with-incense scent coming from the house and I did find Orion and two different cars went by playing that song that was everywhere that summer but I don't remember the whole story, not exactly, because the story didn't seem as important as the teller or the stars in that moment when it was being told. It seemed like something else. Not something you could hold on to like an opaque plastic cup or someone else's hand.

If I'm even remembering it right. I don't know anymore. I'm pretty sure I remember her, at least.

I remember we laughed a lot and I remember I'd been upset or sad about something or other before we'd started talking and afterward I wasn't.

I remember I kind of wanted to kiss her but I also didn't want to ruin it, and I didn't want to be the drunk girl who kisses everyone at the party even though I've been that girl before.

I remember wishing that I'd gotten her number but I didn't or if I did I lost it.

I do know I never saw her again. I would have remembered. She was hot.

She had pink hair.

THE SON OF THE FORTUNE-TELLER is guided by giant bees down a staircase within a dollhouse to where a basement would be though rather than a basement there is now an expansive ballroom made of honeycomb, shimmering and gold and beautiful.

It is ready Mister Rawlins there is not much time left but here you go here is the place that you wanted the dancing talking place the story sculptor is waiting for you inside tell her we said hello please thank you.

The buzzing quiets, drowned out by the music as Zachary descends to the ballroom. Some jazz standard he recognizes but could not name.

The room is crowded with dancing ghosts. Transparent figures in timeless formal wear and masks conjured from glitter and honey, luminous and swirling over a polished wax floor patterned with hexagons.

It is the idea of a party constructed by bees. It doesn't feel real, but it does feel familiar.

The dancers part for Zachary as he walks and then he can see her across the room. Solid and substantial and *here.*

Mirabel looks exactly as she did the first time he saw her, dressed as the king of the wild things, though her hair is its proper pink beneath her crown and her gown has been embellished: The draping white cloth is now embroidered with barely visible illustrations in white thread of forests and cities and caverns laced together with honeycomb and snowflakes.

She looks like a fairy tale.

When he reaches her Mirabel offers her hand and Zachary accepts it.

Here now in a ballroom made of wax and gold, Zachary Ezra Rawlins begins his last dance with Fate.

"Is this all in my head?" Zachary asks as they twirl amongst the golden crowd. "Am I making all of this up?"

"If you were, whatever answer I gave you would also be made up, wouldn't it?" Mirabel answers.

Zachary doesn't have a good response for that particular observation.

"You knew that would happen," he says. "You made all of this happen."

"I did not. I gave you doors. You chose whether or not you opened them. I don't write the story, I only nudge it in different directions."

"Because you're the story sculptor."

"I'm just a girl looking for a key, Ezra."

The music changes and she guides him into a turn. The incandescent ghosts around them spin.

"I don't remember all of the times I died," Mirabel continues. "I remember some with perfect clarity and other lifetimes fade one into the next. But I remember drowning in honey and for a moment, smothered in stories, I saw everything. I saw a thousand Harbors and I saw the stars and I saw you and me here and now at the end of it all but I didn't know how we'd get here. You asked for me, didn't you? I can't really be here since I'm not dead."

"But you're . . . shouldn't you be able to be wherever you want?"

"Not really. I'm in a vessel. An immortal one this time, but still a vessel. Maybe I am whatever I was before again. Maybe I'm something new now. Maybe I'm just myself. I don't know. As soon as there's an unquestionable truth there's no longer a myth."

They dance in silence for a moment while Zachary thinks about truth and myth, and the other dancers circle them.

"Thank you for finding Simon," Mirabel says after the pause. "You set him back on his path."

"I didn't—"

"You did. He'd still be hiding in temples if you hadn't brought him back into the story. Now he's where he needs to be. It's sort of like being found. That was all unforeseen, they did so much planning to have me conceived outside of time and no one ever stopped to think about what would happen to my parents after the fact and then everything got complicated. You can't end a story when parts of it are still running around lost in time."

"That's why Allegra wanted to keep the book lost, isn't it? And Simon and his hand."

Zachary glimpses another couple out of the corner of his eye and for a moment it looks as though the glimmering man in the coat quite similar to his own dancing next to them is missing his left hand, but then it catches the light, transparent but there.

"Allegra saw the end," Mirabel says. "She saw the future coming on its wings and she did everything she could think to do to prevent it, even things she didn't want to do. She wished she could preserve the present and keep her beloved Harbor the way it was but everything got tangled and restricted. The story kept fading and the bees wandered back down to where they started. They followed the story for a very long time through Harbor after Harbor but if things don't change the bees stop paying as much attention. The story had to end closer to the sea in order to find the bees again. I had to trust that someday someone would follow the story all the way down. That there could be one story to tie all of the others together."

"The bees said hello, by the way," Zachary tells her. "What happens next?"

"I don't know what happens next," Mirabel answers. "Truly, I don't," she adds, in response to the look Zachary gives her. "I spent a very long time trying to get to this point and it seemed such an impossible goal that I didn't give much thought to what waited beyond it. This is a nice touch, back to the beginning and all. I didn't think we'd get to finish our dance. Sometimes dances are left unfinished."

Zachary has a thousand questions still to ask but instead he pulls Mirabel closer and rests his head against her neck. He can hear her heartbeat thrumming, slow and steady, in time with the music.

There is nothing now save for this room and this woman and this story. He can feel the way the story spreads out from this point, through space and through time and so much farther than he ever imagined but this is the beating, buzzing heart of it. Right here and right now.

He's calm again. Relieved to have his Max back and even though he knows they both have other people they belong with there is still this room and this dance and this moment and it matters, maybe more than any of the others.

There is a humming noise all around them beyond the walls. The dancing ghosts fade one after another until only the two of them are left.

"I don't know if you will ever understand how grateful I am, Ezra," Mirabel says. "For everything."

The music falters and the ballroom begins to shake. One of the walls cracks. Honey seeps up from the floor.

There is not much time left Mister Rawlins sir you had your dance the story is over we really must be going.

The buzzed warning comes from all around them.

"I missed it," Zachary says. "I missed so much." He is not really talking about the story.

"You're here for the end," Mirabel says. It doesn't make him feel better.

"What happens now?" Zachary asks, as *now* seems suddenly more meaningful than *next.*

"That's not up to me, Ezra. Like I said, I don't make things happen, I just provide opportunities and doors. Someone else has to open them."

Mirabel reaches out and traces a line in the honeycomb wall with her finger and then another and another until they are roughly the shape of a door.

She draws a doorknob for it and pulls it open. There is a starlit wood beyond it, the tree branches heavy with leaves. The waves of honey around their feet lap at the grass but do not pass through the door.

"Goodbye, Ezra," Mirabel says. "Thank you."

She gives him a bow. The end of a dance.

"You're welcome, Max."

He bows to her in return, slow to rise again, expecting her to be gone by the time he looks up but instead she has come back and she is right in front of him and she kisses him, a brief, light brush of her lips against his cheek like a parting gift. A stolen moment before the end laced with honey and inevitability. It is not entirely sweet. Then Mirabel turns and walks through the door.

The door closes behind her and melts away into the wax wall, leaving Zachary alone in an empty, collapsing ballroom.

It is time to go Mister Rawlins sir.

"Go where?" Zachary asks but the buzzing has stopped. The honey swirling around Zachary's feet is getting higher. He makes his way to the stairs and up into the dollhouse. The honey follows him.

Back inside the dollhouse the bees are gone.

The porcelain doll has vanished from the sunroom.

Zachary tries to open the front door but it has been sealed closed with wax.

He climbs the dollhouse stairs and passes unoccupied doll bedrooms and closets until he finds another flight of honey-sticky stairs that lead to an attic filled with forgotten memories and within the attic there is a ladder, leading to a door in the ceiling.

Zachary pushes it open and climbs out to the top of the dollhouse. He stands on the widow's walk, staring out at the sea. Honey bubbles up through the paper confetti, turning the blue sea golden.

The bees are swarming over the roof below him. They buzz at him as they begin to fly up and away.

Goodbye Mister Rawlins thank you for being the key you were a good key and a nice person we wish you well in your future endeavors.

"What future endeavors?" Zachary yells at the bees but the bees do not answer. They fly off into the darkness, past models of planets and stars, leaving Zachary alone with only the sound of the sea. He misses the buzzing as soon as it is gone.

And now the sea is rising.

The honey sweeps over the paper grass and mixes with the sea. The lighthouse falls, its light extinguished. The honey steals the shore away and pulls the buildings down, insistent and impatient.

There is only one sea now, consuming the universe.

The sea has reached the house. The lock on the dollhouse breaks as the waves sweep through the open door and up the stairs. The facade falls, cracking open the honeycomb interior.

The rowboat is floating, not near enough to reach easily but Zachary is out of options. The world is sinking.

Being dead should not feel this perilous.

The honey is up to his knees.

This is really the end, he thinks. There is no world beneath this world.

There is nothing that comes after this.

The reality of it all is setting in as the dollhouse sinks below him.

The end is here and Zachary fights it.

He pulls himself up on the guardrail and dives for the boat. He slips, falling into the honey sea and the honey embraces him like a long-lost love.

He grabs for the edge of the boat but his honey-coated hands are too slippery to hold on.

The boat capsizes.

This Starless Sea claims Zachary Ezra Rawlins for its own.

It pulls him under and refuses to let him surface.

He gasps for a breath his lungs do not require and around him the world breaks.

Open.

Like an egg.

RHYME STANDS ON the highest step on a flight of stairs that once led down to the ballroom and currently descend into an ocean of honey.

She knows this story. She knows it by heart. Every word, every character, every change. This tale has buzzed in her ears for years but it is one thing to hear and quite another to see the sinking.

She has pictured it in her mind a thousand and one times but this is different. The sea is darker, the surf rougher and foaming as it clings to the stone and pulls books and candles and furniture down in its wake, stray pages and bottles of wine finding their way to the surface again before succumbing to their fate.

The honey always moved more slowly in Rhyme's imagination.

It is time to go. It is past time, but Rhyme remains standing and watching the tide ebb and rise until the honey reaches her feet and only then does she turn, the hem of her robes sticky and heavy as she walks away from the sea.

The Starless Sea follows Rhyme as she winds her way through rooms and halls, creeping at her heels as she takes these last steps, bearing final witness to this place.

Rhyme hums to herself as she walks and the sea listens. She pauses at a wall carved with vines and flowers and bees that does not appear to contain a door but Rhyme takes a coin-size disk of metal from her pocket and places the bee on it into the bee-shaped carving and the gateway into the Archive opens for her.

The honey follows at her feet, pooling into the room, stretching through the hidden stacks and shelves.

Rhyme passes the empty spot on the shelf where *Sweet Sorrows* would have been were it not stolen by a rabbit a long time ago and another vacancy where she pulled *The Ballad of Simon and Eleanor* from its place in the Archive, not so very long ago at all, comparatively.

Rhyme considers whether giving people pieces of their own stories is somehow cheating Fate or not and decides that Fate probably doesn't mind one way or another.

Two volumes misplaced over so much time is not that bad, Rhyme thinks, looking up at the shelves. There are thousands of them, the stories of this place. Translated and transcribed by every acolyte who walked these halls before her. Bound together in volumes of single narratives or combined in overlapping pieces.

The stories of a place are not easily contained.

It sounds strange and empty now, in her head. Rhyme can hear the hum of past stories though they are low and quiet, the stories always calm once they have been written down whether they are past stories or present stories or future stories.

It is the absence of the high-pitched stories of the future that is the most strange. There is the thrum of what will pass in the next few minutes buzzing in her ears—so faint compared to the tales layered upon tales that she once heard—and then nothing. Then this place will have no more tales to tell. It took her so long to learn to decipher them and write them down so that they bore any resemblance to the way they unfolded in her ears and in her mind and now they're almost gone. She hopes whoever wrote these last moments did them justice, she did not write them herself but she can tell from the way that they buzz in her ears they have already been recorded.

Rhyme takes one last walk through the Archive, saying her silent goodbyes and letting the stories hum around her before she continues upward.

She leaves the door to the Archive open, to let the sea inside.

The Starless Sea follows Rhyme up stairways and through halls and gardens, claiming statues and memories and oh so many books.

The electric lights flicker and die, plunging the space into darkness, but there are enough candles for Rhyme to see by. She lit her path earlier, knowing she would need the flames to guide her way.

The scent of burning hair greets Rhyme as she reaches the Heart. She does not knock on the door to the Keeper's office as she enters, nor does she comment on his clipped-short hair or the tangle of braids burning in the fireplace, their strung pearls charring and falling into the ashes.

One pearl for each year he has spent in this space.

He never told her that, but he did not have to. Rhyme knows his story. The bees have whispered it to her.

The Keeper's robes are folded neatly on a chair and he now wears a tweed suit that was already out of fashion the last time it was worn which was quite some time ago. He is sitting at his desk, writing by candlelight. This fact makes Rhyme feel better about having taken so long, but she always knew they would wait until the last moment to depart.

"Are all of the cats out?" the Keeper asks without looking up from his notebook.

Rhyme points at the ginger cat on the desk.

"He's being stubborn," the Keeper admits. "We shall have to take him with us."

He continues to write while Rhyme watches. She could read his rushed inscriptions if she cared to but she knows what they are. Invocations and supplications. Blessings and yearnings and wishes and warnings.

He is writing to Mirabel as he always has, as he has continued to write through the years she has been with Zachary in the depths, writing as though he is speaking to her, as though she can hear each word as it materializes on the paper like a whisper in her ear.

Rhyme wonders if he knows that Mirabel hears him, has always heard him, will always hear him through distance and lifetimes and a thousand turning pages.

This is not where our story ends, he writes. *This is only where it changes.*

The Keeper puts his pen down and closes the notebook.

He looks up at Rhyme.

"You should change," he says, looking at her robes and her honey-soaked shoes.

Rhyme unties her robes and takes them off. Beneath them she wears the same clothes she wore when she first arrived: her old school uniform with its plaid skirt and white button-down shirt. It did not seem right to wear anything else for the departure despite the fact that it feels like wearing a past life and the shirt is now too small. The honey-soaked shoes will have to suffice.

The Keeper, seeming not to notice the encroaching waves, stands and pours a glass of wine from a bottle on the desk. He offers to pour another for Rhyme but she declines.

"Don't fret," the Keeper says to Rhyme, watching her as she watches the sea. "It is all here," he says, placing a fingertip on Rhyme's forehead. "Remember to let it out."

The Keeper hands her his fountain pen. Rhyme smiles at the pen and places it in the pocket of her skirt.

"Ready?" he asks and Rhyme nods.

The Keeper looks around the office once more but takes nothing save the glass of wine as they move into the next room, the ginger cat following.

"Could you give me a hand with this, please?" the Keeper asks, placing his wine on a shelf and together he and Rhyme move the large painting of Zachary and Dorian aside, revealing the door set into the stone wall behind it.

"Where shall we go?" the Keeper asks.

Rhyme hesitates, looking at the door and then back over her shoulder. The sea has reached the office, lapping at the desk and the candles and toppling the broom that had been resting in a corner.

"We are past the time for vows," the Keeper adds and Rhyme turns back to him.

"I'd like to be there, if we can," she says, each word careful and slow, sitting strangely on a tongue she has not used for speaking in years. "Wouldn't you?"

The Keeper considers this suggestion. He takes a watch from the pocket of his suit and looks at it, turning the hands this way and that before he nods.

"I suppose we have the time," he says.

Rhyme picks up the ginger cat.

The Keeper places his hand on the door and the door listens to its instructions. It knows where it is meant to open, though it could open anywhere.

Waves of honey sweep into the room as the Keeper opens the door.

"Quickly now," he says, ushering Rhyme and the cat through the door and out into the cloud-covered daylight.

The Keeper turns back and lifts the glass of wine from the shelf.

"To Seeking," he says, raising his glass to the approaching sea.

The sea does not answer.

The Keeper drops the glass, letting it spill and shatter on the floor by his feet, and then he steps out of this sinking Harbor and into the world above.

The door closes and the Starless Sea crashes into it, flooding the office and the room beyond. It smothers the fire and the smoldering braids within it and slides over the painting, pulling measures of time and depictions of fates under its surface.

This space that was once a Harbor is now part of the Starless Sea again.

All of its stories returned to their source.

Far above, on a grey city sidewalk, the Keeper pauses to glance in the window of a bookstore while Rhyme stares up at the tall buildings and the ginger cat glares at nothing and everything.

They continue walking and when they reach the corner Rhyme looks at the sign informing her that they are leaving Bay Street and turning onto King.

Perched on the street sign there is an owl, staring down at her.

No one else seems to notice it.

For the first time in a long time, Rhyme doesn't know what it means.

Or what will happen next.

DORIAN SITS ON the stone shore next to Zachary's body at the edge of the Starless Sea.

He has sobbed himself numb and now he simply sits, not wanting to see the unchanging tableau in front of him and unable to look away.

He keeps thinking about the first thing he encountered in this place that looked like Zachary. He doesn't know how long ago it was, he only remembers how unprepared he was, even after multiple Allegras and greater nightmares wearing the skin of his sister who died when he was seventeen.

It was snowing. Dorian only believed for a moment that it was really Zachary and that moment was enough. Enough for the thing that was not Zachary even though it wore his face to disarm him. To bring him to his knees and Dorian does not remember how he managed to dodge the claws that came for him in the blood-soaked snow quickly enough to retrieve the sword and get to his feet again.

The moon had warned him but Dorian does not believe anyone could truly be prepared for what it feels like to wield a sword in deepest darkness and cut through all that you ever cared for.

With all the Zacharys that followed he did not hesitate.

He had thought he would be able to tell the difference when he finally found the real one.

He was wrong.

Dorian replays the moment over and over in his mind, the moment when Zachary remained while the previous creature-worn guises had vanished once they were struck only to be replaced by someone or something or someplace else, followed by the slow, terrible comprehension that this moment and everything held within it was all too real.

And now this moment stretches on and on, interminable and awful, when everything had been constant, dizzying change before, moving too fast for him to catch his breath. Now there are no false cities, no haunted memories, no snow. Only a cavernous emptiness and a seashore littered with the wreckage of ships and stories.

(The darkness-lurking things that hunted him have fled, in fear of such grief.)

(Only the Persian cat remains, curled by his side, purring.)

Dorian thinks that he deserves this pain. He wonders when it will end. If it will ever end.

He doubts that it will.

This is his fate.

To have his story end here in this ceaseless anguish surrounded by broken glass and honey.

He considers falling on the sword himself but the presence of the cat prevents him.

(All cats are guardians in their own right.)

Dorian has no way to mark the time that passes with dreadful slowness but now the edge of the Starless Sea is approaching, the luminous coastline moving closer. He thinks at first that it is only his imagination but soon it becomes clear that the tide is rising.

Dorian has resigned himself to slowly drowning in honey and sorrow when he sees the ship.

I thought about giving this notebook to Z's mom but I didn't. I feel like I'm not done with it, even though it's a bunch of pieces and not a whole anything.

I hope there's a missing piece, maybe even a small one, something that will make all the other pieces fit together but I have no clue what it is.

I told Z's mom some things. Not all the things. I brought bee cookies because I figured she'd say something if it meant anything to her and also because they're delicious because honey-lemon icing but she didn't say anything so I didn't bring it up. I didn't feel like dealing with secret societies and places that may or may not exist and it was nice to talk to someone for once. To be somewhere else and sit and have coffee and cookies. Everything felt brighter there. The light, the attitude, everything.

She also just *knew* things. I think she broke me down a little bit. Or put a crack in my psychic armor that wasn't there before. That's how the light gets in and all that.

At one point I asked her if she believed there was magic in the world and she told me, "The world *is* magic, honeychild."

Maybe it is. I don't know.

She slipped a tarot card into my coat pocket when I was leaving, I didn't notice until later. The Moon.

I had to look it up, I don't know tarot stuff. It reminded me that Z had a deck and read for me once and kept insisting he wasn't very good but everything he said was pretty much on point.

I found stuff that said the Moon card was about illusions and finding your way through the unknown and secret otherworlds and creative madness.

Madame Love knows what's up, I think.

I put the card on my dashboard so I can see it while I drive.

I feel like something's coming and I don't know what.

I'm trying to let all of this go and something keeps holding on.

No, something keeps building. Keeps leading me to something new and something next.

If this hadn't happened I wouldn't have started building my game, I wouldn't have gotten this job, I wouldn't be on my way to Canada right now.

It's like I'm following a string Z left for me through a maze but he might not even be in this maze. Maybe it's not my job to find him. Maybe it *is* my job to see where the string goes.

It felt weird to leave his scarf. I've had it for so long.

I hope he gets it someday.

I hope he has a really, *really* good story to tell me over dinner at his mom's place and I hope he's there with his husband and I'm there with someone or by myself and fine with that and I hope we stay up so late that late turns into early and I hope the stories and the wine go on and on and on and on.

Someday.

AFTERWARD

SOMETHING

NEW

AND

SOMETHING

NEXT

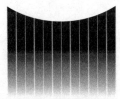

Once, not so long ago . . .

There is a ship upon the Starless Sea, sailing as the tides rise.

Below the deck a man whose name is now Dorian keeps his vigil over the corpse of Zachary Ezra Rawlins while the ship's captain whose name is not and will never be Eleanor navigates the stormy seas.

There is a commotion above, a howling wind as the boat rocks, lilting to one side and then to the other. The flames on the candles falter and recover.

"What's going on?" Dorian asks when Eleanor returns to the cabin.

"There are owls perching along the sails," Eleanor says. One of them has followed her, a small owl who swoops through the cabin and perches on a beam. "They're making it difficult to steer. They're trying to stay afloat, you can't blame them with the sea rising this fast. It's fine, I'll need new maps now anyway."

She makes this remark regarding the table with the maps where they have laid out Zachary's body, blood seeping through paper and golden ribbons and obscuring both the known paths and the unmapped territories where the dragons be, all of it now lost beneath the sea.

Dorian starts to apologize but Eleanor stops him and they stand in shared silence.

"How high will it rise?" Dorian asks to break the silence though he finds he does not care. Let it continue to rise until they crash into the surface of the earth.

"There are many caverns to sail through," Eleanor assures him to his dismay. "I know the ways no matter how high it rises. Can I get you anything?"

"No, thank you," Dorian says.

"This is your person, isn't it?" she asks, looking down at Zachary. Dorian nods.

"I knew someone once who had a coat like that. What are you reading?" Eleanor gestures toward the book in his hands though Dorian is holding it as a talisman more than he is actually reading it.

He hands *Sweet Sorrows* to her.

Eleanor frowns at the book and then the joyful recognition of an old lost friend spreads across her features.

"Where did you find this?" she asks.

"He found it," Dorian explains. "In a library. On the surface. It's yours, I believe." The look on her face almost makes him smile.

"The book was never mine," Eleanor says. "Only the stories in it. I stole the book from the Archive. I didn't think I'd ever see it again."

"You should have it back."

"No, we should keep it for sharing. There is always room for more books."

Only then does Dorian notice the sheer volume of books around the cabin, tucked into spaces between beams and on windowsills, piled on chairs and propping up table legs.

The ship tilts, a particularly rough wave tipping the cabin on an angle before it rights itself. A pencil rolls from a table and disappears beneath an armchair.

The Persian cat that has been napping in the armchair slides grumpily off and goes to investigate the case of the disappearing pencil, as though that was its intention all along.

"I should go back up," Eleanor says, handing *Sweet Sorrows* back to Dorian. "I forgot to tell you, there's someone up on one of the precipices. I saw him through my telescope. He's just sitting there, *reading*. I'll stop for him when the sea level reaches that point. I don't know how he'd get out otherwise, he only has one hand. If the waves get worse hold on to something."

Dorian thinks he should throw himself into the waves and let the Starless Sea take him but he suspects Eleanor would rescue him again if he did.

Eleanor gives Dorian's shoulder a somewhat awkward pat and then she returns to the deck, leaving him alone with Zachary.

Dorian brushes a curl from Zachary's forehead. He doesn't look dead. Dorian doesn't know if it would help if he did.

Dorian sits silently, listening to the crash of the waves against the ship, the howl of the wind and the beating of wings circling through the caverns, and his heart beating in his ears which sounds as though it has an echo because it does and then Dorian realizes where the echoed heartbeat is coming from.

He takes the box from his pack and holds it in his hands.

What is the difference, Dorian asks himself, *between Fate's heart and a heart belonging to Fate?*

A heart kept by Fate until it is needed.

Dorian looks down at Zachary's body and then back at the box.

He thinks about what he believes.

When Dorian opens the box the heart inside beats faster, its moment arrived at last.

Someone left a note on my car.

It's parked in a shopping-mall parking lot outside of Toronto and someone left a note on it. Literally fewer than ten people in the world even know I'm in this country right now and I've checked for tracking devices and I should absolutely not be findable or note-able. I didn't plan on stopping at this mall, I don't even know what city I'm in, Mississomething.

The note says *Come and See* with an address below it.

It's written on a piece of stationery with "Regards from the Keating Foundation" embossed across the top.

The back has a little drawing of an owl wearing a crown.

I plugged the address into my GPS. It's not that far away.

Dammit.

The address is a vacant building. It might have been a school or a library, maybe. Just enough broken windows to cement the whole "abandoned" look. There aren't any signs. The front door is boarded up but there aren't any for sales or no trespassings or beware of dogs. There aren't even any signs to say what it was, only a number above the door so I know I'm in the right place.

I've been parked here for twenty minutes trying to figure out if I should go in or not. The grounds are all overgrown, like no one's been here in years. No one's even driven by.

There's some graffiti but not a lot. Mostly initials and abstract swirls. Maybe Canadian graffiti is more polite.

If I'm going to go in I should do it before it gets too dark. I should probably bring a flashlight.

It feels like it's looking at me, in that old-building creepy way. That space that's had so many people in it but now there's no one so it feels extra empty.

I'm inside now and it was definitely a library once upon a time. There are empty shelves and card catalogues. No books, just random invoices and packing slips and a few stray cards, the old-school kind you had to write your name on.

And everywhere, everywhere there are these paintings.

Like graffiti and Renaissance oil painting had mural babies. All abstract and fuzzy here and there and then hyperrealistic other places.

There are bees swarming down staircases and a cherry-blossom snowstorm and the ceilings are painted to look like night sky, covered in stars with the moon moving across it from phase to phase.

There are murals that look like a city and others that look like a library within the library and one room has a castle and there are people. Life-size portraits that are so realistic at first I thought there were actual people in here and I nearly said hello.

One of them is Z and another is that guy from the bar (I knew that guy was important I *knew* it).

And one of them is me.

I'm on the goddamned wall.

I'm on the wall in the orange coat that I am currently wearing with this notebook in my hand.

What the hell is going on here?

. . .

On this big wall there's a huge owl. Not a barn owl, a barred owl maybe? I don't know my owls. It's gigantic and takes up most of the wall with its wings spread and there are all these keys in its talons hanging from ribbons and it has a crown above its head.

Under the owl there's a door.

It has a crown and a heart and a feather on it, in a line down the center.

The door isn't part of the painting.

It's an actual door.

It's in the middle of a wall but there's no door on the other side, I checked. It's solid wall on that side.

The door is locked but it has a keyhole and hey, I have a key.

Maybe the Time has come.

I'm sitting in front of the door. There's a little bit of light beneath it.

The sun is going down, but the light under the door hasn't changed.

I don't know what to do.

I don't know what you're supposed to do when you find what you didn't know you were looking for and you weren't even certain it existed anyway and then suddenly you're sitting on the floor of an abandoned Canadian library face-to-face with it.

I've been huffing that citrus oil that Z's mom gave me but I don't feel mentally clear.

I feel lemony and insane.

I went outside and sat on the hood of my car and watched the moon rise. There are so many stars. I found Orion.

I put my Moon tarot card in my pocket and I have my feather key. It still has the tag on it. The handwriting is the same as the note that was on my car.

For Kat when the Time comes
Come and See

I'm leaving this notebook here in my car just in case. I don't know why. So someone knows. So there's a record, if something happens. If I don't come back.

So someone maybe somewhere sometime will read it and know.

Hi, person reading this.

Katrina Hawkins was here.

These things happened.

Sometimes it might sound weird but sometimes life is like that.

Sometimes life gets weird.

You can try to ignore it or you can see where weird takes you.

You open a door.

What happens next?

I'm going to find out.

Zachary Ezra Rawlins wakes, gasping, his new heart hammering in his chest.

The last thing he remembers is honey, so much honey filling his lungs and pulling him down to the bottom of the Starless Sea.

But he is not at the bottom of the Starless Sea.

He's alive. He's here.

Wherever *here* is.

Here seems to be moving. The surface he is on is hard but everything around him is oscillating. There are pieces of paper and bits of ribbon and something sticky that isn't honey beneath his fingers.

The light is dim but there are candles, maybe. He doesn't know where he is.

He tries to stand and instead he falls but someone catches him.

Zachary and Dorian stare at each other in bewildered disbelief.

Neither of them has the words for this moment in this story, not in any language.

Zachary starts to laugh and Dorian leans in and takes the laugh from his lips with his own and there is nothing left between them now: no distance, no words, not even fate or time to complicate matters.

This is where we leave them, in a long-awaited kiss upon the Starless Sea, tangled in salvation and desire and obsolete cartography.

But this is not where their story ends.

Their story is only just beginning.

And no story ever truly ends as long as it is told.

Outside what was once a library there is a recently abandoned blue car.

A ginger cat sleeps on the still-warm hood.

A man in a tweed suit leans against the car, leafing through a teal notebook though there is only moonlight to read by.

By the side of the brick building a young woman in an outgrown school uniform stands on tiptoes, peering in a window.

Neither of them notices the woman walking toward them through the trees but the stars do, their light shining brightly on her crown.

She has always known this night would come.

Through centuries and lifetimes, she has always known.

The only question was how to get here.

The woman in the crown pauses in the quiet darkness, watching the man as he reads.

Then she turns her attention skyward.

She reaches her hand up toward the stars. Resting on her palm is a single card. She holds it out at the night sky, displaying it to the moon and the stars with a considerable amount of showmanship.

Upon the card there is an empty void. *The Ending.*

She flips the card over. A bright expanse. *The Beginning.*

She flips it again and it turns to golden dust in her fingers.

She takes a bow. The crown does not fall from her head but it slips and she straightens it and turns her attention back to the ground, back to her own story.

When she reaches the car she is shivering in her sleeveless gown.

"I didn't change," Mirabel tells the Keeper. "I didn't think it would be this cold. Have you been waiting long?"

The Keeper takes off his tweed jacket and drapes it over her shoulders.

"Not long," he assures her, for a few hours are nothing compared to the time they have both waited for this moment.

"She hasn't opened it yet, has she?" Mirabel asks, looking toward the brick building.

"No, but she will soon. She's already decided. She left this." He holds up the bright teal notebook. He presses a red button on the cover and tiny lights flicker around a smiling face. "How is our Mister Rawlins faring?"

"Better now. He didn't think I'd let him have a happy ending. I'm kind of offended."

"Perhaps he did not believe that he deserved one."

"Is that what you thought?" Mirabel asks but the Keeper does not reply. "You don't have to be there, you know," she adds. "Not anymore."

"Neither do you, and yet here we are."

Mirabel smiles.

The Keeper lifts a hand and tucks a stray lock of pink hair behind her ear.

He pulls her closer to keep her warm, catching her lips with his.

Inside the brick building a door opens into a new Harbor upon the Starless Sea.

Far above the stars are watching, delighted.

ACKNOWLEDGMENTS

So many thanks to those who sailed the Starless Sea with me.

To Richard Pine, who I still believe is a wizard, and to InkWell Management.

To Jenny Jackson, Bill Thomas, Todd Doughty, Suzanne Herz, Lauren Weber, and everyone on my amazing team at Doubleday (including Cameron Ackroyd, for all the cocktails).

To Elizabeth Foley, Richard Cable, and company across the star-covered sea at Harvill Secker.

To Kim Liggett for the writing dates, both virtual and in person, at the Ace Hotel or in forgotten corners of the New York Public Library and for the many, many glasses of sparkling wine.

To Adam Scott for everything, always.

To Chris Baty, creator of National Novel Writing Month, who really should have been in the acknowledgments for *The Night Circus* as well. Sorry about that, Chris.

To Lev Grossman for letting me steal the Brakebills bees and keys.

To J. L. Schnabel. Several pieces of the jewelry described in this book, including the silver sword necklace, are inspired by her exquisite bloodmilk creations.

To Elizabeth Barrial and Black Phoenix Alchemy Lab, who truly put stories in bottles. Because of them I always consider what everything smells like when I write.

To BioWare because this book only found its footing once I fell deeply in love with *Dragon Age: Inquisition*.

A note on the naming of things: I borrowed the name Madame Love Rawlins from a tomb in Salem, Massachusetts. Any resemblance to the actual person is coincidental. Kat and Simon are named after Kat

Howard and Simon Toyne because each of them happened to e-mail me while I was hunting for character names. (Kat's friend Preeti found her name in similar fashion from Preeti Chhibber.) As noted in the text, Eleanor is named for the character from *The Haunting of Hill House*. Zachary and Dorian were always Zachary and Dorian, even though I almost changed Dorian's name multiple times. Mirabel was, of course, named by the bees.

ABOUT THE AUTHOR

Erin Morgenstern is the author of *The Night Circus,* a number-one national bestseller that has been sold around the world and translated into thirty-seven languages. She has a degree in theatre from Smith College and lives in Massachusetts.

erinmorgenstern.com